PEOPLES
ON THE
MOVE

"Surprising, is it not, that God declared his intention to bless all the nations of humanity through a covenant promise made to a nomad of sorts, Abraham, whose grandson Israel is forever recalled by his descendants with the words 'a wandering Aramean was my father'. Yet the ancient nomadic peoples of our world seem to be the last to benefit from the great missional dynamic that has sprung from that promise. This unique and timely book, like an oasis in a desert, provides much needed resources in an attractive and accessible format to help us remedy that great omission."

— **Chris Wright,** *International Ministry Director, The Langham Partnership International (former Principal, All Nations Christian College)*

"David Phillips has worked long and hard to produce an excellent resource packed with valuable information, much of which has been gleaned through first-hand experience. *Peoples on the Move* will be invaluable to those wishing to pray in a more informed way. No longer should there be any excuse for ill-informed and general prayer for these neglected peoples of the world, here is all you could hope to know, and more besides! Indeed those writing and researching will also find an abundance of material on which they can draw.

"And for those embarking on service overseas with peoples on the move there should no longer be the impossible task of trying to obtain background information, it is all here ready and waiting to be used. It is sincerely to be hoped that many will feel challenged."

— **John Horton,** *TEARFUND Regional Manager, Eastern & Southern Africa*

PEOPLES
ON THE
MOVE

Introducing the Nomads of the World

David J. Phillips

William Carey Library

piquant

First edition 2001
07 06 05 04 03 02 01 7 6 5 4 3 2 1

ISBN 1-903689-05-8

Published by Piquant
PO Box 83, Carlisle, CA3 9GR, United Kingdom
E-mail: info@piquant.net
Website: www.piquant.net

Co-published in the US by William Carey Library
PO Box 40129, Pasadena, CA 91114, USA
Tel. +1 (626) 798-0819
Website: www.wclbooks.com
ISBN 0-87808-352-9

Cover images: Fulbe in northern Mali drawing water from a water-hole in the dry riverbed
(photo: David Phillips); main photo: the Gabbra move house easily — on camels! (photo:
Malcolm Hunter); Riasiti children in Pakistan — these dispossessed peasants became nomads
during the twentieth century (photo: Genny Feldmann); back and bottom spine: Kirghiz
shepherds moving camp in the Tien Shan Mountains (photo: David Phillips).

Designed and produced for the publisher by
Gazelle Creative Productions, Mill Hill, London NW7 3SA.

Printed and bound in England.

To Freda, my helpmeet in our "nomadic" partnership
who made this book possible in too many ways to mention,
and who is now with the Great Shepherd in the eternal pastures.

CONTENTS

LIST OF MAPS/DIAGRAMS

The maps in this handbook are notional rather than precise. They give approximate and relative positions in order to help the reader have a more tangible visual impression of the distribution of peoples.

AUTHOR'S NOTE

Although the author has made every effort to ensure that the information in this book is accurate at the time of going to press, ethnographic research of this kind requires constant fresh input. Readers who are knowledgeable about a certain nomadic group, or those with additional or updated information, corrections or suggestions, are warmly invited to contact David Phillips via Piquant, PO Box 83, Carlisle, CA3 9GR, UK. Of particular interest is all information regarding the state of Christianity among nomadic peoples. David undertakes to treat the identity of all who wish to remain anonymous as strictly confidential.

LIST OF PHOTO PAGES

Unless otherwise indicated, all photographs are by David Phillips.

FOREWORD BY STAN GUTHRIE

After the AD 2000 initiative during the last decades of the twentieth century, where do we now stand in relation to world evangelism?

While Scripture is available in just under 2,300 of the world's approximately 6,800 languages, some 80% of the world's people do have access to God's word in a language they can understand. Wycliffe Bible Translators hopes to begin work in 1,000 new languages over the next decade so that by 2025 work will have begun "in every language where Scripture is needed."

Meanwhile, the World By Radio initiative, launched in 1985 to provide Christian programming to the 279 "megalanguages" with more than a million speakers, reports that fewer than 100 languages still lack a gospel witness by radio.

The Jesus film has been seen by about four billion people in hundreds of different languages, with millions coming forward to make Christian commitments. Yet such media-centered approaches cannot do the job alone, missions experts agree. "These tools are wonderful when they are used as bridges to presenting the gospel and seeds for planting the gospel, but when they are seen as ends in themselves, they diminish severely the crucial human element in evangelism and discipleship," notes Paul Borthwick of Development Associates International.

One agency, Dawn Ministries, has encouraged an approach known as "saturation church planting," and the 31 countries that have convened national Dawn congresses have started 2.6 million churches, including between 750,000 to a million since 1990.

So, are we winning or losing? On the one hand, Robertson McQuilkin, a former missionary to Japan, says, are the optimists who believe the church is close to fulfilling the Great Commission. On the other hand,

McQuilkin points to the pessimists who see the multitudes of people beyond the reach of the gospel. "Both truths are needed: The task remaining is vastly greater than it ever was before. But the resources and momentum to do it are greater, too."

While the percentage of the world's people that has never heard the gospel has come down steadily over the last century, the absolute numbers remain a staggering challenge — about 1.5 billion of the world's six billion people have still not heard the gospel, according to statistician David Barrett. Adherents to other major religions — Muslims, Hindus and Buddhists — have been largely immune to our witness, and about a thousand people groups have almost no opportunity to hear the gospel because there are few or no Christians present among them.

Among the least reached peoples are the nomads. This, by and large, has not been intentional. Living on the fringes of society, they have been hidden from the evangelical missions' imagination. Our ministry models usually don't fit the nomads. We are comfortable reaching out to people who, whether they live in the countryside or the city, stay where they are. We like to put down roots, learn about a place, and build churches. Nomadic lifestyles are alien to us, and they seemingly run counter to the direction in which an increasingly linked world is heading.

Like few Westerners, David Phillips knows the nomads. This book provides a wealth of indispensable insights and practical information for reaching them in culturally appropriate ways. Any mission-minded person — whether a pastor, cross-cultural worker, sender or intercessor — will profit from it. *Peoples On the Move* is a unique contribution to mission literature, and the author deserves the gratitude of the worldwide missions community.

The task is not done, yet. May this volume play a role in helping us to finish the task and mobilize missionaries to the difficult-to-reach nomads, who, like the Lord who died for them, are truly aliens and strangers on this earth.

Stan Guthrie is Associate News Editor for *Christianity Today* and the author of *Missions in the Third Millennium: 21 Key Trends for the 21st Century* (Carlisle, UK: Paternoster, 2000).

FOREWORD BY MALCOLM HUNTER

"When you can put your Church on the back of my camel then I will think that Christianity is meant for us Somalis." This statement from a camel herder in northern Kenya really grabbed my attention. For 20 years I had been looking in East Africa looking for the most marginalized people. Almost invariably they lived in dry and remote areas herding animals and doing little, if any, cultivation. I also found that they were the least likely to have heard the gospel of God's love for them

I must have come across half a dozen separate ethnic entities before it dawned on me that these were nomadic pastoralists. They did not lay claim to any particular piece of land, as what was valuable to them was their animals. When drought or an enemy raiding party threatened, they readily abandoned whatever crops they had to save their cattle, sheep or goats. They were usually very colorful and resourceful people, periodically fighting with the neighboring tribes over the diminishing amount of grass and water available to them as farmers and government projects invaded their essential grazing areas. The more I studied them and read about them, the more they fascinated me. From my engineering point of view they were obviously technologically backward, but socially they were exemplary as they cared for those within their extended family or clans. Their national governments either ignored or sought to annihilate them. What surprised me most of all was that Christian missionaries did not understand them and their unique world view.

Without exception, these nomads held a high view of God as the one who sends the rain. Every ethnic group has certain ceremonies or individuals to pray to God to send rain and keep disease away. Some offered sacrifices to ask forgiveness when bad things had been done, and peace was restored by killing a bull and eating together. When I saw the Bunna initiation ceremony in which the young boys are "born again" to become warriors, I realized that God knew how to communicate with them. It was Western Christianity in a church building that they could not understand. In fact, if they had ever seen anything of Christianity it was probably on a mission station with a special building in which some people met on a Sunday morning in clean clothes. As that Somali camel herder described his impression, "They go into that building to pray but one man stands in front and talks to God while everybody else puts their heads down and looks as if they are trying to sleep. I am a Muslim because we can pray anywhere, at anytime and we all pray together on our knees and standing up." Most of the nomadic pastoralists I met in southern Ethiopia and Sudan and northern Kenya were not Muslims, but God was far more important to them than to city dwellers.

After 25 years of accumulating questions about what development means to people whose world view is so different, even from farming Africans, I was not finding answers from any expert consultant. So I decided that I should take some time out and do my own research, a dissertation on "Appropriate Development for Nomadic Pastoralists" that was awarded the PhD by the Open University.

When I was invited by the Evangelical Missionary Alliance to present a paper on "The Challenge of the Unreached Nomadic Peoples of the World," I was not surprised that only a few turned up, but one of them was David Phillips. He was the key man that God needed to do the writing and literary research that would take my field experience and glimpses of the global implications and put it all into a book that mission agencies could use. David has done the Kingdom of God a great service by his efforts to collect and compile all the information currently available on the people of the world who think of themselves as significantly different from settled or farming people.

Malcolm Hunter is a consultant for the development of nomadic pastoralists with SIM International, as well as Head of the Institute for Nomadic Ministry at the US Center for World Mission and Chair of the Department for Nomadic Studies at William Carey University in Pasadena.

PREFACE: STRIKING CAMP

Nomads have a special place in God's plans. For most of us, the word *nomad* conjures up the idea of self-sufficient people, who are both resourceful and irresponsible, mysterious and dangerous, who are to be envied for being free from the restraints of ordinary society. We envision nomads as both carefree and stubbornly keeping to an uncomfortable life.

The nomads are an important but often ignored part of humankind. The varied estimates of their numbers demonstrate the difficulty of knowing exact figures, but the total of nomads would be large enough (added together) to populate many countries. The significance of nomads is even greater because many peoples who have a history of nomadism are still in contact with it; some may revert to it; or their culture may still be influenced by this history.

Nomadic peoples represent a unique challenge to Christian mission. It has been said that Christianity has had virtually no success in converting nomadic pastoralist peoples, and this could be largely true of other types of nomad. We must examine why this is so and see whether we need to change our approach.

A number of factors are conspiring against the nomadic life — including unsympathetic government policies, repeated droughts, the end of collectivization in Central Asia, the advance of irrigation and cultivation, the pressure to commercialize pastoralism, the competition of industrial goods and transport, population pressure on common lands, and, more simply, prejudice and bureaucracy. Further, the lure of modern life has challenged them to adapt their life-style or abandon it.

Now is the hour of the nomads! They have been left until last, and time is short. To evangelize these people, we have to serve them spiritually and materially in a way that enhances their identity and maintains a viable nomadism. We set out on what is, for most of us, an unfamiliar journey to understand the nomads and find out how as Christians we can help them. Learning how to reach nomads will challenge many of our well-established ideas. Working with this group of people requires a specialization similar to that required of those working in Christian radio, Bible translation, urban evangelism and among destitute children.

In the first three chapters we will define and describe the nomad's way of life, especially that of the pastoralists, who make up the majority of nomads. Chapter 4 briefly considers how to overcome the prejudice between nomads and the rest of society.

The nomads challenge Christians to understand the gospel and discipleship in a new way — to understand a way of life that is closer to that of the people of the Bible itself. Chapters 5, 6 and 7, therefore, demonstrate that God's interest in these traveling peoples is central, and not peripheral, to his purpose for humankind. In the process of seeking to evangelize them, we rediscover that in God's eyes we also are travelers dependent on him.

Following this biblical overview, Chapters 8 to 10 outline aspects of Christian service sympathetic to the nomadic way of life. The assumption that the best way to reach nomads is to establish a static microcosm of Western Christianity called a 'mission station' is to be questioned. However rudimentary the mission station may seem to Western missionaries, it can give the wrong impression of Christ to nomadic peoples. Because nomadism has shaped the nomads' perception of themselves, the Christian who is to reach them must also in some sense be a nomad.

The second half of this book is a survey of about 200 nomadic peoples. Some are large in numbers, others are insignificant in human eyes. But each deserves to be known to the Christian public as a unique expression of God's image. Our aim is that Christians might hear the call of God to pray for and reach out to nomads with the gospel.

Nomads need Christians willing to be partners with them for their spiritual and material well-being. This involves the dedication to live and adapt oneself to a totally unfamiliar society, often without basic comforts for considerable periods. Ultimately it involves the formation of a network of disciples among the nomads and equipping them to reach other nomadic peoples.

The aim is to portray these different nomadic groups as living human societies, with their names, location, pastoral or occupational life and something of their religious life. Some of the agencies working among nomads are mentioned, and they may be contacted for more information about prayer and service. I know of no other worldwide survey of nomadic peoples, much less from a Christian point of view. This survey is offered by a non-nomad, with the inadequacies of library research, as a

beginning to serve that end. We have found that, in many cases, Christian agencies hold little information about nomads. I am very grateful to the many people around the world who have offered information and corrections from their first-hand experience. The many remaining defects and omissions are entirely mine.

Finally, I want to offer my thanks to Malcolm Hunter who started off my interest in nomadic peoples; also to the Library of the School of Oriental and African Studies at London University, and especially Miss Rosemary Stevens, a former Assistant Librarian, for her help in much of the research; to Patrick Johnstone for his encouragement and for allowing me the time to pursue this specialized research while working in the WEC International Research Office; and to the many workers interested in or busy with outreach to nomads for their contributions, comments and practical help during field visits to nomadic groups.

David J. Phillips
WEC International Research Office
AD 2001

KEY TO MAPS

Country CAMEROON

Province **BAUCHI**

City ● Ouagadougou

River Niger

Natural Feature **Ahaggar Mountains**

Nomadic People *FULANI, Wo'odabe*

Tribal Region

Sea, Lakes

Coastline

Scattered Groups in a Country *Gypsies*

Annual Migration Route

ABBREVIATIONS

ACROSS	Across UK (Doncaster, England)
AERDD	Agricultural Extension and Rural Development Department (University of Reading, England)
AIC	African Independent Church(es)
AIM	Africa Inland Mission
AoG	Assemblies of God
CAFOD	Catholic Fund for Overseas Development (London)
CAPRO	Capro Research and Information Centre (Jos, Nigeria)
CARE (Britain)	Christian Action Research and Education.
CIS	Commonwealth of Independent States
CLC	Christian Literature Crusade
CMA	Christian and Missionary Alliance
COCIN	Church of Christ in Nigeria
CPK Anglican	Church of the Province of Kenya
CRWM	Christian Reformed World Missions
ECWA	Evangelical Church of West Africa
EMQ	*Evangelical Missionary Quarterly*
EMS	Evangelical Missionary Society
FEBA Radio	Far East Broadcasting Association
FMC	Frontier Missions Center (Cimarron, CO, USA)
HCJB	WRMF (Radio HCJB)
IBT	Institute for Bible Translation (Stockholm)
IMA	Indian Missions Association
JGLS	*Journal of the Gypsy Lore Society*
LCCN	Lutheran Church of Christ in Nigeria
LMS	London Missionary Society
MRG	Minority Rights Group
NIDNTT	*New International Dictionary of New Testament Theology*
ODI	Overseas Development Institute (London)
OXFAM	A relief agency (Oxford, England)
Radio ELWA	SIM Radio and TV station (Liberia)

RBMU	Regions Beyond Missionary Union (now merged with World Team, Warrington, PA, USA)
REB	*Rural Extension Bulletin* (see AERDD)
RSMT	Red Sea Mission Team
SALTLIC	Semi-Arid Lands-Training and Livestock Centres (Isiolo, Kenya and Chippenham, England)
SAMS	South American Mission Society
SGM	Scripture Gift Mission
SIL	Summer Institute of Linguistics
SIM	SIM International
SMEET	Société Missionnaire de l'Eglise Evangélique au Tchad
SUM	The SUM Fellowship (Sidcup, England)
TDNT	*Theological Dictionary of the New Testament*
TEAM	The Evangelical Alliance Mission
TEAR Fund	The Evangelical Alliance Relief Fund (now Tearfund)
TOTC	Tyndale Old Testament Commentaries
TWOT	*Theological Wordbook of the Old Testament*
TWR	Trans World Radio
TynBul	*Tyndale Bulletin* (Cambridge)
UBS	United Bible Societies
UBSWR	*United Bible Societies World Report* (Stuttgart, Germany)
UCCF	Universities and Colleges Christian Fellowship (Leicester, England)
UNESCO	United Nations Educational, Scientific and Cultural Organization
UNFAO	United Nations Food and Agriculture Organization
VSO	Voluntary Service Overseas (London)
WBT	Wycliffe Bible Translators
WEC	WEC International
WTPR	World Translation Progress Report (UBS)
YWAM	Youth With A Mission.

Part I:
Characteristics of Nomadic Lifestyles

Jesus at Home in the Tents

The blacksmith's invitation

In the hubbub of a crowded street in a town of North India, a slim woman, looking older than her years but still attractive, crouches by a tiny forge and anvil. The family works together as a team. The mother holds the red-hot metal with tongs, the teenage son swings the sledgehammer, and Granny squeezes the bellows to give a draft to the little six-inch forge. The father crouches behind, very sick with malaria. Together, they mold the scrap iron into a useful instrument — a hoe, shovel, pick, plow, knife or sickle, to help support their family of five children. All of the children were born and are growing up in, under or beside the heavy wooden ox-cart. The mother is proud to be one of the Traveling Oxcart Blacksmiths (*Gadulyia Lohar*). They are a people set apart — not like those noisy town people!

It's a hard life, living and working continually at the roadside. They need all the help that Kali, the goddess of destruction, can give. "The bad-tempered Lady owes us a favor," the mother thinks to herself. After all, her husband and his brothers sing at the Hindu festivals, and she herself has done many *pujas*, or acts of worship. Have they not also given that

white bullock to the Nandiwala, who tells fortunes by the gods moving the "sacred animal"? "Therefore," she reasons, "it's time the gods helped us."

She hitches her floral sari up around her. "What's wrong with that boy? Distracted again!" She looks up at the ring of customers and spectators that always gather around them, for their visits are a minor event. A man has engaged her son's attention. He is dressed just like the rest of their customers, in a long loose shirt. "Mum, this man is a traveler just like us and wants to stay the night!" She glances back at the cart — the torn, dusty tarpaulin stretched over it, the stained, battered mattresses, and the few sacks — that was their home! "Who in their right mind would want to share that, unless he was one of us Blacksmiths?" She turns back to the traveler, for she is streetwise and used to dealing with men. Then she looks at his feet as he stands in the ashes and dust beside her. They have been punctured by nails, and she knows what suffering such wounds cause. His request for hospitality must be to do with that. "Come at sundown and tell us about your feet," she bluntly invites.

The reindeer man's surprise encounter

In the far north, the nomadic herdsman tunes into the telltale sounds of reindeer moving between the birch trees of the Siberian *taiga*. He cannot imagine how the man before him has managed to approach without him hearing. He thought he knew everyone for hundreds of miles around! The man's complexion is too dark for a Russian, but he is dressed as a Nenet, just like himself. The herdsman pours out the

troubles of his people, the Nenets, to the stranger. Through the dark decades of the "People's Paradise," their way of life had been ruined. They had been forced to live in settlements as if they were factory workers. Their children had been taken away to be schooled, learning of such abstractions as "the class struggle." They soon learned that, whatever the ideology, the Arctic peoples were at the bottom of society. The Nenet knew his native Nenets were not benefiting from "progress!" The oil pipelines had polluted the landscape recently, just as they were returning to their old life of reindeer herding. Their Bear-god and the ancestors had not helped much either.

The unknown man listens sympathetically, as if he is well acquainted with the Nenets' way of life. As he talks, the stranger gives the extraordinary impression that he himself is one of them! The herdsman warms to the unknown traveler, who has thrown back his hood to listen. His forehead is scarred as if briars have been crushed down on his head. The stranger turns as if to resume his mysterious journey. The herdsman hastily glances through the trees to the *tepee* of birch poles, skins and canvas where his family has joined him for a brief winter holiday. Soon they will return to the settlement and he will drive the reindeer the long, lonely journey to the tundra for the brief summer. But now his wife is preparing a tasty meal. The herdsman presses his invitation, "Come and share our simple fare and tell us all about yourself." The stranger traveler gladly accepts.

The Tibetan herder finds a friend

The north wind drives grit and sand into our frozen faces and claws at our heavy, knee-length, sheepskin cloaks made from eight fleeces. We stumble across the stony ground, swinging our horsewhips about us to keep the snarling mastiffs at bay. Our cold feet slip on the ice from the spring that thaws around midday to give the camp its only water. The shadowy humps on all sides in the dark night are sheep and yaks. We gratefully slip into the warmth of the big black tent that crouches like a large spider on Tibet's high plateau. Our host motions us to a gap in the close circle around the central fire, and we stretch out our tired legs towards the only warmth. All the neighbors are there, all nomadic herders, but there is a quiet expectancy tonight instead of the usual lively, jocular exchanges on gossip, hunting, religion and the price of wool.

In the half-light, we notice that things are different tonight. Granny is not turning her prayer wheel, the host is not muttering prayers while conversing, and the Buddhist sacred tablets and rosaries on the chest at the back of the tent are covered. Our hostess is busy serving Tibetan tea — tea with "yak" butter and salt. But why is she wearing her finery with her best bright apron, as if she is at the tribal horse races, or about to go on pilgrimage to Lhasa?

A stranger sits in the place of honor, wrapped in a sheepskin coat like everyone else. His face seems familiar, though we have not seen him before. His skin is nearly as brown as his host's, equally grimed with soot from the yak-dung fire and smeared with "yak" butter. Like everyone else he licks his bowl clean, and it is promptly filled again. He is utterly at home with these humble people. He accepts their simple comforts, their rough life, their simple pleasure and problems. He looks around with kindly authority at the faces, young and chubby, old and lined. He has a perceptive look that sees into each life, its hopes and fears and the deep darkness there. It is as if he knows them well.

As the wind howls and clutches at the tent, the stranger raises his voice: "I am the good shepherd and my father is the great herdsman. One day many from all peoples, also the high pasture ones of Tibet, will be tented with my Father and I, the Lamb, will shepherd them."[1] His humble hearers are drawn to his message. "So the future is not endless reincarnations with help from the Buddha, after all," they think. Far into the night, after more teaching from the stranger and after much tea has been drunk and much yak-dung fuel burned, our hostess quietly sobs over her many infidelities and backbiting. We watch in the half-light from the lantern, as two hands stretch over to grasp one another. Our host's hand is tanned and gnarled from a hard nomad's life. It is a hand that has sought ritualized merit for its many sins. The hand of the stranger once worked wood in a land far away and is still deeply scarred by a spike that was hammered through it. Our host has found his master herdsman and the stranger has gained a brother!

At home in the tents

Jesus is among the nomads before us, waiting for our lives and our voices to reveal his presence. Surveys show that most people who have become Christians have done so because they knew another Christian. The nomads need us to live as Christians within the nomadic life, at their level as much as possible. The great Shepherd looks for committed disciples to befriend the world's nomads, to learn the nomads' languages and skills and, through the shared experience of their lives, to make him known. His love needs to be shown in practical ways to enhance the people's nomadism — in education, community health, veterinary and medical help, and range management. We need to understand the nomads' religious practices and unanswered fears, and introduce the nomadic shepherd God of the Bible to them. We need to demonstrate by example that the great Shepherd is really at home in the nomads' tents.

1 Who Are the Nomads?

Self-sufficient, a law unto himself, a roving warrior...the nomad may appear both to have an ideal life and to be a threat to civilization. To those unfamiliar with the life of the nomad, it suggests freedom from routine, from restraints and the entanglements of civilization. It appears to be a simple life that allows one to be in tune with nature. Such a view is influenced by ideas of the evolution of society that assume that the nomad lives according to humankind's earliest and most primitive lifestyle. We have also been influenced by biblical and classical history to regard the Bedouin as epitomizing the word "nomad." With their camels, "the ships of the desert," they are thought to roam free from the restrictions of civilized life. The reality, however, is very different.

Only a few Bedouin nomadic groups, such as the Al Murrah, come near to embodying this idealized concept of the nomad. The Al Murrah, who have little contact with other people, cover vast distances in the center of Arabia and appear to need nothing but a few wells where their camels can drink. They spend the months from June to August living in tents by their wells in the south, allowing their camels to roam freely in search of forage, and returning for water every few days because of the heat. Between September and December, the Al Murrah travel considerable distances for pasture, using nothing but a windbreak for shelter. Finally, in January, they make a rapid march northwards to reach the pasture springing up from the winter rains in the Nafud, a sea of huge sand dunes. Moving further north for the winter, the Al Murrah socialize with other tribes and supervise the calving of their herds. In March they return slowly southwards, as the grass grows, moving about 10 kilometers (6 mi.) every few days until they reach their wells again. Such a lifestyle was possible only with the camel, but the limitations of the camel include its being: a temperamental beast, an expensive investment, difficult to breed, and, now, difficult to market and redundant as transport.

The Al Murrah's "freedom" is in fact limited by their natural environment. To sustain their herds of camels, or flocks of sheep and goats, these Bedouin are constantly on the move, seeking more of the limited pasture in a terrain that often receives little or no rain for years. Most Bedouin have known long periods of thirst and famine, and their diet is monotonous. Their movement is also limited by having to make contact for supplies, marketing sheep, finding work opportunities and schooling for some family members, as well as by government forces and by feuds with other tribes. Modern reality is such that most of the Bedouin are now settled in villages, but their sense of identity and their subsistence is still shaped by pastoralism. Some of the family members travel with the family's flocks to seek pasture, while others supplement the family income by working in the towns or on farms or by periods of employment in the oil industry.

Nomads are distinctive

The term "nomad" was originally used only for those, like the Bedouin we have described, who lead animals progressively to different pastures.[1] Today, "nomad" is used to refer to all societies whose culture and way of life is centered on the need to systematically travel to find a means of subsistence. They support themselves by moving to use resources of pasture or commerce that are marginal, and that the majority of society does not, or cannot, use. This movement leaves important marks on their culture and society.[2] The nomads' chief aim is to maintain their distinct identity as a

1a

1b

1 Nomads are resourceful and adaptable:
   a. Inadan or Tuareq craftsman sitting on the frame of a camel saddle, the traditional proof of their skill.
   b. Like other nomad craftsmen, many Inadan have adapted by moving into cities as far afield as Europe to work as joiners or in other trades.

people by supporting themselves with their skills or animals. This leads them to be different, in varying degrees, from the surrounding society. This type of work that requires systematic travel shapes their view of themselves and their way of life, as well as much of their culture and values.

The ideal of self-sufficiency, therefore, is a more fundamental characteristic of the nomad than even their travel. So while nomads favor a principal method of support — such as, say, raising cattle or blacksmith work — they also supplement this with other economic activity. All nomads show a great versatility in adopting secondary methods of subsistence such as cultivation, trading or truck driving. They use limited opportunities to the full, in complete contrast to settled peoples tied to agricultural land or other property. Nomads may, in fact, even settle for a time. They are resourceful and not the stubborn remnants of an out-of-date way of life that cannot adapt to the modern world.

Each nomad is a member of a whole people — whole families and larger groups either move together or are at least involved with the migrations in some way. They are to be distinguished from various individuals (such as drovers, cowboys, traveling salesmen, airline staff or seamen) who belong to sedentary peoples, but whose occupation or other circumstances may cause them to travel regularly. Nomads belong to a society whose identity and culture is based on nomadism, even when they have settled for a time and may have taken up other occupations (suitable to their sense of independence).[3] Neither does the term "nomad" include the many displaced persons and refugees who are removed involuntarily from their homelands, residences, societies and livelihoods because of discrimination, persecution, civic unrest, war or natural disaster.

The nomad may sometimes be forced away from his nomadism because of war, drought, or new laws against traveling people, but a nomad is not defined by this displacement. Neither is the nomad a tramp, who though he may have a regular itinerary

for subsistence has no social organization. The nomad is not homeless simply because she may not have a house or land. Nomads are at home within the migratory life of their society.

Three main types of nomad

There are three main types of nomad, differentiated by their chief means of subsistence. These are the hunter-gatherers, the pastoralists and the peripatetics. The Aborigines of Australia and the Bushmen and Pygmies in Africa are examples of hunter-gathers. The boat nomads, such as the Bajau of Southeast Asia and the Boso fishermen on the Niger River, are a special kind of hunter-gatherer. There are also shifting cultivators, who move to cultivate because of the limited fertility of the soil. These include the Iban of Kalimantan, Indonesia or the people of the Bijagos Islands, Guinea-Bissau, who move to different islands to grow their rice crops. The hunter-gatherers need to move because of the changes in, and limited quantities of, the natural food supply and raw materials, according to the seasons. Their migration allows for the natural replenishment to take place. But we are concerned with the other two types of nomad — the pastoralists and peripatetics.

The nomadic pastoralists' subsistence and culture is based on keeping domestic animals and seeking pasture for them. The Bedouin of the Middle East and North Africa, the Sami of Scandinavia and the Fulbe of West Africa are examples of pastoralists. The pastoralists are less directly involved with the wider society, because pastoral systems can be self-sufficient and their pasture is often remote from centers of population. Because they are dependent primarily on natural ecosystems, and only partially require human resources, they develop a considerable measure of autonomy as close-knit societies.

Many of them combine other means of subsistence with their pastoralism. The Mursi of southwest Ethiopia, for example, combine a shifting, slash-and-burn cultivation during the rains and a flood-plain crop in the dry season, both of which are done by the women. Meanwhile, the Mursi men alternate between the plain and the hills with the cattle. The Mursi skillfully use the different environments according to the seasons.

The peripatetics are the traveling craftsmen, entertainers and traders — such as the Gadulyia Lohars of India and the Gypsies of Europe. Many other names have been suggested for this varied group, including "commercial nomads," "travelers" and even "Gypsy-like" peoples. But peripatetic gives the idea of movement to reach wider markets for occupations that would otherwise be practiced at the local level.

Both the pastoralists and peripatetics travel systematically and not in a random fashion. This movement is illustrated by the term *parytan*, used by the peripatetics in Pakistan to describe their life as deliberate, thought-out patterns of movement to use their specialized skills.[4] The nomadic pastoralists and peripatetics operate an industry which, although a part of the "informal economy," is systematic in its use of labor, economic opportunities and marginal resources, and must be taken seriously. The lives of both the pastoralists and the peripatetics are shaped by their experience, whether it is the skill of interpreting the environment to maintain livestock, or a craft or service. This skill and lifestyle are the source of their social distinctiveness.

Both the pastoralists and peripatetics have assets to use and resources to find and develop. The fundamental difference between the pastoralist and the peripatetic is that the pastoralist manages the natural resources of animals and pasture without necessarily having much contact with other people. Peripatetics, on the other hand, depend on commercial contact with people to gain their livelihood.[5] They move to enable their main asset — whether it be livestock or a skill — to find its main resource — whether pasture or customers. Both pastoralists and peripatetics have products for their own subsistence or which they can offer for exchange or sale (for what they cannot produce for themselves).

The chief assets of nomadic pastoralists are their domesticated animals, which give them products that enable them to enjoy considerable self-sufficiency — wool, hair, meat, hides, manure and especially milk, cheese and other dairy products. This economic independence, however, is not complete. They must have contact with markets to exchange these products and any surplus livestock for those things they cannot produce themselves. Many of them may also hunt and grow limited crops.

The peripatetics *are* their own asset, with whatever training, skills, experience and mobility they have. The entertainer has his props, the craftsman his tools, the trader his pack animals or cart, and the hawker his goods, but above all he has his own and his family's abilities and resourcefulness to develop a number of skills. From this point of view the peripatetic may be called a professional or service nomad, using "profession" in the sense of having skills to offer a service to others who lack either the skills or inclination. The tools and resources for his profession are easily accessible to him or carried with him, so that he needs no long-term or involved ties with others in society.

The resources the pastoralists need are pasture and grazing to maintain their livestock assets. Along with most hunter-gatherers and subsistence agriculturists, they are concerned with the *natural* resources of the land, such as its fertility, moisture for crops or pasture, and available game. The nomadic pastoralist is nomadic because each part of his territory only produces limited grazing at particular times, in areas too arid for permanent grazing. "We only move when we feel we must," they say. The seasonal changes of the natural resources necessitate the mobility. In contrast, the sedentary pastoralist or rancher has access to sufficient fertile land within tolerable distance of his settlement, and so does not have to travel. For many pastoralists the commercial prospects from their animals are secondary or even non-essential, but the peripatetic must have human customers.

The peripatetics' primary resource, that

requires their travel, is the *human* demand for their trade, craft or entertainment. They travel because: 1) the demand for their service as craftsmen, or as traders or entertainers, is small or seasonal; 2) with low overhead costs they can undercut any attempt by local people to provide the service; and 3) they have the inclination and skill to serve seasonal or scattered clientele.[6] They have to be resourceful in changing occupations and skills, to meet the opportunities of changing markets. If the demand increases to sustain a permanent service in one locality, the peripatetic will settle for as long as there is a demand, or alternatively the local population will begin to provide this service for themselves. The peripatetics exploit established contacts and festivals, markets or harvest times when more people and more money are available. They have no control over the competition of industrial substitutes or changes in fashion in society. They also have to gather raw materials for the articles they sell.

The nomads' movements, therefore, are governed by their need for resources to sustain their main assets — pasture or the demand of the market. Thus pastoralists are best described not as pastoral nomads, which would imply that their movement is primary. Rather, they are nomadic pastoralists, because subsistence by their livestock is their *essential* characteristic. The skills of breeding and herding domestic animals shape their lifestyle and self-identity. Similarly, peripatetics are better described as nomadic professionals, because the service they provide shapes their lifestyle. Being a pastoralist or a craftsmen is a more important element in how the nomad sees and supports himself, than is the degree to which he or she is mobile.

The migratory system

"Here all my troubles I leave behind." The children leap across the flames of the small fire, chanting these words. Their parents finish packing the family's large square tent and their belongings on donkeys. It is March, the Persian New Year, and the nomads are beginning to migrate from the chill and damp of another winter near the Persian Gulf. They have experienced months of struggle to find feed for their flocks of sheep and to move them to higher ground to stop hoof rot. Now, after the arduous journey through the mountains, they will spend the summer in the mountain pastures. This is the happy time. The girls who are of an age to marry dress in their best clothes and travel on a horse or camel to catch the eyes of prospective bridegrooms and fathers-in-law, for arrival in the summer pastures is the time for families to negotiate marriages.

Nomads do not travel just for the sake of it. They move as and when it is necessary for their livestock or skill assets to find their main resources of pasture or customers. Most nomads are static for one or two seasons of the year, and many move not very far or often. The fact that they acquire property or even settle does not mean they are no longer socially distinct or not ready to move again. Being mobile or static are both strategies to be used according to need. When the conditions are favorable, they will remain in one place for long periods.

The numerous motives for nomadism include: 1) as we have said, it is the preferred means of subsistence; 2) it maintains ethnic-cultural independence; 3) it resists outside interference; 4) it is a way to avoid war or ethnic hostility; 5) it is the only lifestyle known and compatible with their view of themselves; and 6) no one area provides resources all year round. Nomads can be divided as follows, according to different patterns of movement, including nomadic, semi-nomadic, semi-sedentary and agropastoralist:

1. There are groups that are continually nomadic, with an established seasonal movement between different grazing or customer areas, usually alternating between two or more areas. Among the pastoralists are the Al Murrah Bedouin, the Tuvans in Siberia, Tuareqs, Maasai, Beja in Africa, the Qashqa'i of Iran and the Rabari of India. Many pastoral peoples, such as the Fulani, make long-term changes of location over great distances because of drought or war.

Some have made great historical migrations from one area to another, such as the Gypsies and the Kyrgyz. Many peripatetics are "true" nomads, living in mobile dwellings and moving systematically and seasonally to exploit their markets, such as the Gadulyia Lohar of India and many Roma in Europe. Some are attached to a pastoralist people, such as the Waata and Inadan of Africa, or the Ghorbati of Iran.

2. Most nomads are semi-nomadic, but this term has a number of meanings. Either part of each family travels, while the rest stay in one place, or the whole family is resident in one place for a part of the year and travels only for particular seasons. Semi-nomadic families may have permanent dwellings in order to enjoy the facilities of modern life, such as education for the children. They may supplement pastoralism with cultivation, or jobs in a neighboring town, while other family members travel with their trade or herds. The Gaddi of India are making the transition from being nomadic to semi-nomadic, with most of the family choosing to live all year round in their villages that they previously closed up for the winters. Having a house or a permanent main camp does not mean nomadism has been abandoned. Many Gypsies live in a house for long periods, and even sleep in their caravans alongside, but travel throughout the summer.

The term semi-nomadic can also be used for a society that has a settled section and a nomadic section, such as many of the Bedouin. Sometimes the term semi-nomadic is used when 50% or more of people migrate, and "semi-sedentary" when less than 50% migrate with the animals.[7] Some families are wholly sedentary in agriculture and others wholly in pastoralism, or they are divided by gender, as the Mursi and other East African peoples.

3. Semi-nomadism can become agropastoralism when cultivation is the main subsistence activity, but with pastoralism still being culturally or economically important. In fact, the pastoralism of an agropastoral society can function as a form of semi-nomadism, as

part of each family or village travels to distant pastures for part of the year. The Lur and the Bakhtiari in Iran have been forced into this semi-sedentary type of pastoralism, cultivating near their villages, while some of them have returned to nomadic pastoralism. Many Kazaks have converted to ranch pastoralism, as some livestock are fed from crops, while the rest are pastured on the steppe or in the mountains in a revival of nomadic pastoralism. Ancient Israel in Canaan also followed this lifestyle.

4. Many nomadic and semi-nomadic pastoralists can be called multi-resource nomads.[8] There are whole groups that move with the animals at different times during the year, and then stop for the growing season to cultivate particular crops, such as dates or millet. While continuously herding and pasturing their animals throughout the year, they also have sedentary periods, at locations or settlements they consider their own. The Fulbe have traditional models of adapting to semi-settled or settled periods to combine agriculture with pastoralism.[9] The Hawazma are nomadic, but they stop to plant and harvest crops. The Karimojong and Somalis separate into domestic and herding camps for part of the year. The families migrate slowly, giving them opportunity for small-scale horticulture, while the herders move with the herds.

The Lur traditionally practiced this type of nomadism, growing two crops in both their summer and winter locations, while the whole people migrated. The Yarahmadzai (Shah Nawazi) Baluch in Iran make trips away from their flocks in the summer for the grain harvest, and in the autumn they travel over 160 kilometers (100 mi.) to their palm date groves. Many pastoralists use other resources in some way or other, so that planting crops, gathering fruit, smuggling, raiding, and military service can be economically important to some nomadic tribes, and these activities have become part of their traditional pastoral migrations.

Peripatetics are particularly ingenious in exploiting many resources, some working as craftsmen in one season and salesmen in another, or as herders and hunter-gatherers, such as the Waata. The Ighyuwn among the Moors are craftsmen and musicians, specializing in political commentaries in their songs. There are a number of Bhotia groups in Nepal who are both pastoralists and caravan traders. Many, like the Fuga in East Africa, are ritualists and magicians as well as blacksmiths.

As we are beginning to see, these terms are not very precise and cover a variety of patterns, so using them to describe a people does not always convey very much. It is more useful to describe a typical migration pattern. Two examples here illustrate just how imprecise the terms are. Among the Berbers, there are those who live in high-altitude villages near their summer pastures and who migrate to temporary dwellings at lower altitudes in winter. Other Berbers live in villages situated near their winter pasture in the valleys and migrate into the mountains for pasture in the summer. Still others live in villages at a medium altitude and travel lower in winter and higher in summer. All could be considered semi-nomadic, and all are examples of transhumance.

The third type of Berber is similar to the Gaddi of India. They have villages that the families leave for the winter to live in tents on the plains with the flocks. Many take winter employment in nearby towns. In the spring, while the men take the flocks to higher pastures in the mountains, the women and children reopen their houses and stay in the villages to cultivate their poor fields in the brief growing season. The men could be described as "true" nomads and, as the whole people make seasonal movements, they too are nomadic. However, as many of the families are now staying in the villages throughout the year for schooling and cultivation, the Gaddi are also "semi-nomadic." With winter jobs in the towns, cultivation and transhumant pastoralism, they are also multi-resource pastoralists.

The peripatetics are nomadic, semi-nomadic or semi-sedentary. Many like the Inadan, a part of Tuareg society, and the

Ghorbati and Luti in Iran, travel with nomadic or semi-nomadic pastoralists all year or only part of the year, providing services as craftsmen and minstrels. Others seek their customers independently, such as the Kalderash Gypsies of Europe, who were originally coppersmiths; the Khyampa of Nepal as traders; and the Lohar as blacksmiths. Many of the Rom Gypsies specialize in crop-picking, visiting fairs or asphalting, and these determine their movements.

5. Finally, there are those who are sedentary but whose ethnic identity, values and history are still shaped by nomadism. These include many Fulbe and Arabian Bedouin who have lost their flocks or herds and may work as laborers, drivers or as beggars, with the aim of returning to pastoralism as soon as possible.[10] They have been termed "nomads in waiting." It must be borne in mind that those that are not practicing nomads would still prefer that lifestyle and see themselves still as nomads. Many return to nomadism when the political or environmental conditions permit.

There is a spectrum, therefore, from true nomad, through semi-nomadic, to settled. Societies can change their lifestyle, wholly or in part, either way. There are nomadic peoples who were once settled and vice versa. To befriend and serve such people, it is vital to understand how they see themselves, and also to understand the way of life with which they are at home, or which they see as an ideal. We must treat them as a nomadic people, rather than judge them by their present circumstances.

A universal similarity as nomads

Pastoralists and peripatetics can still be grouped together as nomads, in spite of their differences. Both the pastoral and peripatetic peoples are distinctive, with a different ethos and world view from outsiders. The nomads are ready to move, even when they have been stationary for a long time. Peripatetics, like pastoralists, see a house as a prison and set themselves off as part of the world of travelers distinct from those "who live in houses." If they have a house they will use it for storage, not for living in.

Nomadism is their *preferred* lifestyle, because they are not tied to limited areas of land and the resultant issues of ownership, and because they have developed a measure of self-sufficiency. The traveling life is seen to be superior because it gives them social and economic autonomy to manage their own affairs. The most numerous nomadic pastoralist people are the Fulbe, with eight million, although only a portion of them is nomadic. Mongolia may have more actual nomads. The Gypsies are the largest peripatetic society with 42 million, and not all of them are actually itinerant. But both these peoples value the traditions of independence that nomadism brings. Nomadic people want to be free to be themselves.

Most African pastoralists consider themselves independent peoples, separate and superior to others. The Drok-pa of Tibet's Chang Tang consider themselves pastoralists or keepers of animals, rather than nomads, even though they live in tents and move constantly, seeking pasture. They regard themselves as the animal-rearing section of the wider Tibetan society, but they have their own customs and dialects. The Mongols have found nomadism to be the most viable method of subsistence on the grasslands of the steppe, and so they have a great love for horses. Most nomads wish to maintain their social exclusiveness and do not want to be absorbed into general society.

The nomads' lifestyle is often given a supernatural or moral origin. A surprising number of peripatetics have legends that blame their nomadic life on their misbehavior in the past. These myths often imply that they were once settled folk and their wandering is the result of either a vow or a curse. The Gadulyia Lohar of India have an oath never to settle, because of their alleged cowardice in war centuries ago. The Ghorbati in Iran, Jogi of Afghanistan, Watta of Kenya and the Chenguin of Turkey also carry this idea of past guilt.[11] The Luti

musicians of Iran failed to accept the generosity of the king to settle down as farmers, and so they were condemned to wander.

Many of the pastoralists have myths concerning the divine origin of their people. Some believe they are descendants of some biblical person. The Idaksahak, for example, believe themselves to be descendants of Isaac. The Gaddi say that the god Shiva commissioned them to be shepherds. The Gypsies reinforce their social separation from others by the practice of their rules of purity. The non-Gypsy is considered "unclean" and polluting.

These attitudes are also colored by more mundane reasons that include not being accepted by the surrounding society; their inability to own agricultural land or houses; their avoidance of war or taxation; or simply that other economic opportunities have been denied them. The Riasiti of Pakistan, for example, were peasants made land-less in the twentieth century. The Donkey-cart peoples of South Africa are another example from recent history.

Definition of a nomadic people

We describe nomads, therefore, as people with a sense of identity distinct from that of the rest of society, which they maintain by having occupations that require systematic traveling to marginal resources. The peripatetics maintain their social independence by providing services that the settled population does not provide and traveling to market opportunities for these. The nomadic pastoralists meet most of their needs with the products of the flocks or herds of domestic livestock with which they live and travel, usually seasonally, to use natural or unenclosed pasture.

A nomadic people is
1. a social group conscious of its own distinct identity,
2. whose social structure, way of life and values are formed by a method of subsistence
3. that involves the whole or part of them traveling systematically

3a. only as necessary for subsistence,

3b. usually according to the seasons.

4. They travel in order to bring their main assets -

   4a. livestock in the case of the pastoralists (sheep, goats, cattle, camels, yaks, reindeer, horses or llamas, with one species often having special cultural value)

   4b. skills as craftsmen, entertainers, traders, musicians, genealogists, etc., in the case of the peripatetics

5. to benefit from marginal renewable resources,

   5a. in the natural environment as pasture and grazing in semi-arid areas or unused land in the case of the pastoralists,

   5b. in the demand for services that the surrounding settled society does not wish to provide for itself.

6. Such a society is usually organized on tribal lines,

   6a. some with, but most without, strong central leadership,

   6b. all living and working as decentralized groups as families, extended families or clans according to the demands of 4 and 5, above.

7. Their goal by this lifestyle is to maintain their distinctive identity and values, including a measure of self-sufficiency.

2 To Where the Grass Grows Greener

The nomadic pastoralist's life is shaped by the search for grass in remote areas not used by settled society. We shall now describe this way of life in more detail.

How many pastoralists are there?

It is difficult to estimate the number of nomadic pastoralists, due not only to their mobility and inaccessibility, but also to the large numbers that have been forced out of pastoralism temporarily. It is often difficult to discover what proportion of a people is nomadic. All we can do is cite the various estimates. *The New Internationalist* of April 1995 estimated 40 million. Malcolm Hunter quotes Robert Chambers as giving the number 100 million.[1] An estimate of practicing pastoralists given by the Agricultural Administration Unit of the Overseas Development Institute, London, is as follows:

> North Africa: 1.2 million.
> West Africa: 6.8 million
> East and Southern Africa: 9.3 million
> Middle East and South Asia: 3.4 million
> Central Asia: 1.9+ million
> Total: 22.6 million[2]

These totals may be conservative. Even if we take an arbitrary mean of around 50 million people active in, or preferring, pastoralism as their way of life, we have a significant number of people equal to the population of Britain, or South Korea, or the combined population of the states of California and New York.

These comparisons bring to mind populations united with highly articulate political institutions to speak for them and to defend their interests. In contrast, the pastoralists are dispersed and isolated peoples, surrounded by indifferent populations, with no one to speak for them. They have learned to live within a marginal environment and continue to survive and even thrive, and should be recognized as having found an efficient way of making the least fertile areas of the world productive. To learn from them and serve them we must consider their chief characteristics.

Attachment to their animals

The pastoralists' animals not only give them subsistence, but they also shape their society and the way they think. Humankind began to domesticate animals around 8000 BC, even before animal products such as milk were used. This fact implies that we have a fundamental need to identify with animals for reasons other than subsistence.

The personal standing of each pastoralist depends on his family connections as well as on the number and quality of his animals. Their animals have enabled pastoralists to survive and to have a considerable degree of self-sufficiency. They still idealize self-sufficiency by using all the products of the herd for food, shelter, clothing, transport and tools — even though it is often easier today to get many items from factories.

Each family or individual has their own livestock, for which they are responsible. Only those who are poor herd other people's animals. To lose one's animals in drought or by pest is a disaster that tends to exclude the individual or household from the nomadic society, leaving them without status or role.

The Kazak's introductory greeting is, "May your domestic animals be safe and sound." The family is referred to second. In Mongolia, visitors ask their host three questions: "Is your family well? Are the cattle fat? Is the grass good this year?"[3] A Somali proverb says: "To be without livestock is slavery," and a Boran would say that "a person without livestock does not have a life-spirit."[4] Sarakatsán of Greece consider their sheep the "guard" of their

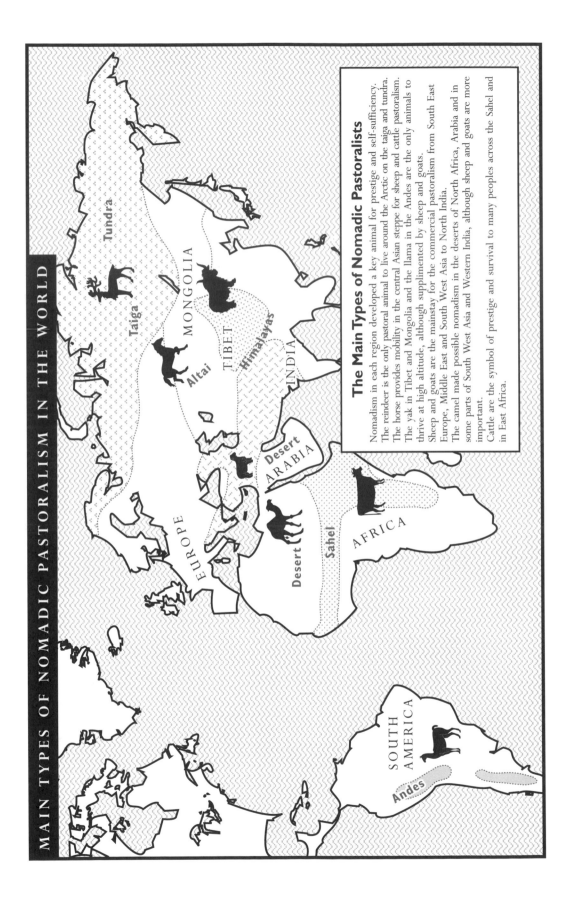

The Main Types of Nomadic Pastoralists

Nomadism in each region developed a key animal for prestige and self-sufficiency. The reindeer is the only pastoral animal to live around the Arctic on the taiga and tundra. The horse provides mobility in the central Asian steppe for sheep and cattle pastoralism. The yak in Tibet and Mongolia and the llama in the Andes are the only animals to thrive at high altitude, although supplimented by sheep and goats.

Sheep and goats are the mainstay for the commercial pastoralism from South East Europe, Middle East and South West Asia to North India.

The camel made possible nomadism in the deserts of North Africa, Arabia and in some parts of South West Asia and Western India, although sheep and goats are more important.

Cattle are the symbol of prestige and survival to many peoples across the Sahel and in East Africa.

family. They are seen as God's animal, displaying ideal characteristics, and to be a shepherd is to be God's image. The "manliness" of the men and a family's prestige all depend on successful shepherding.[5]

The Mursi of Ethiopia see the world as shaped by pastoralism and the nomadic life. Despite their dependence on cultivation, the Mursi continue to have the outlook and values of a pastoral people. All their important social relationships involve the exchange of cattle. More than this, their cattle provide them with a way of looking at the world; the people describe the patterns, shapes and colors of the environment by the color and shape of the horns of their cattle.[6] It is not surprising, therefore, that nomadic pastoralists have a deep emotional attachment to their herds and that their world view has been influenced by them. There are even nomads that name themselves after animals.[7]

Each group of pastoralists associates itself with one key species, even though their herds usually consist of animals from more than one species.[8] The challenge of the natural environment in each region of the world has brought to the fore a particular species that is well adapted to that environment and provides for the basic needs of the pastoralist to live and operate there. Attachment to this key species is their way of identifying themselves with their history and their environment. It is like sports fans who identify themselves with their favorite teams.

In sub-Saharan West Africa and East Africa, cattle are the key animal. In the deserts of North Africa and Arabia it is the camel. In the Balkans, the Caucasus, Southwest Asia and South Asia, sheep and goats have symbolic importance. In the Himalayas, the Tibetan Plateau and northern China, the yak fills this role. Across Central Asia to Mongolia it is the horse; in the Arctic of northern Europe and Siberia the key (and only) pastoral animal is the reindeer; and in the Andes the most important animals are the llama and alpaca. These may not be the most economically important animals today, but in each region they have shaped the way pastoralism has developed.

Cattle confer identity and status in society to most African cattle nomads. In the thinking of the Fulbe or Fulani of West Africa, cattle confer *jawdi*, or wealth, honor and status. The Fulbe are not impressed with practical arguments for pastoralism, such as more protein in the diet, or commercial development. As boys they may have slept cradled by a calf.[9] A Fulani will silently weep for his dead cow. Paul Riesman relates the story of a man who slunk back to camp after his cattle had been stolen. He was berated by his mother, ashamed that he did not fight to the death to defend his cows.[10] In Africa, the loss of one's herd forces a person to become sedentary or urbanized, resulting in loss of self-esteem — even when the person is relatively prosperous.[11] Even the Fulakunda of Senegal, who have been sedentary for a long time, find it a great crisis when they sell their last cow.

When the Boran of Kenya are asked "Who is a Boran?" their response is "people who love cattle."[12] A Wodaabe elder says, "A cow is joy. This is because she gives, she nourishes, she produces. For us a cow means growth, increase. Yes, it is true, a cow is our only security." A cow gives hope, and two heifers are worth more than ten granaries full of millet. "If someone no longer has any cows, he no longer has any friends either."[13] Even Songhai farmers see their cattle as personalities and appreciate having photos of their oxen.[14]

Both the Dinka of Sudan and the Karimojong of northeast Uganda see parallels between the lives of the owners and their cattle. Each man has a particular ox that he imitates in gesture and dance and which bears his name. His well being is thought to be linked to that of the ox, and the ox's fortunes and his own are considered to run in parallel. Thus, when the ox dies, in some sense the man is considered to die as well.[15] The Nuer of Sudan name themselves after a favorite ox. Likewise, they maintain a sharp division between "cattle of women," that are given as a bride-price and never sold, and "cattle of money" that can go to market.[16] The Maasai call their partner "my bull" or "my cow." Generally, African male pastoralists hold agriculture in contempt or see it as work for women.[17] The Fulbe combine it with cattle raising, only reluctantly, seeing their millet-based diet as a way to avoid slaughtering their animals.

The camel is the principal animal right across the Sahara and through Arabia into southern Iran and South Asia. The Bedouin have a special regard for the camel, and the Siraiki of India can not only identify the tracks of each camel, but also memorize eight generations of each animal's ancestry.[18] The camel was first used for caravan transport on the edge of the Arabian Desert. Desert nomadism developed later than shepherding. Various political and commercial factors encouraged some people to develop a subsistence life in the desert, using the camel's full potential as the only animal able to survive in the desert.

Camels can survive up to two weeks without water, but cattle need it every three days. Camels also are less damaging to the environment than cattle or goats, both in grazing and in scuffling the top soil.[19] Away from the Middle East, the Gabbra of north Kenya and the Rabari of west India would not survive without their camels to give them the mobility to get to the rain and the pasture. Today the camel's usefulness has been replaced by the truck and it is more profitable to keep sheep and goats, but many Bedouin still keep some camels for sentimental reasons.[20]

Sheep and goats have enabled minorities enclosed in powerful sedentary states and empires to maintain their distinctive identities. This has been true for nomadic peoples from southeastern Europe to India, and along the southern borders of Russia; including such peoples as the Sarakats·n in Greece and the Turkic tribes of Iran. Repeated attempts to forcibly settle and assimilate these peoples have failed, because their flocks are an essential means of subsistence and trading. The horse is seen as transport suitable for a man, and camels and donkeys for the rest of the family, but these animals do not have the status they have elsewhere. These nomads pride themselves on being self-sufficient as shepherds.

The yak is a high-altitude animal and makes human life possible on the Tibetan Plateau. Like the *dzo*, a cross between the yak and the cow, the yak is a general-purpose animal that can survive at the highest inhabited places on earth. It produces over ten times the milk of a sheep or goat and does so all the year round. The Tibetan drinks its milk, has its butter in his tea, and makes his tents from its hair. Some yaks will be dedicated to the gods in each herd. Sheep and goats are also a vital component of their herds, and traditionally six of them were considered the equivalent of one yak. The yak cannot be grazed with sheep and goats because it pulls up grass by the roots and the pasture takes two or more years to recover.

The galloping horse is the emblem of Mongolia and fermented mare's milk, called *airag*, is the Mongolians' favorite drink.[21] The Tuvinians have their horse buried with them, and a man who does not have a horse is considered not to have a name.[22] The horse gives the pastoralist control of the vast grasslands so that he can raise sheep, yaks and cattle as his main subsistence animals. The horse has enabled the Central Asian nomad to be a formidable adversary. When the Great Wall of China was built to keep the Mongols at bay, the Chinese described these enemies as having the hearts of beasts beating in their breasts.[23] It would, perhaps, be more accurate to ascribe to them the heart of a horse.

The Kazaks and Kyrgyz are also attached to the horse, and they also drink fermented mare's milk, which they call *kumiss*. They will cut off a lock of the hair of a dead animal to continue some contact with it, until they leave the lock at an *ovoo* or sacred cairn as an offering to the gods. However, the Mongols and Kazaks are less emotionally attached and have a functional attitude to their animals.

The reindeer is the only animal that can be domesticated to survive in the *taiga* and *tundra* of the Arctic. To the nomadic Sami,

2a

2b

2 A visit to a Mongol camp:
   a. Erecting a Mongol *ger*. The *ger* is an amazing piece of simple engineering. Covered in felt and canvas it is
      warm in sub-zero winters and acts as a cooling tower in hot summers.
   b. Mongols, as most nomads, are glad to see visitors.

2c

2d

2e

2f

2   c. A love of horses prevails across Central Asia in spite of the adoption of motorcycles and trucks. Here a
       horseman lassos horses in the curral.
    d. Two weather-beaten herders drop in to see the visitors.
    e. Lambs and kids under a month old have to spend the night in the *ger*, but are reunited with their ewes the
       next morning.
    f. Felt boots are still made and worn in winter.

their reindeer represent not only their wealth, but also their whole reason for being.[24] Each Nenet in Siberia keeps a sacred reindeer, to which his well being is linked. Domestication and pastoralism developed from hunting as a better way of managing the reindeer. This is possible because the reindeer herd close together like sheep and follow an older doe as their leader. In this environment little or no cultivation is possible, and the only alternatives to sustain human life would be hunting and fishing. Other pastoral animals need to be sheltered and given a continual supply of imported fodder, while the reindeer survive on lichen.

The llama, alpaca and the guanaco are high-altitude animals of the Andes that were domesticated long ago and no longer seem to exist in the wild. The llama is a pack animal and provides wool and hair as well as meat, although it is temperamental like its cousin, the camel. The Quechua llama herders understand that by caring for their herds they are helping to maintain the order of the cosmos, and that if they failed the world would come to an end.[25]

The pastoralists have a great knowledge of these animals and how they fit into the ecological order. They have an attitude of gratitude and sympathy towards them. However, one cannot assume that even neighboring peoples have the same attitude towards their livestock. Some, like the Nuer and Fulbe, have special cultural concepts about their cattle. Others, such as the Komachi of Iran, who identify themselves as being occupational pastoralists, have a more pragmatic view of their sheep. The animals are as dependent on the pastoralists as the pastoralists are dependent on them. It appears that domestic animals have lost the ability of wild animals to find pasture and water over long distances, so their survival depends on the skill of the pastoralists.

A balanced herd gives security

The composition of the herds is decided according to the quality of pasture, the climate, the species' products, their durability and the herding manpower required. Nomads are able to raise some animals in environments that are not naturally suitable for them, such as horses in the desert, but in general the environment limits the herds to particular types.

The pastoralists can specialize in one species, but most have a variety of animals. Those specializing in only one species tend to have to travel much further to find suitable pasture, and they may suffer the loss of all their animals if conditions are unsuitable for their particular species. Most have responded to diminishing grazing by the diversification of their species. Having a mixture of animals with different grazing and watering requirements — usually cows, camels, sheep and goats — ensures that when conditions are disastrous for one species, the whole herd is not lost. Keeping a mixed herd of different animal types helps to maximize the use of the different browse and fodder available, and also improves the chances of survival in a drought.

Sheep browse on the leaves of the grass, while goats eat the whole grass plant — leaving nothing to grow later. Sheep prefer to be together in large groups of as many as 200 or more — otherwise they scatter and join other flocks. There is some evidence that sheep in small flocks tend to feed less well than those in large ones, with a resulting loss of weight and wool production.[26] Sheep will bunch together and destroy pasture if a billy goat is not there to lead them on. Sheep also need more water than goats, so migration ranges are more limited. Sheep can also lose considerable weight on migration, while goats maintain theirs. Sheep, however, are able to paw away the snow to uncover the grass for the goats.

Goats, like camels, can feed on plants with a bitter taste and a higher salt content than sheep can. Goats are also hardier than sheep, feel the cold less, climb better and can go to higher altitudes.[27] They give warning when threatened by wild animals by bleating, while sheep stay silent. Goats will graze roughly twice the pasture of a sheep, and a buffalo eight times as much. But the goat can give double the amount of milk of a sheep, and for longer periods. In the Himalayas, sheep and goats are used as pack animals, because larger animals have difficulty on the narrow tracks.

As cattle need better grazing material than camels to give milk, cattle produce less milk than camels in the same conditions. Less milk means that fewer humans can be supported, so herds of cattle need to be far larger to sustain the human population. An average family of Gabbra needs 64 cattle or 28 camels to subsist.[28] A few camels may also be kept as symbols of status, beyond the time that they might have any practical use.

Sheep and goats are relatively easy to reproduce to build up a flock after a reversal (loss of stock due to drought, snowfall, disease, etc.), compared to cattle. It requires a long period to build up a herd of camels, but they have always been valued for their ability to carry much heavier loads than any other animal.[29] Many Bedouin in Arabia have switched from camels to sheep. Camels drink more water, but they can go longer without. Sheep breed more quickly and can now be transported to pasture and markets. Mutton is also more marketable than camel meat, and water tankers can take the water to wherever the sheep are. With roads and motor vehicles there is less demand for the camel as a beast of burden, but camels are making a comeback in Mongolia because of the cost of motor fuel.[30] Camels give milk in the dry season, and their milk has a higher vitamin C content than cattle milk.

The products (wool, milk, butter, yogurt, blood, leather, hair, carrying capacity and meat), as well as the demands of prestige and ritual, determine the composition of herds. Commercial exchange of the herd's products has been always more important in Asia, but there is now a large market for mutton in the Middle East, and a growing demand for beef in Africa.

Diversification has the disadvantage, however, of needing more herders, since each species has differing needs. Nine people need to work nine hours a day, all year round, to support an average Gabbra family.[31] Clearly, co-operative systems between families are needed — especially for families with fewer working members.

Having different species in a single herd, therefore, gives security in meeting the different conditions and available pasture or forage because at least one species will thrive while another merely survives. Also, the various products of the different species can be bartered or sold to meet changing markets.

Systematic migration for pasture

Nomadic pastoralism is an industry, because it is organized activity for the manufacture or extraction of animal products. The movement of migration is not random, but involves the systematic use of natural pasture. The nomad sees the fertility of the land as a free resource to support those who understand how to manage it. Land is not so much possessed as it is held in common, for use according to the seasonal renewal of its natural vegetation. Pastoral migration is planned use of these seasonal and local variations of growth. On the other hand, to the cultivator, the land itself is the main asset — social position is determined by land ownership, which involves the right to decide its use (usually to the exclusion of others).

Although the pastoralists do not usually desire to own land, there are inevitable conflicts with farmers. Irrigation has made possible the extension of agriculture into grazing lands, which has disrupted the migratory pattern of many nomads. The use of fertilizers has also broken the reciprocal relationship of the cattle fertilizing the fields in return for grazing on the stubble. But there can be conflict when the animals break into the fields to eat the young plants of the crop. Use of chemical fertilizer means the farmer plows in the stubble and fences off the fields so the nomad cannot use them. Bush burning is still practiced and is detrimental both to farmers and to the herds that could graze on the bushes.

Most nomads and individual clans or tribes have a traditional or ideal route, with grazing areas allocated by tribal custom or by agreement with neighboring leaders.[32] These routes or territories often take on a cultural meaning. But environmental conditions often dictate changing this in

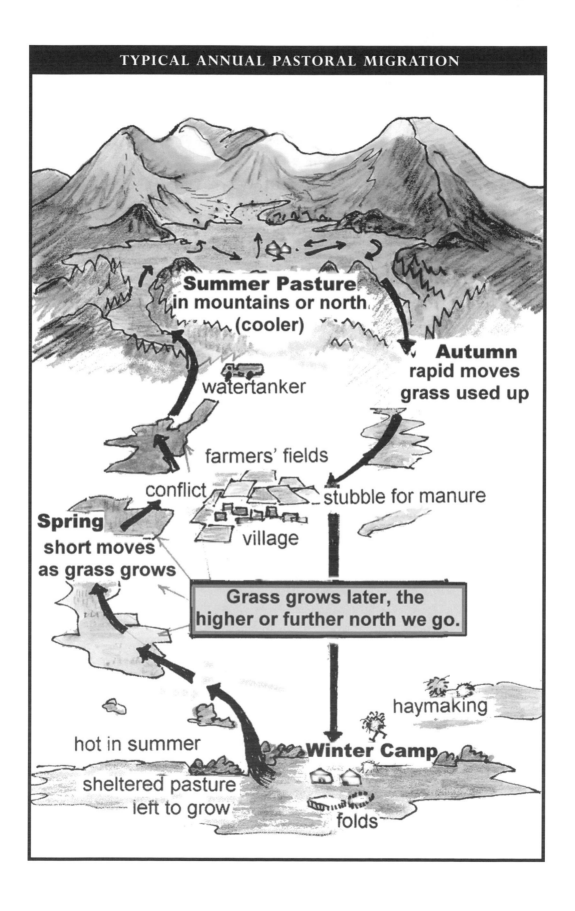

TYPICAL ANNUAL PASTORAL MIGRATION

Summer Pasture
in mountains or north
(cooler)

Autumn
rapid moves
grass used up

watertanker

farmers' fields

conflict

stubble for manure

village

Spring
short moves
as grass grows

Grass grows later, the
higher or further north we go.

haymaking

hot in summer

Winter Camp

sheltered pasture
left to grow

folds

part — and sometimes tribes have to move right out of their traditional area. The less fertile the area, the greater the annual variations of route and distance covered. They also have areas that they do not use for long periods but that they keep as reserve pasture for times of drought.

Most pastoralists have an annual pattern of migration, usually moving between two main areas that provide winter and summer pastures and making use of the seasonal differences of climate and vegetation growth. The grass grows later in the year in the more northern regions and at higher altitudes, and these areas are cooler in summer. These types of migration can be described in general terms as follows:

1. *Vertical migration* is movement between lower and higher altitudes to benefit from the fact that spring comes later in the mountains, so that after the grass on the lower plains has grown and been grazed, the herds move higher for other, later growing, grass. Moving between the two altitudes also avoids excessive heat, cold or rainfall, which are detrimental to the health and feeding of most species, but especially to cattle and sheep. The horizontal distance between low and high pastures may be as short as 15 kilometers (9 mi.). Characteristically, winter is spent in a lowland area, and camp may be changed a number of times as pasture is used up, or the animals may be kept in shelters and fed with hay or other feed.

As spring advances the pastures on the route begin to grow, and migration is gradual according to that growth. Some nomads have a spring pasture location at a moderate altitude or distance before moving higher or further for the summer. On arrival in the summer pastures, periodic changes of camp may be necessary as the grass is grazed. Local factors, such as using southern slopes to shield the animals from north winds, or using a particular pasture before it withers in the heat, also affect the location of the camps. Autumn migration is usually more rapid in order to arrive in the lowland or more southern area before the onset of winter, and because after the hot summer

the pasture on the route has already been used up. In Mongolia, however, pastoralists spend the winter in a sheltered part of the mountain to avoid the heavy snowfall below, and then move down to the valley in summer.

2. *Horizontal migration* occurs when the seasonal change is due to local rainfall or floods, or the movement is between northern and southern areas. The Nenets move between the *tundra* in the summer, away from the boggy birch forests of the *taiga*, where they shelter in the winter. They may have to travel as far as 1,900 kilometers (1,180 mi.) to get the change in pasture (as do the Basseri in Iran and the Al Murrah Bedouin). There are exceptions to this pattern of migrations between north and south. The Al Murrah Bedouin spend the summer in the south, close to their wells in the Empty Quarter, making forays for pasture out and back again. But they move north in winter because the rains near the Iraqi border provide the best forage for their range. The Macina Fulbe move out of the Niger Delta when the Niger floods, and then move back when the grass has grown as the floods recede.

3. Alternatively, in some areas there are no physical features (e.g. flood areas or mountains) that give different seasonal growth periods. These "horizontal" nomads have their camp at a central point and graze the pasture systematically in rotation around it. This rotational pattern is followed in East Africa, where a central camp is established with huts for the families and a *kraal* for the livestock. The animals in Africa need to be defended from large predators, as well as from thieves, far more than in Asia. The herds are taken out each day in different directions and often the men will take them a considerable distance, setting up a temporary camp in order to avoid moving the main camp. As the pasture is used up over a period of time, however, the main camp has to be moved to a new location. But the huts are left to be re-used when the pastures grow again.

A similar pattern is followed by the Drok-pa, in the very different environment on the Tibetan Plateau. Here, any climatic change affecting the growth of forage would mean migrations of great distances. A central camp is established, from which the herds travel out to distant mountain pastures in the summer, leaving the pasture closer to the camp for the winter. At this altitude there is no agriculture and the area can be grazed systematically.

Whatever the system, natural pasture is usually found on the migration route. Stubble from farmers' fields may be available in return for the natural fertilizer of the animals. The increase in cultivated land at the expense of natural grass in northern Syria has increased the size of the flocks for a time, as more stubble from unprofitable barley crops replaced the natural grass. The nomads move to cultivated areas for the stubble, rather than search for natural pasture. Trucks are also able to transport animals, water and fodder to parts of the steppe that otherwise would not be reached.[33] Conflict with farmers en route, and even with other nomads, is common when the routes are crowded — as, for example, at mountain passes.

A migration route usually includes a place for social gatherings such as weddings, festivals or co-operating in some task, such as well digging, tent making or carpet weaving. In Iran the spring migration is the time for the eligible girls to ride on camels in their best clothes, and they negotiate marriages upon arrival at the summer pasture. On the other hand, many of the Drok-pa may not see members of the same clan for an entire lifetime.[34]

The different species are often separated to graze or browse in different areas to provide nourishment most suitable for each species. Cattle must graze before sheep, because the latter clip the grass too short for them, while goats and yaks are taken to higher altitudes than sheep. Water and pasture are often not found in the same place. Even when, at a particular stage of the migratory cycle, there is good pasture where the animals can stay for a time, the herds may still have to be taken between pasture and water at regular short intervals. This interval varies according to species and time of year, as well as to whether a water tanker is available! Fifty years ago the Fulbe Jeeri in Senegal moved more often, but since the introduction of boreholes for water they have been able to stay in one place for longer.[35] Lambing and calving, milking and shearing also must be taken into account as part of the migration pattern. Tibetan shepherds (even children) must constantly look out for ewes about to lamb. The ewe hives off away from the flock and the lamb needs to be carried back to the flock, before the wolves or eagles attack.

The pastoralist's mobility helps him to avoid areas of drought, the extremes of heat or cold, stormy weather, waterlogged ground and various causes of infection such as the tsetse fly. Detrimental conditions can soon affect the livestock such that the nomad's fortunes go into catastrophic decline. The nomad is always alert for local changes in rainfall and other conditions that differ from year to year.

Variations in local conditions due to weather and other factors mean that the direction, distance and timing of any given migration will vary, and much depends on the experience of the leadership of each camping group.[36] Wrong decisions can be made. In the drought of 1972-73 the JeerikooBe sought to stay by their wells, but the lack of pasture, in spite of the continuous water supply, resulted in the loss of a great number of animals. In the next drought, in 1983, they followed the migration pattern they used before the wells were dug, using the pasture and previous water supply. They were not diverted off their course to the abundant water supply from the wells, and they fared far better.[37] Some peoples, such as the Qashqa'i in Iran, have set times in the spring to move from winter to mountain pastures. The whole peoples of many tribes move in the same period. In the Zagros Mountains, the police have often interfered to set timetables for the migrations, irrespective of pastoral conditions.

There is a critical size of herd — above which it is difficult to sustain pasture, and below which independence as a nomad is difficult. Sometimes surplus wealth from pastoralism is converted into buying farmland, to be used as an insurance against hard times, but that can result in nomads settling. The loss of mobility results in the breakdown of the elaborate system that balanced the potential of the environment with subsistence.

The efficient use of the least fertile areas

Nomadic pastoralists are the only people to productively use the arid or semi-arid *one third* of the earth's surface.[38] Nomadic pastoralists live in seven main areas of the world:

1) The 4,800 kilometer-long Sahel (3,000 mi.), covering parts of Mauritania, Senegal, Mali, Burkina Faso, Niger, Chad and western Sudan.
2) Eastern Africa — in such countries as Ethiopia, Sudan, Somalia and Kenya.
3) The Middle East, including Africa north of the Sahara.
4) Southwest Asia (Iran and Afghanistan, with areas of the Caucasus).
5) Central and inner Asia, from the Caspian through the Turkic Republics to Mongolia, and the north and west of China. 52% of the land area of China is classed as pastoral grassland.[39]
6) The Himalayas, South Asia and the Tibetan Plateau and related parts of China.
7) The Russian and Scandinavian Arctic.[40]

Europe and Latin America have limited areas where nomadic pastoralism can be practiced, such as the Andes and the Balkans.

These lands can rarely be developed for agriculture or for enclosed grazing, because of the low or unreliable rainfall. In the Andes and Tibet, the high altitude and very short growing season means there can be no competition from farmers to use the land. In the area of reindeer nomadism, the ground is frozen or too cold for any meaningful agriculture. So the main environmental reason for nomadic pastoralism is the limited fertility of the ground.

Lack of water is not the only

consideration, for sometimes too much water disrupts the careful balance needed for pastoralists to utilize the natural grasslands. The drilling of bore holes to provide a constant source of water, where there was little or none previously, has encouraged farmers to invade the grasslands. They exhaust the soil with irrigation cultivation and then move on. Such irrigation has destroyed pastures by salinization in places as far apart as West Africa, India, Turkey and Central Asia. A constant supply of water has also persuaded pastoralists to change their migration patterns, sometimes with disastrous results, because although the animals have water, the mere presence of water has not produced sufficient grass.

The Fulbe of West Africa move away from the rain because of the threat of the tsetse fly infecting the cattle. In the steppes of Asia, water in the form of swift rivers proved to be a barrier to pasture. Kazaks became skilled bridge builders using the limited available materials of reeds and inflated sheep-skins. This involved the co-operation of large numbers of men.[41] Excess water can also be a problem in southern Iran during the winters, because the plains become too marshy and the sheep can suffer hoof rot. But the Basseri and Qashqa'i, for example, have experienced winters when the rains fail and they have had to rely on government supplied fodder.

Snow is a threat across Central Asia. In northwest Sichuan, in early 1996, 31 days of snowfall with temperatures of minus 45°C, after five years of drought, killed 50% of the livestock — including 35,000 yaks and 21,500 sheep. Seven hundred Golok nomad families lost all their herds. Nomads in Siberia revere fire, but it can also be a hazard, destroying the grasslands. In early 1996, 72 different grass fires raged across 13 of Mongolia's provinces, destroying eight million hectares (20 million acres) and thousands of cattle. Only a heavy snowfall finally extinguished the fire.

Until recently, pastoralists have had no competitors wanting to use these lands. But today they face invasion from agriculture or from mineral and oil exploitation.[42] The nomads are the only people able to extract subsistence, and often commercial production, from land that would otherwise be unproductive.

The use of non-pastoral resources

We have seen that the nomadic pastoralists are pastoralists by preference and nomads as necessary. Being nomadic gives them an ability to adapt to various conditions and resources and temporarily or seasonally adopt other lifestyles.

Nomadic pastoralists often mix sedentary and migratory periods, and this is especially true when part of the family has settled for agriculture, casual work or schooling. In Syria during the 1960s the Bedouin took the opportunity to become sedentary by investing in barley cultivation, which also made more fodder and stubble available for their flocks.[43] Nomads can make a transition from nomadism to various forms of settlement or back to nomadism, according to economic opportunity or pressure from war or officials. Families in the same clan or village can have differing strategies — between full nomadism, semi-nomadism and settled pastoralism. Only a few peoples have been able to rely exclusively on their herds, such as the Sami (Lapps), Maasai and Bedawib Beja.[44] Nomads have been counted as settled (as having abandoned nomadism) because they have a house, grow crops for a season or two, or because members of the family seek employment in other activities.[45]

In Central Asia and Mongolia there is evidence of a return to nomadic pastoralism, as an answer to the uncertainty of the new independent economies. After being compelled by force to turn themselves into agricultural villagers, their tents having been burned and their leaders exiled by the first Shah, many nomads in Iran, such as the Lur and Qashqa'i, reverted to nomadic pastoralism years afterward when the Shah was deposed. In Saudi Arabia the Bedouin are asking the government to give small-scale agricultural plots for individual ownership where they can grow alfalfa and other feed products to fatten animals and provide a security against drought.[46]

Some of the cattle peoples of Africa disdain agriculture as "digging in the dirt." But in practice they, like pastoralists elsewhere, reluctantly take any opportunity to grow various crops, from millet to date palms, to provide food for themselves and fodder for their animals. This prevents them from having to trade precious animals for these commodities. The Jallube Fulbe in Mali, for example, have learned to grow millet — and the combination of millet and cattle are a strategy for survival. In drought, when their herds are lost, the millet not only keeps them in their lands but also gives them time to build up their herds again.[47]

An example of a flexible response to economic opportunities comes from Southwest Asia. Salzman lists six sources of resources used by the Shah Nawazi Baluch: sheep and goats for milk, butter, meat, wool and hair; camels for transport; date palms for fruit and rope fiber; trade caravans and raiding peasant settlements for food, jewelry, carpets and slaves; irrigation agriculture for grain (this work was formerly done by slaves, but is now done by migrant non-Baluch labor); and in hunting and gathering that yields both game and wild vegetables. All of these except raiding, and to a certain extent hunting, continue.[48] The Yarahmadzai (Shah Mazazi) Baluch of Iran also co-ordinate the three resources of goat, sheep and camel pastoralism, date palm cultivation and dry land grain cultivation.[49]

There are other examples of combining resources. The Nuer combine fishing and horticulture with cattle herding, as do the Buduma on the islands in Lake Chad.[50] The Tibetan Drok-pa are well-known for gathering salt from the lakes on the Chang Tang, using their sheep for transport. The salt has been sold into Nepal as far as the Indian border. Goats were of less value among Tibetan and Mongol nomads until the international market in cashmere expanded.[51] The Borana choose two sons for continuing as herdsmen and send the others to school to prepare for non-pastoral jobs. The Sherpas were originally yak herders from Kham Tibet, who in the early twentieth century developed a reputation as

Inuit

Inupiat
Napaaq turmuit
Yupik
Innu

Kaale

Scottish Travellers
Irish Travellers
English Travellers
Gypsies

Gyps

Gypsies
Irish Travellers
Carnival Workers

Gypsies

Gypsies
Merche

Moussa

Vlack Rom

Mu'allmin
Ighyuwn

Imraguen
LawBe
MaabuBe

Nemadi
Inao
Somono
So

LawB
'Yan gog
Akw

Fleteros

Vlack Rom

Patagonians

The Peripatetics or Commercial Nomads

All over the world there are distinct societies, that travel to satisfy limited needs for their services. They are found on the streets, in markets and fairs, or attached to a nomadic pastoralist people. They work as black and silversmiths, wood-carvers, tanners and leather workers, musicians, acrobats, caravaners, fortune-tellers, magicians, hawkers of herbal medicines, toy makers, genealogists, drapers, snake-charmers, scrapmetal collectors, weavers, snake charmers, bear and monkey trainers, and even ear-cleaners.

Nganasans

Komi   Yukaghir

Ømstreifere   Yupik

ttare   Itel'men

izigers   Udeghe

Gypsies

Gypsies   Kowli

nisch   Mughal

Gypsies   Karachi   Sinte

Lom

Chingene   Luti

Tahtaci   Badakhshi

Ghorbati   Sheihk-Mohammadi

Nawar   Kouchi Jats   Be-Da

Halebi   Luti   Siraiki   Humli-khyampa

Halebi   Qalandar

Ghagar   Mirasi   Gadulyia

Lohars

Azza   Dorze

Fuga

Hauda   Bazigar   Bajau

Manna   Yibro   Kanjar

Waata   Midgan   Jogi

Tumalod   Marwari

Chungar

Charan

Churigar

Rajis

Bajaniya

Sarwa   Siyar Marwa

Kalbelia

Nandiwalla

Birhor

Kewats

Luri

The Hunter-Gatherers (underlined on map)

These are societies that rely on the natural provision of food and other materials within a reasonable distance for their means of travel. The resources are naturally renewable with the seasons, and not competed for by other humans. These peoples opt not to domesticate or cultivate. They are hunters, fishermen, and collectors of fruit, roots and materials to make their cloths, utensils and homes. They travel regularly to exploit differing growth seasons and animal and fish migrations. There are hundreds of peoples who are, or have been, hunter-gatherers, but we show only those mentioned in the text.

porters for Western mountaineers, although they themselves had always kept away from the mountains. Today half of them live from tourism and hire local Nepalese to do the portage.[52]

The nomads often consider raiding a legitimate activity rather than a crime. Raiding the herds of other tribes is, or was, depending on policing, a common method of replenishing herd numbers lost in drought. The deliberate raiding of farmers' crops to feed their cattle is also common. Raiding develops skills that make them good recruits for armies. Eighty per cent of a sample of Bedouin families had one member in the Reserve National Guard, perhaps to catch the raiders. Other nomads may organize smuggling and caravans, or, as is increasingly the case, become migrant unskilled laborers on behalf of settled villagers, gathering firewood or working as masons or road builders.[53]

Nomadism creates an ability to adapt to changing opportunities created by new resources and markets. Nomadic pastoralists can make a considerable number of adaptations in their lifestyle in order to preserve their society and culture. The nomad has the traditions of experience of his relatives or forebears having adapted to different lifestyles, in which nomadism is an ideal, rather than the regular reality. This may involve a change of territory, species of livestock, or a measure of settling in order to preserve what is considered more essential to their identity.

3 Who You Know, not What You Own

Nomads keep themselves distinct and ready to move when conditions dictate. They therefore emphasize relationships with their own kind — especially their close relatives. Their identity and security is in who and what they can take with them and in their relationships with others on the route. This identity depends on belonging to a mobile society with its social relationships, customs and even concealed rites and terminology. These are in contrast to, and sometimes in conflict with, those around them.

Sedentary people stress what they possess, particularly the ownership of a house and land. This gives them location — not only geographically but also socially — as part of a neighborhood, town or country. Nomads stress the use of the naturally produced resources of the land, as provided for all. They do not focus on the abstract concept of ownership that inevitably limits who has the right to use it. We turn now to consider a number of characteristics held in common by pastoralists and peripatetics.

Interdependence with settled people

The concept of interdependence appears to contradict the ideal of independence the nomad cultivates, as well as the stereotype most people have. We have seen that peripatetics or commercial nomads naturally have to depend on the surrounding society.

But pastoral nomadism, with few exceptions, has also usually been practiced in conjunction with the surrounding settled society. From biblical times, pastoralists have formed part of an economic system linking cultivators and commerce with themselves. Pastoralists need stable relationships with their neighbors — for peaceful land use, and for grain and other products of town and village — if they are not to deplete their herds.[1]

Like the Bedouin before them, forced into the desert by political interference and commercial opportunity, the Maasai, Turkana and Wodaabe became pastoralists in the mid-nineteenth century due to European colonization.[2] The Wodaabe became more nomadic to avoid being integrated into Fulbe states. The different forms of nomadism are responses to wider human events as much as they are responses to the environment. The Fulbe have managed to be a people apart, even when semi-settled, because of their alliances and trade and market relationships with farming communities.[3]

Today the "nomads of the nomads," the Al Murrah, in Arabia depend on their sedentary neighbors or less mobile nomads for dates, mutton, clothes, tools and weapons. The Bedouin in Oman, some of whom, like the Harasis tribe, live in a part of the Empty Quarter, trade daily in the markets in a number of towns on the edge of the desert. Many of the men also work in unskilled jobs in the nearby oil industry. Their livestock products are exchanged for fodder, fish, clothes and other goods.[4]

In Kalat, in Baluchistan, three groups co-exist: farmers cultivating cash crops, semi-nomadic villagers who carry out subsistence cultivation and migrate with livestock, and Brahui who are true pastoralists. Workers and produce are exchanged between all three. When the Brahui descend to the Kachhi plain they rely partly on the stubble and fodder of the non-Brahui to see their flocks through the winter.

An interesting example of these interrelationships is the trade contact between Nepali semi-nomads and the yak herding nomadic Dolpo of western Nepal. The latter trade barley and corn for salt with the Drok-pa nomads in Xizang (Tibet). The Dolpo then return to central Nepal with the salt and exchange it for more grain from the Rong-pa, who are shepherds using sheep and goats as carriers. They in turn trade with

India to the south, so that Tibetan nomads, Nepali nomads and Nepali farmers all co-operate to serve further sedentary populations. Between them there is suspicion and disdain, as each considers itself better than the other, but together they form part of an economic system. This trade also involves interaction between Shamanism, Lamaistic Buddhism and Hinduism.[5]

Many, such as the Fulbe and Shuwa Arabs, combine nomadic herding groups with semi-settled agropastoral villages of their own people, in a system of interrelated economic and lifestyle options. Various groups of the Fulbe have had dependent peoples, either as slaves or as client peoples, providing agricultural products and even participating in aspects of pastoralism and securing pasture.[6] Others have regular contact through middlemen who are of the same or a similar ethnic group, in a village or town near to their migration route.[7] The middleman stores fodder and other goods, provides stores and advances loans for the pastoralists.

Other nomadic societies see themselves as the pastoral section of a wider society. In some countries, like Tibet and Mongolia, nomadic pastoralists form an integral part of the country's economy.[8] The Tibetan Drok-pa provide the wool and meat for the Rong-pa, or valley people, as the latter provide barley and other goods for the nomads. Down in the valley the nomads become subject to government regulations and agencies. In Kazakstan, most Kazaks became sedentary due to the Soviet policy of collectivization. These Kazaks include the clan and horde leaders to whom the few remaining nomadic Kazaks are subject. Although there is pride and disdain on both sides of the nomad/non-nomad divide, there is still an essential economic interdependence.

The Khans of the Iranian nomads and the Imirs of the Bedouin live a sedentary life in the large cities and serve as the traditional intermediaries with the political system of the country. Today, in Iran, these leaders have been marginalized because of the hostility generated between the tribes and the state by the Shahs. Today permission to migrate has to be gained from government officials, but the social dynamics between the former nomads who are sedentary and the remaining nomads is a vital link both for them and for those who wish to contact them.

Although migratory herdsmen frequently enjoy a standard of living comparable, or superior, to that of the adjacent settled agriculturists, the latter depreciate them as "hill-billies."[9] Both cultivators and pastoralists utilize land that is marginal in terms of its water supply, which results in considerable tension between the two groups — especially when cattle trample or eat the crops. Such incursions may be tolerated because the cattle do provide much needed fertilizer for the fields' crops.[10]

Today, the symbiotic relationships between farmers and pastoralists are undergoing change in many parts of Africa. Because what was once pasture is becoming cultivated land, cultivators are using profits to invest in livestock (and thus are competing with pastoralists). Also, as money replaces barter, trade between farmers and pastoralists is becoming less stable.

Nomadic pastoralists are usually interdependent with sedentary agricultural communities, having a customary trading relationship with either a group of their own people or with another people group. Although they gain their main subsistence for most of the year from domestic animals living off natural forage and must move wherever pasture and water is available, they do not form an isolated social group.[11]

For kith and kin

A nomad's present-day relationships are defined by his ancestors. Most nomadic societies can be described as tribal, and this means that their unity is based on real or assumed relationships by descent. This affiliation with larger related groups gives protection or power to settle disputes, because nomads spend most of their lives in small isolated groups.[12] "Kinsmen should be as the thorn fence protecting the encampment," says a Somali poem. Without kin a person is helpless, and this is particularly true in the herding groups and camps.[13]

Many nomadic peoples are decentralized or segmental tribal societies. They may have traditions of an elaborate structure, but in practice, and often because of the conditions of their nomadism, there is little co-operation beyond the extended family or lineage. The traveling groups consist of one or two related families, and they meet as a lineage or clan perhaps once a year, but they consult more often if necessary. This is becoming the norm as the modern state resents any alternative political structure to its own bureaucracy. Whatever the present structure, kin is still very important to nomads whose lifestyle means they do not have close neighbors.

While the local groups in East Africa are related by descent, there is no political hierarchy outside these local groups to unite them or make decisions for them. The Gabbra of Kenya and Ethiopia have survived in their harsh environment due to nomadism, hard work and social co-operation. The social cohesion is based on the leadership exerted by the local elders.[14]

The nomad spends life in a small group, or in a temporary village of related families. The composition of a group has to balance close family ties with the practical demands of the means of support. All the family is involved with the work as a way of life, from the youngest to the oldest.

Pastoralists may work with each family or extended household caring for its own animals, or they may co-operate with other families to share the work.[15] The size of the "household," even if living in a tent, varies, but usually consists of a nuclear family of three or four generations. The practical pastoral work requires that camp groups vary in size and composition constantly, according to the season or the stage of migration. When the pasture is poor or patchy, even the smallest groups will disperse over a wider area. The composition of the herds themselves is another factor. Mixed herds require more labor, as each species has different breeding and grazing requirements. More herders are needed for the winter care of the animals and for the migrations than for summer pasturing.

The Gadulyia Lohar form small family traveling groups determined by the number of patrons on each circuit. They meet together twice a year when traveling is not possible, when outstanding affairs are decided by their council of elders.[16]

To ensure security on the migrations from stock thieves and predators, a number of groups will usually merge to travel together. The distance between pastures, the weather and quality of grazing sites can also affect the size of the groups. The rights to various pastures also have a bearing on the composition of the groups. Some pastures may be permanently assigned to the larger group or family, while others may be allocated annually. In some cases the grasslands are grazed in a competitive way, on the basis of "first come first served," and those who come later may not find sufficient grazing.[17] Generally, the pastoralists that do not have a prejudice against doing some agriculture also tend to stay together better.

Regular watering places become opportunities both for social encounter and for co-operation in well digging and drawing the water for the herds.[18] This co-operation means that nomad women can have a greater importance than women among sedentary peoples. The influence of wives is sometimes far greater than the formal conception of the society and the initial studies made by outsiders would indicate.[19] Certainly the restrictive aspects for women in Islam are usually more relaxed in nomadic camps. The division of tasks between men and women can also affect the composition of the group.

The herding groups may often include people who are not related, but who are willing to live together. Poorer nomads or even outsiders may be hired as shepherds and herders and join the camp. Pastoral peoples vary considerably on the measure of equality or support they give to their less fortunate members.

The Komachi have a class system based

on the size of their flocks and the number of poor shepherds they employ. The system of contracting the shepherds tends to perpetuate the shepherds' poverty, and referring to them as "servants" or "slaves" reinforces a class-consciousness. This grading is also expressed by poorer gifts being given to them at social gatherings, while the wealthy have imported goods. The shepherds' tents, clothes and diet are poorer, and their infant morality is higher.[20]

The Bororo in West Africa, like the rest of the Fulbe, have no castes, and the family is very important to them. They loan animals to both kin and friends, irrespective of their present wealth or status. And, because they do not have the extra help of servants or slaves, they tend to keep one species, their cattle. Not being able to rely on another species, their response to famine or conflict is to move to another area. But they are also more flexible to do this, because families move independently.

In Iran, the Qashqa'i encourage poorer relatives to work for them and so stay in pastoralism. But their neighbors, the Basseri and Lur, have no tradition of helping those of their people who have lost their animals. Such people are compelled to leave and live in the towns and become "nomads in waiting."

Both the Tuareq of Mali and the Komachi of Iran have had stratified societies according to wealth. The Tuareq have a caste system in which the *imajêghên*, or warriors, have the largest herds and many servants working for them.[21] They used to draw these servants from their slave and vassal castes (although with the impact of French colonialism and modern life, and with the end of slavery and feudalism and with economic changes, Tuareq society has loosened). The Tuareq also mix different species in their herds that require more herders to manage — this used to be possible because they had subordinate workers. This enables them to survive better in a famine. If necessary they will loan animals, but only within their caste. The advantage of the warriors is that they have almost exclusive land rights.

Leadership

The traveling group forms around the headman or leader and may be named after him, and most of the group will consist of his relatives and those of his wife. Leadership of a camp is primarily determined by a man's skill in pastoralism (or, for peripatetics, his commercial skill) or hereditary leadership within the family. His authority depends ultimately, however, on being right in his decisions concerning pasturage and on his ability to resolve conflicts. Such a man among the Baluch, for example, is considered a man of "riches and good speech."[22]

Decision-making may be done at almost any level, according to the custom of the people. The decisions to move may often be taken by one individual leader, but usually seeking the consensus of the heads of families or clans in the group. An individual's decisions are limited by the collective decision making, which may be divided between household or camp, or clan. Consensus helps to hold together sufficient numbers of families for security. Individualism is also found among some nomads, for example in Saudi Arabia, where the Bedouin insist that government help is given to households rather than to tribal groups, because "even brothers will fight." The headman may oversee the practical management of the pastoral work, such as interpreting the weather, the move to pasture and water sources and distance to markets, but often in consultation with the heads of households in the group.

Some of the key decisions involve when and which way to migrate and the allocation of the pastures. The Fulbe in Niger elect a *ruga*, or manager, who decides the routes, times and animal types for the pasture. He also settles disputes between the Fulbe and other peoples, especially farmers, on the migrations.[23] Pasture may be allocated by custom, or according to who arrives first, or by a higher authority such as a Khan. Increasingly in some countries, such as Iran, the state is directly, or indirectly, taking over decisions about migration and the allocation of pasture.

The Turkana of Kenya have no hierarchy of chiefs. Each individual owns his herd and decides his own migration route. When there is a dispute, the "older men" arbitrate for them. Among the Yarahmadzai Baluch, decision making is a contractual arrangement of consultation between equal heads of households. This includes deciding which families settle to do agriculture and which continue in pastoralism. But lineage elders make political decisions.[24]

Larger than the nomadic family group is a hierarchical structure of the tribe or tribes of the people. Many peoples have a traditional hierarchy of leadership that links all the local family groups together. Local extended families are related in a lineage, and a number of lineages form a clan, and the clans form a tribe. A number of tribes may also be united as a confederation.

These elaborate hierarchical structures only developed to maintain political control when nomadic societies had to contend with, or join, powerful empires. Barfield shows that the hierarchies tended to be adopted by peoples living further east, across the Middle East to Asia and Mongolia.[25] The Arabs and the pastoralists across Central Asia were in constant contact and conflict with sedentary powers. For a period the nomads, with either the horse or the camel, were directly involved in these power struggles. The Bedouin extracted "protection" money from the cities around the Fertile Crescent, and the Mongol and Turkic peoples formed Genghis Khan's cavalry to advance across Asia.

In the nineteenth century, with the struggle between the British, Russian and Ottoman Empires, the nomadic tribes of Iran and Afghanistan formed big flexible confederations. With the rise of the independent nation-states, these nomadic confederations have lost power, sometimes after a fight, and their political and administrative role has been taken over by police and other agencies of the national governments. Probably the development of strong leaders by the Asian and Middle Eastern pastoralists in confederations, who were usually wealthy and politically powerful men in the towns, has helped them to have a role in the wider society.

When visiting a small holding in Central Asia, with now only six sheep instead of hundreds, with only two cows and three horses, my Kyrgyz host showed me, with much enthusiasm, a book classifying the tribal structure of his people. He pointed around the room to show me the directions of the parts of the country where they were settled. The trauma of two generations of brutally enforced collectivization had not diminished the significance of this social system to this young man who had never experienced their original nomadism.

Nomadic peoples, like the Tuaregs, the Bedouin and the Turkic and Mongol groups, used to have elaborate political structures, in confederations under ruling families at the different levels. But these have usually been either co-opted into national administration or removed in the course of changes brought about in the twentieth century. Today all nomadic peoples have to deal with the bureaucracy and police of the country in which they are situated. The local clan or extended family group has become more important, because the tribal and confederation organizations have less power and influence.

The Mongols complain of lack of co-operation in the post-Communist era, and they regret the passing of the collectives and state farms that imposed organization on them. Their own solution has been to form traditional *xot ayl*, that is, co-operative pastoral groups of three to twelve closely related families. They work together and camp together if there is sufficient pasture. Unrelated families can join by being "adopted" as kin. They say that being merely neighbors, using the same natural resources, is not sufficient to "bring us together." This adoption was the only way to create the mutual trust for economic co-operation.[26]

The authority of these groupings varies considerably. Because nomadism requires leadership at the local level, these larger social groupings only have an influence on marriages and other liaisons between families, the allocation of pasture, relationships with outside authorities and the settling of disputes. The system for leadership and meeting together varies according to need, since only a small percentage of the people may have any need to know each other. But these larger groupings do play a part in giving a sense of wider identity to the people.

However, both tribes and confederations of tribes are created according to political need. They are not as ancient as the traditions and supposed genealogies might claim. In actual fact, the identity of ethnic groups undergoes change from time to time. Some groups have been formed quite recently and may include a number of people from different ethnic origins. The more removed one gets from the local pastoral groups, the more political the unity — without any pretense of biological relationships. There is a tension between the needs of nomadic work that requires relatively small groups moving semi-independently. This formal structure, therefore, is not always long lasting or stable. Tracing one's descent, and therefore loyalty, through the male line, only marrying cousins etc., makes the bond across clans and tribes a fragile one, and feuds are common. The higher levels of leadership are needed to settle these disputes, or allocate pasture, and negotiate with outside authorities.

The situation in Tibet was different, because a feudal system operated there before 1959. The land was under the control of powerful people who were not of the nomadic society. The majority of nomads were pastoral "peasants," not tribes. They were loyal to, and economically dependent upon, a noble landlord or monastery who allocated their pasture and to whom they had to pay tribute. They were not free to move. The nomads themselves were divided into classes according to wealth and the poor, who had few animals, worked for the more fortunate. These classes persisted until Communism enforced an equality of livestock in 1981, but they have reappeared since the abandonment of the communes.[27]

The societies of nomads vary considerably, but it is still true for most that the ties of the larger circle of relatives and the demands of the lifestyle combine to produce a close-knit society.

In tune with the supernatural

Religion is a fundamental motivating influence in the life of nomads — in their culture and morality. Peripatetics often adopt and adapt the major religion of their "host" society. The vast majority of the pastoralists are Muslims or Lamaistic Buddhists, but they are often lax in their observance and have added their own adaptations.

The pastoralists accept their animals and the environment in a sense as divinely-given, and the livestock is slaughtered sparingly. The animals are understood to be a key part of the order of the world. The pastoralists believe that, in some way, they are accountable to a personal power or powers, and they see themselves as stewards of nature.

Quechua llama herders believe that they are maintaining the cosmic order by caring for their flocks. The continued existence of the world depends on animals, so that when there are no more animals the world will come to an end. The gods of the mountains are considered to be the supernatural "owners" of the herds.[28] The Maasai regard themselves as the chosen people of their creator god, Engai, and all other peoples as "pagan." Since he created all cattle particularly for the Maasai, raiding others' herds causes no moral problems for them. The Bedouin argue that any overgrazing is not a result of increased herd size, but due to lack of rain, and therefore caused by the will of God.[29]

The Mongols and Tuvans understand the universe as an integrated system, supervised by *tenger*, or Heaven, in an overall harmony. Each creature, including human beings, has the right to take what it needs to exist, but not to abuse or waste resources. In the case of domestic animals, human beings must guide them, so that the harmony is maintained.[30] The Mongols believe that nature suffers if they mismanage their herds.

All natural objects are believed to have their spiritual "owners," which defend their part of nature by afflicting the offending humans. Heaven is like a *ger* (tent) roof that opens to send sunshine, rain or disasters. When this happens, a nomad may pray with appropriate ritual for benefits.

The concept of a journey has great significance to nomads. Many nomads, such as the Fulbe and Kyrgyz, have histories of long one-way migrations, just as Israel migrated from Mesopotamia to Egypt and then to Canaan, as well as traditions of key leaders like Moses. Many see their nomadism as divinely authorized, while others see it as divine penalty. Tibetans go on pilgrimage because they see the real landscape as a sort of mandala of the mythical landscape of their beliefs. The physical route is transformed in their minds as a progress towards salvation, that is marked out by the seasons and the phases of the moon linked to the gods and the cosmic order. The Tibetans have a special term for a fellow pilgrim, *nedrog*, that implies a shared bond of spiritual experience on the path.[31]

The Tibetan culture and the Lamaistic Buddhist world view form an all-embracing system called *chö*, within which the nomad sees him or herself as an integral part. Faith in a *boddhisatta*, that is a saint on the verge of Buddhahood and with merit to spare, helps to gain this "grace." Lamaistic Buddhism stresses the individual's life of faith. Religious truth has to be realized by an inward quest for enlightenment within the individual. This gives a greater freedom for the individual and for women, and sometimes has the result of weakening family and marriage ties.[32] Sin is usually thought to be violence, especially against animals.[33] As the Buddhist understands the material world to be an illusion, each person has an unquestioned commitment to gain permanence beyond numerous reincarnations. This permanence is found in the supreme reality known as *Kön Chok*, consisting of the triad of the Buddha, his teaching and the monks. Most confuse this Buddhist supreme reality with the Shamanist sky god.

It is not usually difficult to discuss religion with nomads. The religion of the nomad is sensitive to the varied and hostile aspects of divine providence and the problems of natural evil. The pastoralists' faith in the supernatural is colored by their dependence on the precariousness of rain and other environmental factors.[34] They have ample reason to reflect on the meaning of hardship and the injustice of natural disasters. The Maasai are aware of the inequalities of life and, although their high god is remote, he can be blamed for disasters and natural injustices. Vincent Donovan tells of a troubled Maasai elder who said, "If I ever run into God, I will put a spear through him."[35]

The lives of many nomads are precarious, and death can often be close. Death may mean not only the end of an individual, but also the end of a lineage, and so affects entire families. The fate of the living and the influence of the dead on the living concern them as much as, or more than, life after death. When a parent loses a child, in some sense the parent is also considered to die. Also, a new baby is thought to represent the presence in the society of a deceased parent, continuing the family line and honor associated with it.

The nomads' actual practice is highly syncretistic. Many African nomads accept the idea of a high god or being who they usually consider to be remote from human affairs. This high god is not the transcendent Creator of the Bible, as revealed by the nomads' dependence on many spiritual intermediaries and powers. In conjunction with their adherence to Islam or Buddhism, the nomads continue to observe their original Shamanism, Bonism or African traditional religion. The most devout Muslims still use charms and other forms of magic and, in the Andes, a thin veneer of Catholicism covers a suppressed but thriving indigenous religion that dates from before the Iberian conquest. While some in East Africa tend not to use local shrines, holy places across Asia are sites of intercession and pilgrimage.

The Mongols need to placate the

spiritual "owners" of mountains by prayer at cairns or *ovoos* by burning juniper leaves and attaching strips of colored cloth to trees or rocks. In practice, the world of the nomads of Tibet and Mongolia is riddled with the occult, and they depend on specialists with secret powers to deal with the local nature gods and demons. This world has to be negotiated and manipulated so as not to hinder the inner individual quest for religious merit, which all but supersedes the ethical ideals of compassion, kindness and non-violence.

In Central Asia and Siberia, Shamanism continues to be an important part of the life of the pastoralists, helping them express their unity with the natural world. In fact, in some Turkic areas the understanding of Shamanism is more important than the study of Islam. The shaman can heal by expelling spirits, cursing people, divining the future, and engaging in spiritual warfare between spirits. Rituals range from animal sacrifice to laughter therapy. Their drums are considered to be their "mount" to ride into the spiritual world, and they depict symbols of the helper-spirits of that particular shaman.

In Siberia, the shamans opposed the medical and educational advances that the Soviets offered. The Communists campaigned against the shamans, at first unsuccessfully, because they thought the destruction of drums and other paraphernalia was sufficient to rob them of their influence. They failed to understand that the animistic world view of the Siberian peoples was interwoven with their pastoralism. Even the Marxist rhetoric and phrases were reinterpreted in a supernatural sense.[36]

The nomadic life is so important that nomads are more willing to convert to the religion of their nomadic enemies than to that of their sedentary friends. The Tuareq have adopted Islam more seriously, though still superficially, because French colonialism in North Africa drove more devout Muslims southwards into contact with the Tuareqs. Instead of a mosque, they mark out with stones a rectangle of ground in their camps

as a prayer place. Lloyd Briggs likens Islam to a varnish on the surface of their minds, which has not impregnated their thought.[37]

The Waso Borana of north Kenya have converted to Islam in the last forty years following the model of the Somalis. Since then, they have judged the Somalis to be unworthy Muslims, because of their brutal attacks on Borana settlements. They have also rejected Catholicism, whose priests have helped them in many material ways but did not give them the gospel that could have delivered them from vices such as chewing *miraa*, or chat, that has become a debilitating addiction. In East Africa there is a division between the majorities that continue to follow their traditional practices and Christian minorities.

Some nomads, such as the Fulani and Tibetans, have often actively propagated their faiths. Belonging to one of the major world faiths gives the pastoralists their relationship to the outside world. Both Islam and Buddhism give a measure of social cohesion, but they are faiths that stress the individual's responsibility in achieving his own "salvation." Islamic law does not require a central authority, and the literature and language enshrine "the individualistic spirit of the nomad."[38] It is said that the Bedouin are too independent and difficult to lead, except when they are inspired by a prophet or a saint.[39]

Nomadism resists the sedentary life

The nomads see themselves as masters of their environment and are proud of the way of life such mastery provides.[40] "It is the mobility that engenders the qualities that so distinguish them — tolerance, wiliness, independence, courage, wit."[41]

A number of reasons contribute to settling — including misfortune, forcible settlement and collectivization programs, or the difficulty of sustaining large families through pastoralism. As we have seen, losing one's herd or flock entails a loss of status and esteem that is not easily replaced by the possession of land or wealth from agriculture or urban work. The sedentary life is therefore feared for many reasons, including a perceived threat to male status through the effect it might have on the behavior of wives and daughters — either to restrict their freedom as Islamic rules are applied more strictly, or to allow them an unacceptable degree of social independence.[42]

Nomads forced out of the nomadic life have been called "Nomads in waiting," because when there is opportunity they revert to their familiar life. The nomads' experience of towns and agricultural life is often that of being unemployed and living by begging. It has been estimated that 500,000 nomads have settled in the shantytowns of six West African cities.[43] Fulani from Burkina Faso have also invaded towns in Ghana to beg.

The attitudes and values of a people, and how they perceive themselves, does not necessarily correspond to their present economic reality. Although only a tiny minority of Arabs have contact with the nomadic life, the cultural ideas that give unity to the Arab world have the mobility of a nomadic society built into them. Even after a generation of enforced settlement, former Bedouin have a bond with their traditional grazing grounds and the tribal and family structure. A number of semi-nomadic Arctic reindeer pastoralists, although sedentary due to Soviet collectivization, still have a deep bond with their tundra homelands.[44] After twenty years of enforced commune living in Communist China, Tibet's nomads have returned to nomadic life.[45]

The Kazaks have a strong attachment to their traditional grazing lands, and the collective farms have largely corresponded to these territories. Their clans and families have been able to maintain their links to particular areas. Many a pastoralist today in Central Asia will live on an isolated outpost of a former collective, with responsibility for thousands of sheep. In mid-May he will take the sheep perhaps 200 kilometers (125 mi.) to the former summer pasture of his clan, staying there until the end of September.[46]

Another example of pastoralism persisting after a radical change of circumstances is that of the Kyrgyz refugees from Afghanistan who arrived in Turkey via Pakistan. They brought their valuable saddles and some sheep with them and in spite of difficulties, including the higher temperatures, sought to buy swift horses to "fit" the saddles.[47]

Many return to nomadism in some form; the changes that we see are probably only stages in a continual process of adaptation to changing conditions. When a family is large and co-operative, and its livestock has to be kept within limits, it can maintain its essential pastoralism not only by semi-nomadic adaptation, but also by what might be called a generation-shift system. This means that the phenomenon of young men apparently turning their backs on the old ways for good is very misleading.

In various places there seems to be a pattern in which younger men, who are not needed in their family's herding activities, seek work in factories or in agriculture, or study for a profession. This is particularly true when the younger men are married and have young families. By the time they are forty, their employers often want to replace them with younger men. They have already gained the financial advantages of their employment, and now their fathers are old and need help to maintain the flocks. Many of them revert back, in mid-life, to pastoralism (or at least to agropastoralism), and reintegrate themselves into the tribal structures, now as elders, and reactivate their Islamic or other traditional religious allegiances.[48] It appears that pastoralism will continue in some form, especially as other types of subsistence in or near the semi-arid areas of the world are tried and fail.

Gloomy predictions that nomadic pastoralism is destined to come to an end, therefore, are probably premature. While grasslands last and other economic and political conditions are unfavorable, the traditions of nomadic pastoralists will keep alive the option of returning to a pastoral life with a measure of nomadism. There is a great need to assist pastoralists who are forced to settle — not only in a material way, with alternative means of support, but also in helping them maintain their self-esteem and values as former pastoralists.

Such are some of the characteristics of nomadic pastoralists that make them different from the majority of people in society. The nomadic pastoralists are a hidden, but widespread and unique, type of society, expressing the enterprise of being the image of God.

Invisible Peoples

Rrrrrruh! Rrrrrruh! Put, put. The sound of the chainsaw echoes down among the sunlit trees, as we climb up the mountain. On an imaginary visit to Anatolia, in Turkey, it is early summer and cooler here than down in the valley. We turn off the track to find a small hut made of branches covered with canvas. A man tends the fire while his wife and son are above, operating the saw.

"I am a Tahtaci." Surprisingly, the lumberman admits the identity of his people and invites us into his humble, temporary home. He would not have been so welcoming if we had been Turks. We had discovered a hidden people, so unknown and keeping such a low profile that estimates of their numbers range widely between 100,000 and 400,000. Many people doubt their very existence, "Who has ever heard of these people?" Those who know of them are prejudiced against them. "Why would you want to meet such people?" they wonder. "They are the lowest, like the Gypsies." Even when we pass them in the street, they try to suppress any distinctiveness and appear like the Turks who despise them and pretend they do not exist. The Tahtaci are but one example of many nomadic peoples that are "invisible." There are two reasons for this — their lifestyle and their religion.

Our new friend explains, "Our ancestors came from Persia in the Middle Ages, and like all Travelers, they only got the work that other people did not want to do. Our name means Plank-men or lumbermen. We travel and work as families, and the women do some of the tree work. We start at the bottom of the mountain in spring, camping on our way up, until in the hottest months we work in the cool air higher up. The Forest Agency drags the trees we cut down to tracks to be cut up. Some of our young people today do other work, but tree-felling still pays better."

"In winter we go back to our houses. We like to live together, as many as 300 families together, and separate from the Turks." He paused, because he was about to tell us the heart of the difference between them and the Turks. "You see, our customs and religion mean we must be separate. The Turks are proud to be Sunni Muslims, but they do not know the path to the true experience of Allah. They only know the way of duty, so we consider them ritually 'unclean.' If one of them came here, I would have to wash his cup forty times." Here our Tahtaci friend stopped and showed us his tools. Then he added with a smile, "But Christians are welcome, you can stay with us if you like."

The Tahtaci are Shiite Muslims of the Alevite sect. They follow Ali, the son-in-law of the prophet Mohammed, and believe in a trinity of Allah, Muhammad and Ali. They prefer Christians because of their faith in a trinity and personal experience of God. The Tahtaci believe they are born onto the mystical path leading to the direct personal experience of God. Their meetings are at night in homes or in the woods, with much music, dancing and drinking. Outsiders are not allowed. Alcohol is poured out to celebrate Mohammed's return from heaven. There is no known Christian witness to these people.

As we come down from the forest we remember a better known "invisible" people, who are all around us in Europe and the Middle East — the Gypsies. They see themselves as a people set apart, for Rom and Romany simply means "Man." They too have a system of ritual cleanness, something like that found in Leviticus. Non-Gypsies are "unclean" to them. The Nazis classified them as a primitive race, and more than a third of Europe's one million Gypsies were exterminated in the Holocaust. Still misunderstood, they are constantly harassed across Europe. Today, many live in houses but spend their nights in their caravans behind the houses, and they take to the road at the first opportunity. Over the last thirty years, many in Spain, France and Britain have come to believe in Christ. These rejected peoples can identify with Jesus.

4 The Need for Understanding

Throughout their long history, nomads have had different relationships to the rest of society, but today they meet with much misunderstanding and prejudice. They are forced into conflict more frequently than ever before because they no longer have the freedom of their traditional areas. This is due to factors like the pressure of the world's population, the improved technology to extend agriculture and the power of nation-states to police their territories and borders. Christian outreach to nomadic peoples has to take account of these tensions in their lives.

Tension with the surrounding society

Nomads usually have different ethnic origins from the dominant peoples, and racism takes various subtle forms. Everywhere nomadic peoples are considered as misfits who must be made to submit to the settled way of life. They are subjected to abuse in schools and on the streets, suspected of being backward or criminal. They are judged according to a concept created by the non-nomad which sees their life as paradoxically both romantic and lawless. Nomadism is confused with vagrancy, and anyone who does not obviously own property is suspected of criminality.

There is prejudice based on the assumption that sedentary or urban life is a higher stage in the development of humankind. The notion that nomadism was an evolutionary step between savagery and civilization persists. This is now discredited by scholarship as well as by common sense, for there is evidence that nomadism has often been adopted by previously sedentary people.

Nomads are often considered "second class" by sedentary peoples, and both have a mutual contempt for the others' lifestyles. "These people are 'uncivilized,' they must live like us," is often the attitude of settled people. The assumption is that any lifestyle that requires the sacrifice of "normal" laborsaving comforts and more than ordinary physical effort must be backward. Many still think that civilization means living in houses and cities. Settling and being subordinate to an employer and other authorities are considered part of being a good citizen, or even essential for being human.

The basic premise of this attitude is that what is outside the majority's experience must be eliminated or, patronizingly, be made to conform to the majority's lifestyle. Nomads are also sometimes treated as exhibits for tourists, as the Sami are, and in many cases that is the only way that they are allowed to contribute to the country's economy. The cost of being different is forced conformity, being made an exhibit or being excluded from society.

It is also *assumed* that nomads are doomed by progress to die out.[1] Nomadism is *assumed* to be nonviable, both economically and socially. Society thinks that nomads suffer deprivation, are underdeveloped and live on the verge of starvation. The only support for this opinion is the fact that pastoralism is a precarious lifestyle, due to its dependence on the environment in what can be considered marginal territory (an environment that usually cannot be used for anything else).

It is assumed that commonly held land and other resources are exploited without any regulation, when in fact most nomads have a system of allocating them. Although it has been suggested that a privatization of pasture encourages owners to care for the pasture, often overgrazing, high administrative costs and concentration of resources into the hands of the rich have resulted. Commonly held and regulated land lowers the risks to individuals, and all gain when sufficient numbers co-operate and relations with other ethnic groups are regulated.[2]

Settled people fear insecurity due to the nomads' presence. Like the Gypsies in Europe, most nomads are always suspect of crime because they are different and exclusive. Gypsies have been rounded up or deported in Europe in the last few decades. Their harassment has been compared to the treatment of Jews and Gypsies during the 1930s in Nazi Germany. They have been exiled from some towns in the Czech Republic, for example. Right across Europe, but especially in the East, people feel economically and socially threatened by most migrant communities. Those without a government to take up their cause, such as Travelers and Gypsies, are often considered as not even requiring human rights.[3] The Czech President Havel claimed rightly that the Gypsies are the "litmus test of a civil society," but such warnings go unheeded.

The assumptions of modernization

Nomads are often hostile to any outside intervention because of past experiences with governments, farmers and even development agencies. Many development projects have tried to encourage, or enforce, settlement.

The nation-state, almost by definition, requires the administration and control of persons and resources within a carefully defined territory. In the West we have become used to this over the course of five centuries, so we do not realize that passports and boundary controls are mostly inventions of the last century. Boundaries have divided peoples who were once united, migration patterns have been broken and overgrazing has resulted. Nomadic pastoralists have routes and traditional pasture rights that have nothing to do with national boundaries and sometimes present a security hazard.

A cynic might suggest that the only use a nomad has for an international border is for smuggling, which is a secondary source of income for many pastoralists. But borders arbitrarily divide nomadic peoples from their legitimate interests. For example, the Shahsevan pastoralists are being divided between Azerbaijan and Iran, and the Hindu Qalandar nomadic entertainers are now denied access to festivals in India by the India-Pakistan border.

Administrators have been influenced by concepts of development into which nomadic peoples do not fit. There is prejudice against nomads because they resist being registered for births, education, employment, and so on, and therefore there is no bureaucratic control over them, and they do not fit into economic, security and fiscal policies. A money economy with taxes and endless statistical controls requires people to have fixed addresses. By contrast, nomads favor social fragmentation in order to respond to limited resources, and they resent central controls that are ignorant of local conditions. Planners seem to ignore the fact that settlements in the Third World, without proper water, sewage and power services, are less hygienic than nomadic camps, and to the nomad the settled life is very monotonous and out of touch with nature. It was not understood that a subsistence way of life was both employment *and* a culture.[4] At best, nomadism appears "untidy" to both well-established and relatively new national bureaucracies.

In order to earn respect, nations must appear to be modern, progressive and capable of governing. Development policies, fueled by nationalistic competition, are thought to depend on visible and fixed infrastructure. Emerging nations frequently fear having a reputation for backwardness, and nomads are thought to contribute to this image. In his attempts to modernize Iran, Reza Shah had the black goat-hair tents of the Lur and Qashqa'i in Iran collected and destroyed because he thought they symbolized backwardness, and he forced them to abandon pastoralism and practice agriculture instead. The people were compelled to cultivate in one place only and so, for climatic reasons, they have only one crop a year instead of two. The land was thus used inefficiently.

It is the deliberate policy of some governments, in order to increase agricultural land or to maintain ethnic control, to resettle people on the traditional pasture areas of the nomads. In both the Ganges plain and the Thar Desert in India, valuable pasture is being lost due to faulty irrigation schemes that soak the land and raise the salt content. The desert is being irrigated in order to produce cash crops for the economy. While these give income to the farmers, they cut into the limited pasture for the cattle. This is traditionally an area of semi-nomadic cattle rearing and rainy-season cultivation. As more than 500,000 hectares (202,500 acres) have been transformed into fields, pastoralists are being denied their traditional pasture rights because they are not "permanent residents"! Many dams are dramatic gestures to win elections and use vast sums of aid, but the resulting irrigation leaves the ground saline.[5] This is a gross injustice to people who have been in the area for centuries.[6] Governments encourage internal migration of their dominant people to further political control, to the detriment of minorities and especially nomads. The Chinese government has settled Han Chinese in Inner Mongolia, Tibet and Xinjiang, in order to make the Mongols, Tibetans and others into minorities in their own lands — they thus have greater control, and they have also changed the use of the land. In Inner Mongolia the four million Mongols are now outnumbered by 20 million Chinese.[7]

In the 1960s, the Sudan government attempted to modernize the pastoralists' livestock. They claimed that they integrated them into the life of the nation and enabled them to contribute fully to national progress. The stated motive for the Israelis settling the Bedouin in 1978 was that they might receive all the services the state provided. The Somali government once attempted to settle 120,000 camel herders into four villages on the coast and train them as fishermen and farmers.[8] Usually the pastoralists lose out to the farmers, as is the case in Senegal, where an Islamic sect that has much political influence has forcibly

settled farmers with peanut plantations in two areas of pasture belonging to the Fulbe. The sect's poor farming methods have degraded the sandy soil of the land that they previously seized.[9] Nomads are therefore motivated to rebel. In the civil wars of Chad factions of Goran, the Tubu and Zaghawa took over and transformed a Socialist movement with their own nomadic values.[10]

The Newfoundland government's attempt to turn reindeer hunter nomads, the Mushuau Innu of Labrador, into commercial fisherman, has been disastrous. They were moved from their 6,000-year-old hunting grounds to the Davis Inlet. This resulted in a high suicide rate and an increase in drug abuse, alcoholism and social disintegration — even though families were provided with separate huts and cable television![11]

Collectivization in the Soviet Union did more to destroy nomadic pastoralism than any other policy. Nomadism was presented by the Communists as backward, unhygienic and failing to give the nomads a secure standard of living. It was presented as feudal, exploitative, and as creating extremes of wealth and poverty. This was a meaningless interpretation in many cases, as collaboration and sharing is common among nomads. The enforced collectivization of the Kazaks in the 1930s resulted in the death of about half their population. A Chukchi Communist Party official only succeeded in persuading his fellow nomadic reindeer herders in Siberia to join a collective by telling them it would fulfill their own ideals of co-operation that they had always practiced!

The Communists, like many other "Moderns" of the era, assumed that the modern urban environment was the pinnacle of human development. The motive for forcing the nomads to settle was always claimed to be philanthropic.[12] But it had more to do with bringing everyone under the ideology and administrative control of the Party. In Siberia, collectivization and industrial development took over and destroyed the fragile environment. Newcomers came to work in jobs without any knowledge of, or interest in, the local peoples. To the central planner, the indigenous people were a labor resource who could be moved out of outmoded pastoralism and into the bright future of industrial humankind.

Many projects still assume that the best use of marginal land is to convert it to agriculture, with massively expensive irrigation schemes, rather than considering grazing management projects. Many agricultural projects have failed because of insufficient water supplies. Foreign aid has been used to establish agriculture in locations where there is only salty water. This has had the effect of drawing more people into the Sahel and driving meat prices down, and so posing the greatest threat to the Tuareq's pastoralism. Ill-considered schemes of food distribution near towns like Lagos, Dakar, Bamako in Mali, Niamey in Niger and in the camps in Mauritania have only produced dependency.

Governments and aid agencies have not understood the pastoralists' expertise in balancing herd size with the renewal of pasture. It is assumed that land that is not privately or state owned, and without the economic controls that ownership is supposed to bring, will inevitably be overgrazed. In Kenya, overgrazing only occurs when the migratory freedom of the pastoralists has been restricted or otherwise interfered with.

Development projects, such as the drilling of boreholes, have disturbed migration patterns and herd numbers.[13] Improved veterinary care has increased herd size, but there have been no balancing projects to improve pasture and nutrition. Also, the increase in herd size beyond that sustainable by the available pasture has been forced on the pastoralists to encourage them to participate in the market economy. The result is the dispossession of the pastoralists in many countries, including Kenya and Tanzania.

Only a few countries, such as Mongolia, recognize the pastoralists to be economically important and have given them corresponding political influence to participate in decisions deciding their contribution to the economy. Free from outside pressures, pastoralists have sophisticated systems to manage common resources — including the land.[14] In Mali, 60% of the herds are owned by non-pastoralists as an investment.[15]

There are now some signs of a more enlightened attitude towards pastoralists in terms of decision making. At a conference sponsored by Save the Children Fund, Ethiopian representatives admitted to their government's abuse of nomadic pastoralists in the past. Botswana is now beginning to recognize the validity of nomadic pastoralism within a multicultural economy. Supranational economic unions and agreements, with the mechanisms to facilitate migratory labor and relax border controls, should now change the situation of the nomad — recognizing that reasonable administration can be done without disrupting pastoralism or other itinerant occupations. Electronic means are now available to administer, police and provide essential services of communication, commerce and education without everyone having a fixed address.

World Bank projects are increasingly requiring the establishment of Pastoral Associations for the pastoralists to participate in and to own development projects.[16] Appropriate development involves using only the technology which the people can adopt and maintain themselves, and it requires their participation at both planning and operation phases.[17] Saudi Arabia has had development plans to remove the anomaly that the Bedouin have abundant livestock, which could be used to feed the urban population, while the country still imports most of its mutton.[18] It is ironic that the livestock has increased through government subsidies. This, says Cole, is because they get the subsidy without the organization for marketing their animals. The market system is too complex, so pastoralists prefer to let their animals die rather than sell them.

Another matter that affects the relationship of pastoralists to governments is policing. Security is vital for successful grazing. Nomadic pastoralists are being increasingly threatened — not only by cultivators taking their grazing land, but also by the raids of other pastoralists, who do not hesitate to use modern weapons.[19]

In northern Kenya and countries of the Sahel, it would be ideal if the governments could first recognize the traditional grazing rights of different peoples, although in some cases this might include arbitrating between claims. Secondly, these governments should provide small-scale military and air patrols to enforce these grazing rights and give security to the pastoralists. Most governments will find many reasons why they cannot give priority to this — including the expense, the unwillingness of personnel to serve in such conditions, friction with neighboring nations in border areas, and the ethnic prejudice of military commanders. In fact, the equipment does not have to be very sophisticated, and it would be possible to use pastoralists themselves as troops. The alternative is that each pastoral group would soon invest in their own automatic weapons and even military vehicles, and so risk escalating age-old conflicts and provoking new ones. This would not only be detrimental to successful pastoralism, but it would also heighten the negative attitudes of governments.

Re-education is an uphill task in the schools, government departments and among the nomads' neighbors. Self-centered assumptions and prejudices have to be examined so that they will not bias policy against any group, especially nomads. Equally, the nomads themselves have to learn that isolation is not practical, and that to maintain their distinctive way of life they have to be seen to be able to contribute to the cultural ethos and economy of the nation.

The world's nomads are a little known, but enterprising representation of the image of God. Their nomadism and measure of social autonomy has a right to be considered objectively as part of the overall economy and society of their countries and regions. The trend towards regional and international economic integration will tend to open borders, allow freedom of movement, and enable the land to be used as an integrated whole. Nomads have the right to demonstrate their skills in some viable pastoralism that contributes efficiently to the economy.

Nomadic prejudices

Nomads also have their prejudices. Nomadic people seem to see sedentary life from an ethnocentric viewpoint, and not simply from the perspective of their own love of the traveling life. Nomads consider all settled people to be alien, and they think that contact with them is detrimental to their society and lifestyle. To the nomad, sedentary life appears claustrophobic and distinctly unhealthy; a Fulani or a Gypsy will see the non-nomad as "unclean" or "unholy." The Nuers' experience of life means they are unable to grasp a view of life based on love and reconciliation, so that even their worship is full of songs of revenge on their enemies. The Siberian peoples also have a need for reconciliation with the Russians.

The Alevite sects of Islam encounter a particular problem of prejudice beyond the normal tensions between Shiites and Sunnis. As we saw at the end of Chapter 3, the Tahtaci in Turkey are said by the Turks not to exist, and they are considered the lowest form of life, along with the Gypsies. The Tahtaci for their part will hide their identity when away from their own settlements, refuse to speak freely or invite in a foreigner if a Sunni is present. This barrier is due to their beliefs and renders them almost socially "invisible" in the minds of the surrounding society. But the Tahtaci usually welcome those who are nominally Christian.[20]

The deep misunderstandings and prejudices between traveler and house-dweller, cattle owners and cultivators, also affect their perception of Christianity. Nomads need to be assured that their way of life, or the fertility of their herds, will not be threatened by their becoming Christians. The system of power and government is biased against the traveler and all settled society is associated with it — because, the nomad might hasten to add, they cannot get away! Christianity has to be modeled for them by another nomad, in order to overcome the perception that the gospel is only for settled people.

God has to break down the prejudice between nomads and sedentary peoples as much as that between Jew and Gentile (Eph. 2:11-22; Acts 15 etc.). Human sinfulness quickly changes variety of experience and custom into the competitive pride of one people against another, just as Israel changed her God-given message for the world into an ethnocentric nationalism against the Gentiles. Jesus opposed this by teaching that righteousness with others is part of a personal relationship with God. Both sides of this barrier between the nomad and the settled have been erected by ethnocentric views, including their view of God.

Communicating the gospel counters the ethnocentric and henotheistic notion held by many peoples of a supreme god who is very remote from life and has no purpose or interaction with humankind or creation. A faulty idea of God also leads to personifying the powers of nature as agencies or spirits that have to be ingratiated and manipulated by humans. Even for modern Kazaks, a rumble of thunder provokes the fearful response, "The spirits of the clouds are angry." Not only is there no clear morality in these powers, but this belief puts society under the influence of marabouts, witch doctors, lamas or shamans, and other "experts" who have been key people in their cultures. But, as moral agents accountable to God, we cannot be subordinate to either the personified powers of nature, or to their supposed human controllers.

Christian prejudice towards nomadic peoples

Christianity is perceived by most nomadic peoples to be a religion for settled people. Regrettably, much of the missionary witness has tended to reinforce this misconception — especially where Christians have been

part of well-intentioned attempts to introduce agricultural projects or institutional programs. Christianity is then perceived to be synonymous with settling down, to involve buildings and property and abandoning the values precious to nomads. But this misconception goes further, because we ourselves have misunderstood the Bible and read it with the assumption that God's people are sedentary. We are guilty of presenting its message as implicitly recommending the settled life.

The prejudice or assumption that nomadism is unacceptable or inconvenient is found not only among governments and ordinary people who dislike what is unfamiliar, but also among Christians. Christians often assume that a wandering lifestyle is somehow uncivilized and, therefore, non-Christian. They think nomads can be Christians, provided they cease to be nomads. Christians can be influenced by evolutionary theories, like those of the great Presbyterian missionary in Alaska, Sheldon Jackson. He justified the importation of reindeer and Sami trainers to the U.S. government in the 1890s by arguing that pastoralism was one "great step from barbarism toward civilization," and therefore toward Christianity, for those he described as "wild hunters."

The prejudice against nomads is but part of the hidden assumption that the church of Christ must inevitably take the Western form that is being reproduced in the major urban centers around the world. Unfortunately, any educated or Westernized person, whatever their lifestyle or beliefs, is considered "Christian." This misconception also shapes the nomad's attitude to the gospel.[21]

This prejudice is also found among national Christians, who one might expect to lead the way in reaching the nomadic peoples near to them. The history of local conflicts between farmers and cattlemen, as well as the system of class distinctions, may have to be overcome. Some African Christian leaders consider nomads to be "unreachable" due to their apparent inaccessibility. In Kenya, a deputation of Christian pastoralists visited the nearby churches for prayer and financial support. They were not initially successful because of this prejudice. Later, the churches did respond more positively. Evangelicals in one Eastern European country shoo Gypsies out of their churches because they are thought to be dirty, to carry disease and to be thieves. The missionary vision of the national churches is growing enormously, and often puts Western churches to shame, but it still needs to be stimulated to respond to the needs of the world's most unknown peoples.

Some will question the effort and sacrifice required to reach many of the nomads, who can be dismissed as not "strategic." The misconception here is that if a ministry is surrounded by millions of people in a large city, it is more "strategic." In fact, however, this ministry may have realistic contact with only a few hundred people out of those millions. Such a ministry, considered from the point of view of what it achieves, would be just as effective in a village or nomad situation. But then, it may be argued, will not those few hundred reach the millions? The answer often is, probably not.

The isolation of the nomadic environment is deceptive; they have whole networks of contacts both among themselves and with others. The Roma move around Europe, and the Arabs moved from the Middle East to the Sahel. Nomads were instrumental in spreading Islam in West Africa and the Middle East, and Buddhism in Inner Asia. Establishing the gospel in a number of camps could result in the nomads themselves spreading the message not only to their own, but also to others over a vast area.

The need to evangelize people groups, especially the more remote ones, is often countered by stressing the New Testament unity in Christ (Eph. 2:11-22; Gal. 2:11-17, 3:28; Col. 3:11). The New Testament does not tell us of mission beyond the relative homogeneity of the Roman Empire, except for God's action at Pentecost (Acts 2:8-11),

but there are indications of real differences that the early church encountered (Acts 15:19f.; Gal. 2:14). There is still a debate in New Testament studies on the measure of diversity in the earliest churches. We do not, therefore, have a record of how the early church would have reacted to vastly different ethno-linguistic groups.

God's desire is for diversity in the unity that is in Christ, with saved representatives from every people. The Christian needs to respond to both pastoralists and peripatetics as those who are in God's image. Christians need to learn from them as much as they need to give them material and spiritual help — thereby forming a partnership for the benefit of both.

The result of this prejudice or reluctance is that the settled peoples are evangelized during decades while nearby nomadic peoples are left without the gospel. The Maasai elder's puzzled rebuke to Vincent Donovan must ring in our hearts: "If [the love of Christ] is why you came here, why did you wait so long to tell us about this?"[22] A Banjara Gypsy in India said, "We've neither accepted nor rejected Christ. We have never heard about Him."

Nomadic peoples *are* accessible to the gospel

Church history should warn us that the English-speaking missionary culture, that has beneficially reproduced itself worldwide, is only a passing phase of the last one hundred years. Just as influential in heaven will be Tibetans, Fulbe and Nenets with the saints from first-century Asia Minor. Our goal must be to teach the Bible in a form appropriate for the evangelism and discipleship of each nomadic people, so that they can contribute to the diversity within the worldwide unity of the body of Christ.

The Christian's primary task is to demonstrate God's concern for them as nomads, and to communicate that their lifestyle, far from being a barrier to Christ's grace, is compatible with Christian living. In Chapter 5, we shall present the biblical evidence of God's concern for travelers and nomadism. The cause against endemic injustice between settled people and nomads must be taken up, as well as the nomad's right to hear and respond to the gospel.

The main purpose of the Bible is to change our idea of God and our concepts of ourselves and other peoples.[23] A Christian's greatest contribution to the people among whom he or she works is to give them a true idea of God.[24] Learning a new concept of God can be a painful, psychosomatic shock, as Donovan describes with the Maasai, but it can lead to reconciliation with God and with individuals and peoples.[25]

To reach nomads with the Christian message involves more than finding a few points of common ground between them and the Bible. For example, there are the many prophets accepted by both Christianity and Islam, and the Tuareq have a preoccupation with seeking forgiveness, even in the mundane activities of life.

"Show me how to put your church on my camel before you talk to me about Jesus," protested a Somali nomad.[26] The nomad has experienced a world in which God is rough and tough. It is crucial for us to enter into the nomad's way of thinking and to interpret these biblical contact points from their point of view. This was not only necessary for the evangelization of the nomad, but it is also necessary for Christians everywhere.

For the Bible's contact, and therefore Christianity's contact, with the nomadic life is more profound than merely a number of common points. The discomfort and upheaval of the nomadic lifestyle discourages many from considering working among them. It is easy to stress the practical difficulties of reaching and maintaining a sustained contact with the nomads, and it is tempting to consider other areas and peoples as more "strategic." Our tried and true methods of evangelism and teaching depend on buildings and timetables, and we find it difficult to conceive of working differently. But to force these methods on the nomad is as foolish as the suggestion, once made, that if we taught them all English we would not need to do Bible translations!

We must ask the question: what place have traveling peoples, peripatetics and pastoralists, had in God's purpose?

Pilgrim's Purpose

Looking like a giant inchworm, a Tibetan pilgrim raises his weary arms, then kneels on the ground, and stretches full length on the mountain path, then stands again and repeats the process. Covered in dust, he rhythmically progresses over the stony path. Pieces of tire tread the rocky ground where no wheel could pass, tied on to protect his knees and hands. His padded jacket and denim trousers are torn, for the sacred path tests the determination of pilgrims crossing a varied terrain. Here boulders embedded in sand, behind him painful slopes of shingle, chilling frozen streams, narrow tracks between the cliff where fat pilgrims get stuck. "They get stuck because of their sins!" the man thinks.

"All because of my karma," he thinks to himself, as he rises to his feet again, his whole body aching. All his life he has breathed an atmosphere of the constant quest for merit. As a baby, he had been conscious of his mother holding him with one hand while muttering prayers, her body gently swaying as the other hand turned the prayer wheel.

The life of the Tibetan nomad is hard and monotonous, but his family's yak herd had made them prosperous. The Chinese in the village are jealous. The gods had smiled on his family; they had not lost many sheep in the blizzards last winter, like other nomads in the northeast, who lost all their herds. He had driven his yaks around the stupas, the holy pillars shaped like chess pawns, to get the blessing. He had left his scarf and some of his hair in sacred places to remind the gods of his devotion. The wind had fluttered his prayer flags to shreds. Surely the gods had heard him? He did not waste any part of the few animals that he killed. Blood for sausages, milk, butter, cheese and fat, wool, skin and meat, dung for fuel — he had used everything frugally. He slaughtered sparingly, muttering special prayers of forgiveness — for a Buddhist, there is no greater sin than killing another creature. He had cheated the Rong-pa, the Valley People, in trade for barley to make *tsamba* and to buy tea, but he thought that was a good deal — not a sin. He looks forward to this staple food of flour from roasted barley, hungry from his exhausting day of pilgrimage.

"Go on pilgrimage, to Lhasa, or better to Mount Kailash. The holy mountain is the abode of the gods of our land. The blessed Buddha descended from heaven where he had been to visit his glorified mother," his mother had said. There are many holy places around which a devout Tibetan should make a circuit — the *stupas*, the holy city of Lhasa — prostrating oneself along the ground to gain more merit. But the holy Mount Kailash is best of all. It's in the remote west of the country, where the traditions say that Tibet began and the hero King Gesar of Ling lived. For over a week he has been making his way. Many just take the less virtuous method of walking the 32 miles in a day or two. Aching in body and dazed in mind, he wonders, "Will this gain me a better reincarnation?"

His brother had carried their camp gear ahead; he would do the pilgrimage another time. "To help a pilgrim is merit anyway, they say." His brother always found a good spot for camping, with a good sight of the majestic mountain with its sheer slopes and cliffs permanently covered by a thin layer of snow. Its white-domed top gleams against the sky, a mighty outward form representing what he knows to be the real world of holy men and women who have attained nirvana. The rest of the moon-like landscape is populated by Drok-pa and their herds, as well as by dragons and demons.

At last he reaches the simple camp, but his brother, who normally calls out cheerfully to other pilgrims and teases the girls, is embarrassed into silence. He has company, and the stranger is a foreigner. The pilgrim collapses, exhausted, as his brother prepares the simple meal of *tsampa*. He had seen quite a few foreigners along the path. Many are sick with the altitude (as high as 5,600 meters, or 18,500 feet). They come starry-eyed, wanting to benefit from the ancient wisdom. This man speaks reasonable Tibetan. "I was telling your brother about a man. God became a man called Jesus."

"That's not new. Most of the gods of Tibet behave like men. I want to hear about the Buddha and get help from the gods," the tired and breathless pilgrim replies.

"This divine man was a pilgrim too. He told people: 'Follow me constantly!'"

"Ha! He must have had a lot of merit to say that!"

"Because he is the highest of Gods, higher than the Buddha, he did not need merit. His whole life was a journey to help people, but also to demonstrate his commitment to die in the place of others."

"Yes, no one can arrive at perfection without suffering," the pilgrim says, as he offers the stranger some *tsamba* and tea. He had already been careful to flick some away as an offering to the gods. "Hey, I thought you said he was already divine. Once one is perfect, one does not come down to suffer."

"He died to give forgiveness as a gift, so that we do not need merit."

"You mean for nothing? Do you mean all the prayer wheels, prostration, pilgrimages and offerings are worth nothing? No one can be sure of that. How can I be Tibetan without seeking merit? I cannot conceive of Tibet without the Lord Buddha, the Buddhist Scriptures, the monks! How can I follow this God-Man Jesus? Pah! His Bible fits in your pocket! Why, the Buddhist Scriptures fill whole libraries — the holy monks read this wisdom of many every day!" The pilgrim struggles to grasp these new ideas.

Part II:
The Missionary Challenge of Nomadic Peoples

5 A Journey with God

Hope drove a man and his household to abandon his relatives and familiar surroundings for a life in tents, and to travel some 700 kilometers (450 mi.) to an unknown land. Four thousand years ago, Abraham set out — not knowing his destination, but traveling with God who had given the promise to establish him as an independent people. When God indicated that he had arrived, he and his people continued to live in tents as traveling shepherds for two centuries. He did not own the land, and most of the time he moved according to the need for pasture, depending on the natural resources that God provided. This small company traveled in the open land between the Canaanite cities and their surrounding fields, vulnerable to attack in the midst of a potentially hostile society. They only came under the jurisdiction of settled people temporally, when drought forced them from the pastures of the Promised Land.

This nomadism was the way God began his saving purpose for the world. Many nomadic peoples have similar traditions of long journeys to their present locations, which contribute to their sense of ethnic identity. They, too, travel detached and often misunderstood, sometimes meeting with hostility from the surrounding society.

Reading the Bible from a nomad's point of view leads us to see that God's people, both settled and nomadic, are to have the mentality of travelers being led by God, trusting him as their herdsman. God's calling and leading of Israel demonstrates his desire to befriend traveling peoples and to use them to reach others. The early Christians also considered themselves to be God's travelers, aliens and pilgrims in an unfriendly world. They were a people united by loyalty to one another and to their Shepherd Lord rather than by the ties of nation and property. God calls us today to be much more "nomadic" in our attitudes towards God's plan and the Christian life.

Christian theology has concentrated on various biblical themes — including covenant, law, people, kingdom of God, etc. — as the key to understand the whole Bible. But little attention has been paid to the underlying theme of a traveling people in a pastoral relationship with God. When we examine the biblical evidence, we are sometimes surprised to realize that God has a special place in his heart for nomadic peoples.

From this we can learn two things: first, that faith in the God of the Bible is pre-eminently compatible with nomadic peoples and, second, that all God's people should have the outlook of traveling peoples and understand salvation in terms of the nomadic life.

God's people: A traveling people

The book of Genesis presents, in miniature, the themes that influence the rest of the Bible.[1] It forms the basis for teaching much about God's character and purpose, about human beings as individuals and about society being God's image. It also tells about humankind's disobedience.

First, Genesis demonstrates God being evenhanded to all people, irrespective of their lifestyle. This includes the two main ways of supporting oneself directly from the environment — pastoralism and agriculture. The episode with Abel and Cain rejects the common assumption that hunter-gathering was the primitive evolutionary state of human beings, and that pastoralism is a stage on the way to more "advanced" agriculture. It is the farmer, Cain, who is condemned to wander (Gen. 4:12). The cultivator's attitude towards the pastoralist is the problem, rather than his sacrifice (Gen. 4:6-7). A traveling life seems at first to be the punishment, but Cain was spared that to become an urbanite (Gen. 4:17). Cain's journey was away from God, but God is found with the pastoralist. The relationship with God is paramount — rather than human culture and achievement.

Genesis also reveals God's purpose of salvation as a journey with God. The book has little interest in the events of surrounding societies and empires but concentrates mostly on a nomadic family maintaining its separate identity by the pastoral care of God. God's missionary purpose for the world began with the promise to Abraham (Gen. 12:3; cf. 17:4,5; 18:18; 22:18; Gal. 3:8; Heb. 11:8) and leads Abraham on a lifelong journey.

The promise that *"all peoples on earth will be blessed through you,"* actually an oath, is the "motor" of history. It starts the detailed mission task that each part of every lineage, kindred or clan (*mishpahah*) should receive God's blessing. It refers both to the ethnic diversity of the human race in general *and* to each subdivision of the tribes and nations. Further, it is a promise that each part of every people group should receive God's word. This is of particular significance to nomadic societies, who live and work in small scattered groups. This promise and the history that unfolds from it are God's solution for nomadic peoples as misunderstood minorities keen to maintain their identities.

Secondly, this promise meant that Israel became a revelation of God to the nations as the first step in providing redemption from sin and the formation of a people walking by faith with God (Gen. 12:3; Mt. 12:15-21; Acts 15:14-17; Rom. 1:5,16; 2:9,10; Gal. 3:8).

The impulse of the divine promise turned Abraham and his descendants into a small group of travelers, differentiated from all others, under the direction of the heavenly Herdsman who would "show" their route both geographically and spiritually. Abraham may not have been a nomad to start with, but God chose to use nomadism to call and mold a people for himself. It was through being travelers, supporting themselves as nomadic pastoralists for at least two centuries, that

Abraham's descendants responded to the promise.

Even after arriving in the Promised Land, Abraham and his family were no more than a traveling people, for they did not settle or possess the land or belong to its people. The only lasting signs of Abraham's passing through the land were the altars he built as the promise was renewed (Gen. 12:7-8; 13:14-18; Heb. 11:8-9). But the fact that they did not own property or live in houses was of no importance (Gen. 17:8; 28:4; 36:7; 37:1); the land was theirs as far as the purpose of God was concerned. Like latter-day nomads, they were "at home," not homeless, even without the legal trappings of land ownership (Gen. 13:17). For social and economic autonomy, a religious separation would be an important part of their possession of the land. Although the patriarchs also knew that four centuries of temporary residence in Egypt were predicted for their descendants (Gen. 15:13), nomadism gave them a measure of this independence.

In fact, Abraham's experience as a traveler with God and the self-sufficiency that pastoralism gave him formed a basis for his trust in God, which was essential for the fulfillment of God's promises and covenant (Gen. 17). Abraham traveled with God for 14 years, demonstrating and developing his faith with obedience. During this walk, God justified him (Gen. 15:1ff.). The apostle Paul shows that the relationship of faith, even prior to the structuring and fulfilling of the covenant, is fundamental for acceptance with God (Rom. 4:9-12). The covenant merely confirms the relationship. Therefore the walk of faith with God, whether literal or metaphoric, is required of all believers. The nomad shows his own commitment as a model of sacrificial living. We can learn from each other. Faith understood as a journey illustrates faith's progress, joys, trials and perseverance.

The nomadic pastoral God

The reason for this traveling is the character of God himself. God's freedom over his creation in his transcendence, and yet fulfilling his purpose in his immanence, is expressed in the metaphor of the divine pastoralist. Transcendence means that the nature of God is supremely "nomadic;" he has no need of creation, and is not limited by any aspect of it. God is free to choose his commitments and make them effective as he wishes, surmounting human and physical boundaries.

As Creator-Shepherd, he has elected to have fellowship with a people traveling with him through time. His freedom is demonstrated, paradoxically, by his involvement in leading the patriarchs and Israel. We do not know to what extent God was known to Terah's clan (see Gen. 31: 29, 30; 35:2; Josh. 24:2).[2] What is presented in the Bible is this transcendent, free God who takes the initiative "out of the blue" to call one member of the family, Abraham, to transcend family ties and geographical borders and trust him for what is, humanly speaking, an impossible mission. The promise that God will "show" the land clearly implies that he will "go with" Abraham. This explains how Abraham knew that Canaan was the destination (Gen. 12:4f.; see Heb. 11:8).

This transcendence is emphasized by the Bible's prohibition of idolatry. Some nomads carry idols in an attempt to control the supernatural — at special locations, or by special people or ritual. The biblical God cannot be controlled; there are no "handles" on him to be manipulated. God achieves the ideal of self-sufficiency that the nomad cultivates in a different sense. This independence maintains the deeply personal unity of the Trinity, just as nomads guard their own people's identity. The self-sufficiency of God shapes the life of the believer to travel with him and depend on his provision, rather than on human plans and resources.

God is known as the herdsman of the patriarchs (Gen. 48:15), an idea that continues throughout the Old Testament, although it is sometimes obscured in English translation. The expression "God of Jacob" extends the concept throughout Israel's history.[3] "Herdsman" or "pastoralist" is a better translation than "shepherd" for the Hebrew word describing God, because the word refers to leading and providing pasture for all domestic animals — such as asses (Gen. 36:24) and cattle (Gen. 46:6) — and not just sheep (Gen. 30:36). God leads, feeds, tends, keeps, herds and provides for Israel as a pastoralist cares for his herds and flocks, both collectively and individually (2 Sam. 5:2; Ps. 23; 28:9; Is. 40:11; Jer. 3:15; Hosea 4:16), and this develops the personal relationship.

Only this chief herdsman knew the route (Ex. 40:34; Dt. 2:3, 9, 15, 18, 24, 31, 37; 3:2), the weather, the pasture and water conditions, and the endurance of the people and herds in a dangerous environment — for this was no arbitrary test of obedience. Continual personal encounters with God gave the assurance that the transcendent God was invisibly present all along in their traveling (Gen. 17:1, 22; 35:13; Ex. 13:19-20). God's providence in the material aspects of life was made explicit in his direction of Israel in the wilderness with the fiery cloud (Num. 9:15-23). God chose campsites (Dt. 1:33). Even the details of hygiene were vital, because God "walks" in the camp as he did in Eden (Dt. 23:14). God also used the figure of a warrior and horseman riding in the heavens to further his people's cause (Dt. 33:26; Ps. 104:3; Is. 19:1); he vindicates his servants (Ps. 18:10); enables them to ride with him (Dt. 32:13); and implements justice for the vulnerable (Ps. 45:4; 68:4, 33). The saddle and the sandal are not inconsistent with the temple and throne as God's places of action.

The special nature of God's accompanying them in a unique way was part of Israel's identity, compared to being led only by an angel (Ex. 23:20-23; 33:2-3, 15): *"unless you go with us? What else will distinguish me and your people from all the other people on the face of the earth?"* The character of God is demonstrated even to other peoples as free of earthly limitations. Yet he provides in detail for those who trust him (Gen. 20:3ff.; Num. 14:14; Jos. 2:9ff.). The privilege of Israel's being led by God followed even their disobedience with the golden calf.[4] Through

God's provision of material things, trust and obedience were learned for their spiritual needs too,which reveals principles for every Christian's walk of faith (Mt. 6:25-35) in following Jesus (Mk. 8:34). The image of following turns faith into practical obedient trust, not mere mental and emotional assent.

God's "nomadic" freedom from human and physical barriers, coupled with his commitment to his people, requires that the people be holy, set apart from others (Ex. 19:6,10; Lev. 18:2-5). The patriarchs, the Exodus generation and Israel (throughout her history) were misunderstood minorities under constant cultural and military threat to undermine their distinctive identity. This is also the lot of many nomadic peoples. For centuries, ancient Israel had the ethos of a traveling people united by God's purpose, rather than by ties to a place or the surrounding society. Following God's purpose results in a lifestyle which, if not constantly on the move, at least requires a readiness to move according to his direction. The Passover illustrates the message of a people traveling in haste according to God's command throughout the centuries (Ex. 12:11).

Nomadism isolated the Israelites from others so that they could be alone with God (Ex. 19:4; 33:15-16; Lev. 20:26). This formative experience taught Israel that faith — trusting in and obeying God and receiving his provision and protection — had to be their chief characteristic (Dt. 4:6-8). They had to learn that, after their experienced pastoral assessment, the situation could only be resolved by God's solution. The life of faith is a journey with God marked by God's actions rather than by dates — as much as nomads remember their lives not by dates but by migrations and environmental conditions.

Nomadic pastoralism used by God

Some biblical scholars suggest that the patriarchs were not nomads, arguing that true nomadism did not develop until the first millennium BC, centuries after Abraham.[5] However, this is only true if one identifies nomadism too closely with the particular brand of nomadism of the later Bedouin using the camel. The ass was the common beast of burden in patriarchal times. The camel was probably domesticated in the second millennium BC and used for slow transport across the desert to facilitate the caravan trade between the various civilizations of the Fertile Crescent, especially for the incense trade from southern Arabia. The biblical Midianites may have had to dismount to fight (Judg. 6:4-5). Desert pastoralism resulted from the later development of the camel saddle, but only as the pressure arose to do so.[6]

Yet, irrespective of camel nomadism, at the beginning of the second millennium before Christ and throughout biblical times, there were traveling peoples, including the ancestors of the later Bedouin, who supported themselves with cattle, sheep and goats. They lived on the steppe near settled populations, and not in the desert like the later Bedouin who would rely on camels.[7]

The patriarchs were called Arameans (Gen. 28:5; Dt. 26:5), which implies that they may have already been pastoralists among the semi-nomadic peoples in Mesopotamia.[8] Certainly Abraham's relatives in Haran appear to be pastoralists, which in the environment probably required seasonal movement or nomadism (Gen. 29:6, 10; 31:1, 19-22). Abraham's servant, seeking a wife for Isaac, recognized not only Rebekah's generosity in watering his camels, but also her strength and experience because she would have had to lift over a ton of water for his ten camels (Gen. 24:14).[9] Also, Laban is not too successful as a pastoralist until Jacob turns his fortunes around for him, which he was able to do based on his pastoral experience in Canaan (Gen. 30:30; 31:18, with v. 1).

It has also been suggested that Abraham was not a nomad because his flocks are not mentioned on the journey from Haran and his journey would have kept him within a day's march from well-inhabited and watered localities. But Abraham's many "possessions" (Gen. 12:5) must have included animals, as the term used does refer to animals both earlier and later (Gen. 4:2, 20; 13:6; 15:14; 31:18; Job 1:3). Abraham gained much livestock in Egypt as well as silver and gold (Gen. 12:16; 13:2), and the terms used distinguish sheep and goats from cattle and imply great wealth. Abraham and Lot separated in Canaan because the pastures proved to be inadequate for their increased livestock (Gen. 13:5-12). Later, Isaac's wealth "on the hoof" provoked the envy of the Philistines (Gen. 26:13), and we know that Jacob had both cattle and sheep (Gen. 33:13).

Various details of pastoralism are recorded in the stories of the patriarchs (Gen. 12:8-9; 13:5-12; 21:22-34; 26:27-33; 29:1-10; 31:38-40; 37:12-17; Ex. 2:16-25; 22:10-13). Therefore, even if Abraham did not start out as a pastoralist — and perhaps leaving his family did require him to leave behind his livestock — he soon became one on the journey in order to obey God's call. His life reflects the nomad's ability to adapt his lifestyle according to need and, in addition, his livestock represents his wealth. There is sufficient evidence that the patriarchs were, or became, nomads living in tents, who confined their wandering to the settled lands and their fringes.[10]

It is clear that nomadic pastoralism was God's way of preserving the patriarchs' independence from the neighboring pagan powers of their day so that he could fulfill his purpose. When the method broke down through enforced contact with the surrounding societies by famine, God tested the patriarchs' faith in his protection (Gen. 12:10; 15:13; 20:2; 26:1; 41:1). Jacob's life as both a traveler and a pastoralist is instructive, as it shows God persevering with him to continue his plan. God could have chosen to send Abraham as a merchant to live in the cities of Canaan, but this method kept him and his people separate from these baneful influences. We have only to remember the story of Lot and Abraham's experience with Abimelech and Pharaoh (Gen. 12:10ff.; 19:ff.; 20:1ff.), as well as Israel's later entanglements with Canaanites, to realize how necessary it was to maintain the patriarchs' spiritual and material independence. Nomadic pastoralism was one of God's "secret weapons" to keep the people separate to fulfill his redemptive purpose. It also demonstrates the importance of the nomads in Christian mission.

For the patriarchs and for Israel, traveling in faith with God, supported by nomadic pastoralism, was the means to develop trust in God for both material support and spiritual understanding of God himself. There was something compelling about the encounter with God himself for Abraham to express his faith in a journey, even before the details of God's plan had been revealed. Faith as a journey with God is both progressive and testing, bringing knowledge of both God and oneself. This journeying was the fundamental relationship within which God unfolded his purpose for the world's peoples.

6 The Pastoral God of a Traveling People

The particular method God chose to sustain his traveling people and reveal himself to the nations was nomadic pastoralism. The influence of this nomadism was not limited to the early stage of the patriarchs, but extends throughout the history of God's people and therefore affects the message of God conveyed in the Scriptures.

Nomadic freedom to meet with God

Nomadic pastoralism was still God's chosen lifestyle for his people later, when the Israelites were in Egypt. Joseph and his brothers could describe themselves as nothing else but shepherds to Pharaoh, in spite of the prejudice the Egyptians had against such people (Gen. 37:2, 12, 17, 47:1-4; 46:34). In Egypt they continued in pastoralism as hired herdsmen for the livestock that passed into state ownership as a result of Joseph's policies (Gen. 47:1-6, 17-18).

After Joseph's time the agricultural land may have continued in state ownership and it is unlikely that the Israelites, treated as a powerful and suspect immigrant community, would have been able to own land in Goshen (Num. 11:5). During the four centuries in Egypt, they may have only been allowed to be specialist herdsmen. The Israelites forced into Pharaoh's building projects can be compared to modern "nomads in waiting," forced temporarily into a settled life. Like such people today, they maintained a reputation for having a faith associated with the desert (Ex. 5:1; 8:25-28).

The next revelation for humankind at Sinai was also given in a context of nomadic pastoralism. Moses insisted to Pharaoh that the wilderness was the appropriate place for Israel's God to be worshipped, because he is a God who scorns the elaborate human constructions of an environment like Egypt.

They could support themselves in the wilderness, although the numbers (however interpreted) would stretch the resources of the limited pasture (Ex. 7:16; 8:25, 27; 10:9, 26; 12:31f.). With their animals they would be self-sufficient on the journey to Canaan (Ex. 34:3; Num. 3:41, 45; 15:3). And, because the direct route was closed to them, it was crucial that they could sustain themselves by methods known to them (Ex. 13:17).

The Exodus journey was one for which the Israelites, as pastoralists, were well-equipped. They spent 40 years in the wilderness as shepherds, not as urban or agricultural refugees (Num. 14:33). "Wilderness" (*midbar*) does not refer just to a hostile desert, for it is also a place for pasturing flocks, that is, steppe or grassland. The Israelites were pastoralists with considerable herds of cattle and flocks of sheep (Ex. 10:26; 12:32, 38). Like many pastoralists since, the Israelites had a detachment of pastoral coppersmiths traveling with them. These were Kenites (meaning "smith"), a branch of the Midianites, under the leadership of Jethro, who joined Israel. One of them became Israel's desert guide, or scout (Gen. 15:19; Ex. 2:18; 3:1ff., 18:1-12; Num. 10:29; Judg. 1:16). At the end of the migration, the tribes of Reuben and Gad were criticized for making a typical pastoral decision by choosing the good pasture in the Transjordan (Num. 32:1-15). The Transjordan tribes may have taken their cattle along a different route in the wilderness, as they were more committed to cattle pastoralism.[1]

Moses' management of such a vast migration, with the need for guidance about the route, the provision of water, the gathering of natural food and the arrangement of the camp can be appreciated by a nomad more than by a Westerner. Just the sheer numbers of people and their flocks would create enormous problems in such an arid landscape.[2] The manna and quails would have been necessary to preserve the livestock as mobile assets, and Moses reacted with a typical pastoralist reluctance to any thought of slaughtering their livestock for the short-term gain of feeding the people in the wilderness (Num. 11:22). The livestock would have been used sparingly only for sacrifice, that would also involve a meal.

Even the rebellion of Israel against Moses, which is interpreted as petty moral weakness in many a Western sermon, is better understood when we realize how modern nomads question their leaders when faced with the stark probability of starvation and death. The headman of a herding group has to make decisions that can lead to rapid disaster if pasture or water is not found at the right times and in the right places. Among most pastoralist groups, such failures in leadership result in the exchange of the leader for a man with greater proven experience. The Israelites were men of considerable experience, not just petulant urbanites. They had genuine reasons to complain, because their pastoral expertise told them that such an undertaking was threatened with the probability of failure.[3] All of this describes a people whose natural lifestyle was pastoralism, with experience traveling through the desert.

For both Abraham and Israel, God's method for developing trust and the fear of the Lord was to take them on a journey as nomads, and in this context to reveal his purpose further (Gen. 15:6; Ex. 14:31). One has to question whether either the patriarchs or Israel, or indeed many modern nomads, have a destination in the sense that their traveling is merely a necessary means to get somewhere by the shortest route. Rather, their traveling is all part of living out their tradition and ideals as a people.

Faith tested in the wilderness

The Exodus and wilderness journey were to leave an indelible mark on Israel's spirituality, to be alluded to time and time again (Gen. 47:9; Ps. 39:12; 119:19, 54).[4]

Israel's destination was God himself, not the land (Ex. 19:4-6). The Exodus was an escape from slavery, but it was also for the purpose of learning faith and making them a living message to the nations (Ex. 19:4; Lev. 20:26; Dt. 4:6-8).

The traveler and pastoralist relationship developed over the course of 14 years and predated the covenant. Abraham followed God, and was justified by him, before their relationship was given the form of a covenant (Gen. 17; see Rom. 4:9-12). Similarly, Israel trusted God to flee to the Red Sea, saw God open it before them, received manna and quails and water from the rock — all before there was any suggestion of a covenant (Ex. 13:14 — 19:5). Israel's faith developed through the formative experience of nomadism in the wilderness and was not replaced, but rather expanded, by Israel becoming a covenant nation (Ex. 19:5-6; Dt. 5:3). Their life under the law in the Promised Land, long after the wilderness experience was over, was still to be motivated by recalling God's provision and testing on that journey (Dt. 8:2-5).

God revealed enough of himself to compel the patriarchs and Israel to travel in faith before the more detailed arrangements of covenants were actually made. Recognizing this fact curbs any temptation to forget that every stage of the people's journey with God was entirely on his initiative. He told Abraham about this journey six centuries before the enslaved Israelites cried to him. The fundamental call of grace, and faith as a response to that call, were established long before there were any formal religious institutions.

Israel continued to be a people on the move, in a developing relationship with God, long after they had settled. The promise of the land, therefore, was not so much about the provision of a national territory as it was about giving Israel a *place* in God's purpose and *space* for a relationship to develop as the nation came to know him. To further this, God's character as previously revealed in the nomadic experience continued to be revealed in the law's regulation of society (Ex. 20:2; 22:21f.;

Dt.1–4; 5:15; 24:18; Lev. 11:45; 19:33f.;
Num. 15:41).

The structure of Deuteronomy, with the
foundation of the nation at Sinai falling
between Moses' narration of the wilderness
journey (Dt. 1–11) and the threat of exile
and return (Dt. 27–34), suggests that Israel
was on a perpetual spiritual journey. "Rest"
did not refer to ceasing to travel, especially
in the metaphorical sense of advancing with
God, but rather to a divinely given security
from enemies (Dt. 25:19; Josh. 1:13f.).
Enjoying the responsibility and blessing of a
divine allocation of natural resources
depends on human obedience to God. God
requires that each generation pass on to the
next the moral challenge of loyalty to his
covenant and law in exchange for blessing
and security. Israel's residence in the land
depended on her response, and exile finally
was her experience (Dt. 15:4-6; 26:14-15;
28:1-68).[5]

Israel's journey parallels the need of
many minority peoples for freedom from
oppression in a dominant society. This
freedom can only be found by a "walk" with
God and can lead to behavior that wins the
respect of the wider society. God's purpose
for each people group is that it might know
him, and his standards for its society, and
enjoy the freedom to practice both faith and
life expressing his character. In Israel's case
the Promised Land was an essential part,
and yet only a part, of God's promise. Her
ultimate destination was freedom — to
express a new identity by trusting in God.
To reach this, she had to travel both literally
and morally.

Israel's faith failed when the people
refused to advance into the Promised Land
— the route that even all their experience
indicated was the right one — because of
their fears of being a large, slow-moving
target in the pastures of Canaan, without
the freedom to move further into the
wilderness away from danger. They opted
for the more familiar trials of nomadic
pastoralism. Israel's history parallels that of
many modern nomads, who see their
wandering life as punishment for some past
moral failure (Num. 14:33). The wilderness

came to represent a place of divine
revelation and testing, as well as of spiritual
danger.[6] Israel was to fail repeatedly to learn
the lessons of faith in the pastoral life of the
wilderness.

The New Testament is clear that Israel
never entered the promised rest and was
driven into exile (Josh. 1:13; 2 Sam. 7:10;
Heb. 4:8). The one person who should have
entered the Promised Land, Moses, was
condemned to die outside it.[7] Israel failed to
fulfill God's role for her and was superseded
by a believing missionary remnant, the
multi-ethnic New Testament church (2 Cor.
6:16; 1 Pet. 2:9).

The Bible sees God's people as travelers,
motivated by a trust in a "traveling" God,
ever ready to obey his will and purpose,
unhindered by the commitments and
conventions of the surrounding society. The
New Testament, understood within its Old
Testament context, shows Christ to be the
God-given means to fulfill Israel's role to the
world's peoples by dealing with her spiritual,
social and moral failure.[8] The journey of
God's people is now by faith in God's grace
in Christ, who is the way to be reconciled to
God. The Christian believer continues to be
a pilgrim or nomad (Heb. 4; 1 Pet. 1:1, 17;
2:11), constantly moving in obedience
towards God's final goal.

The pastoral relationship in the covenant

We have seen that God has revealed his
redemptive purpose to the world by creating
a traveling people sustained by pastoralism.
This pastoralism continued to be important
throughout the people's history as it gave
them a measure of separation from others
and dependence on God. Pastoral images are
thus prominent throughout the Bible. We
suggest that this is so because the pastoral
relationship with God of a traveling people
lies implicit beneath other biblical concepts,
like that of the covenant. Faith in the
transcendent, yet immanent, pastoral guide
of a traveling people gave Israel her
distinctive identity.

Therefore, the basic understanding and
experience of a journey of faith with God
was augmented by the varied concepts of

covenant, law, temple (with its ritual), ethnic separatism, prophecy, kingdom and the monarchy. These biblical institutions reinforced the distinctiveness of Israel that was already explicit as they traveled as nomads. They also gave Israel a moral unity as a witness to other nations (Ex. 19:6).

God's purpose was that he might be known by all the nations of the world. Israel was to be God's special *segulla*, that is, a "property abstracted for special use" (Ex. 19:5). The goal of God's choice of Israel is expressed by the phrase "for all the earth is mine." This does not simply make a comparison between Israel and the world, but it expresses God's purpose to make Israel the model and means to bring God's knowledge to the nations.[9] Israel had to become a "showcase" society by fulfilling God's instruction, or *torah* (Ex. 19:6; Dt. 4:6), and show forth the moral character derived from her knowledge of, and obedience to, God (Dt.4:7).

The genealogical structure of Genesis emphasizes that Israel is part of the world through creation, but more important is her declared missionary role in many texts (Ex. 34:10; Dt. 4:6-8, 32-34; 1 Kgs. 8:41; Ps. 22:27; 67; 86:9; 117; Is. 2:2; etc.).[10] Israel's nomadic experience under the guidance of God was to demonstrate God's character and plan for humankind to the nations. Therefore the view and experience of God as gracious and pastorally caring was a vital part of being his people.

The covenant-God is often described as a pastoralist in a way that unites his roles of creator and covenant-maker, so that he has command of both human history and the cosmic ecosystem. The creator-God fulfills his covenant with Israel like a shepherd because he made and possesses everything, including the cattle on a thousand hills (Ps. 50:10; 95:7; 100:3; Ezek. 34:26-27). *"I myself will search for my sheep and look after them."* Understanding God as shepherd expresses most appropriately his covenant grace or steadfast love (*'hesed*), which is the outworking of the relationship. This grace is the undeserved favor of God, who faithfully fulfills his covenant even with a disobedient

people. Gathering the sheep, leading them to good pasture in all conditions and weathers, seeking the lost, binding up the injured, establishing folds and places of rest are all mundane duties of the shepherd — but they are images used to cover the whole range of God's activities in living out this relationship with his people. He has an amazing ability to find good pasture and water in the same place; in real life they are often one or more day's journey apart (Ps. 23:2).

From before Israel's time, gods, kings and other leaders were likened to shepherds (Gen. 49:24; Num. 2717; 1 Kgs. 22:17; Is. 40:11; Jer. 31:10), so that the biblical image of the shepherd also has much to do with the authority to provide, protect and judge. The counting of the sheep and cattle grazing in the mountain pasture are signs of God-given prosperity (Lev. 27:32; Jer. 33:13), as also of his judgment (Ezek. 20:37; Jer. 9:10). As God has helped men to defend the flock against predators, so he also defends Israel against her enemies (1 Sam. 17:34-36). God can provide for, protect and lead the individual as well as the group (Gen. 49:24; cf. 48:15; Ps. 23; 77:20; 78:52; 80:1; Jer. 25:34-36).

The reality of God going before the patriarchs and Israel in the wilderness leads to his requirement that the people should "walk in his ways" by conforming their lives to his will. The "way" of the earthly migration and God's guidance in the wilderness makes an easy continual transition to use the same term for God's conduct and the responding conduct of his people. Because they traveled "in his footsteps" in the wilderness, all their life is a journey with him, even after literal travel has ceased. Their relationship with God is repeatedly described as to "walk in God's ways" (Ex. 16:4; 18:20; Lev. 18:3; 20:23; Dt. 8:13-16; Ps. 5:8; 23:3; 27:11; 31:3; 77:20; 80:1; 139:24; Neh. 5:9; 9:12-19; Is. 40:11; 63:11), even long after any literal traveling was finished (1 Kgs. 2:3f.; 3:14; 6:12; Neh. 5:9; Is. 2:3, 5; 30:21; Ezek. 11:20; Zech. 3:7).

Therefore righteousness that exalts a nation is expressed in nomadic terms. To "walk" was to journey, to arrive or depart on travel, such as the patriarchs' journeys or the wilderness journey for Israel. It was to progress purposefully, just as nomads travel with a systematic purpose according to the seasons, obeying their sense of calling within the conditions of the environment. This walk leads to blessing and prayer being answered (Dt. 1:30f.) as well as success in war (Dt. 20:4).

Deuteronomy especially links walking in the wilderness (Dt. 2:7) with walking in the Lord's ways, that is, obeying his commands (Dt. 5:33; 8:6; 10:12, etc.). One can trace links in the narrative (Ex. 13:18, 21 with 18:20; Dt. 8:2 with v. 6; 17:16 with 19:9; 25:17, 18 with 26:17; 28:7). Other links include Israel's disobedience as departing from the way (the episode of the golden calf: Ex. 32:8 with 33:13; Dt. 9:12, 16 with 10:12; and, generally, Dt. 1:22, 25 with 1:33; 3:26 and 5:32-33). Many of the Psalms also connect the earthly way with walking in God's ways (Ps. 1:1, 6; 18:21, 30; 119). This walk of faith was expressed by trustworthiness and love toward God, with imperfect keeping of the law requiring sacrifices to reconcile to God.

God's concern for justice in society is shown in pastoral terms. The refusal of hospitality and celebration at sheepshearing time is implicitly condemned (1 Sam. 25:2-8, 36; 2 Sam. 13:24-39). The custom of allowing a poor pastoralist, who has lost his own flock, to rear orphaned lambs and so start again, is still practiced today. This is the likely background to Nathan's parable that condemned David's adultery against Uriah, that speaks of the poor man's only ewe lamb reared among his children being stolen by the rich man with many flocks (2 Sam. 12:1-6). This is a poignant image to modern nomads like the Fulbe who lend or share livestock in difficult times. God is as concerned with justice in pastoralism as he is with adultery. Ezekiel describes God judging Israel like a shepherd dividing his sheep. Sheep that grow fat by butting others away from the fodder and trampling down the pasture are a picture of injustice and inequality in society (Ezek. 34:17-21).

The Exodus was a redemption from the consequences of sin and social oppression. Redemption from the guilt and power of sin was to come later, although in anticipation of this any Israelite could receive justification by God (Gen. 15:6; Ps. 32:1-5; 1 Kgs. 8:30). One can often go astray, fall short or rebel, resulting in a ruptured relationship with the Shepherd. In the Old Testament, forgiveness is sought (Ps. 25:18; Num. 14:19a; 1 Kgs. 8:30; 2 Chr. 6:21; etc.), received (Ps. 32:5; 78:38; 85:2; 99:8; 103:3; Num. 14:19b; cf. Ex. 32:32, where forgiveness is refused) and promised (Jer. 18:23; 31:34). Yet Israel was disobedient and unbelieving in the wilderness and later practiced social oppression herself, like that she had experienced at the hands of the Egyptians. A generation were forgiven but refused entry into the land (Num. 14:20-22).

Even if pastoralism may have receded somewhat as a major economic activity during Israel's history, it continued to be given prominence in the Scriptures as expressive of Israel's relationship with God. Israel learned that God was their herdsman leading the migration, often on the edge of survival, environmentally or militarily. The images of nomadic pastoralism integrated the walk of faith and obedience with the great revelation given. The covenant relationship made socially explicit the relationship of trust and obedience already established by the journey with God. It needed to be completed by its fulfillment in the relationship of Jesus to God as Father, for leadership was a crucial weakness in Israel.

God's dwelling

Central to this walk in the Lord's ways was his presence. Appropriately enough God's place of worship was a tent, the tabernacle; he had "no house" (Lev. 26:12; 2 Sam. 7:7). It represented the God who "traveled" with his people, who is not only too great for permanent buildings, however grand, but too "mobile." His character is purposeful nomadism, a God on the move leading his people! This situation continued for three or more centuries, even after settling in the land.

Temple building among Israel's

neighbors was undertaken by the state or a priestly elite in order to honor a god who had given victory to the nation. The building was a prestigious structure in a major city.[11] In contrast, the "nomadic" Yahweh takes the initiative to liberate a people of shepherds and slaves at the Exodus and encounters them in the desert to dwell among them. This begins at the burning bush in the context of desert pastoralism (Ex. 3). His presence, confirmed by covenant, made them into a nation (Ex. 19:5-6).

The tent is no status symbol compared to the elaborate buildings of the surrounding gods. The permanent institution of this tent seems strange when one considers that the journey from Egypt to Canaan was originally intended to have taken only weeks, not 40 years! It is stranger still when we consider that God knew that the journey would be longer. The collection of the elaborate materials underscores this. If the aim was a temple building, why not wait until arrival in the land? It appears that a portable structure was an enduring part of the plan, even after they came to the land.

The building of the temple appears to be a concession, related to the permission to have a king, which departed from the earlier ideal of God pasturing his people through judges (2 Sam. 7:2-29). It was David's fear to go to the tabernacle after his disobedience that instigated the preparations for an alternative (1 Chr. 21:28 — 22:11). There are a number of negative contrasts between the temple and the tabernacle. The temple was only built after the king's palace, and a shorter time was given to its construction, while Moses and the people never built anything for themselves. God seems to make a distinction, calling the temple "this house that you are building," while the tabernacle was built according to a pattern God gave (Ex. 25:8; 1 Kgs. 6:12).[12] At best it was a human project, motivated by a sense of guilt derived from the prosperity of the king (2 Sam. 7:2-7).

The temple, furthermore, was built with forced labor, while the tabernacle was built from the gifts of the people, by craftsmen gifted by the Spirit (Ex. 31:1-3; 35:20f.; 36:3-5). The simpler materials used for the tabernacle contrast with the gold and timber from foreign sources from which the temple was built (1 Kgs. 5:6). The temple may have relied on defensive walls (following the parallel with the vision of Ezekiel [Ezek. 40:5ff.]). The tabernacle, on the other hand, was defended by the threat of divine judgment (Ex. 40:35). The temple and its treasure was a target for invaders and "raided" by Israel's kings, while the tabernacle was never attacked in its "480 years" history (1 Kgs. 6:1). On this calculation, the tabernacle lasted longer than the 375 years of Solomon's temple.[13] Although the second temple after the exile lasted 500 years after Malachi, God passes over it in silence. It was replaced by Herod's structure, which was condemned by Jesus.

Solomon reiterates that God could not dwell there, but only his "name," and prayers would be answered from heaven (1 Kgs. 8:27). We are told that the poles that carried the ark of the covenant, although easily removable, were left in place for centuries — even though they were incongruous in the setting of this grand building. They protruded through the veil that only the high priest could pass through once a year (1 Kgs. 8:8; cf. Ex. 25:12-15). This was hardly because the builders forgot to measure the poles, for God himself gave the plans! The ark was placed with the poles pointing forward and backward as if being carried permanently on the march with the congregation following behind. While Israel had completed the geographical journey to the land, the people's relationship was still to be a spiritual pilgrimage to the "rest" promised (see Heb. 4).

The prophets heaped scorn on the false confidence derived from the apparent permanence of the magnificent building and its elaborate ritual. They predicted the temple's destruction together with Israel's exile from the land for disobedience. Israel had lost sight of God's nomadic character and dynamic purpose, and had replaced it with a mechanistic ritual relationship. Such a false confidence contradicted the complete trust in God that he had taught them as pastoralists in the wilderness. So God had to drive them out to travel again to relearn the lesson.

Israel's spirituality continued to speak of God's protection as like being put in a pavilion, tabernacle, tent, or even behind a windbreak or sunshade — all of which are, physically, very flimsy structures.[14] The emphasis is on the relationship with God himself as protector. Similarly, nomads have little to hid in, but rely on the protection from those they are related to. One's relationships are vital, and physical structures are of limited value.

Pastoralism in the land with God

After arrival in the land, the Israelites became settled and were no longer nomadic, but neither God nor Israel abandoned pastoralism. The land was known as a land for shepherds from before biblical times, and being a shepherd was the most common occupation there.[15] As a land of "milk and honey" it was a pastoralist paradise, being suitable for both sheep and cattle raising as well as for the gathering of natural produce (Ex. 3:8, 17; 13:5; 33:3; Num. 13:27; 14:8; 16:13; Dt. 6:3; 11:9; 26:9, 15; 27:3; 31:20; Josh. 5:6, etc.). Every seventh year was a Sabbath for the land and a return to a hunter-gatherer and pastoral economy. The agricultural and urban features of the land, that contrasted with the harsh wilderness, were merely a bonus and secondary to the God-given natural abundance (Dt. 8:7-9, 15).

Immediately after the conquest, the Israelites' limited agricultural production would only have supplemented their pastoralism. The Israelites must have had some experience as cultivators in Egypt, just as many pastoral peoples today engage in seasonal agriculture without this undermining their essential pastoralism. Although Israel took over terraced fields that were already constructed and vineyards that were already planted, the livestock grazing the pastures around the settlements must have continued to be a major means of subsistence.

Every village of the Israelites continued to have its flocks of sheep and goats and herds of cattle. Most families had members working as herders pasturing near the village, or going considerable distances within Israel's territory to open pastures, beyond the large areas then covered in forest, thus practicing "enclosed nomadism" ("common lands," Lev. 25:34; Num. 35:2, 3, 4, etc.; Josh 21:2; 1 Chr. 6:55). The shepherds passed on their skill and knowledge within their family and, if working for others, their remuneration took the form of a share of the young animals they had reared.

Although settled and no longer nomads themselves, the Israelites were in constant contact with tent-dwelling nomads who living permanently on the steppe with small livestock.[16] Foreign shepherds also passed through Israelite territory, grazing their flocks on the stubble of the fields in return for fertilizing the fields with the dung. They also provided their skills as shepherds to the Israelites, or alternately posed a threat as tricksters, raiders or spies.[17]

The nomads who appear in the Bible, such as the Amalekites and Midianites, are usually presented as hostile, and most references to them are negative (Ex. 17:8ff.; Num. 14:43ff.; Dt. 25:17ff.; Judg.3:13). The Midianites launched what were considered to be the first recorded rapid camel-mounted attacks in war, but they were in fact related to Abraham and Moses (Gen. 25:6; Ex. 2:21). Gideon led the victory of agriculturists against the "legitimate" raiding of desert-dwelling pastoralists (Judg. 6–8). It would not be difficult for nomads to see the Bible as prejudiced against them.

Social and economic changes came when the monarchies of Judah and Northern Israel created centralized courts with wealthy retainers who became the absentee landlords of large estates. But in spite of the abuses created by a powerful court, the decentralized pattern of society, based on the village or the small town with its attached pastoralism, would have continued as the way of life for most of the population. When Israelites "went home" to their houses, the expression is often literally "they went to their tents" (1 Kgs. 8:66; 12:16, etc.), but on other occasions "house" is used (e.g., Judg. 20:8). Other metaphors refer to tents and their ropes in contexts where tents had passed out of use (Is. 33:20; 54:2; Jer. 10:20).[18]

Israel's cities were tiny and very crowded, and most of the population lived in the country. Even the inhabitants of the cities took to the countryside to live with their relatives and to help with the harvests or livestock for the summer months. In Israel's thinking, cities did not carry the connotations of citizenship, culture and human achievement that they did for the Greeks. Cities were considered to be useful for serving the rural population around them for administration, trade and defense — not for living in. As the religious center of the whole country, Jerusalem was a special place for pilgrimage and worship — but it was not necessarily the place to live, and God's influence spread out far beyond the city.[19] The spiritual ideal saw the city as containing a symbol of God's presence and blessing.

Israel's highly developed pastoralism was vital for providing the animals for sacrifice from the best of the pastoralist's assets (Lev. 1, 3–6). Being a pastoralist and being able to sacrifice defined the "poverty-line" (Lev. 1:14f.; 12:8; Lk. 2:24). The system recognized its own limitations and could have required something other than livestock. But the offerings represented not only human sin, but also the moral sacrifice God made in redeeming a disobedient people to himself (Ex. 32–33; Dt. 1:34f., 43; 9:5-21), and pointed to a greater sacrifice he would make in Jesus (Lev. 17:11).

These considerations imply that, in spite of having become agriculturists, at heart the Israelites saw themselves as semi-nomadic pastoral people — at least in the early part of this period. As they continued in this lifestyle, they should have carried on learning the lessons of dependence on God's provision that they began in the wilderness. So pastoralism continued to be an integral part of Israel's experience and history.

Israel's concept of God's land

Israel's concept of land was a nomadic one. Land should be accessible to all and allocated by the Lord according to use and produce, rather than giving outright ownership (Num. 34). This view of the land contrasted with that of Israel's contemporaries, who believed that land was owned by the monarch, or by private landlords to use as they wished. The Promised Land was God's gift or inheritance because of Israel's sonship (Ex. 4:22; Dt. 32:5ff.). However, God retained overall ownership — even when he had "given" it to Israel — because he owns everything (Ex. 19:5; Dt. 10:14).[20]

We are told that the Israelites were God's aliens in the land (Lev. 25:23; 1 Chr. 29:15). They could not be forcibly removed except when he should so decide.[21] The divine allocation guaranteed the inheritance to each tribe and clan, down to each household, in contrast to having a fickle human landlord (Lev. 25:23).[22] Yet being God's aliens also meant that they themselves were accountable to him and not free to dispose of it, as human landowners could, by right of purchase.

The land was not to be subject to commercial or political transactions (Gen. 17:8; 48:4; Lev. 25). The sale of land was not a transfer of ownership but of its temporary use for a number of harvests (Lev. 25:14-16). The original family to whom it had been allocated had a right to redeem it back from the buyer. Further, the jubilee law allowed land to revert back to the original family, thereby undoing any subsequent commercial transactions (Lev. 25:13). On the other hand, "mere" town houses could be bought and sold permanently, since they were of lesser consequence (Lev. 25:29f.). All this was true for the agricultural land around the towns. Presumably there was similar freedom to use the common or open pastures beyond the fields, on which Israel would depend in the sabbatical year, and which must have been of considerable extent.

Benefit from the land was to be shared. Israel's experience as "outsiders" in both Canaan and Egypt also meant that they knew how insecure an alien could feel. Their society was intended, therefore, to be open to all who had a similar faith and were willing to make their home among them. In a similar way, many nomads gradually accept others with a similar lifestyle and experience. They were told to make the alien welcome among them, and even to allow the alien to participate in their worship (Ex. 12:19, 48-49; 22:21; 23:9; Lev. 19:33; Dt. 1:16; Jer. 7:6, 22:33; Ezek. 22:29, etc.). God's promise was to bless each ethnic group with his revelation to Israel and through Christ, and this holds true today for nomadic peoples, who often are a minority in the modern nation state. Right from the beginning the nomadic life was not marginal, but central, in God's revelation.

The land, too, must have its Sabbath year as an independent entity (Lev. 25:1ff.). Every seventh year, Israel abandoned agriculture to return to a hunter-gathering lifestyle and pastoralism to survive. God provided a bumper harvest in the sixth year (Lev. 25:21), but otherwise wild produce from the extensive common lands, and not from cultivated fields (v. 4), had to sustain them (Lev. 25:6-7, 12, 19). This sabbatical year was inadequate as a fallow period, and it appears to be a token return to the pastoral situation (Lev. 25:5-7). It possibly also implies that agriculture is necessary toil for the land as a result of sin (Gen. 3:17-19), from which the land must rest as human beings do. The Sabbath year was a measure of self-sustained natural renewal of the environment, but was inadequate as a fallow period. It appears to be a token return to the pastoral situation (Lev. 25:5-7), and possibly implies that agriculture is necessary toil for the land as a result of sin (Gen. 3:17-19), from which the land must, like human beings, rest. Debtors were freed at the beginning of this year (Dt. 15:12. All this implies a symbolic return to the situation on entry into the land with the same trust in God to fulfill his promise.

Israel's residence in the land was conditional on their faithfulness to God, and they saw this as a continuation of the patriarchs' experience (1 Chr. 29:15; Heb. 11:13). Israel's security was only in God's allocation and disposal, which she could forfeit through disobedience at any time.

Israel's God-given concept of the land maintained the dynamic relationship of her nomadic past even after being settled as a non-nomadic people for centuries. As with nomads, permanence in the form of residence in one place did not depend on ownership of land so much as on maintaining a right relationship with the right people or person — in their case God.

Israel's relationship with God and the land was dynamic, for there was constant tension between its being permanently given and the condition of the people's response to God. Israel was aware that the previous occupants were judged and had lost the land. God's purpose included the land as Israel's resting-place (Dt. 12:9-11), where they could live demonstrating his character by obeying his laws, and so be a witness to the surrounding unbelieving nations (Is. 11:10; 66:1). This involved God finding a resting-place with his people (1 Kgs. 8:56; Ps. 132:8, 14), and entry without God was unthinkable as fulfillment of the promise to the patriarchs (Ex. 32:13). The temple fulfilled this requirement, with Solomon praising God for giving rest to the people (1 Chr. 28:2). But their subsequent history demonstrated a tenuous hold on the land, as the dynamic of the divine relationship turned against them.

Faith, in a fragile environment

The fact that the land was a fragile environment gave them further opportunities to develop their faith, as is the case for many modern nomads. Agriculture depended on the limited rain and dew in the right quantities at the right seasons, using terraced fields, run-off cultivation and cisterns. Without terracing, the topsoil was soon washed away. The development of cisterns was essential for settling any significant population in the Judean hill country.[23] October, with its rains, was the season most looked forward to after the heat of summer (see Is. 41:17-20). Barley was more important than wheat, because of the semi-arid conditions, as it is in Tibet. In time of drought Israel's survival often depended on its pastoralism, since the animals could be moved considerable distances to where there was pasture.

The threat of drought was connected directly to Israel's unfaithfulness. The temptation to rely on the Baals, of the Canaanite fertility religion based on agriculture, often undermined their faith. Israel's continued residence in the land depended on her loyalty to God, who had proved himself in the pastoral situation of the wilderness (Dt. 28:12, 23; 33:28; 1 Kgs. 18:17ff.). With time, the environment was ruined as the forest cover was destroyed and the soil eroded due to overpopulation and war.[24] This was also due to the large commercial estates replacing the stewardship of the local households to whom the land had been originally allocated.

Land ownership was more a matter of divinely-sanctioned occupation for stewardship, than outright possession (Lev. 18:28; Dt. 24:4). The covenant highlighted the conditional nature of this gift, that the land was not merited in any way or owned by right. Its enjoyment depended on grateful, worshipping obedience (Lev. 25:18; Dt. 1:35; 4:1; 6:3, 24; 8:5-7; 9:28; 11:17; 26:9ff.; 27:1-68; Josh. 1:8; Is. 7:20; Jer. 11; Ezek. 20:10-15, 23). If Israel failed to obey God as the wilderness generation had failed to do (Ps. 95:11; Micah 2:10; Heb. 3:11), then the threat of expulsion hung over them (Lev. 18:28; 26:14-25; Dt. 4:26-27; 11:17; 28:15-68; 29:18-29; Josh. 23:13). The fertility of the land could be sustained by God's promise of plenty, on condition of Israel's obedience. With Israel's sin the land became exhausted. Israel's exile was seen as a renewal and rest for the land, as if agricultural activity was toil or a violation of the earth, and a return to natural growth and pasture was the more appropriate state (Lev. 26:34-35, 43).

The Israelites actually only realized the fulfillment of living in the land for about 40% of the time between the giving of the promise and the coming of Christ. This fulfillment was increasingly precarious as the threat of exile hung over Israel. The promise of the land was a means to maintain the dynamic relationship with God already established in the wilderness journey, and it was conditional on their putting into practice God's pattern for society. It was not to be treated as a permanent national territory, but rather as evidence of their trust in the grace of God.

In spite of what we have said about God being the pastoralist God of a traveling people, much in the Bible story is about sedentary societies and apparently only parts (of the Bible) are relevant to nomads. Although the patriarchs were nomadic pastoralists, their *God-given* goal was a sedentary life in the Promised Land. It would be easy for nomads to see Israel as an essentially agricultural people living in houses — and therefore as being irrelevant to them.

But, far from advocating the sedentary life, Israel's experience resulting from her reoccurring disobedience demonstrated all the disadvantage of the sedentary life. These included conflict with neighbors, drought in the fields, high taxation, corruption of culture and religion, exploitation of the poor by the rich, criminality in rape and murder, and invasion and colonization. The spiritual dangers of that life appear the same to nomads today, and the solution the same. The prophets often called for a new exodus experience.

Israel was in no way a nomadic people at this stage of her history. Still, her relationship to God and to the land was more akin to that of the nomads, with a stress on renewable natural growth and the allocation of resources, than it was to modern notions of land ownership and national territory.

Pastoral leadership for God's people

God's shepherding was an exacting model for human leaders. He delighted to use leaders who were pastoralists, such as Abraham, Isaac, Jacob, Joseph and the founders of the twelve tribes, Job, Moses, David and Amos (Amos 1:1-2, 7:14-15). Joshua's commissioning was such that the people might not become as sheep without a shepherd (Num. 27:17). David as king had a covenant to be God's shepherd over his people (2 Sam. 5:2-3), and Jeremiah used so many pastoral images that it would not be surprising if he had worked as a shepherd.

Israel's human leaders who broke God's law were likened to irresponsible shepherds who had failed in their duties (Jer. 2:8; 10:21; 11:3f.; 12:10; 22:22, 24; 23:1-4; 25:35ff., etc.). When this happened, God himself had to step in to shepherd the people (Jer. 23:1-2; Ezek. 34:1-16).[25] God will judge the people as a chief shepherd dealing with under-shepherds. As a shepherd has to give account for sheep lost to predators by saving part of the carcass, so God will give account for his judgment of Israel (Amos 3:12). The shepherds or leaders of Israel will not be able to stop the judgment any more than shepherds can frighten a lion (Is. 31:4).

Invaders will occupy Judah like alien shepherds stealing another's pasture with their flocks (Jer. 6:2), and they will do it casually like a shepherd who flicks grass from his cloak (Jer. 43:12). The camp guard dogs will fail to keep watch. And enemies, no better than dogs themselves, will triumph (Is. 56:9-11; Job 30:1). The effect of God's judgment will be like trying to put up a tent single-handedly, or like a pasture withering in the heat, or like sheep that are lost, or going to slaughter, or like a well going dry (Jer. 10:20; 12:2-4; 14:2-6; 50:8). God's judgment is completed by the exile, but it will not last (Ps. 74:1).

A second exodus to liberty and a return journey to the land will come. God will enable Judah to lead the captives of other nations to liberty like a billy goat leading the flock (Jer. 50:8; Ezek. 34:1-17). The two prophetic oracles of Zechariah 9–11 and 12–14 describe God's shepherd, who would destroy the evil shepherds, and who would then be struck down while the sheep was scattered. Jesus related this to himself and his cross. God will finally dwell with his people (using terms here for being in a camp of tents) and, paradoxically, this implies security and permanence (Ezek. 37:27; Zech 2:10-11).

Israel's future spiritual pilgrimage was constantly expressed in pastoral images, regardless of the lifestyle of most of the Israelites and the later Jews. Isaiah, the urbanite prophet of the Jerusalem court, also uses images that are relevant to pastoralists. Describing this future like a new exodus, in chapter 40 he describes the improvement of migration routes across the mountains (vv. 3-4). He goes on to mention the withering of pasture (vv. 6-8), the careful shepherding of young animals (vv. 10-11), the wisdom of the heavenly herdsman in understanding the ecosystem (vv. 13-14), the pastoralist's disdain for princes and khans (vv. 18-20), the destructive effect of the wind on vegetation (v. 24), observing the stars and birds of prey (vv. 25-26, 31), and the earth made into the habitation of human beings with the sky being spread like a tent and curtain (v. 22). God gives strength for what is usually a very hard life (v. 29-30). All of this is part of Isaiah's picture of a greater exodus, beyond the judgment by Assyria and the other world powers of the day, that will fulfill God's promises to Israel.

God requires a relationship of trust and obedience to him as the free and faithful Creator. He also requires that life and society be shaped according to his character. Israel became a sort of ethnic minority, with her ethos established by a divinely led migratory journey. She had to maintain her distinct identity by her internal spiritual and moral resources. In this she was like many nomadic peoples. Her existence among the settled, well-established territorial nations, with their territorial deities, was dependent on her loyalty to the non-territorial, transcendent God.

Israel was to be God's witness to the world. Their pastoral experience demonstrated God's provision and protection, and revealed God's grace, faithfulness and righteousness, that establish the foundation of the gospel. Israel's history provides an authoritative model of revelation and redemption that challenges all peoples to travel with the "timeless" God, who intervenes in our lives to develop our trust and obedience. What was required to complete this relationship was an act of transcendent, "nomadic" redemption in Jesus.

7 Come, Follow Me

The Bible's message is one continuous whole, initiated and sustained by God's revelation. But the coming of God as a man forms the crucial fulfillment of all that had gone before. While the Old Testament appeals to the interests of the nomads, we live as the disciples of Christ and must consider the New Testament and how we are to apply this nomadic emphasis in the Bible in our lives and ministries. As David Livingstone said, God had only one Son and he made him a missionary. The nomads need to follow the Good Shepherd, both to understand their own itinerant life and to share in an eternal destination. Jesus was, by his choice, the supreme peripatetic — and we lose much of his meaning if we ignore this. Jesus invites us all to come and follow him.

Christ fulfills God's pastoral relationship

The purpose of God began with the journeys of the patriarchs and Israel to develop their faith. God promised a good shepherd, "my servant David, and he shall feed them" (Ezek. 34:22-24; Jer. 23:1-6), who would lead his people into a new era of redemption. Jesus fulfills this pastoral role in the New Testament.[1] The shepherd takes the initiative at every stage of the journey, both in nomadism and in God's purpose for humankind.

The only *public* announcement of his arrival in his first 30 years was to otherwise unknown shepherds. These were probably not local men (possibly with their wives), but they were living with the sheep and migrating around the land, only returning to the owners of the sheep once or twice a year. They became the first Christian missionaries (Lk. 2:8-19). Jesus began his journeying early, spending a period in Egypt and so identifying himself with Israel's formative experience of being in Egypt (Mt. 2:13-15).

Jesus' parents were artisans like the modern Inadan, Waata or Ghorbati and, like many of these people, they were too poor to have a flock to provide a sacrifice (Lk. 2:24). The carpenters formed themselves into guilds and their sons inherited the trade, making doors, roofs, furniture, bowls and spoons, boxes, plows, yokes, carts and threshing sledges (Mk. 6:3; Mt. 13:55). But social prejudice is implied against such craftsmen by the people of Nazareth (Mk. 6:3), and manual work was despised by Greeks and Romans.[2] His trade would give the growing Jesus contact with everyone in a rural society.

Jesus is the Way to travel to the Father (Jn. 14:6). John the Baptist preached repentance as the preparation of the Way of the Lord (Mt. 3:13; Mk. 1:2; Lk. 1:76, 79; 3:4-5). He did this by quoting Exodus 23:20 and Isaiah 40 (the latter containing many nomadic themes of a new exodus). In line with this, John identifies Jesus as the Lamb of a new Passover (Jn. 1:29, 36). These echoes from the Old Testament prepared his hearers to make the path of the coming Savior straight, by a believing response and obedience. This can be understood as a challenge to all classes to support Jesus on his way that will lead to the cross, and to "travel," morally, with him.[3]

Jesus left the settled life of a carpenter to be an itinerant preacher. He was "tented" among humankind, as a transition between coming from and returning to the Father rather than having permanent residence (Jn. 1:14). After he declared his "manifesto" in Nazareth, based on Isaiah 61:1-2 as one "sent," there was an attempt on his life. From this time Jesus is presented as always on the move on a mission.[4] He had no lodging place he said, even as the solitary fox has, or the temporary nests of the birds, despite the fact that his family were offering one (Mt. 8:20; 12:46; Lk 8:19; 9:58). His ministry fulfills the Way predicted by John the Baptist — not as road-building, but as a traveling preacher having an impact by performing signs and experiencing either acceptance or rejection (Mt. 11:10-15). In the parable that is given an interpretation, the sedentary sower is portrayed as very inefficient if he sows on the highway, for the term usually refers to well traveled roads, not to narrow track on the edge of a field-strip (Mt. 13:4; Mk. 4:15; Lk. 8:5). This makes sense if it alludes to Jesus' own traveling ministry.[5] Jesus goes on his way by betrayal and the violence of the authorities, yet it is integral to his whole life as prophesied (Mt. 26:21; Lk. 22:22; Mk. 14:21). He lived an itinerant lifestyle by choice, a complete transient in a sedentary society. He rejected home and family in order to fulfill God's will.

As we saw with the patriarchs and with Israel, the journey was not considered as only a means to getting to a destination. It was, rather, about following God and waiting for his direction. The numerous historical details appear to refer to more than one circuit of Palestine (Lk. 9:51, 53, 57; 10:1, 38; 13:22, 33; 14:25; 17:11; 18:31; 19:11, 28). This pattern is similar to that of nomads who can be said to have a "circular" destination by fulfilling their annual circuit of migration, perhaps arriving at the summer pasture with the social goal of celebration. They travel to maintain their freedom and identity, with overtones of a mandate from the supernatural. Many nomadic peoples also have traditions of their original migration, perhaps over some distance, but their ultimate destination is seen in otherworldly terms. They are aware of the precariousness of earthly life.

While topographically Jesus' route was indirect, morally his progress was direct (Mt. 16:21; Mk. 10:33; Lk. 9:31, 51). Each event contributed both to his fulfilling his mission and to our spiritual understanding of him (Jn. 14:4-6). Jesus traveled to identify himself with God's purpose for Israel. Like Israel crossing into the land under Joshua, Jesus, the latter-day Joshua, was associated with the Jordan in his baptism. His journey might be seen as a spiritual re-conquest of the land, leading to an ultimate Passover pilgrimage to Jerusalem, a new beginning or exodus for the people of God (Lk. 9:31). The term "conquest" is not used in the Old Testament, rather the idea is to occupy or receive the land from the Lord.[6]

Jesus' ministry symbolizes a re-establishment of the ways of the Lord in the land as disciples receive his word of the Kingdom of God. Like Israel, Jesus was led into the wilderness to be tested, and he often returns to desert places in his ministry, to be tested and confirmed in his obedience to his Father.[7] As Israel learned to obey in the wilderness and to continue, spiritually, to "walk in the ways of the Lord," so Jesus was to use the same model and metaphor relating a physical journey to the way of faith in him. There are many allusions to aspects of the Exodus and wilderness journey in Jesus' Galilean ministry, as described in the first three gospels.[8] Jesus appears to have lived within this thought world and sought to fulfill it.

For example, the transfiguration parallels Moses taking three companions with him up Mount Sinai. The difference, however, is that Moses was a spectator of the glory and receives the plans of the tabernacle, while Jesus was glorified as the Son in anticipation of his return as the Son of Man (Ex. 24:9-16; Mt. 17:1-8; Mk. 9:2-8; Lk. 9:28-35).[9] This lifestyle certainly identified him with prophetic figures like Moses, Elijah and Elisha, who never settled in God's service. This implies that his traveling was symbolic of his commitment to his task and his disassociation from the contemporary religious conventions and institutions.

Jesus (Gk. for Joshua) sees himself as fulfilling Joshua's role as shepherd to Israel, who are sheep without a shepherd (Num. 27:17; Mt. 9:36; 10:6; 12:11-12; 15:24; Mk. 6:34; 14:27; Jn. 10:10; 21:15). All human beings since creation need the Creator as shepherd, but their present state as sinners is like the disorientation, straying and dying, of lost and leaderless sheep (Mt. 9:13, 36). Even spiritually privileged Israel was in the same state (Mt. 10:6; 15:24), arousing the compassion of Jesus (Mt. 9:36; Mk. 6:34).

Jesus' empathy or care for each person is likened to the search for one lost animal (Mt. 12:11-12; 18:10-14). The Fulbe and Turkana do not count sheep to know that one is lost; each shepherd knows them individually.[10] We notice that the man who lost one in a hundred did not count them either. Most nomads know the habits and character of their animals individually, in a flock or herd of over a hundred, by their markings and behavior (Mt. 18:12f.; Lk. 15:3-7; Jn. 10:4).

Jesus also traveled because of his interest in the ordinary classes, rather than in the religious and social elite (Mk. 1:38; Lk. 9:52; 10:1). Jesus showed God to be egalitarian in his choice of companions, as he spent time with unimportant, or even despised, individuals, and as he sacrificed himself for his friends. Pride of position, rank or expertise has no place in the church. Jesus became despised because he mixed with the ordinary people, the poor and the religious outcasts. The Gospels and the rest of the New Testament, as influenced by Jesus' teaching, have to be re-read from the point of view of the interests of all vulnerable minority groups, not just the economically poor. For example, Jesus' teaching on inner cleanliness would be of interest to the Roma (Lk. 8:37-41). Initially, Jesus only had 120 in hiding as a result of his ministry to multitudes. Small, if not beautiful, is fulfilling to Jesus.

His traveling was not only for him to reach people, but also so that they might make the effort to reach him. Faith needs an outward expression of trust and obedience. Crowds sought him from considerable distances (Mt. 4:25; 12:15-16; Mk. 1:37-39; 2:2, 13; 3:7; Lk. 6:17-19; Jn. 6:2; 10:42). Even the uncommitted were obliged to travel along with him to hear him, when stopping would have been more convenient for teaching (Mt. 8:1; 12:15; 14:13; 19:2; Mk. 3:7-8). His course was so unpredictable, that on two occasions the crowds could not provide food for themselves. In relation to people, Jesus' travels were an object lesson,

because Jesus expected people to follow him (Mt. 8:20; Lk. 14:33), much like a pastoralist with his flock or a peripatetic plying his craft.

Jesus' life and those of his disciples were to be journeys of obedience to God and missionary service to others. We can discern multiple motives for this: first in relation to God, second in relation to Israel's history and third in relation to his contemporaries. As an expression of his commitment to God's purpose and to people it did not matter how circuitous the route may have been.

Jesus' journey for righteousness

Jesus described his coming in relation to God as fulfilling righteousness and the Law, and his traveling lifestyle was the expression of his total commitment to fulfill his Father's will (Mt. 3:15, 17; 5:17). The four Gospels present Jesus' ministry in the form of his traveling to the cross. In the first three Gospels, this is stressed from the time of the inquiry about his identity and his revelation that the Son of Man must suffer (Mt. 16:13-20; Mk. 8:27-30; Lk. 9:18-21). Mark and Luke particularly emphasize the idea of "the way" of Jesus (Mk. 8:27–10:52; Lk. 9:51–19:44).

Jesus defined discipleship in Mark in the context of his journey (Mk. 8:27–10:45).[11] Discipleship and the cross are interrelated by the practical commitment of both Jesus and the disciples to travel around together. But the disciples could not accept that this involved suffering and death. It has been suggested that Mark organizes his Gospel around the idea of Jesus bringing a second spiritual exodus for God's people as predicted in Isaiah.[12] This implies that Jesus saw his journey to Jerusalem as an enactment of God returning to his people as foretold in prophecy.[13]

Much of Jesus' teaching that only Luke gives us is set in the framework of his traveling towards Jerusalem, as the place of decision for Israel's leadership and his own obedience to the cross, which he described as an exodus (Lk. 9:31, 51–19:44).[14] The parable of the banquet has the king inviting people from the roads and under the hedges — that is, those who are denied access to the town for reasons of poverty, disease or social prejudice, and who live on the margins like nomads. While this teaching can be arranged in some topical order, the original context of the Teacher as a traveler is important for Luke.

In John's Gospel, Jesus is declared to be the Lamb of God and he immediately asks men to follow him (Jn. 1:36, 43) and, as in the other Gospels, his ministry is a journey that is directed towards the cross. The Father works through an itinerant Son as he did with Abraham and Moses (Jn. 5:20, 45). Jesus identifies himself with Israel's experience by journeying within the Promised Land like Abraham and, like Israel, by not finding rest in the land. John concludes with Jesus' commands to loyalty in terms of pastoralism and following (Jn. 21:15f., 22). This suggests that traveler and pastoral metaphors have priority in our Lord's mind.

His traveling was an expression of his obedience to the Father, as a divine redemption of Israel's story. Jesus' itinerant lifestyle may have made the arrest more difficult since he was a "moving target," but he could have settled in Capernaum, Bethany or Jerusalem and still have been arrested and crucified (Jn. 7:1, with v. 10; 8:59). The very abandonment of his home and family and his circular traveling was, in Jesus' mind, to have the cross and a return to the Father as his goal (Mt. 10:37; 12:46-50; Mk. 3:31ff.; Lk. 2:43-51). Jesus saw his destination beyond death, in the redemption of this world through his resurrection.

A traveler whose goal is human sacrifice is considered a scandal, and the cross can be rejected on these grounds. The purpose of Jesus' journey is that the shepherd might lay down his life for the sheep. He goes to his death as a lamb to slaughter (Jn. 1:29, 36; 10:11, 15; cf. Mt. 26:31; Mk. 14:27). In the context of the Passover lamb, his blood is the basis for a new covenant (Mk. 14:24; cf. Acts 8:32; 1 Pet. 1:19). Christ's death is likened to that of a sacrificial lamb as representing a people united to him (Jn. 1:29, 36; 10:15, 17f.; Acts 8:32; 1 Pet. 1:19). But he also describes the circumstances of his death as like sheep-thieves killing the shepherd in order to seize the sheep (Mt. 26:31; Zech. 13:7; Jn. 16:32), and his final return is as Shepherd (1 Pet. 5:4). The disciples objected to it in principle (Mt. 16:21f.), yet the Tibetans and Mongols have a tradition of a human scapegoat who took the curse on behalf of the whole people.[15]

Like a nomad, Jesus' earthly migration pattern was a crucial part of his task. But his ultimate destination was where he would supremely be both Great Shepherd and Lamb on the throne (Rev. 5:6-12, passim). It was Jesus' journey that joined the call to follow him and to be a disciple to the fact of the cross.

Following as faith in Jesus

Jesus takes the initiative to call people to be disciples in a personal relationship with him. Discipleship involves following Christ. In all four Gospels, terms describing following or coming after Jesus are used equally as those for faith or believing, and they are used more than terms for conversion or repentance in Matthew, Mark and Luke. Only John's special emphasis on belief overshadows his similar stress on following Jesus, but even here to be a disciple means to follow Jesus. At the beginning and end of his ministry Jesus gives the challenge to follow (Jn.1:37f., 54; 21:19-22). This emulates the Old Testament models of key people that "followed" God (Ex. 14:15; 1 Kgs. 19:19-21).[16]

There is an initial or fundamental commitment to Christ that is the basis for the progressive and continual following (shown by the tenses in Mk. 8:34; Mt. 10:38; 16:24; Lk. 9:23; 14:27). Justification and the forgiveness of sins are crucial elements in salvation (Lk. 1:73; Mt. 6:12; 12:31f.), but they are not dependent on the sacrifice or *quality* of our following, because this following is an expression of trust in unmerited grace. In other words, behavior or works that are evidence of a sinner's trust for salvation in the work of another cannot be meritorious in themselves. Forgiveness is given to a paralytic before he can walk (Mt. 9:1-8; Lk. 5:20-24). There is an instantaneous acquittal for the guilty that produces a sense of indebtedness that also enables us to forgive others (Mt. 6:14-15; 18:21-33; Lk. 7:43-49; Jn. 8:11).

Yet this faith and relationship is lived out in a lengthy "walk" of faith as perseverance in the face of suffering (Rom. 8:39; Heb. 2:1, passim). This is shown in the crisis that Habakkuk faced and in Abraham's case that Paul quotes (Hab. 1:3f; 2:2-3; Rom. 4:18ff.; Heb. 11:17-19; Jas. 2:21ff., etc.). Such a life is characterized by deeds of obedience that have nothing to do with intrinsically meritorious "good works" that would render faith and forgiveness irrelevant. The disciple follows Jesus and lives the spiritual peripatetic life out of gratitude for a reconciliation effected with God as Father and a desire to realize his will in society (Mt. 6:9–7:34; Jn. 14:6); through this God deepens and completes the pastoral relationship.

Jesus called individuals and challenged all who would be disciples to deny themselves, identifying with him as if they were to be crucified (Mk. 8:34; Mt. 10:38; 16:24; Lk. 9:23; 14:27). His geographical traveling was, for many, a literal challenge to travel with him — testing their commitment, trust and obedience to God and missionary service to others. Indeed, martyrdom would be the end for many of them. In Jesus' conception, faith and being a Christian is to *follow* him on his journey, learning something of the same sacrificial commitment from his example (Mt. 4:19-20; Jn. 8:12).

Faith is no longer, then, only believing *about* Jesus or trusting in something. To be a disciple is to openly identify with him for all that he is, all that he does, and to depend on him utterly. Spiritual following, like being a literal traveler, requires sacrifice, leaving conventional comforts and sin, and suffering hardship and abuse with him. To be a follower, one needs to be as close as possible to him in fellowship and service. As reality for the twelve, and metaphorically

for the rest of us, following means that we become like him. His journey is a model for the Christian life as a "walk" with him. All of us may have a crucifixion experience, some in martyrdom, but all will have trials on the way that test and strengthen our faith in him.

The Gospel of Mark uses the concept of "the way" as the key to discipleship. Disciples are challenged to lead a life of self-denial, to not conform to the surrounding sinful generation (Mk. 8:31-38). The spiritual and physical "following" become fused (Mt. 19:27-28) so that life, and everything in it — possessions, relationships, etc. — are limited to what furthers our relationship with him. They are given as a temporary stewardship. The challenge of literally leaving the security of family, fortune or the familiar brings into sharp relief whether we trust and obey him above the comforts of conforming to social conventions of home life (Lk. 9:57-62).

Pastoral images, recalling the Old Testament, describe Jesus' ministry to his disciples. In John 10 he "expels" the sheep from the fold for their own good to feed on the available pasture, which is not near the fold, but in an area of danger from "pastoral" enemies (Mt. 7:15; 26:31). He knows that the sheep will respond to his call, and each flock separates to gather around its shepherd (Jn. 10).[17] He judges according to the behavior of the species (for example, sheep and goats must be separated because they tolerate different forage and go to different pastures), just as one's knowledge of God gives different spiritual appetites (Mt. 25:32ff.). His choice of being despised and rejected by surrounding society throughout his ministry and of being forced to travel on his way identifies closely with the experience of many nomadic peoples.

The Gospels as we know them probably circulated years after the Lord's ascension, and yet the apparent circumstantial detail that Jesus has no "settled" home was retained as a major part of his life and teaching to challenge the early church of settled people (Mt. 8:20). His example of being a mission and "seminary" constantly on the move challenges the way that Christians embrace the conventional standards of sedentary life. But the main thrust of following Christ was metaphorical — it was about giving exclusive priority to Christ, his teaching and salvation so that these things would shape the disciple's life and give him or her a new identity distinct from the surrounding sinful society.

The Christian life is compared especially by Paul to a peripatetic (*peripateo*) lifestyle in moral contrast with the world (Rom. 6:4; 8:4; 14:15; Gal. 5:16; Eph. 2:2; 4:1; 5:2, 8, 15; Col. 1:10; 1 Thess. 2:12; 4:1). There is a contrast between the new life and the former way of life. The latter is rejected due to darkness and willful ignorance of God (1 Cor. 3:3). The Christian walks by faith (2 Cor. 5:2; "in the light" Eph. 5:8f.), according to the knowledge of Christ (Col. 2:6), and in the Spirit and life (Rom. 6:4; 8:4; Gal. 5:16). This parallels the nomad's life, who lives often contrary to the ways of the dominant secular society, but sees his own values and way of life as superior, and even as representing human life at its best.

Paul alludes to the patriarchs and the Exodus journey as prefiguring the Christian's walk of faith because of the spiritual continuity between Israel and the church. He also, however, stresses the changes that Christ brought (e.g., 1 Cor. 5:13, cf. Dt. 17:7; 1 Cor. 9:8-19, cf. Dt. 25:4; 1 Cor. 10:1-13, cf. Ex. 32; Dt. 32:21; 2 Cor. 3:7, 13f., cf. Ex. 31:18; 34:27-35; 2 Cor. 8:15, cf. Ex. 16:18; Dt. 8:2-3). Christ is later the Rock for Christians, as God was to Israel (Dt. 32:4, 15, etc., cf. Rom. 5:14).[18] The Gentile Christians are expected not only to know of Israel's formative experience, but also to consider themselves on a similar journey with Christ (Rom. 4:23, cf. Gen. 15:4, etc.).

The Christian's destination is otherworldly, as it is according to the nomad's religious view, aiming for paradise, nirvana or the ancestors (Phil. 3:10f.; Heb. 11:39). Therefore the challenge to be a Christian is as radical as the challenge Abraham and Israel faced in embarking on their journeys, leaving the familiar comforts to trust God alone. The message of being a traveler or a shepherd has been largely lost in the Western understanding of the Christian life.[19]

Pastor my sheep

Like the Old Testament prophets, Jesus condemned irresponsible leaders. The background of John 10:1-6 is the condemnation of Israel's leaders (Ezek. 34:24; Jer. 25:32-38). The hired man in John 10:12 has to be interpreted with care, as many pastoralists are hired as shepherds.[20] The term simply means wage earner, and he is specifically described as "no-shepherd," possibly an agricultural worker, introduced to demonstrate the worth of the true shepherd.[21] He is a comic figure, for when left in charge of the flock and danger threatens he hesitates, uncertain what to do. He then runs away from a solitary wolf, which would not normally attack men. A real shepherd would drive off or wound such a threatening animal with stones from a sling and then, if he were able to get close enough, he would club it to death. The shepherd's life, literally and spiritually, is not for well-meaning novices without genuine concern and experience!

The analogy from nomadic life is that a true shepherd has affinity with his sheep and has experience defending them against all threats. Jesus, as the only true shepherd, has to be the model in his life and ministry for any leader among the disciples. Jesus uses pastoral images to describe how all the world's ethnic groups are accountable to God (Mt. 25:32f.). Jesus is saying that he alone is the person qualified to lead believers for he is morally and emotionally bonded to them, and even ready to die for them. Such a sacrifice of the Shepherd for the sheep had worldwide consequences as it was the very foundation of the church itself.

8   Mission of Pilgrims

Out of Jesus' ministry came the band of disciples that had witnessed his life on the road from the beginning. These disciples in turn formed the apostolic church that continued to see the Christian life as a journey and that should still have had the character of spiritual nomadism. The apostles and many other early Christians traveled to proclaim the good news. To fulfill Christ's great commission still involves much literal travel with limited belongings.

Mission of travelers to travelers

Israel's missionary task has been described as centripetal — that is, the prophets envisaged the nations being attracted towards Israel to worship the true God.[1] The missionary task of the chosen people can be summed up by Johannes Blauw's conclusion that "the whole history of Israel is nothing but the continuation of God's dealings with the nations… to be understood from the unsolved problem of the relation of God to the nations."[2] With the coming of redemption in Christ, the mission of the church became centrifugal — a going out to the nations to make disciples. Like nomads in an unsympathetic dominant society, Christians must go out to the peoples, while maintaining their own spiritual identity among them — "in the world but not of the world."

The worldwide mission extending Jesus' ministry is also described in pastoral terms (Jn. 10:16; Heb. 13:20; 1 Pet. 2:25; 5:4). Jesus' disciples are likened to sheep as they set out on his mission, because they are in constant need of him as a shepherd in their ministry (Mt. 10:16; Lk. 10:3; Jn. 10). The disciples were called to an itinerant life, and they relied on the hospitality of those God provided for them (Mat. 8:20; 10:10). Peter, the fisher of men, is transformed into a shepherd (Jn. 21:15-17) even in the context

of his familiar ground of fishing. What we know of the apostles' lives after Pentecost shows that they learned the lesson from their itinerant Master, of constant travel in commitment and sacrifice, even martyrdom.

Jesus' solidarity with each people

Jesus represented all the ethnic groups of the world in his redemptive work. He fulfilled the promise to Abraham and to all the clans and families on earth. He also fulfilled the role of Israel for the blessing of all ethnic groups (Gen. 12:3; Mt. 24:14; 28:19; Gal. 3:9). The original terms signify clans (Gen. 12:3; 28:14) and nations (Gen. 18:18; 22:18; 26:4); which means that every subdivision of the human population is to be blessed. The Old Testament promises and prophecies, as well as the New Testament commission, use the terms "all the ethnic groups" to signify the blessing being presented to the groups differentiated by descent, social organization, culture and language.[3]

The genealogies of Jesus demonstrate his credentials to act on behalf of Israel (Mt. 1:1-17; Lk. 3:23-38). Jesus was the son or "seed" of Abraham, the predicted son of David and the Anointed, or Messiah, to act on behalf of Israel (Mt. 1:1; Rom. 1:3; Gal. 3:16, etc.). This fulfilled God's purpose, that through Israel his blessing might reach every section of humankind. He also used the title "Son of Man" as representing humankind. Christ's emphasis on Israel, however, does not have to be "universalized" for humanity, because by the promise to Abraham it was already for "all the ethnic groups" of the world (Lk. 24:45-47; Rom. 1:5).

Christ's solidarity with each people group offers what is appropriate both for individuals and for the future of that group. However, his work is only effective for those who actually unite themselves to him in faith. This is important for societies like those of nomads that seek to maintain their distinctive identity in a dominant culture, and among whom the group honor must be maintained against outsiders and members who offend that honor. Some nomadic peoples call themselves by names that just mean "man" and see their own people as the "real" humankind. Christ's redemption offers a transformed identity for the people group through the individuals who trust him, and who through Christ show love for their people.

Christ's atoning work is for the world, but his grace is distributed to each people and sub-people group in the world for their welfare and future. No strategy for mission can successfully treat a group of nomadic people as if they were merely absorbed into a larger population. We should bring the gospel to each as a distinct entity.

In Western theology the incarnation has been understood in a metaphysical way — God became man and is interested in humankind as a whole and individualistically. But peoples with tribal social structures are more inclined to see the incarnation in terms of solidarity and corporate responsibility within a family or clan. The disobedience of one member brings consequences for the whole, and another member may be able to atone for the offense by substituting him or herself for the whole group (Rom. 5:12-21). In a sinful world, such an offense leads to expulsion or death of the offending member, or to indiscriminate revenge on other groups. By dying on behalf of the people, Jesus fulfills the blessing of the promise to all peoples.

In terms of this corporate responsibility, the Father as Creator or "High God" is the ultimate basis for the people group's leadership and is therefore concerned for its standing and honor with himself (cf. Acts 17:26; Eph. 3:14-15). Therefore God the Father, as "High God," as the highest authority in every human people or tribe, sent Jesus as the representative member to restore the people's broken honor, or standing, with himself. As Son, he reinterprets and challenges the values and rules of the group to restore its honor and remove its shame. Jesus acts as the brother within each group, to maintain that group's honor with the Father. He takes the penalty of the group's shame and dishonor (usually expressed in the expulsion or death of the guilty) upon himself, in order to satisfy the group's standing of honor with the Father. His cross upholds both strict justice and yet is God's provision of mercy for reconciliation.

From this restored honor with the Supreme Authority in the tribe or people, Jesus also has authority to reconcile tribal members with one another. Jesus' atonement affirms God's honor by being a just penalty for rebellion, and provides justification for both the innocent and guilty victims of revenge attacks. He therefore has authority to arbitrate and determine guilt in inter-group conflict and to see that only the guilty are punished, rather than allowing arbitrary revenge.

An example of this reconciliation can be seen in how the New Testament church worked out the relationship of Christ with Israel and the Gentiles. The reconciliation is with God, but it also affects the relationships between those peoples who are willing to accept him (Acts 11:18; Eph. 2:13-16; 2 Cor. 5:16). Jesus' act counters the ethnocentricity that is the springboard for conflict. Jesus and his atonement have secured the possibility of reconciliation, which has profound implications for the well-being of each ethnic group until his return.

The pilgrim church

The church is universal because the focus of the people of God is no longer the fixed temple, as it had been for Israel. Jesus declared the temple to be superseded rather than "cleansed" (Mt. 21:12-13; Mk. 11:15-17; Lk. 19: 45-46; Jn. 2: 13-17). Each believer was to become a mobile sanctuary wherever they are (Jn. 7:38; 1 Cor. 3:16, 17; 6:19, 20; 2 Cor. 6:16; Eph. 2:19-22). The participation in the relationship between the Father and the Son through the Son's standing and representative work, and the Spirit's intercession, is the "new temple," which the believer carries everywhere (Jn. 14:6, 10, 20, etc.). The new Israel united to Christ has all its spiritual resources in an entirely portable form.

Like Israel of old, the Christian church is intended to be ready to move in obedience to her Master. It is appropriate that both the gospel and the church became known as "the Way" (Acts. 9:2; 16:17; 18:26; 19:9; 22:4; 24:14, 22). To have salvation is to be a traveler or pilgrim trusting the divine Shepherd, involved with the conventions and commitments of the surrounding society only sufficiently to fulfill his service.

The experience of the patriarchs and the wilderness generations was formative both for the faith of Israel and for the beginnings of the church, and this character of faith should influence the interpretation of the rest of Scripture (Heb. 11; 1 Pet. 1:1; 2:11). Very soon after the New Testament was written, the term for "alien residents" was used for local churches. They were seen not as "of" a certain location, but merely as temporally resident pilgrims (1 Pet. 1:1). From this word came the term "parish" — that now conveys a totally contradictory idea of territorial permanence and elaborate ecclesiastical structures.[4]

A nomadic eternity?

The Lord's transfiguration anticipated the end of faith's journey in heaven. It inspired Peter to offer to make tents, dwellings which imply a very transitory lifestyle to us, but which seemed to Peter a permanent, secure and appropriate dwelling for the divine presence (Mk. 9:5; Lk. 16:9, *skênai*). Life in heaven is described in terms of being led by the Shepherd (Rev. 7:15) and living in tents. While terms based on the word for "house" are used to describe God's dwelling in believers' lives on earth, the immediate presence of God is conveyed by using *skênê* and *skênoô*, perhaps as an ongoing allusion to the wilderness camp around the tabernacle (Rev. 12:6, 12; 13:6; 15:5; 21:3).

This idea of tents is symbolic of an intimate, visual and audible contact with each other, for in a camp one's behavior is transparent and life is stripped of all pretense, or insincerity. What is clear is that,

to the biblical mind, the nomadic dwelling in tents does not imply temporary discomfort. Rather, the tent is the natural medium in which to enjoy God's presence, and it must take its place in our minds alongside the figure of the eternal city.

The final destination of life's traveling is a recreated environment of a new earth (Is. 66:22; Rev. 21:1). Israel is described as seeking a city (Heb. 11:16), and we have referred to the different conceptions the Hebrews had of cities. No ancient city's sphere of influence ended inside its walls. It provided security and spiritual focus for a whole rural region, rather than representing a lifestyle itself. It was a center for the rural populations around it and was itself sustained by the freedom of traffic through its gates. The Old Testament visions of the city also include the surrounding land outside (Ezek. 47; Zech. 14:8).

The vision of the New Jerusalem does not imply urban life as the ideal (Rev. 21:25-26) — that might be seen as regrettable rather than desirable to many nomadic peoples. Rather, God is "tented" in the center of the new earth as a New Jerusalem (Rev. 21-22). Some might draw the conclusion that the images imply that the saints are shut within the city, but one has to wonder why there is a new earth outside it and why the city gates are never shut? The point of the vision is that this city is the antithesis of every known fortified city, for it never has to defend itself, nor does it pose a threat to anyone.

The city is a missionary vision, in which the presence of God transforms the whole earth, and access to him is continual through gates that are always open. The foundations are named after the apostles and express the call to faith in the gospel that is the only basis to enjoy eternity and resurrection life. The gates represent the tribes of Israel and remind us both of the fulfillment of the promise to Abraham and of the church's nomadic nature. The vision reveals the freedom of movement in a redeemed environment as God's presence radiates into all lifestyles, including that of the traveler and nomad. The service of God will replace economic necessity as the motive for migration. The false sense of divine disapproval that many peripatetic peoples feel will be finally removed. Every ethnic group on earth has its redeemed representatives to bring homage to God (Rev. 21:26). They do not add to the city's glory, but nevertheless have their fulfillment in rendering this homage. If they did not come in and out continually, the gates surely would be presented as finally and irrevocably shut. Traveling on the new earth is for the purpose of rendering worship to the Creator.

Applying a nomadic theology

Of all the possible methods that God could have used to establish his purpose in the world, the pastoralism of a traveling people was the one he chose. The traveler and pastoral themes of the Bible are not merely a powerful teaching device, but the historical method that God used to reveal himself and to begin the process of redemption.

We have not argued that Israel was a nomadic people. Israel went through various stages of 200 years of nomadic pastoralism, 400 years of settled pastoralism, a formative 40 years of nomadic pastoralism leading to 900 years of agropastoralism with an increasingly urban-based elite, and then into exile. Most nomadic people have not had such a long history but have gone through similar transitions. Certainly Jesus and those in the early church were not nomadic people.

But we have presented a major theme throughout the Bible. For elements of nomadism influence our understanding of the message and our attitude to life and how we approach nomadic peoples. It is not that nomads are more "spiritual," or that the Bible endorses all their values and methods. But the very nature of nomadism has important parallels to the Christian message and life — for example:

- a commitment to relationships rather than to property or place
- maintaining a distinct social identity from the surrounding society

- assigning natural resources according to use rather than exclusive ownership
- maintaining a symbiotic relationship with nature, attributing its resources to the supernatural
- "living by faith," or trusting in the supernatural to provide in an often precarious environment
- radically limiting personal possessions in order to be "ready to move" in a sacrificial lifestyle
- stressing virtues such as perseverance, suffering, self-reliance and initiative, and corporate responsibility.

The nomad's migration cycle is both a practical necessity as well as a formative influence on attitudes and values, aiming at a measure of self-sufficiency from the surrounding society.

We prepare ourselves to evangelize nomads by our own rediscovery of the Christian life in the Bible and theology as a pastoral journey. The Bible's agricultural, political and military metaphors are also more meaningful to nomads than they are to us. Westerners have romanticized the figure of the shepherd, so that the prevailing interpretations of the Bible passages stress such ideas as safety and comfort, rather than struggle and survival. The shepherd's life is lonely and hard, with long periods in the cold or heat, with nothing but a cloak for cover, and with only a sling and heavy stick to guard against wolves or leopards. There is the continual threat of theft of livestock, when fights can lead to injury or death. The loot is often quickly converted into mutton to cover the crime (Jn. 10:9). The Gaddi say, "it is very bad work, too cold, and too dangerous all for two chapattis in the evening." It is easier to appreciate both God's care for Israel and the Good Shepherd laying down his life for his sheep when we understand the practical difficulties of modern nomads.

These metaphors cannot be used patronizingly, however, as if nomads have no other interest besides sheep. Nomads do not consider their nomadism in the abstract, but rather as the framework of their lives.

They are concerned with the identity of their people and their place in the world, which are shaped by nomadism as a matter of course. Just as Israel's travels were to fulfill her identity as God's people, so nomadism has to do with maintaining the identity of the nomadic peoples.

Further, caution is necessary in interpreting pastoral passages such as Psalm 23 and John 10. Kazaks, for example, dislike being compared to sheep! In some circumstances, they *follow*, instead of lead, their sheep. Turkic and Iranian nomads keep billy goats to lead the sheep, and this may be an apt illustration of Christian leadership. While some nomads have developed cultural relations with their animals, many have a more pragmatic attitude. The view nomads have of themselves is broader and deeper, sharing common human needs that also have to be dealt with by other themes of the Bible.

The easily presumed identification between ancient Israel and the modern state of Israel can create problems for Arabs. It is claimed that some parts of the Bible, such as the story of David and Goliath, have to be passed over, because the "wrong" side seems to have won! But it can be pointed out that Goliath was a Philistine, not an Arab, and the special role of ancient Israel has ceased after Christ and Israel's rejection of him. But, on the whole, Muslims appreciate learning about the figures they have heard of in Islam — such as Abraham, Moses and David.

We need a "nomadic" theology for communicating with nomadic peoples that Christianity is compatible with their lifestyle. The Creator's word is intended to affirm and enhance the nomadic life, and we dishonor him and the people if we allow ourselves, by our own assumptions, to dismiss nomadism as "inconvenient," dying out, or even "immoral."

A theology for nomads?

Key elements in such a nomadic theology would be:

1. To recognize God as the transcendent pastoralist of a traveling people can be the beginning of a walk of faith, before a need of salvation is felt or understood. This view is more personal, practical and dynamic than the usual abstract treatment of the nature and attributes of God; the attributes can be treated in illustrative story form. This brings the Creator into the fortunes and trials of human life, countering ideas of God being a will to which one must submit, or a remote high god, or a fickle deity of India, or a supreme state of Buddhism. This also introduces the Bible at the point of most concern in the nomad's life. To change the nomad's concept of God, we must respond to their search for guidance and success.

2. At the Exodus, God presented to Israel a plan for their well-being and service to him. Israel trusted God for political freedom and survival in the desert before salvation from sin was revealed to her. Jesus called the disciples to follow him before they understood his work. In each case the initial requirement was trust and commitment on a journey, involving the mundane needs of survival and life.

3. We see clearly that this journey is only on God's initiative and calling or invitation. The personal character and purpose of God or Jesus draw out faith expressed as obedient following, and from this context of a walk with God the profounder aspects of God's message are taught.

4. With this nomadic emphasis, life is seen as a journey, both socially independent and dependent on subsistence from precarious or marginal resources, and so it requires faith in the providence of God. Providence is the way God fulfills his promises to creation and shapes events, in the direction and care of his people. God's providence reaches the needs of the nomads in sickness, hunger, fear of attack and crime, the welfare of their animals, poverty, shame over their failure to fulfill the aspirations of the group, fear of curses and spirits, and the afterlife. Life for most nomads often rapidly draws to a conclusion in early death. Faith can have small, secret, practical beginnings before an individual makes a specific commitment as a Christian.

5. Faith treated as a journey with God

stresses the necessary motivation, commitment, trials and progress. To start the journey one must leave behind what is incompatible or a hindrance — that is, one must repent. There is the sacrifice of not conforming to the world in lifestyle and possessions, for one must travel light. God and Christ determine the route, the stopping places and the destination. The traveler must also trust God for the provision of needs (versus wants). There are many dangers and temptations to overcome in the course of a journey. The journey requires commitment and consecration to Christ and his standards — that is, holiness. We have to keep close to Christ for instruction and fellowship — otherwise we will miss the way.[5] Without this biblical metaphor, stressed along with other images such as war, building and athleticism, faith becomes spiritually "settled" and static.

6. When we begin with life as a journey with God (as the Bible begins), the other themes and concepts of the Bible become more relevant. The pastoral-traveler theme has to be completed by the other biblical themes — including God's fatherhood, covenant lordship and law, priesthood and reconciliation, and prophecy and kingdom — all in the fulfillment of God's purpose. A rediscovery of biblical Christianity in these terms, lived out in practice, lays the foundation for introducing the gospel themes.

7. By his life and death, Jesus fulfilled the biblical "nomadic" ideal of the person who is utterly committed to trust God's providence and purpose. This is a master model of the Christian life for those identified with him by the "walk" of faith. Being a Christian cannot be abstracted from its biblical context of spiritual nomadism and being a follower.

8. Being a disciple requires a readiness to "move" with God in Christ, spiritually and morally — and often geographically as well. God requires a simpler lifestyle that derives its sufficiency from trust in providence. The message of nomadism is that one must have wisdom and trust to move according to the provision of resources for each season and

circumstance. There can be no settled life for either nomadic or settled Christians. There can be no commitment to worldly interests, or to static Christian structures set up to last, that supersedes a commitment to God himself.

9. The "rugged" nomadic interpretation of the Bible and Christian life emphasizes the individual's walk of faith with a measure of spiritual self-sufficiency in his or her relationship to Jesus, taking the authority of the Bible as primary over ethnic traditions.

10. The biblical emphasis on God as pastoralist should guard churches formed of nomads against imitating the sedentary churches, and it should encourage them to express their faith with an appropriate discipleship structure in keeping with their way of life. God and Christ as head pastoralist is a model for leaders. A church that is "nomadic" in its attitudes will be a missionary church.

11. The themes of biblical nomadism show that God cares about the identity and fulfillment of despised, disregarded and misunderstood peoples and gives them a place in history, economically and geographically. We need to think through what God's purpose for a people group might be, and learn from the solidarity and corporate responsibility that lies behind much "tribal" behavior.

12. Many nomadic peoples have a history of defensiveness and revenge because of the hostility of the surrounding society. Others have a sense of guilt built into the traditions of their origins. The gospel must be shown to be the solution to these attitudes. A people's ability to pass on God's blessing and the gospel is the true measure of its greatness — following Israel, a people created to be a blessing to other peoples. The followers of Jesus in a people group have to stand against the sort of disobedience and injustice that lead to a people's disintegration and God's condemnation. A nomadic theology must convey both God's place for nomads as well as the importance of building good relationships with other peoples and with the environment.

13. The moral changes that God requires in the nomad's life and society should be taught from the perspective of God as shepherd leading in the journey of life. Israel can be used as a paradigm of God's purpose for all peoples (Mt. 28:19; Rom. 11:17ff.), showing how a people group can be blessed by God, through faith and obedience. The points of contact between the nomads' values and the Bible's ethical teaching need to be found, in order to know what to affirm and what to renounce in their culture.

Often nomads can identify themselves with the Bible's message without any prompting. A Gypsy woman who owned nothing but an old baby carriage found a Sunday School lesson book thrown away in a hedge. She was illiterate, but from the pictures she came to identify herself with Jesus. For, she said, he was poor like them, he came to crossroads and wondered which way to go, he was moved on by the authorities of the day, he had no knife and broke his bread, and he had only a candle for light. She concluded that Jesus was a Romany like them, a traveler before them.[6]

The supreme lesson is that we must not fail in the challenge to demonstrate Christian love to the pastoralist and peripatetic peoples for their spiritual and practical benefit. The nomads recognize that they should be better teachers of the Bible to us! In fact, nomads like the Tuareq and Kazaks have pointed out the irony in the fact that Westerners, who know nothing about pastoralism, have to teach them a message that is based so much on their own pastoral experience. When converted nomads begin to minister to us, Christians who mostly belong to the sedentary world will gain fresh insight into the Bible and their journey with God. Cross-cultural evangelism is ultimately a partnership of learning from each other.

It's all Go!

Nomadic missionary living among the Fulbe

The missionary yawns and prayerfully starts to think about the new day dawning. Fifty yards away the cattle are getting restive, laboriously getting to their feet. He looks out of the tent. He sees two girls moving rapidly to do the morning milking, their bright African clothing looking dull gray in the half-light before dawn. He and his wife serve the Great Shepherd among these unevangelized nomadic cattle people. Many such peoples - shepherds, yak-people, reindeer herders, Gypsies - have no one to live alongside them to demonstrate Christ and give them practical help. He crawls outside and sits on the straw mat, continuing in an attitude of prayer. The missionary muses that many see their work among these nomads as too sacrificial and non-strategic. But if anthropologists and journalists can do it, then certainly Christ's messengers must. A motto comes to mind, *if Jesus Christ… died for me, no sacrifice is too great…* The challenge is to trust absolutely that God will bring a harvest; perhaps spiritual calving might be a better metaphor?

His wife and children are stirring in the tent. His wife is home-schooling the eldest, at a little folding wooden desk. But he and his sister prefer to play in the water hole with the local children or ride bareback on the donkey. Sacrifice? "The children love it," they had been told by a couple who had raised their family with the cattle people, in a hut without electricity, running water or refrigerator, and only with an earth oven.

Not what you know but who you know

In the increasing glow of the morning light, women gather at the open ground that is the camp "kitchen." They rhythmically pound the millet with their long pestles, for the first meal of the day. The calves have sucked the rest of the milk and are tied back on their ropes. The sun rises as a red globe low in the sky. The cattle begin to amble out of the camp, forming long lines of wide horns and humped backs. They leave the characteristic areas of dung in a Fulbe camp that, with the heat of day, will attract many flies. The young herders in their conical straw hats talk to each cow and ox by name, encouraging them in the right direction for each of the herds.

"Did your night pass in peace?" The dark, dignified, blue-robed head of the camp greets the family on the mat. "In peace," the missionary replies. Unhurried, lengthy greetings are important in this culture. The missionary is grateful for the "authorization" of this man, for it clears the way for fruitful contacts with hundreds of others all around. The missionary family is "accepted." Working this way, living in the camp for a month at a time, being able to move to the next camp with the people, means they are able to identify with their way of life.

"I have to journey," the headman says.

"We, like you, have to travel also. We will see our countrymen and study your language more," replies the missionary.

"We will be back in two weeks."

"Of course we understand, for we like to go and visit our distant relatives, too. The camp is due to move 30 kilometers to the Moors' Ruin. There is more water there," the headman explained. "I will see you there!"

People, not possessions or places, are vital to the nomad. But for the missionary and his family, the breaks in their house in town are vital for recuperation, study and Christian fellowship.

Busy life in camp

Visitors from the camps around them occupy the missionaries. One woman comes with a medical problem; others want to sell colored mats they have woven. An older man, who has shown some interest in the Bible stories, asks for worm medicine for his cattle. Learning to tell the Bible, like the people tell their own stories, had been an effort. But it was proving to be worthwhile. Another man has walked for miles over the flat dusty plain. He does not say yet what he wants, but lengthy polite conversation in the increasing heat of the day proceeds. So the morning is usefully spent.

"Guess what's for lunch?" asks Junior. "Probably millet and milk, or is it milk and millet?" Two small heads peer under the lid on the big bowl the neighbor has left. "Oooh! There's chicken, too!" The people overwhelm the family with hospitality and continual gifts of milk.

"Who is coming to visit our mission herd?" asks the missionary.

"We all are!" cries Junior. "I like watching the Global Positioning System; think of those satellites it uses out in space!" The Land Rover rolls across the plain for an hour. There are no roads, only the tracks of the previous vehicle - which may or may not be going where you want to go! At first, it is difficult to distinguish one herd from another, for more than a dozen are in sight around the horizon. Not all the herds come back to the camp every day, for this would tire them unnecessarily.

When they drive up, their herdsman cheerily tells them, "We gained a new calf in the night. Black-neck-born-of-crooked-horns has given birth!" As they picnic in the hollow where the herdsmen sleep, the missionary thinks of some of his past problems. There was the day the car broke down in the middle of nowhere, another time their daughter was sick and had to be driven for 24 hours over rough tracks to an inadequate medical center, and then every day they have to resist the insidious temptation to give up because of the heat and flies. But he knows this is the best way to work with people who do not yet know Christ. How the missionary craves new spiritual calves among his friends. So far there is one precious believer, who loves to read the few portions of the Bible in their language.

9 Christian Nomadic Partnership

The nomads, like the rest of us, are an expression of God's image. Being made in that image, we all have responsibility to respond to the Creator and the creation around us by the way we live, the relationships in the society we form, and by our goals and values. The nomads have had to respond to the environment in ingenious and creative ways to develop their way of life and society, using marginal resources and conditions. However, like the rest of humankind, they have shut God out of their lives and have sought other ways to get what they consider supernatural help.

The knowledge of God and the gospel should enhance the self-respect and well-being of nomadic peoples, and contribute to their nomadism. We can hope to do this by a presentation of the Bible's message consistent with their lifestyle, together with discipleship training that is not shaped by a sedentary church structure. It should also, of course, lead individuals to become disciples of Christ. How can we present the Bible's message in a form relevant to the nomads' lifestyle and society? How do we overcome their misconceptions that Christianity is only for sedentary people and that nomadism is unacceptable to the Christian faith? What follows are some suggestions to begin thinking about the answers to these questions.

It takes a nomad to reach a nomad

The churches of sedentary peoples have evangelized nomads and gained initial converts. For a time, Dogon Christians in West Africa sought to evangelize the neighboring Fulbe, even after a period of great tribal tension caused by the Fulbe cattle eating the crops of the Dogon and the death of a Dogon farmer in the ensuing conflict.[1] In Nigeria, a few national Christians are now living with, and reaching, nomadic peoples. Settled Christians among the peoples with whom the nomads are interdependent can, therefore, be the means to reach them.

But often the cultural barriers are too great for these people to bring Christianity to nomads. Experiences in Africa have shown that, while there may be long-term economic ties between them, there is often a mutual latent hostility between sedentary and cultivating peoples and the nomads.

National Christians of an agricultural or urban background often do not, therefore, provide an effective Christian witness to nomadic peoples. The outreach of sedentary Christians produced no results in northern Kenya, and in southwestern Ethiopia some have been martyred for having dared to tell the nomad about Christ. This barrier between nomad and sedentary continues to exist even between those pastoralists who have become sedentary, but still consider themselves belonging to the nomadic lifestyle. The Kazaks and Kyrgyz, for example, consider Christianity to be a religion only for Russians.

It is often said that a nomad may convert to the faith of his nomadic enemy, but never to that of his sedentary friend. A more fruitful method of reaching nomads, therefore, may be evangelism by Christians from other nomadic peoples. There is a great need for Christian nomads to be evangelists. In southern Ethiopia, the church is now strong enough to consider training nomads or people with a nomadic background to be evangelists to other nomadic groups. Elsewhere it may be some time before converted nomads are serving the Lord by bringing the gospel to other nomadic peoples. But beyond the affinity of lifestyle, ethnic affinities and similarities of language are important. Koreans, who originated in the Altai Mountains centuries ago, find acceptance among the Turkic peoples of Central Asia. Navajo Indians can take advantage of the ethnic affinity between the Amerindian and the Mongol.

The expatriate missionary, living "out of a suitcase" and "without roots" in the country, may find greater acceptance among nomads because he or she is not involved in the local cultures. An outsider's commitment to the nomads can demonstrate that the nomad is valued in his or her own right. But this can also be interpreted as a way of the expatriate gaining "merit"! The expatriate could even be a catalyst for helping those on both sides to overcome their prejudices, especially as the presence of Christ enables them to forgive and love one another as brothers and sisters. Thus it is essential that we do not present a Westernized Christianity and that we resist bringing in a Western lifestyle.

God's love for travelers engaged in nomadic pastoralism should encourage us to prayer. He has sometimes worked independently of any human Christian influence. He used repeated famines and the loss of their animals to force many nomadic pastoralists of a well-known tribe into contact with the gospel. Gospel cassettes were played over and over, until two brothers felt compelled to look for Jesus in a local market and so came into contact with missionaries. The result was that, in the short space of time between 1990 and 1995, a church was established among them. They had spread the message among themselves with recordings before any Christian worker visited them, and they soon established a way of meeting together at a well for fellowship and mutual encouragement.

An appropriate strategy

The peripatetic's or pastoralist's attachment to the migratory cycle has to be a basic consideration in our approach. Finding a "strategic" spot to "set up shop" and expecting the "customers" to come for what we offer — whether medical, spiritual or other help — appears practical from our sedentary point of view, but actually reveals the depth of our prejudice or bias. The result of such endeavors is that the gospel becomes associated with buildings, literacy

and technology to peoples who do not have, and perhaps even prefer not to have, those things.

Malcolm Hunter and Debra Braaksma urge the rejection of what they call the "mission station" approach, because the simplest missionary house or base gives the impression that the gospel is not for nomads. A house soon gains a garage, a clinic, a generator hut and workshop to form a tiny "village." This was the experience of the Braaksmas among the Orma in Kenya. Experience shows that such an establishment, which appears very basic to Westerners, proves a magnet to all to settle around it. Being fixed, it soon also attracts sedentary neighbors, for whom various ministries can also be established — leaving little time for a traveling to contact the nomads.

What is needed is an approach that meets the nomads more than halfway, and encourages the migratory cycle to stay as intact as far as possible. Nomads are grateful for aid in an emergency, but they reject it as part of their aspiration for the normal life. Development projects like gardening, or schooling, though perhaps grudgingly recognized as useful, can have a negative recommendation for the gospel, because they implicitly recommend leaving the nomadic life.[2] The gospel has to become nomadic — not merely mobile — in the perception of the people. "The gospel will be best communicated to the Gabbra in Kenya by someone who appears to them to understand their situation and has demonstrated that he shares their same lifestyle and world view... who can enter the obligations of Gabbra life to demonstrate how Christianity can be lived as a Gabbra."[3]

The golden rule for missions, the missiologist H. Kraemer urged, is to have a genuine and untiring interest in the whole of the peoples' lives — their ideas, sentiments, religion and institutions — for Christ's sake, and for the sake of the people themselves. One identifies oneself with the people by repeated contact with them. Servants of the shepherd-God should be ahead of the anthropologists and journalists, who have lived among nomads for extended periods for their own purposes.

Catholic missionaries have lived among Kenyan nomads in tents for a few months at a time.[4] The priest Vincent Donovan's stay among the Maasai is very instructive. He left the mission station and started to visit elders and simply talk about God — not about education or development. After five years, 3,000 people showed evidence of changed lives. Donovan became ashamed as he observed the Maasai witch doctors. Their power and rituals seemed so similar to his own as a priest in the Catholic Church. He realized the Maasai could be led to trust the gospel as if it was a simple matter of trusting another sort of witch doctor. Donovan reflected that Jesus was not a priest and never offered sacrifice — except in the one supreme event of his death, where he made a sacrifice that brought together all the meaning of priest and sacrifice and did away with the need for a priestly caste.[5]

We need close personal contact and opportunities for a two-way understanding. Effective witnesses of the gospel need to share in joys and troubles, in sickness, bereavement and celebrations. This is not to imitate a lifestyle for its own sake, nor merely to gain access, but to demonstrate Christian love by living in close contact with them. The relationship must be mutual. Since the Fulbe value honesty and integrity, for example, the Christian among them needs to be in a relationship in which forgiveness for mistakes in the culture and language can be sought.

The Christian has to demonstrate that a biblical faith does not require the trappings of secular sedentary life, but is sympathetic to many aspects of the values and lifestyle of the nomads. This would fulfill, as far as is practical, Kraemer's golden rule. We need to join them on their "journey" rather than implicitly or openly attempting to change their way of life because we simply have not bothered to understand it.

Partnership is God's way

Our relationship perhaps should be seen as a partnership between Christians and nomads.

One comes not as an outsider to give material help, but as a Christian. The ideal is that the only offense should be the gospel itself — not our lifestyle, method, technology, cultural clumsiness, or the nomad's misconceptions of Christendom. Then we can be accepted as friends, and even partners, of the people group in the shared experiences of life. It is not just a cross-cultural adventure for a few hardy Christians. Three aspects of God's character — his being a creator, Trinitarian and transcendent — encourage us to have a partnership with nomads.

In the act of creation God fulfilled a purpose entirely his own without outside materials or help — *ex nihilo*. Every part of his creation finds its being, with its unique characteristics and ability to relate to others, without any effort on its own part. This means that every person and thing has the nature of undeserved gift from God to each other. Creation out-of-nothing means that every person and thing not only has the gift of existence but has that existence as a gift to the other persons and things around them. They are set into relationships by the Creator to be appreciated and to serve those around them. In all of our actions we respond to God's gift of ourselves, other people, things and creatures. We should accept all of these as gifts of great worth within God's purpose that he seeks to fulfill through us. Therefore the nomads, and the way they have responded to a difficult environment — however insignificant in human eyes and in spite of their sinfulness — are to be approached as gifts of God.

God's gifts of nature, health, work, or other people bring a responsibility for treating them correctly. The commandments for human conduct given in the Bible are not mere rules that require individual compliance. Rather, they express God's definition of what it is to be a human being and what sort of society reflects his character and purpose. Love of God and our neighbor means forming a moral community in which we should seek to help, support and encourage one another to fulfill God's purpose. Our obeying or disobeying the commandments affects not just our relationship with God, but also the lives of others around us. Our actions either further or frustrate God's purposes for them. This view of creation brings us closer to the situation of the nomads with their ideas of a close interdependent society and dependence on nature.

Our relationship to people unknown to us is also based on God's Trinitarian character. God is not only independent of creation, he is also a self-contained "society" of three Persons, who are united as one in perfect fellowship. All moral perfection, including love, are perfectly realized within God because he is a Trinity, a community of three. Each Person both gives and receives care and fulfills the others, so that God is love (1 Jn. 5:8). This interaction is perfect, complete and continuous. Love in any form can only be known by being influenced, however indirectly or imperfectly, by this community of Persons.

In the Trinity we see that God himself is an autonomous and independent "nomadic society" which maintains its integrity as holiness, but which nevertheless enters into voluntary but costly commitments with humankind. In this respect, God is a "true nomad." The love of others for us, and our love for nomads, is an extension of this love within the Trinity, experienced directly or indirectly through Christ. He came to reconcile us to participate in a community of love. This is a challenge, an invitation, a faint stirring in the heart that, regrettably, most resist or ignore.

The oneness of God that Muslims are concerned about does not undermine the Trinity, but rather upholds the *uniqueness* of God, reiterating that there are no others and that nothing can be added to God. Some see the Trinity as a hindrance to evangelizing Muslims. But the uniqueness or oneness of God would only be undermined if his love "needed" humankind. Within himself the one unique God is three Persons in a community of love, a love so united in action towards creation that often the Persons are not distinguishable one from the other, and their actions appear to be performed by one. The distinction of the Persons in this love was revealed when the Son became a man and identified himself with unbelieving, disobedient humankind. The Trinity's love for humankind is but an indication of the love within this threefold community itself.

In his transcendence, God is free to have fellowship with anyone, anywhere, without contact with special places, persons or rituals. He is "at home" in high mountain pastures or on the arid plain, over the horizon of the steppe or in the crowded cacophony of a market or city street. No mediators or intermediaries from within creation or created by humans are necessary to encounter this God. He is at home in any humble, lonely nomad camp. Are we able to be there as his hands and mouth? Our task is to share this love with people whose lifestyle and values may seem, at least initially, totally alien to us.

Jesus in his own human experience was more at home with shepherds and poor itinerants than he was with those with a more comfortable standard of living. At the human level, he would be more at home in a camp with a group of Fulani or Qashqa'i, than he would in our Western churches. The ideal is to bring nomads to the point that we become observers of their relationship with Jesus. It is impossible to wrap God exclusively in terms of Western, or any other form, of Christianity. We cannot claim to know him in the sense that he is "possessed" by us.

In the close-knit society of a nomad camp, this life of trust in God and his providence would be constantly observed, to see whether Christianity has something better to offer than the nomads' own traditions. The Christian here would demonstrate how God transforms our lives, and would show the real love that is often lacking in their lives — this would be in contrast to their impression of Western culture.[6] Nomads are watching Christians more than they are listening, and initial conversions often occur among those who have traveled and met Christians elsewhere living ordinary lives. The missionary is "to

3a

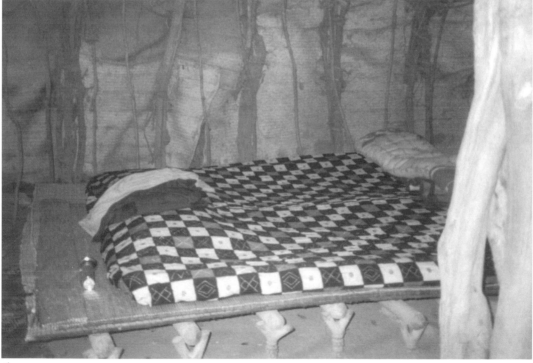

3b

3 Living with nomads:
  a. Missionary home among the Fulbe not too far from Timbuctoo.
  b. The bedroom.

3c

3d

3 c. Living in a *ger* among Mongols.
  d. Early one cold morning the chimney of the *ger* has to be cleaned before lighting the stove, the only source for warmth and cooking.

live a life of faith and prayer among them so that they see the reality that God is near and hears us and is so faithful that he can be depended on in the crises, as well as in the ups and downs of life."[7]

Answered prayer is one example of God's pastoral providence. There is a misconception among Muslims that Christians do not pray often, so the Christian worker should make his or her daily prayer habits known to the people in order to alter this. Our desire not to display our piety probably needs to be modified to show that God and prayer are as important to Christians as they are to Muslims.

This partnership means becoming accepted by them as a member of their society at some level, or in some category that they understand favorably. The Christian among them should make a contribution and not be considered as a permanent outsider. Like the apostle Paul, we can in some measure be "all things to all men" (1 Cor. 9:22) by a sympathetic sharing of experience that does not compromise God's message and the Christian worker's ability and health. Establishing meaningful relationships and finding a role, at least as a partial insider, requires regular personal contact for shared experiences to develop. It will take time, and there will inevitably be failures. Ultimately, there needs to be a role model of a Christian living their lifestyle without material possessions, buildings and comforts. But it is the people themselves who decide to accept the outsider into a relationship or role that they are familiar with.[8]

Many of these peoples are tired of the surveys and cameras of visiting anthropologists and tourists, and of the unrealized promises of material help. To fulfill Kraemer's golden rule, the Christian needs to be constantly discovering as much as possible about their way of life and thinking by having closer contact than most outsiders have had. Much has been done from ecological, economic and sociological perspectives, but there is a great need to understand and record from a biblical and Christian point of view. This biblical view results in a different understanding of the people, their aspirations and problems — for as we have seen, their lives are in fact quite close in many ways to the life portrayed in the Bible.

Befriending nomadic peoples

Many nomads can be contacted regularly at wells and at seasonal camping grounds where they gather for trade, limited agriculture and social contact. These may be points for offering literacy, medical and veterinary help. This is useful, because initial surveys in preparation for living with a nomadic people can be done at these focal points. The danger is that these local points can develop into mini "mission stations." Traveling or camping with the nomads for regular short periods is advantageous if one is to know and be accepted by the people. The key idea is to appear as mobile as the nomads are, so that any material help offered does not encourage a change in the migration pattern and thus undermine the subsistence methods. Swedish pioneers among the Afar walked their whole migration range to find the best location for their base.[9]

A family of six of the Christian Reformed Church, after a decade of church-related ministry, saw the needs of the unevangelized cattle people. They planned to live in a village of the pastoral Fulbe for increasingly longer periods.[10] Their agency supported the idea but insisted that they also have a home in town, a four-wheel-drive vehicle and a two-way radio. The village was on a hot windy plain and was a day's journey from any town. It was semi-settled near deep wells, which meant a third of the people stayed in the village while the rest migrated with the cattle.[11] The family lived in a typical grass house built for them by the people, without electricity, running water or refrigerator, and they cooked on an earth oven. The mother also home-schooled her children in the village until they were old enough to go to boarding school.

Initially the villagers expected the family to bring them more modern technology. They overwhelmed the family with hospitality and continual gifts of milk. The constant attention and visits during every hour of daylight were a trial at first, and this was only resolved when the women of the village decided that being so hospitable was stopping them from doing their own work. Later, a severe attack of dysentery laid low all the family except for the mother. The villagers were very concerned about them and offered their own remedies before persuading them to make the difficult journey for medical help. When they all recovered, they returned to live in the village. The people were then convinced that this expatriate family really cared for them.

After two years in the village, the family found that agricultural experiments, teaching and medical work had left them no time for language learning. They therefore changed to cattle breeding and started their own herd, using herdsmen from the village to look after it. The father took on the role of a "Jesus marabout," and he became accepted by the leaders of the village as a religious teacher, although unlike such teachers in the culture he also engaged in projects such as well digging. The rainy season, when the pastoral work was lightest, was a good time for teaching.

He prayed every day in public for the village. When he had attempted to help them with agricultural development they did not consider him to be one of them, but once he started owning cattle they accepted him as one of themselves. Today all members of this team are encouraged to own some cattle and wear African dress. They are aware that they are not reaching the more nomadic clans of Fulbe, with whom a more "nomadic" method will be necessary, camping in different places as the people move.

A town base with some Western amenities is necessary for recuperation and for doing those aspects of ministry that cannot be done in the camp or nomad village, such as language study, translation, administration and gaining support and fellowship from other Christians. But only 40% of one's time would be spent at this base, and the rest of the time is to be spent among the nomads. This has proved to be an ideal that has not been realized for a whole range of reasons — from travel difficulties to bureaucracy. The team's policy statement says the method is "to incarnate the Gospel among the people, by identifying with the lifestyle of the people, that is to live in the people's housing, eat the people's food, wear the people's clothes, learn their language, participate in their daily life, strive for a sympathetic understanding of their culture… to let go of the comfortable, familiar attachments of our culture."

Cash Godbold rode on horseback and took his wife and children in a cart pulled by a camel to visit the Tuareq camps north of Tahoua in Niger. They carried their own food, which the Tuareq had prepared for them. They ran a sort of pawnshop for the Tuareq to loan them money for food etc., and gave them medical treatment. They also had a local mud-brick house in Kao because the market was a good place to contact not only the Tuareq, but also the Hausa and Fulani. They later switched to using a Land Rover, but the early years of being willing to use resources known to the nomads paid off in gaining their confidence.

To live in an indigenous hut or tent may be considered the ideal, and it requires that for short periods we limit our resources to those available to the nomads. There needs to be a balance between identification with the people and their common sense expectation that if you "have it," you should "use it." What is needed is a disciplined limitation of gadgets and comforts to those that are essential to maintaining one's health and effectiveness in daily contact with the people.

Providing one's own mobile accommodation can be understood by the people and gives a measure of privacy. A specially modified Land Rover, like that used among the Fulani in Niger, can be designed as a mobile home.[12] The Hunters used a small tent on top of a Land Rover. It had the advantage of being above the mosquitoes, snakes and scorpions, and it gave privacy at mutually understood times. The people did not expect the outsider to be completely "native," and they appreciated the unhurried friendship. A vehicle is also useful to find a highly mobile group, when the "ideal" of indigenous transport on a mule or camel may result in frustration in not making contact. The people did not resent the modern vehicle, but they did think the outsiders were extremely poor because they did not own a single goat![13]

A young couple working with WEC has lived in a bell tent for periods of two weeks for over a year with a nomadic family of Fulbe in the Delta area of Mali. Finding their host each time was a problem, due to vague directions and floodwaters forming a barrier to their Land Rover. In the camp, they cover the vehicle with a tarpaulin both to protect it from the sun and to symbolize their willingness to stay. Far from being isolated, they have found that camping brings contact with many other nomadic families around them who would not necessarily be contacted in any of the villages.

Peripatetics in urban areas, such as the Gadulyia Lohars of India, also need a dedicated approach. A town where groups of these people visit customers could form a base, and the first step would be to survey the itineraries of particular groups or families. A ministry within a church in the town would constantly bring the missionary challenge of the Lohar to the local Christians. The Lohar could then be visited in a number of locations in the region, and a sustained contact could be maintained that does not interfere with their work.

There are many secular examples of the issues and problems to be encountered. Although anthropologists and Christian workers have mutual misgivings about each other's motives, they can learn from each other. An anthropological research project, even without academic backing, gives a basis for sharing their life for a sustained period and gaining a disciplined understanding of the people.

There would be some advantage in traveling with a group for a short part of the itinerary in order to appreciate their way of life. To find particular families on their itinerary can often be difficult, as Satya Pal

Ruhela found, and only by asking different Lohar groups was he able to find them. During his short journey with them he witnessed childbirth and worship at the roadside, as well as the routine of hard blacksmith work. But only after much patience did he get recordings of their Hindu songs.[14] At particular times a dozen or more families withdraw from their itineraries and camp together. This was an opportunity to camp with them if they gave him permission. But was only after many of these contacts was he able to gain their confidence to achieve one of his aims, to record their Hindu songs.

Marion van Offelen and Carol Beckwith integrated themselves with a camp of related Wodaabe families for seven months. During this time Carol received an offer of marriage — as a second wife. The women decided her hair was too short, so she grew it long and had it braided and greased with butter as theirs was. They found walking for five hours a day across the desert in the great heat, with nothing but muddy, sandy water to drink and milk for food, very exhausting. They discovered that buying a jeep did not create a barrier with the families, and the men took turns in acting as their "map-reader," which meant "reading" the hard-to-see marks in a trackless desert. The transport meant that their food and equipment was not a burden to the people's animals and they could carry extra food to return their hospitality.[15]

Traveling with the Dolpo and Rong-pa in the Himalayas, Diane Summer found that the concentration of sheep or yaks on the mountain route meant that dung covered the camp sites and polluted the streams from which they drew their only drinking water.[16] The Tibetan families camped and slept all together in the open, using some of the baggage as a windbreak. When her four-year-old daughter had a fever, the people were greatly concerned and interpreted this as the work of envious demons and offered an exorcism.

Such a ministry needs to arouse the awareness of the local churches to these groups. It cannot be assumed that local

Christians will have the time or vision to reach them. In fact, there can be such mutual prejudice between the nomads and the local people that Christians living nearby may have difficulty in being accepted.

In cultures that are traditionally nomadic but have been forced to settle, such as the Kyrgyz, it is important to identify with this past. It should not be assumed that, because they have lived in village houses with small farms for two or more generations, they have renounced their traditions and now aspire to a Russian way of life. The local people talk fondly of visits to the mountain pastures where the shepherds tend the flocks of the village. The Christian should do the same and perhaps own a few sheep as nearly every family does, and hire a horse to ride from time to time.

Reaction and acceptance

The first hurdle in some countries is to get government permission to visit areas where the nomads are. Two years of negotiations were necessary to arrange a visit to the Kazaks in the Altai Mountains in China.[17] Melwyn Goldstein had three years to wait and a further year of negotiations before he gained approval to live with the Chang Tang nomads in Tibet. But once permission has been gained, how do the nomads respond to an outsider living among them?

A request to camp or travel with them is often met with unbelief. The nomads may have preconceived ideas about the position of a foreigner in their midst. One needs a reasonable explanation for one's interest in the people, even if this may be different from that given to the authorities. An introduction by an outsider, with whom the people have regular dealings, may be needed. Most of the cases above depended on an invitation from a particular leader to accompany and become part of that group. Ilse Köhler-Rollefson spent seven months driving to visit various camps of the Rabari, but they refused to give her information until she was introduced to them by a Rabari veterinary surgeon, who translated directly into English for her.[18]

The foreigner usually receives the protection or hospitality of one key man and his household. One gains a measure of acceptance as part of the social group, and to that degree comes under the authority of that host. Foreigners should obey the leadership on migration and in camp, and should ask permission to leave.

Marie Herbert, a secular travel writer, traveled alone with four Sami men in northern Norway. She had some difficulty in overcoming the initial hostility created by their past experience of patronizing tourists and journalists. She made a prepayment for expenses. The men queried the adequacy of her modern clothing and equipment, and especially her motives for making the trip. The Sami were very concerned to ensure that she wrote an accurate, non-romantic assessment of their life and problems.[19]

Robyn Davidson found that the Rabari of India did not take her request to migrate with them seriously, and they made every excuse to refuse her.[20] Like Herbert, she found she needed an introduction from an outsider with whom the nomads were used to dealing. She took her own pack-camel on the migration but found that she had too much equipment for it to carry. The women teased her about being too weak, saying that she would abandon the journey, and that the police might accuse them of having kidnapped her. They even accused her of being a man in disguise. They taunted her about being childless and sick. Behind all this, she found out that they were genuinely concerned about her happiness.

The headmen took personal responsibility for her safety during her eleven weeks with them. She found all the meals to be identical, and the loneliness was unbearable. Often she got only two hours of sleep a night, because of the coughing and wheezing of the sick animals next to her camp bed. Years later, she continues to visit her Rabari family. Isabel Fonseca found that the Gypsies considered her barren, because at thirty she was single, childless and therefore "condemned" to travel the world, even to visit Albania of all places and, worse still, to have to stay with complete strangers like them.[21]

The Fulbe distrusted Paul Riesman and his wife when he asked permission to live with them, mainly because of their past experience of Europeans. Without any display of emotion, their leader stressed the hardness of the life. It took six months to overcome this until, by the end of their stay, they felt fully accepted. The reason they gave for their work was to study the language, although the real motive was to write an anthropological thesis.[22]

Lois Beck, like the others, had to be introduced by an outsider. Armed with a research scholarship and with the recommendations of the U.S. embassy and the Iranian government office for tribes, she first stayed with a Khan and taught English to his children. But later she was very fortunate to get a spontaneous invitation from a nomad, while they were merely waiting for the animals to pass them in the road.[23] A Qashqa'i headman of a sub-tribe took the initiative by first inviting her and a companion to have tea, then to an evening meal with him, and finally to travel with them. They spent twelve months, including six months on migration, in the tent of the headman. They got to know most of the one thousand nomads traveling with him.

Brian Hugh MacDermot lived among the Nuer with only a local guide and "translator." He showed that even a brief visit, in his case to make a television documentary, is useful to get closer to the people and to understand more of how they think. He discovered that previous anthropological studies had been done by people who had not lived with the people. Nevertheless, he found reading these studies sharpened his own awareness and observations to help him correct some of their erroneous conclusions.

He became overwhelmed by the demand for his untrained medical help.[24] A prophet of one of the Nuer deities initiated him into the tribe. After his ox was sacrificed, he received a new name, which identified him with the ox. When a marriage was arranged for him, he decided it was time to leave. Clearly there are limits to one's identification!

Close contact often requires one to change one's daily habits, including those helpful for one's work. Over a hundred years ago in Mongolia, James Gilmour found that the best way to learn the language and win the confidence of the people was to live with a Mongol in his tent. The Mongols considered that Gilmour brought them bad luck, because he went for a walk a few yards up-hill "for no purpose." He went simply for a few moments of solitude and fresh air. He found that taking linguistic notes was also thought to bring bad luck to the camp. The foreigner, he concluded, must not only adapt to close confinement with people who have bad health, bad hygiene, and bad habits in a smoke-filled environment, but must never go for a walk, write or hunt for a better diet, if he wants to win their confidence.[25] He also found that, with his apparent wealth and gadgets, he was expected to have powers of divination. Modern Mongols may be different, but we have to anticipate their surprising reactions.

Joseph Berland spent 14 months traveling 5,200 kilometers (3,250 mi.) with the animal trainers of the Qalandar and Kanjar in Pakistan. He gained entry to the camps by saying he wanted to study how children learn their peripatetic skills. The settled people resented this, however, until the Qalandar themselves suggested that he pretend to study the monkey and bears. Berland slept in a bender tent made of branches bent over in a semi-circle and covered with cloth, at the roadside. He carried his equipment on three donkeys, and he bought and learned to train his own bear. He also had a flat in Karachi where a Qalandar family might stay with him to discuss in depth some features of their thinking and culture. He found there was nothing romantic about traveling with these people.

Once the Qalandar were convinced that he really cared to know about their feelings and aspirations as well as the material aspects of their life, they accepted him as their "student," and they made every effort to point out new facts about their life. The people were a mine of information about the sedentary societies they "worked," and some of them had a working knowledge of five different languages. He found his relationships were full of tension, as these closed societies both accept and remain aloof towards the outsider. However, in this way he ultimately had contact with 800 families, which is more than many missionaries have.[26]

Judith Okely accompanied a posse of Gypsy women in southeast England on their rounds of hawking, fortune-telling, collecting scrap and even reselling thrown-away household goods.[27] A family usually traveled alone in an old trailer or truck, camping at the roadside. She had initial access as a temporary local government warden of a campsite. She soon learned that formal anthropological interviews were almost useless for getting real information. Shared experiences and prolonged companionship produced more volunteered information in comment, gestures and actions in the natural context of Gypsy life.

Over about ten months, Okely allayed their fears that she was a police informer by staying with them, doing chores such as reading letters and clearing rubbish. She also changed the way she dressed, and so gradually built up friendships. This apparently informal curiosity about their customs and beliefs was finally recognized as genuine interest.[28] Yet, after months of acquaintance in close contact, there was still reserve and suspicion of her as an outsider. She found that only by marriage to a Gypsy and adoption of the cleanness ritual would full acceptance into the group be possible.

Christina Noble traveled with her own tent and food and two trekking guides among the Gaddi shepherds in northern India. She walked nearly 600 kilometers (375 mi.) in the Himalayas, usually faster than the average nine kilometers per hour of the flocks. This meant she overtook the sheep and the shepherds and kept pace with the families of the shepherds who always went on ahead to set up camp before the arrival of the flocks each night. While she and her guides had their own tents, the shepherds they camped with often spent the night in a cave or a stone shelter.[29] Married to an Indian and sympathetic to Hinduism, she entered into their beliefs and aspirations and encouraged development projects to help maintain the viability of the Gaddis' pastoral way of life.

This effort of traveling with the people, once accepted, brings great rewards in winning the respect of the people, as well as providing first-hand experience of their concerns and interests. Such contact affords opportunities to laugh and cry with the people, as well as insight into their interests and knowledge of their heart language.

Impact on the nomad's life

The presence of the outsider can create strains in the host's relationships with others, as well as economic problems. The rules of hospitality may mean that the foreigner becomes part of the leading extended family. This adoption has the advantage of closer contact, but it also means limitations. Returning the favors indirectly is often necessary. Although often vitally needed, health or development projects can take all one's time, have short-lived results, and achieve little real friendship with the people. It may take time for one's motives to be believed, but genuine friendship and even offering to pray for the people can help. As so many have grotesque misconceptions of Christianity, praying and Bible reading in public view can help to create a new attitude.

Richard Tapper found that, as a guest and "dependent" of the Shahsevan chiefs, his desire to travel with an ordinary nomadic camp was not taken seriously. They thought this was not "proper" for a foreigner.[30] At first he found his car useful for interviewing otherwise elusive members of the group. However, when he became "taxi" man for taking the nomads between camps he gratefully exchanged it for a horse. He found he had few of the small status symbols of wealth that they had and, as an anthropologist, he was actually poorer than many of the nomads.

The headman treated him as one of his many sons, was concerned for his health, and tried to persuade him to become both a Muslim and a permanent member of the family. However, the headman was also blamed for having an "infidel" in the camp. In this situation, the nomads' concepts of hospitality to guests and their ideas about the polluting influence of non-Muslims conflicted. The mullahs (Muslim clerics among the Shahseven) were divided between those who persuaded the nomads to have nothing to do with Tapper and those who at least tolerated him on the basis of hospitality.

Tapper and his wife had a small tent alongside the Shahsevan family tent and so maintained a measure of independence. He found it best to accompany family members on visits to other camps or households rather than have a research program of his own. He also could not hire an assistant, as this was incompatible with his status as a "son." Many of the Shahsevan were reticent to give him information, but his wife was able to gather information from the women. Government officials and the police were uniformly hostile and harassed his hosts (this was in 1964).

Any outsider residing with nomads not only learns a lot and gains acceptance from them, but also has an impact on their life, as Tapper found out. Anthropologists, Beck says, fail to realize the impact their "impartial" observation has. The headman she traveled with was concerned for their comfort, and he invited them to be present when he entertained guests and to go with him when he was invited out. She realized that her presence could affect his position politically and economically. He was already heavily in debt due to the expense of maintaining his prestige as headman. She smuggled food to his wife as a way of compensating for their hospitality, and helped by driving his pickup truck for him and paying medical expenses for his relatives. She encouraged the children to use the school system set up for them (cf. Qashqa'i entry in ch. 13, below). Aware that an anthropologist can never return the hospitality, she gave gifts of things from America that they could use in the nomadic life, yet could rarely afford.

Politically, the headman seemed to gain status by having two Americans with him — although he had rivals to his position and the headman deposed before him traveled with him. Beck's presence helped to deflect threats, demands for bribes and criticism of his leadership that he would otherwise have suffered. He delighted in amusing his guests with questions about American life. Above all, he appreciated their interest in Qashqa'i life and history. Beck saw no reason to accept invitations from other headmen, and it would have been impolite to have done so. She herself was competent in Persian, Qashqa'i Turkish and Arabic, and her companion was able to learn enough of the first two languages to communicate with the nomads who preferred to speak their own Turkish and knew no English.

Although the nomads live without walls, they have their own ideas of privacy and Tejinder Randhawa, who has traveled with many nomadic groups in India, stresses that photography must be by consent.[31] Daniel Bradburd stresses the limited social universe of the nomad camp in which one meets the same few dozen people day after day, and where the anthropologist may himself be dragged into controversies about relationships, such as arranged-marriage negotiations.[32]

Even with the potential difficulties, it is possible to fulfill Kraemer's golden rule. It requires patience and much time, making oneself available and showing a measure of commitment by regular visits. Necessary absences should be explained as contact with one's family, a traveling society can understand. This is better than implying that they are because of difficulties with the camp environment, which the people are quick to suspect. To return regularly, even after sickness or other difficulties, can help to prove one's commitment to the people.

Special skills required of workers

A young Kyrgyz stared in horror at a visitor traveling on foot and by bus: "You haven't got a horse?"[33] It was inconceivable to him that someone could not ride a horse. This initial perception of the people can be important. The Fulbe may consider a person who arrives in a Land Rover as someone to be exploited, but a person who rides a horse is someone to be respected. Unfortunately, women do not ride horses in that culture.[34] The reindeer-herding Koryaks accepted Robin Hanbury-Tenison because he had been a deer farmer in Britain.[35] The nomads are also amazed when an outsider can herd cattle correctly; but it is just as important not to pretend you know how when you do not! It is easy to discredit oneself trying to handle camels without previous experience!

We need some knowledge of animals, or our ministry among pastoral groups will probably be limited. "The Christian evangelist will be challenged by the need to relate the Christian message to Gabbra concern for their animals. He will need to articulate a 'Theology of Herd Management'."[36] Knowledge of estate management, dairy farming, shepherding, soil analysis or any other such related skill would be useful. One agency needed to recruit a Livestock Management Specialist, a Community Health Educationalist and a Alcohol Abuse Counselor for Mongolia in one year. The Agricultural Christian Fellowship of the UCCF or related bodies elsewhere could help here, both in finding experienced workers and in giving some orientation to non-specialists.[37] In most cases, short periods of familiarization with animals would be sufficient for non-specialist workers. Obviously, to gain visas for particular projects professional qualifications are needed for some key workers. Training and skills learned through military service or any experience of camping and hiking are an advantage.

An important way of identifying with the people is to own some animals yourself, using local people to herd them and yet being seen to be involved in the same problems.[38] Often a person accepted as a religious teacher loses respect if he herds his own animals. It is common practice for wealthier members of a society to hire herders. The full adoption of orphaned or abandoned nomad children can also help in

gaining acceptance into the tribe, but it obviously raises much wider issues.

Peripatetics do not necessarily need Christians who have the same skills as themselves, but other skills to help them. But being willing to learn their skills, and perhaps having some previous training in an appropriate craft such as blacksmithery or basket weaving, will help us not only to appreciate the problems of the work, but also to perhaps begin a development project to make their work more viable. The nomads also need someone who is able to do what they cannot do for themselves.

Most important for working with nomads are linguistic skills, anthropological observation and the ability to make friends cross-culturally. We have to be amateur anthropologists in some sense, because so little is known of most of the peoples' society and way of life. A diary of initial observations that can be compared with later experience is very useful, because with familiarity our observation and learning soon become dulled, and we can habitually ignore whole areas of the people's thinking and life. We need to be creative Bible students to be able to show them how relevant its message is.

The thought of additional training may be discouraging, but a willingness to learn is as important as professional qualifications, which may be of limited use in developing countries. A nomad often believes himself to be superior to the outsider, and the outsider's ignorance and poverty in not understanding and owning animals just proves this! In allowing them to teach us, we learn from the nomads themselves about their way of life, language, skills and thought forms — and this honors their culture.

More fundamental still is the ability to incarnate Christian living among the nomads, in a way that they can appreciate. Those who have experience among nomads see a clear need for orientation courses beyond the training provided by most missionary college courses and mission orientation periods. Many feel the need for an internship that tailors the formal missionary training to the nomadic situation, with a testing of the practical commitment to the people. Suggestions for training include desert camps similar to WBT jungle camps in temperate climate conditions to teach appropriate skills in real life situations, and "adventure" treks into the Sahara. YWAM organizes Safari Trips.[39] The Christian College Coalition runs a Middle East Studies Program with 13 weeks in Cairo for service projects, lectures and conversational Arabic and visits to Israel. This gives North Americans an experience of Muslim urban life, between academic years at various Christian colleges.[40] A few years ago the Christian College Coalition ran a similar course involving experience of pastoral and nomadic life in Africa and the Middle East.

Prayer journeys and experience assignments can be difficult to organize for students in remote areas, but they can prove rewarding to support and recruit. Again, there are several secular examples. A student of Trent University, England, made a lone journey on horseback to the Khusgul Lake area of Mongolia to study the effect of tourism on both the nomads and the wildlife. She submitted her study to the Mongolian National Parks Authority.[41] Philip Andrews-Speed made six visits to Xinjiang during a four-year period and traveled mostly on foot, seeking out communities of herdsmen in the mountains in different parts of the province. He later published a number of articles.[42]

A sustained Christian commitment

Partnership requires a realistic commitment, demonstrated by the size and duration of a missionary team. When, in the people's experience, workers have remained only long enough to "murder" the language and make all the inevitable cultural mistakes, the impression is left that they had no real interest, or found the people too difficult to get along with. Two or three years in the nomad environment may seem to be a very long time to the unaccustomed outsider, but it is a transitory novelty in the lifetime of the people. The short sacrificial stint can be

interpreted by the Fulbe as the missionary topping up his or her own merit to get to heaven, rather than as a real desire to convert the nomads. A Bozo marabout angrily complained to us that foreigners have come and done surveys and left, but the people have never benefited from them. We can justify our spasmodic visits, interrupted by home or sick leave or other mission business, but such a limited involvement must necessarily undermine the personal relationship that is the beginning of confidence. In the eyes of indigenous peoples, the missionary, even with a decade or more of service, is seen as both a foreign and a *temporary* phenomenon.

Many years of contact to overcome the nomads' suspicion and fear, with few or no visible results, is difficult. It has been said that evangelizing an African people takes 50 years. The first 25 years may result in 25 converts, but the harvest only comes in the second 25 years.[43] The assumption that goals can be accomplished in a decade never gives the workers, or the changing of the world view of the people, a chance. A Tuareq commented that without real commitment and a more explicit presentation of the message, when there is opportunity to do so, we can give the impression that we do not really believe the message ourselves.

This factor of commitment also touches on the greatest fear of the nomads when considering conversion — that Christianity will lead to their being socially isolated, without someone to care for, marry or bury them. But the lesson from Christ is clear. The incarnation is permanent, the Son remains a man forever. Even his absence in the ascension is a continuation of his commitment, and he has only left temporarily to deal with his adopted people group's best interests as their representative with the divine paramount Chief of all peoples! He will return. The missionary or, failing that, a team in relays, could be a visible sign of God's commitment to the people. When the worker can no longer live in the country, the people should be assured that the absent worker continues his or her interest in prayer and any other means to promote their spiritual interests, including perhaps contact with expatriate communities of the people.

It would be beneficial to have teams called and trained together. To achieve the best results in sport and in warfare, teams are trained together before going on an assignment. The bonding between the workers will be more apparent to the people, and the absence of some members of this missionary "family" will be better explained as family business. The arrival of workers who have hardly known each other before that missionary assignment must seem a strange and unconvincing "tribe." A team provides for relays of workers being present as well as meeting the needs of the scattered groups of a nomadic people.

These teams probably require a range of generations to be convincing. Younger women have problems in being accepted as religious teachers among Muslim peoples. Older workers, including women, are often more respected as "holy" or wise. This is illustrated by a Wodaabe man who regarded his thirty-five-year-old daughter as no longer a "woman," but rather as an "old man," because she had arrived at a mature understanding of life through her experiences of suffering.[44]

Partnership by Christians with nomadic peoples must enhance their society and their nomadism in realistic ways. We shall now turn to some practical ways of doing this.

10 Working with Nomads

Our strategy is to make sure that our presence and friendship not only does not disrupt the nomad's way of life, but also that we contribute to maintaining a viable nomadism in the modern world. The aim of the gospel is reconciling people to their Creator so that they live lives worthy of him in the environment and society in which he has set them. The nomad's ingenuity in using a difficult environment effectively is one of the many ways that humankind fulfills its responsibility to the Creator. The defects in the nomad's expression of the image of God are not in being mobile, or in being on the fringes of society, but in being as unbelieving and egocentric as settled people. In order to reach out to nomads we need to understand their values and family relationships, and also how to give them practical help so that they can sustain themselves.

A witness to biblical and nomadic values

One major contribution of Christian partnership with nomads is the reform of moral attitudes and norms. Many a Christian has been puzzled that while the gospel message is about the cross (and rightly so), most of the Lord's ministry was spent correcting his contemporaries' misunderstanding of God's law. The Beatitudes encourage people (who may themselves be economically poor, either by choice or by injustice) to give priority to right relationships rather than to possessions. The ultimate goal is not only to have a group of disciples, but also to create a more caring society within the nomadic herding group or family, resulting in limited resources going further and work relationships being fairer.

Many nomads have their own behavioral codes and values, like the Fulbe *pulaaku*, by which they consider their culture superior in order to maintain their identity. The cattle are thought to have belonged to the Maasai long ago and therefore they, like many pastoralists, consider stealing cattle as a legitimate method of returning them to their rightful owners![1] It is easy to hastily judge these systems and practices, and so reject the entire value system. Even presuming to try to alter the methods and morals of another culture appears to be arrogance. We have to be careful not to justify any unjust practice as acceptable because it is "culture." We need to examine our motives for wanting to conserve the customs or suggesting their modification.

The basis of the Bible's moral standards is the covenant relationship with God, but many of the details were adapted and modified from the contemporary practices of the day. How God corrected and enlarged Israel's life by his instruction or *torah* is a model for teaching modern people. God corrected contemporary standards and much of the behavior exhibited by people in the biblical narratives. This should encourage us to see that a gradual transformation of the people's culture is possible. The apparent simplicity of some Christian interpretations of biblical commands often fails to take into account the context, especially in the Old Testament. The points of contact between the nomads' values and the Bible's ethical teaching need to be found, to know what to keep and what to renounce in their culture. For example, Christian Gypsies are already modifying their customs — prohibiting fortunetelling but continuing their custom of the bride-price as biblical.

These moral issues are often complicated, because they also affect how the people see themselves. The pastoralist will be concerned not only with how a Christian should live, but also with how this impacts on his or her place in society and the future of the people as a whole. The challenge to

Christians is to learn what the Scripture says, or does not say, about many areas of life.

We have already suggested that the Bible's teaching can be introduced through its nomadic themes. Ultimately God's standards for all people are the same, so they can be found in some form in the values of societies that do not know the Bible.[2] Modifying the people's rules is often sufficient to lead to a greater moral change, just as many of the laws in the Old Testament seem to be provisional changes of contemporary practice with an eye to further improvement later.

Moral instruction must be accompanied by the gospel, just as grace was present with the Law. Salvation restores us to fulfill our responsibility, but it also assures us of forgiveness and reconciliation with God as a motive to change. It follows, therefore, that Christians are the only people who have been given the full vision and motivation to serve others for evangelism as well as for social and environmental development. As General William Booth said, we need the gospel and good works like we require two legs to walk. We begin in the key nomadic unit of the family.

Nomadic women have special needs

Women may be the unreached among the unreached, for a number of reasons. They often form a sub-society within nomadic society. They are not only sometimes difficult to contact, but they are also devalued and literally overworked. And yet, they have enormous influence. Many studies of nomadic groups fail to mention women and their roles. The first task would be to understand precisely how women's relationships work within the culture, getting beyond outsiders' judgments as well as the stereotypes of both men and women within the culture itself.

Pastoralist women rarely leave camp or have contact with outsiders or even their own relatives. The men, who pick news up from trips to town or outsiders, are more likely to share it with their male relatives than with the women. It is a fallacy to think that nomadic peoples can be evangelized by speaking to the men in the markets and towns. Even contact with the male heads of families in the camps does not mean that the women also hear.

This lack of contact with outsiders means that some Fulani women in northern Burkina Faso have never seen white people. Qashqa'i women look forward to the migrations, when other families may travel with them, and to such chores as gathering wild fruit or collecting water. In these ways they have contact with women from other camps. They also welcome visits from peddlers and others with whom the men want no dealings.

Women have little or no opportunity for education, and consequently they have a higher illiteracy rate than the men. Many women do not even learn the trade language well enough for contact with outsiders. Husbands do not necessarily pass on information or teach their wives; the women may have developed other ways of getting news about the outside world and learning useful information. For centuries Mongol women were considered ritually impure and condemned to be illiterate, but Communism forced a change in these attitudes. Fulani women learn better by encountering concrete illustrations and situations throughout the day, than they do by listening to teaching and trying to absorb it as the men do. Literacy can transform the lives of women and give them self-esteem, but it can also create tensions in family relationships.

Women develop social relationships between themselves that are different from the more formal relationships among men. Among the Turkic nomads of Iran, the women and children form a camp-wide fraternizing group when the men are away herding. When the men return, they revert to staying separate in their own tents as dutiful wives and daughters. In Africa, the women do not have the attachment to cattle that the men have. They are more concerned with, and work harder for, the more practical subsistence of their household.

4a

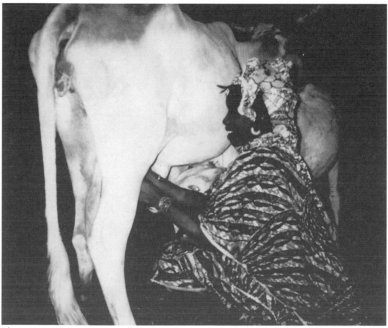
4b

4 Among nomads women do much of the work but often have more equal status with the men than in surrounding settled societies:
   a. The Fulbe women pound millet to be eaten with milk.
   b. Milking among the Fulbe.

4c

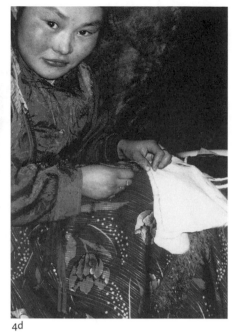

4d

4e

4 c. Mongol woman milking a yak – if winter is not severe, the yak will provide milk for most of the year.
   d. Nenet woman hand-sewing furnishings (Photo: Mark Dotson).
   e. Rashaida women in their tent.

Women often know more of what is going on in the camp than the men do, and they have a greater loyalty to each other than to their husbands. In some nomadic societies the women have solidarity against the men. In East Africa, Maasai wives defend each other against the sexual freedom that the men have to take any women in the rank or age set after their own. When they have affairs themselves, the wives do not consider this to be the result of mere lust but rather a deliberate protest against the male-dominated system.[3]

Although undervalued, some nomadic women will join in a fight to defend either their pasture or their men. Lois Beck tells of how 30 Qashqa'i women drove off 130 Luri shepherds on one occasion. On another occasion a sheep thief, who had killed a Qashqa'i, was summarily executed by the men because they feared what the Qashqa'i women would do to him. In the Sahel, the men complain because the women are becoming more active in community matters outside the family.

Usually there is a division of labor between the sexes, and the descriptions below mention some of these. This appears to outsiders as subordination of the women to the men, but the women often see their roles as complementary to those of the men. Western ideals tend to see hard domestic work as demeaning, but in a nomadic society a division of labor is necessary and is not considered to confer lower status. The women may be solely responsible for constructing or assembling the tents, or milking and dairy production, and the men take care of the herding. Among the Somali and the Toubou, the women often do the herding. The Bedu men herd the cattle or the camels and the goats, the less prestigious animals, are left to the women.

But the division of labor is often unequal, and the women frequently do most of the work. Davidson described the Rabari women that she traveled with as being "made of iron." The women had little free time, even to wash clothes, and they were often beaten. Many of the men, on the other hand, were ineffectual and alcoholic.

Among Golok Tibetans, the women are bashful and stand when men or strangers are present. The Fulani have a strict segregation between men and women, so that a wife may be more accountable to her mother-in-law than to her husband. It is considered shameful for a couple to speak together in public.

Nomadic women are undervalued in many ways. Often the women eat last, and in times of hardship they go without. Qashqa'i women are not allowed to slaughter animals, and in times of hunger they have resorted to eating dead animals — which is against Islamic custom. Only when they are cooking may they take a share for themselves. Muslims consider contact with women to be a hindrance to devotion to God. Women are not thought to have religious understanding, and so many women have an ingrained habit of not thinking of, or discussing, religious matters.

A man can be loyal to his father rather than to his wife, which undermines the nuclear family (Gen. 2:24). But not all nomadic women are downtrodden. Women both in the Bible and in nomadic societies often have greater influence than their formal status appears to allow. Shuwa women, for example, are responsible for marketing the milk, while the men stay to herd the cattle. But modern change can also have the effect of limiting the freedom of women. Syrian Bedouin women became nostalgic for the camels when they were replaced by trucks because milking, loading and riding them gave the women greater involvement and social interaction. Working with the trucks has become a male preserve.[4]

Peripatetic women are not confined to remote domestic situations like the pastoralists. Among the Lohar of India and the Ghorbati in Iran, the women take an equal share in working as blacksmiths and contacting customers. Ghorbati peddler women of Afghanistan inherit permanent customers from their mothers and make decisions, even in contradiction to their husbands. Romany women have a talent to use the aura of mystery that surrounds them to "ask" (beg) or hawk from non-Gypsies.

This talent is highly valued by their men, although the contact with non-Gypsies renders them "unclean."[5] But the non-Gypsy stereotype that Romany women are immoral is contrary to the facts. For the Gypsies have a strict code of contact between the sexes, and virginity at marriage, and fidelity afterwards, are highly prized.

Pastoral women who have settled in towns, because of marriage or abandoning nomadism, may find the stricter adherence to Islam there results in them being shut in their houses for months, without even the variety that camp women have. Many yearn for the privacy of the camp, away from the gossip and constant contact with unwelcome neighbors. There is a need for specialized outreach to nomadic women in the villages and towns.

Women and their children, particularly because of their insular outlook and limited opportunities for outside contacts, have many special needs. These require a special strategy, that does not offend the men, in any serious outreach to a nomadic people. We need to understand how the women relate together and to whom they look for authority and advice.

Masters and wives

Societies vary considerably on the economic value they attribute to a bride. In many very different societies, including the Maures, Qashqa'i, Wodaabe and Nuer, the woman may be allowed to own her own animals, but she is not always allowed to make decisions concerning their sale or slaughter. Among the Sami, a daughter may own a significant number of animals in her own right — so her marriage depletes the family herd and the bridegroom has to compensate the father to get her. In India, however, the bride-price is paid to the bridegroom to persuade him to take the "unwanted" asset — that is, the daughter.

Most nomadic peoples practice exogamous marriage — that is, the girls marry husbands from another clan, which means a wife is isolated from all her relatives for most of the year. Rebekah's faith and courage to leave home would be well understood by nomadic women (Gen. 24:5, 8, 38, 61). Newly married women may have to live with, and work for, an unsympathetic mother-in-law or sisters-in-law and are often very miserable.

A wife's greatest disaster is to be childless, and many wives have little status until they have given birth to a son. A marriage without children is frequently likened to a tree without fruit and even to a living death. As we have seen, children are thought to be the continuation of the presence of the parent after death. Among the Wodaabe a childless women may be considered to be of less value than a dog, and is often abandoned by her husband, or greatly humiliated by his taking a second wife.

Mothers transmit the values and superstitions of the society. In many cases women have different attitudes and religious practices from the men. The Fulbe women's religious practices are often more superstitious and animistic than those of the men, and it is unlikely that they would follow their husbands in becoming Christians, even though Islam offers very little for women. Women in nomadic camps usually do not have the same religious restrictions placed on them that sedentary women, or those who have never been nomads, have.

Regardless of the controversies in Western denominations about the role of women, the Bible gives plenty of evidence of the influence of women so that we can rediscover an appropriate Christian balance of rights and responsibilities between the sexes that fits within the nomadic society. The Bible starts by stating that man and woman together form the image of God and the second chapter of Genesis demonstrates that the entire creation was incomplete until woman had been created (Gen. 2:23). Eve, Sara, Rebekah and Rachel were hardly without influence on events, not to mention Moses' mother and sister, Rahab, Ruth and many others, including the repeated naming of the king's mother (1 Kgs. 1:11; 2 Kgs. 12:1, etc.).

Nomads can appreciate the protection

that David, as a roving mercenary, gave to Nabal's shepherds (1 Sam. 25:15-16). Their testimony discounts the idea that David was just running a "protection racket," although later Bedouin commonly augmented both their wealth and political influence by this means. This episode reveals the hospitality customary at shearing time, the plans for inevitable revenge (v. 34) and poetic justice inflicted on this very wealthy "Imir." The novel twist is the intercession of his wife to save *David* from blood-guiltiness. Abigail represents the "common sense" faith in God of pastoral women, who wish to leave justice in the hands of God and stem the upsurge of masculine bad temper and pride. She proved to be God's mediator in a male-dominated situation.

Women are less inhibited about the family hierarchy of descent than the men are, and they relate together much more in larger groups. While the women are often confined to camp, and perhaps only move to another camp when they are married, they have ways of communication and influence across families and camps. They have considerable informal influence even on their husbands, but also in the raising of the children, so while in many societies women are subordinate to men, they are the sole influence on the men as sons while they are still young. They often enshrine and pass on the values and traditions to a greater degree than the men do.

Women missionaries should not be dissuaded from seeking to develop a women's ministry, in what is apparently a male-dominated world. Women will often confide in another woman, who is outside the camp network of gossip, in a way they can never speak to their husbands. In fact, the only male they confide in may be a brother. In Fulbe society it is not considered good form for couples even to speak together in front of others. In one case among the Fulbe, women have confided to the missionary about their children who have died as babies or infants; these mothers were still grieving, many years later. Therefore, women have a crucial role to play as disciple-makers, and a ministry among

women may produce fruit in the next generation. It may, in fact, be more productive than the witness to men.

Church planting or discipleship strategies should place a subtle emphasis on the women, or more precisely on the mothers. They provide the mainstay of their family and may even live separately from the men. The men need to give permission for the women's involvement, but at the same time to reach the men does mean reaching the women as well. In time, biblical standards of complementary partnership between the sexes would transform relationships, without disrupting nuclear and extended families.

Our response to the environment

The Christian's task is to encourage people to respond to the Creator and the environment as gifts. This is the role of the image of God (to reflect God's social nature and character, both in himself as a Trinity and in his dealings with humankind) and so is the basis of morality. Our response should not be a passive "live and let live," but rather a seeking of ways to harmonize the varied uses of the environment to maintain its self-sustaining nature. When we cease to respond in love to the Creator and to one another and to the environment, the relationship with God is broken. The gospel aims at bringing humankind to fulfill our role as image of God as a loving society, imperfectly now and perfectly in heaven with Christ, and later in the resurrection on a new earth. We are not to be cosseted individual "souls" in heaven without developed social relationships and responsibilities.

The Bible's emphasis on trust in God for physical subsistence or irregular income is novel to many Western Christians, except perhaps to those who "live by faith" for all their needs. Most of us have grown up in a culture in which everything has apparently been controlled and provided by human beings, and as Christians we see a dichotomy between spiritual life and everyday life. Because of the nomads' intimate relationship with the environment, we need to develop what the Bible says or implies about the environment.

The environment is not restricted to non-human aspects, but includes how the human actors understand it. Some nomads have a sensitivity to the environment, such as the Buddhists who understand killing animals to be sinful, and who are therefore reluctant to do so.[6] But many nomads have a narrower view of exploiting the environment with large herds for their own status and security. The Bible also mentions shepherds who destroy the environment as part of divine judgment (Jer. 6:3; 12:10-11). We need to teach about responsibility for creation and environmental sins alongside the gospel, which should also lead nomads to a clearer idea of what sin is and the need for redemption. From the outside, the nomads' environment appears to provide few alternatives for ways of affecting it. Both the Bible and ecologists recognize that attitudes to the environment vary according to the individual and do not simply follow the cultural norms of a people. There are pastoralists or craftsmen who respect the environment and others who do not. Individuals who have some influence as mentors can learn to examine their motives and goals in their attitude to sustaining the environment so that some can be encouraged to maintain the renewable aspects of the environment.

Development as the nomads' task

Development should be the response of a society to people and the environment as gifts from God. The goal of development, therefore, is to live in harmony as a community with the self-sustaining nature of the environment. But we must ask what is effective, and for whom? The variety of responses to a multifaceted creation is an essential reflection of God's image.

The starting point for a plan of development should be a positive attitude towards nomadism, accepting pastoralism as an efficient way to use semi-arid areas, as opposed to capital intensive and destructive irrigation schemes for converting the land to agriculture. This also applies to many of the economic niches that peripatetics occupy. For they contribute to wider employment and a more varied society than would be achieved by substituting their services with high investment factory products. The overall aim is a sustained nomadism for a significant number of the people, that also maintains their identity and culture as giving subsistence in a way they value. This aim involves, in some degree, their relationship to the surrounding society.

Development, therefore, must be appropriate to maintain this way of life. Some projects are determined by the benefactors' concerns — for example, to relieve population pressure — rather than by the welfare of the beneficiaries. The outsider, who often has a secular, scientific and market economy view of what is desirable, may "objectively" decide what is good for the land or the people. But the "pursuit of happiness," subsistence and lifestyle are all relative ideas. Many projects have been an "unrelieved failure" because the beneficiaries have not been involved in the decisions by "bottom up" planning.[7]

Projects must meet the needs of particular pastoralists rather than having wider development aims, recognizing "that the pastoralists themselves are the experts" and that we need "to learn from them."[8] The misunderstanding of "overgrazing" by planners has led to livestock reduction and the removal of the pastoralists, when the real solution is in fact grazing management. This involves not only stock density but also relating the timing and scale of grazing to the growth cycle of pasture. The pastoralist is already familiar with this, but his knowledge may have been overridden by other fears.

It is now recognized that the pastoralist is sensitive to ecology, and the peripatetic to the economy, in a way that others are not.[9] Nomads have an integrated knowledge of their environment and their livestock and are aware of how a variety of problems are interrelated. Development agents, on the other hand, are specialists in only one area.[10] To bring nomads into the planning process from the beginning is not merely a

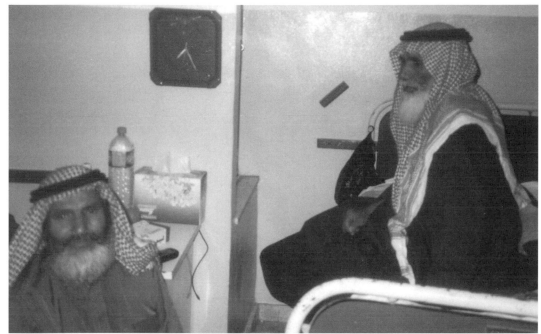

5a

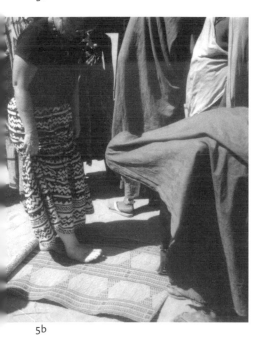

5b

5c

5 Nomads need access to outside services:
   a. Bedouin await medical treatment in hospital.
   b. Indigenous crafts are marketable — missionary feet measure a mat to ascertain a fair price.
   c. Goat breeding project for the Bedouin.

5d

5e

5 d. Bucket irrigation project to help settled Bedouin.
   e. Tent school for Golog children (Photo V. Downes).

good development strategy, but also a fulfillment of God's intentions. Because God's goal is that society be a community of mutual respect and fulfillment, changes such as development should involve wide consultation and explanation.

Enlisting the knowledge and co-operation of the local people in a development project helps towards the greatest of developments — that of a caring society that will sustain the changes. For example, the Evens and Koryaks of eastern Siberia understand, and have a possessiveness towards, their land. This makes them the perfect guardians for control over tourism and natural resources.[11] Many pastoralists constantly show resourcefulness in developing supplementary subsistence strategies, belying the stereotypes that they are only interested in livestock.

Yet there is also a negative side to all of this. Many nomads have a short-term view of resources. Gypsies see the ground beyond their vans as a no-man's-land that can be soiled or littered, especially to keep the non-Gypsy at bay. The Fulbe do not see the need to protect trees, and so they lose interest in planting projects. In many instances, providing wells has resulted in the concentration of livestock until the pasture has been destroyed. Vanderaa tells of a motorized pump, intended to be run for a short time each day to water the local herds, that was run continuously to destruction so that the local men could sell the water to herds from a distance.

Consultation requires an ongoing educational process. This must deal not only with the practical advantages, but it also must touch on the fundamental concepts of the culture. Local "policing" may be needed for those convinced of long-term advantages to monitor those who are desperate for short-term gain.

How nomads participate in development consultations is not always clear in practice.[12] Is the aim merely to gain their consent, or is it for them to decide? The kinds of decision required need to fit in with their forms of decision-making. Is only an

elite among them to be involved, or should a broader constituency of people participate? Many nomadic societies stress the independence of the family and have difficulty in co-operating as a community. Those who have to implement the decisions are not always those making them. Also, this must ultimately mean that the women are at least informed, which may go against the usual cultural practice.

It is often difficult to get a consensus — because of lack of vision or because some projects may only benefit a few. Some projects raise questions that the usual leadership does not normally have to deal with, so the consultation may have to involve more than those traditionally involved in decision-making. In some cases, pastoral and peripatetic associations need to be set up. Discussions, therefore, must be in their language and with their leaders.

What the people expect from the project may change during the consultation, as they see the potential of the development.[13] Often a "guinea pig" recipient is needed to demonstrate the advantages before the whole community becomes convinced. Any changes have to be planned so they will be accepted by a new generation, rather than being confined to the shorter time scale of the projects themselves. How far can such a consultation become part of a long-term politicizing process?

Motivation according to the world view of the people is crucial. The tradition of the Fulbe is not just looking at the past. They have, rather, many different models by which they adapt to different lifestyles according to changing conditions, and yet they remain assured that these changes are culturally acceptable.[14] They are therefore able to adjust to new concepts of land use.

Projects must use local resources and be within the management skills of the people. A project in Kenya failed because it attempted to make milk producers into meat producers. The Chinese government attempted to limit grazing on the Chang Tang by forcibly moving families and ordering unnecessary herd culls of 20%, without any evidence of overgrazing.[15]

Restocking the livestock is one of the most appropriate ways to help pastoralists, if not imposed from the outside without reference to local practices.[16] But it should be done in such a way that it reinforces the traditional loaning and giving of animals as practiced by many pastoral peoples. Christians were involved in this long ago, when the reindeer of St. Lawrence Island off Alaska were all killed by white hunters, leaving the local Yupik people destitute and reduced to drunkenness. The herd was restarted with reindeer shipped in from Siberia by the Presbyterian missionary Sheldon Jackson. This has resulted, indirectly, in the local people evangelizing the donors in Siberia.[17] Western charities also helped to replace yaks lost in heavy snowfalls in Qinghai, China. It was necessary to replace them with the right sub-species matching the experience of the nomads, with the right milk yield and feeding habits.

One of the major problems that pastoralists have is getting their product to market. The new private companies among the Mongols failed to establish suitable structures, and nomads have been reduced to bartering pastoral products for other goods from traveling peddlers and merchants. Some are fortunate to own their own vehicles and are able to reach customers further afield.[18]

Nomads are not necessarily conservative in their attitudes, but they must be convinced of the overall benefits of a new method. The Bedouin abandoned their revered camel for the truck on their own initiative, because of the benefits that have revolutionized their lives. The greater mobility has meant that migrations to get to pasture that took two months now take two days, with the family spending more time at home with schooling and other services. The middlemen that kept the shepherd in continual debt-dependence can now be by-passed as livestock, wool and other products are taken to various markets to get the best prices, and goods and fodder can be bought at lower prices. The wool is sold to Japanese dealers and producing milk has become a commercial operation, as it is sold directly to dairies. The trucks can be hired to farmers at harvest time, and younger people can get transport to work in the fields or towns for the day.

The profits have been invested in land for pasture, because of the pressure of encroaching cultivation and market gardens. It is also rented to farmers in a "turning of the tables" on the traditional hostility between the two ways of life. The disadvantage is that the sheep are in the Baqa'a Valley for a longer period and have to rely on bought fodder for the second half of the summer. But life has materially improved through this one initiative without changing the family life, values and pastoralism of the Bedouin.[19]

One important development need is to care for the soil. The notion of the advancing edge of the desert is not proven, and the reasons for land degradation are complex.[20] Overgrazing and fuel gathering, as in Africa where 201 million people depend on firewood, are some of the problems. Solar ovens may be one solution. Over-cultivation also leads to erosion, and over-irrigation leads to a salty ground with decreasing crop yields.

One method for caring for the soil is tree planting. Trees save the topsoil from being blown away, provide organic material to improve the soil, and create micro weather benefits — especially shade. Where rainfall is higher the trees reduce the impact of raindrops on the soil. This stops the soil from becoming clogged and unable to absorb the water, lessening run-off and erosion and the washing away of nutrients. The trees contribute organic material to the soil that in turn helps water absorption.[21] Trees also provide fodder for goats and cattle and cash crops of fruit as well as serving as a source for fuel.

There are tree-planting projects in Kenya, the Cabo Verde Islands and the Sahel run by OXFAM, Christian Aid, CAFOD, CARE (Britain), and SOS Sahel. Trees are being planted in Somalia and Niger to stabilize sand dunes and to act as windbreaks. In Niger, SIM has planted acacia trees as windbreaks as part of Operation New Leaf.[22] China has completed a belt of trees 7,000 kilometers (4,350 mi.) by 1,000 kilometers (620 mi.).

Sam David, a Methodist, has recognized that ground temperature has much to do with infertility. The restoration of woodland for shade as well as for fruit, combined with a well digging program, are contributing to reversing this trend. He has been involved in projects for many years in Gambia.[23] A Spanish engineer, Antonio Ibanez Alba, was experimenting with 30,000 trees made of polyurethane, 10 meters high, in the Libyan desert in 1991. The desert air cools at night to cause a heavy dew. The shade of the artificial trees prevents this from evaporating, creating a micro-climate in which real palms can be planted and grow.[24]

Nomads, as part of a wider society, need to be heard where political policies are made, so that all those involved may participate in the decision making. They cannot be dismissed as having few votes or being insignificant. Yet, on the other hand, nomadic peoples can no longer use large tracts of the environment without contributing economically and socially to a nation's life. There is a moral case to be made for nomads being involved in the commercial production of meat, dairy and other products, to repay at least some of the investments of outsiders. How nomadism contributes to the national life needs to be clarified — whether as part of the economy or as a subsistence strategy that more than keeps people out of urban squatter settlements.

An example of co-operation between very independent and almost politically autonomous pastoralists and a national government can be found in the development of desert tourism among the Sinai Bedouin. Using concepts of Bedouin law, local men are encouraged to volunteer to be guards of the environment in their area.[25]

The Christian worker, who knows the language and has made a long-term commitment to the people, should know the way decisions are made within the social structures and may already have the confidence of the local leaders. He or she should be able to participate in this consultation far better than short-term development workers. The goal of a more caring, sharing society should be foremost, rather than material improvement as part of a secular "modernizing" trend.

Nomads live on the environmental and economic margins of society, and are resourceful in exploiting new opportunities, even in the face of competition from factory-produced products. Workers with specialized expertise may be able to do economic surveys and establish businesses for marketing pastoral or handicraft products. However, establishing a relationship as a business, even buying handicraft objects for a private collection, can undermine friendship — so it is important to decide what sort of relationship one wants to establish.[26]

Vital veterinary care

Veterinary specialists should play an important role among the pastoralists and among the peripatetics who also have animals. It has been found that an effective program for the nomads' animals can give credibility to all the non-veterinary members of team. This can lead to interest in other things the missionary can offer. Any team working among pastoralists should have at least one veterinary worker.

Many basic services do not require a veterinary specialist and it is considered better to use "para-vets," or less well trained assistants drawn from the ethnic group, rather than outside development workers.[27] In northern Pakistan it was found that, while these services are provided at Dir and to the northeast in Kohistan, they reach only 10% of the stock at present. There was a need not only to provide vaccination and other health services on a wider basis, but also to carry out the research for such a program.[28]

Both the Veterinary Christian Fellowship in the UK and the Christian Veterinary Mission in the USA, along with similar bodies in other countries, have members who could be involved in furthering mission work among pastoralists.[29]

Medical and health assistance

Since nomadism requires good health in an unhealthy environment, health education is as important as medical treatment. Close proximity in small tents and huts results in the spread of infection, deformity and death, and resistance to common childhood diseases is low. Patients disappear over the horizon before treatment is complete, because staying in one place is alien to the nomad's thinking. The rigor of the nomadic life in areas such as East Africa means that sick or handicapped individuals may be abandoned to die, and being an outcast from one's tribe can also have such a detrimental effect as to hinder recovery.[30]

Nomads are not noted for using too much water because it is scarce. Basic hygiene is therefore lacking, which results in chronic health problems. Goloks never wash their cups, except perhaps for a guest. Mongols are reputed to lick their dishes clean, and they never wash their clothes, wearing them until they rot.[31] The Maasai use sand and urine to clean their food pots, or the dogs are allowed to lick them clean. There are several pastoral societies in Africa who use cow's urine to wash their utensils, their hands and even their hair, to acquire an odd golden color. Dogs generally eat anything from human feces to animal and human corpses — the path of cross-infection is clear.[32]

Illness is often considered to be the result of having broken a taboo. Gilmour cites the case of a Mongolian Buddhist who thought his tuberculosis was the result of having killed worms when digging a hole many years before as a boy. Vandevort describes cases of psychosomatically induced illnesses among the Nuer, resulting from their fear of death, which is synonymous with fearing "God." Death is considered inevitable and the person dies — even of a treatable condition.

Health education programs can be devised that at least meet halfway the thinking of the people as well as their mobility. Novel teaching materials such as songs, plays, pictures and talks can be used. A community health program in Mongolia not only needs the civic leaders to co-operate, but also has to persuade the elderly who are highly respected, so that they in their turn win over the younger generations.

A mobile medical service can reach more patients, but because of low population densities and the mobility of nomads, fuel costs can be very high. This means that governments only attempt such services where the number of nomads is high and politically significant. In one example among the Maasai, a mobile clinic treated 12,400 people — as opposed to a district hospital that treated only 1,100. Such a service among the Turkana usually spent 25 days visiting the herding groups, alternating with 13 or more days of administration and leave. Eight journeys were made within a year, followed by a staff training period. This mobile unit was made up of diagnostic, immunization, antenatal, laboratory sections and a dispensary.[33]

A medical service has to win the confidence of the people. Most nomadic people will consult each other about a diagnosis and what to do long before they seek medical help. In Somalia, if there is no one around who traditionally helps them to make decisions, such as the male members of the family, the women may delay doing anything at all. Men away on a herding migration may delay seeking medical help because of the difficulties of herding and the cattle having priority in their lives, rather than from lack of communication with the home village or a clinic. They tend to have confidence in health workers they know and are reluctant to seek help at the nearest source.[34] Again, the need for a relationship, something like a partnership, is necessary to make professional skills and equipment effective.

One aspect of medical training that is particularly useful among pastoralists is ophthalmic nursing, because of the eye conditions caused by the dust in arid areas.[35] Trachoma and night blindness due to vitamin A deficiency are also common problems.[36] Long ago, James Gilmour noted that eye diseases were common among the Mongols because of the glare from the dried-up steppe or the snow, and from the smoke inside the *gers*.[37] Michael Wood also describes how the manure covering the ground and huts in Maasai camps encourages many flies that spread eye infection.

The provision of Western medical care can have a negative effect when it does not coincide with the people's own concepts of good health and how to maintain it. The description of the diagnosis and the treatment offered can contradict the considerable popular understanding of these things, and so undermine the confidence of the patient. One way to bridge the gap is to train primary health workers from the ethnic group, who can specialize on a few procedures. Missionaries should have some paramedical training, so they are able at least to look after themselves.

A much-desired education

Education is vital for equipping nomads to represent tribal interests in national affairs, for preparing children to enter other types of work and, perhaps most importantly, for enabling nomads to make their livestock raising and other activities more efficient, using modern resources. Another benefit of education that should not be ignored is a more fulfilling life for the nomad, beyond the limitations of the nomadic life. Much of the work of herding is boring, and literacy enables nomads to know more of the wider world. The psalmist and warrior king of Israel had an education and skills well beyond those necessary for shepherding!

Donald Cole gives a survey of attitudes to education and literacy among Saudi Bedouin. While 95.2% of the sample strongly believed in the value of schools, for reasons such as learning about Islam or practical subjects, over 90% saw nomadism as the major impediment to schooling. A significant minority felt that education was of no use to full-time Bedouin. However, 89.1% of semi-settled and 79.1% of long-range nomads felt that, generally, education

would be useful even if they continued as nomads.[38]

Herding demands often take the children from school — even in the settlements. The Rabari of India consider education necessary for their survival, to learn other languages, to correspond with other Rabari who have left, and to have wider options of employment as this is increasingly forced on them.[39] The Mursi in Ethiopia desire literacy, now that its value has been demonstrated.

Since 1950, governments have attempted educational schemes with limited results — such as those among the Maasai, Somali in Kenya and the Qashqa'i, Bakhtiari, Lur, Baluch and Kohkilooyeh in Iran. There is a description of the highly developed scheme among the Qashqa'i in the Southwest Asia section in Chapter 13, below. Education is probably the most difficult modern service to provide for nomadic peoples, even when they move among settled peoples who have good school systems.

The goals of the government and those of the nomads can conflict, with prejudices and hidden assumptions coming into play on both sides. The hidden intention of many schemes is to get the people to settle. In Kenya, teachers from an agricultural background have taken a patronizing attitude to the nomads. Similarly, the program for the Qashqa'i aimed to make Turkic tribals into Iranians by using material designed for Americans!

Often the schemes have not been thought out clearly. Education is organized according to local government territorial divisions, which are meaningless to nomads, and restricting them to these territories merely brings pressure to settle. Educational systems are also tied to buildings. Officials seeking to provide education for a remote tribe of Bedouin were amazed that there were no villages, but they still went ahead with a scheme based only on the existing school building. The Bedouin were flexible enough to adapt to the scheme by boarding some of their children at the building.[40]

The success of an educational program may depend on whether the government feels the people make a contribution to the national economy. But while cattle raising is important to Nigeria's economy, the Fulbe are a deprived minority as far as education is concerned.[41]

A population following its chosen way of life is content. Any curriculum for education and literacy must be sensitive to the nomadic minority's identity, lifestyle and place in the national unity.

Clear goals that relate to the nomads' social and economic interests are more important than simply providing facilities and services. Consultation with the leaders to find out what the nomads value most for their children is essential. The Qashqa'i project had serious problems in this regard. Nomads need time to discuss the ideas and how to combine their nomadism with the education of some of their children. The nomad leadership needs to support the project, and families need sufficient time to weigh the alternatives. Education may involve considerable expense or take children away from nomadic tasks or other employment.

The curriculum must include material relating to new employment possibilities that can be combined with a family's established lifestyle.[42] Among the Maasai, only the boys least useful for herding are sent to school, and the only employment opportunity afterward is to be a teacher, but Maasai teachers remain a minority.[43] Other projects can indirectly help education, such as the provision of support for the students in the form of a hostel. To support Nenets who come to town for vocational training, funds are being raised to provide one meal a day for those who otherwise go hungry, or who abandon the course or steal to eat.

A literacy and primary school project among the Fulbe in northern Nigeria is not an encouragement to settle, but enables the nomads to make their own decisions about the future. The entire project was considered a partnership between nomads and outsiders, using consultation with every clan followed by feedback to amend the scheme. The nomads contributed to the cost of the adult education scheme. Small primers were produced, which dealt with such subjects as

migration and drugs for cattle diseases. The nomads saw education as enabling them to deal with government departments, to improve livestock raising, including becoming veterinary doctors and nurses, and helping them deal with the purchase of land for pasture.[44]

When the school system tends to encourage the maintaining of their cultural identity, as it did among the Qashqa'i, it leads to enthusiasm and high participation rates, with unschooled adults enrolling. Those in Qashqa'i schools are well motivated, even though lessons are in Farsi, their second language. Teaching in Farsi, however, seems to have been less successful among the Baluch, because their own language was banned and the curriculum was a national Iranian one.[45] A project for the Fulbe in any language besides Fulfulde would be doomed to failure, because the language is such an integral part of their culture.

Schooling overall needs to be decentralized. Both stationary schools at seasonal camps and boarding schools incur expenses borne by the government and can limit the motivation of the nomads. The Qashqa'i project shows that it is possible to have tented primary schools that accompany nomads to winter and summer pastures, except during the actual seasonal migrations twice a year, followed by boarding for secondary schools. Tent schools are also being started among Tibetans. Most of the projects have a high teacher turnover, probably because of the remoteness of the schools and because the teachers are not from nomadic backgrounds. An idea for a mobile teacher among the Bedouin foundered on this difficulty.

Meeting the needs of children sent away to boarding schools is an area in which Christians could play an important role. The alienation from their own culture and their families, without acceptance into another culture, requires a careful and compassionate response.[46] It is necessary to provide the best education for pastoralists as near as possible to their traditional environment.[47] Home-schooling techniques are well developed for missionary children, and it is time to turn our attention to developing a similar scheme for nomads. Cassettes and even videos and radio programs need to be developed. Such a scheme of home-schooling could be accomplished by first teaching an adult, who could then supervise a group of children.

The development of a literary culture

Many oral cultures, such as the Pathans and Kazaks, are now seeking to establish their culture in literary form. Christians with the right academic skills may be able to help in this.[48] Kyrgyzstan, for example, has recently celebrated the millennium of the epic poem about Manas, a legendary Kyrgyz warrior who died defending their mountain pastures. This epic poem is being promoted as a national symbol. There are at least 18 different oral versions of this very long epic — it takes three weeks to recite — and the Academy of Sciences is promoting research into its history.

The Tibetans tell, and retell in many versions that take weeks to tell, the legend of King Gesar of Ling.[49] Another Tibetan god is Anye Machen who lives, it is thought, in the mountain of that name in Qinghai. The name means something like "Great Holy Peacock," but he is often depicted riding a white horse, with the sun and moon on either side. The Jangar Epic, of the Weilat Mongolians in Xinjiang, is now a subject of international study. It mixes history with legend and gives an insight into Mongol social history.

The Buryats have their *uligers*, or poetic epics, telling of prosperous heroes with their horses, struggling against evil forces. One of these describes the creation of the world. It is found in various forms across Siberia, and therefore is not of Mongolian origin. The god commanded a bird to bring up earth from the bottom of the sea, and the god made the forms of a man and a woman from clay and covered them in fur. A fur-less wolf was made to guard these still lifeless forms, but the Destroyer came near and tempted the wolf, who was shivering with cold. The Destroyer spat on the human forms, and the wolf got his coat of fur. The god returned and cursed the wolf, but shaved off the fur from the man and the woman.

Pastoralism is also "explained" by myth. The Chukchi of the Russian Arctic describe how the Creator first made man a very fleet carnivore. To reduce his power, he was remade naked and slow, with reindeer and dogs especially created to support him.[50] The Bedouin have itinerant poets, and an American at Tel Aviv University studied their unwritten poems for 23 years. As this poetry is composed for particular contexts such as exchanging news, expressing political views, or settling a quarrel, visiting the camps regularly was essential.[51] These various tales can be used to retell biblical truth.

The Fulbe see the skill and knowledge in their riddles, proverbs, allegory and myth as part of *pulaaku* — that is, these are part of being a true Fulbe. Pure research in anthropology and development studies can provide an entry into the nomad area. This could be related to helping the people group maintain their distinct identity by recording their techniques, knowledge and cultural values for their own benefit as well as for academic institutions. Certainly there is a great lack of missiological studies of the culture and world views of nomadic peoples. This gap must be filled by those few with experience in the field.

Abraham went on a journey to rediscover God. That journey became the story of his life and has continued to this day as God's story with humankind. We must lead other ethnic groups in their own journey of discovery.[52] Partnerships between Christians and pastoralists and peripatetics involve making the gospel known to people, and in the next chapter we consider some of the problems involved in doing this.

Of Heroes and Horses!

We humans have always felt attachments to favorite animals. The Jungle Book, Tom and Jerry, Rupert the Bear or Winnie the Pooh, as well as national symbols like the British lion, Canadian beaver and the American eagle, all testify to this truth. Stories about animals are appealing because the animals express human characteristics and people become heroes going through adventures with animals as faithful companions.

Nomads identify themselves with their livestock — not only as a means of subsistence as in Asia, but also with special affection as many African nomads have for cattle. The Fulbe of West Africa describe the world in terms of the colors of their cattle or the shape of their horns. To be accepted as a "real" Fulbe, a man is expected to be a wise herder, and the death of his cattle is a matter of shame. In Karimojong society each man has a ox name, for example, "Father of the ox with the heavy horns." This gives the man adult status in society. When the ox is sick or dies, the man is considered to be "sick" or "dead."

Around the world, other species have special cultural significance, such as the llama to the caravaners and herders of the Andes, and the camel to the Bedouin across North Africa and the Middle East. The reindeer is special to the Nenets and other peoples of the Siberian Arctic. The yak is very important to the Tibetan nomads, who dedicate one animal in the herd to the gods, and leave it to graze and do no work. A white yak appears in their myths as a divine animal. It is considered auspicious to have such an animal in the family's herd. All these species have earned an honored place in the culture of these peoples — because they survive in difficult climates, provide milk and dairy products, hide, hair, bones, stomachs and sinews to meet most of the nomads' needs and give them self-sufficiency. Today, most of these species have been replaced as the main commercial stock by the ubiquitous sheep and goat.

But there is one species above all — the horse — that has given the nomads their mobility and a heroic image. The horse enabled Mongols, Kazaks and Kyrgyz to leave the overcrowded valleys of Central Asia and to develop a nomadic life on the vast grasslands of the steppe. Out in the open, without fortifications, the horse also provided the nomad with his only security, by rapid movement and by helping him to unite into tribes. The nomad relies on relationships, not possessions — except for his horse! From Arabia to China, the mounted nomad became an admired and feared war-machine. This combination of tough herder and rugged small horse formed the cavalry of Genghis Khan, which created an empire from China to Eastern Europe. They would ride 100 kilometers (62 miles) in a day, often without food, and mounted dummies on their spare horses to give the impression of a larger force. Today, Mongol and Kazak children learn to ride almost as soon as they walk and take part in cross-country horse races.

Heroes are considered to have gained a personal power or grace, through their exploits, to help others in time of need. Genghis Khan has become a national hero to the Mongols, through the exploits of his horsemen, and today he is a cult figure who is worshipped. The Tibetans tell many versions of the legend of King Gesar of Ling, a sort of King Alfred or George Washington icon figure. He was born, it is claimed, by magic. His mother was a yak herder girl, who was once a water sprite. After defeating the murderous attacks of a jealous queen, the king's steward and a wizard with a piercing look, he and his mother were banished to the high plateaus, where he grew up into a perfect nomadic hunter. He became king by winning an extraordinary horse race. Tibetans believe that he is still alive to assist them in the troubles. Some Tibetan exiles are trying to develop a more secular view of being Tibetan, by using an original version of the Gesar epic, without its Buddhist elements.

The hero is, above all, a way of spiritual salvation. To the Muslim, Mohammed's life and times are often considered a Golden Age to be imitated. But more important to the nomadic peoples of Central Asia is the pursuit of *baraka* — a quasi-physical power or grace that resides in holy people. This can be gained by pilgrimage to *pirs*, holy men often claiming to be descendants of Mohammed, or to the tombs of dead *pirs*, and carrying clothing or other objects to absorb the *baraka* and "bring" it home again.

The Tibetans often say that "The Dalai Lama is our hero and the living Buddha." Buddha and those on the verge of Buddhahood have achieved "grace" by their good works to dispense it to those struggling through their incarnations. More subversive are the various tantric gods that the lamas visit in trance to learn new rituals of liberation from the karma. The Tibetans and Mongols have a non-stop quest to gain merit with rosaries, prayer wheels and devotions.

In India, the Gaddi shepherds of the Himalayas and the Rabari camel breeders of Rajasthan are both devoted to the god Shiva, who, they believe, gave them their animals to care for. The Oxcart Blacksmiths, living and working at the roadsides, are devoted to Kali, the goddess of destruction, because of their supposed cowardice in the face of a Muslim attack centuries ago.

The Fulbe have a cultural code of behavior that admires the virtues of patience, respect and modesty, fortitude and courage, solidarity and loyalty. Fulfilling this as a wise nomadic herdsman, each herder is his own hero!

God revealed himself to Israel, using the figure of a warrior and horseman riding the heavens to further his people's cause (Dt. 33:26; Ps. 104:3; Is. 19:1), vindicate his servants (Ps. 18:10), enable them to ride with him (Dt. 32:13), and implement justice for the vulnerable (Ps. 45:4; 68:4, 33). God's place of action is as much the saddle or sandal as the temple or throne. We see clearly the need to introduce to the nomadic peoples the Hero of Heroes, Jesus Christ, a leader of men, who rode in humility on the foal of an ass, declaring his coming in peace and reconciliation. In place of magic, he gives undeserved love and grace. Instead of aggression, he gives moral courage in the face of suffering. In place of uncertain merit, he gives complete pardon. He is a friend to the despised and seals his care with his sacrificial love to all who trust him.

11 Communicating the Gospel to Nomads

The nomad has the right to hear the Christian message in a way that is clear and non-threatening. As we have seen, the Bible and the gospel have a lot of affinity with nomadic peoples — perhaps more so than with the Westernized world. We need to sympathetically discover the nomad's point of view and misconceptions about Christianity. We must rediscover God's ways of communicating (as revealed in the Bible itself), as we reach out to societies that, for example, rely on oral communication and have a greater solidarity than Western societies.

Because the nomadic lifestyle is alien to most Christian workers, evangelizing the nomads is a radical challenge. Our knowledge of the Bible and Christian witness and worship has been formed for centuries according to the thinking and needs of sedentary people. We have passed over much of the Bible's teaching that is appropriate for pastoralist and tribal societies.

We start communicating the gospel by recognizing that God used nomadic pastoralism and a traveling people to reveal redemption. The patriarchs had close connections with the settled peoples in the Fertile Crescent and also maintained their independence — just as today most pastoralists live close to settled populations and form a part of their economy, and yet conceive of themselves as distinct. The covenant, the law, redemption and the challenge to be a holy people were all revealed to Israel — a people on the move who were already socially separate.

To reach the nomads involves a twofold task: to rediscover how to follow the biblical model of a traveling people as well as to understand how the people see themselves. We have to appreciate how the nomad may present himself — exaggerating his self-sufficiency and yet having close connections with those he apparently dislikes. These attitudes of self-sufficiency and separation from others can cause the nomad to have misconceptions about the Bible and Christianity, as the religion of sedentary outsiders.

Oral communication in a literate world

The spoken and remembered word predominates among nomadic peoples. Problems are solved, lessons are learned and values are applied not by rational argument, but by digging into the memory and by storytelling. Oral communicators retain information using concrete examples of events and people rather than in generalized facts and ideas, so they should be taught using narrative or biographical forms. They also prefer interactive learning to the monologue. They have learned values and world views by rote from an early age, by the repetition of traditional stories. In general, memory retention is over three times more for the story form to analytical presentation.[1]

Although many nomads are literate, the prevailing culture of most nomads is oral. Even many people in the West who can read prefer not to, and those in oral societies are used to understanding and expressing themselves orally. Many nomadic pastoralists are Muslims and memorize the *Qur'an* orally in Arabic, and mores and religious practice are learned more by peer pressure, so that literacy in either Arabic or the vernacular is not necessary.

In many languages the oral form has priority, and languages like Kazak and Kyrgyz have only been written down in the twentieth century. The Kyrgyz have professional reciters of their Manas epic. Kazaks delight to tell their history and values orally with legends such as *Alash and his Three Sons*. Another is *The Golden Garden*, which tells about the founding of Almati and commends honesty as the basis for a prosperous land. But rural Kazaks are actually dismayed to find some of their songs *written down* in Kazak, for to their mind these songs lose their power when in anything but an oral form. This is also true for Middle Eastern Gypsies, whose Domari is not considered a written language. Printing to them is part of an alien world, and they prefer cassettes.

The Bedouin and many nomadic peoples have itinerant poets. Somali traditions are conveyed orally by complex poetry.[2] Mongols have poetic and narrative legends such as *The Sea of Parables*, *Jangar* and *Badarcha* that convey Buddhist teaching. "Because stories and fables are so much a part of Mongolian culture, Jesus' parables can be an effective means of communicating the truth of the Gospel to the Mongols."[3]

Some nomads have no interest in literacy, and whole civilizations have functioned in the past without it. Literacy must not, therefore, be assumed as an indispensable condition of culture.[4] Oral cultures are not primitive or immature — rather, they are adequate for all the challenges that they have had to face. Many Tuareq see literacy and school only as a way for them to be relieved of their surplus children, by equipping them for a settled life.

It is often assumed that to be a Christian one must be literate, and missionary stress on education has conveyed the misconception that local culture was inadequate to express Christian truth. For many, Christianity is more or less identified with Western education.[5] When a majority of literate young males makes up a congregation, Christianity is seen to undermine the authority of the older generation. But this is a problem also for Islam and Buddhism.

In both Judaism and Christianity, the primary authoritative form of the Bible is its final written form, and writing was an important part of the earliest revelation to Israel. Yet this revelation was first spoken, and it was circulated to most people as oral storytelling, or read aloud. It still retains characteristics of this form.[6] Much of the Old Testament was meant to be read aloud.[7]

Jesus was the master of oral communication, leaving his teaching committed to the memories of the apostles and their friends. Jesus taught through many vivid images and repetition, and he probably left nothing in writing. If this is true then it was an extraordinary step of faith in oral communication, by a religious leader who was highly literate himself (Mt. 12:3, 5; 19:4, etc.; Lk. 2:46; 4:4; 16-19; Jn. 8:6-8).

Israel and the New Testament church, with their literate leadership and the value they placed on traditions in written form, must have nevertheless operated successfully within an oral society. The New Testament church would have been partly illiterate, in a society that relied on the oral performance of all types of communication. The gospels were oral teaching by mobile teachers, long before copies were ever made. Based on his modern experience of oral traditions and storytelling in Middle Eastern villages, Kenneth Bailey suggests that the traditions about Jesus' teaching and ministry would have been accurately transmitted from those who first heard them until they were written in the New Testament texts.[8]

Yet the church produced much literature and contributed to the development of the codex form more than its pagan neighbors did.[9] In apostolic times, the gospel was spread by oral testimony, which was later endorsed by the written version. We have to start with the written text to form various oral presentations. The memorized Bible is as fully inspired as the written text.

In New Testament times, both oral and written methods of communication were used — for spreading the message as well as for teaching within each congregation.[10] This is the situation of most nomadic societies today, in which indigenous oral traditions with a more circular view of history have adopted, to various degrees, religions with written traditions and a more linear view of history. Since the New Testament church transmitted the gospel message both orally and in written form, it should be no surprise that we are called to do the same in the missionary task today.

We need to rediscover and use the varied literary forms that the Bible itself uses, such as narrative, proverbs and poetry. The parts of Scripture less popular in Western theological history, such as the historical narratives and the wisdom books, may well be the key to reaching nomadic peoples.[11] In Western culture we are more concerned with content than with the way that same content is conveyed. While the overall idea of a traveling people in the Bible can be found applied, other biblical concepts, such as redemption and covenant, may also be explained by stories from within the local culture.

Wisdom and verse

First we consider the biblical wisdom literature. It conveys many practical truths that are universally valid to all peoples, and it presents them in practical, pithy forms. Wisdom is based on creation and draws its lessons from the observation of human experience and nature. Proverbs 30 defines wisdom as a knowledge that is from God, and it goes on to mention more than a dozen human activities and failings, referring to 11 animal species. Wisdom is often likened to walking in Proverbs — it is not so much a journey to a destination as it is the habitual conduct of normal life according to righteousness and the knowledge of God (Pr. 2:20; 14:7, 8; 15:12, 21; 20:7; 30:29-33). The nomad is not going to a particular destination either, but is engaged in activities within his traveling that maintain his distinctive independence, identity and character.

The Westerner's relative depreciation of the wisdom literature is the result of a selective blindness to important aspects of life. Wisdom poses the problems to which salvation is the ultimate solution, as the redemption of God's human creation. Christ used popular accepted knowledge to show himself as wisdom's ultimate and complete fulfillment.[12] It is possible to gather the proverbs of the people and use common sense to convey biblical truth. We note that oral culture can understand proverbs better within a narrative context.

The Gospels give such a context for Jesus' wisdom.

God's response to the crisis of Israel's spiritual decline was in verse — perhaps preached and certainly written — by prophets. Nomads hold much important information in verse. The Kyrgyz find their identity expressed in the Manas legend that, with over a million lines, takes three weeks to recite. Kazak poetry is of two different types. The poetry of the traveling courts of the khans was influenced more by the outside world and the Sufis. The poetry of the humbler *akyns*, or itinerant poets who moved among the *auls*, on the other hand, reflected the life of the nomads and is more easily understood by the Kazak. These were transmitted only in oral form until the last century.

Somali traditions are transmitted by poetry. A Somali child learns the traditions, mores, history and genealogies of his tribe and clan — first from songs and verses from his mother at work, then from the work-songs of the men sung while riding, herding and plowing. This gives him a considerable vocabulary, simple ways to compose his own poems, and a well-developed ability to memorize.[13] Poetry may well prove to be the way the Fulbe can express themselves in worship. The Bedouin have traveling poets that transmit news, political comments and tradition by their verse. This might also be a way for those with suitable skills and gifts to communicate the gospel.

Visual images communicate in a way that respects illiteracy and indigenous storytelling. The system of biblical pictures pioneered by Gunnar Kjaerland among the Borana enabled illiterate older men to be leaders in the nomad churches and so fulfill Borana culture. A picture Bible enabled them to retell biblical narratives, in a similar way to the storytelling that communicated Borana history. In the Central Asian world of Buddhists, the *thanka* is used to recall the life of Buddha. A similar version has been produced on the life of Jesus. The Baluch entertain themselves on migration by telling proverbs and riddles and transmit their traditions in ballads.[14]

Music also helps all people both to worship and to listen to Scripture — especially when it is the sort of music that they can identify with most deeply. Handel's use of Scripture in his oratorios has been an inspiration to millions. Scripture itself uses songs in many places (Ex. 15; Dt. 32; 2 Sam. 1:19-27 and, of course, the Psalms). Other sections of Scripture can be set to music — including prophecy, that is mostly poetry, and much of the Gospels, which were probably in verse in their original Aramaic.[15] There are a number of cases in which indigenous music is now being used to convey the Christian message, such as for the Tibetans and the Tuareq. It takes years of living in the culture to master the form of music, but is very rewarding.

The *His*-story of Scripture

How can biblical truth be taught to nomadic peoples? Three quarters of the Bible is narrative, and Western Christians have difficulty in interpreting much of it because it often leaves its readers to draw their own conclusions. But, within its own culture, this narrative contains clues and allusions that conveyed its message to its hearers. Different cultures perceive different lessons and values from the same biblical text, and this can give missionaries insights they have not noticed before. They must discover the range of meaning consistent with the immediate and larger context.

A method that stresses the value of storytelling and narrative is needed — especially for oral or pre-literate societies. We have to learn not only the message, but also the methods of communicating that message from the Bible.[16] There is a need, therefore, to bring together both the narrative or story form of the Scripture and the local skills of storytelling.

One way of teaching the Bible is the chronological method. This well-known method uses the historical progress of revelation to communicate the whole Bible. There are two main tools for teaching this chronological method that are now widely used. One, *God and Man* by Dell and Rachel Schultze, consists of 35 lessons. Twenty-two of these are from the Old Testament, of which the first 19 are from Genesis and Exodus.[17] The other was developed by Trevor McIlwain and David Rodda of the New Tribes Mission. The Old Testament is rightly seen as an essential preparation for conversion.[18] They believe that the message of the Bible can only be learned by retracing the chronological order in which it was revealed. Basic Christian teaching is studied using the historical framework of the narrative parts of each Testament. They approach the prophetic and wisdom books and the epistles in chronological order, according to their place in the historical narrative, rather than in the order of the modern Bible.

The chronological method rightly raises a number of important points both about the nature of the Bible and the content and historical development of its narratives. It delays introducing the gospel by first correcting the student's views of God, creation and the need for moral change in one's life and society, and gives opportunity for the personal conviction of unbelief and sin before the solution in the gospel is offered.[19] The chronological method confirms God's control of history by stressing that messianic prophecy is fulfilled. It makes clear the nature of sin, before introducing Christ. It concentrates on presenting truth through concrete examples of people in real life situations, instead of in discursive and analytical language, and so appeals both to the people's use of storytelling and the importance of personal relationships.

The method gives far more religious teaching than the hearers have ever had, but this is done in a biblical framework rather than re-teaching them their own religion. A common criticism is that it takes too long, especially among nomads, who are usually not in one place long enough for more than three or four lessons. Also, many hearers are convinced of the need for a Savior before the appropriate lesson is reached. Reduced courses of six or eight lessons have been tried, in concentrated sessions of a week or so, but shortening it does not give the preparation from the Old Testament that the method wishes to teach.

The chronological method cannot be used with a people until most of the Bible has been translated into their language. One has to recognize that many of the books of the Bible reiterate basic truths of the overall scheme of revelation, so that it is not *necessary* to work through it. Many of the fundamental doctrines of Genesis at the beginning of the courses are to be found in Romans towards the end. Further, an outline of the progress of revelation in biblical history can be given in the same session. Yet the ideal of building up the sense and authority of God's progressive revelation, as he did for Israel, is still desirable.

These courses do not use storytelling or narrative as the actual method of teaching.[20] Although this method stresses chronological order over canonical order, the Bible itself tells its story more with biography linked by genealogy — rather than simply following the course of events. The chronological emphasis fits the Westerner's idea of historicity — that is, if we can accurately "date" something, it must have really happened. But most peoples look at personal and ancestral connections to events and wonder in what sense they are heirs and descendants of the people in the Bible, irrespective of the number of years in between. Such connections are also an aid to memory in predominantly oral cultures.

Understanding Bible narrative

We need to understand both how the Bible tells its story and how nomads tell their stories. We have already referred to the poetic epics of Manas of the Kyrgyz and Gesar of the Tibetans. The Tibetans have their own storytelling styles, including alternating narrative and song and also dialogues of questions and answers. We need to connect the biblical story to the nomads' lives in a form they can relate to. In order to do that effectively, we first need to learn how nomads use storytelling to communicate their identity and values, and how the persons and events in the stories are related to the hearers.

While stories communicate cross-culturally, because they engage in common human experience, their value is in interacting with things and situations within the real world that also affect the lives of the hearers in a later age. They can be typical cases that are lessons for individual lives or about specific events that have influenced all of us since, such as major acts of God. It is important to know how the people understand the historicity of their own stories. If the biblical stories are conceived of as being merely hypothetical and having never happened, then their authority is undermined. We can accentuate the tendency not to see biblical stories as historical fact by isolating the life of Jesus from Old Testament history and from the relevant history of the church up to the outreach to that particular people.[21] Most nomads are Muslims who already believe that the church has falsified the Gospels. While events such as past migrations are part of their histories, many nomadic peoples have a circular view of history, derived from the cycles of nature. And, like the Qashqa'i, they think more in terms of repeated seasons than in sequences of years.

We are convinced of the historicity of something when we see that it is connected to a belief we already accept. The New Testament answered this by demonstrating how Christ fulfilled the promise and prophecies of what God had already started with Israel. In addition, most non-Western cultures are concerned not with the argument, but with establishing trustworthy personal relationships through experience. This is seen in the importance they give to genealogies. What importance do we attach to the genealogies of Jesus?

As history, the Bible is not *just* a story told as a heuristic device, as many traditional myths are. The Bible shows the progress of a divine purpose from creation through the fall to the promises to Abraham and the revelation to Israel leading to Jesus and pointing to world mission and the second coming. But we do not encounter this linear sense of history outside the Bible. The biblical narrative is God's own

6a

6b

6 Abraham's servant, sent to find a wife for Isaac, met Rebekah whose name means "calf rope". She symbolized God's answer to prayer for the future people of God and the fulfilment of the promises that led to the gospel. A Kazak nomad once remarked, "We should really be teaching you the Bible because it is all about our life."

   a. The calf rope, onto which the young animals are secured, represents the success of the pastoralists work here in Mongolia.

   b. Among the Fulbe of West Africa there is a taboo about stepping over the calf rope, as it is believed to be detrimental to the well-being of the herd.

explanation of his *actions*, and through the means of this message we are able to understand and respond to receive personally the benefits of his actions. Biblical narrative concentrates on the interaction of characters as moral agents. God's actions establish a "chain reaction" of human responses that affect people's actions generations later. It is in this interaction with God that we introduce a more linear concept of history from the Bible. Nomads need to learn of God's purpose as progressive history being worked out through the Bible until the gospel reaches their lives to include them.

This means that the biblical stories are not merely illustrations or examples, but must be seen as *previous chapters of our own history*. Our lives and decisions are an extension of the same history that began in the Bible. We have a responsibility for the next "chapter" in *His*-story with humankind, and this in turn has consequences for others. Grace, fortunately, can reverse past mistakes and give new opportunities to rewrite the "story" in God's direction. Seeing life as a story stresses the personal relationship with God and gives value to any witness of a lonely discouraged worker among nomads as being part of a chain reaction of faith and service running through history.

These three things: the use of story to convey truth, the historical progress of the purpose of God, and life as personal relationships, are all involved in teaching narrative and history. Humankind's history, and the history of every people group, is the story of an ongoing personal relationship with God that is either broken or being rebuilt. Nomadic peoples have their own chapter to write in response to their Creator. This they can do by efficiently managing a difficult part of God's creation, by developing the image of God within their particular type of society and lifestyle and, most of all, by being included in the redemption of creation as believers in Christ. Each individual's life is a linear development of a relationship with God, of receiving his gifts for life, of responding

with unbelief or possible faith and reconciliation. Each of us is a small part in the chain reaction of personal events in the on-going development of *His*-story.

We need to understand how the Hebrew and Gospel writers told the biblical history in ways that their contemporaries understood, for often the application that would have been clear to them can only be inferred by us. To be able to distinguish the structure of the story — its characters, scenes, plot and themes — helps us to discover what the author intended, which is more helpful than rushing to read our own ideas into it.

The recent theological emphasis on Narrative Theology may be helpful in developing an oral method of teaching the Bible.[22] It helps us in two ways — to interpret the narratives of the Bible and to recognize the story quality of human life. This scholarship has produced a variety of theories and has been used to sidestep the historicity of the events of the Bible. Yet, as evangelicals, we can use this study to interpret the narrative texts of the Bible. To cast truth in the form of a story leads the hearer or reader to pay closer attention to it, to be shocked into reconsidering what otherwise might easily become a truism.[23]

The vital role of cassettes, film, radio and TV

How are widely dispersed nomads to be disciples of Jesus? Biblical narrative, poetry and wisdom can all be communicated through audiocassettes, radio, TV and videos. These can reach people everywhere as oral presentations of the gospel, and at present they are the only way to reach many nomads. Battery-powered tape recorders are increasingly found nearly everywhere, and hand-wound machines are also available.

The recording of portions of Scripture on audiocassettes is well underway for most languages. Monologue reading is not as suitable for an oral culture as dialogue and dramatization, and tone and expression also need to be used carefully. *The Dramatised Bible* in English gives an example of overcoming the monologue.[24] Cassettes including basic Bible teaching with an interactive element, prepared by a mentor who the people know, would be useful to disciple nomads between missionary visits.

The number of radio programs available is still very limited. Transistor radios are common among nomads, from the Fulani to the Gypsies. Kazaks and Mongols have radios and televisions in their *gers*. Thousands of 100-watt DC wind turbines are in use in Inner Mongolia and Xinjiang to charge truck batteries, and also for light and television.

There is a growing number of ways to broadcast the gospel. Language Recordings have produced a portable transmitter with a five-mile range. Buying time on commercial radio can be more effective. Already in the Middle East, people in the cities can choose from some 80 television channels. SAT-7 is a satellite TV channel that began a regular schedule of programs in 1997.[25] There are no such programs for many of the people groups discussed in this book because of the lack of Christian native speakers of their languages. Most only have only fifteen-minute programs on certain days of the week.

The *Jesus* film certainly attracts people to consider Christianity, and it continues to be translated into different languages. But the people's previous experiences of films, and their perceptions of stories from outside their culture, need to be considered. When the film was first shown in Senegal, the audience laughed all the way through it, especially at the crucifixion, because they had previously seen only cartoons in which the characters come alive again after grotesque misfortunes! Many Chinese films are tragedies, so Jesus may be seen as yet another fictional hero coming to an unhappy end. This excellent tool needs local explanation, therefore, to maximize its effectiveness.

A church is *only* people

Christ's Great Commission does not mention building or "planting" churches, but emphasizes the importance of being witnesses and making disciples. Discipleship

means developing a close relationship with Christ, with a growing understanding of salvation and the progressive assimilation and practice of his teaching. The call of the itinerant Jesus was away from institutions and towards dynamic relationships in small groups. He focused on the Master mentoring the disciple, like a shepherd with his sheep.

It is extraordinary that the first evidence of Christianity that people have today is an institution called a church. Unfortunately, the word "church" carries connotations of elaborate buildings, well-established timetables and rituals, hallowed traditions and unfamiliar structures of leadership — as if they are to last as part of this world forever. Most mission agencies are committed to reproduce the accumulated wisdom in the church structures of their home countries as the ultimate desirable result. This idea is congenial to the workers and entails a ready-made package to overcome the inconvenience of the converts' slow learning.

The Western-style church is time- and property-orientated. Christian activity centered around a building with a weekly timetable is alien to people who live according to where the grass is growing. This structure therefore reinforces the nomads' misconceptions of Christianity. The relationship of the members and leaders can be conveyed, rightly or wrongly, by the seating arrangement — even in an informal camp meeting. Many times the building of a special meeting place or mission "station" (meaning something stationary) can be the death knell to work among nomads; it could either be ignored or distort or destroy the nomadic cycle, and demonstrates the workers' ignorance of the value of nomadism to the people. Christianity could easily become synonymous with disrupting their way of life.

This mistake has already taken place in a number of places. The gospel has spread in a remarkable way among some European Gypsies, but the resulting churches and forms of worship have been imported from non-Gypsy churches. This may well be the reason why large numbers of the second generation are growing up as nominal evangelicals.

Similarly, Eleanor Vandevort records the struggle of the first Nuer pastor to relate to the culture of the missionary rather than to create a Christian Nuer culture. The missionaries brought not only the gospel but also their possessions, which the people wanted more than the gospel. The mission insisted on the people wearing clothes — these people who considered their bodies "full" when they wore only a string of beads around the waist and had no word for "naked." They introduced formal education in an oral culture, permanent rectangular houses among their own round huts, and a sedentary life in a society that was mobile. A full Presbyterian church government was established in a society whose structures of authority were totally different.

Ideas of individual property were inadvertently introduced in a society that thought all things were shared, including the property of the missionaries. In trying to find a Nuer word for "conscience" Vandevort suggested to her informant, "If you took some of my money would your heart peck at you?" "Yes," was the reply. Checking later, she found out that the heart would be saying "go back and get some more." The result of this lack of sensitivity to the culture was to put the first Nuer pastor continually in debt.[26]

Nor can it be assumed that an expatriate's experience of the joyful fellowship of Christians crowded together in a room, singing and expressing their emotions in worship, can be reproduced among nomads. The Fulbe, for example, disdain the public expression of emotion, consider singing only for women, and resist being entangled with unnecessary commitments. They value stoic independence and are taught to suffer and make decisions alone.[27] They do, however, sing and dance in the bush for the girls as part of celebrations.[28] How much does our own spiritual experience depend on the thrill of large congregations, professional music in comfortable buildings, surrounded by friends who do not disturb our

convictions? Christianity is perceived as a therapy, when the Lord predicted suffering and persecution.

Is our dependence on familiar practices and structures due to a lack of faith? Vincent Donovan expresses this by saying that the gospel may be preached and the church may well result, but it might not be the church the missionary had in mind. However different that church is in its structures, from any church that we might know, it must be recognized as the church of Christ among that people.[29] While this is significant coming from a Catholic, it is also necessary for evangelicals, whose emphasis on the gathered church still smuggles in Western ideas of organization and social structures that have their origins in the seventeenth century. Fortunately for us, the Lord is also divine and so is able to accommodate his humanity to our weaknesses, as we conceive the church as we have experienced it in our own culture. But why make his task more difficult? The ideal is expressed by the second objective of the North Nigerian Programme to reach Fulani as "To help them find suitable ways of worship within their cultural structures with minimal disturbance to their life-style."[30]

For both nomadic and settled Christians there is no place for commitment to worldly interests, or for static Christian structures set up to last. The nomadic theme of the Bible totally disregards what most of humankind considers of great importance, which is to fulfill the conventions and ambitions of the surrounding society.

Disciple development

Our assumptions about the nature of both the church and worship have to be examined. Christians do not *belong* to a church, but the church is derived from the relationship of the disciples to Christ. A conscious attempt to "plant a church" and then make disciples gives priority to an abstract concept with a lot of extraneous content. We then forget that all the New Testament says applies to each individual Christian. The accountability of each disciple is diminished by much that is only tenuously derived from Jesus, and the authority of church structures can also substitute the Lordship of Christ.

We have to recognize that Christ himself is more at home in a nomad camp, with its humble hospitality, its small group fellowship and its storytelling way of exchanging news, than in a Western church. We should not look for the pattern of the church in a separate doctrinal treatment entitled "Ecclesiology," but we should rather start with the nature of God himself.

Jesus' example is that worship is a total lifestyle of submission and service to his Father, and not something done once or twice a week.[31] He derived his strength from his private walk as the incarnate Son with the Father. This was a continuation of the Trinity or Community of self-sustaining love, committed One to the Other and self-affirming in holiness. God, as Trinity, is an autonomous community or fellowship that also reaches out to others, extending fellowship to believing humankind.

Jesus allowed God's love to be observed and shared with the three, the twelve, and also a wider number of disciples. This itinerant and autonomous band of disciples, united by each individual's acceptance of Jesus' instruction and the uniqueness of his Person, was the basis for the church. Discipleship is to receive the teaching of Christ, that was modeled by Jesus himself in ordinary life encounters and situations that demonstrate the teaching in practice. Christ separated himself from both the honored establishment and the religious leadership of his society. He concentrated on a wide range of "ordinary" people.

As we have already noted, the gospel and the church were first called "the Way." A church among nomads has to start with individuals practicing the walk of faith. This faith necessitates trusting the Creator alone, who is transcendent and provides the renewable natural resources, and includes wise stewardship and contentment with having what is sufficient for one's needs. This leads on to teaching that God loves and expects love in return, towards himself and others, and that God judges unbelief and individual and social wrongs. We have to start with the isolated Christian, who needs to develop the ability to nourish his faith for periods independent of others. Most of the problems in the Christian life grow out of an inadequate knowledge of God.[32] We fail to rely on the teaching and reminding role of the Holy Spirit (Jn. 14:26; 16:13, 14). Do-it-yourself packs of Scripture and instruction, prayer guidance, and even songs, are needed on cassette. In many cases these are also needed in literary and graphic form. Discipleship has to be learned within the herding or peripatetic group, ideally with at least one other sympathetic companion of the same sex.

Other religions also recognize the role of the lonely individual or pilgrim fulfilling his or her own religious quest, even to the detriment of the family or business. The Muslim prides himself on praying anywhere, although the practice of Islam is lax where there are no mosques. Lamaistic Buddhism also emphasizes the quest of the individual to work out her or his own "salvation." Some peoples, like the Fulbe, value independence and reserve in company. They are also used to the idea of older people withdrawing from active life for religious purposes.

The lonely aspect of Christ's ministry is a model here, as he met with hostility and misunderstanding from his friends and family. The greatest fear is that Christianity will bring social isolation, leaving the Christian without marriage, family or burial. In Islam it is the duty of the family to kill the apostate. Patience and protection and prayer are the key words! The convert needs patience as he or she wrestles with the practice of new basic religious concepts of God, sin, faith and works. He or she needs protection from exposing still-fragile faith to conflicts of loyalty and fear. The convert also needs prayer, that God will demonstrate himself practically in his or her affairs and give conviction of his reality.

All we have suggested concerning Christians befriending the nomad, living alongside and demonstrating that the Christian life can be lived within the nomad context, leads to mentoring. Individuals who are pondering the gospel of the pastoralist Creator through the traveler Son need to be mentored. The dispersed and mobile nature of nomadic people will require traveling to regularly visit a number of these individuals. This was the norm in the New Testament church as leaders and members constantly moved between the local churches, transmitting both oral and written teaching. Most journeys would have been on foot and taken weeks.[33] This is not uncommon for many nomads today. In this way the nomads should be aware that they belong to a universal community of Christ. A judicious use of examples of Christians from biblical and church history should demonstrate that fellow disciples form a long line from the past to the future, just like their own ancestors and tribal history.

"The Way" church again?

The Western concept of conversion as instantaneous and involving a "decision," or act of the will, is usually only understood among people who already have a background of Christian knowledge and are, in effect, lapsed church attendees. Among people with no such background, a period of pre-evangelism and even covert discipleship is necessary. Perhaps a person should only be declared to be a Christian when there is a minimum number of Christians for a group to be formed. Among the Somalis of northern Kenya and in the Middle East, a deliberate strategy of waiting for the conversion of a number of close family relatives before baptism has been adopted.[34] We must have the faith to expect results as members of a younger generation, who have secretly absorbed some of the gospel teaching, grow to accept leadership in the tribe or clan. Christian moral standards have to be presented as furthering the good of society and its nomadic lifestyle. They cannot be taught as just things that a Christian does.

Jesus' own worship with the Father and Spirit found adequate expression not in a church chancel or seminary, but at the roadside or in pastoralist locations (Mt. 4:1).

The implication of Christ's ministry is that the church is a company of people who do not need specialized sacred places or buildings, and so the church has used secular places for convenience. The universal church was formed by Christ's death and resurrection, not from the organization of local churches. The latter express the universal church, but they depend on the quality and opportunity of local believers. The local Christian assembly does not have to have a location, but is "local" in the sense of being a "face to face" community, based on personal commitment to the Lord and to each other, wherever the members might be.

The early church seems to have grown for more than two centuries without any special church buildings. There is no sacrifice to be offered any longer on earth, and therefore there is no longer a need for sacred places. Among nomads the only ecclesiastical furniture might be a cloth spread on the ground with bowls of milk and millet or *tsampa* for the communion, just as Christ used the common food that was available at the Passover. The nearest river or water tank is sufficient for baptism. The place of the church is incidental, according to circumstances.

In the Bible, it was often households that worshipped together (Ex. 2:3; Acts 16:39). The New Testament churches were groups of no more than 40 persons, who met together in a family home (Acts 20:20; 1 Cor. 16:19; Col. 4:15). This was probably the structure even in cities. The epistles are concerned with how Christians should relate to each other and to the world, and not with organizational details, which is why it is both easy to "read in" our favorite ecclesiology and become frustrated over not getting "proof" of the details that seem so important to us. Such an "egalitarian" and decentralized company appeals to the nomad who, while feeling the need to belong to a body wider than his own people as Islam, Hinduism and Buddhism provide, still needs a practical devotional life that is flexible and independent of outside structures. The evangelism of the nomads provides an opportunity to get back to the basic ecclesiology of the gathered church.

The nomad is already used to a social life that may consist of close contact with no more than a few dozen people for most of the time, and long lonely periods with only two or three companions. Developing personal relationships is more important than organization. Nomadic people also have their larger gatherings and celebrations, often only once a year, involving religious observances and extended family rites of passages such as circumcisions, initiation rites and weddings.

A similar social pattern of small groups, with occasional larger gatherings, should be possible for the church among nomadic peoples. We will see small groups meeting with cassette recorders for months at a time and only coming together with other believers a few times a year. These gatherings can take the place of pilgrimage common in Islam, Buddhism and Hinduism. But the local nomad church, consisting of the scattered believers perhaps within a few nearby extended families, will have to learn in time to develop evangelistic and fellowship contacts in the wider nomadic society of clans and tribes. It will then have to adjust to the dynamics of both small groups and occasional larger meetings.

A new model of the church, like the cell church, needs to be worked out. But most of the concepts of cell and house group churches have been developed in large urban settings, to make large impersonal congregations more personal and interactive. In the nomad's situation, the entire church may consist of only small groups meeting together occasionally, and requiring greater participation from each member. Jesus used dialogue with small groups (Mt. 16:13, 15; Mk. 14:17-19; Lk. 22:24ff.; Jn. 3:2-14; 4:5-29; 14:5-8). Full participation works in groups of up to a dozen; the question and answer method with double that number, and monologue from the "expert" takes over in groups of more than 35 people.[35]

Each member contributes according to how they have remodeled their thinking, allegiances and behavior in response to the training received. Every disciple within the group is drawn into making decisions to apply the teaching. However, the lowest level of faith can dominate, trying to get help for its own problems and be unhelpful for others. Christ himself experienced this (Mt. 8:26; 16:23; 26:40). Church history illustrates the dangers of both institutional structures as well as of small groups. Mature members need to emphasize the authority of Jesus in the Scriptures. Missionaries need to try out such small group for worship and fellowship among themselves, envisage how it would relate to family and tribal structures, and try to anticipate the potential problems.

What form the church among nomadic peoples will take is one of the crucial questions that still has to be resolved, and we pray that the Holy Spirit will show the answer. We move now to consider an important aspect of nomadic societies — the obligatory sense of responsibility for one another. For this will have to be taken into account by the church.

The solidarity of the people

One of the strong characteristics of nomadic societies that affects Christian living is their solidarity. This goes beyond the voluntary involvement of individual Christians allowed in Western society because of the separation between church and state, to Christians being obliged to get involved in what they should not. Most nomadic individuals identify themselves almost completely with their social groups. Decisions are taken either by the head of an extended family or herding group, or by consensus of all the adult males. All members defend the group's reputation and standing and take responsibility for it in the face of insults, offenses against life or property, and especially in the violation of its women. This often leads to a tit-for-tat "balance" of offenses with, for example, revenge killings. The men face ridicule if they fail to maintain their honor. This concept is found in such diverse groups as the Muslim Bedouin, with their *ird*, and the Greek Orthodox Sarakatsán with their *timê*.

This solidarity affects their perception of Christianity and how a convert to Christ is treated. Being a member of one's people and practicing its religion are the same thing to most nomads. To be Tibetan is to be a Buddhist, to be Kyrgyz is to be Muslim. The only Christian nomads are the Sami and Roma. For a person to step "out of line" by being a Christian, or even by showing interest, often results in a sense of bringing shame on the group, leading to persecution and his or her expulsion from the family. The inheritance of livestock, carts or tools for their trade might also be denied. Christians, who are now "outsiders," might be "fair game" for cattle raiding. Even today conversion can result in death or threats of death. The majority of believers will leave or be killed soon after conversion.[36] Underneath their hostility, the family will be thinking of and longing for the excluded member, and reconciliation is usually possible in time.

For an immature believer to stay in the camp can also be a source of great temptation, morally and ritually. The easy option would be to persuade the converted nomad to leave the nomadic life, move to a town and join a sedentary church. Yet leaving the family results in the convert being considered part of the missionary "family," or becoming a sort of non-person outside the tribal structure.

Whatever the immediate difficulties for nurturing the first converts, plans must be laid for a church that takes responsibility for its people group. We have to counter the accusation that the missionary, his message and method has made the convert reject his or her people and their way of life. In time it might be possible to form a Christian herding or peripatetic group, but as hostile tribal authorities assign clientele or pasture rights, this could be difficult. The nomad church must be seen to care about the people and the continuity of their lifestyle in a viable nomadism.

While the gospel stresses the individual's faith and obedience, most of the Bible's moral instructions consider how the individual contributes to or participates in a group and affects it positively or adversely. We find the idea of corporate responsibility in ancient Israel with its tribal, clan and extended family levels of society. Her faith was lived out in small, semi-autonomous agropastoral communities. The individual was accountable for the well-being of the group, as the group was responsible for the welfare and the behavior of its members (Gen. 3:16-19; Ex. 20:5, 32; Num. 16:26; Dt. 5:9; 13:12ff.; 21:1-9; Josh. 7:10-12; 22:18, 31; Judg. 20:8; 1 Sam. 14:27ff.; 1 Kgs. 2:31; 9:6-9). Jesus also taught that one's obedience to divine law should have a social impact (Mt. 5:19), and Paul compared the influences of Adam and of Jesus on humankind's relationship with God (Rom. 5:12ff.).

The actions of any individual affect others with whom they have special bonding. This idea of corporate responsibility is hardly mentioned in Western Christian thinking, but it is important to the nomads with their concern for their own people and their co-operation and hospitality, for which they are famous. Redemption brings into practice the positive aspects of the solidarity of the people, as love is being totally committed to the well being of those with whom one is linked.

The supreme example of a member acting for his social group was Jesus. He also models not only the responsibility of the Christian nomad for his people, but also the missionary's responsibility for his adopted people. Jesus voluntarily joined himself to the fortunes of humankind, and remains man forever (1 Cor 15:28). By being identified with the destiny of Israel he also fulfilled the promise to Abraham that through his seed all the families or clans of the earth would be blessed. He made himself a representative of every people group and of their destiny in the plans of God. He identified himself with their guilt in order to die for them.

Sacrifice in the Bible can be offensive to Buddhists, but the Hindu Gaddi and the Muslim Turkmen still sacrifice lambs. The atonement is not an impersonal way of dealing with sin, for Jesus personally put himself in the place of others. He did this so completely that he was treated as the guilty person. He identified himself with all people, but especially with the believers who have morally identified themselves with him by faith. Taking such a responsibility does not mean being a participant in sin, but it does mean being identified with the sinners before God out of concern for their well being as a group.[37]

To be a Christian is to participate in a joint responsibility with God for his purpose for Christians, and to be concerned for the well being and conversion of one's people. This involves holistic mission in the sense of both evangelism for conversions and concern for the social, moral and material well being of the people or clan. The call to serve a particular people means not only partnership with them for a period of service, but an identification with them for life, in intercession and any other way promoting their Christian interest. We have lost this sense of corporate involvement that the Israelites knew and that is found in the atonement.

The nomad as missionary

The social structures of nomadic peoples vary, and in some the independence of the individual is stressed, while others stress interdependence. Some have a social hierarchy that has to be consulted, while in other groups each family or herding group has virtual autonomy. According to Art Everett, the Navajos insisted on sitting in a circle rather than in rows, so that no one had prominence. This had the effect of encouraging the natural indigenous leadership to show itself and develop.[38] In some societies the local religious leader may have more practical authority to get things done than the formal tribal structure of leaders. This is true of the Fulbe, among whom the heads of families have most of the authority, and only the marabouts have enough influence to get co-operation.[39]

All Christians are on the same level, and there can be no imitation within Christianity of the world's executive structures, or of the dependence on leaders as found in some religions. Being saved by undeserved grace removes any aura of sanctity of special powers in the case of Christian teachers. All are directly dependent on Jesus, who modeled leadership by mentoring in a small group. The election of a replacement for Judas shows that a larger number of unknown disciples besides the twelve were continually with Jesus (Acts 1:21). The qualification for leadership was learning from Jesus on the road right from his baptism, and the implication was that Joseph, the one not chosen, was just as able for leadership.

Christians pastoring these small groups may be able to fit partially into some local tradition of religion teacher. Traveling holy men and peddlers visiting the camps are common, and similarly an evangelist or catechist visiting to encourage the tiny groups would be possible. Their authority is not based on constitutional or traditional institutions, but comes from a knowledge and conformity of character to Christ himself, as well as from their ability to meet the practical problems of faith and moral issues. They need to be taught so that they can re-teach others through storytelling and other aids that convey both basic truths and further applications later.

A church that is "nomadic" in its attitudes will be a missionary church. This new nomadic pattern of the church is already taking shape. The Christians of a particular nomadic people meet together at a well, without any church building, and read and pray wherever they travel. No missionary can claim to have started this work. The gospel has spread among them by audiocassettes played over and over. Two brothers, under a God-given conviction of sin, came to a market looking for the Messiah, a man called Jesus, who could forgive their sin. They came across a short-term missionary worker who, with a limited knowledge of their second language, was able to tell them how to find him. The result is that these few Christians have spread the witness not only to their families, but also to many more people than would have been possible if they had been based in one place.

The Fulani is trained from his culture to overcome the vicissitudes of nature, to take pride in enduring pain, hunger and thirst and to never express emotions. He values his independence, is ready to be alone for long periods, and makes his decisions on his own. This highly developed concept of the resilient lonely cattle man helps the convert to be independent, while the solidarity of the wider group and family in Islam would counter this with spiritual hardship and persecution.

The nomad would make an excellent evangelist. He or she has the experience of constant personal interaction within a small social group. Depending on circumstances beyond human control and learning the management of uncertainty lead Christians to a life of dependence on God. Such a person often has had to make the most of opportunities in life that others would not notice.

The nomad has learned to live with few personal possessions, is accustomed to being mobile and has experienced poverty, hunger and long periods of hard unpaid work. He or she has also known despair and fatalism and what it is to be despised. Such a Christian would be able to reach the largest sectors of the two-thirds world. One wonders how the modern missionary movement has got so far without a special effort to reach nomadic peoples, and without the participation of Christian nomads!

Jesus himself had an effective ministry as an itinerant teacher (Mt. 8:20). The New Testament churches were very mobile, having contacts with each other and having a much more uniform understanding of the gospel than is often thought. Nomadic Christians are already able to be mobile. Sooner rather than later we shall not be able to do without the nomad, not only as Christians but also as messengers of the gospel.

12   Moving On

We have discovered that nomadic peoples are a unique representation of the image of God with a lifestyle that either profitably uses the least fruitful areas of the earth's surface, or that provides marginal services to the settled society. They see themselves not so much as always on the move, as peoples set apart who base their values and practical living on a readiness to systematically travel. These societies value personal relationships more than property, resourcefulness and self-reliance more than dependence on society, and they see the earth and its produce as resources to be shared and used, rather than owned.

The nomads represent some of the remaining peoples who are most unreached for Christ. They cannot be left out, or even left to last. The gospel of Christ is also for traveling peoples whose way of life is close to that of the nomad Abraham, through whom God chose to give his promise of blessing to all peoples. One can hear a long list of contemporary objections: the cities are more strategic; nomads are difficult to access; it is not possible to work outside church structures; nomads do not have class mobility to reach the wider society; there are too few of them; workers will become isolated from fellowship and "control" — these are just a few of the possible excuses. So often the word "strategic" means giving up masses of people to concentrate on work elsewhere, or is a disguised way of saying we do not have the resources to reach the world. Perhaps the problems we face in reaching these peoples has as much to do with the expectations of missions and supporting churches, as with the real problems of discomfort and threats to health. The objections have the weight of biblical evidence against them.

We must therefore dedicate a considerable effort to bringing the gospel to nomadic peoples. For every people listed in this book, there should be Christians who are willing to fulfill Kraemer's golden rule of having "an untiring and genuine interest" in them for Christ's sake and for their sake. Teams for nomadic people should be seen as essential branches of a work to reach a whole country or region, thus recognizing the relationship of these people to the rest of society. Such a ministry does not compete with others.

The commission to reach nomadic peoples is urgent in two ways.

First, nomadic peoples should be reached with the gospel and shown Christ's love.

Second, we need to learn from them this lesson of being spiritual nomads — before they and their churches, which are sure to emerge, learn the wrong lessons about Christianity from us. Nomadic peoples are a challenge for Christians, who should be truly "nomadic" in not conforming to the conventions of lifestyle and prejudices of the society around them. We should learn to make do with less, so that we can do more.

In addition, Christians all over the world need to imaginatively and fervently intercede for the nomads regarding each aspect and season of their lives, their families, their being able to maintain a viable nomadic way of life, their relationships with governments and other outsiders, their health and educational needs. We need to pray for the translation and supply of Scriptures, development projects, the growth of groups of believers, with the moral reform of many individual lives, and the countering of the occult. God has reached peoples initially without outsiders to help them materially and spiritually, and such a commitment to prayer will also bring missionaries to engage in partnership with them.

Further, this is a challenge for Christians dedicated to the spiritual and material needs of these peoples. Such workers need appropriate orientation and skills to identify themselves with the concerns and world view of these peoples. The biblical evidence shows us that nomadism is a legitimate way of life and self-identity, and the settled life organized as a nation state is not the only way the image of God should express itself.

Christian love requires that a partnership be formed with these peoples, to encourage them to have caring societies, with appropriate development to maintain a viable lifestyle, either as a symbiotic relationship with animals in a fragile environment, or as offering services which others cannot match. The Christian who is willing to provide services without consideration of cost-effectiveness is in a better position to meet the needs of the nomad.

Secular patronizing attitudes have suggested that the impact of Christianity destroys such cultures. But nomads have independence of mind and the right to make their own decisions, as they constantly do in the many variables of their nomadic lives. The danger is that they may consider abandoning their nomadism for a short cut to what they perceive as a superior, or more convenient, way of life. The dangers lie not with missionaries, but with the insidious commercial propaganda of "international" culture and government and other pressures that are against nomadism as "backward" or just administratively inconvenient. Much depends on the strength of their own self-identity and culture.

Outreach to nomads must work to maintain the ethos and practicality of the nomadic life in some form. In some cases the missionary may be the only one to consider whether there has been an infringement of human rights in the way the nomad is marginalized, harassed or legislated against. The way human rights are interpreted locally may presuppose an urban, sedentary, lifestyle as the ideal. For example, insisting that nomad children should have a conventional education, as a "right," can destroy all that the nomad believes is worth living for. The Christian must root out the prejudice that assumes that a Christian nomad must become "like us." Being a disciple of Christ is more compatible with the nomadic life, than it is with urban, settled, property-owning life, and it must be demonstrated to be so.

These peoples present a crucial challenge to Christians to rediscover the meaning of their faith in its proclamation across one of the least understood cross-cultural barriers. The evangelization of the nomads is the ultimate test of whether we can make Christ known outside our urban and individualistic Western culture. To reach the nomad we need to rediscover Christianity and its biblical sources. We need to learn a lot from the nomads themselves before we can gain their respect enough to recommend a Christian way of living as a nomad. We can therefore control whether the impact of Christianity destroys or transforms and enhances a people's life and identity. When Christ wins them to himself, we will wonder how the church could be without them.

Part III
Nomadic Peoples Survey

13 A World Survey of Nomadic Pastoral and Peripatetic Peoples

Over 250 traditionally nomadic peoples are described here — many more if we count the subdivisions of the larger people groups. It is difficult to estimate what proportion of these peoples are actively nomadic. There is a more extended description of some of the peoples simply because more information is available. These serve as illustrations for others, about which little is known. Please note that where alternative spellings exist for a group name, the author has used all forms in order to show up the diversity that exists in literature, rather than imposing his own system of standardized names. All alternative spellings are listed in the Index.

Nomadism

The descriptions illustrate that the term "nomadic" does not refer only to movement, which is relative to need, but also to a culture and society shaped by a traveling life, either with animals or to seek customers. Terms like semi-nomadic have been avoided because, as described above, such terms can mean very different things. A description of the actual lifestyle is more meaningful. In some cases the majority of the people have become settled, but their self-identity is still shaped by their nomadic past. We briefly list the sedentary sections of large peoples, such as the Fulbe and Gypsies, for completeness.

Names

Most peoples are known by a variety of names. As often as possible, we list the name that the people use to refer to themselves. This honors them, especially as the common names used by outsiders can have derogatory connotations. Some common names are occupational, like Baggara and Lohar, and can cause confusion by being applied to a number of unrelated groups. Other names refer to the language spoken, so that the people can be confused

with a much larger population that happens to speak the same language. Similarity of names can confound two very different groups, such as the two Hazaras and the Iranian Lur with the "Gypsy" Luri.

In general the following convention has been used in the text: ALL CAPS BOLD refers to the main Name for a people group, followed by italic bold to indicate the alternative name or alternative spellings of this people group title. Subsequent names in bold refer to subgroups, tribes, or related groups found in neighbouring countries or in geographically removed regions.

Regions

The world has been divided into regions and the peoples within each region are listed from west to east, and from north to south. This arrangement is for convenience of reference and does not imply any historical or ethnic relationships. The survey begins with West Africa, moving in turn to East and Southern Africa, North Africa and the Middle East, followed by Southwest, Central, Inner, South and Southeast Asia. Then we survey in turn the Russian Arctic, the Americas and finally Europe.

Divisions

Each regional section has been divided between pastoralists and peripatetics, although in the case of some peripatetics who use animals for transport, such as the Bhotia, the distinction is difficult to maintain. Groups have been included not according to any rigid concept of ethnicity, but because they can be identified as a distinct mobile social group needing special Christian involvement.

Peripatetics

The craft castes of the larger pastoral societies, such as the Lawbe and Inadan in West Africa, or the Ghorbati in Iran, have been given separate treatment as peripatetics, so that their special needs might be considered. This does not imply that they are considered as separate "peoples," although some of them may have had separate ethnic origins. But they often have a distinctive sub-culture and are considered as socially different by the pastoralists. Many peripatetic groups are small and appear to merge with the urban population in markets and streets, but their distinct identity needs to be recognized.

It is hoped that Christians will use these limited descriptions for prayer, and that the information will challenge Christians to identify themselves with the needs of many remote and overlooked peoples. For various reasons, up-to-date information on Christian work among these peoples is difficult to include here, but further information can be obtained from the mission agencies and sources mentioned.

WESTERN SAHEL

This area includes Senegal, Mali, Burkina Faso, Niger and the countries to the south such as Guinea Bissau, Guinea, Côte d'Ivoire, Ghana, Togo, Benin, Nigeria and Cameroon. Northern Chad is part of the Sahel but is treated below with the Sudan. Much of the earth's surface is desert, half of which forms the Sahara (which means "deserts" in Arabic). The Sahel is an area of semi-arid steppe on the southern border of the Sahara. Pastoralists are found in 20 countries of West Africa, roughly between 9° and 16° latitude in the Sahel and savannah areas, and also in the grasslands extending across central Cameroon and the western part of the Central African Republic.

The *World Directory of Minorities*[1] estimates a population of about 4 million nomadic or semi-nomadic peoples for this area. But the ODI lists 5.6 million pastoralists for Northwest Africa as follows: Algeria 500,000; Morocco 200,000; Burkina Faso 800,000; Mali 1,500,000;[2] Mauritania 1,500,000;[3] Niger 800,000; Senegal 3-400,000.

A number of factors have affected the pastoralists in West Africa over the last few decades. Pastoralism is now increasingly commercial, as the people supply meat to the growing urban centers and for export; nomads have learned to change their stock to breeds that produce what the markets want. Farmers are moving north and taking up pastoralism, while the pastoralists have moved south and some have taken up farming. Some of the pastoralists have taken up settled residence so as to establish ownership of their pastures. Many of them have moved south to avoid the periodic droughts or have given up pastoralism altogether. Only some pastoralists continued, with greatly reduced herds, after the drought between 1968 and 1973. Many nomads died or lost between 40% and 80% of their livestock during another drought that coincided with a fall in the demand for meat in 1984.[4] These changes have fragmented the ethnic peoples, and their social structures have loosened. Families are losing their young men to work in the towns and have to hire outsiders to herd the animals.

We have listed the Maccube, Lawbe and Inadan separately from their Fulbe and Tuareq societies as deserving special consideration as craft nomads, because with the loosening of these ties they are finding their own independent areas to work. This separate treatment will be controversial to some people.

Christianity has had hardly any success among pastoral peoples in West Africa, and the contacts these people have had with more zealous Muslims to the south have tended to deepen the Muslim faith of the hitherto nominal pastoral nomads.[5]

Nomadic Pastoralists of the Western Sahel

TAMAJEQ, *Tuareq* or *Taureg* (*sg.* Tarqi)

They only refer to themselves as Tuareq when outside their own region, and many consider the name derogatory. They call themselves the **Kel Tamajeq** (*sg. Aw Tamajeq*), or the people who speak the Tamahaq language in Niger and **Kel Tamahaq** in Algeria. **Tamasheq** is the French translation of this.

The estimates of their numbers vary considerably, but the following are probably fairly accurate: Mali 800,000; Burkina Faso 100,000; Niger 600,000.[6] North Africa has

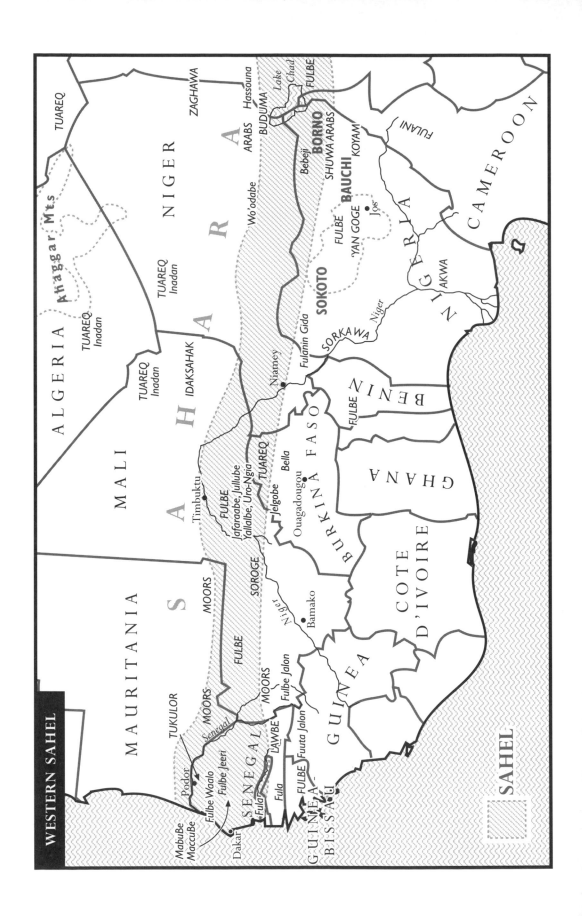

between 25,000 and 76,000 in Algeria and 17,000 in Libya, but we discuss them here. The total number, then, is 1.3 million. However, the *Survie Touregue* estimates a total of three million, with 1.5 million in Niger; one million in Mali; and 500,000 in Algeria, Burkina Faso and Libya.[7]

History

In the past, the Tuareq or Tamajeq were warriors on camelback, with their faces veiled. The Hawwara or early Tuareq, a Berber people already known to people passing through in ancient times, lived in the remote Fezzan, of what is now southern Libya. The name Tuareq is thought by some to come from a word implying "forsaken of God," and to refer to the fact that they initially resisted conversion to Islam. But others think that the name is derived from *Tarqi*, "a man of the Tarq," the old name for the Fezzan.[8] Their special script is related to that of an ancient Fezzan kingdom around 500 BC. While most of the Berbers prospered under the Roman Empire, the Hawwara stayed independent of Roman power and influence. Some of them were converted to Christianity in the sixth century, and it is thought that a cross design that appears in their art dates from this time. Christianity did not have a lasting influence, as there seems to have been no attempt to translate the Bible into their language. The Christianity of that time, therefore, continues to be associated with Greek and Byzantine culture.

When the Arabs invaded North Africa in the seventh century, the Berbers were hemmed into large enclaves widely separated from each other as they are today. But unlike the Romans, the Arabs spread across the Sahara and the early Tamajeq moved away southwards and took up desert pastoralism, many moving over 2,000 kilometers. Some of them took over the fortress-like Hoggar Mountains in 1050 AD and the rest occupied the area to the south up to the Niger River. No place could be more remote than the center of the Sahara desert, in what is today southern Algeria and northern Niger and Mali. The Tamajeq used their skills as camel

riders and fighters to dominate the region militarily, demanding tribute and protection money from all around them — not only from caravans crossing the desert, but also from farmers who moved into the area. These practices produced a powerful and wealthy elite of Tamajeq warriors.

This domination by the Tamajeq continued until French colonialists came with modern weapons at the beginning of the twentieth century. The Tamajeq nobility quickly lost political control and their ability to sustain their wealth by raiding. They had to move south to get better pasture for their herds, while at the same time the Fulbe and others migrated north into the same areas. French colonial policies did not favor the pastoralism of the Tamajeq, and a rebellion against the French army resulted in the deaths of many of the nobles. Since the independence of the nations of the Sahara, the division of the desert by national boundaries has divided Tamajeq society. Still later, the droughts in 1973 and the following years seriously harmed the conditions for nomadism.[9]

Nomadism

Those that are still nomadic keep herds of camels, cattle, sheep and goats in over a million square miles of the Sahara and Sahel. Many of these are nobles whose wealth has enabled them to survive, because they have the largest herds and flocks while the other castes own a few animals, and have suffered greatly. For the nobles the camel has been the "key" or prized animal, but they also keep large herds of cattle and sheep as well as goats and donkeys. The typical herding group consists of five or six family tents with about two dozen persons. The northern Tamajeq use tents made of goatskins.

The men are often away from the camp caravaning, leading camel caravans carrying salt from Taoudenni in northern Mali to exchange for food, cloth and utensils in the south. They leave their wives to tend the Tamajeq flocks. The Ahaggar, a sub-group, used to travel south with their flocks and load salt and carry it to the Nigerian border in July, returning north again in January.

Many Tamajeq have settled, because they have too few animals to sustain nomadism. Many men move to the towns, or work in the mines, to earn enough for a bride-price, or to re-establish themselves with animals. Unfortunately, AIDS is now being transmitted back to the Tamajeq areas.

In Niger and Mali the Tamajeq, who were once the masters of the southern Sahara, find themselves the most underprivileged in two countries that are underprivileged. When Niger became a one-party state under military government in 1974, many of the Tamajeq were out of the country, having gone to Algeria and Libya to escape the droughts. Later, 18,000 Tamajeq returned to Niger and, by 1990, friction had developed between them and the government. A heavy-handed response from the authorities resulted in the arrest of a number of innocent people, which provoked their friends to force their release from jail and in the process a policemen was killed and guns stolen. There were further reprisals, which resulted in a large number of Tamajeq being killed.[10] Many thousands of Tamajeq are now living in Niamey, the capital of Niger.

Similarly, pro-democracy protests in Mali encouraged the Tamajeq to revolt to present their own grievances, and Tamajeq rebels attacked a World Vision base and killed the Malian workers in 1991.[11] Peace talks later resulted in Tamajeq being offered jobs in the Malian army, police, civil and customs service. Fifty thousand Tamajeq are refugees in southeast Mauritania, supported by the World Food Programme.

Society

The Tamajeq are made up of a number of confederations of tribes and are not one people. The tribes are called drum groups, because a large kettledrum, one meter in diameter, used to be beaten to call the warriors together and also became the symbol of authority of the chiefs. The term drum group now refers to the leaders, the tribes and the lineages of related families within the tribes. The tribes have grown or waned in power and numbers over the

years. The Northern Tamajeq are the *Kel Ahaggar* or *Ihaggaren* tribes who occupy the Hoggar (or Ahaggar) Mountains. The *Kel Ajjer* and *Ganet* occupy the territory to the southeast of Hoggar and southwestern Libya.

The Southern Tamajeq are in eastern Mali and western Niger, and consist of the Eastern and Western *Iwellemmeden* or *Tewellemet*, the *Kel Adrar*, the *Kel Geres* and the *Kel Ayr*. The *Kel Insar* are situated west and south of Timbuktu and southwards into northwest Burkina Faso. Most Tamajeq trace descent through their mother, *Iwellemmeden* through the male. The *Iwellemmeden* split off from the others over the method of tracing descent and moved away from Timbuktu after a war in 1640.

Each of these *Kels*, or "peoples," is really a confederation of tribes of warriors that are in turn subdivided into clans and lineages. Each tribe has, or had in the past, its own dependent peoples or castes working for them, who also still take the name of the tribe and of the confederation. The vast majority of the Tamajeq are in these southern groups. The *Iwellemmeden* make up more than half of all the Tuareq.

The original Tamajeq dominated the region by developing a feudal or caste society. They themselves formed the *Imajaghan*, or the noble or warrior caste. Each family of Tuareq nobles or warriors had vassals called *Imrad* who were also organized into tribes. In this way the nobles maintained their leading role in the region by incorporating other peoples into their society. There was even a distinction of "color." The original Tamajeq were considered to have "white" skin, but today they are a mixture of skin colors. The *Kel Ahaggar* called their *Imrad* the *Kel Ulli*, meaning "the goat herding people," who supported the warriors by paying tribute and "protection" money as well as providing milk and meat. This left the warriors free to raid and fight on their camels, moving rapidly about the desert. The nobles often feuded with each other for the contributions of the vassals, in what was an exploitative system.

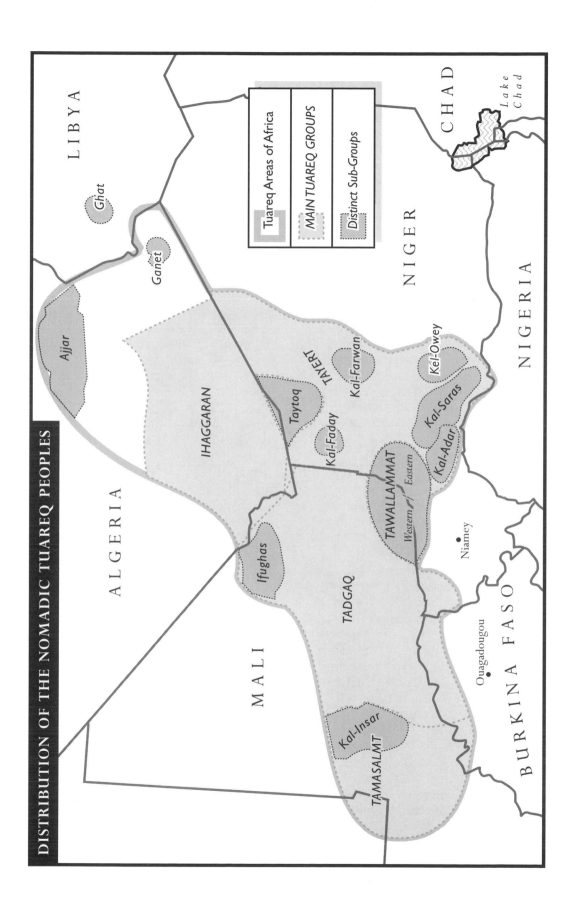

DISTRIBUTION OF THE NOMADIC TUAREQ PEOPLES

Tuareq Areas of Africa
MAIN TUAREQ GROUPS
Distinct Sub-Groups

LIBYA

Ghat

Ganet

CHAD

Lake Chad

NIGER

NIGERIA

Ajjar

IHAGGARAN

ALGERIA

TAYERT

Taytoq

Kel-Farwan

Kel-Owey

Kel-Faday

Kel-Saras

Kel-Adar

TAWALLAMMAT
Western / Eastern

Ifughas

Niamey

TADGAQ

MALI

Ouagadougou

BURKINA FASO

Kel-Insar

TAMASALMT

The *Kel Ahaggar* also had a second group of 14 vassal tribes called the *Isekkemaren*. Together the vassals outnumbered the few hundred warriors by about twelve to one. Only in the mid-twentieth century has this unfair social hierarchy broken down, but the *Imrad* continue to form part of the Tuareq people. They have become fragmented, mixed among other peoples, but the names of the divisions are still used. Sharing the language and culture is what determines who is a *Tarqi* today.

The Tamajeq also have a caste of religious teachers called *Inselman* (sg. *Aneselem*) or marabouts, who are organized into tribes. They officiate at weddings and other ceremonies, act as mediators in disputes and interpret Islamic law. They are not necessarily those who claimed to be descendants of the Prophet Mohammed, as some of the nobles claimed to be.

The *Inadan* (sg. *Ened*) are the craftsmen, musicians and magicians of Tuareq society and are listed with the non-pastoral peoples below.

The *Iklan* (sg. *Akli*) were the slaves, divided between each drum group of nobles. The term means "black," because they were captured in raids on the peoples to the south. They were domestic servants, leaving the Tamajeq nobles and their wives free of routine chores. The slaves adopted a fictional kinship relationship in their masters' families, and many referred to their master as father and his children as brother and sister. Some women became wives of the nobles, and the male slaves were able to become a class of freemen. All the *Iklan* were emancipated around 1960, and there is a movement among them called *Tamadraya*, that campaigns for them to have their own political representatives and tax-gatherers.

There was also a class of subordinate sedentary cultivators or *Izeggaren* (sg. *Azeggar*). They were called *Harratin* in Arabic, which means "fruit of the Acacia tree." These people migrated into the Hoggar Mountains in the nineteenth century and now outnumber the Tamajeq. Before that time the Tuareq had no agriculture. In return for "protection," these farmers were allowed to keep only a fifth of their produce. They constituted the lowest strata of society and were held in contempt for their digging by the nobles, who nevertheless enjoyed their produce.

Tradition

The Tamajeq have a concept of *takarakayt*, or a sense of reserve and dignity that must be maintained in relation to elders, in-laws and inferiors. Since the nobles' descent was traced through the mother, the Tamajeq treat women almost as equals. The women go completely unveiled and have far greater freedom in contact with other people than they would in most Muslim societies. They can choose their own husbands and own animals, vassals and slaves. Most domestic chores such as cooking are done, or used to be done, by slaves.

One of the distinctive things about the Tamajeq is that the men over sixteen years of age veil their faces. The *Tarqi* wears the turban and veil not only when in company, or when women approach, but also when he is asleep. This custom predates Islam, and there have been many suggestions as to its origin and original purpose. Practical explanations, such as keeping dust or the sun off the face, would apply to women too, and only when riding in the desert. Perhaps it started as a practical device to mask the individual's identity in warfare, but the *Tarqi* understands the turban and veil today to show that he is both a mature man and a Muslim. It seems to have something to do with covering the mouth before anyone they respect. According to Keenan, who has a chapter on the subject, men finger it in conversation, raising and lowering the cloth as a way of expressing their varied attitudes to the subject, or the company so that, whatever its origin, it is part of masculine *takarakayt*, or dignity.

Burkina Faso

Fifty-five thousand Tamajeq live in the extreme northern province of Oudalen. The three tribes of nobles are decreasing in size as many seek work elsewhere. There are three groups of former vassals (*Imaghad*) and two groups of marabouts. There are also groups of former slaves, and *Inadan* craftsmen, all named after the tribes of nobles or marabouts for whom they worked. The *Bella* people, as the Songhai call them, are scattered across the north of Burkina Faso. They are *Iklan*, or former slaves, and identify themselves by the names of the Tamajeq marabout lineages in Timbuktu with whom they were previously associated. These Tamasheq or Tuareq in Burkina Faso have varied occupations, from nomadic pastoralism and millet growing to town work. Many are semi-nomadic, planting millet crops in their villages in the wet season and migrating in small family groups with their animals for the rest of the year. In the early 1990s there were many Tamajeq refugee camps in various parts of Burkina Faso due to famine and the war in Mali and Niger.

Language

The Tuareq language is called Tamahaq, or Tamasheq, and has eight dialects that are mutually intelligible: Eastern and Western Tewellemet, Taggadart (of the Kel-Ader), Tayert, Tadghaq, Teneslemt (Kel-Ensar), Tahaggart, and Ghat and Ganet. The people are proud of their ancient script, called *Shifinagh*, which is being revived. Biblical portions are available in this script from SGM, and a New Testament translation is in progress in Niger.[12] There are a number of Tamajeq Christians.

Outreach

SIM has been involved with the Tamajeq since the 1930s, when the pioneer Dr. Frances Wakefield lived in Tamanrassett, Algeria, for 30 years and made the first New Testament translation in one of the three main dialects. An outreach was later established in Niger and Mali. SIM is continuing with church planting and translation work in Niger. Maurice Glover has composed Christian songs in the Tuareq style, and singing these songs is an effective method of evangelism.

The Tamajeq have a habit of asking for forgiveness for any possible offense caused,

and this is a point of contact for Christian witness. A Tuareq has assisted the Glovers in England in translating the Bible and Christian classics such as *Pilgrim's Progress*.[13] Cassettes of about a third of the New Testament are available, and the synoptic Gospels and James have been printed. The complete New Testament should be available very soon.[14]

World Horizons works in Burkina Faso, Mali and Niger with a small Tamajeq church. The tragic events surrounding the revolts in Mali had the effect of strengthening the Christians there. In 1994, YWAM was involved in implementing low-cost measures to conserve the meager rainfall and produce small areas of pasture and cultivation in Niger. YWAM also ran an animal loan scheme involving 1,000 animals. New Opportunities anticipate helping this people.[15] The Baptist International Mission, Porte Ouverte and a French couple from another organization work in Niger. There are African workers in Timbuktu and Gao. The two small Tamasheq-speaking congregations consist of a *Bella* extended family and Tamasheq young men without families. The Burkinabe, Costa Rican and French Assemblies of God and the Chilean Presbyterian Church also work among the Tuareq.

IDAKSAHAK or *Belbali* or *Dawsahaq, Dausahaq*

There are 1,800 in Algeria and 25,000 to 35,000 in Eastern Mali. The Idaksahak, which means "Sons of Isaac," used to be herders for the Tuareq nobles in return for their protection. This relationship has now broken down and there is less mixing of the two peoples, except that they use the same water holes and trade at the same markets. Some have become settled farmers.

Nomadism

As nomads, the Idaksahak have few material possessions other than their animals, and donkeys and camels carry their tents from camp to camp. The average annual rainfall in this region is around 200 millimeters. The rains fall from July to September, when the

7a

7b

7 Idaksahak:
   a. Two Idaksahak shepherds of the Sahara. The name means "sons of Isaac" (Photo A. Lake).
   b. The Idaksahak originally were shepherds in Tuareq society (Photo A. Lake).

Idaksahak are on the move with their animals up to the northern salt plains, in search of the best grazing. They sometimes cross into Algeria and Niger.[16] Later they return south to within 200 kilometers of Menaka, where some of the people have built mud brick buildings for grain storage and for holding literacy classes where there is a permanent water supply.

They trade with Arabs or the Songhai in the towns, selling their cattle in return for agricultural products. There are only a few dirt roads in the area and traveling is mostly by camel and donkey. This trade depends on transport from the south. Trucks supply two or three of the larger market towns, but even this slowed down considerably during the 1990s because of civil unrest in the area.

Language

Their language, Dausahaq, is related to Songhai, but about a quarter of its vocabulary is from the Tamahaq language of the Tuareq. Many of the men are bilingual and speak the Western Tewellemet dialect, for example, because they lived with these Tuareq for a long time.[17] But the women and children are isolated in their camps and understand very little of any other language. SIL is doing a language analysis of Dausahaq. Formal schooling in French is available only in the towns, so many of the nomad children have no access to education. Some adult literacy work in their language has been carried out in conjunction with a Christian development agency, and this has been fairly successful among the nomads. Some evangelism is possible using French and Tamasheq.

Outreach

The droughts of the 1970s and 1980s severely reduced their traditional grazing areas, and a large proportion of their herds were lost. Some Idaksahak groups have become dependent on famine relief and development aid. Christian aid programs have helped them with herd reconstruction, nutrition and health care. By 1994 the situation had improved and they had become more self-sufficient again.[18] They

have mixed animistic beliefs with Islam and consider themselves descendants of Isaac, not Ishmael. They claim to have had a knowledge of Old Testament leaders before the coming of Islam. There are only two known Idaksahak Christians.

FULBE or Fulani

Fulbe is what the largest group of nomadic pastoral people in the world call themselves; *Pullo* is the singular and is from a Fulfulde word meaning "new" or "created new." *Fulani* is the usual English-speaking name, which is derived from the Hausa, and *Peul* is the French. *Fula* is a Mandinka form used for the Fulbe in Senegambia-Gambia. In the Sudan, the Arabs call them *Fellah*.[19]

The Fulbe have an estimated total population of between 6 and 19 million; the higher figure might be higher still if all the settled groups were included. The Fulbe people is so large and so scattered across West Africa, that their attitudes and sense of identity vary considerably from place to place. There are various suggestions concerning the origin of the Fulbe. Some say they are descendants of a prehistoric pastoral people of the Sahara before 1800 BC, who are thought to have initially migrated first to northern and eastern Senegal, and then spread out eastwards along the Niger around 1000 AD looking for pasture for their large herds.

The Fulbe could be of mixed Caucasian and Negroid or Tukulor and Berber origin, since they are lighter skinned than their neighbors. Some groups have intermarried with various peoples, while other groups have refused to do so — resulting in the variety of modern Fulbe groups. These physical characteristics, together with their pastoralism, their cultural concept of *pulaaku* and Islam, have helped them maintain their distinctiveness. Some, like the Wodaabe and Fulbe Jeeri, have maintained this culture more than others, such as the Fula in Senegal.

The Fulbe have four main branches, each descending from a common ancestor: the *Wollarbe* or *Dayebe*; the *Ouroube*; the *Yirlabe* or *Yillaga*; and the *Férobe*. But normally the

Fulbe identify themselves by their local territorial lineages, within which are the migratory groups they belong to, led by an *ardo* or "guide." The Fula or Fulani society also has three castes. The *Rimbe* caste consists of the Fulbe proper, who raise cattle and who have the political power. Two other main groups are the *Neeybe*, who are craftsmen and include the Maabube and the Lawbe, who are also praise singers and genealogists and are mentioned below among the non-pastoral nomads; the *Jeyaabe* or *Muccube*, who are the former slaves, some of whom are weavers among the Tukulor, also described below. Other descriptive terms used of various groups are:

Fulbe Mbalu, or Sheep Fulani, are small groups in various countries herding sheep rather than cattle.[20] *Fulbe Ladde* or *Na'i*, or Bush or Cattle Fulani, are found in different areas. There are a few clans that are completely nomadic, with grass or mat huts. Many migrate between rainy season and dry season villages. Some are semi-sedentary, and rely on the crops of the surrounding farmers. Some are prosperous with small herds; the men migrate with the cattle for part of the year and leave their families at home.

Fulbe Ouro, or Settled Fulani, have settled for various reasons including farming and education. In Nigeria they are called *Joodiibe*, or *Fulbe Gariri*. Those that have lost their cattle are the poorest and are despised by other Fulbe.

Some Fulbe were converted to Islam early in the fourteenth century and are proud to have spread it by the jihad movement in the nineteenth century in Nigeria and other parts of West Africa. While the majority of Fulbe continued in nomadic pastoralism, some called *Toroobe* specialized in reading Arabic and settled as Islamic scholars and teachers in the courts of pagan or nominal Muslim non-Fulbe leaders to the south. The *Toroobe* may have been slaves who adopted Islam to emphasize their difference from surrounding animists, broke free from their masters, and lived by begging — or they may have just been Fulbe who lost their cattle, or became different by intermarriage.

Whatever their origin, through the influence of the *Toroobe* the Fulani soon had a loosely united empire for a short time in the early nineteenth century that extended from Futa Jalon in the west through Mali, northern Burkina Faso, southern Niger, to Nigeria and Cameroon, that gave them greater self-respect and autonomy. Usumanu dan Fodio, who led the jihad in Nigeria, came from the Toroobe. Many of the pastoral Fulbe did not convert to Islam until much later.

The influence of the Toroobe paved the way for the pastoral Fulbe to move south into these areas for pasture. The Fulbe do not take to agriculture, although many do it, but prefer cattle and trade in hides, meat and dairy products in return for agricultural produce. They are both despised and feared by others, especially by the farmers who complain of damage to their crops caused by the Fulani cattle.

Tradition

The Fulbe consider their culture superior to that of others. Their code of behavior, called *pulaaku*, is central and enables them to maintain their identity across boundaries and changes of lifestyle. *Pulaaku* has been described as "Fulaniness," and includes their language and pastoral chivalry. It involves important virtues such as *munyal*, which is patience, self-control, mental discipline and prudence; *semteende*, which is modesty and respect for others, even for enemies; and also *hakkillo*, or wisdom, forethought, prudence in managing one's personal affairs and giving hospitality. The *Pullo* is trained to be stoic, never to show his feelings, to even appear introverted to outsiders and to have a deep emotional attachment to cattle. He maintains his respect by keeping a distance from others. It means that one is a better person if one is self-sufficient and relies on few personal possessions and comforts.

Pulaaku implies one can manage one's herd well. The *Pullo*, or Fulbe male, sees himself as having a priestly role to maintain the triangular relationships of interdependence between himself, his wife and his cattle. His cattle give a man milk

8a

8b

8 Fulbe:
   a. The Fulbe of West Africa are the largest pastoral people.
   b. They live for their cattle.

8c

8d

8   c. Water supply is a constant preoccupation in the Sahel.
    d. The calves are secured in the camp or village.

and prestige and they are treated like an extended family rather than just an economic asset. In return he gives them pasture, water and protection. The wife looks after food preparation, dairy production and bears children. Therefore the man has to show skill not only as a herder but also in wisdom and character to fulfill his responsibility.

Pulaaku must be passed on by each generation — otherwise it will disappear, which it seems to do when herds are lost and clans break up to look for work in the settled society. It is taught by any Rimbe relative, or perhaps by the parents and also by *maudo laawol pulaaku*, a leader of the clan.[21] To be a true Fulbe, and described by terms such as *O waadi*, or *banti*, or *teendru Pulaaku*, means a man not only speaks the language but also knows how to live as a Fulbe.

Wodaabe (see below) have their own form of *Pulaaku* called *Mbodangaaku* that unites them or "holds their hands together." A sense of responsibility to their fellow Wodaabe, involving hospitality and generosity, binds them together. They have a kind of fear or respect for others, especially old people, that includes a fear of uttering names, and this practice reveals who each individual respects most. Even an unwelcome guest is treated as if he were a god, as their proverb says, "Your guest is your god." For all the Fulbe, *Pulaaku* means that adults should show children a "black" or stern face so that they are respected.[22]

Language

The Fulani are proud of their oral culture with its poetry, myths, proverbs and riddles. They are also proud of Islam and are resistant to change.[23] Their language is called Fulfulde in most of the region and Pulaar in western Mali and Senegal. The different Fulbe groups across West Africa speak many different dialects. Fulfulde is written in Arabic characters, but there is also a version using European letters.

Outreach

SIL has a Computer Assisted Dialect Adaptation program to facilitate translation into several Fulfulde dialects. New Testament translations are in progress in Benin, Burkina Faso, Guinea, Mali, Niger, Nigeria and Senegal.[24] A provisional translation has been in circulation in the Jelgoore dialect since 1997, and the Fulakunda translation should soon be in print. The Fulfulde Bible in one of the Adamawa dialects of Cameroon is complete.

An International Fellowship of Fulani Christians was projected, to be based in Jos and to bring Fulani Christians together from all over West Africa, but it has never met. Joint Christian Ministries in West Africa brings together some fifty organizations for consultation about Fulbe work. The Watkins of the CMA began work among the Fulbe in Guinea in 1923 until 1967, with few visible results, but in fact had an influence on many who were converted later. WEC works among the Fula agropastoralists in southern Senegal. In Burkina Faso there is a small response through five SIM teams and the AoG. The Christian Reformed World Missions and the United World Mission are reaching out to the Fulbe in Mali.

There are less than a thousand Christians among the ten million Fulani in northern Nigeria. Christians are usually rejected by their families, lose their cattle and their wives and children. A program has been set up to help them, providing a booklet entitled "Let's Help the Fulani" and cassette players with Fulani tapes and suggestions to develop their trade contacts with Christians of other peoples.[25] Nigerian missionaries of the Church of Christ in Nigeria and the Evangelical Reformed Church of Christ have outreach programs to the Fulani in northeast Nigeria. COCIN and ECWA have extensive veterinary programs for the Fulani.[26] The *Jesus* film is available in the Cameroon dialect, but is not understood in Nigeria or elsewhere.

In 1974 there were an estimated 1,500 converts in Benin, but it has been claimed that 2,000 have responded to SIM outreach in Benin. At that time, a 30-minute gospel broadcast was the only one in Fulfulde. The Baptists, Evangelical Free Mission and Orebro Mission are also working with the Fulfulde in the Central African Republic.

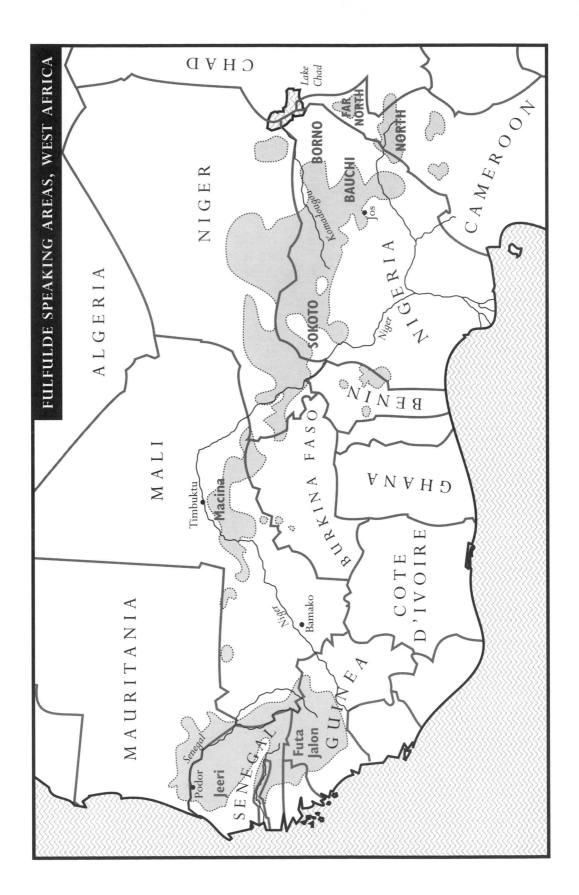

FULFULDE SPEAKING AREAS, WEST AFRICA

Subdivisions of Fulbe

We divide this very large, diffuse people into nomadic and settled sections, some of whom have been settled for a long time and have no intention of changing. About a third are semi-nomadic or nomadic. However, there are various strategies of combining agriculture with cattle herding, and periods of settlement with nomadism, which are options within Fulbe culture.[27]

1. Nomadic groups — about 20%

a) Mauritania

Estimates of the **Fulbe** population vary between 12,000 and 100,000.[28] Thousands have moved to Mali.

b) Senegal

Fulbe Waalo and Fuuta Tooro

There were 80,000 in the early 1980s. They are the pastoral Fulani of the Senegal Delta and Valley. The *waalo* is the flood plain on the south bank of the Senegal River where crops can be grown as the floods recede each year during October — November. This is distinguished from the *Jeeri* or *Ferlo*, which is the slightly higher ground south of the Senegal River that stretches south to include the course of the Ferlo River. In its center is the town of Lingeer (Linguère). On the *Jeeri*, crops can be grown only in the rainy season.

Two dams were built in the 1980s on the Senegal River — one at Manantali in Mali and the other at Diama in Senegal. These now provide irrigation along the river and the government has promoted rice as a major crop. These changes have been detrimental to the pastoralists, because they have turned the best pastures into cultivated fields for wealthy farmers and have stopped the floods that created pasture in the delta area, as well as lowered the water level which turned the ponds salty where the cattle used to drink.

The *Fulbe Waalo* and the *Fuuta Tooro* are difficult to distinguish, because they have not stopped moving between these two areas from east to west and vice versa. The Fulbe Waalo inhabit the region of the delta, and Richard Toll is their center. In the delta

the Fulbe groups are situated near the Lac de Guier, and along the road between St. Louis and Richard Toll, and are mixed with Moors and Wolofs.

The *Fulbe* of the Fuuta Tooro region mostly live in that region now known as La Région du Fleuve of the Department of Podor. It is a lowland, some 250 kilometers (150 mi.) long, along the south side of the Senegal River, just southwest of Podor with Matam to the east. Many have moved to Richard Toll to find work at the sugar factory.

Both the *Fulbe Waalo* and the *Fuuta Tooro* have five descent and political groups each that can be distinguished, and some of these groups are also represented among the Fulbe Jeeri to the south. They migrate to the *Jeeri* with their herds of Zebu cattle during the rainy season from June to October, where they plant a crop fed by the rains. After the harvest they return to the *Waalo* and *Fuuta Tooro* to plant again as the floods recede. The distances of the migrations vary between 30 and 70 kilometers (20-45 mi.), according to the group. The Fuuta Tooro group of the *Ururbe* travels the furthest — from near Njum to between Mbidi and Yaare Law.

The Fulbe have attempted to maintain both their pastoralism and also engage in cultivation, for keeping one's herd is security against poor harvests. They have tended to divide the family, with the father cultivating the fields and the children looking after the cattle. But with changing conditions in the lowlands, neither can be done successfully, and many Fulbe farmers and sedentary herders are being forced to move into the Ferlo, the area of the Fulbe Jeeri, so there is a degree of conflict between these two groups of Fulbe.

Fulbe Jeeri

There are 350,000 in the center of northern Senegal, and a large number of diverse lineages still follow a semi-nomadic life, but this total possibly includes the Fulbe of the *Waalo*.[29] Cheikh Bâ gives a total of 236,000, or 40% of all the Fulbe in Senegal. They are named for the *Jeeri*, or central region of dry higher ground south of the Senegal Valley, where most have lived since the fifteenth century. The Fulbe Jeeri can be divided between those groups who live in the areas of the old pre-colonial kingdoms nearer the coast, and those on the *Jeeri* further into the center of Senegal. There are 40,000 Fulbe Jeeri in Mali, and probably others in the west of Gambia.

The *Jeeri* is a windswept, semi-arid area that receives sparse rainfall. It is crossed by the valley of the Ferlo River and numerous dry valleys and riverbeds that have pasture only during the rainy season. The town of Lingeer (Linguère) is the center around which the various groups of the Fulbe are found. The Fulbe on the *Jeeri* are divided into two major groups called *Laccenaabe*, or Fulbe of the Lacce area, and the *Jeenglebe* or *Jengeloobe*. The former has twelve clans. Some of these are related to the *Waalwaalbe*, with whom they have contact when they migrate northwards in the dry season. The *Jeenglebe* consists of three groups located south of the railway between Louga and Lingeer and southwards to the Saalum Valley.

Nomadism

The Fulbe Jeeri living on the *Jeeri* are family groups linked together by descent who are still nomadic, or semi-nomadic, as cattle raisers with flocks of sheep and goats. During the month of April the Fulbe Jeeri plant crops of millet, peanuts and beans on the *Jeeri*. In the following months, during the rains, they care for their animals and maintain their camps. After the harvest in October, when the rains are over, they move out of the *Jeeri*, because the watering holes dry up in this season. They move either to the north towards the Waalo or south to the peanut basin, and then return to the *Jeeri* the following April.

This movement was modified in the 1950s when artisan wells were drilled at intervals of 30 kilometers on the *Jeeri*. The constant supply of water is making it possible to cultivate fields where the ground was previously too dry. Sedentary Fulbe and Wolof farmers have been encouraged to

settle on the *Jeeri* and graze their herds close to the wells, so that the wells near the Ferlo valley are becoming surrounded by such settlements. The pastoralists are finding it increasingly difficult to move their herds close to the water. The water from the wells does not guarantee pasture close to the villages, as the pastoralists found out in the drought of 1972-73 when many *Jeerinkoobe* decided to stay by the wells to have water. They soon ran out of pasture and lost many animals.

Having learned this hard lesson, the Fulbe Jeeri have continued to be highly mobile, owning large herds of cattle and, more importantly, sheep and goats, of which they have flocks of five hundred to a thousand animals. The rainfall has been better since the drought, so that in most years the majority of the Fulbe Jeeri are able to stay some 15 to 20 kilometers from the wells in the dry season and get better pasture than the farmers close to the wells. This has enabled them to adopt a semi-nomadic lifestyle with semi-permanent camps for the families in reach of the boreholes, while the men travel with the herds looking for pasture. In this way the herds get the best of the pasture before the herds of the sedentary peoples, and they only need to go to the wells every second day. This means they move camp several times in the year to "rotate" the herds over the pastures. But other Fulbe Jeeri continue to be truly nomadic with whole families traveling outside the *Jeeri* in the dry season for pasture. They live in straw huts, which they take apart to carry with them.

In the past, the Fulbe Jeeri have found dry season pasture in forest reserves established by the French to the south, where agriculture was banned. There is no alternative to these reserves for the pastoralists, because the surrounding country is heavily populated and cultivated by Serer and Wolof peoples. Unfortunately, one of these reserves, the Mbegué Forest, has been taken over for peanut plantations by the Mouride Islamic Brotherhood, driving out the Fulbe. The Brotherhood is one of three Sufi movements seeking to dominate

Senegal. They teach their members that physical work is a means to gaining paradise, and the work of establishing peanut plantations in virgin grasslands fits into this belief. Young men are sent out, deliberately ignoring legal and customary land rights, to plant the peanuts in lands that hitherto were used for Fulbe pasture. In the spring of 1991, they drove out 6,000 Fulbe pastoralists and their 100,000 cattle, and five million trees were cut down to be replaced by a vast plantation of peanuts.

The government fails to see nomadic pastoralism as an efficient response to varied pasture in a semi-arid region, which has limited use for cultivation. While peanuts are a cash crop to contribute to the economy in the short-term, they deplete the fertility of the soil and give nothing back, for the whole plant is pulled up since money can be made even from the dried plant. One response of the Fulbe herders is to file legal claims as the owners of parcels of land, since some local authorities are favorable to people other than the Brotherhood.[30] The pastoralists' aim is not to restrict the use to individual herders, but to exclude cultivation so that they can use the plots all together as common pasture.

West and south of the *Jeeri* region is the area once occupied by the ancient kingdoms of Njambur, Kajoor, Bawol, Siin and Saalum. Here are other groups of Fulbe Jeeri. The region of Njambur has 16,500 Fulbe in six different groups. The Kajoor to the south and 100 kilometers east of Dakar has 50,000; Bawol, immediately to the east, has 20,000. Nearer the Gambia border, Saalum has 78,000 and Siin has 8,200. These people have had greater contact with the farming communities and so have more incentives to settle.

Outreach

There may be a number of Christians among the Fulbe Jeeri. The Finnish Lutheran Mission has three medical and literacy workers in some villages. The Evangelical Lutheran Church of America is working in Linguère, east of Louga. This includes some veterinary work.[31]

c) Mali

There are about 90,000 *Fulbe* in western Mali, including 40,000 *Fulbe Jeeri* around Nioro and Kayes and 100,000 Tukulor. The estimates of all Fulbe in Mali is between 8 – 10% of the total population. There was no work in the Pulaar language with these people in 1990.[32] Ten thousand Mauritanian Fulbe have moved into Mali and have received refugee status and are being contacted by New Opportunities. The few believers have since been contacted by CRWM.

Fuuta Tooro Fulbe, Ségala and Nioro

Many of these originated from around Podor, in the Fouta Toro area of Senegal, but there are other villages of Fulbe that have a different origin. They spend the rainy season in about thirty villages within a 30-kilometer radius, mostly southwest of Nioro around Govmané. In the dry season they migrate some 200 kilometers southwestwards to the area north of Bafoulabé. Others are based around Ségala and migrate southwards to the Senegal River Valley, northwest of Bafoulabé. Others are found 50 kilometers northeast of Kayes, close to Kontela. They speak Pulaar. There is no known Christian work among them.

Fulbe around Nara and Dilly

These are probably *Wolarbe* and migrate southwards some 150 kilometers to Didieni or southeast to the rice plantation area around Niono. There is no known Christian work among them.

Maasina (Macina) and Nampala Fulbe

These Fulbe occupy the central part of a number of interrelated areas of Fulbe, from Dilly and Nara through to northern Burkina Faso. They use, or have used in the past, the flooding of the Niger in its delta in central Mali as part of their migratory pastoralism. The estimated numbers of Fulbe in the Maasina vary between 600,000 and 1,000,000, but these are possibly 50% Maccube. There are around 100,000 nomadic or semi-nomadic Fulbe.[33]

The Fulbe live among many other

9a

9b

9c

9d

9   Fulbe (continued):
    a. Portable reed mat huts used in the Niger Delta, Mali.
    b. Fulbe huts in Senegal (Photo: M. Seitz).
    c. Once they spread Islam and now still hold to their own version.
    d. Framework for a Fulbe hut (Photo: M. Seitz).

peoples, including thousands of Bella, Moors, Tamasheq, Bozo, Songhai and Dogon, and the estimate of their population may be affected by the fact that their social organization, called the *wuro*, or a residential community, often includes more than the Fulbe.

Each *wuro* (Fr. *ouro*) is under the leadership of a *jooro* or *dioro* who negotiates the use of the pastures with other Fulbe *wuro*. The *wuro* may have 30,000 head of cattle, so reciprocal renting of pasture between the *wuros* is often necessary in the dry season, during May to July. At this time the Fulbe get permission at "gates," such as those near J'Afarabe and Yuwaru, to move into the flood plain of the Niger River to use the fresh pasture until July.

When the river floods from August to December, the Fulbe migrate northwestwards into the Sahel to avoid the mud and flies from August to October. They go as far as south Néma in Mauritania, a distance of over 300 kilometers. In the 1990s many turned to the south into farming areas, because of the threat of attack by the Kel Tamasheq. They return to the Niger flood plain in November and so begin the cycle again. Nomadic groups including the Cookinkoobe, Naasaadinkoobe and Sonnaabe migrate from the north. Others have abandoned going into the delta and pasture their cattle in localized areas instead.

The Fulbe live in semi-permanent villages, with one or two families of a craftsman caste, probably Lawbe or Inadan, working in wood, leather, and gold and silver. There are also ex-slaves called *maccube* living among them, who nowadays have to be paid to do menial work such as cultivation, sweeping and carrying. Although the Fulbe claim that milk is their mainstay diet, in practice they eat a porridge of millet and trade milk and butter with their farming neighbors.[34]

Jallube herders (sg. Jallo)

In the Douentza or Haayre region of Mali, they live in camps a few miles from villages of the Riimaybe, the former slaves of the Fulbe, who are sedentary cultivators of millet. The Riimaybe either belonged to individual Jallube or to their clans, but these arrangements were abolished in 1945. The Jallube themselves now grow millet during the rainy season and trade milk with the Riimaybe for more millet, spices and other goods. They also herd the animals of the Riimaybe.

The Jallube migrate for the dry season, north towards the delta or southwards. Some move the short distance to the fields of the Riimaybe; the rest travel some 30 to 100 kilometers (20-62 mi.) to the fields of Dogon farmers. They return before the rainy season (July through September) to plant again.[35] The men are responsible for both the herding and the cultivation of the millet. The women are responsible for the milking. According to *pulaaku*, Jallube fathers neither eat with, nor speak to, their sons. Even though the sons do all the cultivation and herding for them, instructions have to be passed by intermediaries.

The Fulbe see the practice of folk Islam, combined with their animistic world view, with its superstition and magic, as meeting all their material and spiritual needs. Many of the men can read Fulfulde in the Arabic script, but only the better educated can understand Arabic.

The Christian and Missionary Alliance started work among the Fulbe in 1923, but left them to work among people who were more responsive to the gospel message. In 1982, they encouraged Dogon Christians to reach out to their "Samaria" — the Fulbe. CMA are now working in the BaKo region of Mali and have given short-term veterinary help.[36] RSMT and United World Mission have started an outreach. Christian Reformed World Missions have a team working in the Maasina area. There about 60 believers.[37]

d) Burkina Faso

There are over 700,000 **Fulani** in the northeast of Burkina Faso.

Jelgoobe, Djibo, northern Burkina Faso

The Jelgoobe claim to be descended from two chiefdoms that migrated from the Hairé region of Mali before 1750. According to their oral traditions, they arrived from Maasina in Mali in the seventeenth century. They were driving the cattle of the Jallube in the seventeenth century because of famine and the political struggles in that region. But they did not escape these entirely, for in 1824 they became the western edge of the Islamic Diina kingdom of Aamadu Seeku, based in Maasina. When they rebelled they had their Jelgoobe leaders killed. They appealed to the (non-Fulbe) Mossi king of Yatenga, who attempted to impose Mossi rule. The Jelgoobe threw off both until the French arrived in 1864.

They continue to be a very independent group. Many Fulbe who have migrated eastwards to Oudalan, Liptako, Yagha and into Niger continue to call themselves Jelgoobe. These and other Fulbe of different origins and varied dates of arrival are called *Fulbe Jelgooji*, like the *Fulbe Kelli*, who became subject to the Jelgoobe.[38] But some of the *Riimaybe*, ex-captives, who possibly gained their freedom in the conflict with the Mossi around 1834, live in the town of Djibo and speak the language of the Mossi. The town is about 25% Mossi; a further 18% are also Riimaybe-speaking Fulfulde.

In this region, 72% of the population are Fulfulde speaking and maintain the Fulfulde culture. But only 44% of these are Fulbe, the rest being Riimaybe former slaves who now have independent farming communities. The Fulbe living in the surrounding hamlets speak Fulfulde and insist on keeping cattle to have status as cattle owners in the Fulbe tradition. Many migrated south during the droughts of the 1980s. But, since then, those that remained have prospered better than the farming population. New water holes and a cattle market in Djibo have helped to enable this prosperity.[39] They have an Inadan craft community, *maabube*-griots, living with them. Griots are West African ballad singers who accompany themselves with stringed instruments.

SIM has a team in seven centers in Burkina Faso. SIM also works in Nigeria and Niger, reaching the Fulani with the hope of three more centers soon. The COCIN works with Action Partners in veterinary work and friendship evangelism. Many Fulani have transistor radios to receive programs from Radio ELWA when it was transmitting. World Horizons has two workers in Burkina Faso; the Evangelical Missionary Society of Nigeria have recruited other pastoralists to work among the Fulani; and the Assemblies of God are working among them as well.

Queguedo Fulbe

To the west of Tenkodogo in southeast Burkina Faso, the *Queguedo Fulbe* are an example of small groups of Fulani who are settling among other ethnic groups and taking on a specialized pastoral role. They number 300. They came from Maasina in Mali and work as herders for the Mossi, as well as having cattle of their own. While both sides profit from the arrangement, they tend to mistrust each other — the Mossi claim that the Fulani tend to "lose" only Mossi cattle. The advantages to the Mossi include keeping their cattle separate from their crops. They also used to keep the cattle hidden from the tax inspector! But this tax had been abolished. These Fulbe migrate with the cattle herds, going north out of the area during the growing season. The Fulbe also do some cultivation, but they live in portable houses that can be moved.[40]

e) Niger

Niger has 825,000 Fulbe, including the Bororo, right across the southern part of the country and west and north of Agadez. A few dozen of them have responded to the gospel. The SIM team in Niger helps with community development, animal husbandry and other ministry.

Wodaabe, Bororo, M'Bororo or Wooda(a)be

The singular is *Bodaado*. Wodaabe means the "People of the Taboo" or the "People to Avoid." They are a migratory clan of the Bororo. There are 45,000 in Niger and others in the Central African Republic, Cameroon and Chad — 100,000 in total.[41] There may be 50,000 in southern Chad.

History

The Wodaabe claim they are descended from two brothers in the upper Nile valley in Ethiopia, but this contradicts the idea that the Fulbe originally came from Senegal. It is possible that they do have a separate origin, since they have no contact or intermarriage with Fulbe or other peoples. They became nomadic, or reverted to nomadism, to escape incorporation into Fulbe kingdoms. Colonization pushed them northwards into semi-arid areas during the nineteenth and early twentieth centuries, but today they are threatened by the southward advance of the Tuareq and by the advance of millet planting farmers to the south.[42]

Nomadism

The Wodaabe have specialized in cattle, especially red cattle, rather than having mixed herds of cows and goats. They have to rely on movement to survive the repeated droughts, and so they are scattered across 250,000 square kilometers (96,000 square miles). During the dry season, from October to May, the men lead the herds out in small groups to use the pasture around the wells in rotation. The wells serve as a central gathering point for the family camps to which they belong. Every second or third day the herds return and both men and women are involved in the heavy work of drawing water from the well for the cattle. If the rains are delayed the Wodaabe have a difficult time, for there is little milk and pasture, and water and millet supplies are also short. At such a time the nomads may begin to sell their beloved cattle, in exchange for millet, just to survive.

When the rains finally come the Wodaabe move constantly, "following the clouds," as the fresh grass is produced wherever rain falls. For a brief few weeks, the once-dry landscape is swept with sudden storms. The herds gradually move northwards in larger groups, because of the greater amount of pasture after the rain.

During this period they can go considerable distances from the wells because the temporary pools are full of rainwater. While the men herd the cattle on foot, the women ride with all their household belongings on the backs of selected cows. In September the rains cease and they return to the wells once again.

At the beginning of the dry season the clan congregate, and the families camp in a strict order according to the generations. The camp as a whole is considered to look west, which is "front," and the older generation camp on that side. Within the camp, each family camp is divided by a leather rope, the *daangol*, into "front" to the west as the male and cattle part called the *waalde* in the center of which a fire of cow-dung burns. This is the focus of many myths associated with cattle. The east side of the rope is for the women. The wife is head of the "house," and all inside it belongs to her. Although the *Bodaado* is master of the camp, she is responsible for the transportation and care of her own hut and camp. The hut, or *suudu*, is covered in palm leaves or grass. Depending on the season, it is often left without a roof. It can be easily dismantled and carried on a cow or ox's back, as it is made of woven mats covering bent sticks. Their food is milk and very little else.[43] The women prepare the food, make butter, and pack and unpack camp, and the men milk the cows.

Society

Today the Wodaabe have 15 lineages and many sublineages, or clans. A *Bodaado* is permitted to marry only a cousin from his own clan — any other marriage within the clan is considered adultery. However, a man may take up to three secondary wives from other clans. Four wives is the limit at any one time, and divorces are common to change wives. Apart from this, they also have many promiscuous liaisons at the special festivals. A woman's status symbols are highly decorated ceremonial calabashes that she displays on a stand on special occasions. Often a large part of the herd belongs to her, although it is referred to by the husband's name. Children are considered a gift of Allah and give women status; a women without children can be considered as less than a dog. A girl is of little value to her clan because she is to be married into another. When the children die, in some sense the parents are considered to die, too.[44]

The Wodaabe are found in Bongor, in Western Chad, during the dry season and move to the Kanem Prefecture, north of Lake Chad, during June for the rainy season. At the end of August, or early September, they start their journey south with cattle, to take advantage of all the new growth of grass. Some travel 800 kilometers (500 miles) as far south as the Central African Republic. As well as fine cattle with huge horns, the Bororo in Chad have long-legged sheep that have white hindquarters and a black front half.

The Wodaabe are renowned for their wide-ranging nomadism, their immorality, and their practice of witchcraft and supernatural medicine. Their magical talismans and other magical arts have given them a reputation far beyond their own area. They believe they have a special magic to make themselves attractive to women. The Wodaabe fear spirits, so they keep their real names secret. Their art is famous for using motifs not only from their way of life, but also from the modern world. Celebrations are a time for dancing and singing. The women are tattooed, and the men decorate themselves and paint their faces to dance. They spend long hours in storytelling, for the Wodaabe do not use written Fulfulde.

The Wodaabe are the Fulani who have been least influenced by Islam and follow their own traditional religion.[45] They would probably be thought as the last society in Africa to be interested in Christianity, yet God is working among them. Working among the Wodaabe are: the Chadian Ba Illi Missionary Training Centre; the Lutheran Church of Christ in Nigeria (LCCN-SUM in Denmark) in the northeast; and the Southern Baptists work in the southwest and northeast. CAPRO has had five workers in

Borno and Taraba. World Horizons are in contact in Burkina Faso, Mali and Niger. SIM works among them in Niger, with some 80 believers. SIL is carrying out an intermission multiple translation project for related dialects called the Fulfulde Harmonisation Project. Bible portions are available and a New Testament translation is in progress.

f) Chad

There are 32,000 *Fulbe* living in Kanem, northeast of Lake Chad, southern Batha and northern Baguirmi Prefectures. They arrived in Chad from Nigeria, Niger and Cameroon during the 1920s and 1930s.[46] Many raise flocks of sheep, herds of Zebu cattle and some camels. Some of them have settled as farmers, and some as town traders. Action Partners reported progress in spreading the gospel among settled Fulani in 1995.

g) Benin and Togo

Fulbe in Benin number over 300,000, including about 30,000 *Gannunkeebe*, or former slaves. Togo has 48,200. They are herdsmen and supply milk and cheese to the settled population. Christian work by the SIM is in progress with about 1,500 Christians.

h) Nigeria

Fulani in Nigeria total between 9 and 11 million. The Fulbe arrived in Nigeria in the seventeenth century. A division developed between the sedentary "Fulani," or *Fulbe wuro*, who became an urban religious and military elite in the Hausa kingdoms of the region and increasingly spoke Hausa, and the *Fulbe Na'i*, who continued in the pastoral way of life. However, they joined forces to overthrow the Hausa with a jihad in the early nineteenth century.

The pastoralists benefited from the defeat of the Hausa by being able to move southwards with their herds into Nigeria and Cameroon during the dry season and return north again in the rainy season to avoid the tsetse fly. Better veterinary services under colonial rule enabled the herds to go further south to pastures in Oyo State. With the spread of cultivation northwards during the 1960-1980s, and the demand for beef in the urban centers, the Fulbe have moved even further south into Rivers State.[47] Today pastoral Fulbe are to be found all over Nigeria. The Fulani supply 90% of Nigeria's beef and cattle hide, represented by 15 million head of cattle.[48]

Bebeji, a clan of true Fulbe nomads with large herds, are found around Gombe, in southern Borno and eastern Bauchi States, Nigeria. This group has stayed in the same place for some years, but could move when circumstances dictate. CAPRO has two workers living and moving with them. The workers live in temporary huts or booths like the people and keep their own goats, with a view to eventually purchasing cows. They are learning the language and give simple veterinary advice.[49] There is also much contact with fully nomadic *Fulani* that stay for a few days and then move on with their cattle. To really befriend these cattlemen, workers are needed to travel with them.

Fulbe pastoralists first visited the Jos plateau in the dry seasons for pasture, migrating from Bauchi and Zaria in the north. Then the Fulani launched a jihad in the nineteenth century and finally won the battle of Panyam. Thereafter, the pastoral Fulbe were free to come more frequently. The British development of mining in the region, beginning in 1910, created a market for dairy products. This encouraged more pastoralists to migrate with their families and settle on the plateau for the first time. However, by 1946 the plateau had become overgrazed, with about a million head of cattle. A short-lived policy to cut the herds to a third only caused the Fulbe to migrate away. Subsequent policies have had the effect of making the heads of households more independent of their Fulani leadership.[50]

There are about 2,000 Fulani Christians in Nigeria. A number of agencies are helping these people, including COCIN, ERCC, LCCN and CAPRO in the north, and the Baptists and SIM or EMS under ECWA in the southwest. There are Linguistic Recordings cassettes in three dialects. Every two years,

the agencies consult on projects to help the Fulani.[51]

i) Sudan

Fellah or *Fellata*: There are 90,000 Fulbe or Fulani Na'i in western Sudan.

2. Settled Fulbe groups

Toucouleurs, Tukulors, or *Futa Toro*

They live in Senegal and number some 700,000, with 140,000 in Richard Toll and Podor areas and bordering the Senegal River. They are agriculturists who speak Pulaar, and they use the name Tukulor to distinguish themselves from Fulbe, the name they reserve for the cattle people.[52] However, there is evidence that they may be a mixture of Serer people and Fulbe, for they readily intermarry with Fulbe. They despise the Fulakunda as recent converts to Islam. There is a tendency in the face of domination by other ethnic groups for all Pulaar speakers, whether Fulbe or Tukulor, to identify themselves as *Haalpulaar*, or Pulaar-speakers. WEC works among them in the Senegal River Valley and aims to expand the team, and a few Tukulor have showed some interest in Christianity. The Tukulor New Testament translation was finished in July 1998. Tukulor shepherds near Ndioum have been contacted by Finnish and U.S. Lutherans. The *Jesus* film is available in Futa Toro.[53]

Fulakunda, Senegal, Gambia and *Guinea Bissau*

The Fulas were cattle and sheep herdsmen who gradually entered the land from the fifteenth century. Some settled to pursue agriculture and adopted the social organization of the Mandinkas, thus they were called Fulakundas. They created a class-stratified society, the Fula Forro being "free" Fulas. The Fulakundas were the peasants, and other assimilated captive peoples were slaves or "blacks."

The 700,000 in Senegal make up 17.8% of that country's population, with 450,000 in neighboring areas in Mauritania and Mali. Many are concentrated around Kolda as subsistence farmers, though their roots as cattle people are very evident in their culture. There is no sense, however, of regret or desire for the nomadic pastoralist life. The herdsmen travel short distances from the villages to find pasture, but the people are sedentary. They consider selling a cow to be a crisis, and selling the last cow is very serious indeed.[54] Polygamy is normal. Both the Fulakunda and Tukulors are sedentary.

WEC has worked among the Fulakunda over a number of periods between 1936 and the present and completed the New Testament translation in July 1998.[55] WEC founded two multi-ethnic, Pulaar-speaking churches with Fula converts. One is in Velingara (pop. 14,000), and the other in Koukani, 30 kilometers away. There are cassettes of the whole of the New Testament, which also have been used in Guinea-Bissau, Gambia and Mali. The *Jesus* film was dedicated in February 2000.

In Gambia, each village usually has one or two Fula families who serve as the cattle herdsmen for Mandinkas and other farmers, finding pasture nearby. They were estimated to number about 155,000 in 1993, and there are 32 Fulbe Christians in eight WEC churches.

The *Fulas*, with 223,000, or 23% of the population, are the second largest people group in Guinea-Bissau, after the Balantas. They see themselves as divided into the following groups: *Fula di Gabu* (Fulas of Gabu); *Fula Preto* (Black or Slave Fulas); *Fula di Baka* (Cattle Fulas). They live in the interior eastern half of the country centered on Bafata and are the largest Muslim group. They are agropastoralists, being settled into the villages and towns. But a Fula's cattle are still his wealth. In the villages, those men who own herds of cattle will migrate during the dry season, November to May, or send their stock out in search of suitable feed and water with their sons or hired herdsmen. Of all the people groups in Guinea-Bissau, the Fulas are the most technologically advanced in agriculture. They import single-furrow steel plows from Senegal, as well as small five-point scarifiers and single-furrow seeders, all of which are used behind oxen. Many of the young men are moving into the larger towns.

Animistic practice continues beneath the veneer of Islam. They respect the *mouro* or iman of the mosque, but also the *mouro dos demonios,* or priest of the demons. They speak Fula Forro with five dialects in Guinea-Bissau. The *Jesus* film in Tukulor and cassettes of the New Testament in Fulakunda are used with great effect. The *Look, Listen and Live* Bible stories, prepared by Gospel Recordings for Fulas in Burkina Faso, are also being used. There are now at least 12 Fula believers, but there could be as many as 20 in the whole country. WEC and the Kairos Group from Brazil work in Bafat·. Southern Baptists, YWAM and AoG of Brazil work in Gabu.[56]

Peul or Fulbe Futa Jalon, Guinea

The population estimates vary between 800,000 and 2,550,000. Most live in Fouta Djallon and are concentrated in the Labé, Pita, Calaba and Mamou districts. There are 100,000 in Senegal who "spilled over" from Guinea. The entire population is scattered throughout the country.[57] The *Futa Fula* of Guinea have a distinctive mark similar to the figure "11" on both temples, acquired at the time of circumcision. The Futa Jalon are also in southwest Mali and in Falea and Faraba, south of Kenieba — having moved into the area around 1926.[58]

They moved into Guinea before 1700 and lived as pastoralists, moving among the agricultural peoples, herding the local herds, exchanging dairy produce and fertilizing the fields in return for grazing on the stubble. Those with a stronger allegiance to Islam refused to be submissive to the local leaders, provoking the jihads between 1725 and 1776. More Peul entered the area, forcibly converted the local people, and became settled stock-raisers and cultivators. For a time the Fulbe imposed a feudal system. After Guinea became independent, the government's beef monopoly, with a 10% slaughter quota on the Fulbe, seriously limited their power. Many lost their herds, being forced to sell them to the government at low prices. The small herds left could not reproduce quickly and were a source of shame and humiliation to their once proud owners. The former vassals of the Fulbe became free. Christian Missionary Alliance started work in Labé in 1923, and CRWM came in 1985. A Bible translation in the dialect has been started.[59] A few Christians converted from outside the area.

Fulbe or Fulakunda

There are 3,000 in several villages of northwest Guinea, near Sareboido. They also speak the Fulbe Fuuta-Jalon dialect.[60]

Bamana Fula

These people are so called by the Bambara, among whom they settled and lost their Fulbe language and culture. A number of peoples in the Bambara region of west Mali were probably Fulbe who have lost their original identity.[61]

Khassonke

These people number 120,000 in Mali; 6,000 in Senegal; and a few in Gambia. They are probably Fulbe who lost their language and culture by mixing with others. They are found in the towns of Bafoulabé, Kayes, Kita and Yélémané. The Norwegian Mission to the Santals and New Opportunities work among them.[62]

There are 1,200 Peul in scattered groups in the Ivory Coast, working as herders for other peoples. There are estimated to be between 7,300 and 36,000 Fulani in Ghana.

Fulbe-Borgu

There are 224,000 in four groups who live in Parakou district, Benin, near the Nigerian border. Since 1980, between 40,000 and 50,000 Fulani have migrated into the Banikoara area. There is evidence that many are resistant to the Muslim missionaries and would welcome the gospel. The Assemblies of God have had contact with them.[63] There are 2,000 who have responded to SIM and AoG ministry. There is a Christian radio broadcast every day in the Fulani language, and SIM is working on the northern Benin dialect.

Fulanin Gida or Fulani and Sokoto Fulani

There are 452,700, in Sokoto State, in northwest Nigeria. They are possibly the same as the Western Fulani in Niger, between the Niger River and Dogondoutchi. They have a distinct dialect of their own.[64] The name Fulanin Gida means "house," or settled, Fulani. They initially settled in camps outside the Hausa towns, and were nominal Muslims. However, with the preaching of Islamic reform by the "jihad" movement in the last century, they set up Fulani-led Muslim states in Sokoto, and other places, and restrictions on women were imposed. Most of the Fulani in Sokoto, Kano and Katsina are subsistence cultivators and have adopted both Hausa language and culture. In north Borgu State most still speak Fulfulde, although the younger generation is adopting Hausa.[65]

Fulani zaure

These people living in Sokoto, northwest Nigeria, are an aristocracy with a mixed history of Arab and Fulbe roots. Originally they were preachers of Islam and took part in an Islamic revolution in northern Nigeria, with the support of their pastoral clans.[66] The urban elites in Bida speak Nupe, and the settled farmers in Oyo speak Yoruba — yet they still insist on their identity as Fulbe.[67]

Fulbe in Kwara State, Nigeria

The very first Christian converts among them were probably poisoned in 1963. Twenty years of Christian ministry followed, with continual disappointment. But when Christians among the neighboring Batou people distributed New Testaments in their own language, a Pullo asked for a copy for his village. A number of young Fulbe from two different villages learned to read it and consider themselves Christians.[68] They also received the ministry of a converted Pullo from Benin, and two churches were formed as separate Fulbe congregations. Southern Baptists, Gospel Recordings, Christian Reformed and SIM, among others, have also contributed to the work among them.

Toorobe (sg. Tooroodo)

These people were Muslim Fulbe who were attracted by Hausa culture and settled in towns of northern Nigeria. They forgot Fulfulde and intermarried with the Hausa. They became the clerics, teachers and judges, while often continuing to own herds of cattle. They ruled over the Hausa states for a few years, following the jihad of 1804. They have two clans, the Lido and the better known Tal.[69]

Walawa

There are various groups of dominant clans of Walawa in Nigeria. CAPRO has two workers among them near the town of Jalingo, Taraba State, Nigeria.

Adamawa Fulani

The Adamawa Fulani, in Cameroon, total 669,000, or 7% of the population. They arrived in the eighteenth century and joined the jihad in neighboring Hausaland. Non-Fulani peoples were enslaved, and the state of Adamawa was established early in the twentieth century. The Fulbe here continue to speak Fulfulde, although they are settled and many other surrounding ethnic groups use it as a second language.[70] In northern Cameroon, to the west of Rei Bouda, the Fulani still had slaves until 1970. A Norwegian Lutheran missionary successfully campaigned against this and harem keeping, and some 50,000 slaves were emancipated, helped by a land reform that gave them a measure of independence.[71] Evangelism by Hausa Christians is not accepted by the Fulani, who consider themselves superior to these "farmers," while the Hausa national churches expect the cattle people to adopt a Western-style church life. The Bible is in the Maroua dialect. SUM, RBMU and Worldteam are working in the Adamawa and North Provinces, and the Lutheran Brethren in the North and Extreme North Provinces, Cameroon. The Evangelical Lutheran Church broadcasts from TWR.[72] There are a number of Christians among them.

SONGHAI

Burkina Faso 122,700; Mali 600,000; Niger 390,000.[73] At Oursi in Burkina Faso there are 600 Songhai farmers mixed with Fulani and Tuareq pastoralists, with 12,000 head of their own cattle. The Dendi, a subgroup of the Songhai who number 28,000 in Benin, are not nomadic but are partly pastoral, and SIM hope to work among them.

BEDOUIN

There are 10,000 Bedouin in Burkina Faso.

SHUWA ARABS

There are 1,773,600 in Chad, Cameroon and Niger. Five hundred thousand of them are in the Chad Basin, and 100,000 are in the northeast of Borno State, Nigeria.[74] The Shuwa fit the "romantic" idea of the nomad since they have a reputation for being warlike — attacking and retreating into the desert on horseback. As they are found from the Nile to Borno, Nigeria, they are the most westerly of the Baggara groups. The total of all the Baggara groups from Nigeria to Sudan is estimated at three million.[75]

History

They call themselves Arabs, and Shuwa is the name given to them by the sedentary Kanuri. They probably originated from the Juhayna tribe, which migrated from Yemen into Egypt. They left Egypt for Sudan in the seventh century after the Muslim conquest. But they seem to have been troublesome subjects, for the Sudan appealed for help against them. They moved on, or were deported, and finally migrated from the Darfur region of Sudan to Kanem in Chad, in the sixteenth century. They moved south into the Borno area of Nigeria around 1800. Therefore the Shuwa in Borno are related to the Arabs of Chad, where they make up 30% of the population.

The Shuwa have maintained their independence throughout their history as nomadic pastoralists. They have resisted governments in Egypt, Sudan and Nigeria and avoided having political relations with other groups. The Shuwa near Lake Chad continue to herd camels. But others moved in the seventeenth century to the less arid areas and adopted cattle raising from the Fulbe, combined with millet cultivation.[76] This was a case of nomad adaptability.

Society

The Shuwa have not integrated into the local society of Borno and are considered imperious and even exploitative by the sedentary peoples. The only people they have close associations with are the Kanuri, but relations were often difficult due to conflict over the use of land, until after the 1980s. Most of the Shuwa have permanent settlements, but they are divided between the *hallal*, or "village people," and the *nas al-diran*, or "cattle-camp people." They mix the two lifestyles as there is need. They can practice close pasturing using the village as a base, transhumant herding further afield, or distant nomadism, according to the conditions and the size of the herds.

They are organized into some 31 clans in Borno under an elected clan leader called a *Fugu*. These clans are divided into smaller groups of related brothers and their sons for co-operation in herding and for defense. These clans maintain contact, even when herding groups divide or amalgamate due to the leaders making bad decisions about where to herd and environmental conditions. The patriarchal leader of each group is called the *Jauro* and is considered a father figure and both law and judge, although most decisions are taken in consultation with the heads of households. He is also champion of the group and should be willing to sacrifice his life for the well-being of the groups if necessary.[77]

Nomadism

The basic herding unit, or *da'n*, consists of a man over forty years of age, with his wife or wives and their children, and, on average, between 60 and 100 heads of cattle. The sons are considered part of their father's household and do not participate in the political life of the wider group. They are married at age twenty and have considerable responsibility herding their father's cattle

and building up their own herd, on which their own status depends. The women sell milk in the towns, while the men tend the cattle. Both men and women plait their hair. The cattle are housed during the day, because of the prevalent tsetse fly. Each family lives in a round hut about 10 meters across, with their cattle. There is a raised inner room for the family, and the outer part is for the animals. The Shuwa bought hundreds of children as slaves from the Wulla or Matakam during a famine in 1930, but eventually most of them were returned home.[78]

Religion

They are Muslims and sacrifice a cow or goat after a death, which is believed to help the dead go to paradise. There are no Shuwa Christians. The New Testament is available.[79] CAPRO has two workers between Ngala and Wulgo, in the extreme northeast of Nigeria, near Lake Chad.[80] Attempts were made to reach them by introducing agricultural projects and medical clinics, but with no visible results. Action Partners have passed this work over to the Nigerian churches, but CAPRO knew only of their own two missionaries working among them in 1995.

ARABS

In Niger, north of Lake Chad, there are 12,000 Arabs in close contact with the *Toubou*. They have adopted their lifestyle and culture. They have not been reached with the gospel.

KOYAM or *Keletti*

They are a cattle-raising tribe of the *Kanuri* people in Borno State, Nigeria. They once owned the camel caravans connecting Kanem in Chad with Tripoli and the Sudan and traded in Saharan salt to the south. The Koyam have their own dialect and style of dress and have maintained their distinctive identity for a thousand years. They are now situated between Lake Chad and Maiduguri, around Bama, Dikwa, Munguno, Kukawa and Baga. Others further west, near Illela and Hadeija, have apparently integrated with the Fulani.

Nomadism

The Koyam follow an annual migration route moving southwards and westwards during the dry season and returning northwards to their farms for the rainy season. Today the families travel in trucks rather than by pack animals. The Koyam can often be found in the market at Shattaram, west of Gajiram. The rise in meat prices has created extra income to encourage many to settle their families around Maiduguri, although they still return to their homelands for special occasions. The women buy butter from the Fulani near Jos and sell it on the streets. They use the extra income to invest in more long-horned cattle.

Religion

The Koyam are staunch Muslims and may well prove to be the last to consider the gospel. They prefer to send their children to Qur'anic schools, rather than use the government schools. After many years of witness by SUM and others in the area, there are only about 20 Kanuri Christians and no Koyam Christians. COCIN have started a Kanuri Project of outreach with a Bible translation, films, and medical and literacy programs.[81]

Non-Pastoral Nomads in the Western Sahel

LAWBE, or LaoBe (sg. labbo)

The Lawbe are itinerant Fulbe woodcarvers found in Senegal, Guinea, Mali, Nigeria and elsewhere in West Africa. They are part of the craftsmen caste of Fulani society and speak Pulaar, but many live and work independently of the cattle Fulbe. Also, since the Fulbe in Niger, Chad and Nigeria use carvers of other ethnic groups, they merit separate treatment.[82]

History

The Lawbe tell a myth that illustrates their relationship to the Fulbe. The ancestors of the Lawbe, the herder Fulbe and the *Bambaabe* Fulbe minstrels and praise singers were three brothers. The spirits gave each of them different gifts, but the cattle Fulbe, having received all the cattle, have been under obligation to give the Lawbe free milk. Within Fulbe society, and to a degree among others societies among whom they work, the Lawbe have a low but intermediate status. For since they have no right to inherit cattle they are "poor," although in fact they can own some animals. But they are free to move independently with their work, which the former slaves were not allowed to do.

The Lawbe are considered to be in touch with the spirits and have the ability to pass on blessings or curses, through the objects they make, to their customers. Their power to utter incantations gives them protection, which they are thought to pass on to others. So while they may be considered inferior by the cattle Fulbe and similar classes among other people, their contact with the spirit world means they will be sought out for blessings, healing or "luck" when thing are not going well. They offer prayers to the spirits of the trees they fell, and their ability to turn wood into objects is considered a spirit-given power. Each lineage holds to myths conveying belief in a *taana*, an animal who is their protector.

Their ancestors appear to have accompanied the Fulbe westwards towards the Senegal area, before the Fulbe made their historic expansion eastwards again. The Lawbe were once more nomadic than the cattle Fulbe, either migrating with the pastoralists or traveling independently through the Sahel looking for both suitable wood for carving and for customers. The Fulbe herders increasingly use calabashes instead of the wooden bowls carved by the Lawbe; this seems to have led to the Lawbe seeking work with other peoples.

There are about seven million Lawbe scattered in small communities of two or more families from Senegal to Chad — including Guinea, Burkina Faso, Mali, and Cameroon — often completely independent of the Fulbe. The Lawbe usually only marry other Lawbe, preferably close cousins. They need to be distinguished from many other groups that do similar work.

Nomadism

The Lawbe migrate either to find suitable trees or to travel with various cattle groups — whether Fulbe, Moors or Tuareq. In the past they used large troops of donkeys to carry the wood, but now they use other transport. The head of a family may travel on his own to fulfill a particular order. Some migrate to Europe as traders. Although they are usually settled in towns today, they often travel to camp on the edge of a village for a time.

They make pestles and mortars for grinding millet, bowls for storing food, water troughs, dugout canoes, stools, spoons, tool handles and saddle packs according to local demand. Some families are able to specialize in making particular artifacts. Their tools are few, consisting of axes, adzes and gouges, which the father hands down to his son. Their wives make love potions and perfumes, in addition to doing some carving.

Because of their status as low "caste," they are not permitted to own or inherit land but have to rely on a patron giving them the use of a plot of land. Other people, such as the Wolofs in Senegal, also treat them as low-caste. This means they are never permanently settled. Those who consider themselves "true" Lawbe, with the power to bless, disdain to cultivate the land, believing they should rely on their trade to receive the produce they need.

In Senegal the Lawbe are found in the cities and at the crossing points of the Senegal River, fulfilling orders for both farmers and herders. Some migrate with the Fulbe herders in the dry season. Most are makers of domestic utensils, but many have retrained as sculptors to meet the demand of the tourist trade and for export to France. These are called *Lawbe-yett*, who, in contrast

to other ethnic groups working in cooperatives, have formed the National Union of the Lawbe of Senegal. Lawbe who have become purely traders are called *Lawbe-dyala* and are distrusted by the *Lawbe-yett*. There are a number of sub-groupings that are distinguished according to region but also because of suspected non-Fulbe origins. There is a subdivision that makes dugout canoes for fishermen, and they consider themselves superior to the others.

Language

Being part of the Fulbe, they speak Pulaar.[83]

Outreach

Those who bring the gospel to the Lawbe will need to take into account their distinctive traditions and way of life, and not assume that they are assimilated into their patron's society.

BAMBAABE

These people are the praise singers at Fulbe and Tukulor naming ceremonies. They are also genealogists, recording and passing on the traditions of clans and lineages. They are walking archives in a non-literate society and are considered able to heal the sick. Their traditional instruments are five-stringed *halams* and one-string *rites*. Since they also are allowed to live by begging, they are considered of very low social status. Formerly they were attached to families, but they are now itinerant and travel to find customers.[84]

MAABUBE and *Maccube*

The *maabube* are weavers of the Tukulor, or Toucouleur, people in Senegal. They are part of the Fulbe people. Among the Tukulor, the weaving of cloth is a male occupation and the weavers are nomadic, traveling to their customers for at least part of the year. The moveable parts of the loom are readily transportable and carried over the shoulder. The main frame can be set up from timber found in the bush or in the street, so that it takes only two hours to set up the loom in a new place.

The *maabube*, also called *maaboobe*, are

10 Fulbe weavers, like other *nyeenbe* or craftsmen, work away from the cattle men, who stay in the "bush" (their term). The craftsmen will move between towns and other areas where they find customers outside their own Fulbe society.

part of the middle caste of *nyeenbe*, or craftsmen, which makes up about 10% of Tukulor society. The freemen look down on the *maabube* as "beggars" who perform tasks in return for a gift, and they consider them somewhat footloose and unreliable. There is evidence going back four centuries of the *maabube* being itinerant weavers scattered in the various empires of West Africa, exploiting the opportunities of the urban centers that these powers created. But with the coming of French colonialism they concentrated again in northern Senegal and Dakar. They restrict membership to their sons. They can recite their line of descent going back as many as 16 generations. They only marry within their own group and their wives work as potters.

Nomadism

The weavers, the *maabube sanyoobe*, divide their time between working in a weaving shed in their own village and traveling to visit a number of regular patrons in other villages, in whose houses they set up their looms and receive hospitality. But this itinerant work is often limited to the harvest time after the rains (from October to June), so they visit the towns of St. Louis, Podor, Diourbel, Matam and even Dakar, to meet the permanent demand of the cloth merchants. They bring their families and stay with the established groups of *maabube* traders and weavers. At harvest time they revisit the villages, accompanying people from the towns going to help their relatives with the crops.

Beliefs

The *maabube* are aware of modern innovations but tend to be conservative in their technique, because of their beliefs about the loom. One legend says that fishermen gave the loom to the Tukulor, not seeing any use for it themselves. But the *maabube* claim to have a semi-divine ancestor, Juntel Jabali, who received the first loom from the spirits. The loom is considered to be the meeting place between the spirits and man, and each part of the loom has a divinely-given name. The weaver represents humankind in contact with the spirits, and the loom's frame is made according to the weaver's proportions and ideally should be set so that the weaver faces east. The front pair of posts is thought to be the entrance for humankind, represented by the weaver, and the rear pair is the exit for the spirits. The weaver must be ritually clean and remove his shoes before weaving. The spirits are thought to live in jinn-towns to the northwest and southeast, so millet seeds are planted under the posts corresponding to these directions, to propitiate the spirits. The spirits are thought to haunt the frame at night, so all the moving parts are taken away with the weaver each night.

Because of this association of their craft with the spirit world, the *maabube* weavers are considered experts in magic. They use special incantations to protect their position both as craftsmen and as itinerants traveling alone. They identify themselves with the hyena, which even they consider, like all Tukulor, as unclean. They act as healers and diviners, as well as slaughterers. They are also employed as praise singers. Their women specialize in hair styling. Therefore, like peripatetic craftsmen in caste societies elsewhere, they are both despised and feared for magic and yet respected for their craft skills.

There is a sub-caste of *maabube*, the **maabube jaawambe**, who are praise singers and genealogists. They often do not know how to weave and do not mix with the weavers but work entirely as griots, minstrels and singers to enliven the festivals and parties organized by the *maabube*. There are also the **maabube suudu Paate**, who are entertainers among the sedentary Fulas.

The **maccube** differ from the *maabube* in that they are bonded workers, descended from the lowest ex-slaves in old Tukulor society. They do, or did, weaving and other tasks for wealthy leaders and landowners in the Senegal River Valley, and up until recently they were tied to the village of their master. They are clearly distinguished from the *maabube* by being called *maccube-sanyoobe*, or "weaver-slaves," but they prove that the *maabube* do not have a monopoly on weaving. The *maccube* form part of the lowest caste of *rimaybe*, or bondsmen, which make up about a quarter of Tukulor society. Many bonded weavers are now emancipated to set up as weavers in the towns, but because the merchants are often freemen, or *maabube*, the *maccube* cannot escape their servile status. But their competition tends to limit opportunities for the *maabube* and causes them to move away. Because the demand is seasonal, the *maccube* need a number of locations to visit through the year. They also able to sell cloth on market stalls, or hawk it around the streets on Fridays.[85] The custom of giving cloth at weddings and child-namings provides much work for them.

Sanyaobe

The Sanyaobe, or Fulbe weavers in western Mali, are an example of the regular migration of the artisans well away from their pastoralist people. Some fifty from Nioro du Sahel have, for many years, moved to Kayes for the dry season because of the better trade prospects. They set themselves up on vacant lots in the town, with the more senior craftsmen having the best places. They send money to their families and move back home to plant their crops for the rainy season. They get their thread from Segou, Mali, although the better quality thread comes from Côte d'Ivoire and France. The elaborate association of their looms with the spirits is not always confirmed by questioning some of them.

INADAN (pron. Inhadan; sg. Enad)

The Inadan are blacksmiths of Tamajeq society in Mali and Niger, totaling perhaps 10,000. Many still work as an integral part of Tamajeq camps.

The two chief characteristics of an *enad* are his craft, with its association with magic, and his persuasive sales talk. They delight in describing their goods as being associated with a special place, person or event, which might enhance their value to the buyer. They make jewelry, silver ornaments, saddles, camel bags, various tools, bowls and utensils of all kinds. They manufacture

swords and spears and many are stone- and woodcarvers.

They consider their most prestigious work to be the making of the highly decorated saddles of the Tuareq. In the past they established their importance by being able to fully equip the Tuareq warrior and his camel for war. The Tuareq think that craftsmanship is "in the blood," so no one can practice it except an Inadan. Anyone else who attempts to practice these crafts is attacked or harassed. When the Inadan settle they hold on to their culture and often return to blacksmithing. They are also to be found working well away from the pastoral Tamajeq, settled in the larger towns as well as mobile artisan teams serving the surrounding non-Tamajeq population.

Society

Their relationship with the Tuareqs is a complex one of interdependence and vassalage. They are considered to be socially inferior, due to their obscure origins and darker skin. They claim to be descendants of King David, because in some early Islamic legends David is said to be the first blacksmith. It is possible that the Inadan are descended from Moroccan Jews. They believe they are condemned to subjection to the Tuareq nobles and misery because of ingratitude to the prophet Muhammad. They cannot form tribes as the Tuareq warrior caste can, but they are free to travel as they wish, which the Tuareq slaves were not allowed to do.

The Inadan also possess their own camels as pack animals. They are remunerated by gifts rather than by wages. When the Tuareq travel, they always make sure that they are within reach of the Inadan camps. The Inadan adopt Tuareq or Moor style tents. The women do a lot of the craft work, especially making leather items such as scabbards and belts. The women are also midwives for the Tuareqs. They are left at home for as much as six months of the year when the men are away with the caravans, or itinerant, selling the women's leather work and their own crafts.

11a

11b

11c

11 Inadan, craftsmen of the Tuareq society:
  a. On camels the Inadan are indistinguishable from their Tuareq masters.
  b. Inadan take pride in making Tuareq saddles.
  c. The Inadan tent is distinctive, here closed as the family is away.

11d

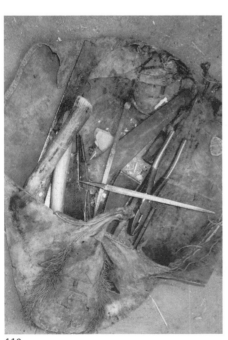

11e

11f

11 d. The Inadan men are metal workers.
   e. A metal worker's typical tool bag.
   f. The Inadan love music and, from a young age, all join in.

Inadan men wear the veil like the Tuareq, but their wives do not. This is to fulfill the concept of reserve and dignity with women, elders and especially one's in-laws. Because this reserve is supposed to be less among the Inadan, they can be used as negotiators to arrange marriages and mediate other delicate matters between the Tuareq. The Inadan also act as masters of ceremonies, drummers and caterers at Tuareq nobles' weddings and circumcisions, and they have great ability as poets and storytellers. Although nominally Muslim, they are feared for their black magic, which is associated with working with iron and fire.

Language

The Inadan speak the Tamajeq language, but in some areas they seem to use a private dialect called Tenet.[86] Riesman found that the blacksmiths with the Jelgoobe Fulbe in northern Burkina Faso spoke Tamasheq and poor Fulfulde, although they had been in that situation for a long time.[87] They are found in Mali well away from Tamajeq camps.

Outreach

There is no known Christian witness among them specifically, and while they can have contact with the gospel as part of Tamajeq-speaking society, it is necessary to see that they are not overlooked — especially where a specialized outreach relating to their crafts is practical.

WEST AFRICAN ITINERANTS

There are numbers of groups who are not strictly nomadic peoples, but who nevertheless travel constantly, such as *Pilgrims to Mecca*, or Fellata who often settle for long periods in Sudanese towns on the journey. *Marabouts*, like the Indian Sadhus, travel for a few years and sustain themselves by begging, before settling down to establish a teaching center.

CHILDREN OF THE BOWED LUTE, or 'Yan goge, Northern Nigeria

They are not a nomadic people, because they do not form a complete family-based society. The members are highly mobile individuals, drifting off to other lifestyles.

They are probably hundreds of traveling entertainers in troupes of between 20 and 50 musicians and dancers. *Goge* music is associated with escapism and moral license, and these troupes arose in the period of independence as part of the *dandi* culture. The *dandi* are settlements of bars and brothels on the edges of towns, and are associated with breaking out of the restraints of Islamic society, or escaping from unhappy home situations. This lifestyle has been described as "Western," or "modern" or "free." Most of the troupe members are young, individualistic "dropouts." The music is claimed to give "strength of heart" for people to either forget their troubles, or to remove the sense of shame for their vice.

The performances are given in the open-air, in the courtyard of a hotel or outside a bar. A praise-singer collects contributions from the audience and relays requests for music to the musicians, or sings impromptu songs about the audience or local events. The instruments are made by the musicians and are the calabash, drums and the *goge*, a lute made from a gourd and played with a bow of horsehair and scrap metal. The dances are formal, synchronized and erotic free-style in character. The dancers are both male and female. During the day the men clean shoes or do similar work, and the women serve as prostitutes. Many of the women are also involved with the *bori* spirit-possession cults, mimicking the supposed movements of the spirit in their dance.[88]

They are highly itinerant, each with a manager who travels ahead of the troupe to arrange a schedule across Nigeria and into Niger. They are found in towns like Kano, Zaria, Funtua, Kaduna and Jos. The spiritual need is obvious, and most of the members have a troubled past.

AKWA

They are itinerant smiths of the *Ibo* society, in southeastern Nigeria, named after their hometown. They settle in one place for a long period and then move again, or return to Akwa. At any one time, half of the population of male smiths is traveling, or staying in work sites, while the others work or farm in Akwa. Even when apparently living and working away for long periods, they still consider themselves to belong to Akwa. They are reputed to be specialists in rituals, such as divining and circumcising.[89]

SOROGE, *Bozo, Sebbe*

These people are semi-nomadic fishermen and boat builders in Mali, with a distinct culture of their own. They are found on the Niger and Senegal Rivers and other places where there is water, and they soon colonize the new lakes formed by dams. Sebbe is the Fulfulde term. Bozo is the outsider's Bambara term for those speaking a group of four languages, one of which is Sorogama, which has six dialects. Estimates of the numbers of those who speak these languages vary between 20,000 and 200,000.

Society

The situation is actually more complex, because all four of these languages are spoken by people of four different ethnic origins. Soroge (sg. *Sorogo*) is the name one group uses to refer to itself. Others are Marka, one of the original peoples of the Niger Delta before the arrival of the Fulbe, considered to have been Soninke farmers who changed to fishing. Another people among them are the Somono fishermen. The fourth group are people of mixed descent from the Bambara, Dogon, Malinke and Soroge.[90]

Nomadism

The Soroge villages are close to the rivers Djaka, Bani and Niger, upstream from Lac Debo. They are often cut off by water and difficult to find. Typically they consist of compounds of driftwood fences joined to each other, with low barrel-roofed huts made from palm leaves or woven mats. Usually they lay fish out on the roofs to dry in the sun. The Bozos eat fresh fish themselves, but they sell or exchange dried fish with outsiders for their other needs. They use various types of nets and traps to catch the fish. During the droughts in the 1970s and 1980s the Soroge and Somono fishermen started farming and many have adapted to it well, with irrigation pumps to grow rice all year. They prefer rice to the millet that the Fulbe and others prefer.

When the Niger Delta floods from October to February, the fishermen move to temporary camps to follow the fish. There are some 130 species of fish in the delta. During the dry season all the rivers except the Niger dry up, so the Bozo villages are accessible by car. Otherwise, the villages must be accessed by boat.

Another important occupation of the Bozo is building a distinctive style of boat for sale to other peoples for river trade, ferrying and fishing. It is flat-bottomed with flat sides, ideally of one plank made waterproof by caulking with a local glue and cotton. The boats have long, slender pointed ends. Each shipwright paints his own pattern of colored lines and eye shapes on the bows as a sort of trademark.

The Bozos have migrated to where ever they have found fishing and boat building opportunities, such as to Senegal and Côte d'Ivoire. Bozos work both as ferrymen and boat builders in Kayes, and have come from Ségou.

In Kayes and Ségou there are annual boat festivals. Groups in the boats dress up as animals, such as lions, hyenas, birds, crocodiles, snakes and, of course, the all-important fish. Spectators have to guess the identities of those behind the animal masks. There are popular stories of Fulbe and other non-Bozos being drowned by water spirits, while the Bozos can swim like fish and have plenty of practice in repairing their traps and nets. Fear of water and inability to swim is the cause of death, say the Bozos, who say they have no fear of the water or its spirits. The Bamaras, not the Bozos, offer sacrifice to the water spirits.

Pulaar Bozo

One group migrated to the Kayes area late in the nineteenth century, but the Sonnike drove these people into Senegal. In the Senegal Valley they intermarried with Fulbe and lost their Bozo language to speak only

12a

12b

12c

12 Soroge or Bozos:
    a. The Soroge or Bozos are nomadic boat builders and fishermen.
    b. A typical Bozo boat ferrying goods or fish on the River Niger, Mali.
    c. When the floods recede the Bozo live in temporary villages on the sandbanks.

12d

12e

12 d. Bozo children are very lively.
    e. Bozo homes use the thatch to sun-dry the fish.

Pulaar. They appear to call themselves "Bozo-Fulbe." They have since migrated back into Niger, living in small groups by the river and migrating to temporary camps as necessary according to the fishing. There may be a few hundred people in this group.

All the Bozos are nominal Muslims, although it is claimed they have little time for religion. One marabout at the village we visited became irate with our guide, saying that these foreigners always come asking questions, but no help ever arrives. There are very few Bozo Christians. One said that Christians should come live like Bozo, learn the language and learn to fish, in order to gain acceptance among them. The language

is Sorogama, and SIL have a translation project in one dialect. The people resist education and literacy in French and Bambara, so the Sorogama project is crucial to them. The German Allianz Mission have one family working among them and the CMA has had a ministry among the Bozos.

SORKAWA, West Africa

The Sorkawa are migrant fishermen on the River Niger who travel annually between the delta in Nigeria and Gao in Mali. They barter their fish for millet and their other needs. As "outsiders" from the local culture they are often used as mediators and negotiators in disputes.[91]

EASTERN SAHEL

The eastern part of the Sahel is made up of Chad and the Sudan, with 3,800,000 square kilometers (2,361,300 sq. mi.) — equivalent to western Europe or half of Australia. There are an estimated six million pastoralists in these two countries.[1] The northern 40% of Chad is covered by the mountains of Tibesti surrounded by the desert, and 60% of the Sudan is desert. Only the southern fringes of these countries are fertile for agriculture, so that "nomads and semi-nomads control about fifty per cent of Chadian territory, although they represent only twenty percent of the population."[2]

Chad has been at war with Libya in the north and with various dissident movements throughout its period of independence, as the government attempts to move towards democracy. Goran, Tubu and Zaghawa peoples have all contributed leaders in the civil wars in Chad in the 1970s through the 1990s.[3]According to the 1984 census, Sudan had 2,192,000 nomadic pastoralists, or about 20% of the population.[4] While the populations of other types of animals have remained stable, the number of sheep increased two and half times by the mid-1990s. Since the early 1980s, Sudan has been racked by civil war as the government has attempted to impose a fundamentalist Islamic state on the Christian and animist south. The southerners have split between those demanding a secular Sudan and others seeking a completely independent south. Millions have been reduced to starvation or have become refugees.

The peoples below are listed moving from west to east and then southwards.

Nomadic Pastoralists of the Eastern Sahel

TOUBOU or Tebu and Daza

These are a group of similar peoples, who are sometimes called *Teda* (pronounced *tedá*), after one people among them. Toubou means "People of Tibesti," Chad, but only about 10,000 now live there. They do not have a social or even a genealogical unity, but they are scattered across northern Chad, eastern Niger and the southern oases of Libya.

They are divided roughly at the eighteenth latitude into two main groups: 72,500 *Teda* to the north, who speak Tedaga; and 282,300 *Daza* to the south, who speak Dazaga. There are 40,000 Teda and 15,000 Daza in northeast Niger. The Dazaga language, however, is also used by both groups as the medium of their common way of life that they refer to as "Teda" culture.

History

The Toubou have had a long history as desert warriors controlling the caravan routes across the Sahara. They were free to do this because both groups used to have a caste society with vassals and commoners who worked for them. These included the smiths called *Azza*, black serfs called *Kamadja*, like the Haratin among the Moors and Saharawis (see below), and slaves. For a description of the Azza see the separate entry below, as they are non-pastoral nomads. The Kamadja are sedentary and live near Borkou, south of Tibesti, and number 3,600. They were once vassals of the Toubou and paid them tribute, but now they are paid for their produce and have their own camel herds.

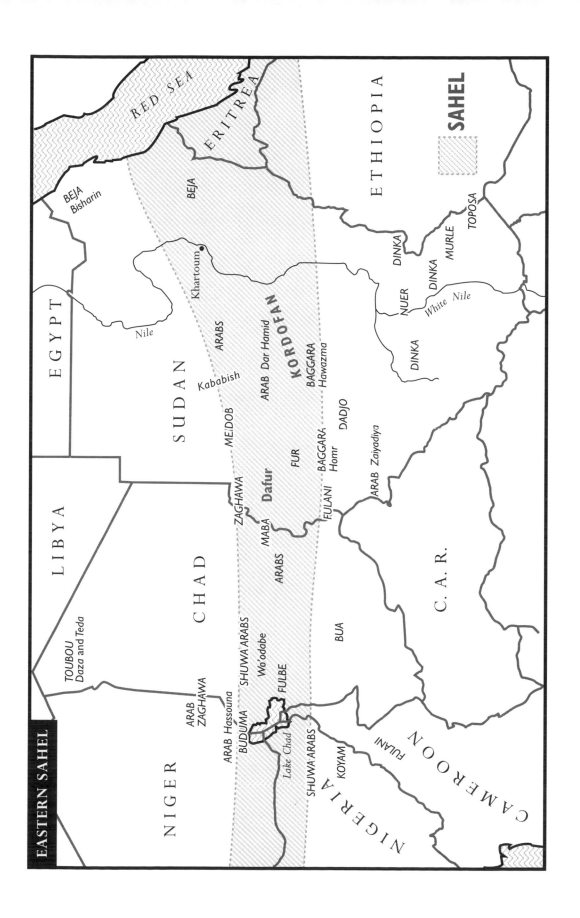

EASTERN SAHEL

SAHEL

RED SEA

EGYPT

LIBYA

SUDAN

CHAD

NIGER

NIGERIA

CAMEROON

C. A. R.

ETHIOPIA

ERITREA

BEJA
Bisharin

BEJA

Khartoum

Nile

ARABS

Kababish

MEIDOB

ZAGHAWA

Dafur

MABA

ARABS

ARAB Dar Hamid

KORDOFAN

BAGGARA
Hawazma

FUR

BAGGARA
Homr

DADJO

ARAB Zaiyadiya

FULANI

BUA

NUER

DINKA

DINKA

White Nile

DINKA

MURLE

TOPOSA

SHUWA ARABS

Wo'odabe

FULBE

BUDUMA

ARAB Hassouna

ARAB
ZAGHAWA

TOUBOU
Daza and Teda

Lake Chad

SHUWA ARABS

KOYAM

FULANI

Society

The Toubou have a very decentralized or fragmented society, with clans breaking up and reforming frequently, and so the main social unit is the nuclear family. Close links are maintained with other families on the male side, rather than through the mother or sister. Boys may choose their wives, but girls cannot choose their husbands. Yet the birth of a daughter is considered as joyous an occasion as the birth of a son (in contrast to the reactions of many peoples). Women can own property, including livestock, and when their husbands travel they act on his behalf. Helping relatives in need is obligatory, and blood feuds are common. To take revenge requires not only that murderers are killed, but also one of their close kin as well.

The Daza are also called *Gorans*, or *Booboo*, by the Arabs in Chad. They number 159,000 in Chad and 23,000 in Niger.[5] They make up about 90% of the Toubou and are divided into 14 subgroups. Their clans appear to be linked to territory rather than to ancestors, but these in turn are divided into lineage groups with a male ancestor. The *Kreda* is the largest clan and is found in Bahr el Ghazal, 200 kilometers (120 mi.) northeast of Lake Chad. The next largest are those also called *Daza*, with two smaller groups in Kanem, closer to the lake. Further to the north in Borkou are five more groups. To the east in Ennedi, parallel with the Northern Darfur of the Sudan, are the *Ounia*, *Gaeda* and *Erdiha*. The *Char'Afarda* are in Ouaddai, south of Abéché. The *Dowaza* are a group of Teda who live in the oases and practice animal husbandry. *Wajunga* is a smaller group.

The Daza are cattle and camel herders who also have sheep and goats, horses and donkeys. They live in villages of small domed mat huts close to wells, which they occupy only from July to September, the rainy season, to plant seasonal crops. They scatter to various pastures during the other nine months, moving from well to well, some traveling as far south as Lake Chad. The women do the herding while the men go to market. Divorce is common and does not carry a social stigma. They have adopted Arab ways and some live in the towns. They were in rebellion against the Chadian government during the 1980s.

The *Teda*, or *Teda-Tou*, are the second largest group of Toubou. Fifteen thousand live in Tibesti, northwest Chad, and 3,000 live in Niger and Libya. They call themselves *Tedadaga*, or "the people that speak Tedaga." The Teda are divided into about 40 clans, and many seem to have an ancestor that is described as a rebel who has fled from somewhere else. The *Tomaghera* is the dominant noble clan, and their leader is considered the nominal ruler of Tibesti, distinguished by the symbolic green turban he wears. The *Arna* live in Borkou, and the *Gourous* and *Mourdia* live in Ennedi. Their language is Tedaga (actually a dialect of Dazaga), in which all Teda songs and poetry are written and which their smiths speak. Around Bilma and Djado in eastern Niger, the Teda speak Kanuri and have adopted Kanuri customs and are called *Guezebida*.

Nomadism

About 3,000 Teda practice agropastoralism in Tibesti, but the rest are nomadic. Agriculture has declined for three reasons: first, due to the increased aridity of the area; second, because their slaves have been emancipated; and, third, because the Teda consider the work too degrading to do themselves. This has meant an increased emphasis on camel and goat pastoralism. The camels are kept for milk and transport and are left to roam free when not used. The goats provide milk, meat and leather, and are herded close to camp.

The Teda live in simple huts of bent sticks covered in mats or hides about 5 to 8 meters long and 2 meters wide, with a narrow entrance. Years ago they used to wear a leather tunic called a *farto*. The Teda men travel with butter and animals for sale or transport, and in return they bring home grain, cloth, salt and other goods. The women also gather nuts and berries. The women do most of the herding, because the men are often away doing their trading.

Religion

The Teda are Muslims, but their world view is essentially animistic. Some of the Teda acknowledge some early Christian influences in their culture. Demons are conceived of in very human terms, although they are invisible. They are thought to live in the north, at the foot of mountains or in sandy places. The Teda never pitch their tents, therefore, to face north. Black and white objects are thought to bring protection from evil. They believe that the dead are still alive and affect the living for good or ill. Each clan has a taboo animal associated with it. The Teda like large gatherings for feasts and most occasions, such as rites of passage, call for goat sacrifices. At least once a year, a scapegoat is sacrificed with a general confession of all the faults of the village.

Language

The two dialects of Dazaga and Tedaga are distinct enough to merit two separate Bible translations, but they appear to be mutually intelligible. Bible translations in Daza and Teda are in progress.[6]

Outreach

One Christian attempt to reach the Teda was by four Roman Catholic nuns who migrated with them living in tents. AIM has a medical team among them and SIL and TEAM work in Bardal, Chad. They seek to contact the Teda through reaching the Daza first. SIM, SIL, World Horizons and New Opportunities also have teams in Niger.[7] A Christian Chadian soldier witnessed in the area, with the result that a congregation has begun to form. The Teda have contact with Fulani and Toubou in Galmi, including the hospital staff.

SHUWA ARABS

The Shuwa Arabs, in Chad, form the second largest ethnic group there. They first moved into Chad over the long period between the fourteenth and nineteenth centuries. Estimates of their numbers vary greatly, between 30,000 and 450,000, because their mobility makes a census impossible. Similar groups of Arabs are found outside Chad, including the Shuwa (see entry for Nigeria, above) and their dialect is spoken by half the population as Chadian Arabic. See the entry for Nigeria, above.

Nomadism

The Arabs are to be found between the twelfth and fourteenth parallels of latitude, and they can travel as far as 1,600 kilometers (1,000 mi.) northwards into Libya.[8] But they normally leave the north to the Toubou.[9] Although born in Chad, many are not registered with Chadian nationality. More Arabs have also come westwards from the Sudan into Chad over many years, as camel drivers or cattle herders. As true nomads, they have tended never to accept territorial government. Politically they have been fickle in their relationships with the local Sultanates, refusing to pay the large sums of tribute demanded by the Sultans' representatives. Their involvement in Chadian politics has been spasmodic, and they have tended to be concerned with their own independence and have been reluctant to accept education, technology and employment.

Yet the Arabs have played a key cultural role because until colonization Arabic was the only written language, and also because of their knowledge of Islam. In this way Arabic became the language of both trade and religion in Chad. The Arabs have exercised influence through their commercial contacts in the markets, exchanging cattle, milk and butter for food and fabricated goods. In spite of some intermarriage with local peoples, the Arabs have not been assimilated.

Society

The Arabs are divided into three major tribes. The largest is the *Djoheina*, consisting of the *Ouled Rachid*, *Ouled Hemat*, *Atié* and *Salamat*. Ironically, they are named after an ancestor who was expelled from Arabia in the seventh century for not accepting Islam. The *Hassouna* includes the *Assahé*, *Assala* and *Dagana* in the west, north of Lake Chad. Those situated on the west bank of the Chari are called *Gawalmé*. The *Ouled Sliman* is the smallest group. They were once commissioned to spread Islam to North Africa.[10] They include the *Missirie*, *Mahamid*, *Awazme* and *Khozam* tribes.

These tribes have a patriarchal structure of leadership, but they have split up over time because other contenders constantly challenge the leadership of the clans and other groups. They no longer make concerted migrations, because of differences of opinion on how to survive in a fragile environment.

The basic social unit consists of extended families called *kochinbet*, or "mouth of the tent or house." These consist of a group of tents or houses, each with a family, set up around the chief's tent. They practice arranged marriages, without consulting the bride, and with a bride-price set according to the wealth and status of the bride's father. Weddings are great celebrations for the two extended families, rather than for the couple. Polygamy is common, and each wife has her own household. Divorce is common, especially if there are no children. Having sons and grandsons is as important as possessing large herds.

ARABS in eastern Chad

The Arabs in eastern Chad consist of tribes with either cattle or camels, or with mixed herds, who describe themselves as Arabs. They speak Arabic and most seem to have no second language. They also have goats, along with donkeys for the women to ride and horses for the men.

The *Hawazme* number between 6,000 and 13,000, with separate sections with camels and cattle. Along with the Khozam and their camels, they are a true nomadic tribe, migrating over a distance of 600 or more kilometers (400 mi.). Their chiefs have a base in Abougoudam, southwest of Abéché.

Other tribes of Arabic nomads with their chiefs based in Abougoudam are the *Wuled Zed*, the *Zaghawa* (who have darker complexions), the *Wuled Rashid* (with lighter skins) and the *Missiriye*. The *Mimi*

do not migrate, and the *Nuwabye* only migrate short distances. These tribes live in round grass huts.

Nomadism

During the dry season, the Hawazme are found in the far south of Chad in the Salamat, an area of seasonal flooded marshes, which provide good pasture. In a very dry year they will travel further south into the Central African Republic. After the rains begin, they move northwards, through Abougoudam, and then onwards to near Arada or even beyond to Qum Chalouba. When the rains and floods in the south abate, they again retrace their way to the south. Each camp might have a dozen "Arab houses," or huts. These consist of frames of arched poles with grass mats tied over them, with blue plastic sheets over the mats.

A French NGO has sunk a number of wells and offered animal husbandry courses, which have had disappointing attendance. UNICEF have plans for an education program.

ARABS in the Sudan

These Arabs may total 5,000,000. The Arabs crossed the Red Sea before the first century AD, but the main influx of the Bedouin into Sudan took place from Egypt between the thirteenth and fifteenth centuries, when they occupied the savannahs. They are of mixed origin, because they have intermarried with local people. Some were of Berber origin but have adopted Arab ways. They engaged in a slave trade to the Arab world in the nineteenth century.

Society

Arab society is divided between two main groups of tribes, the *Gaalin* and the *Guhayna*, according to social class, lifestyle and claims of descent. The Gaalin, who settled in the towns, claimed descent from an uncle of Mohammed. The Guhayna, who concern us, are those who continued to be nomadic pastoralists. They are divided in turn between the Jamala camel nomads in the north and the Baggara cattle pastoralists to the south. The Jamala include confederations such as the *Kababish* (see below) in northern Kordofan and Darfur, and the *Sukriyyah* in south Kassala near the Beja. The *Baggara* include the *Rizaygat* and the *Taaisha* in the Darfur and the *Homr*, the *Messiriyyah* and the mostly settled *Hawazma* and *Selima* in southern Kordofan (see below). The Baggara number about three million across Nigeria, Cameroon, Chad and Sudan.[11]

The VSO is involved in herd restocking projects, but the Arabs of Sudan have received no specific Christian outreach. The Societé Missionaine de l'Eglise Evangelique au Tchad (SMEET) works with Action Partners on a water development project with wells for nomads and sedentary peoples in the area. This also includes medical work, especially leprosy treatment.[12]

ZAGHAWA

There are 105,000 of this ancient people, living northwest of Kutum, over 200 kilometers (125 mi.) northwest of El Fasher in Darfur, Sudan. Thirty-five thousand live in northwest Niger and 17,500, including 3,000 of the *Badiyat*, or *Bideyat*, live in the area of the Ennedi Mountains, northern Chad. They are nomads with herds of camels, sheep and goats and some cattle. Their ancestors were in the region before the Arabs arrived, but they have largely adopted Arab ways. However, this has not stopped them from being long-standing rivals of the Kababish.

Their *gom*, or traveling groups, are feared for camel stealing. Their land is semi-desert in northern Darfur. This region was badly affected by drought in the 1970s, and many have either moved south with small herds or abandoned pastoralism to go to the towns, such as El Fasher, constructing shantytowns around the markets. Their own language appears to be dying out, and they speak their own version of Arabic.

They have a distinct caste of mobile *gunsmiths* traveling with them, carrying their equipment on camels. All they need to make a gun is an imported barrel, and they make the rest in camp. They claim that modern weapons are easier to repair because

the parts are more standardized. Although the Kababish and other peoples are enemies of the Zaghawa, the gunsmiths are able to work for them all, because their skills are held in high regard.[13]

MEIDOB, *Midob*

This group consists of 30,000 semi-nomadic pastoralists keeping sheep, goats and camels in the Meidob Hills, about 60 kilometers (40 mi.) west of Hattan, in the northeast of the Darfur, Sudan. A 1997 survey had estimated that there were only 1,800. To stop the raiding between them in 1922, the British prohibited the Kababish from going into the hills. They have a large salt deposit in their area from which they also benefit commercially. The Meidob also have some settled communities.[14]

KABABISH

This is a confederation of 19 tribes, situated in northern Kordofan, northern Sudan between Khartoum and the eastern border of Chad. They number perhaps 100,000.

History

Most of their ancestors came from Arabia before the eleventh century. Others of them, of Beja and Moorish origin, form sections of their tribes. The Arabs originally came as mercenaries of local rulers, and when these rulers dispensed with their services they moved back to pastoralism and formed the Kababish confederation by 1300. The name comes from *kabish*, meaning "a ram."[15]

The Arabs west of the Nile married into the Christian Nubian kingdom and, as Nubians can inherit through daughters, the Arabs gained control of the land through their wives. Another tribe, the Awlad Sulayman, were Bedu who had settled in the Fezzan in Libya and lost a battle with the Tuareq. They moved into Chad in 1850, and from there some joined the Kababish in Sudan. They used to serve as guides and suppliers of camels to the caravans on the routes passing through between the Nile and West Africa. They succeeded in claiming their area of North Kordofan by pushing the Zaghawa, Bani Jarrar and Dar Hamid southwards. They have became more united as the modern state extended its control during the twentieth century.

Society

The Kababish are organized into economically independent households. A tent to the Kababish symbolizes a married couple, and by implication the giving of hospitality. Hospitality and food are synonymous — called *karam*, from *karama*, or food offered in sacrifice. Each tent belongs to a wife, and the women are kept secluded in their tent. Single men do not have tents, because they do not have a wife to cook for them and so give hospitality. The tents are usually pitched under a nearby tree for shade and are open to the east. They are made of *shugga*, or woven camel hair, with some goat hair. Two posts support the tent, with a ridge in between and the outer corners supported by more poles. The Bedouin in Arabia prefer to use only goat hair. Outside the tent a small shelter made of loose wood, called a *tukul*, serves as a kitchen. Usually the only belongings inside the tent are the folding bed (about 30 cm. from the ground), some large camel bags and a camel frame for carrying the tent.

Nomadism

The Kababish consider themselves Jamala, or camel nomads, but they soon learned to keep sheep and goats and some cattle. Donkeys are used to carry goods, including water. The Kababish breed their camels to sell them in the markets of northern Sudan. They are then resold in Upper Egypt. The shearing of the camels is a time of celebration at the end of winter, and they invite all the neighbors to a feast. The Kababish do not rely on camels for their regular diet but eat millet porridge, with meat or milk when they are available. Their clothes will often be rags, but their camels and their saddles will be carefully maintained. The Kababish consider themselves naked without a shotgun or rifle and a dagger strapped to their left arm.

The scarcity of grazing means the herds have to move rapidly, and careful pastoral decisions have to be made. During the dry season they stay near their *damars*, or permanent wells, or dig new holes in the dry watercourses. Some spend the dry season in the southern Libyan Desert. Rainfall is very limited and falls only between July and September. In these months the men take the herds over 100 kilometers (60 mi.) away from the main camps.

DAR HAMID

This is a confederacy of Arab tribes, now sedentary, in the Qoz region of central Kordofan, Sudan. This is a transition zone between the nomad and the cultivator. The 164,000 Dar Hamid are descended from camel herders who migrated from Egypt, and were nomadic until 1890 when they lost their herds in conflict with the *Baggara*. Some are pastoralists. Their sons learn to herd the livestock, starting with the goats and progressing to cattle and sheep, and later going a greater distance with the camels. The majority have a meager existence, combining some cultivation with small herds and collecting gum arabic. The ground is not very fertile and the fields increasingly become more distant from the limited sources of water. They have to change their fields every few years, and therefore they are nomadic in the sense of being shifting cultivators. They practice Folk Islam.[16]

BEJA or Bedawi

Between 951,000 and 1,500,000 Beja live in northeast Sudan and Kassala Province, Ethiopia, between the Nile and the Red Sea. One hundred and twenty thousand live in Eritrea, and 77,000 in Egypt. They call themselves Bedawi and speak To-Bedawie, which is unwritten. They have been in the region for 4,000 years and may be descended from the ancient Egyptians. They came to dominate the area in the third century, until the Arabs invaded Egypt in the seventh century.

The Beja are being pressured politically and militarily in Sudan, Eritrea and Egypt. Their pasture is being taken from them, and some have been interned into camps. They migrate only short distances between the Red Sea Hills and the coastal plain in the dry season, keeping close to their wells. Only 3% are town dwellers.

Society

The are four major Beja tribes — the *Hadendowa*, *Bisharin*, *Amarar* and *Beni-Amer* in Eritrea all have the To-Bedawie language in common.

The *Hadendowa* in northeastern Sudan were called "Fuzzy Wuzzies" by Kipling. There are 30,000 in Sudan, living along the deltas of the Gash and Tokar. They were originally situated around Sinkat, but they have moved southwards. The Hadendowa are always short of food, which must be bought to supplement the products of their camels and goats. They grow cotton and invest the profits in livestock. A Sudanese government scheme to grow cotton and castor is operating, but few have settled in the associated villages, preferring to hire others to cultivate their land for them while they continue with the nomadic life. In their culture each woman receives a permanent tent when she is married, which is inherited by her daughters.[17]

The *Bisharin*, *Bishariyyan* or *Abadan* are a Beja tribe, but of mixed Bedouin and Beja descent. There are 15,000 in northeast Sudan, along the Atbara River, with camels, sheep and goats. There are 58,400 living in southern Egypt, in the hills and on the coast of the Red Sea. They still live in huts of logs and branches or tents of woven palm-fibers.[18]

The *Amarar* live in the center of the Red Sea Hills and are semi-nomadic.

The *Beni Amir*, a name used of all the Beja but also of this group within the Beja, live on the border of Sudan and Eritrea moving according to the rainfall.

Religion

The Beja became Folk Muslims in the fifteenth and sixteenth centuries. This has changed their society and made them politically active in Sudan on behalf of Islam. They were originally matriarchal,

with inheritance coming through the mother. Women administer the household and can own goats and camels, but they are not allowed to milk them. They do not need permission to travel. The men do much of the heavy work. The women can divorce their husbands.[19]

Outreach

There is no Bible translation for the Beja. An Arabic version of the *Jesus* film is available.[20] New Opportunities anticipate helping this people and a Red Sea Mission Team works in the area, but two organizations have been expelled. There was one baptism in 1991.

YEDINA, *Buduma* or *Boudouma* and *Kouri*

Their own name is *Yedina*, meaning "the people of the Lake." Buduma means "people of the grass," referring to the papyrus reeds they use for their boats and houses. The surrounding peoples, from whom they differ considerably, use the name in a derogatory sense. The Yedina migrated from the Middle East with the Kanji. There are 25,000 in Chad, 4,000 in Niger and 3,000 in Borno State, Nigeria.[21] They are divided into five or six clans of fishermen and the *Guria* clan, who are semi-nomadic pastoralists.

The Yedina live on the northern shore of Lake Chad and on its 2,000 real and floating islands. Because of the relative isolation of these islands, the Buduma have succeeded in maintaining their identity, and they have a long history of raiding the mainland and then retreating to their islands. They have villages of papyrus huts on some of the more permanent islands. But if the lake floods the islands, they simply carry the huts to higher ground.

Nomadism

They can be considered as a nomadic people, by their seasonal movements and by the trading trips they take. Their lives center around their cattle, which are not for meat but for milk and sacrifice. So the Yedina's diet is based on cow's milk and fish. They also plant millet and maize. The Yedina men pasture their herds, each with about 100 head of cattle. In the dry season, they move from the villages to establish temporary camps on the floating islands to fish from their papyrus boats called *kadai*. Some of the larger boats can carry cattle.

The men go to distant Kanem to sell fish, or to sell dried fish to be sold in markets in Nigeria. This is an example of a subsistence strategy being turned into a commercial operation, but it has also endangered their way of life by over-fishing.[22] Many Buduma, both the fishermen and the Guria pastoralists, are migrating into Nigeria. They have two settlements, Baga and Mallamfatori, in Borno State. They speak their own language and some Kanuri or Hausa. They intermarry with the Kanuri.

The men only herd cattle or fish. The women build the houses and do the rest of the work, for such work is considered beneath the dignity of the men. Marriage is arranged, but with the couple's consent, and the groom pays a bride-price in money and cows. The couple lives with the groom's family for the first year before setting up on their own. Polygamy is permitted and divorce is common. Adultery used to be punished, but a more relaxed attitude allowing divorce prevails today. Children are not named for some time after birth since infant mortality is high, and they are given both a secret name and an everyday name. Male children are initiated into the society at the age of five. This requires cutting seven or more scars on the face. They are circumcised at seven and receive gifts of cows.

Religion

The various clans have their own religious rites, mixed with a superficial Islam. Most of them worship the spirit of Lake Chad with sacrifices and believe in a frightening creature that is supposed to live in the lake. Their language is unlike the others around them, and so a Bible translation is in progress. An initial medical work among them in Chad by SUM was halted by persecution. About this time, many of the people were converted to Islam. COCIN and Action Partners work among these people in Mallamfatori and Baga, Nigeria. There are no Buduma Christians. TEAM and SMEET are in the area but, according to Patience Ahmed, no group is specifically reaching the Buduma. Evangelistic cassette recordings are available in Buduma.

BUA, Boa, Boua or Bwa, Chad

There are 20,000 Bua, although the 1993 census listed only 7,700 — divided into two groups of farmers and herders. They live 150 kilometers (80-100 mi.) north of Sarh and east of Kono and Korbol. The pastoralists travel great distances for weeks with their large herds of cattle, sheep and goats. The Bua were forcibly converted to Islam by the Rabas around 1900. Those who refused were killed. Many have reverted to their own form of animism, although 20% would claim to be Folk Muslims. There are no Christians among them, but there is some interest in contact with Christians among Chadian government workers sent there. AIM also have a family among them. The Bua have a very limited knowledge of Arabic, and so a Bible translation is needed.[23]

OUADDAI or *Maba*

There are 300,000 in northeast Chad. They are semi-sedentary agropastoralists based in 200 villages, many within a 150-kilometer (95-mi.) radius of Abéché. The Maba occupy their villages for three to four months during the rainy season to grow millet and sorghum, their staple food. Each village consists of about 500 people living in a hundred straw huts within small courtyards, with passages linking them to a central meeting place. This meeting place consists of a shelter about eight meters (30 ft.) square that serves as mosque, village hall and courthouse.

The young men (16 to 25 years old) are away from December until April, the dry season, with their herds of cattle, sheep and goats, going great distances for pasture in the south. Meanwhile, the parents and younger teenage children move to gardens bordering the dry riverbeds, where they live in temporary shelters. Other young people seek manual work in Abéché and the Sudan.

Their migration cycle is such that, for part of the year, only the old or very young are in the villages.

They live on a knife-edge in an increasingly arid region, as most of the limited rain runs off the region and dams are needed to replenish the water table. Even new and deep wells may run dry after two years. In 1984 the drought caused many to starve to death and villages to be deserted.

The language is Bora Mabang, and SIL have started a translation. WEC had contact with the urban Maba, who in turn have contact with their villages.

DADJO or *Daju*

They are thought to have migrated from the Nile valley in the thirteenth century and established a Sultanate in the Darfur region, before being displaced by the Fur. They now form isolated groups still speaking their language in both Darfur and Chad. They are sedentary cultivators and cattle herders. In Chad, the *Dar Daju* call themselves *Saaronge*. They total 23,100 and are semi-sedentary around Mongo and Eref. They speak Shuwa Arabic as well as Dadjo and trade with *Missirié* Arabs. The *Dar Fur* number 90,000 and live 40 kilometers (25 mi.) northeast and southeast of Niyala, Darfur Province, and also in western Kordofan, Sudan. The *Dar Sila*, who call themselves *Bokoruge*, total 33,000 in Goz Beida, Chad and Darfur, Sudan. They speak both their own language and a dialect of Arabic. They have no Scriptures in their own language. Their Sultans lead them in a mixture of Islam and their folk religion, which involves the reverencing of sacred stones and trees.[24]

FUR, *For(a)*

There are 500,000 living in the Darfur, or land of the Fur, western Sudan and 1,800 are found in Chad. The Fur have been in the region for 2,000 years and had an independent Sultanate reducing the surrounding peoples to vassalage. They dominated the region from the villages in the Marra Mountains. This ended when the British came. The Fur like to distinguish themselves from the Arabs, who are relatively recent arrivals.

They live in houses made from lava rocks, surrounded by terraced fields that go up to 3,000 meters, for there are heavy rains on the mountains from July to September. Their diet is mainly millet porridge and vegetables. They trade fruit from their orchards and other produce in the markets of Nyala, El Fasher and Kutum. The Fur failed to dominate the Baggara and Dar Hamid in the Qoz to the south, and they now trade with them. They buy their calves and resell them at five or six years old to supplement their limited income from cultivation. Each man is a separate economic unit and usually has two wives who live in separate houses. The men eat together in their communal house. They are Muslims.[25]

ZAIYADIYA or *Zayadiyya*

They are nomadic Arab camel herders in western Sudan, who spend the winter in Bahr el Arab, between Darfur and Bahr Al Ghazal, and pass the summer to the north in the Darfur. Little is known about them.[26]

BAGGARA, or *Baqqara*

Their name means "cattle raisers" and so could be applied to a number of groups. They live in southern Darfur and southern Kordofan, Sudan, to the south of the *Kababish*. They are a related group of Arab peoples who have intermarried with Nubians. They have a prejudice about having a lighter skin. The Baggara consist of the *Rizaygat* and *Taaisha* in Darfur, and the *Homr, Hawazma, Messiriyyah* and *Selima* in southern Kordofan. Their territory was defined by natural and political factors at the beginning of the twentieth century.

Nomadism

Each tribe is divided into clans, down to subgroups called *surras* or camps, which travel together. Each man has his own herd and the *surras* are flexible in composition. They can divide up because of limited pasture, or families can leave and join another. Cattle are the center of the life of the Baggara and provide most of the diet of milk and meat; only the cattle about to die of disease or age are slaughtered. The cattle also provide transport for the family, are self-propagating and self-transporting, and are a form of currency for all sorts of business between the Baggara. They are also the only basis of social status, for the size of the herd decides the influence of the man and his family. Any cash from other business is spent on obtaining more cattle. This preoccupation with herd quantity rather than quality, for motives of social status, is causing severe overcrowding on the limited pastures. Since they do, however, believe in having sleek cattle, keeping some bulls as symbols of quality, it may be possible to change attitudes.

A large herd confers status because it implies that the owner is a skilled stock manager, and it gives a man the means to be hospitable and to influence business. The men carry a spear and an amulet containing portions of the *Qur'an* at all times. The women have an important role in the camps and neither veil themselves nor are segregated (as with the Bedouin Arabs).[27] They migrate southwards in December with their cattle herds and return northwards in April, to arrive in their most permanent camps in June where the women cultivate millet while the men take the herd further north.

Homr (sg. *Homrawi*) are the largest and most conservative of the Baggara; they number 55,000 and live in the Dar el Homr, between El Fula and Bentiu in southern Kordofan, central Sudan. They claim in their traditions to have come from Arabia, crossing the Red Sea and the Nile to settle south of the Sahara. They remained mobile for a long time to avoid falling under the power of the Sultans, and only established themselves in Kordofan in about 1775, attacking other Baggara tribes in the process. They are divided into two sub-tribes, the *'Ajaira* and *Felaita*, which in turn have five clans each, and today the clan leaders are paid by the Sudan government to maintain order.

The *Homrawi* lives and works as part of a group of related families called a *surra*, or camp. The camp itself consists of a circle of domed portable huts. His cattle provide his self-sufficiency and his skills as a herdsman determine his survival and status in the group. His ability with cattle also attracts women to become his wives. Marriage is commonly between cousins, or at least within the *surra*, and the wives have responsibility for milking and making butter, that is sold in the markets. The *Homrawi* will work for others in their fields to earn cash. They prefer to invest this in more cattle, rather than in other goods. This leads to the threat of overgrazing.[28]

The *surras* spend the summer in the north between El Muglad and El Fusa. Fortunately this is the rainy season to replenish the pasture, because space is restricted and the grazing has to be shared. They migrate via Muglad to the south of the town, where they harvest the crops of millet that they sowed earlier on the way north. They take the journey further south slowly over a number of weeks. The herds use the pasture en route and they wait for the insects to die down in the southern pasture. In the Bahr el Ghazal, where they stay from December until spring, each *surra* bases itself near its own well for the dry season.

Hawazma: This is a confederation of two tribes — the *Halafa* in eastern Kordofan, Sudan and the *Hawazma* proper in central districts of Southern Kordofan. Among the Hawazma there are nomadic pastoralists, settled agropastoralists and those beginning to settle as well as those restarting nomadism — apart from those settled in towns who also form part of a constantly changing social network. More than half of the Hawazma have settled as farmers or government workers in the towns.

There is a constant interchange between the sedentary families visiting the nomadic groups and the nomads who are settling. Most of the settled farmers have small herds of about 20 cows, as well as other small livestock. There are young men of the settled families who are seeking to return to pastoralism by building up their own herds. They form temporary groups who will herd their livestock north during the rainy season, leaving their wives to tend the crops. Often they do not have the experience of the nomads, and it can be a risky business. But if a man is successful, his wife may join him on migration and become part of a new nomadic group attempting to establish itself. This is a clear case of some sedentary pastoralists returning to nomadism, while others stay settled. The nomads can leave their children with sedentary relatives for education. The arrangement gives security for when either cultivation or pastoralism fails.

Society

A camp is called a *fariq* and consists of a number of families. The camp members are closely related, although unrelated families are often incorporated as equal members. The members often intermarry, and they co-operate in pastoral tasks and are expected to be loyal to each other. The layout of the camp is circular, symbolizing the egalitarian relationship between the men. A man leads each family with a number of tents managed by wives or sisters with the younger children. Within the circle of tents there are *kraals* of thornbushes constructed by each family. In the center is a meeting place for the men. Portable wedding and mourning houses made of sticks and thatch are situated outside the tents. Most of the nomadic lineages have at least one family that remains all the year in camps, to take care of their crops in their absence.

From this central camp they make journeys to rainy and dry season pastures in different directions. The pastoralist families have on average herds of 100 cows and more sheep and goats, and usually only those with more than 30 cattle, in addition to sheep and goats, migrate. Oxen, donkeys and camels are used for transport. The migration routes have to be scouted first as not only do the water supply and grass growth have to be checked, but also the cultivated areas and barriers due to water courses have to be avoided. The Hawazma spend the long dry season of the year in camps near permanent sources of water on the clay plains of the Nuba Mountains in southern Kordofan.

For the rainy season, from July to September, the nomadic pastoralist camps move north to the sandy soils south of El-Obeid, North Kordofan. The journey takes about six weeks, and the return takes three weeks. Five different routes are used, taking advantage of the paved roads and watering places. The Hawazma also plant crops of sorghum, sesame and cowpea along the route at the beginning of the rains, and they harvest them on the return at the end of the rainy season.

Religion

The Hawazma have a close relationship with their livestock and their values are a mixture of beliefs and myths about cattle and Muslim ideology.[29]

FELLATA, *Fulfulde* or *Fulani*

This group lives close to the Baggara in southern Darfur. There are 90,000 Fulbe or Fulani Na'i in western Sudan. They are an offshoot of the *M'bororo*. Many speak Arabic as well Fulfulde. The Bible in the Fellata dialect of Fulfulde was available from 1983.

DINKAS

There are 320,000 in southern Sudan, divided into 20 tribes that live in an area of 250,000 square kilometers.[30] There are four major groups: 400,000 Padang; 250,000 Bor; 250,000 Agar; 450,000 Rek (total 2 million).[31]

Nomadism

Cattle predominate in their culture, with each man having a favorite ox. They see parallels between the lives of the cattle and humankind. A man's identity is wrapped up in his ox, so that the status of his manhood depends on the ox's presence in the herd. Without cattle, a man has no place in society. He can neither marry, appease the dead, nor settle disputes and debts. People without cattle, like missionaries, are considered to be almost subhuman. The cattle have rights and are not considered property. They are slaughtered as sacrifices and only secondly for food. The Dinka do

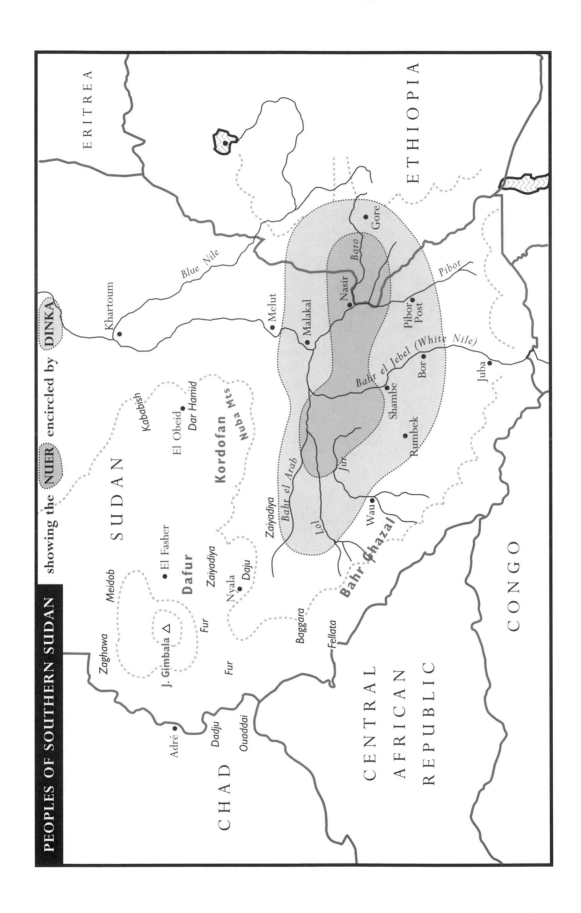

PEOPLES OF SOUTHERN SUDAN   showing the   NUER   encircled by   DINKA

ERITREA

ETHIOPIA

Khartoum

Blue Nile

Melut

Malakal

Nasir

Baro

Gore

Pibor

Pibor
Post

Bahr el Jebel (White Nile)

Bor

Shambe

Rumbek

Juba

SUDAN

Kababish

El Obeid
Dar Hamid

Kordofan

Nuba Mts

Zaiyadiya

Bahr el Arab

Jur

Lol

Wau

Bahr el Ghazal

Meidob

El Fasher

Dafur

Zaiyadiya

Nyala
Daju

Zaghawa

J. Gimbala △

Fur

Fur

Adré

Dadju

Ouaddai

CHAD

Baggara

Fellata

CENTRAL

AFRICAN

REPUBLIC

CONGO

not rely entirely on cattle, however, but also grow millet and vegetables and catch fish.

They have permanent settlements of a few round huts near which, with the first rains from March to May, they plant their crops. They have few personal possessions. In June and July the swampy land near the rivers floods the pastures, causing the younger men to migrate with the herds. They build cattle camps where both men and younger animals are housed in temporary shelters, which are little more than windbreaks. The rain ends in October; some of the men return to help with the harvest and when this is gathered the cattle are brought back to the original pasture, with its new growth of fodder. November is the time when the Dinka gather together for religious, social and creative activity. But in January, as the homestead pastures are used up, the herders return to the rivers with the cattle.

Religion

The Dinka claim to know the universal deity called *Nhialic*, who they say is also the Nuers' Kuoth, the Muslim Allah and the Christian God. But it is to the lesser gods, such as Deng, Garang, Macardit and Abuk, or, among the Agar Dinka, a key deity called Loi, to whom sacrifice is made. Some of these gods are not known by all the Dinka. These deities can only be active when invoked by their correct names. Men called "masters of the fishing spear" have hereditary functions like priests and often are buried alive so as to continue their powers after death. There are also seers, or *tyet*, who claim to be divine. G. Lienhardt was able to demonstrate that a seer whom he and his companions consulted was predicting general events from information he had picked up in conversation. A *ran wal*, or medicine man, sells fetishes like bundles of roots and twigs, which are considered powerful medicine against a man's enemies. The power of it is supposed to threaten a man with evil consequences unless he puts right his alleged wrong deeds.[32]

The Dinkas have led the southern rebel coalition against the Muslim government of the north. In 1992 the Nuer and others rebelled against this leadership, allowing the government army to advance as far as Juba. In 1995 the Dinkas were again leading the rebel coalition and aiming for independence, rather than for a secular Sudan, with the help of northern rebels. Their society is structured according to the cattle camp, with families working together as convenient. A number of these camps form larger camps that in turn form the sub-tribes.

They are animist, with 4% Christian and 1% Muslim. The Padang, Bor and Agar have Bible portions. The Dinka Padang translation of the Old Testament is 14% complete.[33] The Rek New Testament translation is underway by SIL.[34] The Dioceses of Bor, Rumbek and Wau of the Episcopal Church in the Province of the Sudan are largely Dinka.[35] ACROSS works with both local churches and Action Partners. SIM and Sudan Interior Church are also involved with the Dinka. A radio broadcast in Dinka has been broadcast since 1996.

NUER

The Dinka call these near neighbors Nuer, but they call themselves Naath ("people"). They number 40,000 in Ethiopia and 740,000 in Sudan.[36]

The Nuer are surrounded by a ring of Dinka groups. They have so many cultural similarities with the Dinkas that it has been suggested that internal conflict among the Dinkas led to a differentiation giving rise to the Nuer about 400 years ago — or perhaps much earlier.[37] Both the Dinka and the Nuer consist of so many separate groups that it is not clear how far they see themselves as one people.

Society

The tribes tend to consider themselves distinct communities. They are divided into clans and lineages, the latter taking responsibility to administer grazing and migration. As there is no overall authority to arbitrate, disputes tend to be decided by conflict at the local level. Feuds are therefore common. Compensation is the basis for settling disputes. The local courts are now said to take over arranging settlements. On marriage, cattle are given in exchange for a bride to her family.

Nomadism

The Nuer share with the Dinka a basin of grasslands in southern Sudan that has natural barriers of the desert in the north and woodland to the southwest, south and east which makes grazing difficult and harbors cattle diseases. The Nuer are enclosed in a smaller area than the Dinkas' more open situation, and so they are forced to use pasture more efficiently. This means they can move less and require more co-operation between themselves.

Each family owns its own cattle. The Nuer's status and interest is in their cattle, and they despise those without them. A boy is initiated into manhood by parallel scars being cut on his forehead. An ox is given to him as his companion and he leaves behind the world of his mother, of milking and domestic chores. To marry and to count cattle is expressed by the same word, because the bride-price in cattle gives the women her worth.

The center of their land is around Lake No, which is often flooded from June to August. Except for those living in a few scattered villages on higher ground, the people have to move to avoid the floods. In late August, as the floods recede, the tall grass is burned to encourage new growth. In the dry season the clay soil retains sufficient water for the cattle to graze. The herds tend to stay near the rivers that still have water. When this pasture is used up they travel across the plains to find grass. In this season the milk diet has to be supplemented by hunting and fishing. As the floods return the herds are moved to the higher ground further from the rivers and near the villages, if possible.

Religion

Many Dinka have been assimilated to the Nuer, including sharing their religious myths and rituals. These involve "the spirits of the air" or *diel*. *Kuoth nhial*, the god of the sky, is the supreme deity associated with breath or blowing. The other gods, or *kuth*, include the snake deities Lual and Deng. To atone for sin, a sheep will be cut in two by a prophet. The prophet and prophetess claim to have trances while dancing to reveal the divine will to appease the gods and have the power to heal. The dead can demand sacrifices or even levirate marriage. As spirits, the dead can communicate with the living through dreams.[38]

Outreach

United Presbyterians have been involved with the Nuer for most of the twentieth century. There are dozens of churches among them. The first translation of Bible is in print.[39] Since the 1960s, the Muslim government has driven Christians into exile. A Christian radio broadcast in Nuer started in 1996. The Salvation Army was involved in redeeming Nuer Christians sold as slaves to northern Sudan in 2000.

MURLE

There are 60,000 in Sudan and 6,000 in Ethiopia. In Sudan they are cattle nomads and live in hills along the Pibor River, near the border with Ethiopia. This is a very remote area, but even so it has been greatly disturbed by the civil war in Sudan. They constantly raid the Anyuak agricultural communities in Ethiopia for cattle, fishing and even children. A Bible translation project began in 1976, and a team from a number of missions has provided medical and veterinary services and literacy classes as well as evangelism. The civil war disrupted the work, the missionaries were taken hostage for a few months, and the translation was finished in Kenya. A church has been formed among them. New Testament and Scripture Gift Mission portions are available.[40]

TOPOSA

There are 95,000 who are semi-nomadic pastoralists in southeastern Sudan, and 10,000 living in the southwestern tip of Ethiopia. They inhabit a swampy plain in the Eastern Equatorial Province. A Bible translation is progressing and two sets of evangelistic cassettes are available.

Non-Pastoral Nomadic Peoples of the Eastern Sahel

AZZA or *Haddad*

These are a people or an artisan caste among the Toubou. They are scattered in small groups among both the Daza and Teda, working as potters, rope makers, weavers and tanners. There are also smiths who, like other artisans, live in scattered groups in different parts of the north of Chad — but about a quarter of them live in Kanem. The Teda consider iron to have a magical quality that offers protection from demons. The Azza are also butchers, dyers, tanners and shoemakers, minstrels, orators and weavers. Briggs treats them as a caste in Toubou society, and he is particularly describing the Teda in Tibesti. He says they are more integrated with the clans that they serve among the Teda and Daza, although even those who live among the Teda of Tibesti speak Dazaga. But this language seems to be a lingua franca among all the Toubou group of peoples. Weeks and Godbold consider them a distinct people. Traditionally, they wear leather clothes or a leather belt with a fringe as a sign of their caste. The term seems to also include the minstrels and hunters. They are both despised for their occupations and feared for their contact with the spirits.[41]

EAST AFRICA

This area includes Ethiopia, Eritrea, Somalia, Kenya, Tanzania and Uganda. We add southern Africa to this region for convenience. This is the area of the world in which we find the greatest number of nomadic cattle pastoralists. Cattle are bred here for social rather than for commercial or subsistence reasons. The permanent camps developed because of the need to have kraals to keep the cattle from the large predators common in the region. This permanence also gives opportunities for supplementary cultivation. ODI lists the following numbers for pastoralists: 1,600,000 in Ethiopia;[1] 1,700,000 in Somalia; 1,500,000 in Kenya; 500,000 in Angola; 14,000 in Botswana; 100,000 in Tanzania (Maasai only).

Ethiopia appears to have the greatest number of domestic livestock in Africa, and 40% of the land area is pasture. Fifty-seven per cent of the land in Eritrea is suitable for pastoralism, and another 3.6% of the total land area is suitable for agriculture. Pastoralism is the main way of life in 11 districts of Kenya. These districts represent about 70% of the land area but support only 8% of the population. There are 3.5 million pastoralists in Kenya occupying the northern half of the country and in the south and west. The Kenya Pastoralist Forum was founded in 1994 to urge that development and relief be evenly spread so as to help the pastoral north of the country.[2]

Nomadic Pastoralists of East Africa

'AFAR or *Danakil*

They are semi-nomadic pastoralists and settled village dwellers divided between Djibouti (170,000), Ethiopia (450,000), Somalia (488,000) and Eritrea (300,000).[3] They prefer to be called 'Afar, which means "the best" or "first," and they consider the term Danakil derogatory. They probably came from Arabia but have been in the Danakil desert for ten centuries. They have been able to maintain their independence; the Italian invasion of Ethiopia never defeated the 'Afar. Most of the 'Afar now live in towns. The 'Afar are divided into the *Asahiyamara* (*Asiemba*), or "reds," in the region of Assayita, and the *Adohiyamara* (*Asiemra*), or "whites," living deeper in the desert. Those living along the coast combine fishing and trading to Yemen with keeping sheep and goats.

Nomadism

The 'Afar form *kedos*, or herding groups, consisting of a number of related families. They usually have more goats than sheep, but they still need mutton for the Muslim feasts. The Somalis, on the other hand, tend to have more sheep than goats. In Ethiopia, the 'Afar spend the time of rains, from November to February, on the higher ground just below the escarpment to avoid the mosquitoes and mud. They move down as the flood abates until they are settled around their permanent water sources to await the rains again. In Djibouti, the 'Afar practice a horizontal nomadism, going short distances in different directions according to the pasture and rainfall. Many have been helped to use their water resources better for vegetable gardens and some now grow grass as fodder.

Society

In the camp, each wife or mother is the head of her own household and lives in a domed hut called an *'ari*, made of palm-frond mats covering curved stems of the palm leaf. The hut is made by all the women and given to a new bride on her marriage. When this hut is reassembled on a new site, the hut's contents are laid out on the ground first in the position that they occupy inside, then the hut is assembled over them by the woman owner. Most women are married at the age of fourteen and to cousins so that little or no bride-price, with the subsequent loss of herd stock, is necessary. There is a very high divorce rate. The women usually milk the goats, make the ghee, or butter, and lead in music-making by singing and drumming. The women also collect firewood and water.

A man's prestige depends on his bravery and livestock. Status among the 'Afar is assigned according to how many people a warrior has killed, because war is fundamental to their way of life. Bravery in circumcision, hunting and warfare are measures of prestige and virility for marriage. When the boys are circumcised, they gain as many cows or bulls whose names they are able to call out, in spite of the pain. The 'Afar tend to be suspicious and reserved, even of other 'Afar they do not know. The clans are competitive, and constant feuds and conflict have been common. The scarcity of water at the end of the dry season is one of the most frequent causes of friction. Quite often the animals will be watered before the families. The only collective decision to be made is when to migrate. While pasture is shared, water sources are owned exclusively by each clan and jealously guarded. Groups of warriors called *fi'ma* have a detached existence guarding the herds and water holes. The men always herd and milk the camels.

The 'Afar trade livestock with the Galla or Oromo agriculturists in the highlands, who keep dairy cattle. Many trade salt from Lake Karum in the Danakil Depression for grain grown in the highlands. Salt becomes more valuable the farther one goes inland into Ethiopia, and young 'Afars are in effect peripatetic camel caravaners. The 'Afar use their male camels only as pack animals, and they never ride them unless they are too sick to walk.

The **Harsu**, who live in the foothills, are probably of 'Afar origin, and they act both as hired herders for the Galla and as trade intermediaries between the two peoples. The total number of speakers of the language include 400,000 in Ethiopia and Eritrea and 300,000 in Djibouti.[4] The groups of blacksmiths traveling with them appear to be outcasts from other clans, but they do not follow 'Afar customs.

Religion

The 'Afar are Muslim but have an elaborate ritual system involving the right and the left. The right signifies "clean" and "male," and the left signifies "unclean" and "female." There are no Christians among them. The RSMT translation of the New Testament was published in 1994, and the first draft of the Old Testament is complete.[5] A hymnbook and cassettes are available. The RSMT have established clinics in three towns, with visits traveling out from them. An agricultural project has been carried out as well. The Southern Baptists are also working in Ethiopia, TEAR Fund has helped them with projects, and the 'Afar can hear a daily broadcast from FEBA Radio. There is a Christian witness among them in Djibouti.

RASHEIDA, or *Rashaida*

The Rasheida are nomadic Arabs with camels and goats. They migrated from Saudi Arabia in 1846, under the leadership of a man called Rasheid. They are distributed along the Red Sea coast of Eritrea and the estimates of their numbers vary between 3,500 and 10,000. They used to use their camels as pack animals and walk alongside them, rather than ride them. Today they carry the sheep and goats to the pasture in pickups, and the male camels are kept more for prestige. The female camels are kept for milk and to increase the herd. The Rasheida camp with just a blanket or sheet on poles

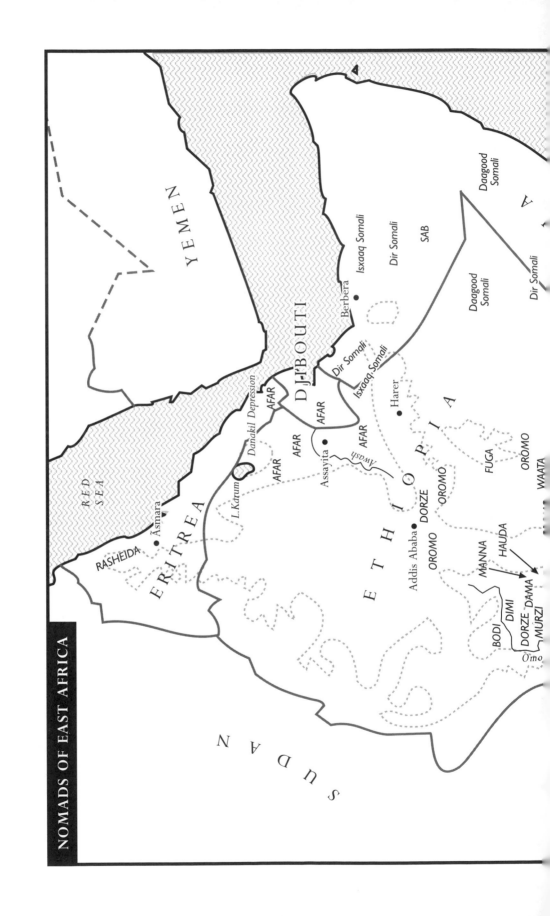

NOMADS OF EAST AFRICA

YEMEN

RED
SEA

Daagood
Somali

Isxaaq Somali

Dir Somali

SAB

Daagood
Somali

Dir Somali

Berbera

DJIBOUTI

Dir Somali

Isxaaq Somali

Harer

ETHIOPIA

FUGA

OROMO

WAATA

AFAR

Danakil Depression

AFAR

AFAR

AFAR

OROMO

Awash

AFAR

Assayita

L.Katum

OROMO

DORZE

HAUDA

ERITREA

Āsmara

Addis Ababa

OROMO

MANNA

RASHEIDA

BODI

DIMI

DORZE-DAMA

MURZI

Omo

SUDAN

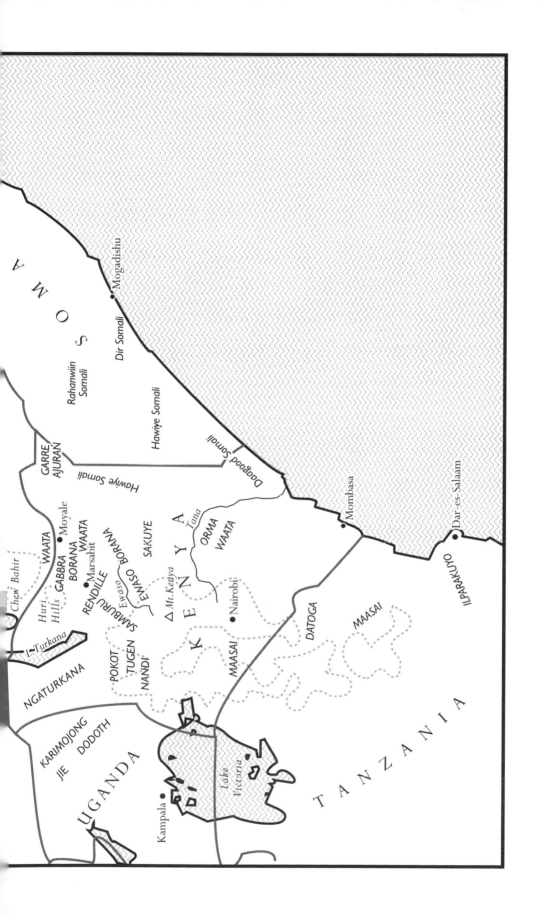

13a

13b

13 Rashaida:
   a. The Rashaida live in a very arid part of Eritrea (Photo: M Hunter).
   b. A Rashaida family group in their tent.

(as a windbreak or shade). They are an extroverted people, although they keep themselves to themselves and have not assimilated. The political changes in the region, however, are making them more open to outside influence. They speak their own version of Arabic and Scripture portions on cassettes are available. RSMT had two clinics during the 1970s, but since then the Kale Heywet Church of Eritrea has worked among them.

SOMALIS

They may have traveled from Yemen in the seventh century AD to settle in their present area. The name is derived from Arabic and means "wealthy," that is, in livestock and especially camels. There are 290,000 Somalis still living in Yemen, mainly in camps near Aden. Today there are over 7,000,000 Somalis — the majority live in Somalia, with 2,000,000 in Ethiopia, 380,000 in Kenya, 180,000 in Djibouti and about 30,000 on the border of Tanzania. Culturally and linguistically they are related to the 'Afar and Oromo and Borana.[6]

History and distribution

Each Somali belongs to one of five major clan confederations. The *Dir*, consisting of the *Esa* and *Gadabursi* clans, are scattered throughout the four countries. The *Daagood* are the largest clan and are situated in northeastern Somalia and the neighboring Ogadan, Ethiopia and southern Ethiopia and northeastern Kenya. The *Isxaaq* are found in northeast Somalia, Djibouti and Ethiopia. The *Rahanwiin* live in southern Somalia. The *Hawiye* also live in southern Somalia and Ethiopia and northeastern Kenya. They partly mix with two other confederations of clans called Digil and Rahanwin, who are of more mixed descent and are primarily cultivators in the southern third of Somalia between the Shabeelle and Jubba rivers. Because they are farmers, the pastoralist majority calls them Sab, although the term is used elsewhere and by northern Somalis to refer to itinerant hunters and craftsmen.

These major confederations have little political cohesion, as they are nomadic groups by practice and tradition. The elders or adult males lead each clan, and central leadership with a chief is rare. This makes Somalia unstable as a nation, and is an example of the decentralization and democratic structures that nomadic pastoralism creates. The nation's symbol, a five-pointed star, alludes to other divisions caused by colonialism rather than by the clan confederations. Tensions between these groups caused the United Nations to intervene militarily during 1993-94, to attempt to bring peace between the three warring factions. The north of the country declared its autonomy and a few countries are beginning to recognize it as Somaliland.

a) Somalia

The differences between the northern and southern Somalis create a culture of disdain and mistrust. The *northern Somali* constitute 77.5% of Somalia's population, and two factors have shaped their culture: nomadic pastoralism, as the only feasible means of livelihood in this arid area, and their adoption of Islam in the tenth century. In contrast, the *southern Somali* have mixed with the agricultural Bantu between the Jubba and Shabeelle Rivers, and this has led to a different lifestyle than in the north. In the extreme south of Somalia two groups, the *Maxamed Zubeer* and the *Herti*, moved in to establish a partnership in exporting livestock out of the region, which illustrates how international trade affects pastoralism. The Maxamed Zubeer of the Ogaadeen clan occupy a large section of land stretching into Kenya to the west. They have dominated the southern part of Somalia for a century, having forced out the Orma to become the main cattle herders of the region. The Herti are camel herders with experience in trading, and after a period of conflict they settled in the ports and formed commercial alliances with their former enemies. The trade builds up local herds to provide beef for the local market and for export. In the 1980s they exported both Kenyan and Somali cattle to Saudi Arabia. They lost this market to cheaper Australian exports, but they compensated for the loss by building a trade exporting to Egypt and Yemen, and then to Kenyan markets.[7]

b) Ethiopia

Somalis in Ethiopia are represented by clans such as the *Ogaadeen* (4,000) and the *Murille* (4,000). Somalis in Djibouti total 215,000, divided between the *Issa* (103,000), the *Gadaboursi* (48,000) and the *Issaq* (41,000).

c) Kenya

Somalis represent a third of all pastoralists in Kenya, totaling 400,000 there, according to the 1979 census. They form about 90% of the population in the districts of Mandera, Wajir and Garissa, along the eastern border with Somalia and Ethiopia. Kenyans see them as a threat and in 1989 the Somalis were forced to register as residents without full citizenship.[8] The *Ajuran*, one of five divisions of the *Hawiye*, number 17,100. They migrate in groups of loosely related families, with their herds of camels, sheep and cattle. Few of them can read, but evangelistic cassettes are available. The Mennonites and Anglicans are involved, with their work among the Gabbra establishing a base for further work.[9]

The *Gurreh* are another clan of the *Hawiye* and total 30,000, but this number includes many who have intermarried with the Borana. Sixty per cent are nomadic pastoralists, and they are similar to the northern Somalis. There are 400,000 in refugee camps in northern Kenya.[10] The *Degodia* are another group of Somalis in northern Kenya totaling 40,000. They are the wealthiest of the Somali group with the largest herds. Conversions due to hearing the gospel on cassettes have taken place mostly among this group. Their Sunni belief in the return of Isa or Jesus contributed to the conversions.[11]

d) Tanzania

There are about 34,000 Somalis in Tanzania, in the Maasai country around the border town of Namanga. They have many camels and probably consider themselves to be in Kenya. The Moravian Missions have an interest in this group. There is also a group west of Lake Natron, to the west of Namanga, who are considered raiders and formerly of the Somali army.[12]

Nomadism

The Somali men rear camels and prize them as their wealth, and only in more favorable conditions do they keep cattle, sheep and goats. The women and children herd the sheep and goats. The Garre and Gaaljacel clans have developed marketing for their camels' milk, which has integrated them into the national economy of southern Somalia.[13] They continue to be nomadic, seeking pasture and traveling in groups of related families forming a reer, or camp. In the rainy season the herds can be kept near the camp because of the greater amount of pasture. This is the season for relaxation and ceremonies, such as marriages. As a Muslim, a Somali man may take up to four wives, but there is a distinction of status between the wives. With his first wife and her children he forms what they call the "great house," and the other wives the "little house."

Religion

The Somali Bible was translated in 1979, but there are only 1,000 copies in circulation. The *Jesus* film is available in Somali. There has been a SIM radio program in Somali for over 20 years, from Nairobi and FEBA, and many letters and correspondence courses have been received. This mission needed more staff in 1995. AIM has seconded SIM workers in Garba Tula, Lokichogio, Moyale and Wajir, and is forming a Training and Outreach team. There are about 2,000 Somali Christians, who have been persecuted in Somalia. Lokichogio was once a small village with a church, dispensary and primary school, but it has now become the main base for sending supplies into southern Sudan.[14]

BODI or *Podi*

Pastoralists in southwest Ethiopia, they live on the bend of the Omo River to the north of the Mursi, whom they call *Dama*. The Bodi have a history of attacking and raiding all the surrounding peoples, to replenish their herds that die from quite common diseases. All the men are obliged to participate, and they leave no survivors among those they attack. But the Mursi eventually drove the Bodi out of their southern pastures on the east bank of the Omo and, in the 1970s, a war between them resulted in their retreat from the Mara valley as well. Gofa and Wallayta evangelists have proclaimed the gospel to the Bodi for many years, as have Western missionaries on occasional visits to them. The Bodi killed a Dimi evangelist in 1990 and Nana Shaga, an evangelist from the Wolayta people, was stabbed to death by a Bunna in 1991, while working among the Bodi. The Bodi speak Me'en, a language related to Mursi, which they share with their neighbors, the Tisheni farmers. The chronological method has been instrumental in the salvation of thousands of these farmers. Many of these farmers are now Christians and there is hope that one day the Bodi might be evangelized by their witness. SIM and WBT are working closely together, and the Bible translation is progressing.[15]

DIMI or *Dime*

The Dimi live in Kefa, Ethiopia, near the Omo River and next to the Bodi. They now number only 2,100, due to untreated diseases. SIM established a medical clinic at Bako in 1954, where a dying Dimi patient made the first gospel recordings in this language. Meanwhile the man's father had a dream about the "the Word of Life" coming to the Dimi. A Dimi evangelist was martyred by the Bodi people in 1990.[16] There are also Aari and Gofa evangelists among them. There are three churches among this nomadic people, but they have no Scripture in their own language and the people are not bilingual.

MURSI

The Mursi call themselves *Mun*, and there are between 6,000 and 7,000 of them situated in southwest Ethiopia between the Omo and Mago rivers. They were until recently a relatively remote nomadic people, never subjected to invaders or taxation. Now

both government and tourism are entering the area. They are related to the *Chai*, across the Omo to the west. Many of the Chai have taken up residence among the Mursi because of famine and warfare. The Mursi seem to have moved to this area during the late eighteenth century, crossing the Omo from the hills they call Dirka in the west. They could not settle on the western bank of the Omo because it becomes waterlogged during the rainy season. They crossed the river and displaced the Kwegu, a hunter-gatherer people, and fooled the first European explorers in the area by hiding their cattle to give the impression they were hunters, because their herds were weak due to an outbreak of rinderpest.

The Mursi are divided into three tribal groups or *buranyoga* (sg. *buran*), called **Dola** (with three sub-divisions of about 1,500 each), **Ariholi** (500) and **Gongulobibi** (1,000). These groups move about the territory, but they are distributed in this order from north to south along the Omo River in the dry season. They practice not only cattle pastoralism, but also flood cultivation and shifting hill cultivation, all in an annual cycle.

Nomadism

Pastoralism shapes the Mursi men's thinking. They are so fond of their cattle that if a man is not fascinated by them he is considered delinquent. But they depend on two forms of agriculture worked by their women. Rainfall is very erratic, and in most years water is found only in the Omo and Mago rivers. They occupy the bank of the Omo in the dry season, and in the rainy season they cultivate the grassland valleys of tributaries. They have no permanent settlements or huts.

The Omo River floods in August and refertilizes the riverbanks, which are more reliable for cultivation than the hill clearing crops. When the floods recede in September, the Mursi families divide and live apart from September to February. The women and girls live on the riverbanks tending the fields of sorghum, planted in narrow strips along the riverbank. This can be harvested in about

14a

14b

14c

14 Bunna and Mursi:
   a. A group of the Bunna children (Photo: M. Hunter).
   b. Mursi have a precise division of labour — the men have cattle (Photo: M. Hunter).
   c. Mursi women preparing a meal (Photo: M. Hunter).

ten weeks. Each *buran* of the Mursi occupies different flood cultivation areas along some 80-100 kilometers (50-60 mi.) of the Omo River.

Meanwhile, the men and boys take the cattle to grasslands in the Arichukgirong and Dara Hills, and the Elma Valley in between, some 15-25 kilometers (10-15 mi.) away. The cattle cannot be kept on the flood plain near the Omo because of the tsetse fly. They live in temporary camps, depending on the milk, blood and meat of their cattle for a major part of their diet.

In March the main rains come. The whole period until November, when a second period of rains fall, is called the wet season. This is the beginning of the Mursi year and migration cycle they call *bergu*. The people come together, the women and girls moving inland to the valleys of some seasonal tributaries of the Omo and the men moving the cattle westwards down from the hills to within walking distance of the fields. These tributaries only contain water for about two weeks during the rains. But the rains vary considerably, and the Mursi have to create new fields by clearing the scrub about every four to six years. The places of recent rainfall give sufficient pasture and a second crop of sorghum. This means that during these months all the people can benefit from the milk of the cattle. June is the time for social gatherings such as weddings.

In September they split up again, the women to cultivate their strips on the east bank of the Omo and the men to graze cattle on the grasslands. Before leaving at the beginning of the rains, the Mursi burn off the last year's growth, to allow fresh grass to grow in the Elma Valley. If this is a success the cattle may find enough pasture. Otherwise, the shortage of water in the hills often means they have to bring the herds down to the tsetse-infested Omo Valley.

These seasonal nomadic separations mean that the fortunes of their economic activity increasingly determine the composition of their social groups, rather than family ties or descent. The Mursi come together to discuss co-operative actions,

such as defense against cattle thieves. Otherwise, the people tend to live separately with their herds.[17]

History

The whole period since 1970 has been one of tension; the Mursi have now acquired automatic weapons. A conflict with the Bunna was resolved by them "eating each other's cows together" in peace ceremonies.[18] Some of the Dola Mursi occupied the Mago River Valley, to the east of the Mursi pasture grasslands, which was Bodi territory in the 1970s. Other Mursi occupied the valley of the Mara to the north. These action provoked war with the Bodi to the north in 1952, 1971-75, and again in 1997-98. The Mara has become the boundary between these two pastoral peoples, as 200 Mursi have settled there. But these Mursi have had to leave their cattle in the grasslands, to be herded by others, because of the tsetse.

The Mursi are an example of a pastoralist society undergoing successive adaptations to changing conditions. They use two forms of cultivation with transhumant pastoralism and only about 20% of their subsistence comes from their cattle, because of the low numbers of cattle for the population. Many of the Mursi died in the famines of the 1970s and, when the cultivation fails, their survival depends on exchanging cattle for food. The rains for the second crop along the tributaries often fail, and space for new clearings for the shifting crop cultivation is running out. The areas fertilized by the floods of the Omo are also getting smaller because the level of Lake Turkana, into which the river runs, has been falling over the last 100 years. These lower floods also result in valuable dry season pasture by the Omo being lost because of the growth of dense thickets of bush. This is why the Mursi will need to continue to adapt their methods of survival.

Religion

The Mursi follow their traditional religion. Their society is divided into age-sets and clans. Attempts to establish schools to teach

Amharic have failed, and only one person was literate in this language in 1998. SIM has a medical center on the Mago River. A meningitis epidemic on the grasslands in 1992 was successfully treated. Regular veterinary and medical visits are made to the herding camps, and there are ongoing attempts at literacy training. Another man was taught by SIM missionaries to read and write Mursi. His ability to communicate from cattle camps to the base on the Mago has created a new positive attitude towards education. Trials of other crops and projects to improve the cultivation areas are being carried out.[19] Evangelists of the *Aari*, a people in the hills to the east, are living in the area but are not free to travel among the Mursi.

DAMA, Dhuak, Suri or Surma

The Dama, numbering between 20,000 and 40,000, have a similar lifestyle to that of the Mursi as transhumant pastoralists and swidden agriculturists. They live in southwest Ethiopia, to the west of the Mursi. Language analysis is in progress and the Mekane Yesu Evangelical Lutheran Church is working among them.

HAMER and BANNA or *Bunna*

These are two distinct pastoral peoples, each totaling 25,000, in southwest Ethiopia. They live northeast of the northern end of Lake Turkana — the Hamer to the south, and the Banna to the north. They both speak the same language.

The Hamer women stay in the camp, each family cultivating a field of sorghum. The young men are often away with the cattle and goats in distant pastures until they marry. When they marry, both women and men are counted as "elders," and the men describe their time as divided between their wives in camp and their favorite ox in the pastures, and between a grain diet in camp and a milk and blood diet with the cattle. Two African evangelists, both called Peter, who had worked with the Mursi, were killed by the Hamer.

The Banna have been evangelized for about 30 years by SIM. Two veterinary doctors from SIM and national evangelists of the Aari, an agricultural people to the north of the Banna, are working with them. There may be the beginnings of about eight different churches. Cassettes and records are available, and a Bible translation is underway.

ARBORE

The Arbore are a small people, numbering about 5,000, situated to the east of the Hamer-Banna and north of Lake Chew Bahir, Ethiopia.

DAASANICH or Daasanetch, *Merille, Glena, Reshiat,* or *Shanhilla*

They live along the lower reaches of the Omo River and the northern end of Lake Turkana, south of the Hamer-Banna. There are 27,500 in Ethiopia and 2,500 in Kenya. The Turkana, who they have constantly attacked, call them the *Merille*. Shanhilla is their name in Amharic. They are composed of eight small people groups, both pastoralists and cultivators. In Kenya, they are mostly spear fishermen. The largest people are the *Inkabelo*, numbering 7,000.

Nomadism

The *Daasanich* are pastoralists who supplement their subsistence with agriculture and fishing. Their lifestyle is semi-nomadic, because cattle are central to their society as well as their survival. At birth and at every stage of life, their children receive gifts of livestock, each building up the basis of their status and wealth with a herd. A daughter is highly valued, and when she is seven or eight years old the ceremony of *dimi* is held, during which her father sacrifices a cow from his herd in order to increase her fertility. A man must kill many cows for his daughter, for this increases his prestige and status as an elder, even if it makes him poor.

The rains upstream in Ethiopia descend the Omo River and cause floods in the delta during October and November. As these floods recede they leave a fertile silt, so that the nomads can plant their crops of sorghum, millet and tobacco, and these are ready to harvest in April. During April and May further heavy rains herald the coming of the dry season again, and this is the time for the people's ritual sacrifices and feasting. These and the *dimi* have the effect of culling the herds, which must be made up by raiding and rustling from the Turkana, Gabbra and Rendille herds. During the dry season the men take the herds westwards for pasture.

Language

The Daasanich or Geleb language is a dialect of Ormo. The people practice both their traditional religion and Christianity. The transition from boy to manhood is by late circumcision and participation in raids. They take great pride in killing an enemy, and afterward perform a "cleansing" sacrifice during which scars are cut on their chests. SIL are involved with others in the Bible translation that should be available soon. In Ethiopia, the development projects started by missionaries were halted for a time by the Marxist government, but they have now been resumed. The SIM and its related Kale Heywet Church and African Inland Church have some believers among them.[20] Linguistic Recordings also have evangelistic cassettes available.

OROMO or *Galla*

In southern Ethiopia, this is a large group of peoples that may constitute between 25% and 40% of Ethiopia's population — about 15 million people. These peoples include the *Arusi* (1,330,000), *Guji* (380,000) and *Salale* (1,946,000). The 1,077,000 *Harer* people speak Eastern Oromo. The *Wellega* (8,000,000) speak another form of Oromo.

The Oromo originated as pastoralists in southern Ethiopia, but in the sixteenth century they took advantage of the conflict between the Christian Habesha kingdom and Muslim forces, and expanded northwards to occupy most of the highlands. Many of them became assimilated into the culture of those they encountered, took up agriculture, and some even married into the imperial family.[21] A feature of their society is the *gada*, or an organization of generations of men who are set into a hierarchy, each with rights and responsibilities in society.

The Oromo in different regions follow their traditional religions. Waka is considered the supreme deity, but Ataytay, the goddess of fertility, and the male god Astaro are important to the Oromos' lives. Ataytay is important to sick or barren women, for offerings are made to appease her and the blood of a sacrificed goat is poured over the woman, followed by a smearing of butter. Others, like the Harer and Arusi, have converted to Islam or to the Ethiopian Orthodox Church.

Outreach

There are only a few Oromo believers. Swedish and German Lutherans were the first to reach the Oromo, and today there is a church among the Wellega. There are about 30 small SIM-related congregations among the Arsi.[22] The 380,000 *Guji* follow their traditional religion. An old man among them had a vision about 50 years ago before any Christians arrived, of a road in the sky and white men coming. There are about 200 believers, although this small but significant growth has been at the cost of the martyrdom of an evangelist. A few of these believers have been trained as evangelists. SIM has also been involved in water supply projects among them.

BORANA or *Born*, Kenya and Ethiopia[23]

The Borana are one of the Oromo speaking groups, but the Borana do not consider the term "Oromo" as referring to themselves — to them it implies someone who is hostile. An opportunity to unite them inside what later became Kenya was lost when the border with Ethiopia was drawn by the British. The majority of the Borana, perhaps 150,000, live in Ethiopia. There are a number of groups among them, including a group recently identified by Malcolm Hunter as the *Wato Wando*. In Kenya, the Oromo peoples speak Southern Oromo, or "Gallq," and consist of 69,000 *Borana*; 30,500 *Gabbra*; and 6,500 of the *Sakuge* or *Sakuye* (see below).[24]

Nomadism

The Borana are cattle herders in a very arid area. They migrate constantly in small groups of 10 to 30 families, called *ollas*, to find pasture. An *olla* consists of households or *waaras* belonging to different clans. The *waaras*, or households, are usually economically independent — with the man managing the livestock and the wife responsible for the milking, food preparation and feeding the calves. She is also in charge of marketing dairy produce. The Borana keep camels and small stock as well, but they have a system of grazing that gives priority to the milking cattle over the other animals.

A number of *ollas* group together to share pasture and water resources. Like other East African pastoralists, they classify land according the water supply, vegetation and soil type as "camel country," "sheep country" or "cattle country." This, part of their conscious management of the land, can be disrupted by drought, by other tribes raiding the herds and by official and voluntary pressures to settle. The *olla* usually has a well-established system of gifts and loans to help the impoverished *waaras*, even to the point of self-denial themselves. This system is called *maaro*, or "mutual concern."[25] Restocking the herds of the poor is traditionally the clan's responsibility. The clan does this by asking its members to pledge animals to the poor member.

In Ethiopia, the Borana inhabit the southern area of Sidamo, which is formed by hills 1,000 meters (over 3,000 ft.) high in altitude, but the only river is the Dawa. The heavier rainfall occurs on the higher ground in two periods, from March to May and then from September to November, with cloud cover, fog and mists in between. In the dry season from November to March, cattle have to be brought to a well on at least every third day. The centuries-old wells are often very deep and have a ramp down which the cattle walk to get closer to the water level. The Borana go down the shaft in relays to lift the water up to troughs at the lower end of the ramp where the cattle can drink. In the 1990s the Somali Garre drove the Borana away from the wells, and this threatened their survival. The Garre speak Borana, indicating that they were once in close association with the Borana.[26] CARE International has repaired and reopened some of these wells.

The Borana moved south from Ethiopia into Kenya at the end of the nineteenth century. The Borana in Kenya reject the term Oromo for themselves, because they associate it with the Orma to the south of them. They are divided between the Northern or Obbu Borana around Debel and Moyale, and the Southern or Ewaso Borana in Merti and Garba Tula, with the Rendille in between. The Borana first settled in Wajir in northeast Kenya near the Somali border (although even when the border was fixed the Somalis did not necessarily respect it).

The *Ajuran* and *Garre* Somali tribes accepted the presence of the Borana as the water supply was plentiful, and they adopted the Borana language. The arrival of the Degodia, however, another Somali group, was too much and so the pasture and water supply became untenable for all of them. Because of this the Borana were resettled by the British, first in Buna to the north in 1908, and then in 1933 in the Ewaso region, which had once been occupied by the Samburu. In this way the Borana in Kenya became divided into two, and the Somalis spread westwards. This division also involved a division of religion.

The *Northern*, *Gutta* or *Obbu Borana* in Kenya inhabit the slopes of the Badha Escarpment that forms the natural border between Kenya and Ethiopia. For generations the herds have been able to cross the border for water and pasture, but in the 1990s this was being restricted. Because of drought and other difficulties, many *waara* now only have about ten head of cattle. These northern Borana have begun to diversify their resources and become market-oriented by selling milk in the markets in Sololo. They have also diversified to farming. Since the rains come between April and May and then between October and December, two crops a year are possible.

But the Borana, being pastoralists at heart, accept farming as only an opportunistic supplement to cattle. Many men have left to work in the south of the country.[27]

The **Ewaso Borana** were moved by the British in the 1930s from the northeast to the semi-arid pasture lands they inhabit. This area depends on the water from the slopes of Mount Kenya forming the Ewaso Nyiro River, crossing to the southwest. As the Somalis move westwards, they are encroaching upon their pasture. Yet during the 1960s, in the civil war between the Kenyan authorities and the Somalis, the Borana, surprisingly, sided with the Somalis. This is another example of pastoralists who would rather unite with their pastoral enemies than submit to the rule of farmers. Many of the Ewaso Borana were killed, their families died in concentration camps, and others lost their cattle. In the midst of these traumas they submitted to the Islam of the Somalis rather than to the nominal Christianity of the Kenyans. In 1979 there were 21,000 Borana in Eastern Province, of whom 41% were pastoralists.[28] Their adoption of Islam has also changed their marriage habits, since traditionally they were monogamous. Today, however, divorce and polygamy are common.[29]

Borana society is structured according to the Gada system of five generation groups, each of which consists of all males born over an eight-year period. According to this system a Borana cannot marry until his generation group has reached its thirty-second year, which is not necessarily his own age. A man is not permitted to have a son until his fortieth year, and the desire to keep these rules may result in infanticide or adoption outside the society. This system at least has the advantage of keeping the Borana population low.

Religion

The Borana believe in a supreme deity called Wak. Their priests, the *Qallu*, keep black cattle and are considered reincarnations of their first priest. According to the myths, the **Wata**, a hunter-gatherer people living in the mountains on the border with Ethiopia, discovered the first priest (see below) and secured his services for the Borana.[30]

Outreach

Christian outreach to the Borana started in 1931 in Marsabit. Borana culture requires older men to lead, so Gunnar Kjaerland developed a system of biblical pictures so that illiterate elders in Borana churches can tell biblical narratives, in a way similar to the storytelling that the Borana use to recall history. In this way the church is able to grow without the difficulty of teaching literacy to older people. The first complete Borana Bible was published in March 1995. A local man, David Diida, completed this translation after the translator died — but not without some difficulty. In the process of preparing the translation David survived a bus crash, was trampled and severely injured by an elephant, and was held up by robbers who stole his literacy materials. Fortunately, the robbers saw no value in learning to read, and the materials were later found.[31]

AIM International are working among the Borana in Garba Tula, Marsabit, Moyale and Wajir. Crosslinks has handed over to the Church of the Province of Kenya (CPK Anglican) and its work, which is largely self-supporting through Diocesan Missionary Associations. SIM also works among the Borana. There are about 6,000 Borana worshipping in 42 congregations of eight different denominations.

KARIMOJONG, or *Karamajong*

There are 370,000 Karimojong living in the northeast of the Karamojo District of Uganda. The men have a particular attachment to their cattle, and the people introduce symbols and allusions to their cattle into every aspect of life.[32] Each man has an ox name, prefixed with *apa*, meaning "father of." So, for example, *Apaloraianjiran* means "Father of the ox with the heavy horns."[33] His name gives a man adult status in Karimojong society as being responsible for the herd, but having the same name does not mean the man and the ox are identified with one another.

During the late 1980s, the Karimojong were noted for cattle raiding right across the north of Uganda, principally against the *Teso*, and into Kenya. Military forces were unable to contain them.[34] Agriculture is also important to them, and Barfield shows that they have a low ratio of cattle to people, compared to others who depend on their cattle more, but they are semi-nomadic. This also applies to the Jie and Dodoth, and all three peoples speak Karimojong.[35]

There are both Christians and those who follow their traditional religion — and there are no doubt some who have mixed the two. The Revised New Testament was published in 1996.[36] The local Anglican church now has responsibility for the former Crosslinks ministry.

DODOTH, or *Dodos*

The Dodoth are one of five peoples related to the Karimojong in northeast Uganda. There are a total of 370,000 Karimojong speakers. The Dodoth arrived in the area about 1000 AD. They have a decentralized society of cattle camps. The men grow their hair long and warrior status is important. They receive the name of the ox given them on initiation. Dodoth or Dodos is counted as a dialect of Karimojong, with 90% lexical similarity. They share a legend about creation that says that people originally lived in heaven with the Great God. Some remained in heaven, but others came to earth.[37]

JIE

There are 50,000 Jie. They are related to the Karimojong and speak their language. They practice their own traditional religion.

NGATURKANA or *Turkana*

There are 250,000 Ngaturkana living in the desert between Lake Turkana and the Uganda border, in northwest Kenya. They are one of the Karimojong or Ateker group of related peoples, which originated in northeastern Uganda. Their myths relate their claim to be descendants of a woman of the Jie people. There are 200,000 Turkana living in the Turkana and Samburu districts

of the extreme northwest of Kenya where, in 1979, they formed 96% and 17% respectively of the population. The Turkana have lived in this, the driest area in Kenya, for between 100 and 150 years.[38] In the early twentieth century, the British fought against them to stop them moving further south.

Nomadism

The Turkana are herders of cattle, but they also have camels, sheep and goats. They spend the rainy season on the plains and the dry season in the highlands. At the start of the dry season, they migrate in groups of about five nuclear families from the plains. They move progressively up the valleys into the hills, the cattle pasturing first, and the sheep and goats following to browse the same areas. During the dry season the herds have to be divided into smaller and smaller groups to find pasture, so that not only do the families separate from each other, but even the families themselves will be divided up as members take part of their stock to different pastures. As herds of camels, cattle, sheep and goats are kept by the same family, and have to be pastured in different areas, each family needs a number of herders. The cattle thrive on pasture in the higher grassland, while the camel herds keep to seasonal vegetation on the plains. Their territory contains about 67,000 square kilometers (42,000 sq. mi.) of sand and gravel plains in the Rift Valley.

The Turkana then migrate back to the valleys when the rains come, from April to July, and in a good year they will have more milk than they can drink. This is the season for social events, such as feasting, dancing and marriages, when the animals are corralled. It is also the time for calving and lambing. They supplement their diet with fast-growing sorghum cultivation and fishing.[39] When the milk runs out they will drink the blood of their animals. The poorer animals are slaughtered first, and the head of a goat is considered a delicacy. They are said on occasion to eat crocodile and lion meat.

After severe droughts in the 1980s the Turkana were able to successfully re-establish their nomadic pastoralism. Some of the poorer Turkana abandon pastoralism for the dry season. But the free food that was distributed as aid in the camps during the droughts had a bad social affect, according to Terrence McCabe.[40] Cattle stealing from other tribes, such as the Pokot, is common.

Society

The family is the most important social unit, and each individual family owns herds. The head of each family takes decisions about the pasturing, and family members are set out to scout for forage. They have no chiefs, and disputes are settled by discussion among the older men. Each section, or *ekitela*, has its own territory. While pasture is shared by the whole section, wells belong to the families that dig them. In the north the ground is more arid and the sections have to share their territories as they move greater distances to find adequate pasture.

Polygamy is encouraged, and for a man to have five wives is common. To have many children is considered necessary to be a successful pastoralist. In the camps, each woman has a daytime shelter and sleeps in a dome-shaped hut of skins called an *aki*. The women have responsibility for much of the security of the family, for providing the food and for caring for the livestock.[41] The children grow up with the animals and drink milk straight from the goats, which they also help herd. In contrast to other societies, a daughter is a source of wealth — for on marriage a bride-price of animals is demanded, thus increasing her father's herd.

Religion

The Turkana believe that most illness is caused by their supreme god and that they are able to treat it by native medical remedies. Many of these remedies take the form of a purge that is thought to drive out the illness. To deal with more serious complaints they resort to an *emuron*, or diviner or magician. They are open to Western medicine. The African Medical Research Foundation provides a "flying doctors" service in East Africa, and has set up a Specialist Outreach Programme with a mobile clinic.[42] The Turkana believe that the recently dead must be appeased by killing an animal that belonged to him. The blood of the animal is then smeared on the bodies of all his family members.

Outreach

The Turkana New Testament was published in 1987 and the complete Bible was at the press in 1999.[43] The estimate of the number of Christians is difficult, perhaps 30%. The Africa Inland Church is working in the area at Eliye Springs, Loiyanggilan and South Horr and Roman Catholics are also present. Literacy classes.[44] AIM works in Gatab, Kalokol, Lokichogio, Lokori and Napuu, and is involved in a hospital in Kalokol and a girls' secondary school in Lokori.[45] United World Mission have a team among this people.

GABBRA

The Gabbra are a Cushite, Oromo-speaking people who live in the Marsabit District, northern Kenya to the east of Lake Turkana. Previously, they were forced out of Somalia. They are 30,500 strong and were by tradition camel herders, as distinct from the Oromo who have cattle — though in practice they also have cattle, sheep and goats.

Nomadism

During the rains, the Gabbra live with their herds in the Huri Hills while the pools are filled, but there are no permanent sources of water there. Then they descend to the Chalbi Desert, where the camels are able to graze in about an 80-kilometer (50-mi.) radius of their camp. They return to the springs at the foot of the hills about every five days. Their villages (*ola*) are made up of about 10 to 15 huts and are moved frequently, as many as ten times a year. Everything can be packed, and loaded on camels, in five hours. Their moves are often made to accompany the rain. The milk yielding animals are kept in the camp. The camels give milk even through the dry season, while the cattle give only when the grass is good. The dry animals are sent with

15a

15b

15c

15 Gabbra and Borana:
   a. The Gabbra move house easily — on camels (Photo M. Hunter).
   b. Borana receiving mission visitors before the house is finished! (Photo M. Hunter).
   c. A Borana grandmother (Photo M. Hunter).

the warriors to distant camps (*fora*) to avoid overgrazing of their local pasture. The herds are often raided by other tribes, who can be chased off by Kenyan army helicopters. The Gabbra draw water from deep wide wells, which require a chain of men to pass buckets up to the surface.[46]

Society

The Gabbra are divided into six clans that are linked to the Borana moieties, but Gabbra men who are born during a certain number of years are grouped together, and this determines their roles as warriors and elders as well as who they may marry. In their special calendar the years are counted in sevens to correspond to the days of the week, with 100-day periods and other periods dividing the year. Many have settled in Maikonas, North Horr, Sololo and Marsabit. The people were caught up in the war on the border with Somalia in the 1960s and lost many men and animals. They have a system of redistribution of cattle to help poorer pastoralists, like the Jubilee Year practiced by the Israelites.[47] The wealthy cannot bank or hoard their assets, so they prefer to redistribute them. It is difficult to know who owns what, because of various methods of loans and redistribution. They gather three times a year, and families that have been separated for months because of their pastoralism are reunited.

Religion

The Gabbra used to be Muslims, but in the 1970s they revived their traditional monotheistic belief with the expectation that their high god would reveal himself to them in the near future. They worship the camel in many rituals. Each family sacrifices goats and sheep, and bracelets of hide are made from the animals. An Islamic spiritist cult is also gaining influence among them.

The Roman Catholics and the Anglican Church work among the Gabbra. The latter has a number of evangelists, and there has been at least one Gabbra bishop. AIM has workers in contact with the Gabbra in Kalacha and has conducted extensive water supply and tree planting work. SIM and SIL workers seconded to the AIC also work among the Gabbra.[48] Linguistic Recordings have produced four sets of cassettes and commentaries on tape for two picture series.

GARRE and AJURAN

The Garre and Ajuran are semi-nomadic Somali pastoralists in the extreme northeast of Kenya, totaling 96,000 and 32,000 respectively. Their languages are related to Somali but understood by the Borana.

RENDILLE

There are 22,000 Rendille, with 9,000 *Ariaal*, who are camel herders in Marsabit District, North Kenya, southeast of Lake Turkana. The migration patterns have changed and become progressively restricted during the twentieth century. The Rendille used to take their herds up to Mount Marsabit, but this has been turned into a wild animal park for tourists and the pastoralists have been banned from entering. Today they are located to the south in the harsh Kaisuit Desert.

The Rendille live in clan-based groups, called *gobs*, of 20 to 70 persons, with a few milk camels. The camels carry the frames of their small dome-shaped huts on their backs, giving a characteristic crescent-shaped silhouette as they move across the landscape. The main herds are guarded at some distance by the young men who move *fora*, or camp, frequently. The camels find limited fodder, although they can go far greater distances from sources of water, so the camps have to move often. The human population is limited by the level of subsistence from the camels, which in turn depends on the slow reproductive rate of the herd. They combine different livestock to overcome these limitations, so the girls tend herds of sheep and goats. UNESCO has a project to restock their herds of camels, cattle, sheep and goats.[49] Because of this slow reproductive rate, the younger sons of the Turkana often cannot inherit their share of the family camel herd, and therefore they move to join the Ariaal or the Samburu.

There are about 6,000 Ariaal, or southern Rendille, who are cattle herders. The cattle need grass that is longer than that which other animals will graze, and they need water every second day. The Ariaal Rendille have an interdependent relationship with the Samburu, and so some also speak Samburu.

The Rendille are related to the Maasai and speak the same language. Some parts of the Bible have been published in Ki-Rendille, a language akin to Somali, following from SIL's work.[50] AIM works in Gatab, Laisamis and Loglogo. The CPK (Anglican) has taken responsibility for the Crosslinks work here. AIC churches at Kiturun, South Horr, Nguronit and Soriadi probably have contact with this people.[51] The *Jesus* film is available in Ki-Rendille.

POKOT or *Pökoot*

The Pokot, in western Kenya, are one of the Kalenjin peoples like the **Tuken**. Most of the 175,000 Pokot are agriculturists, "the corn people," living in the Cherangani Hills. But about 29,000 of them are semi-nomadic herders on the dry plain of the great Rift Valley between the steep Tiati Hills and the Karasuk Hills on the border of Uganda. There are 5,000 in Uganda near Kupsabing. The population may be larger, and more than half may still be pastoralists. There is a smaller group of the pastoral **Kadam** who live with them.

Nomadism

The Pokot have the pastoralist's love for cattle, which give not only status but help to overcome the limitations of the individual, because they are exchanged in most transactions to establish stable relationships, reconcile disputes, ensure an inheritance, or to demonstrate the generosity of their owners. Whole villages can lose their cattle in raids either by the Pokot or against the Pokot. If the Pokot raid other tribes, the government takes livestock from any Pokot to make restitution. The Pokot pastoralists prefer to kill with the spear, rather than with the agriculturists' bow and arrows, and neighbors are killed indiscriminately to get their cattle. If a man kills a Pokot he has to surrender all his livestock to the bereaved family.[52] The Pokot

have often been in conflict with the Turkana to the north for pasture.

When she gets married, each Pokot wife is allocated sufficient livestock for her needs. This livestock is passed on to her sons to serve in turn as their bride-price.[53] The Pokot will eat the meat of almost any animal and supplement their diet with cow's blood and honey. The women already have sufficient tasks, so to introduce agriculture, which the men dismiss as women's work, would only increase their workload.[54] Their houses are temporary structures made of woven sticks and leaves. Boys are circumcised in groups that form an age-set.

Religion

The Pokot believe in a vague and remote creator called Tororot, but not in an afterlife.[55] This god is said to listen to their prayers. Ilat is the spirit of the wind sent by Tororot to cool the earth, bring rain and blow away dust. Ilat is also the divine messenger sent to warn humankind, so drought or floods are explained as rebukes against human misconduct. The Pokot believe that humankind has responsibility for the environment, and a harmony between the environment and humans, as well as between humans themselves, is the ideal.

The Pokot's prophets, or messengers, have dreams or trances to encounter the divine. They seek to give advice on how to counter misfortune by claiming to travel in the sky, or to interpret entrails or how sandals land when thrown in the air. These omens must be obeyed. Misfortune can be the result of others being selfish, such as hoarding food that others need. Sickness can strike like the wind. Witchcraft is not always directed at the victim, but also against his or her family and friends, so that the enemy is left alone.

The British colonial administration curtailed the Pokot's pastoralism and, in the late 1940s and 1950s, they turned for help to a version of the banned Dini ya Msambwa sect. Elsewhere it had encouraged violence and arson against Europeans, but among the Pokot it was transformed to involve singing and praying. Many believed that it would rid them of colonialism, and in particular of the loss of pasture and freedom of movement. The goal was a "promised land" where pastoral herds and travel was unhindered, and where the advantages of the Europeans would be given to the Africans. It encouraged people to be possessed by a spirit and so to reveal the divine through their strange behavior. This was induced by hymns invoking Tororot as "Our Father," until they shook and fell to the ground, uttering strange speech, including speaking in other tongues. People would go to the meetings hoping to be possessed, but they believed that this only happened to those who were relatively good.[56]

Outreach

Language Recordings have made cassettes in Pokot, and the Bible was ready in 2000. AIM have workers at Alale, Amaya, Liter, Loruk and Orus. The Africa Inland Church among the Pokot is at Maron, Kipchere and Yatia.[57] Crosslinks served among the Pokot for many years. The Anglican Church of the Province of Kenya, B.C. Faith Churches, Africa Gospel Church and Faith Homes of Kenya are also working among the agricultural Pokot.[58]

NANDI

There are 262,000 Nandi included in the Kalenjin people living in western Kenya. They have scattered homesteads rather than villages, without any central social organization. These are situated at 6,000 to 7,000 feet, west in the Rift Valley Province where there is good rainfall. Their lives center on their cattle, although they also cultivate a wide range of vegetables. Both men and women practice their own traditional religion, with magic and witchcraft.[59] Some Nandi are Christians, and the Bible is available in Kalenjin.

TUGEN

There are 131,000 Tugen in southern Baringo District, Kenya. They are part of the Kalenjin, related to the Nandi and Pokot, and are divided between the Arror, or Northern Tugen, and the Samorr, or Southern Tugen. About a third of the Tugen live on the plains, which were vacated by the Maasai at the end of nineteenth century, and took up pastoralism with cattle, sheep and goats. The rest live in the Tugen Hills and are agropastoralists, but prefer keeping livestock to agriculture.

Early in the twentieth century a struggle developed between pastoralists and European settlers, who took the best dry season pasture for cultivation. The Tugen have varied their emphasis on cultivation and pastoralism according to the conditions. Each family was allocated between 30 and 50 hectares of land in the 1970s. President Moi of Kenya, a Tugen, has been president since 1978.[60] The Bible is available in Kalenjin.

SAMBURU or Loikop

Their name means "the People" (of the White Goats). There are 85,000 of them living in northern Kenya between Lake Turkana and the Ewaso Ngiro River. They are cattle, sheep and goat herders who live dispersed over an arid land. They divide up their herds so that the milk-cows are pastured near camp, and the goats and sheep are also nearby, but the young warriors take the other cattle some distance for pasture. The husband allocates pasture to each of his wives and their children so that they can build up their own herds.

Religion

The Samburu, like the Maasai, believe in one benevolent high-god, Nkai, who created the landscape to provide all the needs of the pastoralists. Spirits inhabit the landscape, and each person and animal has a guardian spirit, or *nkai*, to give moral guidance. Diviners predict the future. Children are valued and polygamy is the ideal.[61] They have a group of blacksmiths who are believed to have especially powerful curses. The Samburu are relatively unusual in that they avoid an aggressive posture toward other tribes.

Outreach

Language Recordings have produced evangelistic and other cassettes in Samburu. In the towns of Laisamis, Loglogo, Marsabit and Orus, AIM International works among the Samburu. There are AIC churches at Kiturun, Loiyangilan, Nguronit, South Horr and Soriadi. At least 13 different denominations are working among the Samburu.

SAKUYE or *Sakuge*

Various estimates for the Sakuye camel herders range from 1,800 to 6,500. They are one of the Oromo-speaking peoples. According to their legend, they came from Arabia and traveled through Ethiopia to arrive around a place called Saku, which is possibly Marsabit. They lost many of their camels in the civil war between Kenya and the Somalis. Today they are found in the north of Kenya with the Gabbra, where they accept the religion and priests of the Boran. Others are found along the Ewaso Ngiro River in Isiolo, where they are Muslims. Those around Merti and Garba Tula are adopting cattle and settling. Children are named after the time or conditions of their birth, such as "morning," "drought" or "new moon." They speak Borana (Southern Oromo), and the Bible has been available since 1995. Those in Isiolo are Muslims, but those in the north accept the priests or *qallu* of the Borana. The CPK has a ministry from Moyale, and the AIC has a group of Christians in Debel in the north.[62]

ORMA

There are 37,720 Orma in the Northeast and Coast Provinces of Kenya. However, unofficial counts estimate that there may be as many as 50,000. They are another of the Oromo-speaking peoples, situated to the south of the others on both banks of the Tana River in southeastern Kenya.

Nomadism

They pasture their cattle, sheep and goats along the lower Tana valley in the dry season, but move westwards to the higher ground of the Kitui area for the rains. It is ironic that they are able to use the tracks abandoned by oil exploration teams. For if these teams had found oil, they would have turned the area into an oil field. It is claimed that some of the Orma are sedentary, but since all of them depend on their livestock in this semi-arid area they are probably pastoralists who have sufficient water to stay near the Tana River all year round. Those that are nomadic remain in the valley for six months of the year.

The Orma are considered the most successful pastoralists in Kenya, being an example of a society subsisting from cattle milk, meat and leather. Their life is permeated by references to cattle. They give names to all their cattle, and men who own more than a thousand head of cattle have a special status — as well as a great ability to choose names! Their diet is mostly milk, butter, ghee and meat. The crops they plant are not very productive, being sufficient to support a family only once in four harvests. But because of the drought in 1984-85, they are putting more effort into cultivation.

A man can gain status not only from having a large herd, but also for killing five men, lions or buffaloes with a spear and sword. This status does not secure a lifestyle that is any different from his poorer neighbors, but rather gives a man influence and the ability to lend or give cattle to help the poor, or to support community projects like building a school. A poor client herding the cattle of a wealthy pastoralist can keep the milk and male calves in order to re-establish himself. This help for the poor is usually decided at the corporate level of the elders of a lineage group. The despised castes of *Wata* (see below), *Boda* (former slaves) and *Tumtus* (blacksmiths) are excluded from any help.

Society

There is a strong egalitarian aspect in Orma society, because all decisions are made collectively by elders, including the poor men. Family life and children are important to the Orma. Marriage is accompanied by sacrifice, and an expectant mother receives many gifts of food. On an auspicious day decided by the diviner, the father publicly names the child and bathes it in milk. The parents are referred to as the father or mother of their eldest son (rather than by their own names).

Religion

Their language is Afan Oromo or Ilma Orma. Their traditional belief is in a high sky god called Wak, whose will must be revealed by divination. They believe in humankind's stewardship of the environment and the possibility that the sky god can destroy what he has created if humankind abuses natural resources. They became 99.9% Muslim in the 1930s, and there are no Christians among them. Mission work has often been disrupted through attacks by the Somalis.

Outreach

The CMS was the first to evangelize the Orma in 1844, but the small church soon died out. Christian cassettes are available. SIL are undertaking the Bible translation, and the New Testament was to have been ready by 2000. AIC and the Reformed Church in America have sought to reach them in the Kitui District. Del and Debra Braaksma have established a veterinary service and made a study of mission-based development among this people.[63]

MAASAI or *Masai*

The Maasai number 382,000. The 1979 census reported 250,000 Maasai in Kenya, living mostly in the southern districts of Narok and Kajiado, where they make up about 60% of the population.[64] There are 327,000 Maasai in Tanzania.

Nomadism

The Maasai are cattle nomads with a highly organized society. Most of the villages are semi-permanent, and remain in one place for about four years, before moving closer to new pasture and water sources, and away from the mud and flies generated by the old camp. In each camp live anywhere from one or two families to about twenty. The huts are surrounded by a thorn fence or hedge — not only to keep out predators, but also spirits. The cattle, goats and sheep leave for pasture in the early morning with the young men and return in the evening. When they use more distant pasture, the men and some of the women will establish temporary camps there. The milking cows are left near the village. The people co-operate in herding and consider the land to be jointly owned, but individuals own the livestock. Women are given cows on marriage, which they raise to give to their sons, who also receive animals from their fathers. Women have rights over the milk and its products and the cowhides, but otherwise the men make the decisions.

Both the British and Kenyan governments have seen the nomadism of the Maasai as a threat. The Maasai and Kalenjin people groups are related to the government's political party, which appears to favor an ethnically partitioned Kenya.[65] Most of this people are no longer nomadic due to a government agricultural settlement program.[66] This scheme removed 1,000 square miles from the Maasai, and in 1968 the pastures were divided into "Group Ranches," that is, construed as belonging to particular communities of Maasai. This has resulted in the more powerful individuals gaining the land for their private use, with the ordinary herders usually being left with nothing. Wealth that used to be shared is now concentrated in the hands of a few individuals.

The notion of private ownership of the land does not allow for the varied yield of pasture and the need to vary the size of herds as well as move them constantly. As the ranches were divided up, most plots became too small for pastoralism and the cattle died because of lack of rain or overgrazing. This led to the plots being sold for cash to outsiders, including corrupt officials.[67] The final result is that an estimated 300,000 Maasai are squatting in the towns, as "nomads in waiting." Some have jobs that they hope will give them enough money to return to their traditional lifestyle, and Maasai organizations are working for a return, in some measure, to pastoralism.[68] Their land is being ineffectually cultivated by mechanized farming and destroyed as pasture, and then abandoned by the farmers. Some of the Maasai are putting their land together again, by buying up the now degraded fields. The Maasai attacked Kikuyu farmers in early 1995, claiming that the Rift Valley area northwest of Nairobi was Maasailand.

Society

Maasai society is divided by rank, sex and age-sets. Men are divided between elders, who are married, the *moran* or warriors who are not allowed to marry, and boys. The women are divided between the uncircumcised girls and the circumcised, who are usually wives of the elders. These ranks form a hierarchy in which women are considered inferior. The male ranks do not eat in front of, or have sex with any but the females "below" them. The age-sets, or *olporror*, include all the men born within approximately a 14-year period. They maintain a special relationship throughout their lives and even share their wives.

Men seek "wealth," which means not money but rights over livestock, women and children. Women are considered as a complement to the cattle, rather than as equals. Such "wealth" guarantees immortality to a Maasai elder, and death is considered to be falling asleep. Usually the men herd and care for the cattle; the women care for the children, the camp, milk the cattle and carry water and firewood.

Maasai society is regulated by a concept of *enkanyit*, or respect, dignity or correct relationships within the status of individuals in the hierarchy. To infringe the rules results in *enturuji*, or shame and embarrassment. The Maasai have prophets or diviners called *oloiboni*.

Outreach

They speak Maasai, and there is a Maasai Bible translation available. AIM has run a Bible college at Norok, a child care center for disabled children at Kajiado. They also have workers at Siyapei and Sajiloni. In addition to this, AIM has begun an outreach to the area around Osupuko in the northern hills, among Maasai previously unreached, among whom witchcraft is still strong. There has been a remarkable work of God's Spirit in that area.[69] There are many AIC churches among the Maasai. The unconventional Catholic ministry of Vincent Donovan among the Maasai has demonstrated many points of contextualizing the church among pastoralists, but the local Catholic hierarchy abandoned this work after he left.[70] There is a Maasai version of the *Jesus* film. African Enterprise, World Horizons and the Assemblies of God are all involved in working among them. SALTLIC provides training and livestock improvement projects, mostly led by local people.

DATOGA

There are 400,000 Datoga, living mostly in Arusha, northeast Tanzania.[71] They are semi-nomadic pastoralists who have lost much of their pasture to a wheat-growing project funded by the Canadian government.[72] They had 485,000 head of cattle and 265,00 small livestock in the 1970s. They consist of ten sections, widely scattered in the region, and they are losing their identity by being assimilated into neighboring peoples. They were resettled under a special scheme during 1978-81, but the social services provided as part of this scheme were never completed, and the little there are have made the Datoga areas attractive to sedentary neighbors who also use these services.

The **Barbaig** are a 76,000 strong section of the Datoga, who have traditionally raided the cattle of the Maasai to the north, and the Maasai appear to have driven them southwards. They have a reputation for murder, because every non-Datoga is considered a potential cattle thief, and therefore an "enemy." The Barbaig reward any warrior who kills an enemy with 5 to 25 head of cattle. This was the way for young men to get recognition and status. They observe both Christianity and their traditional religion. A Bible translation is in progress.

ILPARAKUYO, *Baraguyu*

The Ilparakuyo is a 30,000-strong pastoralist people in Tanzania, just north of Dar es Salaam. They were driven away from their own territory by the Maasai in the nineteenth century, and they now live dispersed in 20 different districts. They live among agriculturists, and the spread of cultivation is forcing the Ilparakuyo closer to the bush that contains the tsetse fly. Although they are seen as backward by the farmers and the government, they tend to be wealthier than the local cultivators. Their traditional dress declares their identity, district, social and marital status, but the government has tried to get them to change to European-style clothing.

In Bagamoyo, a state ranch took over much of the dry season grazing area without paying the Ilparakuyo compensation, because it was said to be "under-utilized" by a "few pastoralists." Yet the government also told them to reduce their herds due to overgrazing! The ranch placed a similar number of cattle on the land, but its staff did not have the local expertise that the Ilparakuyo have. The Ilparakuyo have constantly moved because of cattle disease. Only a few of them have gardens, and they tend to hire cultivators to look after them.

The government has provided a village, called Mindu Tulieni, exclusively for pastoralists. There is also a veterinary service, which the pastoralists used, but most of their children failed to attend the schools provided because the curriculum was biased to cultivation. This scheme did not work because farmers stayed in the area that had been allocated to pasture and because the tsetse fly was prevalent.

The Ilparakuyo prefer to have small kraals and camps to make use of small grazing areas. They drive cattle, some bought from other people, about 150 kilometers (90 mi.) to Dar es Salaam for sale. They are polygamous, which means that they have large families.[73] The women raise chickens and sell eggs to neighboring peasants, although they do not eat either themselves, and they also use their knowledge of natural medicines to gather and sell them. The Ilparakuyo are an example of a small community forced into "enclosed" pastoralism in restricted areas, and they have maintained their pastoral life and identity partly because the government has recognized it as distinct. They have managed to maintain their herds. They need to constantly find new areas for pasture and find ways of eliminating trypanosomiasis. They speak Maa, or Maasai. Gospel message cassettes are available from Language Recordings and SGM.

Peripatetic Nomadic Peoples in East Africa

FUGA

Fuga is a term used in southern Ethiopia by the *Gurage, Kambata, Yemma, Oromo* and *Wolayata* agriculturists for their associated groups of craftsmen. The term *fuga* is derogatory. They may have originated either as one of the early hunter-gatherer peoples of the region, or by specialization within their host peoples.

It is estimated that about 1% of the 1,860,000 Gurage are *Fuga* — consisting of the *N'Afarä* blacksmiths, the *Gezha* tanners and the *Fuga* woodworkers, who fell trees and construct houses. They often have a client relationship with a wealthy Gurage, who controls their access to other customers in his village. They speak the language of their host people groups, but the women also have their own ritual language called Fedwät. They lead their young women in a secluded retreat to initiate them into a special society and teach them Fedwät, which the men do not understand.

The 1,000,000 *Kambata* call their potters *Fuga*, their leather workers *Awada* or *Faki*, and their smiths *Tumanu*. They support themselves as woodcarvers, musicians, ritual experts and hunting. They own some goats and chickens and are only able to rent small gardens. They have their own specialized vocabulary or cant, with many loan words from neighboring languages.

The *Yemma* or Janjero, who are half a million agriculturalists in southeast Ethiopia, call their 4,000 potters, smiths and tanners *Fuga*. They also perform circumcisions and funeral rites. Among the Jangero they are allowed to do some gardening, but not to own land or cattle. The Fuga in the Jimma district to the southwest may speak a separate language from the Yemsa language spoken by the Yemma, but this has not yet been established.

The *Oromo*, or Galla, and the Wolayata have *Fuga* as musicians, ritualists and makers of amulets and charms. The *Fuga* are also the executioners. The Orma call their smiths *Tumtus*. They are despised as irreligious because they do not, or are not allowed to, keep the food taboos of their host society.[74] They cross tribal boundaries according to the opportunities to practice their trades, and sedentary farmers who host them consider them nomads. They are described as "mobile," and presumably they are itinerant without any systematic routine of migration. They have their own ways of speaking the languages of their host societies, and use many loan words from other languages. They settle temporarily in flimsily built huts, just outside their host village on a plot of ground set aside for them.

Nomadism

The Fuga lead an itinerant lifestyle because their host society denies them ownership of land and the freedom to practice agriculture. The Fuga are both feared for their magical powers and despised for not being farmers. They are thought to make houses and food unclean and the fields infertile. If anyone visits the Fuga, such as Christian workers,

these visitors are then considered contaminated, and their host people will refuse to have anything to do with them. The Fuga move to find marriage partners or a place where they are respected. They only marry other Fuga.

DORZE

There are 3,000 Dorze, itinerant weavers who are scattered across southern Ethiopia. They have their homes in the Gamu highlands of Gamo Gofa Province, southwestern Ethiopia. While their families stay at home, the men migrate regularly to seek customers in the towns and cities of southern Ethiopia. They are also found in the rural areas at harvest time, particularly in the coffee growing areas. A craftsman travels together with one or two apprentices, staying in rented houses with other Dorze weavers on the edge of town. There is a significant Dorze community in Addis Ababa. After ten months away they return home for the Maskal feast, the most important celebration of their year. They speak Dorze, or Dorzinya, in Genu-Gofa Province, which is possibly a dialect of Wolaytta.[75]

SAB

The Sab are the bondsmen of the Somali pastoralists in northern Somalia. *Sab* is a derogatory term, which implies that they do not belong to the Somalis. The main groups are the **Yibro** and the **Midgan** hunters, leather workers and barbers, and the **Tumalod**, or *Tumaal*, blacksmiths. Their origin may have been in Arabia and they have a tradition of descent from a pagan priest who, they claim, was killed by the Muslims. Blood group research, however, shows them to be related to the Somalis.

The Midgan believe they are descended from the Somali Dir clan. But they are indistinguishable from the Somalis because they often call themselves by the name of the clan to which they are attached or by their own lineage name. In general they have no rights or influence in Somali society. A few who have independent wealth through trading or government service can now participate in local Somali assemblies.

But Somalis treat them as inferior and do not allow intermarriage. It is said that no Somali ever enters the smithy of a *Tumalod* or shakes hands with him. The different Sab groups intermarry and socialize only among themselves and have their own leaders, or sheiks. They tend only to relate with the Somalis through their individual patrons.

The Yibro (sg. *Yibir*, *Jebir*, or *Ebir* or *Jiber*), who number 1,300, are itinerant soothsayers, makers of talismans, magicians, blessers and circumcisers. Each lineage of Yibro is associated to a Somali sub-tribe and speaks the dialect of the Somalis to which they are attached. It is not known whether they have their own dialect or just a specialized vocabulary. The Somalis think that they have great magical power and can even fly away after death!

They are supported by gifts given in exchange for their religious services and also by begging. They interpret this gift as repayment for the death of the ancestor, and they threaten to curse any Somali who does not give it. This is another example of a nomadic lifestyle interpreted as the result of misfortune in the past.[76]

WAATA, Wata, Wasanye, Ariangulu

The Waata in Ethiopia and northern Kenya are hunters and craftsmen living among the *Borana*, *Oroma*, *Pokomo*, *Somali*, *Sidamo* and *Amhara*. Each of these peoples gives them different names. "*Wata*" is also used by the Oromo for all hunter-gatherers. They live in the mountains west of Moyale, just inside southern Ethiopia and along the Tana River. There are others on the coast, and they probably all have their own suppressed local ethnic identity.

The Waata are scattered in small communities as woodcutters, tanners, garden watchmen, wine makers and ritual experts, and their hunting seems to be only a small part of their means of subsistence. They live in small domed grass huts that can quickly be dismantled. They are mobile enough to fulfill tasks for the pastoralists and farmers as well as to return to hunting and gathering. They maintain a measure of autonomy and move according to the opportunities of the pastoral and hunting environments.

They have an important role in the Borana rituals, and are said to have found the Borana priest. The Waata's host societies despise them and have traditional stories as to why they are in this unfortunate situation. The Waata have their own myths about their origin and low status. They tell of how the sky-god called a meeting of peoples to distribute livestock, and the Waata's ancestor either refused to attend or arrived late, and so they were condemned always to be beggars.

Alternatively, the story relates that the sky-god was taking a walk and tripped and stumbled. While the others rushed to help, the Waata merely laughed. The Orma believe that the Waata foolishly chose against being cattle herders to become hunters.[77] For this "reason," the Waata are denied the ownership of cattle. These myths again demonstrate the typical pattern of peripatetics, believing that a past misdemeanor was the cause of them being subordinate and nomadic. They appear to have a jargon of their own.[78] Their language is a version of Sanye, distinct from Boni and Dahalo.

MANNA

The Manna in southern Ethiopia are craftsmen associated with the *Koorete* or *Amarro* people. Koorete is their own name; Amarro is the mountain area where they live. The Manna have a myth that says that one of their ancestors was so poor that he only had scraps of raw meat to offer to a tired and hungry Amarro king. Because of this poor hospitality, the king banned them from being full members of Amarro society.[79]

HAUDA

The Hauda live in southern Ethiopia and are associated with the *Komso* in western Sidamo Province. They are banned from owning land and from agriculture. As craftsmen they are considered to be nomads, moving according to the dictates of the trade and often trying to find somewhere where they are respected.

CAMELEERS and TRUCKERS

These people, in Ethiopia and Djibouti, are occupational groups that consist of individuals from various peoples. Camel trains carry salt from Lake Assal, Djibouti, and the Danakil region in Eritrea, up to Ethiopian markets. They return with grain, metal and stone, spices and manufactured goods. Most of these people would belong to the various pastoralist groups listed above. Three hundred trucks travel between the Ethiopian highlands and the port of Djibouti each day, and local churches are providing refreshment and literature for them.[80]

SOUTHERN AFRICA

There are a few nomadic peoples in Southern Africa. The region consists of Angola, Namibia, the republic of South Africa, Zimbabwe and Mozambique. Basically the region is dry to the west with desert and desert-like scrub; to the east savanna and scrub predominate. The Portuguese reached the Cape before Columbus discovered the Caribbean, and Europeans were trading in the seventeenth century with the nomadic Koikhoi or Hottentot people for cattle. Cattle were an important asset in the early history, as the Dutch *trekboers* also adopted a semi-nomadic pastoralist lifestyle in the interior. When the local population was absorbed to provide labor, they changed to settled ranching. Today much of the land is cultivated.

Nomadic Pastoralists of Southern Africa

HIMBA or *Zemba*

They are a 5,000 strong sub-division of the Herero people in Namibia and Angola, who preserve much of the early nomadic pastoralist way of life. The Hereros migrated from the north of Africa and arrived in their present area around the seventeenth century. In the last century there were about 100,000 Herero with about 150,000 head of cattle on the Kaokoveld of northern Namibia.

The Herero established trade with the Europeans in the Cape Colony, seeking and adopting European goods in exchange for cattle. German colonization from 1884 brought unjust laws and provoked a revolt in which the colonial administration attempted and nearly succeeded in exterminating the Herero with machine guns. A public outcry in Germany stopped this, but many Hereros fled to what is now Botswana. The Herero have been in the forefront of those seeking independence for Namibia.

Society

A man's status was, and still is, determined by the size of his herd and by his genealogy, which is traced through both his mother and father. The men also have military-style ranks to reflect their position in society. The lives of the Himba are centered on their cattle, and they still migrate for pasture. During migration they live in domed huts made of branches covered with dung and clay. Their traditional diet is sour milk, prepared in a wooden pail that is passed around the camp. Because they are reluctant to slaughter, meat is eaten often when the animals die or are killed by predators.

Religion

The Herero had a monotheistic belief in a Supreme Being who takes both humans and animals to heaven. This Being created the first Herero couple from a tree and they chose to become cattle herders, thus becoming superior to all other peoples. They had priestesses who maintained a holy fire that was used for the sacrifice of specially bred Holy Cattle. Today, most Herero are Lutheran and Anglican, and the women wear colorful long dresses and turbans said to have been originally copied from the dresses of the missionaries. Most Hereros are settled, but the Himba continue to be pastoralists.[1] There are Bible portions in the Herero language, and AIM and other organizations work among them.

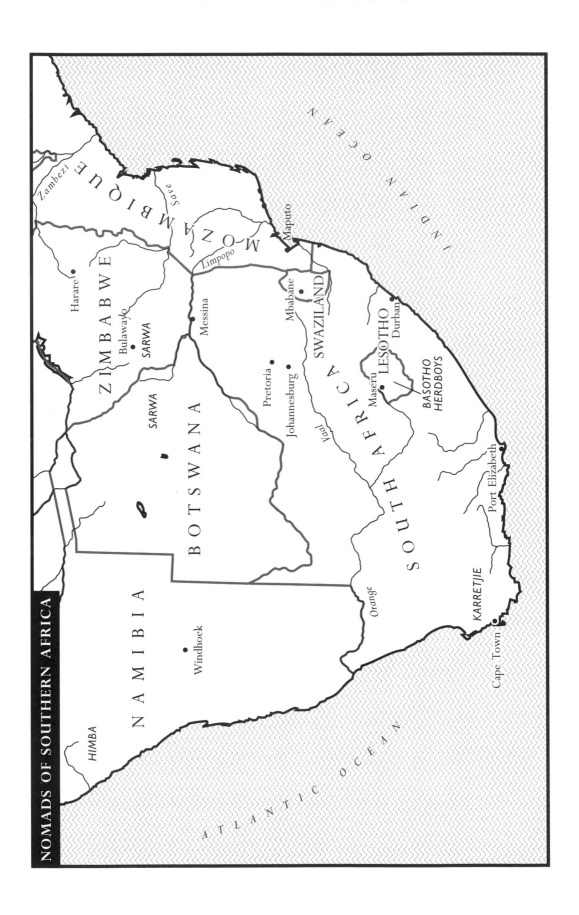

NOMADS OF SOUTHERN AFRICA

BASOTHO HERDBOYS, Lesotho

These are boys and young men of the Basotho population, so as a British colony the country was called Basutoland. This is a pastoral occupational subculture of a sedentary people. Young boys are "rented" to shepherds at about five years of age and they become part of the flock owner's household, in return for livestock or money given to their parents. They often herd for urban stock-raisers. As they grow older they spend longer periods in the mountains with the sheep and goats, living on a diet of maize and wild plants, building their own stone huts to survive in all kinds of weather. Exposure to strong winds and snowstorms can kill both the stock and the boys.

This separation from home also disadvantages the boys from skill and education for future employment after their herding careers are over. Girls have a higher literacy rate than the boys, but the distance-learning scheme provides materials for the boys to take into the hills.[2] The Basotho worship their *badimo*, or ancestor spirits, as the only way to get in touch with the supreme god. One former herdboy who began his personal search for God while meditating on the mountains is now director of a mission showing the Jesus film among his people. The herdboys are also being contacted by AIM workers.[3]

Non-Pastoral Nomadic Peoples in Southern Africa

SARWA, Botswana and Zimbabwe

There are about 4,500 Bushmen, or *San*, who were originally hunter-gatherers but who adapted their lifestyle to what some consider to be peripatetic groups. The Sarwa attach themselves to a *Kgalagari* or Tswana village for about nine months of the year, where they work for their patrons watering the cattle, fetching firewood, cleaning the *kraal*, treating the sick and dancing for rain, or hunting and bringing back objects for trade with the villagers. The Kgalagari consider the Bushmen to be "uncivilized" because they do not possess cattle. But this fact means that, as the Sarwa are of the wilds, they are thought also to be more susceptible to magical powers for healing or dancing for rain. Many other San move with their entire families from farm to farm as laborers, cowherds or fence builders. They live in villages near the farms, but in the wet season they move in scattered groups in the bush for hunting and gathering.

The *Tswana* are an agropastoral people living mostly in South Africa, but there are about 850,000 in Botswana. Traditionally they migrated in family groups from their main village to their fields from November to June. The pioneer missionary James Moffat first translated the Bible into Tswana, and about half the people consider themselves to be in some sense Christian. The Sarwa understand Tswana but speak Iiechware themselves, with 3,000 speakers in Botswana and 1,600 in Zimbabwe. They practice African traditional religion.[4]

KARRETJIE, Cape Province, Republic of South Africa

Their name means "donkey cart people," and they support themselves as itinerant sheepshearers in the season and by doing other casual farm labor. They are descended from the original inhabitants of the Karoo region, the Koikhoi (Hottentot). They were nomadic pastoralists who resisted the European colonists but were finally reduced to farm laborers and, more importantly, became landless. They are treated as the lowest rank of society and have been discriminated against for 200 years. The Karoo, meaning "thirstland," covers 260,000 square kilometers (100,000 sq. mi.), but the farmland is owned by a few thousand sheep farmers. Most of the Karretjie have lost their positions as farm workers or surplus labor and have been forced into a precarious itinerant life seeking what work the dominant white farming community might give them. There are thousands of them, and they represent about 1.5% of the region's population.

Nomadism

The Karretjie camp, in groups of five to a dozen families, either on farm land with the permission of the farmer or on the verges of the roads — which one can do legally for 24 hours before being moved on. They construct small shanties for each family group. The families are often divided up since both parents, and especially the men as shearers, will leave the younger children with the grandparents to travel or camp separately. They travel considerable distances, perhaps hundreds of kilometers, for a few days of work. They use donkeys and donkey carts, but they also walk and hitchhike with trucks. Families will often use the same site on the road as their "home."[5] Any Christian witness among them would have to overcome the suspicions of both the people themselves and the of the farming community.

NORTH AFRICA

The countries of Mauritania, Western Sahara, Morocco, Algeria, Tunisia, Libya and Egypt form this region and have long been associated with the civilizations of the Mediterranean, rather than with sub-Saharan Africa. Since the invasion of the Arabs in the seventh century, bringing Islam, this region has also been orientated to the Middle East and was part of the Ottoman Empire for centuries. Algerian wheat, rather than pastoral products, was indirectly responsible for French intervention and colonialism, followed by Spain and Italy in the twentieth century.

Nomadic pastoralism is practiced both in the northern Sahara and in its transhumant form on the Atlas Mountains. This lifestyle has enabled some societies to maintain a measure of independence from the main trends of the region, and to develop links with the south. Those in the Sahara both participated in the caravan traffic across the desert and raided it as well. Motor vehicles and modern weapons introduced by colonialism have limited the autonomy of the nomadic societies. Since Islam crushed the early presence of Christians, North Africa has had a long history of resistance to Christianity.

Nomadic Pastoralists of North Africa

MOORS, or *Maures*

There are 1,200,000 Moors living in Mauritania and in other countries. Over 200,000 have left Senegal for Mauritania following unrest in the early 1990s.

The *Sanhadja*, or Desert Berbers, were probably some of the original inhabitants of this region. They resisted the invasions of the Arabs for centuries, but in the Cherr Baba War of the mid-seventeenth century they were finally defeated. They intermarried with the Arabs and the result was the *Bidan*, or White Moors, who developed a lifestyle derived from both the Bedouin and the nomadic Sanhadja. They lost their Berber language, adopted Hassaniya Arabic and learned Arab ways.

The Bidan are divided between a noble class and their former vassals, and they make up over half of Mauritania's population. The noble classes are made up of the warriors, called *hassan*, or "the people of the sword," and the marabouts, or *zawiya*, who are the holy men, also called "the

people of the Word." The *hassan* were mainly of Arab descent and monopolized the use of weapons. The *zawiya* were a cultural unifying force, compensating for the disunity among the *hassan* political leadership, or emirs.

When the French intervened to transfer all Saharan trade from Mauritania to their colony of Senegal, they undermined the political power of the elite. The *zawiya* benefited most from education, and they occupy positions of power in Mauritania. They have traditionally had the greatest influence and wealth — owning the largest herds, organizing caravan trade and digging the wells. The result is that Mauritania is one of the few states that does not see nomads as "backward" or as a threat. The second-class are the vassal pastoralists, or *zenaga*, who used to pay tribute to the nobles and were not allowed to own arms.

The other Moors are the **Haratin**, or Black Moors, who are the farmers, herders, fishermen and craftsmen and are descended from African slaves from the south. The

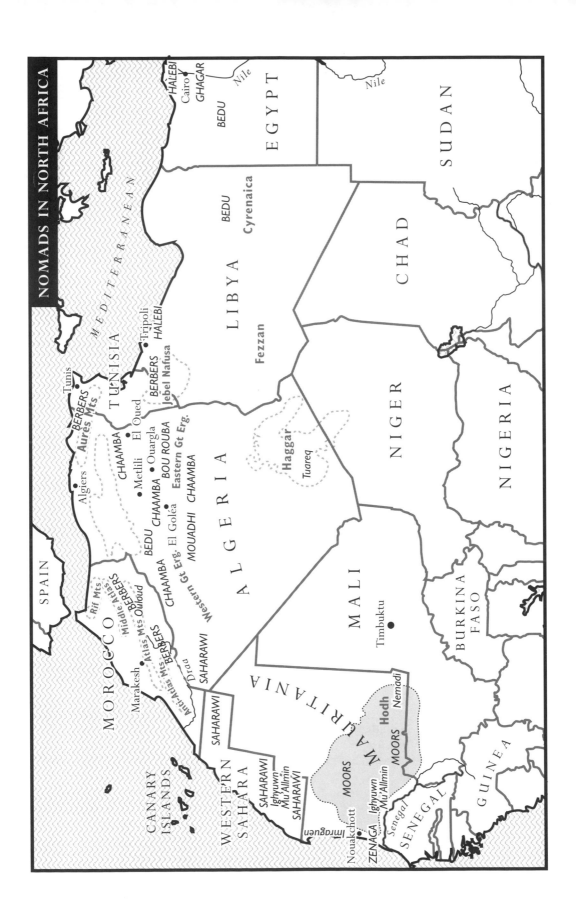

NOMADS IN NORTH AFRICA

Bidan still discriminate against them socially. The Black Moors are now classed as *haratan*, or freedmen, but many continue in a servile position, cultivating fields for noble landlords. The Moors are great tradesmen and poets, but it is often only the women who make music. For the attached craftsmen and musicians see the **Mu'allmin** and **Ighyuwn**, below.

The Moors are organized into over a hundred *qabila*, or patrilinear tribes, each being either *hassan*, *zawaya* or *zenaga*. But traditionally, within these tribes, there were also specialized castes, or the craftsmen, musicians and slaves. Each tribe paid tribute to others more influential in the hierarchy. But this social structure is fairly fluid and has broken up somewhat due to French colonial policies and the inroads of modern life. The tribes have become loose political groupings of the more permanent clans of related families.

Nomadism

The Moors have in the past been nomadic, and 80% were still active pastoralists in 1960. But the great droughts of the 1960s killed most of their herds, and they sold the rest. This meant that 80% of them settled, took up agriculture and built new villages. They are still proud, however, to have been nomads. The successful families can be described as agropastoralists — often they like to stay in tents near their houses and keep flocks of sheep and goats. The new irrigation dams on the Senegal River and changes in the land laws have helped them. But many settled in Nouakchott and other towns and live in great poverty. Large groups of Haratan live in the towns on the Senegal River such as Podor, Richard Toll, Rosso and St. Louis that also have twin towns on the Mauritanian side of the river.

Only about 12% of them are nomadic pastoralists at the beginning of the twenty-first century and live in the deserts from the River Draa in South Morocco and southwards to Senegal.[1] Many nomads are still to be found in the remote Hodh region of southeast Mauritania. Some tribes or clans have specialized in cattle rearing and others

in camels. Thus closely-related clans may be separated from one another because of the differing pasture needs of their livestock. The animals are owned by individuals, both men and women, and status and wealth is decided by the size of a man's or a woman's herd of camels and goats. Each family herds their animals together. The camels are set loose, but sheep and goats are always accompanied.

The Moors move in widely scattered small groups many kilometers apart, because of the limited pasture and water. They form small camps, or *frigs*, of as little as five tents; the size depending on the quality of the pasture nearby. Each tent, or *khayme*, represents a married couple and their dependents. Camels are used to transport the tents and household goods with the women and children. They live in barrel-vaulted huts of woven grass, called *tegits*. The area is so arid that the herding groups have to move frequently and carry their water supply with them; each family has an oil drum carried on a camel for water. They spend the cool months from October to December in the north, in Awker. The Moors then move southwards every few days and reach their most southerly area for the rains, during June to September. Those that have date palm plantations harvest the dates in July. In times of drought they will move further south, into Mali. The typical nomadic response to recent droughts is to migrate temporarily to Mali, or to settle for a short time and then to continue the pastoral life as conditions improve.

The Moors tend to co-operate together in the various tasks, which has not always been the case among all nomadic pastoralists. They also make loans of livestock to poor relatives, just as the Fulani do. Pastoral associations have been set up to improve the viability of the nomadic way of life with veterinary care and other services and with funds from international organizations. Malnutrition is common because they rarely eat meat. Their diet consists of milk, yogurt, butter and sour cream as well as bread and millet. In order to buy other goods that they need, they have to sell animals on a widely fluctuating market.

Society

Families always desire to have a number of sons, because the men do the herding and milking of the animals. They also draw water both for both humans and animals. It often takes a journey of many days to reach the wells. Because of this, the men may be away from the camp for days.

The women care for the camp, the cooking and children, and they also do the dairy work. The women marry at about twelve years of age, and they often spend as much as a year with their parents after marriage, being visited by their husbands. Monogamy is the rule among the Moors and women have relatively great influence among them. A bride receives a bride-price in cash from her new husband, instead of receiving camels, as in former days, and also a wooden chest filled with clothes and perfumes, which she gives to the other women of her camp. The women do not veil the face and can mix freely with men, in contrast to women in other Muslim societies. Women may own animals and other property and they can also buy a divorce. Although the clans are patrilinear, often a husband may be adopted into his wife's family and clan.

The tent, or *khayme*, represents a family — the word in Hassaniya is the same for both. The tent is assembled, repaired and taken down by the women because it belongs to the wife, and it is usually made by her mother prior to marriage and stays with her if divorce occurs. This makes it permissible for her to live alone. The tent consists of cotton cloth, rather than the traditional woven goat hair, covering semi-circular wooden hoops. It has open sides and is always pitched facing west. Inside each tent on the north side there is usually a four-legged frame or *rhal* (like a table upside down with the legs in the air) that serves as a platform for their belongings. It also serves as a baggage frame on their camel, and this is a distinctive feature as a camp moves across the desert. Camel saddles are status symbols and are placed on the south side of the tent. The packing and loading can take up to two hours.

Each clan has some families who live in market towns to facilitate the exchange of goods for their pastoral relatives. For example, since 1981 the *Hammunat* tribe has constructed the villages of Numal and Tuwiln with schools and clinics, because of their awareness that they are disadvantaged within Mauritanian society due to lack of education and health care. The dams along the Senegal Valley have enabled agriculture to develop considerably. There are 55,000 *Haratins*, who have settled in towns of the Senegal River Valley because of the advance of the desert.

Religion

The Moors are religiously motivated by the mystical Sufi form of Islam and by magic. Among them there are many brotherhoods of disciples following a living or dead "saint," who is considered to have much *baraka*, or a magical divine power to bless and heal. This power can be gained by touching them or, if they are dead, by making a pilgrimage to their tomb. The marabouts, or "holy men," are intercessors who teach their disciples and also practice magic. Fear of spirits, the *djin*, is still prevalent among the Moors. They believe that the world has a hierarchy of these invisible but human-like spirits who stalk at night, especially near cemeteries. They also believe that the *djin* are the cause of most misfortune, and an excuse for human failures. Both the marabouts and African magicians are used to counter them. The spirits are thought to come from the north and the father of a family will sleep near the *rhal* in the tent to protect the family, who sleeps to the south of him in the center of the tent. Inauspicious days and certain actions and objects can bring possession by these spirits. Uttering special formulas, reciting verses of the *Qur'an*, never being alone at night and wearing talismans on different parts of the body are all believed to ward the spirits off. While the spirits may cause mental illness, both supposed and real, sorcery and curses are thought to cause physical illness or misfortune. They are also preoccupied with countering the evil eye.

16a

16b

16c

16d

16 Moors:
  a. The Moors form 60% of the Mauritanians but have also spread south (Photo: M. Seitz).
  b. Moors in north Mali.
  c. Moorish hospitality in the Senegal River area (Photo: M. Seitz).
  d. The Moors have their own distinctive style of tent.

The different tribes have various practices and taboos, and practitioners in the occult have reputations either for effectiveness or for extortion. Poisoning due to feuds is common and constantly feared.

Outreach

The Moors are in great need of practical help in development because the droughts of the 1980s caused them to lose their flocks, and most have no other employment. Mauritania became an Islamic Republic in 1958, with the result that evangelism is possible only in Senegal and Arabic, rather than French, must be used. They reveal their limited knowledge of Christianity by calling Christians "Nazarenes," and "Catholic" is used of any person of ill-repute. They can also be reached with the Christian message in the capital and towns. There are WEC churches established in Senegal, and World Horizons is involved among them. Language Recordings cassettes are available in Hassaniya.

ZENAGA

The Zenaga are pastoral Arabs, perhaps 25,000 strong. They live in southwest Mauritania, between the coast and Mederdra, with both white and black or former slaves among them. They appear to have engaged in caravan trading. They speak a Berber language.[2]

SAHARAWI

The Saharawi or Sahawari are a mixture of the Berbers and the Bedouin Arabs, probably from the Yemen, who arrived in the Western Sahara in the thirteenth century and intermarried with Berbers and their African slaves. But the Saharawis are distinct from the Berbers to the north, the Tuareq to the east and the Moors and black Africans to the south. The Saharawi had the dubious distinction of being the first slaves of the modern European slave trade. The Portuguese, in an otherwise commendable program of discovery, captured thousands of the "Azengues," "Sanhaja Tuareq" or "Berbers" from 1441 onwards, and took them back to Portugal.

The Saharawi total about 200,000 in tribes such as the *Reguibat*, who claim descent from Mohammed, the *Ould Delim* or "people of the gun," and the *Tekna*.[3] Peoples Database estimates 93,400 *Reguibat* and 105,000 *Delim* in Mauritania, and 91,000 in the Western Sahara. The Tekna total 50,000. Other tribes are the *Izarguien* and the *Ait Lahsen*. The Tekna are semi-nomadic, in the north along the Moroccan border. Some tribes, such as the Ould Delim, called "sons of the gun," do not claim descent from the prophet. Many of them served in the Spanish Colonial Army. Others, such as the Reguibat (the largest tribe), claim to be "sons of the prophet."

Once the Saharawi dominated the western desert and were called "the sons of the clouds," referring to the great distances they traveled on camels in the desert. As camel nomads, they have an unerring sense of direction across the desert that has contributed to their skill as raiders. They formed the resistance to the colonial powers and have provided many troops for the Polisario independence movement. They move in small groups because of the meager vegetation and water, between southern Morocco and Mauritania, in an area where there are almost no oases. They are not able to supplement their diet by growing barley, and so they have to trade for cereals, tea, sugar and salt.

Their social unit is the *friq*, a group of about 50 tents. The women are usually unveiled. Their society was once divided not only into tribes but also into castes, like the Tuareq. There were also small groups of vassal shepherds, slaves and *haratin*, or farmers. For the attached craftsmen and musicians, see the **Mu'allmin** and **Ighyuwn**, below.

History

Towards the end of the Spanish colonial period in the 1960s, many Saharawi settled in the towns. When Spain left the colony, a joint administration under Mauritania and Morocco was set up, but the population resisted this. At stake are phosphate reserves and fishing grounds. When Mauritania renounced its claim to the country in 1979, Morocco invaded and many Saharawi reverted to the desert life to avoid the alien power. There were 170,000 refugees who moved into Algeria, where they have camps that have developed considerable facilities with schools, hospitals and plantations.

As the real inhabitants of the Western Sahara, the majority has supported the Polisario, preferring an independent country. Algeria encouraged the setting up of the Saharan Arab Democratic Republic in 1976, which is recognized by 70 countries. A quarter century of war by about 20,000 nomad guerrillas fighting against the Moroccan army has resulted. Morocco now holds much of the territory after a UN supported cease-fire, behind a 1,500-kilometer (930-mi.) barbed wire and rubble barrier. Talks between Morocco and the Saharawi aimed at allowing a UNO referendum in the year 2000 broke down.

Language

The Saharawi speak Hassaniya Arabic and some Spanish. There are 70,000 who have been refugees in Tindouf, Algeria since the 1980s, and many have gone to Spain. Education in Saharawi nationalism is given in the camps, and literacy has been raised from 5% to 95%. Many are going abroad for university education.[4] There are 75,000 Saharawi who still remain independent in Mauritania. No progress, either material or spiritual, is really possible until the international community is able to establish a just settlement. There are openings for a Christian witness to the Saharawi in Europe.

IMAZIGHEN, or *Berbers*

They live in scattered areas in the Middle Atlas Mountains, Morocco and along the Atlas range into Algeria. They total between 18 and 20 million. *Imazighen* is their preferred name and means "freemen" or "masters" — only outsiders call them Berbers. They are thought to be the descendants of the original inhabitants of North Africa. There is historical evidence for Berbers being Christians and Jews at the time of the Roman Empire. The Arab invasion resulted in this previously independent people being surrounded by Arab settlers, so that they now form a number of separate autonomous peoples. They have had no sense of unity greater than that within their tribe and have little contact with each other, but this is evolving into a greater political consciousness. The pastoral *Tuareqs* and the agricultural *Kabyle* (2 million), in the mountains of eastern Algeria, are also Berber groups.[5] The Berbers speak about 33 different Berber languages.

Rif Berbers or *Northern Shilha*: they live in the Rif ranges, Morocco. There are about 1.5 million *Ishilhayn* or *Southern Shilha*, with three million in the Western and Anti-Atlas Mountains, Morocco. Both groups are settled agriculturists. Shilha is the Arabic name for all the Berber languages. A *rif* is also a group of the tents of related extended families. There are a number of agencies trying to reach the Berbers in Europe, including YWAM, who have a Latin American team working in Amsterdam among 20,000 Rif Berbers.

Soussi or *Shleuh Berbers* or *Southern Shilha*: 2,000,000 inhabit the western High Atlas and Anti-Atlas Mountains, Morocco. The area is called Sous in Morocco. The two ranges suffer extremes of weather; the High Atlas is covered in snow between November and May but the lower southern slopes are arid and without trees. The villagers are agropastoralists and tend terraced fields with irrigation ditches and dams, usually growing two crops a year. In the summer whole families go with their flocks up into the high mountains for pasture, and in winter they may hire shepherds to take the sheep to the plains.

In the Anti-Atlas Mountains the villages are built on rocky slopes, often with three-story houses, the ground floor being a shelter for animals. While each family has some livestock, they do not practice the transhumant lifestyle as other Berbers.

Many Soussi have migrated to the cities, and some families of the *Ammeln* and the *Ait Sonab* tribes of the Anti-Atlas have gained a monopoly in the grocery business in Casablanca, Tangiers and Larache. Others have managed to develop their small businesses into wholesaling and chain store operations. Though their parents are largely illiterate, the younger generation has advanced to university and some even to further education. The Soussi have always had an influence on political events in Morocco, not least in their support for independence from the French. The Berber language the Soussi speak is Tashilhit.[6] New Opportunities is working to help this people.[7]

Central Shilha, ***Middle Atlas Berbers*** or ***Central Morocco Berbers*** are also called ***Tamazight***, which is the name of their language. There are 2,785,000 in Morocco, with others in Algeria and other parts of North Africa and France. They total 3,918,000. Those that live in the Middle Atlas Range rely primarily on transhumant pastoralism of sheep and goats. Some of them are winter nomads, who have villages up in the mountains, and who travel to the valleys in the winter. Other tribes are spring nomads, having their villages in the valleys or on the steppe and taking their flocks into the mountains during the summer. Yet others have a double transhumant lifestyle. They have their village at a middle altitude and travel higher up the mountains in the summer and go lower to the valleys in the winter. Part of each family always remains in the villages during the migrations. All of them practice some limited agriculture and their villages have characteristic granary towers. Each valley has a number of patrilinear-related villages that together form an almost autonomous district, or *ait*. Ten to fifteen extended families form a village.

The Berbers are Sunni Muslims, but the worship of saints, or *igurramen*, is vital to them. The *igurramen* make up about 5% of the population of the tribes, and for this reason the power of any one of them can be limited. They believe that the "magical" holy power of *baraka*, that these men are thought to possess, can heal or resolve other problems. The power is inherited so that saintly families have considerable influence and live separate lives, usually by the tombs of their ancestors. To gain protection from evil, therefore, one should wear amulets blessed by a holy man, or make pilgrimages to the saints' tombs, or consult teachers who are their descendants.

Three Christian agencies are in contact with them. A fifteen-minute broadcast is beamed to this people once a week.

Kabyle Berbers, Algeria, are agriculturists and therefore outside our survey. They have a well-developed dualistic symbolism expressed by the layout of their traditional homes. A half-hour radio broadcast is provided five days a week in Kabyle.

Berbers of Central Algeria — there are 57,000 of various groups, speaking different languages, who live in and around Tougourt, Gourara and Ouargla. There are only 2,000 Berber-speaking people. They are related to the Mzabi, who are traders.

Shawiya, Algeria. There are 450,000 of these Berbers of the Aurès Mountain massif in eastern Algeria. They follow a semi-nomadic lifestyle, which is partly agricultural and partly pastoral. They have occupied these rugged mountains since their retreat from Tunisia during the Arab invasions in the Middle Ages. The Shawiya have lived in isolation with a self-sufficient society and economy. Because of this, they were able to conserve the original character of their people. They have resisted in turn the Romans, the Vandals, the Byzantine Empire and the Arabs. Only the French succeeded in capturing and destroying their villages and put them in camps in the 1850s. This is still resented. There is no Christian witness among them.

Nafusa: A 40,000-strong Berber group in the Jebel Nafusa, western Libya. Their villages, in the mountains, are difficult to reach. They are agropastoralists growing various crops, but in the autumn they take their sheep to graze to the south outside the Jebel. They are also distinguished from their Arab neighbors by belonging to the Ibadi sect. They have contact with the Djerba island community. Many of the men have migrated to the towns.[8]

CHAAMBA

There are 60,000 Arabs living in the northwest Sahara. They may have come from Syria around the fourteenth century and settled in this region of the Great Erg because of the development of caravan traffic. Metlili, on the southern slope of the Atlas Mountains in Algeria, is one of their centers. They are spread to the south and east but retain a loose confederated structure of various groups, such as the *Mouadhi Chaamba* in El Goléa, the *Bou Rouba* in Ouargla, and the *Chaamba Berazga*, all of which have member tribes. There are some tribes of nobles, and some tribes of commoners or vassals. Their society is also divided between sedentary elements and the nomads, who keep camels, sheep and goats. They have a dual political division of society as well, which has lost its real significance, but camps are divided in two.

The camps consist of between four and 30 family tents. Most of the pastoral families also own date palms. They own town houses and rent them out in order to live in their tents. Between September and January they are at their home bases, but they migrate for the rest of the year. They usually avoid marriage with black Africans, but some Negro concubines have meant that there are now some Africans in Chaamba families.[9]

BEDOUIN

The Bedouin are in Algeria, with 130,000 in northeastern Libya and 150,000 in Tunisia. It was common to use the term *arabi* to describe them in contrast to settled people. The Arabs were always a minority in the population, but they had great influence by intermarriage as they settled along the coast and successfully converted North Africa to Islam before the thirteenth century. By contrast, the Bedouin always remained self-contained as endogamous tribes, and they succeeded in driving out the Berber farmers.

The 30,000 *Gafsa Bedouin* live in 19,000 square kilometers (11,800 sq. mi.) of semi-arid so-called "steppe" in central Tunisia. They keep sheep and grow dates and olives, which are the main commercial products of the region, in the oases. The environment is affected by phosphate being mined and transported to Sfax. The Bedouin speak Levantine Arabic, a language in which gospel audiocassettes are available.

The *Bedouin* in Cyrenaica, Libya, have been estimated to total 130,000. The Italian colonization of Libya disrupted tribal life and drove the pastoralists to more arid lands, and in Cyrenaica they never surrendered to the invaders. The tribes claim descent from marabouts and nobles. The Libyan government has attempted to appoint their leaders according to competence, rather than according to the traditional method based on descent and local experience. Most stay in one place during the winter, but they migrate in the summer with their flocks in groups of closely related families called a *bait*, or "house." The tribal area of pasture and wells is called *watan*. The women are usually unveiled and have the duty of carrying water to the camp or village. In the nineteenth century, their Islam was influenced by the Sanusi movement that established brotherhoods in the oases, and encouraged the resistance to European powers. They speak a Libyan Colloquial Arabic.[10] They have contact with a medical clinic.[11] New Opportunities anticipate helping these people.

There are 1,200,000 *Bedouin* in Egypt. There are many tribes, such as the *Awlad 'Ali* along the northern coast bordering the Mediterranean, the *'Amarin* west of Suez, the *Ma'aza* between the Nile and the Gulf of Suez and the *'Ababda* and *Bisharin* to the south bordering the Red Sea. In Sinai there are about two dozen tribes. The *Ayayda*, *Huwetat* and *Ahaywat* are east of Suez, and the *Muzena* to the south and east of Gebel Musa (Mount Sinai). The *Tarabin*, *Azazma* and *Ahaywat* straddle the border with Egypt from the Mediterranean to Aqaba. Their lifestyle is divided between being nomadic, living in goat-hair tents, and being semi-nomadic, using concrete houses for the winter. Most now live off salaried income from tourism or driving trucks, or remittances from urban relatives.

TUAREQ

These people are described in the Western Sahel section. Perhaps 25,000 are in the Aijer Mountains and Ganet and in western Libya around Ghat.

Non-Pastoral Nomadic Peoples in North Africa

NEMADI or *Namadi* (sg. Nemedai)

There are about 200 who live on the southwest border of the Sahara in Mauritania and northern Mali. They are nomadic hunters of antelope, using a pack of dogs. They also hunt wild boar and sell them to Muslims. They trade both with the Maures and Negro peoples to the south. The Nemadi are hunter-gathers, but they are included here because of their travel to trade in dried meat and hides for cloth, firearms and millet. This trade is an important part of their lifestyle, which would otherwise be impossible.

They are very poor, with few clothes or goods, and only some own a camel. They avoid settlements and live in tents made of hides or of woven wool and cloth, but they also sometimes simply make a windbreak of mud bricks. The tents are said to be lowered over the occupants like a blanket at night. Nemadi come into the Nara and Kayes regions of Mali. Some camped in a Fulbe Jeeri village in 1995, with, it is said, about 60 to 100 dogs. They often cause problems because of their dogs, which are said to be kept hungry to hunt; the Fulbe say "they are bad neighbors."

They have a tradition that they were once Moors who chose to be independent, but the Moors deny this. In fact, a recent preliminary survey indicates they are a hunting caste of Moor society. While nominally Muslim, they are said to be completely ignorant of Muslim practices. They speak Hassanya Arabic, but many details about them are unknown — including whether they have a language of their own, although the recent survey discounts the existence of this language.[12]

IMRAGUEN or *Hawata*

They are semi-nomadic fishermen on the coast of the Western Sahara and Mauritania.[13] A number of groups include part-Europeans among them. Some of them are thought to be descendants of the Bafour, the original inhabitants of the region, who were an offshoot of the Soninke near the Senegal River. The original Imraguen are probably a group of 120 situated north of Nouakcott, along 150 kilometers (90 mi.) of the coast north of Cape Timiris. In earlier times they used dugout canoes, propelling them with their legs. The Portuguese explorers of the fifteenth century who first saw them thought they were flying low over the water. A few still use launches, living on them for months with their families, fishing and taking fresh fish to sell in Nouadhibou (Port Etienne).

Most Imraguen live in small groups of huts or tents among the dunes on the shore. The area is desert, without trees or roads. The huts are built of flotsam and other debris and have enclosures for nets and tables for drying fish. The Imraguen men normally do not wear clothes, except for leather leggings when fishing. The normal method of fishing is for two lines of men to wade into the sea with a net between them. They trap the fish, usually millet, between the net and the shore. Sharks are often a danger. The fish is sun-dried for later sale. They also catch dolphins and turtles and turtle eggs. They are reputed to use dolphins to drive the fish shoals nearer the shore. The fishing has to be on a co-operative basis, as the supply of fish caught in this way is limited.

The number of fish caught offshore is ample, and boats from the Canary Isles and elsewhere fish profitably there. The Imraguen need help to get better boats. In the 1960s the Mauritanian government attempted to develop their fishing because the Moors, who make up the majority of the population, have an aversion to such work.

The Imraguen can fish only from August to April, because during the summer the limited freshwater supply near the coast dries up. In spring the Imraguen migrate to live within reach of wells used by pastoralists about 20 kilometers (12 mi.) inland, and peddle their dried fish and fish oil around the camps of the Moors. They are clients of the Moor warrior and marabout classes, especially the Oulad Bou Sba, for they have to pay for their fishing "rights" and are too weak to resist the treats from these nomadic pastoralists. The Moors usually visit the Imraguen during the winter to collect the tribute and exchange goods. They have their own language, which appears to be a mixture of Arabic and Soninke, but some also speak French. They have no knowledge of Christianity.

IGHYUWN

This is the entertainer caste of the Moors of the Western Sahara and Mauritania. They number probably a few hundred and work in small family groups, traveling between their patron tribes.[14] Traditionally they did this for weddings or circumcisions or for visitors among the warrior or hassan tribes. But the *zawaya*, or marabout, tribes rejected them. Both the men and women participate in the entertainment as singers, dancers, clowns and storytellers. The latter will include recounting the history of the tribes or individuals and giving a political commentary on recent events. In this way they used to be the "media" before the advent of radio and the press. Their music draws from Berber, Arab and African sources and uses the *tidinit*, or four- or five-stringed lute, and the *ardin*, a harp played by the women, and drums.

The Moors, like the Arabs and other peoples of Africa, despise the Ighyuwn and fear them as sorcerers, representing all the dubious aspects of the Moorish character.

They are seen as political schemers, spies and extortioners for fees. They are also thought to have occult powers and to be able to curse anyone who offends them, including tribal leaders. In the second half of the twentieth century they moved to urban areas, for greater commercial opportunities. Western guitar music is competing in Mauritania, and the possibilities of commercializing recorded traditional music are being pursued. The Ighyuwn are essentially animists, being more lax in Islamic practice than their Moor patrons. Such groups as this, and the Mu'allmin below, should not be overlooked in a ministry to the Moors.

MU'ALLMIN

The Mu'allmin are a caste of craftsmen working for the tribes of Moors in Mauritania and the Western Sahara. They travel and work closely with one tribe and its dependent castes, like the Inadan of the Tuareq. The women make articles in leather and the men work in wood and metal, making such things as the curved tent poles and camel frames. The Moors despise them. The Mauritanian government has developed an outlet for their handicrafts in tourism and export, and this has helped the Mu'allmin to raise their social status.[15]

OULOUD n'SIDI AHMED or MOUSSA

They are troupes of acrobats that migrate among the Berbers of the Atlas Mountains in Morocco. There are a number of groups called *r'rma*, consisting of 20 to 30 boys and men who are said to have been blessed by the seventeenth-century saint of that name, and from whom they claim descent. The blessing enables them to practice a form of martial arts for entertainment. Many think that they practice magic, steal, demand hospitality and otherwise profit from their saintly connection. They travel on foot or with donkeys. During the day they move from house to house banging their drums, giving blessings and receiving donations and gifts. The entertainment is in the evenings. The gifts received from the women in the morning collection are auctioned back, and are considered to be charged with *baraka*, the magical power of the saint. In August all the troupes come together at the saint's tomb, to give gifts and so guarantee their power to perform for another year. About 100,000 pilgrims attend this festival. Many acrobats "retire" to Marrakech to establish small hotels or cafes. Others are recruited for circuses abroad.[16] It is not a distinct people group.

HARRATIN

These are the descendants of "redeemed slaves" of Black Moors and live in the oases of the Sahara and work for Moor or Bidan landowners. But they are now sedentary.[17]

GYPSIES

Morocco and Algeria: The 2,500 *Xoraxai* in Algeria are Muslim, and the name implies they came from the Middle East. They are said to be also in Morocco. Some may be in Tunisia. Some *Kali* or *Gitan* are probably in Morocco. The *Afrikaya* in Algeria are possibly Manouche, French-speaking, and originating from France at the time of French colonization.[18]

Halebi or *Dom* in Egypt and Libya (33,000), and possibly Tunisia. Some of them travel into the Sudan because of economic hardship.

Nawar: Minorsky argues that Nawar is derived from Luri, or Luti in Iran, and that they therefore probably originated in India.[19] Van de Pijpekamp lists 100,000 in Chad, Libya and Egypt and a literacy rate of less than 5%. They sell animals and veterinary medicines, but they are not pastoralists. The women tell fortunes. They believe that they are condemned to nomadism because their forebears stole oil-lamps at Mecca.[20]

Egypt claims a high degree of ethnic homogeneity, with only the Nubians not speaking Arabic. But the 1,080,000 Gypsies represent 2% of the population, and although most speak Arabic, a considerable number speak dialects of Domari.

The 864,000 *Halebi* or *Dom* are in the Nile Delta in four tribes, and some are said to live on floating islands. Halebi is an Egyptian name for Gypsy. They claim to come from Yemen or Syria, but this may reflect a desire to appear better Muslims. Traditionally the men trade in horses and the women practice folk medicine, fortune-telling and divination. Some of them travel into the Sudan because of economic hardship.

There are 216,000 *Ghagar* or *Ghagar* or *Nawar* (sg. *Nuri*) who migrated back from Europe and came from Turkey in the nineteenth century. They live around or just north of Cairo, working as ferriers, smiths, tinkers or as traveling entertainers. The women are ropewalkers, dancers, musicians and tattooists. They are also found elsewhere in Egypt, in the Maghreb and in the Sudan. The Halebi like to distinguish between themselves and the Ghagar, but both are considered with contempt by the dominant Arab culture.[21]

MIDDLE EAST

The Middle East is where nomadism, both as pastoralism and as caravaning, probably began. The area includes Turkey, Syria and Iraq and southwards to Sinai and the Arabian Peninsula. Peoples were migrating both permanently and seasonally within the Fertile Crescent, formed by Mesopotamia and Lebanon and Palestine, before biblical times. Most of the nomads throughout the region's history have moved close to settled parts. Livestock raising on the open, semi-arid peripheries, that were suitable only as land for shepherds, was part of the economy to support the civilizations based on the irrigated valleys of the rivers. Only under political pressures at particular times was it necessary for nomads to live in the desert. The almost autonomous nomadic band on camels has all but disappeared in this region, but the culture derived from that life continues to persist in different forms.

Today, while irrigation for cultivation has been extended far beyond what it was in ancient times, much of land is still only suitable for nomadic pastoralism. The scarcity of water in this region is being exacerbated by the large-scale development of agriculture resulting in some nations exceeding their supply. Sharing the water of the rivers Euphrates, Tigris and Jordan for irrigation is a potential for conflict between Turkey, Syria and Iraq. The depletion of aquifers could result in a serious shortage to affect the lifestyle of many.[1] Nomads are using machine-bored wells and carrying water in drums on trucks to their flocks in the desert grazing areas.[2]

The nomadic peoples of the region are all Muslims, and nomadism and life on the fringe of the desert would be considered as part of that faith's heritage. Because of the conflict with Israel and the West, who strongly represent settled urban life, as well as the fact that all the Christians of the region are settled, Christianity appears to be the antithesis of the nomad's values.

Nomadic Pastoralists of the Middle East

BEDOUIN or Bedu (sg. Badawi or Bedui)

Bedouin means "desert dweller," which is increasingly a misnomer for many of them. The estimate of the number of Bedouin in Syria, Lebanon, Jordan, Saudi Arabia, Yemen, the Gulf States, Egypt and Israel is 6,500,000. Alan Keohane estimates there are between four and five million. Together with those in Saharan Africa, there are between 12 and 19 million. Both the Jordanian and Saudi monarchies derived their initial political support from the Bedouin. Three-quarters of the population of the Arabian Peninsula claims an origin among the desert nomads and idealize their traditional values, but they often despise the minority who still live that way. The Bedouin way of life has forged values of an essential egalitarianism, self-reliance and generosity in hospitality in a harsh environment.[3]

Some peoples of the Bible, such as the Amalekites, the descendants of Esau living to the south of Canaan (Ex. 17:8f., etc.), and the Midianites, descendants of Abraham on the desert border in Transjordan (Gen. 25:1-4, etc.), were among the forerunners of the

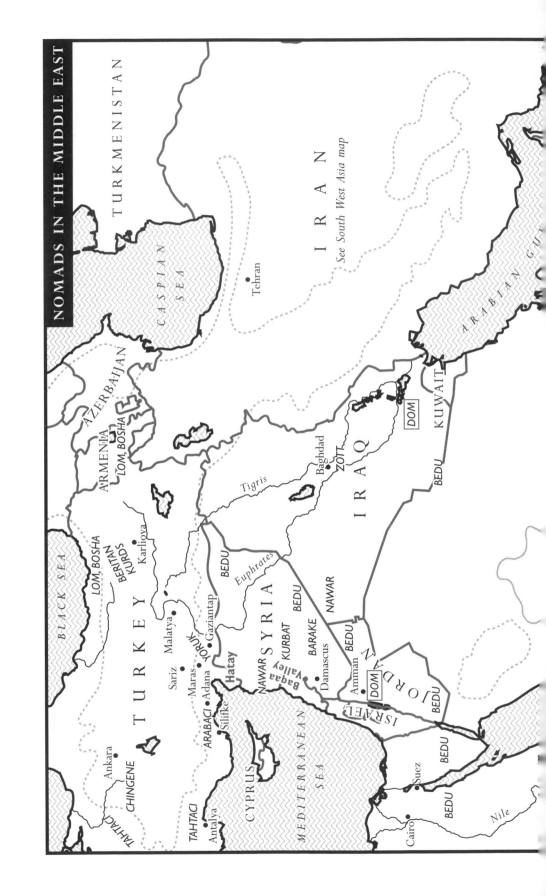

NOMADS IN THE MIDDLE EAST

TURKMENISTAN

CASPIAN SEA

Tehran

IRAN

See South West Asia map

ARABIAN GU

ARMENIA

LOM, BOSHA

LOM, BOSHA

BERITAN
KURDS

Karlıova

AZERBAIJAN

BLACK SEA

DOM

KUWAIT

BEDU

Baghdad

ZOTT

Tigris

I R A Q

BEDU

Euphrates

NAWAR

BEDU

NAWAR

KURBAT

BEDU

Sariz

Malatya

Maras

Gaziantap

YÖRÜK

Adana

ARABACI

Silifke

Hatay

S Y R I A

Baqaa
Valley

BARAKE

Damascus

BEDU

Amman

DOM

JORDAN

BEDU

Ankara

T U R K E Y

CHINGENE

TAHTACI

Antalya

TAHTACI

CYPRUS

MEDITERRANEAN SEA

ISRAEL

BEDU

Cairo

Suez

BEDU

Nile

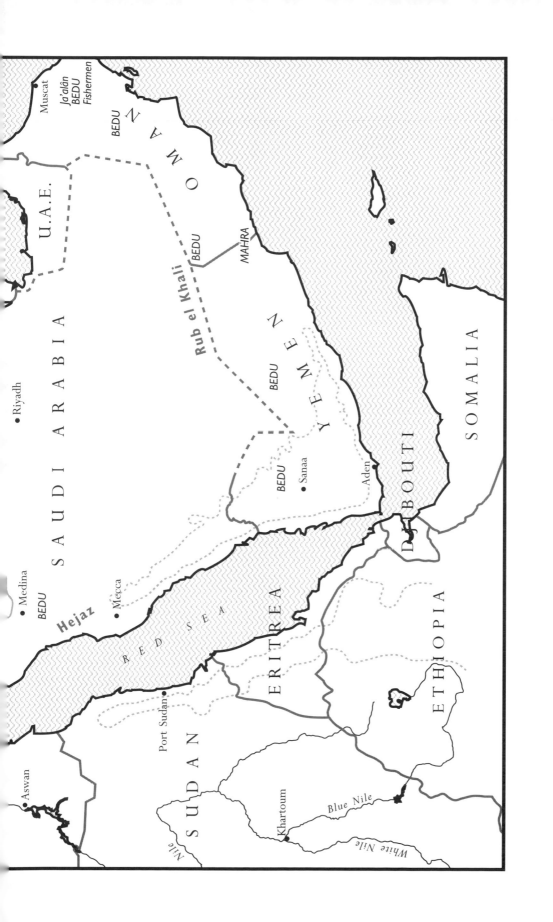

17a

17b

17c

17d

17 Bedouin:
    a. A visit to a traditional Bedouin tent.
    b. The Bedouin are noted for their hospitality (Photo: R. Spraggett).
    c. The kitchen of a Bedouin tent.
    d. Mother and daughter.

Arabs (Num. 22ff.; Judg. 3:13; 6:3f.; Dt. 25:19). While camels were already domesticated in biblical times for transport and warfare, the nomads of that time, as the majority are now, were semi-nomadic and kept mostly sheep and goats. Camel pastoralism developed as an offshoot from the caravan trade using camels in the second millennium BC, and was therefore closely connected with the political and economic complexities of the powers of the Fertile Crescent.[4] The *Rwala* Bedu think they became camel pastoralists to escape the imperialism of Baghdad and so preserve their own values. Therefore the romantic notions of the Bedouin being primal and completely autonomous from civilization is a myth.[5]

The southern Bedu tribes in Yemen claim to be the original Arabs, *Arab al Araba*, descended from Qahtan (Joktan in Genesis 10:25-26). The Jordanian and Syrian tribes to the north, with a more developed pastoralism and tents, are considered to have descended from Ishmael. The tribes in the center of the peninsula in the Nejd, like the *Shammar*, are thought to be descended from an intermarriage between the two lineages. Although the true Bedu make up only a tiny portion of the Middle East's population, they nevertheless have given it its values and sense of history.

Society

A Badawi's whole view of life, sense of honor and allegiance, is determined by knowing who his ancestors were and by belonging to his extended family, clan and tribe. His genealogy is passed on orally from his father and grandfather, being traced back to about five generations, though they would accept that tracing over many generations is inaccurate and mythical, and often has more to do with past political allegiances than literal descent. The individual is subordinate to the lineage and tribe and their leaders, such as the emirs (princes) of a tribe (*kabila* or *ashira*). A clan consists of a number of extended families tracing their descent through five generations (*fakhida*) and is led by a

mukhtar. These groupings are not as permanent as the genealogical claims suggest, and clans may change their affiliation of tribe.

The Badawi's key cultural concept is *ird* — that is, he must maintain the honor or be loyal to the reputation of the living and dead of one's lineage. He, his father, uncles and brothers and other men of his lineage form a mutually accountable unit, or *khmas*, corporately responsible for one another's actions. On occasions a member can be made an outcast (*meshamas*, or "to be exposed to the sun") for a serious offense.[6] He and his fellows assume responsibility for the conduct of the extended family's men, women and children, whose behavior is judged according to whether it maintains the family's or tribe's honor, or offends that of another similar group. Offenses against one's family, lineage or tribe require compensation by a similar penalty being inflicted on a member of the offending group.

This system aims at a balance of damage, viewed as compensation rather than as an appropriate penalty. In the past, this led (and often still does) to revenge raids and killings. But conflicts between parts of the same tribe can be resolved by mediation by the leaders of a higher level in the tribe. There are also ways of forging closer relationships between the families, such as by marriage and hospitality. Sharing a meal creates a special bond between those who eat it. A Bedouin considers that he cannot attack an enemy who was his guest until after three days, when the food shared is considered to have left his body.

Fifty percent of the Bedu are under fourteen years old. At age seven the children start to learn adult duties, under the often harsh instruction of the men in the family. In some places the children receive free schooling with a free lunch. The Badawi's marriage is usually arranged by his father and uncles. Dating is not permitted but young people do get to know each other, when taking the flocks to the well, for example (Gen. 29:9 ff.), and can state their preferences. Marriage to first cousins on the father's side is preferred, and usually takes place between the ages of sixteen and twenty.

Women have been, and still are, subsumed as belonging to the father's or husband's sphere of honor. Girls grow up with a close relationship with their brothers as their protectors. On marriage, a wife lives with her husband's family and only gains respect when she provides him with a male heir. Almost all women are married and divorce, usually followed by remarriage, is quite common. In such cases, the children remain with their father. A woman usually does not inherit, even though this contravenes Islamic law, but the Bedu feel that to allow women also to inherit would result in the dissipation of their limited wealth. That their sons have sufficient to inherit is important, because life expectancy for the nomads is around forty-five years. To reach old age, especially as a grandparent, is to be much respected.

There are three main divisions among the Bedouin:

Hadari

In Arabia, 55% of the Bedouin are sedentary or *hadari*, but they have the mentality of the nomad and often have close relatives who are still active pastoralists. They are considered *fallaheen*, or poor farmers, in a derogatory sense by the "true" nomads, but the semi-nomadic clans have always had contact with both the nomads and the Hadari.

Sharwaya

Some 35-40% of Bedouin are semi-nomadic *sharwaya* or sheep raisers, living in villages with flocks of sheep and goats. Some of these make the distinction that they are not Bedu who have camels, but Arabs. By the mid-twentieth century, the motor vehicle took away the need for camels, so the nomads changed to breeding sheep to provide mutton for the towns. These days, the few remaining camels expect to ride at least part of the way in a pickup! Many of them are not fit for long desert journeys. Even some of the "noble" tribes of camel

nomads, such as the *Feedan* in Syria and the *Howietat* and *Bani Sakhr* in Jordan, have changed to sheep. The reasons for this are that the *Badia*, or the gravel plains in northern Jordan and Syria, are not only more fertile but firmer for trucks to transport both the sheep and water. The market for mutton is far greater than that for camels, and flocks are both cheaper and easier to build up than camel herds. They can recover their investment in a third of the time it takes to do the same with camels. The winter there is also too cold for camels.[7] Most of the Bedu have therefore changed their lifestyle.

The role of semi-nomadic sheep raisers is still economically important, because the limited agricultural land is irrigated and too expensive for pasture.[8] Two or more sublineages may form a *sharwaya*, or village, and the extended families live closely grouped together. The *sharwaya* migrates to find pasture for the flocks and returns to the villages about three times a year. Other family members have the opportunity to have town jobs to supplement their income, and the children can attend school. Many men work in the towns as taxi or truck drivers but "continue to think of themselves as Bedouin," and a number of the men have two families — one in town and another with the flocks.

Bedu (badawijin)

Their name means "the unsettled," "the desert dweller." These are the true nomads who have herds of camels and who are constantly mobile, often living in tents. They make up about 5–10%, that is around 350,000, of the total Bedouin. They show affection for their camels by kissing them, giving them names and composing verses about them. They can recognize the footprints of individual animals.[9] But, even among the nomads, the baggage camels are being replaced by motors, and tents are being exchanged for abode huts. The result is new settlements for seasonal residence and some cultivation of agricultural produce that they can sell in the towns. A household consists of a nuclear family with about six to

18a

18b

18c

18 Bedouin (continued):
   a. A Bedouin plays the flute.
   b. An old Bedouin lady shows the tattoos of her clan.
   c. Camels are increasingly just for tourists.

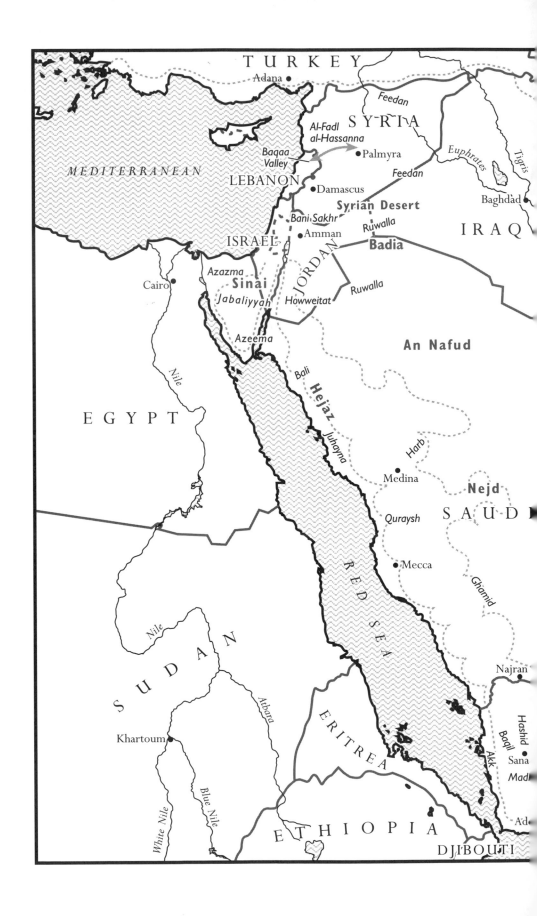

THE BEDU IN ARABIA

AFGHANISTAN

Tehran

IRAN

KUWAIT

Al Kūwayt

ammar

ARABIAN GULF

Beni Khalid

Hajir

QATAR

Dubai

Riyadh

U.A.E.

Muscat

Nizwa

Manasir

Dūru

ARABIA

Rashid Awamir

Sanaw

Wahiba
Sands

wasir

Al Murrah

Adam

Al Wahiba

Rub el Khali

Harasis

OMAN

Awamir

Rashid

Bait Imani

Bait Kathir

Al Murrah

m

Dahm

Saar

Abidah

YEMEN

Hadhramaut

Mahra

Humum

JORDAN
— other tribes include:

*Beni-Hasan, Beni Khalid,
al-Ajarmeh, al-Adwan,
Beni-Attiheh, al-Hajayah,
as-Sleet, Sirhan,
Beni-Hameideh, 'Amer,
Majali, ad-Darawish*
and the *Nueimai*

nine persons, normally owning about 20 camels. The sublineage or clan can consist of about nine households moving together, and this is the permanent unit for the nomads. The tribal structure still persists, with about 60 tribes of a few thousand Bedu each.

Nomadism

The classic nomad is represented by the *Al Murrah* tribe, who number 15,000 and cover vast distances in the Rub el Khali, or Empty Quarter, which is the size of France or Texas. They can travel as far as 3,000 kilometers (1,860 mi.) in a year, covering the whole of the Rub el Khali and even reaching into Iraq or Syria. As few as some 400 persons "occupy" an area of 5,000 square kilometers (3,100 sq. mi.). Yet they also share this huge area with other tribes. The stages of their migrations vary according to the scarce rainfall and its location. In the summer they are found camped by their wells, leaving their camels to roam freely since they need water at least every four days. From September to December they travel short distances constantly in the Empty Quarter, their camels drinking once a week either by returning to the wells or by being supplied by a water truck. They leave their tents at the summer wells because it is not cold enough to use them and so they live "in" nothing but a wind break.

Their winter and spring migrations cover the 650-kilometer (400-mi.) extent of the tribe's territory. In January, they are at their summer wells in the south. When they hear of the arrival of winter rain to the north, by radio or passing visitors, oil company employees or army patrols, they pack their tents and possessions on the male camels and make a rapid march northwards. They travel separately in small groups, the women traveling ahead with the tent to pitch camp before the herd arrives to trample on everything. This journey is swift, traveling up to 60 kilometers (40 mi.) in a day into the Nafud, which appears to be a sea of sand dunes, but gives them adequate winter pasture after a little rain.

Once in the north they make moves of

about 10 kilometers (6 mi.) every few days, pasturing the camels. Here in the north, because they are outside their area, they have contact with other tribes such as the shepherd and village Bedouin. It is also the time for calving. Camel breeding is planned so that the calves are born in the winter, at a time of more milk and pasture. This is a time when they eat meat, as some of the surplus male calves are culled. Only a few males are kept, for breeding and for transporting the baggage. All females are kept, as the Bedouin are primarily interested in milk, not meat. In March they return southwards more slowly to their permanent wells for the summer.[10] The Al Murrah therefore represent what is perhaps the most common outsider's view of the nomad. Other tribes in their area are the *Ajman*, *Mutayr*, *Dawasir* and *Subai*.

In the Eastern Province of Saudi Arabia there is a minority of Shi'ite settlements, each with a *husainiya*, a hall for Shi'ite religious gatherings, alongside the mosque. They are considered of a lower social class by the Sunnis and only intermarry among themselves.

a) Saudi Arabia

Ninety-five per cent of the population has been sedentary since about 1960, but some 200,000 are still pastoral Bedouin.[11] The twentieth century saw the climax of a process of conquest and amalgamation of the country by the Saudi family. The spread of the Wahhabite sect and the development of an army and the loyalty of the tribes became the basis for the foundation of the state of Saudi Arabia. The sect encouraged the Bedouin to believe they were the true Muslims, and that members of other tribes should be treated and defended as "brothers." This helped to undermine the feuding that had been endemic. A Bedouin force that enforced Wahhabism became the Saudi army. Paradoxically, Saudi Arabia has paid grants for settling the tribes, with aid for agricultural equipment. But this has not always been successful.

The *Dhafir*, in northern Saudi Arabia, is a confederation of about nine tribes, each with *badidas* or clans.[12] The seventeenth century saw them expelled from the Hejaz and migrate to the west of modern Kuwait.[13] Together with other groups they settled in villages such as Sufairi, with piped water and electricity in mud huts or concrete houses, but many keep their tents for use part of the year. They keep herds of camels for milk and for sentimental reasons. Their flocks of sheep are the economic stock, and are moved about the desert by trucks for grazing. They also use cars or trucks for carrying water, firewood and tents.[14] They consider themselves "Bedouins," not "settled," which depends more on belonging to particular tribes rather than on lifestyle. Gaining Saudi citizenship is easier for those considered Bedouin than for those considered "settled."

The Hejaz in Saudi Arabia is the ancient holy land of Islam. Tribes of Bedouin camel herders include the *Huwaytat, Bali* and *Juhayna* in the northern Hejaz, *Zahran* and *Ghamid* in the south, and *Hudhayl, Thaqif, Fahm* and *Sa'd* between Medina and Mecca.[15]

b) Syria

In the eighteenth century, the Bedouin from the Nejd in Saudi Arabia moved north into Syria, forcing the local nomads to settle or become semi-nomadic, as more of the land became cultivated. By the 1980s two trends were taking place. Some of the 927,000 Bedouin had become farmers, keeping small flocks of 48 sheep, on average, to a family. These flocks were too small to migrate and were fed on barley, stubble, feed and stale subsidized bread. Other Bedu became based in scattered villages on the steppe and tended to revert to a more nomadic existence, going greater and greater distances because it was cheaper to keep the flocks on natural rangeland or crop residues than to buy feed. These Bedu spend a large part of the year moving between three different cultivated areas for the stubble.[16]

The *Al-Fadl* and *al-Hassanna* are tribes in Syria that were part of that movement northwards from the Nejd over two hundred years ago. By the beginning of the twentieth

century they had become enclosed by agricultural land. The tribes are divided into *beits*, or clans, of related extended families. Two or more *beits* usually camp together — between 30 and 100 households. Included in this is the grazing group, with up to a dozen households, living in both tents and houses. A household of between 8 and 15 individuals is also called a *beit*.

The shepherds of these tribes divide their time between Palmyra, in the desert, and the Baqaa Valley.[17] After spending the winter in the desert, they move into the valley, following the early rain in April. During the summer the men and boys graze the sheep and goats on the mountain slopes, moving first southwards and then northwards on the Anti-Lebanon Range, including the lower eastern slope of Mount Hermon, north of Damascus. During the summer they trade wool, milk and butter for their other needs, using camels in local markets. At the end of June they form smaller groups who have agreements with farmers to graze on the stubble. In November they arrive again in the north of the valley, and when the winter rains commence they turn northeastwards to the desert, where there is adequate grass from January to March when lambing and butter making takes place.

After switching from pack-camels to trucks around 1963, their life has been revolutionized, reinforcing their pastoralism by creating commercial outlets. They have been able to get better prices for their products further afield, a fact that is making them quite prosperous. Camps now have to be set up beside roads that are accessible to the trucks, and migrations that took weeks can be done in one day. And, of course, trucks have eliminated the need for many of the intervening camps and reduced the number of men required to herd. The use of trucks has also changed the role of the women, who tend to have more free time. The cheese and butter making is now done in town dairies. They used to load and unload the camels, but trucks are considered a male domain, so the women are now excluded from this role. Without camels there is also no hair available for the women to weave rugs. Many of the young men work on the farms to save up to marry or buy motorcycles. They value education, and they are willing to sell their sheep to build a school. Tribal leaders also teach the boys to read so that they can read the *Qur'an*.

c) Jordan

There are between 168,000 and 240,000 semi- or fully nomadic Bedouin, or about 6% of the population of Jordan.[18] The main source of income for 22% of the population is in livestock, and it is a major activity for another 33%. The farmers are subsidized according to the number of sheep they have, and the Badia is now overpopulated. Although there are many research projects in this area, a priority need is a program to teach the people how to increase productivity without increasing their flocks. Key tribes in Jordan are the wealthy *Bani Sakhr* and the *Ruwalla*, who number between 250,000 and 500,000 and are also in Iraq. The *al Howietat* tribe is the largest in south Jordan. They have mostly settled and have built cement houses around the town of Ma'an, exchanging camels for sheep. But some families still migrate with their flocks out from the villages and live in tents for the summer.

d) Negev, Israel

After the establishment of the State of Israel in 1948, most of the Arabs fled to Jordan. Tribes in this area are the *Wuhaydat*, *Jubarat*, *Hanajra* and the *Tityaha*, situated north and east of Gaza. The *Zullam* are east of Beersheba to the Araba, south of the Dead Sea. The *Tarabin*, *Azazma* and *Ahaywat* straddle the border with Egypt from the Mediterranean to Aqaba. In 1974 there were 33,000 Bedu left in Israel, with the numbers increasing. The Joshua Project estimates that there are 732,000 in Israel.

These tribes used to have recognized traditional lands with cultivated plots to which they returned annually. The Israeli government has relocated 11 tribes and, since the 1960s, has tried to get them to settle. Seven townships were built for them in 1969. These are the only planned locations for the Bedouin, and about half of them now live there. Primary and secondary education is said to be available for them, and mobile health clinics have reduced the once high infant mortality rate.[19] The Bedouin population of the Negev in 1986 was said to be 60,000 from 30 tribes, with about 30,000 living in planned urban settlements, another 20,000 living in huts scattered in the tribal areas and about 10,000 still nomadic, living in tents with their flocks.

Livestock is still the primary economic source, although many Bedouin now work on modern farms.[20] The Bedu have to negotiate with three different Israeli bodies to find pasture outside their immediate tribal area of 1,000 square kilometers (620 sq. mi.), and this requires the service of special brokers. This results in a patron-client relationship with the usual social and economic dependence of the Bedouin.[21] The *Azazma* were resettled on land belonging to their neighbors in 1951, where they were forced to cultivate rented plots without being able to buy the plots, have long leases or settle permanently. The land is said to be contaminated by chemicals. A mass demonstration of 5,000 Bedouin gained a concession to establish a town on their traditional land.[22]

e) Egypt (east of Suez)

There are 33,000 Bedu from 13 different tribes living in southern Sinai. Although they are Egyptian citizens, they consider themselves a people apart, living according to Bedouin law. They have had considerable autonomy under the Israelis and now under Egypt. They prospered and gained schools and clinics under the Israeli occupation from 1967 to 1982. Israel established the infrastructure for a tourist industry and Egypt is developing it, including tours to gain an insight into the life of the Bedouin.[23] The people combine work as casual laborers at tourist villages with keeping flocks of sheep and goats and orchards. Their pastoral movement is not so extensive as in western Egypt or Arabia, being centered as it is on fairly fixed villages. They produce milk, cheese, fruit, and grain.

The tribes are the *Gebelya* (5,000 in the area of Gebel Musa, or Sinai) and the *Azeema* tribe in Sinai, who are poor — an indication of this is that they still use camels for transport. They are able to supplement their diet with fish. The *Jabaliyyah* in central Sinai, close to the Gebel Musa, number about 1,500. They differ from other Bedouin in that they concentrate on terraced gardens in the wadis high in the mountains. They live in the town of St. Catherine in the winter, and high in the mountains in summer. This is another illustration of pastoralists being economic opportunists seeing their vegetable and fruit gardens as a successful way of making a living in a difficult environment.[24]

f) Oman and the neighboring Empty Quarter of Saudi Arabia

The tribes in this area are the *Al Kathir*, that includes the *Bait Kathir*, *Rashid* and *Bait Imani*. The Rashid live in the Empty Quarter, around the wells in its center. The other tribes live near the coast. Other tribes in Oman are the *'Amir*, *Hikman* and *Mawalik*, and the largest is the *Al Wahibah*. The *Walhibi* and *Bani Yas* do not use tents but live in rectangular huts made of palm fronds, called *barasti*, for coolness. The women look after the goats and the men look after the camels. The Bedouin regularly come to the markets in the towns of Sanaw, Adam and Nizwa to buy palm fronds and rope to build their shelters and supplies of grain and vegetables and to sell livestock. Bedu fishermen on the Oman coast also sell dried shark meat for human consumption, anchovies for fertilizer, and dried sardines to nourish the camels (see below). Many imported goods are changing their lifestyle.[25]

g) Yemen

Yemen is the only place in the Arabian Peninsula that has sufficient rainfall to have regular cultivation. It produces, among other things, the "mocha" coffee. The central mountain range, from 1,500 to over 3,000 meters in altitude, is home to *Hashid* tribes who are surrounded by *Baqil* tribes on both the western slopes and the plateau to the east. The *Saar* live on the plateau and mountains to the north of the Hadhramaut, taking their water from two deep wells. They are a large and powerful tribe, with a reputation for raiding other tribes. They are called "the wolves of the desert," and they are traditional enemies of the *Rashid*.[26] They claim a dispensation from Mohammed himself from fasting and daily praying. The Dahm and Abida are settled farmers that have, in contrast to the usual practice, raided the Bedu.

Religion

The Bedouin are 98% Sunni Muslim, but they do not strictly observe the five pillars of Islam. The call to prayer begins and ends the day at sunrise and sunset, and is responded to by the men. The women have devotions in their tent or house. The will of Allah is considered responsible for events that are beyond human influence. They believe two angels render accounts of every deed of each individual for the judgment day. They also seek protection with amulets and pronouncing Allah's name from jinns that are thought to appear in human form. Many non-Shi'ites accept the idea of sanctity, or *baraka*, in some people or objects. Visits, especially by women, to shrines dedicated to these are therefore thought to bring relief from sickness or other personal problems. There are two nominal Christian tribes near Madaba and Kerak in Jordan claiming to belong to the Roman Catholic and Greek Orthodox churches.[27]

Outreach

The North African Mission sought to reach the Bedouin near Homs, now in Syria, in 1892. They were welcomed by the Bedouin, but were frustrated by the Ottoman authorities. The Saudi Arabs have been chosen as a key people for strategic intercession.[28] Prayer for these needy peoples in the whole area is very necessary, both to help them adjust to the transformation of their lifestyle and also to hear the gospel. Both classical and colloquial Arabic Bible translations, the *Jesus* film and cassettes are available. Arabic radio broadcasts are available, but none are in the Bedouin dialects.

MAHRA, or Ahl al Hadara

Mahra is the Arab name for those Bedouin tribes who are different in appearance to other Arabs, having almost beardless faces, fuzzy hair and dark pigmentation — such as the *Qarra*, *Mahra* and *Harasis*, along with parts of other tribes. The Mahra live mostly in Yemen (294,000), in Saudi Arabia (17,000) and Oman (109,000) in the region of Dhofar, on the southern Arabian coast, just east of Hadhramaut. Other population estimates are as high as 900,000. Many still speak the Mahri language, 76,500; there are 58,000 in Yemen; 15,000 in Oman; 3,537 in Kuwait.

The Mahra country is a huge area between Wadi Masileh and the Qarra Mountains, extending to the Arabian Sea and drained by the Wadi Jiza, which curves in a great arc in a valley with palm groves and small settlements to enter the Arabian Sea near Ghaidat, the largest Mahra village.

The Mahra belong to the Ghafiri confederation of tribes along with the *Durus*, *Bani Ghafiri*, *Bani Amr*, *Qarra*, *Shihuh* and others. The other confederation in the Hadhramaut is the *Hanawi*, which includes the *Rashid* and *Bait Kathir*, with whom the Mahra have a state of armed truce. The Gh'Afaris tribe includes Mahra, Duru and Junuba groups. The division between these confederations in Oman is a religious one. The *Hinawi* follow the Ibadi version of Islam. The *Ghafiri* have been more associated with outside influences, some tribes are Sunni, others have adopted Wahhabism. Wahhabiism is the Islamic sect or emphasis based on an attempt to derive all faith and law directly from the Qur'an alone, rejecting much of later Islamic teaching and practice. The Saudi family adopted it for Saudi Arabia. This allows a surprising flexibility in relation to things not actually mentioned in the Qur'an, such as the innovations of modern life.

The Bait Kathir live like the Bedouin Harasis — not in the traditional tents, but in the open with perhaps a windbreak of blankets on a tree. The Harasis are limited to the Jiddat, the central desert plateau of Oman. As many as 80% of the men are employed with the oil company on the plateau. New water wells have been drilled so that the camels no longer have to rely on water gathered on the ground from the morning fog.[29]

Each family of the Mahra has a few camels and lives in the mountains and on the plateau along the coast. The men wear their curly hair long and have a large ring in their right ear. The Mahra circumcise the male on the eve of his marriage. For special occasions the women paint their faces bright colors, with green and blue stripes.[30]

The Qarra are unusual in that they keep cattle and goats, as well as some camels. They are among the most primitive people of Arabia. According to Thiesiger they resemble the Al Kathir. The Qarra conquered the original Shahara people of the Dhofar, and only 300 remain as serfs. They adopted the Shahara language and customs. They are divided into 15 clans. Similar to the pastoralists of Africa, the Qarra men are obsessed with cattle. Each cow has a name, milk is the most important part of their diet, and only men milk them. They collect their herds together in the valleys for the monsoon and protect them in caves or byres constructed on stones and roofed with grass mats. The women look after the goats and do the plowing. They live in low mud huts and caves. Men wear their hair in braids wound around the head.

Young boys are circumcised by a person of note, such as a sheik. They also practice a crude complete female circumcision at birth. The women are short and attractive. They do not veil their faces, and they paint them red and green for ceremonial occasions. Men marry at fifteen, and the girls at thirteen. A bride can be bought either from her father or from her husband for between 10 to 30 cows. Thirty days after marriage, a scar is cut along the center of the scalp. Divorce and remarriage are easy. Sultan Qaboos of Oman had a Qarra mother.

The Qarra will go through the outward signs of being Muslim when visiting towns and where other Arabs are present, but they despise Wahhabiism, and in their camps they are animists. They consider, for example, that to utter an oath on the basis of one of the local shrines has great power to avenge. They sacrifice a cow and sprinkle the blood on anyone who is ill. They also apply a red-hot iron. Death is attributed to the evil eye, and many women who are thought to be witches are persecuted as a result. Half of a man's cattle herd is sacrificed when he dies. The Qarra eat hyena, which they consider a magical beast, and the jaw muscles are considered a delicacy. They refuse to eat foxes, birds and eggs. The evil eye is considered to cause a fall in milk production, and is appeased with a ritual use of frankincense.[31]

YORUK or Yörük

These shepherds in Turkey number 313,000. The Yoruk are a distinct ethnic cultural group, but they speak the local Anatolian Turkish dialect. They are distinguished from the Turks by having a history of migrating from Iran and Turkistan in the eleventh century, and are probably related to the Turkmen. They live along the Mediterranean and Aegean coasts in villages established by the Turkish government. Whole lineages have settled together, so that all the inhabitants of a village are usually related. The lineages are endogamous, and sons often prefer to marry their fathers' nieces. Polygamy is also approved. There are groups of Yoruk in Macedonia and Cyprus.

The semi-sedentary *çobanlar*, or shepherds, are transhumants. They traditionally wintered on the coastal plains and moved into the Taurus Mountains for the summer. Most of them have abandoned the pastoral life because of the difficulty of getting pasture rights from farmers and buying grain as fodder. As these prices have risen, so fewer families can be sustained by the pastoral system. Pasture has to be rented at high prices and it is very difficult to buy land to settle. But about 20% of them are in agriculture.

Nomadism

Those Yoruk who are still nomadic camp in the winter on the plains of Antaky (Antioch), or Hatay, Gaziantap and Maras. The nomadic Yoruk have relatives who buy and store supplies and market the livestock for them. Each family needs about 270 sheep to be self-sufficient. The Yoruk take pride in being able to recognize all of their own animals. The flocks have to find ample fallow fields, in an area where three or four crops of rice and cotton are produced in a two-year cycle. The villages on the plains have mechanized farms, and the fields are controlled by Kurdish landlords who themselves are descendants of tribes who were once nomadic. But there are also rocky outcrops with sufficient pasture.

In spring the Yoruk migrate some 200 kilometers (125 mi.) over the Anti-Taurus Mountains to summer pastures around Sariz, in central Anatolia, Kaseri Province. The migration requires a change of altitude of over 2,000 meters and takes about six weeks. The shepherds migrate at night with sheep, camels and donkeys and live in black goat-hair tents. Camp groups are formed of up to 20 tents, and they are as much for socializing as for security. They visit each tent in turn for a time of gossip which they jokingly call their "parliament." The men wear a mantle of felt made from the wool of their sheep called a kepenek, that is very effective in keeping them both dry and warm. The migration is difficult, because of the hostility of non-Yoruk villagers and the limited fodder. En route they are dependent on negotiating the rent of the fields. These negotiations have to be renewed every season. Another difficulty is that the animals are weakened by the fast pace without proper nourishment, and a late snowstorm can cause loss in the flocks. Another constant danger is the theft of whole flocks in trucks being carried away to distant markets on the improved roads.

The period from May to September is spent on the summer pastures in the mountains. The Turkmen or Çerkes (Circassian) villagers higher up the migration route and in the summer pasture region are more active in animal husbandry themselves, so they are reluctant to allow the Yoruks to share the pasture. Because of the severe mountain winters, these villagers have only the summer to benefit from the pastures, and so renting them to the Yoruk has to be profitable. The Yoruk tent groups gather together alongside a stream, as the pasture is used up, which can be exhausted by early August unless there are late rains.

The autumn migration is better than spring, because there is much stubble without the danger of crop damage to anger the villagers. The Yoruk are Sunni Muslims. Revenge attacks and deaths in feuds are a serious problem, including attacks due to collective revenge of one family on another.[32]

TURKMEN

There are reported to be semi-nomadic groups of shepherds in Turkey. They are often confused with Yoruks and other groups.[33] Bible portions are available for them.

KURDS

There are 25 million Kurds, including 13 million in Turkey, 2,786,000 in Iraq, and others in Iran, Syria, Lebanon and Caucasus. Their motto is "The Kurds have no friends." The Beritan tribes are migrating shepherds in eastern Turkey following an 800-kilometer (500-mi.) migration pattern. They market milk and other sheep products in nearby markets. Their summer camps are near Karliova.[34] They possibly speak standard Kurmanji. There are also semi-sedentary shepherds in the Kurdish Autonomous Region in northern Iraq, living in the mountains in tents with their flocks of goats and sheep.

Non-Pastoral Nomads in the Middle East

TAHTACI

These people are "those working with planks," a name they have had since they worked as lumbermen in the forests working for feudal landlords in the Ottoman Empire. Estimates of their number vary up to as much as 400,000, but Kehl gives an estimate above 100,000.[35] The Sunni majority discriminates against Muslim nonconformists and suppresses their population figures.

The Tahtaci could be a case of nomads who were once pastoralists, who adapted to an economic opportunity within the Ottoman society by taking up lumber work. But they have a tradition of coming from Khorasan, Iran and it is possible they originated as Iranians, arriving in Turkey in the fifteenth century. They are divided into *obas*, or clans, and these are linked together into a *boy*, or *asiret*, or tribe. The clan is the main social unit, consisting of up to 200 nuclear families that live together based on a settlement.

Nomadism

In winter they are found in these settlements in the mountain valleys of southern and southwestern Turkey, in the districts of Balikesir, Manisa, Izmir, Aydin, Denizli, Isparta, Mugla, Finike, Antalya, Akseli, Manaygal, Anamur, Mersin, Adana, Maras and Malatya. Some groups or clans have been able to buy marginal land, build houses and grow a winter crop of barley and corn, planting it in autumn and harvesting it in early spring. A few of these villages now have irrigated fields of their own, in which they grow fruit and vegetables. Other Tahtaci have tried to do agricultural work, such as cotton-picking, in the new irrigated plantations that have taken over the valleys. The winter is a difficult time for employment for them.

In early spring, small groups of related families move into the mountain forests. Each family has two or three mules to carry the children and the household goods, and the leading man of a group may own one or two horses. They never use camels as the Yoruk shepherds do. They may have a dozen or so goats with them and, because of some magical belief, they also like to have a cat with them.

For felling the trees they have to split up into small work groups of two or three families, being separated by more than an hour's walk through the forest. Older couples stay with their youngest son. They live in rectangular huts made of untrimmed branches, with ridgepoles covered in canvas or plastic. Their tradition says that they once used black tents and a type of yurt like the pastoral nomads. The thresholds of their huts have planks across them, and it is taboo to step on these planks. The women wear head cloths that are decorated with silver and gold coins that can represent significant wealth for them.

Each group works its own *yayla*, or summer territory. In spring, the Tahtaci start felling trees on the lower slopes. They gradually work upwards as the weather gets warmer until, in the heat of summer, they are working at the cooler high altitudes. In earlier times they not only felled the trees, but they also sawed them into planks of specified sizes. Today they usually leave the logs by approach tracks, and trucks take them to sawmills. They did not traditionally use power tools, but they are now beginning to do so. In the autumn they return to the valleys to their *kislak*, or winter territory.

This traditional pattern of work has changed as they now have to work with the government forestry agency. Some Tahtaci now specialize in transporting lumber, but they are still considered the best people to do the felling. However, work is sometimes scarce and many take on, or even prefer, other work when available.

Society

The Tahtaci keep to themselves, even when living in the towns. They tend to be secretive, hiding their identity among the Sunni majority. The Turks are suspicious of them and accuse them falsely of being thieves or of being immoral. This is mainly because the Turks are prejudiced against them being Shiites. They will be evasive with foreigners when a Turk is present, but welcoming when visited alone. Because of the distrust and even harassment they suffer from the Turkish majority, they have supported any movement that counters Sunni power, such as Ataturk and his vision of a secular Turkey, and are said to be vaguely sympathetic to Christianity. They also distrust Iranian fundamentalism.

Religion

The Tahtaci are not only Shiite, but also Alevites. They are considered by other Shiite groups in Turkey to be exemplar *kizilbas*, meaning "redheads," or the followers of Ali, the son-in-law of the prophet Mohammed, and they believe in a trinity of Allah, Mohammed and Ali. Ali is considered a special revelation of Allah himself, but because he is also human his followers who are initiated into a mystical relationship with him can share in the divine nature. This is heresy to the Sunni majority, but one can see parallels to Christ in Christianity. All Sunni, they believe, are merely at the level of duty, but Alevites are born onto the mystical path passing through three "gates" or stages to the direct personal experience of God.

The Tahtaci are strongly communal — the experience of God is only possible as a close fellowship. Their religious gatherings are held at night in homes or in the woods. Outsiders are not allowed. They involve much music and dancing and drinking. Alcohol is poured out as celebrating Mohammed's return from heaven. The leaders who claim descent from Ali visit each group. There is little separation of men and women in their religious and social gatherings, in contrast to their Sunni neighbors. Older women tend to be treated as equals with the men.

They and the Sunni Turks consider each other "unclean," because the Tahtaci do not observe Sunni cleansing rites. If they have to give hospitality to a Sunni, the crockery must be ceremonially washed 40 times afterwards. But a Christian will be welcomed, and even allowed to spend the night. They also refuse to work on Tuesdays and Fridays, which conflicts with the forestry department whose only day off is Sunday.

However, the Tahtaci also have pre-Islamic beliefs and taboos about which they are secretive. A non-Islamic prayer is offered for each tree felled as an apology for killing a living thing. At the beginning of the season a goat is sacrificed and special prayers and rites performed. They refuse to fell old gnarled trees. Water is considered sacred and must be handled with care.[36] There is no known Christian outreach among them.

GYPSIES

The history of the Gypsies seems to be that many moved out of India in the third and fifth centuries, and many were taken to Persia as minstrels and dancers. With the Arab expansion eastwards, many were taken back during the seventh and eighth centuries to various countries of the Middle East. The Seleucid invasion into the Levant caused a further spread into North Africa and Asia Minor. A common Arab name for them was Zott, or Jat.

Chingene, as they are called by the Turks, are 70,000 indigenous *Roma* Gypsies, possibly Xoraxané, in Turkey. According to a legend, the Chingene come from the marriage of Chin (or Chen), their ancestor, to a sorcerer's daughter called Guin. A Muslim saint considered this an unnatural union and put all the Chingene under a curse to be outcasts and wanderers.[37] They spend the winter near Hatay, and they travel each spring and summer in central Anatolia as musicians, dentists, circumcisers, fortunetellers and traders. Dentistry and circumcising are considered "unclean" in Islam. They are despised by the Turks as

"sub-human" and irreligious, because they do not have a book such as the *Qur'an*, and they are also thought to be immoral. In fact they are Muslims.[38] They have a few animals, but they travel by donkey and live in white tents. They have been taught as Muslims in the state schools, although they are not counted as such by the government and therefore there is a greater freedom for them to be evangelized.[39]

The *Arabaci*, in Turkey, claim to be Gypsies from Eastern Europe. They travel in ox-drawn wagons and live by doing various crafts, as above. They winter in Hatay and along the coast. (See the fuller note on them in the European section, below.)

The *Lom*, or *Bosha*, live in Armenia, East Turkey and Iran and total about 100,000. They are mainly nomadic, but little is known about them. Lom is their name for themselves. They still speak an Armenian form of Romani called Lomavren.[40]

The *Dom*, meaning "man," are found in Cyprus, Iraq, Syria, Lebanon, Jordan, Israel, the West Bank and Gaza, Saudi Arabia, U.A.E. and North Africa. Centuries ago, the Arabs took them from Iran. They were then called Zott, or Jat. The Arabs call them "Nawar," with the connotation of contempt. There are said to be between three and five million of them. Such estimates of their numbers are difficult, because they move from country to country. They are not a homogenous group and they have different lifestyles and linguistic practices.

Tsigani: Various Dom have been in Cyprus for five centuries. They call themselves Kurbet, and their language is Kurbetcha, but most speak Turkish. Most were nomadic until the division of the island in 1974. There are 600 in Famagusta and Morphou. Others travel from Greece to hawk their wares. Another 600 are in Turkish Cyprus, where they live in a camp. Twenty of these families crossed over and were settled in Limassol in 1999, and others in Paphos. Because they speak Turkish, they cannot benefit fully from welfare and job opportunities there.[41]

The Gypsies are called *Ghorbati* or *Kurbat* in northern Syria, and *Barake*

19a

19b

19c

19 Dom or Ghorbati:
    a. A Dom family in their tent in a northern town in Jordan.
    b. The Dom camp on empty lots in the towns.
    c. The children live by begging.

elsewhere in Syria. The Ghorbati who work as craftsmen and musicians often distinguish themselves from the Nawar, who tend to live by begging. There are 50,000 Zott, or Ghorbati, in Iraq. There are some called *Zargaris*, who call themselves Roma, who have migrated from Europe.

Many speak Domari among themselves; others claim to have forgotten it and most are illiterate. They tend to encourage their children to speak Arabic. The nomadic families are musicians, metal workers, fortunetellers and dancers, or work doing casual labor in the harvests. Other Dom are settled and adopt a more Western lifestyle. Because the dominant Arabs hold them in contempt, the Dom have adopted the languages and customs of the countries in which they live, and they even declare themselves to be indigenous, although most do not have birth certificates or citizenship. They are considered outcasts.

In Lebanon they number 8,000 or more in Beirut, Jubayal, Tripoli and the Beqaa. In the valley they live in tents, while in the cities they are found in self-made huts.[42]

Nomadism

A number of the Dom peripatetics served the Bedouin in the past. These include the *ageyi*, or camel dealers, who lived in the towns but visited the camps, and the *sunna* (sg. *sani*), or smiths, who attached themselves to the camps of those rich enough to own horses. There were also various traders and peddlers.

Today the Nawar provide various services in the towns. The men work as gunsmiths, jewelers, tinkers and dentists, and the women are herbal doctors, healers, fortunetellers, tattooists and also dentists. But it is still their custom to visit the camps once a year, exploiting the Bedouins' perception that if they are wealthy they must also be generous to visitors like the Nawar, and also that to give alms is meritorious. In contrast, the Nawar show themselves not to be Bedouin by believing that wealth is to be accumulated. But much of the trade with the Bedouin has been replaced by village stores and by the

Bedouin themselves being able to visit towns to buy goods. In Jordan they claim to be Turkmen, of whom there are about 4,000.

Tsoani is the name given to the Dom in Israel. They have been there for over a century. They benefit from education and other ways of integrating more, and want to be known as Arabs. Many have migrated to Jordan during the various wars. The community in Jerusalem numbers about 1,200. In 1999, they formed their own society to promote their education, health care and the place of women.[43]

Other migrants travel with the Nawar today, including pilgrims begging to get to Mecca as well as displaced persons. The "real" Nawar speak Arabic. It is not known whether they are Gypsies, or speak Domari, but they are able to use Gypsy-type networks to travel across Europe to France and other places without documentation.[44]

JA'ALÂN BEDU FISHERMEN

Bedu fishermen are found between Shiyya and Daffa, on the coast of Oman, where the Arabian Gulf becomes the Arabian Sea. Ethnically they are no different from the Bedu listed above, and they belong to clans of the pastoralist tribes nearby. We describe them separately here to highlight their distinctive lifestyle. While many families have members who are in pastoralism with herds of goats, they also support themselves from nomadic fishing and date palm cultivation. A typical family may fish in two places on the coast, 100 kilometers (60 mi.) apart, according to the seasonal movements of the fish, and also migrate to their date palm plantation, 200 kilometers (125 mi.) inland, from August to October.

They use three types of boat in the fishing: canoes for the lagoons behind the beaches and close inshore; modern dinghies for going further out to sea; and the larger motor *lanjes*, with a crew of six or more, that used to trade with dried fish as far as India and East Africa and around the Gulf. Today they trade with the local Bedu and also take fresh fish by pickup trucks to the cities of the Gulf States. The local trade is facilitated by the exchange of manure and fodder dates, as well as fish.

The Bedu see all natural resources, including the fish, as provided by a generous Allah. They have their own ideas about conservation, deciding what are the acceptable sizes of nets and other equipment. These ideas are based on the local knowledge of shoal movements, the underwater terrain and the weather. Conserving the stocks is seen as a moral or religious duty, rather merely economic prudence. Access to the sea is open to fishermen from all parts of the coast, provided they follow the local conservation measures. This is a clear case of conservation and development having to work together with the religious world view of the participants. The catch is shared according to who owns the various equipment, which is financed by loans within a man's extended family.[45] There is no evidence that Christianity has reached these people.

ZATUT

They are a separate nomadic community of circumcisers. They came from the Punjab, India, as Hindus, more than 1,000 years ago. They rank among the tribes of Oman as lower than slaves, but they are accepted and travel unarmed to perform circumcisions for all the tribes. They have their own language.[46]

SOUTHWEST ASIA

Iran and Afghanistan both have large numbers of nomadic pastoralist peoples as well as peripatetic traders, craftsmen and entertainers, but no up-to-date survey has been done. Western Pakistan, consisting mostly of Baluchistan and the Northwest Frontier, is within this region. Baluchistan makes up 40% of Pakistan's area, with only 6% of its population. There are probably an additional 340,000 people living in the Northwest Frontier Province.[1]

The pastoral migratory movement in both Iran and Afghanistan is, in general, towards the high ground in the center for the summer, and back to lower ground around the borders in the winter. Most of Iran is dominated geographically by its central plateau which is mostly desert, but across the north into the central mountains of Afghanistan, and around from the northwest and all along the Zagros range to the southeast, there are numbers of nomadic pastoralist peoples. Twenty-seven per cent of Iran is considered pasture.

In Afghanistan, the nomads have used the central high ground of the Hazarajat and Hindukush for summer pastures, returning for the winter to the lower peripheral regions. Two-thirds of the country can only be used as seasonal pasture, so the future of nomadic pastoralism should be assured, but the limitation seems to be the inability of the cultivated areas to produce sufficient winter fodder. To the south of Afghanistan, in southeast Iran and reaching across into Pakistan, is Baluchistan — another area for nomadic pastoralism. Pastoralists use the variation in altitude and water supply within it or migrate towards the Indus valley.

In Iran, there has been a long-term tension between most of the nomads, who are of non-Iranian origin, and the Iranians and government policies. Many have been forced to settle without adequate means to do so. There are possibly 5,000,000 "tribal" peoples of nomadic pastoral traditions, though the number of active nomads is much smaller. In Afghanistan, there were calculated to be 2,500,000 *kochis*, or nomads and semi-nomads, in 1989. Many were driven into Pakistan refugee camps by the war with Russia and its aftermath.[2] The thousands of land mines laid in that struggle, the continued civil war afterwards, and extreme poverty have disrupted the pastoralism in many areas. One result of the poverty in northern Afghanistan is that many have turned to growing crops to supply the drug trade, which is producing an addiction problem throughout Central Asia and Europe.

Nomadic Pastoralists of Southwest Asia

SHAHSEVAN, *Shahsavan*

They have their home in Azerbaijan Province, northwest Iran. The number of those involved in nomadic or semi-nomadic pastoralism has increased from about 20,000 in 5,000 families in the 1960s, to 5,897 families in 1987 and 7,800 families in 1995.

However, there are also about 80,000 settled Shahsevans. There is another group of 28,000 who have a mixed economy of pastoralism and agriculture, near Zanjan, Qazvin and Saveh, west and south of Teheran. This region is called Khamseh — not to be confused with the tribes in southern Fars. However, part of a tribe of the

Shahsevan from this region joined the Khamseh Confederation in Fars. There are five different regions in Iran with this name.[3] There are 49 tribes of Shahsevan.

The Shahsevan speak Azerbaijani Turkish and are Shia Muslims, who in the eighteenth century resisted the advance of the Ottoman Turks and the Sunni religion. They may have received their name, meaning "those who love the Shah," from Shah Abbas the Great (1587-1629), who is said to have created the tribal confederation to be loyal to him. They have had no love for the Shahs of the twentieth century, because of their policies to settle the nomads. A more likely explanation of the name is that they took the name of a chief called Shahsevan, who led them in the eighteenth century. The Islamic Revolution attempted to rename them the Elsevan, "those who love the people," but this has never been adopted.

The Moghan area, where their winter pastures and camps are found, was divided by the Russian-Iranian border in 1828. At first the Russians allowed the nomads to cross the border on the condition that they paid pasture dues to the local chiefs. The Shahsevan rejected this and seized the pastures by force. For this reason, Russia closed the border in 1884 and about two-thirds of the Shahsevan lost their pastures. This provoked conflict between their tribes and others. A few thousand are reported to still live in the south of Azerbaijan.[4] The Shahsevan have always had a love for brigandage, and this conflict over the pastures created pressure that for a time intensified their raiding as an alternative source of income. The local agricultural Iranian people are called Tats, and their villages still contain the ruins of surrounding walls and narrow alleyways used for defense against the nomad brigands. The final redistribution of pastures on the Iranian side favored the more wealthy Shahsevans, giving them more than they needed. Only in 1966 was a more equitable distribution of land organized.

Reza Shah, in the interests of what he perceived to be the modernization of Iran,

banned nomadic dress and tents and brutally enforced cultivation and house building on the nomads. The Tats were encouraged by the Shahs to expand cultivation into the grasslands and also to buy their own villages and fields in land reforms that curtailed the previous feudal system under which they were tenants of absentee landlords who could claim as much as 25% of produce in rent. However, the farms often did not produce even enough for their own consumption. These changes also affected the nomads because many of the Shahsevan chiefs were also landlords to the Tats. In combating the Shah's reforms, which were biased towards the Iranian peasants and cultivation, the Shahsevan attempted dry land farming to substantiate their own claims to land rights.[5]

With the Soviet occupation of northern Iran between 1941 and 1946 and the exile of the Shah, the Shahsevan reverted to nomadism. The result was that the individual tribes of the confederation gained recognition as distinct political units. The main tribes, according to Tapper in the 1960s, are the *Geyiklu*, with 750 nomadic families; the *Hajji-Khojalu* with over 350 families; the *Moghanlu* with perhaps a thousand families; the *Ajirlu* with 440 families; and the *Talesh-Mikaillu* with over 300 families. Their affiliation to the tribes and sub-tribes provides a cultural identity that is not determined by descent but rather by the location of their winter pasture. A family that loses its pasture is considered "detribalized" and fit only for town life, or to become a Tat or an agricultural peasant. For this reason the Shahsevan consider the theft of grazing land worse than theft of their animals — without land they cease to belong to their tribe and people.

Society

The pastoralists feel their lifestyle is superior to that of the villagers, being healthier and more independent. Their *alacig*, or tent, is symbolic not only of their resistance to the interference of the Iranian state, but also of their identity as nomads in contrast to the Tats or village peasants in the region. These

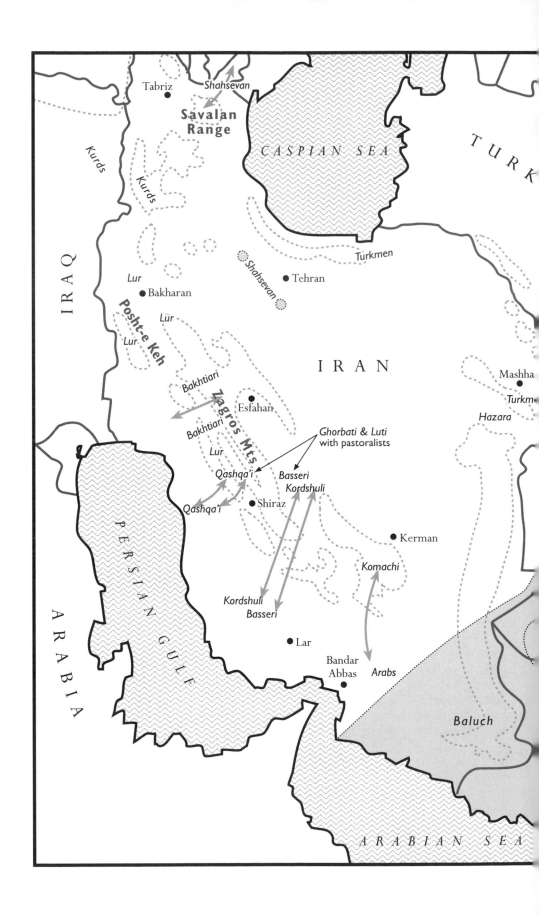

UZBEKISTAN

TURKMENISTAN

KYRGYZSTAN

Badakhshi

TAJIKISTAN

Meru
Baluchi
Brahui

Pamiri

Turkmen

Mazar-e Sherif
GHORBATI

Arabs
GHORBATI

Tajiks

Wakhi

Herat
GHORBATI

Chahar

Aimaks

Koochi

Nuristani

Kalash Kafirs

Hindu Kush

Hazara

Kabul
GHORBATI

PUKHTANA

Jalalabad
Sheikh Mohammadi

AFGHANISTAN

PUKHTANA
GHORBATI

PUKHTANA

GHORBATI

PUKHTANA

Kandahar
GHORBATI

Brahui & Baluch

Quetta

PAKISTAN

Lahore

Brahui

Baluch

Baluch

Indus

Delhi

Karachi

INDIA

tents are dome-shaped and made of bent semi-circular poles, joined at the top by a heavy roof ring (as the yurt in Central Asia), and covered in white felt sheets made in the camp. On average seven or eight persons live in one tent, but they are able to house 20 or more people. Poorer families live in smaller barrel-shaped versions. In recent years they have built mud brick houses, although they retain the nomad's disdain of the settled life that a house symbolizes. But many of this people were being forced to settle and to become mixed farmers.

The Shahsevan emphasize the social and economic independence of the family. A family is called a "hearth," emphasizing its unity, even when a polygamous man may have a number of tents for each wife and her children. The sons live with their father as long as possible. Even after the father's death the sons may continue to live together so as not to divide the family inheritance. Each son is considered to have two shares, and each daughter has one. But on marriage a daughter rarely gives this share to her husband. This inheritance will include a share in the grazing rights, and this she usually gives to her brothers, when she leaves home to be married.

Nomadism

The Shahsevan migrate between low-level winter pastures in the north and high-altitude summer pastures in the mountains only a short distance to the south. The winter pastures are allocated to families and marked by stones or tracks. This allocation is decided by the grazing group of between eight and 15 tents, or families, who are usually related. On arrival at the winter pastures at the beginning of December, the family is involved in repairing the sheep corrals, shelters and underground rooms in which they have to pass the severest part of the winter. Here they store hay and the weakest animals. When the bitterest east winds blow, the family will abandon their houses or tents for life underground. It is necessary to take the sheep from the corral to three different areas each day, and also to take them out after midnight for one or two

hours of grazing. In the daytime, one shepherd can guard a flock of 200, but two or three men are needed at night.

Each Shahsevan household may own from 40 to over a hundred sheep and some goats, six or eight camels and donkeys for transport, with perhaps a horse for the head of the family to ride. A large family with a small flock can barely subsist, since the commercial production of mutton and milk is necessary to buy necessities such as cloth, flour, sugar, saddles, tent frames, lamps and paraffin oil. City dairies go to the winter camps for milk and cheese, and the wool is sold to the villagers. A flock must be constantly renewed, not only because of sales and disease, but also because the sheep must be slaughtered by their fifth year, when their teeth fall out.

March is called "gray month" and "crying-smiling month" because of the variable weather. But it is in March that God is said to send a "wind of promise" to awaken the creation from winter. "Spring fever" spreads through the camps, says Tapper, as each family is involved in making hay to be stored for the next winter and sending some of its baggage ahead to a village near to their summer pasture. On the last Wednesday of the month it is the custom to light a bonfire, and the young people jump over it shouting "my pains and troubles stay here," signifying the end of the hard winter. The whole camp is involved in spring-cleaning, repairing and dismantling the extra covers of the tents and stables used for the winter. They visit one another and excitement rises in anticipation of the migration southwards.

Traditionally on May 5, the forty-fifth day after the spring equinox, the family groups set out. At some point in the journey Iranian taxes are collected according to the size of the flocks, and for this reason weak or poor animals are sold off before leaving. Sheep do not graze well and are prone to disease in the rising heat of spring, so the tribes move out according to the quality of their winter pastures; the Moghanlu leave first, but the Geyiklu leave last because their pasture lasts longer. The women are dressed

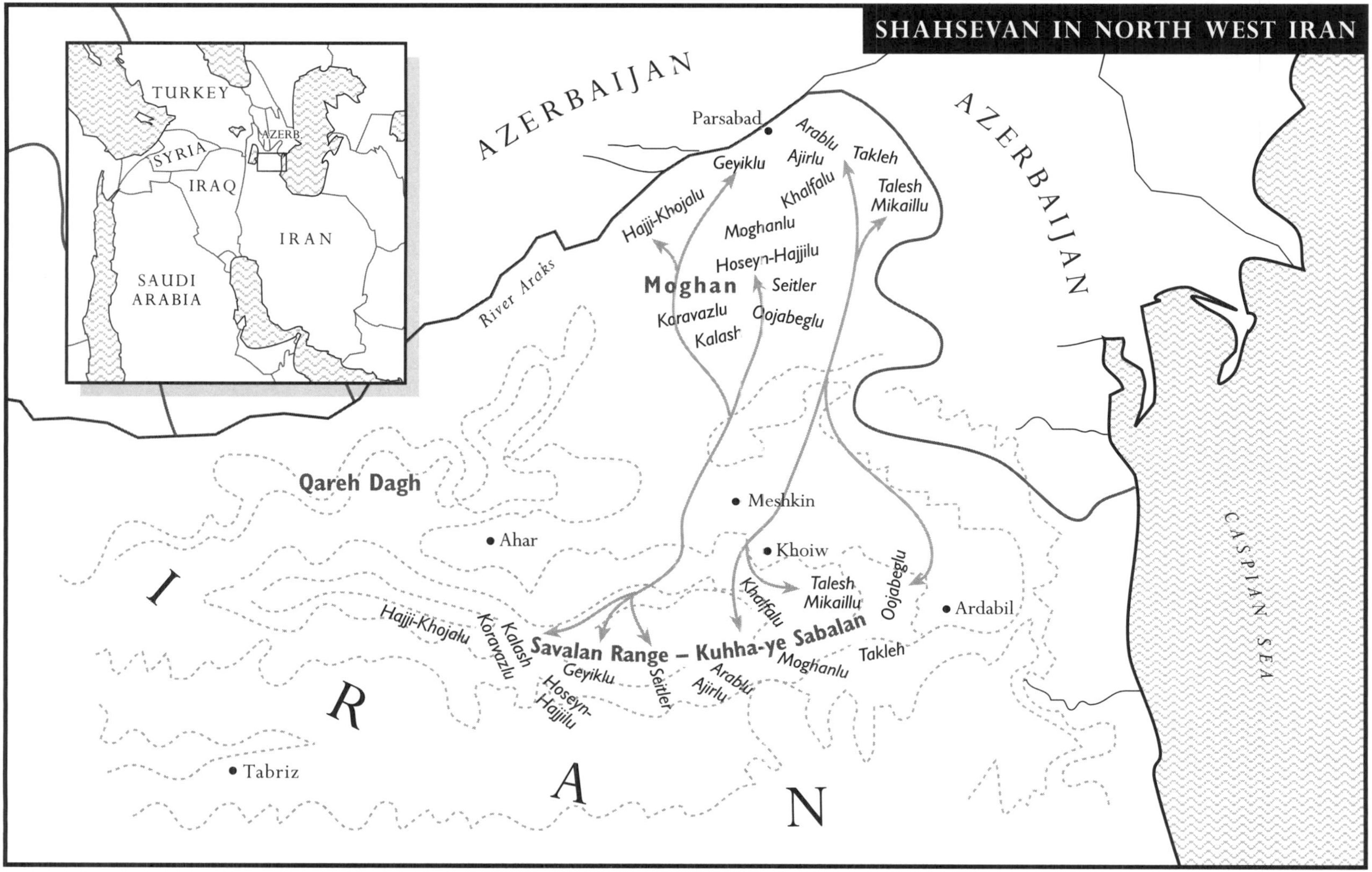

SHAHSEVAN IN NORTH WEST IRAN

CASPIAN SEA

AZERBAIJAN

Ardabil

Talesh
Mikaillu
Takleh
Arablu
Ajirlu
Khalfalu
Geyiklu
Moghanlu
Hoseyn-Hajjilu
Seitler
Oojabeglu
Karavazlu
Kalast
Parsabad
Hajji-Khojalu
Moghan

Meshkin
Khoiw
Oojabeglu
Talesh
Mikaillu
Khalfalu
Moghanlu
Takleh
Arablu
Ajirlu
Savalan Range – Kuhha-ye Sabalan
Seitler
Geyiklu
Hoseyn-Hajjilu
Kalash
Karavazlu
Hajji-Khojalu

River Araks

AZERBAIJAN

Qareh Dagh

Ahar

Tabriz

I R A N

TURKEY
SYRIA
IRAQ
SAUDI ARABIA
IRAN
AZERB.

in the newest and most colorful cloths, sitting on the camels that are also decorated with tassels and bells. The girls in particular are made to look their best on display to attract wedding proposals, which are often made when the camps are established in the summer pastures.

The Shahsevan migrate some 150 kilometers (95 mi.), from wintering near sea level on the Moghan steppe to their summer pasture at 4,000 meters altitude on the Savalan range to the south.[6] It is customary for nomads to "move at moonrise and stop at dawn." Using camels, each camp group moves about 10 to 15 kilometers (6 to 9 mi.) in four hours each night. This way they avoid traveling in the heat of the day and the flocks can graze in the morning and evening. The villagers used to allow each camp a day's stop with free grazing on stubble, but in recent years they have been impatient to see the nomads leave. By the 1970s, however, trucks and pickups had replaced camels for transporting both tents and sheep. When the nomads reach the foothills of the Savalan range, the sheep are able roam freely in an area free of cultivation and abundant in grass. This is also the time for the Shahsevan to have feasts and celebrations.

The summer camps are smaller than the winter ones, as each sub-tribe goes to its allocated pasture. The sheep are sent out to graze three times a day, in three different locations, beginning with the south-facing slopes, since these are the first to dry up in the sun. The sheep are kept in a fold in the camp at night as wolves and other predators abound. In the more rugged terrain of the mountains at over 4,000 meters, three shepherds are needed for a flock that required only one shepherd during the winter. Each herding unit of five or so households must provide at least two men all the time to watch at least 200 sheep and goats. Each animal can be recognized and is counted at least once a day.

Those families too poor to have large flocks can be employed on a six-monthly basis as hired shepherds. Normally they can receive between 4% and 5% of the number of sheep cared for in newborn lambs, so that they have the opportunity to build up a flock of their own again. The camels are also kept together as a herd. By mid-summer the ewes no longer give milk, but there is shearing, tent repairs and the making of ghee to keep the families busy. The camps move three or four times during the summer. By August 5 the sheep are considered to be in peak condition, which is judged by the amount of fat in the tail. At this time the weather becomes misty and sultry and the pasture is exhausted, so the flocks are moved down to the foothills again.

The return journey is conditioned by news of the first rains falling on the winter pastures. This journey is more rapid and without the joy of the spring, as pasture is scarce everywhere and the shepherds must rent village stubble and marginal pastures for their sheep. Soon after establishing their winter camps the Shahsevan celebrate Ramazan (Ramadan), at the end of which they give presents and receive visits from relatives and friends. They consider themselves good Muslims and tend to explain their values in terms of Islam. They are Shiites, and Richard Tapper gives an excellent account of the ritual life of the Shahsevan.

The nomadism of the Shahsevan has been progressively disrupted by the loss of winter pastures on the Moghan to dams and irrigation schemes for agriculture. Many were evicted from their winter homes. The expansion of the villagers, new fields on the migration route and the encroachment of cultivation on the slopes of the Savalan, their summer pasture area (and for which they had to get permits rather than having long-term tenure), are all increasing their difficulties. The Shah's government had no interest in pastoralism and encouraged livestock imports — even though much of Iran, such as the Savalan range, is only suitable for livestock pasture. The Qashqa'i and Bakhtiari, among others, were exploited more for tourism, and the imbalance in Christian interest among Iranian "Tribals" may be a result of this.

The Iranian Revolution called the nomadic tribes "Treasures of the Revolution" and set up the Organisation for Nomadic Affairs (ONA) to give them representation and infrastructure for health, education and pasture control. It established stores, tents and veterinary services in both winter and summer pastures and encouraged the marketing of pastoral products and meat. But by 1993 settlement was still government policy and Moghan was earmarked for industry and agricultural development. The ONA divided the remaining winter pastures into "pastoral habitats" by 1995.[7]

Religion

Shiism accepts as authoritative only the interpretations that come from the Prophet Mohammed and the twelve Imams descended from him. The last of these, it is claimed, shall return at the end of time as the *mahdi*, or "the expected one," to fill the earth with justice. Celebrating the martyrdom of Hussein is a national cult in Iran, and the Shahsevan celebrate it with the construction of a mosque tent around which the young men march dressed in black scarves and smocks, chanting laments and shouting *saxsey*, a corruption of the exclamation "Shah Hussein!" so that in spite of the motives being solemn, it is more like a party.

Shiite Islam is eschatological and otherworldly, such that the Shahsevan believe that by prayer and purification all classes have a chance to enter paradise. Good conduct has to do with rewards in the afterlife and, in contrast to the assumption of many peoples, a person's present material fortune does not indicate the blessing of Allah. However, many of the nomads are impatient with the platitudes of the mullahs about the misfortunes of life. They consider the promise of paradise to be inadequate, and therefore humankind must co-operate with Allah's will through folk medicine and magic. While the men tend to think of amulets against the evil eye as unorthodox they still use them, and they will also put them on their favorite animals.

Circumcisions and weddings are occasions to establish new relationships between the extended families and clans, and there is little interest in the bride and groom or child. Those who have been to Mecca, the *Hadji*, have a prestige among the people to be mediators in disputes. The nomads believe the dying must hear the Qur'an being read. The dead are wrapped in a shroud, strapped to a board and carried by a camel to the burial site. Many try to touch the bier on the way, believing that to do so gains them merit for paradise.

Outreach

Their language is unwritten. No outreach to the Shahsevan has been attempted. Present conditions allow little opportunity to help these people except by prayer, but pray for the radio broadcasts in Azeri and Farsi from FEBA.

TURKMAN

There are 600,000 Turkman living in northeastern Iran, near the southeast corner of the Caspian Sea and along the Turkmenistan border. Many are semi-nomadic. There are 300,000 of the Yomut tribe on the Gurgan Plain, and 30% are Goklan. (See the Central Asia section, below.) One million speak Turkmen in Iran. Elam Ministries, England, is committed to producing a radio program for these people.[8]

AIMAQ or Berberi

There are 800,000 Aimaq living in two separated areas in northeast Iran and northwest Afghanistan as transhumant pastoralists. They spend the winter in their villages in the valleys, where they also weave carpets of traditional designs that differ according to each clan. The largest group, the *Chahar Aimak*, consists of groups of Baluch, Kipchaks and Uzbeks who have united over the last two centuries.

Chahar Aimaks, Afghanistan, are semi-nomadic groups of tribes, totaling perhaps 300,000, in the western central highlands between Herat and Changhcharan. They are a mixture of Caucasian and Mongol peoples and appear to be related to the above entry. In winter they live in permanent villages but migrate to summer pastures to live in yurt-like tents, rather than the black hair tents used elsewhere in Afghanistan.

Their tribes are as follows: *Jamshidi*: 80,000 in the area of Kushk, 70 kilometers (45 mi.) northeast of Herat. *Firuzkuhi*: 40,000 are centered in Murghab Valley, Badghis and Ghor Provinces. *Taimanni*: there are 40,000 on both sides of the Hari Rud, Ghor Province, and so divided into Northern and Southern. The Southern Taimanni have adopted the black tents and some culture of the Pushtuns nearby to the south. The Northern Taimanni are farmers. *Hazaras*: they have no ethnic connection with the other people group in the Hazarajat. There are 50,000 who leave their scattered villages for the mountains with their flocks in summer.[9] They speak dialects of Dari with Turkic and Mongolian elements and are listed as Aimaq with an estimated 800,000 speakers. They are Sunni Muslims.

The Afghan civil war has destroyed their flocks, and the remaining minefields have reduced the *Aimak* to being urban refugees. Many will probably return to pastoralism as conditions improve. They speak their own differing dialects of Dari. They are Sunni Muslims of the Hanafi school: there are no known Christians among them. They have no Bible translation. New Opportunities anticipate helping this people. Daily broadcasts from FEBA are made in Dari.

HAZARA

There are two distinct groups called by this name. They may be related, but they are usually treated separately.

The *Hazara* (*Hazare'i, Hezaesh*) in Khorasan, Iran, are situated south of Mashdad near Torbat-e Heydariyeh. There are others in the Kuh-e Hazari Mountains north of the city. They are semi-sedentary agropastoralists. They are descendants of the many refugees from Afghanistan at the end of the nineteenth century and total 290,000. They are Muslim and there are no known Christians among them.[10] There are 70,000 Hazaras in Quetta, Pakistan.

The *Hazara* or *Hazaragi* live in the Hazarajat, in the western Hindu-Kush, the central mountainous region of Afghanistan.[11] They call both themselves and the region *Azra*.[12] Estimates of their numbers range between two and six million. They live mainly in the provinces of Ghowr to the west (242,000), Oruzgan (370,000) and Bamiyan (241,000) in the center, and Ghazni (561,000) to the southeast. They are heavily concentrated in these areas, where 80% of the population is Hazara. Parvan (88,000 or 18%) and Vardak (150,000 or 40%) west of Karbul form the eastern edge of the Hazara homeland. Hazaras make up 20% of the population of Kabul, the country's capital, with 411,000. Others live in Herat, Qandahar and other areas.

The origin of the Hazaras is unknown, but there are three suggestions: that they are descendants of the soldiers of Genghis Khan's Mongol army; or a mix of Tajiks and Mongols; or that they represent the aboriginal inhabitants of the Hazarajat. Some suggest the name *Hazara* comes from the Dari for "one thousand," probably referring to a military origin.

Their relationships with all the peoples around them was affected by the fact that they are Shiites of both the Ishmaili and J'Afari sects. The Sunni majority in Afghanistan consider them heretics, because the Hazara area was Sunni before Iran became officially Shiite. The majority of the Hazaras probably converted to Shi'ism in stages in the fourteenth and seventeenth centuries. But three Hazara tribes are Sunni.[13] In the past the Shiite clergy has always been paid by the elite and has given religious support to the division of society, and has also helped to maintain Hazara unity against outsiders.

The Hazaras have been fiercely independent throughout their history, being able to defend themselves in mountainous territory and quite capable of launching attacks on passing caravans, armies or towns. The Hazarajat suffers six months of winter but has the best pastures. The Hazara independence ended when the British Empire, fearing a Russian threat to its hold on India, instigated Afghan unity by backing the king in Kabul who finally defeated the Hazaras in 1893. At great cost to the Hazaras, Afghanistan as a country was born, dominated by the Pathans, or Pukhtana. The Hazarajat was divided into three, and the people were enslaved. Sunni clergy and practice were imposed, so that now a minority of Hazaras are Sunni Muslims. Afghan governments have attempted to replace the name Hazara by Shi'ia, and so remove the ethnic identity by pretending that the Hazara are only a religious deviation.

In the 1930s a Pakhtun deposed a later king and, adapting Nazi ideology, imposed Pukhtana supremacy by attempting to destroy Hazara culture and language and encouraged Pukhtana nomads to occupy the Hazara pastures. When the Hazaras rebelled, many were executed. The economic exploitation of their own leaders, as well as the Pukhtana domination of trade, forced many poorer Hazaras to move to the cities to take menial work as domestics, porters and laborers. Hazaras were discriminated against and many hide their ethnic identity, even becoming ashamed of it. They became divided by these outside pressures and some side with central government, others under Iranian influence are strongly Islamic and still others accept a Hazara nationalism. Many declare themselves to be Uzbeks or Tajiks rather than admit to being Hazaras. During the twentieth century, the Hazaras have lost half their territory, most of it in the west.

During the Russian invasion the Hazara fought against the Communists, but they were betrayed by their Sunni allies and 11,000 were killed in the evening of June 23, 1979. Many of them were buried alive. Later the Hazara rebels fell out among themselves and they continue to be disunited. A Hazara Assembly, the *Shura*, was formed in 1979, with all the forms of a national government, including an army. But this failed to unite the Hazaras and it became controlled by Shiite Fundamentalists trained in Iran. Hazara refugees in Iran were also obliged to fight for Iran in the Iraqi-Iranian war. A Party of Unity was organized in 1989, but this exhausted its resources in

three years of fighting and Taliban allies undermined its power. Their own region cannot support them all, so many have been forced to survive as wheat farmers, become squatters near towns or move to laboring jobs in Kabul. The land mines left by the Afghan war have reduced their ability to be pastoralists. Leprosy and eye infections are common in this area, and more medical clinics are required. They are the most materially needy people in Afghanistan.

Society

The typical Hazara family consists of parents and married sons with their families and the unmarried children, but often it includes unrelated nuclear families who have no close kin or land of their own. This extended household lives, eats and works together under the leadership of the eldest father and jointly owns the house, fields, tools, and so on. A number of such extended households live in a *qala*, or castle a joint house enclosed by a high wall with one large entrance gate. All the rooms look into the courtyard, but the best room with a view of the mountains is over the gate. Villages and towns are now developing, with roads linking them together.

The families in a valley are united as a *tol*, with the leading head of household, the *malak*, representing them all in the larger more complex unit, the *tayefa*, led by an *arbab*, or *khan*. The *tayefa* is part of a number of *qaum* that give political and economic leadership, that dominated them as a feudal society up to 1893 and also since 1978. Hazara society used to be divided between an elite of mirs and sultans, who controlled the land and resources, and the lower classes of peasants, artisans and nomadic and other pastoralists. This structure is modified by assemblies, often held in the open air, where ordinary Hazaras can join the leaders in deciding important issues.

Nomadism

The Hazarajat region, northeast of Chaghcharan, is almost inaccessible and consists of arid mountains dependent on melted snow for moisture. The mountains are seen proverbially and practically as representing strength and security. The Hazaras live in mud huts in small villages, or *qalas*, as described. The women and children lead their flocks of fat-tailed sheep into the mountains for several weeks each summer, while the men stay to tend the meager wheat harvests, so that about a third of the population follows a transhumant lifestyle. Each summer, they re-establish mountain pasture encampments they call *aylok*, that have been used for generations and are usually in a well-defended position. Here they live in simple yurt-like tents made of reed mats. They have a few cows and their donkeys with them, and the boys have to constantly protect the few sheep and goats from eagles and wolves. The women occupy themselves in the *aylok*, making both buttermilk and yogurt, and a hard cheese-like *crut* to be stored for the winter. The main meal is in the evening, when the young-men return with the flocks. They rarely eat meat, as the livestock is too valuable and kept for dairy produce, or for exchange as a bride-price or to purchase land in the valley.

Religion

As Shiite Muslims, they are isolated from most people around them, who treat them as outcasts, and they are said to adore Ali as a deity, of whom they would say they are slaves. They continue to suffer discrimination because of this as "infidels" and "extremists." The mosque in the center of the village is the place for decision-making and for accommodating visitors. Some of their homes have a weekly visit from a *Maddah*, a man who recites poems venerating the prophet or nature, carrying the "holy" staff of a local elder. They also make pilgrimages to tombs of martyrs or key religious figures, where miraculous signs are claimed to happen.

Their language is Hazaragi, a form of Dari similar to Tajik, with 10% Mogul words. There is little literature in this language, but there is much oral poetry and many proverbs and philosophical sayings, and outreach in the biblical faith should develop these aspects. The poetry is accompanied by local stringed instruments played by the men, and flutes and tambourines by the women.

Outreach

Only 5% of the Hazaras are literate. Audiocassettes of Genesis, Exodus 1-20, Acts, eight epistles and parts of the gospels are available. A Bible translation is needed. There is a fifteen-minute daily radio broadcast in Hazara. Operation Mobilisation visited them in 1983. New Opportunities and others anticipate helping this people in Afghanistan.

ARAB KOOCHI or *Kuchi*

They are nomadic traders and pastoralists in Afghanistan and are of Arab, and possibly of other, ethnic origins. *Koochi* means "nomad," and there were estimated to be 2,500,000 in Afghanistan in 1978 — although this figure must include many Pukhtana caravaners and pastoralists. The Russian invasion and the resulting minefields have completely disrupted their traveling. For example, one group of 1,000 Arab families used to travel into Pakistan, but now this number is probably less than 200. They have traded animals for Red Cross tents, replacing their traditional tents. Their summer pasture is in Sakardara, northwest of Kabul and their winter pasture is near Jalalabad, 150 kilometers (90 mi.) east of Kabul. The Koochi are also found, as Afghans, in Pakistan — both as pastoralists and caravaners.[14]

ARABS

They live in Kondüz, Takhar and Badakhshan provinces, northeast Afghanistan. Their total number is approximately 29,000, although there are probably now many more. They originally came from Arabia in the eighth century, and became assimilated into the settled pastoralism of the Khanate of Bukkara.[15] While conscious of being Arabs, they did not stay as distinct as other nomadic peoples who also were moving into the area. The Russian invasion in the 1860s caused them to move south into their present area, one that had been previously depopulated by the slave raids of the Turkmen. Being mobile, the Arabs could defend themselves from these raids. The raids stopped with the establishment of the Russian-British border in 1873 on the Amu River, and the Arabs came under the control of Afghanistan.

After they moved to Afghanistan, the Arabs became true nomads to exploit the pasture at different altitudes. Qataghan, where they had their *quishloq*, or winter villages of reed houses, was swampy and notorious for malaria, but the Arabs survived by spending only the winters there, migrating into the mountains during the mosquito season. The swamps have since been drained and become successful cotton fields. Since World War Two, Pathans have moved into the area and the main towns, such as Kunduz, Khanabad, Baghlan and Pul-i-Khumri, now have Pukhtana majorities and Pukhtana nomads also pasture alongside the Arabs.

Nomadism

The 13 Arab clans have become identified with their *quishloq*, in which related families live close to each other. The clans, unlike those of other peoples, have few political roles. This is because the land and flocks belong to each family, and they make their own decisions as to when to migrate, so that each family has a relationship with the Afghanistan authorities. The clan has a representative who usually is appointed by the state, but the Arabs also have *bais*, or wealthy men, who have a greater informal influence to mediate in disputes and a reputation for practical wisdom. Beyond the immediate extended family, Arabs tend to relate according to which mosque they attend, rather than according to lineage or other factors.

After spending the winter in Qataghan on rich pasture near their winter villages, with the coming of spring the Arabs' flocks migrate eastwards across the Kokcha River. The flocks on average consist of about 250 large Turki sheep raised for mutton and their fat tails, or the much smaller Qarakuli breed raised for their good quality carpet wool. A few goats are kept to lead the sheep, because sheep are not confident in the mountains unless they have goats ahead of them. The family sets out a week after the flocks. Social status is shown by which animals the members of the family ride on migration. Only the men ride stallions, the women with small children ride mares, and older daughters ride on top of the household baggage on camels, advertising their availability for marriage. The boys ride the donkeys.

The tent is made of reed mats and felt, both made by the women. The spring is spent in the lower mountains near to Uzbek villages. These Uzbeks were once nomads, but they now support themselves mostly by growing wheat on the mountain slopes. In these spring pastures the lambing is attended to. There is usually only one lamb per ewe each year, but this is sufficient to rapidly change a family's fortunes in pastoralism, compared to agriculture. Traditionally the women looked after the camp and the milking, and they make yogurt but no cheese. The ewes give an average of one kilogram of milk from March to August. The ewes are kept as the capital and the males are castrated and fattened for sale.

For the summer pasture the flocks are driven higher over mountain passes at 2,500 meters into the Shahr-i Bozog plateaus of Badakhshan and Rogh. At this higher altitude there are Tajik villages that also have their pastures in the valleys. Each Arab family owns pasture rights to designated areas that have been recognized by the Afghan government since 1921 on the slopes above and below the Tajiks at up to 4,000 meters. They often need only one shepherd to guard the sheep in these areas. Sudden storms can chill the sheep and kill most of the flock at once, in addition to the losses due to falls, disease and predators. These threats are believed to be *kismet*, or fate. Even on migration, three-day trips to nearby bazaars for salt, tea, sugar, rice and other manufactured goods is necessary. Here the often lonely life of the nomad is brightened by contact with Tajiks and Uzbeks.

During the Cold War, more roads were built in the region. This has meant that the meat or sheep can reach far greater markets, and has in turn created a demand for imported goods. They have changed from being subsistence pastoralists to commercial meat suppliers. Sheep prices doubled after 1965 so that the Arabs could afford to hire shepherds to avoid going on migration themselves, and invest in businesses other than pastoralism, and an economic stratification has developed between them. This has resulted in most of the family living in the *quishloq* all year round, and they have built substantial houses to live in. So while the men may be employed supervising the livestock, the women, without a camp to manage and the dairy work to do, have time on their hands.

Because a man has to earn his bride-price, he usually marries in his mid-twenties while his bride may be only sixteen. Married sons will continue to live and work with their parents, because Arabs only inherit on the death of the father. While it is quite popular to marry Uzbek or Tajik women, Arabs are reluctant to allow their daughters to be married to the men of these peoples.

They speak Farsi, not Arabic, and some are bilingual in Uzbek. Only 5,000 speak some Arabic in villages west of Daulatabad and Balkh, north of Mazar-i Sherif.[16] There are no known disciples of Jesus among them. A number of daily radio broadcasts in Farsi from FEBA and TWR reach the area.

TAJIKS

Living in the Hindu Kush, Afghanistan, the Tajik were originally a Turkic group who now speak Dari and resemble the Hazaras. They migrate between winter and summer pastures on the northern slopes of the Hindu Kush Mountains east and west of Baghlân.

NURISTANI

There are 90,000 living in the Laghman Valley of northeast Afghanistan. They are divided between the Eastern Nuristanis in the Bashgal Valley and the Western Nuristanis in the Ramgal and other valleys. They winter in villages built of stone, but they move to the mountain summer pastures to live in *ailogs*, which are roofless stone shelters.

Their main subsistence is from their cattle, sheep and goats and their cheese and butter. The men are the herders and the women cultivate millet, maize and wheat. They trade with the Pathans. They were treated as kafirs until they converted to Sunni Islam after a long fight of resistance in 1890s, and the area is still called Kafirstan. They speak Kati, a Dardic language, and literacy is 6%. There are no Christians among them. They possess radios, but they have only a limited understanding of the Pushto and Dari broadcasts. They welcome medical and veterinary aid, and help with irrigation engineering.[17]

KALASH KAFIRS or *Ashkund, Ashkun*, or *Wamayi*

These people number 2,500 or 4,500 and live on the border of Afghanistan and Southern Chitral District, Pakistan.[18] This is at the extreme eastern end of the Hindu Kush Mountains. They live in about 20 villages in three valleys. A road has been built to transport timber from one of their valleys. The women tend the irrigated fields near the villages, while the men herd goats, sheep and cattle in the mountains away from the villages. They are primarily pastoralists. Their wealth and status is measured in goats, which produce milk for cheese, long goat hair for rope and rugs, goatskin, meat and sacrifices.

This appears to be a very old society that has withstood the influences of Hinduism, Buddhism and Islam. They are nominal Muslims in the south but polytheists in the north. The latter see their own valleys as "clean" and the surrounding Muslims as "unclean." Everyone that travels out of their territory must undergo purification rituals on return. The seasons are marked with festivals in honor of various deities, in which singing and dancing drive away the spirits. The spirits have their territories, and they do not forgive intrusion by humans. A *dehar*, or shaman, is needed to communicate with the gods and spirits and to heal.

On special occasions the women wear long headdresses down their backs, similar to those worn in Tibet and Ladakh. Childbirth requires separation from the family and involves "uncleanness." There is a hostel in Islamabad for Kalash boys.[19] Their language is Kalasha, and a Bible translation is in progress.[20]

PAMIRI, "Mountain Tajiks" or Galchah

There are 55,000 pastoralists in small groups of people, divided according to their dialects, which in fact may be separate languages as they are virtually mutually unintelligible.[21] Tajik is the literary language. They were first mentioned in history in the Chinese Chronicles of the second century AD, and Marco Polo also mentions them. They have been in constant conflict among themselves and with the Tajiks. After their defeat by the Red Army in 1920, the Gorno Badakhshan Autonomous Province, consisting of 44% of the land area of Tajikstan, was set up. It has only one town, Khorog (pop. 13,000). They are pastoralists in the Pamir Mountains who were collectivized under the Soviet regime:

Shugnis (their name for themselves is *Khugnon*): 20,000; and 2,000 *Oroshur* are related to the 4,000 **Bartangis** (*Bartangidzh*); the 1,500 **Khufis** (*Khufidzh*); the 5,000 *Sarikol* in Xinjiang; and the 15,000 **Rushanis** (*Rykhen*) in Tajikistan (3,000 in Afghanistan). *Yazgulemis* number 2,000 in Tajikistan. There are 500 **Sanglechi-Ishkashimis** in Tajikistan and 2,000, with two and 17 villages respectively, in Afghanistan. There is no information available on the **Badzhuis** or *Badzhuwedzh*.[22] They are Ismaili Muslims, except for the *Bartangis* and some of the *Yazgulemis*.

Wakhi, *Guhjali*, call themselves **Khik**, a formerly nomadic people 29,000 strong:

6,000 live in Tajikstan; 9,000 in the Hunza Valley, Pakistan; and 7,000 in Wakhi Corridor in the Pamirs between Tajikistan and Pakistan; and 6,000 in Xinjiang. In the Hunza Valley they live with the 50,000 agricultural *Burushos*.

In the Corridor, the Wakhi are clustered in villages of stone houses on the fertile valley floors, while the neighboring Kyrgyz live entirely at higher altitudes.[23] The Wakhi can be described as agropastoralists, since they all either cultivate fields near their villages or work on the fields of the others.

Nomadism

A small number of families practice nomadic pastoralism, with large flocks of over a hundred sheep and goats, with yaks and cattle. Some members of the families camp in a yurt with the livestock, often all the year around, spending the summers on the lower slopes of the Pamirs and wintering in the valleys, sometimes some distance from their home village. The families with smaller flocks have a community shepherd to keep the flocks together on pasture near their villages. While both men and women work the fields, the men herd the animals, make hay, shear and weave. The women milk, feed and care for young animals, and spin.

Society

Their society has six castes. The upper two castes claim to have descended from Mohammed or his uncle and are considered spiritual intermediaries for the others, who are "followers." They give their advice and blessings in return for tribute. The upper three castes do not intermarry with the lower castes. *Khik* means "commoner," the lowest majority caste, but the term is also used to distinguish all Wakhi from the Kyrgyz. The Kyrgyz despise the Wakhi for being farmers, Ismailites, for using opium and being economically poorer, but the two peoples have become economically interdependent, especially since the Soviet and Chinese borders were closed. This closure denied them access to considerable pastures to the north.[24] Many have become addicted to drinking tea and opium. The IBT has translated John's Gospel.

KYRGYZ

The Kyrgyz live in the Pamirs, Wakhi Corridor.[25] (Further, see Central Asia section, below.)

PUKHTANA (sg. *Pakhtun* or *Pushtun*) or Pathans

The first name is what they call themselves, the latter is the English name which they consider derogatory. Many like to call themselves Afghans, although this only reflects their domination of all citizens of the country. They make up 55% of the population of Afghanistan and 13% of Pakistan.[26] There are 7,490,000 Pukhtana in Afghanistan and 14,000,000 in Pakistan,[27] but a more recent study estimates 11.5 million for all Pukhtana. They entered recorded history by resisting Alexander the Great at the Khyber Pass.

Over the last 100 years, the consolidation of Afghanistan as a country has encouraged trade and the development of roads, and so caravaning has been adopted by the nomads. Those tribes with long distance pastoral migrations have been able to develop into caravaning, to the point they have abandoned pastoralism. Their trade routes are north to Central Asia and westwards to Iran, with some being able to settle as merchants or landowners with houses in Mazar-e Sharif, Kabul and Jalalabad. The switch to trading has had the greatest affect in some of them deciding to settle.[28]

Most of the people had converted to a sedentary lifestyle by the middle of the twentieth century, but many of the settled villagers also practice the transhumant grazing of their livestock. An estimate in 1991 thought that two or three million are still seasonally nomadic, moving their flocks to higher ground in the center of the country to live in tents for the summer. Only about 100,000 were "pure nomads," called Kouchis, a Farsi term meaning "nomads," living in tents all the year.

The social barrier between nomad and settled society does not apply in Afghanistan. One's links to one's tribe and region are more important than lifestyle. Their tribes are divided between two confederations, the Durani, or Durrani, and the Ghilzais:

Durrani were originally called Abdali, who renamed themselves Durrani in the mid-seventeenth century and some of Afghanistan's leaders have come from this tribe. There are said to be Hazara and Tajiks among them. They are divided again into *Ziraks*, with four tribes, or *kaum*, and the *Panjpaos*, with three tribes. Many are urbanized, living in Kabul and other cities, and others are farmers. About half of them are still nomadic or semi-nomadic, with flocks of sheep. They form camps of up to 100 families and migrate from March to August in the central mountains.[29] They are situated in southwest Afghanistan between Herat and Kandahar, which is an arid area except for the valleys, where cultivation is possible. Many have moved northeastwards between Herat and Mazar-i Sharif, where the hills are so fertile that some have settled there all year round. The women receive status only from their husbands. They milk the animals and weave the carpets, but they have no independent income. The Durrani speak Pushto and have almost identical customs.

The *Ghilzais*, or *Ghaljis*, are in the southeast of the country, mainly south and southeast of Ghazni. There is a popular story that says that Ghilzai means "son of a thief" because their ancestor was illegitimate. They inflicted defeat on British forces in the days of the "Great Game." They are also further divided into two groups of tribes, the Turans and the Burans. Many are settled, but they still have a high proportion of nomads, although traditionally they are less economically dependent on pastoralism than the Durrani, because of their trade and extending of credit to the Hazara in the eastern central highlands.

There are also a number of unaffiliated Pukhtana tribes along the Pakistan border such as the Yusufzai, Afridis and Shinwaris.

The Pukhtana have their own moral code

called *pukhtunwali*, interpreted by the *jirga*, or council of elders, which often conflicts with Islamic laws. It emphasizes the maintaining of personal and group honor, with revenge, male domination and defense of personal property. Settled women are known not by their own name, but as the mother of their eldest son. The *burkha* is the dress that covers the Muslim women entirely, with varied degrees of face cover showing only the eyes: 1) a scarf across the lower face; 2) a hole for one eye; or 3) an embroidered grille covering the entire face. Women are especially guarded from exposure to Western influence, which is considered immoral.

The civil war has disrupted rural life since 1978, and some five million Pukhtana have gone to refugee camps in Pakistan and Iran. Some men have become trading nomads. Some tribes have returned to pastoral nomadism in the Hindu Kush Mountains, moving into Pakistan in October or November. An early return to Afghanistan for the refugees is impossible, because of the destruction of 90% of the villages, the irrigation systems and the resultant erosion. There is still the danger of mines.[30] There is a Pukhtana nationalist movement demanding a Pakhtunistan, to be formed out of parts of Afghanistan, the Northwest Frontier and North Baluchistan. Historically this gained more votes than the Muslim League did in India when it succeeded in gaining the creation of Pakistan.

Powindahs, in Pakistan, are *Ghilzais*. There are estimated to be as many as 500,000. They used to trade from Central Asia through Ghazni, Afghanistan, and down into Sind, the Punjab and even to Calcutta. The ancestors of these pastoralists set up Puktun kingdoms in India in the fourteenth and fifteenth centuries. But the border between Afghanistan and Pakistan has been restricted or closed since 1961, although a small number continued to cross. They rear and trade in goats, sheep and some cattle, and they use camels and donkeys as pack animals. They migrate between South Wazirstan in the summer and Sind and the Punjab in winter. Many work on digging the irrigation canals in these areas during the winter.

The majority of Puktuns consider themselves as *maldar*, flock owners, or *powindah* pastoralists, rather than "nomads." They tend to be disdained by settled Pukhtuns, not so much because of their living conditions as because of their dependence on others to give them permission to pass through their land to their pastures. Today they often use tractors and trucks, rather than camels. They are willing to starve rather than beg. Although Muslims, they have a reputation for usury and their women are unveiled.

The Pashto language has been supplemented with Persian and Urdu, which they resent. There is resentment against Urdu being taught to Pukhtana children, and the Pukhtana are attempting to develop a modified Persian script and record their oral traditions in written form. The Pukhtana are Sunni Muslims of the Hanafi sect, and they consider that to be Muslim and Pukhtana are interchangeable. New Opportunities is interested in working among them.

BAKHTIARI

They are an Iranian confederation of pastoral tribes that live in the Zagros Mountains in western Iran. The Bakhtiari form part of a great chain of traditionally tribal pastoralists using the mostly fertile pastures of lowland winter areas to the west and the high-altitude pastures in the Zagros in summer. These peoples are, running from northwest to southeast, the Kurds, the Lur, the Bakhtiari, the Lur and the Qashqa'i and Khamseh Confederations. There are 680,000 Bakhtiari, of whom about 200,000 were still pastoralists in 1970. Their traditional territory lies between the two main territories of the Lur between Ahvaz and Esfahan, and between Arak and Shah-e Kord. The Lur are on both sides of them and they have contact with the Qashqa'i in their summer pastures in the mountains.

Society

The Bakhtiari are of Indo-European origin and not Turkic. Their traditions tell how they were one people with the Lur until about 1,500 years ago. Like a number of the tribal peoples, they have at times had considerable influence on events in Persia, and they provided both military forces and cabinet ministers until around 1925, when they lost their influence due to their internal divisions. Reza Shah removed the tribal leadership by executions after a civil war in 1925. Their relationships with the Qashqa'i have often been tense as they have had more contact with the Iranian state and sided with the British in Iraq against other tribesmen. At times, however, they have also supported the other tribal confederations against the state.

The Arabs, Lur and Bakhtiari have lost large areas of land in their winter pastures due to the exploration and development of the oil fields. The second Shah, Mohammed Reza, attempted to settle the Bakhtiari in the 1960s. But this plan failed due to the poor soil and the lack of national resources to aid the establishment of agriculture. The Shah attempted to abolish the tribes in 1975, treating the pastoralists as peasants and therefore as clients or peons of the landlords. Their pastures were confiscated and they were forced to settle on small plots that soon became overgrazed and overcrowded.[31]

The Bakhtiari are divided into the *Haft Lang* and *Chahar Lang* confederations, each of which has a number of tribes. Three-quarters of the Bakhtiari belong to the Chahar Lang tribes of settled farmers in the valleys of the Zagros alongside Iranian peasant communities. The Haft Lang are the pastoral nomads. The economic advantages of settlement in villages and moving to the towns are attracting many of them to abandon the arduous life of the nomad.

Political power among the Bakhtiari has always tended to be decentralized, so that the leaders of smaller groupings make the decisions. Today loyalty is increasingly to the nation rather than to the tribe. Each tribe consists of lineages, or *taifehs*, but their smaller units, the sublineage, or *korboh*, and its subdivision, the *mal*, or camp group, have more authority. The *mal* consists of up to ten related families that either migrate together as a camp or form a village. The family is the unit that owns the flocks and land. Sheep enable them to contribute to the outside economy, but the poor make do with a herd of goats.

Nomadism

The Bakhtiari have their winter quarters on the plains of northeast Khuzestan, where hundreds of their sedentary kinsmen live as farmers in the villages. The nomadic groups spend the winter on the slopes beyond the fields in black hair tents. In April this pasture dries up, so they take the difficult routes over six mountain ranges, gradually advancing higher as the pastures grow with the coming of warmer weather. This is a journey of about 400 kilometers (250 mi.), and between one and three months of each year is spent in migration.

The summer pastures are in valleys on the edge of the central plateau of Iran in Bakhtiari and Esfahan provinces, where the nomads remain until October. The more northerly groups have a harder terrain and their routes are longer, which bring them often into hostile contact with the Lur and other tribes, as well as with settled people. The southern groups have shorter routes to their summer pastures, but they can have conflict with the Qashqa'i. They migrate from these summer camps at the end of summer to return to Khuzestan for the winter. This journey is the most difficult, because all pasture on the route has been used up.[32]

Bakhtiari women have greater freedom in the nomadic life. Their dress declares their ethnic identity and social status and outsiders are prohibited from wearing it. Their social world is the camp, but when they settle the physical constraints of compound and house walls make the family a more independent unit. They seem to make fewer rugs and do less tent weaving than other nomad women of this region.

The Bakhtiari language is a dialect of Luri. They are Shia Muslims like their neighbors the Lur and the Qashqa'i, and in contrast to the Kurds, who are Sunni. New Opportunities anticipate helping this people.

LUR, Lors or Lori, Iran

The Lurs are a pastoral nomadic people, possibly of indigenous, pre-Persian, origin such as Elamites or Kassites. The names Lur and Lurs are preferred to the Luri, because Luri refers to any Gypsy-like group in southwest Iran. Therefore to call the Lur Luri is to confuse them with the Luti or Luri minstrels and acrobats who work with them and originated probably in India much later than the Lur. The Luti consider being called Luri derogatory.[33]

There are 4,280,000 Lur, and they live in the Zagros Mountains, in western Iran.[34] The Bakhtiari are a related people and are probably included in this total. They are a key element in the great system of nomadic pastoralists in the Zagros Mountains of western Iran. These can be listed coming southeastwards with the Kurds in the north, followed by the Bakhtaran Province Lur, then the Bakhtiari themselves. To the southeast of them are the Kuhgiluyeh, centered around Yasur, followed by the Qashqa'i Confederation in two areas north and south of the important town of Shiraz. Further south are the Khamseh and the Arabs.

In 1978, 50% of them were pastoralists and they are divided between three areas:

The two Luri tribes in Bakhtaran Province in the northwest are the *Ahmadvand* and *Harsini*.

The Lur in Posht-e Kuh, near the Iraq border in western Luristan, total 600,000 and consist of tribes who are nomads with sheep such as the *Tarhani*, *Jalalvand* and *Hulailani*.[35]

The following six tribes: the *Boyr Ahmed*, *Bavi*, *Behmei*, *Tayebei*, *Doshmanziari* (Mamassani) and *Choram* are in Kuhgiluyeh away to the southwest.

The origin of the Lur is unknown and some suggest that they are descendants of the original people of Iran. But various peoples, such as the Arabs, Kurds and Turks, have mingled in these areas. The first mention of the Lur dates back to the tenth century. As the valleys are fertile for cultivation, the traditional nomadism of the Lur appears to have been forced on their ancestors in the fourteenth century when the Mongol invasions destroyed their villages and terraced fields. Their nomadism, therefore, was a defense mechanism, to avoid contact with outside powers and their invasions.

This independence of the Lur persisted until Reza Shah and his son, from 1925 to 1979. A state of anarchy had prevailed after the First World War, but Reza Shah desired to modernize and westernize Iran, and he considered nomadism as backward. When the Lur rebelled, the Shah's army fought against them between 1922 and 1933 and the Lur lost. The Lur do not have the resources or strategic position of the Qashqa'i and so had not developed a central political leadership. Their tents were burned and the tribes disarmed and forced to wear a "uniform" of western dress. They were forced to settle and farm either in their winter or summer pastures, and this was disastrous. Land was registered in such a way that only the wealthy khans and other landowners acquired it. The majority continued to oppose the Shah's regimes and the authority of their own khans, who had benefited from the Shah's policies. This had the effect of detribalizing the Lur so that the local village, and not the tribe, became the center of political leadership. Many of them moved to the towns, like Khorramabad and Burujird, and many are now porters in Baghdad.[36]

During the Second World War, many Lur reverted to nomadism. Later, the land reforms during the 1960s broke up the monopoly of the landlords to give a wider distribution of the land. But the Boyr Ahmed tribe in the south suffered particularly from the reforms that converted good pastures into indifferent agricultural plots.[37] Education and land reform has encouraged a shift to sedentary agriculture.

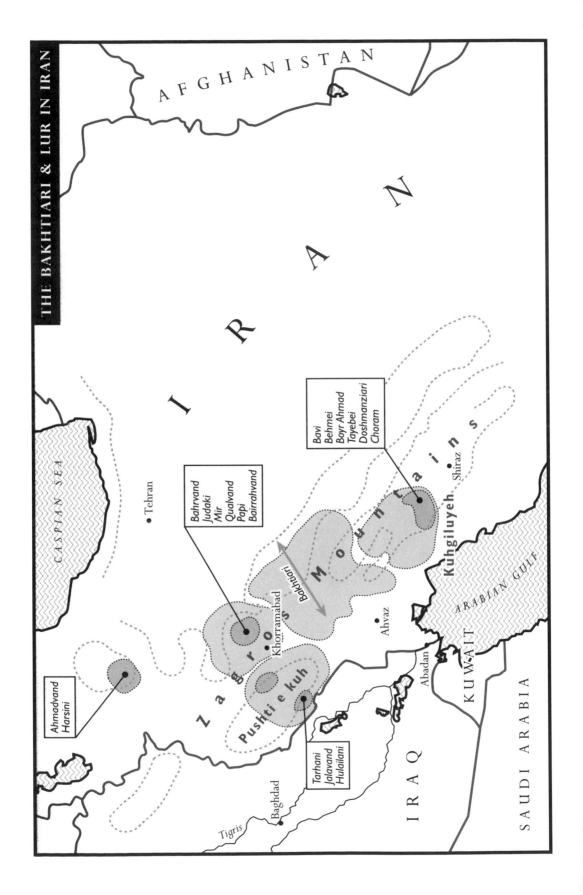

THE BAKHTIARI & LUR IN IRAN

AFGHANISTAN

I R A N

CASPIAN SEA

Tehran

Bavi
Behmei
Boyr Ahmad
Tayebei
Doshmanziari
Choram

Bahrvand
Judaki
Mir
Qualvand
Papi
Bairrahvand

Z
a
g
r
o
s
M o u n t a i n s

Bakhtiari

Kuhgiluyeh·
Shiraz

Khorramabad

Ahvaz

ARABIAN GULF

Pushti e kuh

Ahmadvand
Harsini

Abadan

KUWAIT

Tarhani
Jalavand
Hulailani

I R A Q

Baghdad

SAUDI ARABIA

Tigris

They trade their produce in two towns, Behbakaan and Ardekaan, buying what they do not produce with credit at high interest.[38] The transhumant migration was still taking place in the 1970s.

The **Pish-e Kuh**, in the eastern part of Luristan, include the *Baharvand, Judaki, Mir, Papi, Qualvand* and *Bairanvand*. Inge Mortensen describes these groups.[39] These were forced to become settled farmers, and they have become more assimilated with the Persians. They live in villages between October and April in lowland pasture with some agriculture and pasture for the herds nearby, but in May they journey for 25 days, traveling 250 kilometers (150 mi.) up into the mountains for the dry summer until September.

A Lur knows himself by belonging to a sublineage, or *owlad*, which consists of a number of *huna*, or households, descended from a common ancestor. Traditionally land belonged to the *owlad*, not the households. These lineages were grouped together as *tireh*, which used to provide the political leadership within the tribe, which was led by a khan, who used to control agricultural land, water and pasture.

Nomadism

The Lur have traditionally used three types of dwelling in their annual migrations. In the spring, April and May, they lived in black goat-hair tents called *siah chador*, but in the heat from June to September they used leaf- and branch-covered shelters called *kula*, which were cooler than the tents. While in the higher summer pastures, they plowed and planted a crop. In October they again used their tents. However, for the winter from November to the end of March, they and their pet animals moved into double-ended houses called *zemga*. These were half-buried in the slope of a hill, built of boulders, and two-thirds of the area was covered in branches and sods. One third, at one end, was the family living quarters, and the other covered end was for the animals. The central third was a sheltered courtyard for cooking, for small livestock and for guests. It was usually covered over by the

tent. Winter crops of wheat were grown in the valleys nearby. About eight oxen and mules were used for transportation of one family, and indeed the Lur provided mules for most of Iran at one time. Weaving rugs, blankets, saddlebags and other items has also been a great industry. Some of these are still used by those in pastoralism, depending on the season and altitude.

Language

The Lur speak two dialects of Farsi: Laki is spoken by the Ahmadvand, Harsini, Tarhani, Jalavand, Hulailani and Bairanvand. Luri, on the other hand, is spoken by the Baharvand, Judaki, Mir, Papi and Qualvand. Most men are bilingual in Turkic-Farsi, but the women speak only Luri or Laki. Both Islam and Lur folklore give them their values of loyalty and bravery, including tales of past heroes.

Religion

The Lur are mostly Shiite Muslims, although some are Sunni and others are of the Ahl-i Haqq sect. Because Islam insists on a dictation view of inspiration for the Qur'an, the Islamic Scriptures are considered to only be true in Arabic. This means that people that do not speak Arabic have a limited knowledge of its contents. This is true of the Lur — because of this and their geographical isolation, they were considered as needing a "reconversion" to Islam about 150 years ago. Mosques were few and only in the towns. As with others in Iran, the commemoration of the martyrdom of Hussain and the infant 'Ali Asghar, in the month of Muharram, is important to the Lur, when they stage *ta'ziya*, or passion plays, or parades.[40] Only since the Islamic Revolution has a serious attempt been made for them to be orthodox. Most men wear Western clothing and the women have been encouraged to abandon their traditional turbans and dress for the Islamic *hejab* with a veil.

It is commonly believed that Noah, Abraham, Moses and Jesus will draw into heaven only those who have been on such a pilgrimage. Their own understanding is that to be accepted by Allah, have success and avoid evil, one must gain *baraka*. This illustrates a feature of popular Islam in Central Asia and the Middle East. *Baraka* is "divine grace," considered as almost a physical power or influence, which is transferred by touching or possessing objects endowed with it. The pages of the Qur'an, Mohammed and his descendants, special saints and prophets, sultans and objects in contact with them, can all transfer this grace to ordinary people. In Iran and Central Asia, *baraka* is available at the tombs of the saints, over which *imanzadek* or shrines are built. They worship mystical leaders and make pilgrimages to their tombs. The Lur consider it important to be buried near these shrines, and caravans used to pass through the country to collect all the recently buried dead for reburial at one of the shrines. Cloths, candles, food, prayer beads or other presents are left at the shrine to become empowered with *baraka*. Certain trees are considered to have it, and cloths are left hanging on the branches. The imams shred banners that have been placed next to a shrine and sell the strips to the devotees. If the request is for healing the strip will be tied to the appropriate part of the body. In all this the aim is to mollify or appease the saint with the attitude, "If you will grant me this favor or solution, I will do such a thing for you." *Seyyids*, or claimed descendants of the Prophet, often live near the larger shrines.

Outreach

No evangelism has been done among the Lur. No Christians are known among the Lur, and New Opportunities hope to help them. The language, which has three dialects, has not been reduced to writing. A Bible translation in Lur is needed. One gospel record is available. Radio broadcasts are at present the only way to reach these people, and one may soon be established.

QASHQA'I or *Gashgai*

There are 860,000 Qashqa'i in Fars Province and other provinces to the north, in southwest Iran, but they estimate their own population to be about two million. They form a Confederation, *il-e Qashqa'i*, consisting of some 14 tribes and other affiliated groups. The Qashqa'i Confederation dates from around 1600, when the Jani Agha Qashqa'i was khan.

The Qashqa'i have a mixture of origins and their confederation has only had its present form as a result of outside political and military pressures and the formation of modern Iran during the last 150 years. But the tribes have been in the region for centuries. Some of them originated in the Caucasus, coming into Iran in the eleventh century. The Qashqa'i tribes range in size from 1,000 to 50,000 strong. On average a tribe is divided into 20 sub-tribes, each with its own traditions and history. They consider themselves to be Turkish, in distinction from the Persians and Arabs around them. The sub-tribes consist of lineages that on average consist of between 15 and 50 households of perhaps five or six individuals each. The following are the five main tribes as described by Lois Beck:[41]

The **Amaleh** tribe is approximately 45,000 strong, with about 54 sub-tribes. The name means "workers," that is, the retainers of the *ilkhani* and *ilbegi*, the paramount prince and his deputy of the confederation. Only about 500 of them are actually part of the household. Their traditional winter pastures are near Firuzabad and they spend the summers in Khosrow Shirin.

The name of the **Darrehehuri**, or "Salty Valley people," refers to an area in the mountains they claimed to have once seized for themselves from the rest of the Qashqa'i. They had 45,000 with 44 sub-tribes in 1960. They winter near Dogonbadan, northwest of Shiraz, and camp in summer at the most northern part of the Qashqa'i territory close to the Bakhtiari.

The **Shish Boluki** number 35,000 with 40 sub-tribes, and their name means "Six Families" — probably referring to the six tribal sections from which they were originally formed. They winter near Farrashband.

The **Kashkuil Bozorg** number 25,000 with 40 sub-tribes, and their name refers to the begging bowl of the Sufis. They may be a breakaway from the Kalhor, who were

20a

20b

20c

20d

20　Qashqa'i, Iran:
    a. Qashqa'i on migration sometimes hold up traffic.
    b. A Qashqa'i camp with a fold of thorns.
    c. Men enjoy their tea.
    d. Qashqa'i women have a freer way of life as Muslims.

originally probably Kurds or Lur. Many of them can trace their roots to the Mamassani tribe of the Lurs. They can be found in the winter near Mahur-e Milati.

The *Farsi Maden* seem to have migrated from the Tehran area, first to the Kuhgiluyeh region and then south to Fars, to join up with their fellow Turkic people. They are about 20,000 strong, divided into 21 sub-tribes of varied sizes. Their name means "Those who do not know Persian," which possibly implies the guarding of their independence in their early history when they roamed across Persia. They bought their summer pasture in Padena from the Basseri in the nineteenth century. Their winter location is near Jereh.

There are a number of smaller tribes, such as: The *Qarachahi*, or "Black Well," thought to be a remnant of the first Turkic people to reach Fars (3,000 — 10,000) and dispersed among the other tribes. The *Kashkuli Kuchek* tribe consists of Bakhtiari, Kurd and groups from Lak, Mamassani and Boyr Ahmad of the Luri tribes. But the main group of these smaller tribes are from the Turkic *N'Afar*, the majority of whom belong to the Khamseh Confederation with the Basseri. The Kashkuli numbered 4,300 in the 1970s. The *Safi Khani*, "Those of Safi Khan," number 4,000 with ten sub-tribes. The *Namadi*, or "Felt Rug," number 7,000. There are also a number of still smaller tribes.

The Qashqa'i, therefore, are not ethnically homogeneous, and each affiliated tribe has a vague early history. This means that "Qashqa'i" and "Turk" in Fars have more of a socio-political meaning, consisting of affiliation to that political hierarchy, rather than being ethno-linguistic groupings.[42] As we have seen, many Qashqa'i are of Luri origin. The non-Turkic groups adopted some of the Turkic features of the culture only in the early twentieth century. While these cultures are not uniform, they are sufficient to distinguish those affiliated from those who are not. Having at least some family members engaged in nomadic pastoralism has been one of these unifying features.

Each tribe, or *tayefeh*, used to be led by a family of khans, who live in the towns themselves but have considerable flocks cared for by Qashqa'i shepherds. The *il*, or confederacy, is led by the *ilkhani*. The majority of the Qashqa'i have been, or are, nomadic pastoralists who received the use of their pastures in exchange for their political allegiance to the khans. The military power of the khans gave them protection against other confederations and tribes in the competition for an overpopulated and fertile area. Reza Shah exiled, imprisoned or executed the Qashqa'i leadership in the 1930s, confiscated their pastures and stopped their nomadism by imposing military rule and dress codes on them. This had the effect of making the lower leadership more politically active to defend the Qashqa'i identity, with its cultural and linguistic traditions.

After the Shah's abdication in 1941, and following the Allied Occupation of Iran, the Qashqa'i leadership revived nomadic pastoralism. About this time the distinctive *do gushi*, or "two-eared" felt cap, was adopted as a symbol of Qashqa'i independence. At this time a school and hospital were also established in Firuzabad.[43] By the 1960s, the khans and wealthy elite gained their wealth by owning much of the agricultural land and exploiting non-Qashqa'i farmers. But now the police allocate pastures and give a timetable for the migrations. Because of U.S. influence, education and other benefits came to the Qashqa'i under the second Shah.

Nomadism

Their territory lies between the Luri tribes of the Kuhgiluyeh to the northwest and the Khamseh Confederation, including the Basseri and the Kordshuli, to the southeast. Their migration pattern is northwards into the Zagros Mountains between the summer pastures of the Lur and Khamseh Confederations.[44] The *Boyr Ahmed* of the Kuhgiluyeh Lur are the nearest neighbors, and the Qashqa'i Darrehehuri migrate through their territory. The Qashqa'i territory is remote and defensible, at least until the day of combat helicopters. Shiraz is the center of Qashqa'i political life and lies between their winter and summer pasture areas, so they pass through it twice a year.

A *tireh*, or sub-tribe, consists of a number of the pasture groups, defined by kinship ties and allegiance to a headman or *kadkhuda*, and is often named after him. The Qashqa'i migrate between winter pastures on the plains near the Persian Gulf and summer pastures over the Zagros Mountains in the north to territory north and south of Semirom. The winter pastures are to the northwest and southeast of the town of Kazerun. To avoid the marshy ground due to rain and snow, their winter camps are scattered along the higher ground between the mountains and the plain. Often they have to alternate their flocks between the plain and the slopes. They use thicker tents for the winter that often have a pen for the lambs in the rear. The flocks are put in enclosures at night because of predators and thieves. The Qashqa'i have a number of difficulties during the winter: many have to pay rent to Luri villagers; they have carry water up from the plains; and they need to buy fodder for the animals to get through the winter. The plain near the Persian Gulf is also an area of heavy commercial and military traffic.

In the spring, they migrate diagonally across the high ridges and fertile valleys of the Zagros, as the routes are difficult for the flocks in many places. From the air, this landscape shows its corrugated nature of close parallel ridges separated by narrow valleys. The villagers on the route are often hostile, guarding their fields. Most of the tribes pass near Shiraz. The summer pastures are high in the mountains swept by high winds. However, those Qashqa'i who have settled have chosen to build houses and villages around Semirom, finding the harsh winters easier to face than the dry long heat of summers down on the "winter" plains.

These summer pastures are now largely devoid of vegetation for fuel, so dung has to be collected by the younger girls for the cooking fires. The fields of the Persians and the Luri villagers encroach on the Qashqa'i territory. But this also means there is less cover for predators such as leopards, wolves, hyenas, foxes and bears. Therefore guarding the flocks is easier with only a shepherd and dogs. The summer is a relaxed time for the nomads compared to the rest of the year. However, they must move camp a number of times within each tribe's and clan's territory and fight off, or negotiate, with intruders as the pasture is used up.

Each Qashqa'i household, or *oba*, is independent to control its own economic affairs. Each family has a flock of about 70 goats and sheep. Camels are kept as status symbols and for transport, which other tribes in the Fars Province do not keep. The clans have wheat and barley plantations in their southern winter areas, and they grow apple trees and vegetables in northern summer areas, while sending the flocks to nearby grasslands. They group themselves together in flexible temporary encampments or villages, a number of which in turn form pasture groups to look after the flocks. The Qashqa'i are famous as rug weavers.

Those Qashqa'i without flocks serve their tribesmen as hired shepherds, camel drivers, field laborers, and so on, which has meant that they could continue to be integrated into the tribe and its nomadic pastoralism. This is a different situation from that of other pastoral societies, such as the Basseri or Lur, in which those unfortunate enough not to have their own animals have to leave for the towns to become "nomads in waiting." The Qashqa'i poor are able to stay part of the tribes in pastoralism because the Qashqa'i were more prosperous and better protected. The Qashqa'i also have had no inhibitions about being cultivators as well as pastoralists, in contrast to many nomads. This contributes to their economic resilience.

Society

A notable tribal school system was started by a Qashqa'i, Mohammed Bahmanbegui. He was the son of a retainer on the staff of the *Ilkhani* who learned to read and write only because his father was rich enough to employ a scribe. He was encouraged in

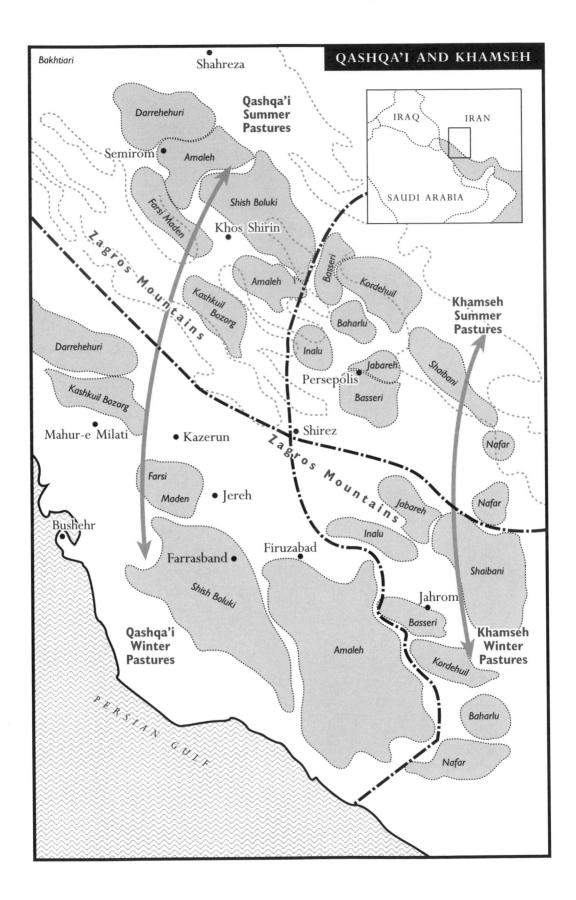

QASHQA'I AND KHAMSEH

Bakhtiari

Shahreza

Darrehehuri

Qashqa'i
Summer
Pastures

Semirom

Amaleh

Farsi Maden

Shish Boluki

Khos Shirin

IRAQ   IRAN

SAUDI ARABIA

Basseri

Amaleh

Kordehuil

Kashkuil
Bozorg

Baharlu

Khamseh
Summer
Pastures

Inalu

Jabareh

Shaibani

Darrehehuri

Persepolis

Basseri

Kashkuil Bozorg

Nafar

Mahur-e Milati

Kazerun

Shirez

Zagros Mountains

Zagros Mountains

Jabareh

Nafar

Farsi

Inalu

Maden

Jereh

Bushehr

Firuzabad

Shaibani

Farrasband

Jahrom

Shish Boluki

Basseri

Khamseh
Winter
Pastures

Qashqa'i
Winter
Pastures

Amaleh

Kordehuil

Baharlu

PERSIAN GULF

Nafar

education and took a law degree in Teheran, and later studied in the United States. Bahmanbegui was a translator in German, French and English during the Second World War and became a liaison agent for the U.S. aid program under the second Shah. He started a Qashqa'i literacy program in 1952, and then another in Farsi. This has been extended by Iranian government and U.S. aid to give a formal education to the nomads with tent schools in every sub-tribe of the Qashqa'i. There were about 212 schools in 1979, and some have been transformed into permanent buildings for settled families. Other tribes of the Lur also gained schools.[45]

A tribal teachers' training school in Shiraz was founded in 1957, serving most of the tribal groups. A Tribal High School with 1,000 students was started in 1967 with Peace Corps teachers. A tribal carpet weaving school and a tribal technical school followed. Lur students complained that the bias was to the Qashqa'i in student placements, and even the carpet patterns taught were promoting the Qashqa'i traditions. Training courses in midwifery, paramedic and para-veterinary skills have also been established. Midwives also worked among the tribes.

Bahmanbegui had great diplomatic skill in getting local chiefs, the Qashqa'i *ilkhni*, the chiefs of other non-Qashqa'i tribes, the Iranian government (already hostile to the tribes) and the U.S. aid administration to all co-operate together in these projects. Local participation was essential to success. Teachers had to teach Persian rather than tribal history and the rest of the Persian curriculum. Some of the textbooks were direct translations of American ones, including illustrations of middle-class American family life! The education had little or no relevance to a nomadic pastoral or rural life, says Lois Beck, because Bahmanbegui thought that tribal life would eventually end.[46] For some reason he encouraged women to wear the most elaborate traditional dress, but the men to dress as Persian town dwellers.

However, at the time, the Shah's land reforms favored non-Turkic cultivators. This meant that much of the Qashqa'i pastures were converted into agricultural land, even in areas beyond the reach of village water supplies. Seventy-five per cent of the uncultivated land, including most of the nomads' pasture, came under state ownership. Irrigation was increased for the fields with motorized pumps that lowered the water table and caused environmental damage. The confederation leaders were dismissed or exiled, and the tribes and sub-tribes were placed under police leadership. Pasture was then allocated by the police, with the nomads being forced to stay on one small plot for the season, irrespective of overgrazing, flock size, and so on. Persian commercial stock-raisers and non-Qashqa'i village pastoralists were allowed to use the pasture first each season.

During the 1970s, 30-40% of the people settled, and 50 settlement areas near new industries were set up. In 1975 the tribes were "abolished," and the nomads had to apply for grazing licenses. They were placed last on the waiting lists, after other land users. Land and grazing rights were distributed to about 25,000 individual families by the pre-Revolutionary government, rather than being concentrated in the hands of chiefs, and the clans were disarmed in the 1970s.

After the Islamic Revolution, the anti-clerical Qashqa'i supported the change of government. At this time the Qashqa'i was the best-armed tribal group. This enabled them to regain the pastures confiscated by the Shah. During this period the prices of meat and milk went up, making pastoralism more attractive even to those who had settled. About 25,000 are estimated to be still nomadic. They are moderate Shiites, but few are practicing Muslims. Their political and military capability, together with their lax religious practice, mean that they are out of favor with the theocratic state. Early in the Revolution the government attempted to remove the *ilkhani*, Naser Khan, and Qashqa'i resistance was revived, again with the *do gushi* as a symbol of defiance. The Islamic Revolution banned co-education and imposed Islamic dress, discouraging the girls from attending school. In town Qashqa'i women had to wear black *chador* (the black overdress used by Muslim women), but they were clearly distinguishable by their brightly colored dresses hanging beneath! The Revolution also prohibited Qashqa'i music and dances.

From 1980 to 1982, Revolutionary Guards attacked the Qashqa'i rebels and their Bakhtiari allies in the mountains with tanks and helicopter gunships. Key battles were fought at Farrashbad in the spring of 1981, and at Jahrom in the summer of 1982. After two years resistance, the leaders were betrayed and the revolt came to an end.[47] The Revolution has proved itself to be biased against non-Persians as much as the Shahs had been, restricting the cultural and political expression of the tribal peoples.

The future appears to be difficult for the Qashqa'i, as it does for other nomadic pastoralists in the Zagros Mountains. Their nomadism is being restricted by land being given to farmers for cultivation, but many are still nomadic into the twenty-first century. They have overcome difficulties many times before. They need both medical and veterinary help.

While they call themselves "Turks," most settled Qashqa'i are bilingual in Farsi and speak it well. But their language is Turkic and close to Azerbaijani, and about 200,000 speak it.[48] There are no Christians among the Qashqa'i.

Outreach

New Opportunities anticipate helping this people. There are a number of radio broadcasts from FEBA and TWR, daily in Farsi, but neither the programs nor the Scripture are in the Qashqa'i language and reception appears to be difficult. The southern Azeri Bible translation is in progress and will meet a need here. The Farsi Bible has been available since 1994.

Families of *Kowli* or *Qorbati* or *Ghorbati* attach themselves as ironsmiths to some of the Qashqa'i bands, or peddle pots and pans among both settled villagers and pastoral groups.

KHAMSEH Confederation, Iran

The Khamseh, or "Five Together," Confederation is about 100 years old and consists of the *Jabareh* (13,000) and *Shaibani* (16,000) Arab tribes, the *Ainalu* or *Inallu* (a Turkic Afshar tribe of 5,000), the *Baharlu* (7,500) and *N'Afar* (3,500) Turkic tribes, as well as the Iranian *Basseri* and *Kordshuli* (see below). Lois Beck says this confederation was formed to counter the political power of the Qashqa'i. It is unknown whether it has disbanded, or whether these tribes are still separate entities. The N'Afar and Inallu are to the west, the Baharlu in the center and the Arab tribes to the east.

BASSERI

There are 16,000 or more in Fars Province, southwest Iran, who form part of the Khamseh Confederation. They are an Iranian people, speaking the Shiraz dialect of Dari, and have no tradition of having migrated from outside the region. They were forced to settle under Reza Shah, but after his abdication in 1941 many returned to the nomadic life. Interestingly, some started the pattern of migration without any animals, the way of life being more important to them than the pastoralism. They raise sheep and goats to sell the meat and wool in the markets, but they have horses, donkeys and camels as pack-animals.

Nomadism

The Basseri emphasize the self-sufficiency of each family, each having about five or six persons to a tent, or *khune*. The family owns the animals and forms the basic social unit. A family has to own a minimum flock of about 60 sheep and goats to support itself, but most have 100 or more. Two to five tents move together and have a limited co-operation in herding and milking. However, these herding groups are not necessarily related and only stay together as long as the heads of the families decide to. If they fail to agree on decisions, the group readily splits up.

Their main traditional migration route,

21a

21b

21c

21d

21 Qashqa'i:
a. The Qashqa'i tent houses one family. Wool, freshly dyed, hangs out to dry.
b. The women are famous for the weaving of their rugs.
c. Water has to be carried and stored in sheep-skins.
d. One of the famous tent schools among the Qashqa'i.

or the *il-rah*, the tribal road, is about 500 kilometers (310 mi.) long and between 30 and 80 kilometers (20-50 mi.) wide, running northwards between the southern Zagros range and the desert near the Gulf of Hormuz.[49] Its pastures, wells and passes are recognized as the people's property and they need to be on the move for three months of the year. The Basseri are true nomads, sometimes moving camp nearly every day. The average tent is struck and re-erected about 120 times a year.[50] The winter camps are dispersed about three kilometers (1.8 mi.) away from each other on the ridges and slopes just above the coastal plain around Lar to avoid the mud.

In spring the health of the sheep quickly deteriorates as the temperature rises, so the migratory cycle is thus necessary to maintain the health of the nomads' herds, quite apart from their requirement for pasture.[51] The Basseri congregate to migrate on the Benaron-Mansurabad plain, between Jahrom and Lar, on Nowruz, the Persian New Year, or March 21. On this day they meet together wearing new clothes and greet each other, and the routine acts of preparing to camp and decamp take on a special significance in anticipation of the journey together. A number of the herding groups camp together on migration to form an *oulad* of ten to forty tents, usually of related families. The *oulad* is led by a "gray beard," but he makes decisions by consulting with each head of family to get unanimity. The "gray beard" has no authority to make decisions himself, and the decision can be influenced by how many of the heads of families are related.

They migrate over the passes, passing near Khafr and Shiraz, where many sedentary Basseri live, into the growing spring pasture of a number of valleys. Northeast of Shiraz some groups pass Takht-e Jamslid, the ruins of Persepolis. Crossing the Kur River, they can have contact with Qashqa'i and Arab tribes also crossing the river, but normally they do not have anything to do with each other except when looking for lost animals. Beyond the river the sections take different routes until they reach either the upper Kur valley or go further up, to the Kuh-i Bul at 4,000 meters (13,000 ft.) to spend the summer. They occupy these pastures at high altitude, which provide the optimum pastoral situation in the summer. The autumn return journey is faster as most of the pasture is dried up and trucks are often used.

Society

The wider unity of the Basseri consists of 12 lineages, or *tira*, with allegiance to their chiefs or khans. The khans do not take part in the nomadic life, but settle disputes, especially with other tribes. The autocratic power of the khan can intervene directly in any family or camp, bypassing the "gray beard." Some of the nomadic Basseri own fields along the route that they rent out to villagers to farm. William Irons describes how wealthier Basseri often invest in land rather than face the losses due to hiring shepherds and theft. Poor Basseri tend to settle, being unable to amalgamate with other households, or become shepherds to the other Basseri. Both trends lead to sedentarization, rather than developing a self-sufficient pastoralism.

There are other groups of Basseri: the **Bugard Basseri** are situated west of the Qashqa'i in northwest Fars, and they migrate parallel to the Qashqa'i. The **Isfahan** (or Esfahan) **Basseri** are a group that defected from the main body at the end of the nineteenth century and migrate between spending the winter in the Yazd-Isfahan plain and the summer near Semirom or Yazd-e Khast. A large group in the desert east of Teheran are recognized by the Basseri as being related to them.

Religion

The Basseri are Shiite Muslims and seem to be familiar with the basic tenets of Islam, but they follow less of the ritual and customs than other neighboring peoples. They have no religious or ritual specialists in the tribe. They confuse the Islamic calendar and pray irregularly and alone, and usually do not observe Ramadan. During the time of the Shahs they had little interest in religion, except the Il-e Khas clan that had lived in the Isfahan area for 100 years, who are considered too strict. This situation may have changed since the downfall of the Shah. The Persian or solar calendar is more important to them than Islamic festivals because they organize their migrations by it. Barth describes the wedding ceremony.[52] They have a number of taboos that appear to have no rational explanation. The belief in the evil eye is widespread, distinguishing between conscious envy that is ineffectual and unconscious envy which is usually by someone close to the family. Salt, mirrors and objects tied to a child or animal serve to turn unconscious envy into conscious, and therefore harmless, thought.

The **Ghorbati**, *Qorbati* or *Kurbat* groups travel with the Basseri.

KORDSHULI, Fars Province, Iran

This is a tribe of the Khamseh Confederation with the Basseri and 'Arab, or the Arabs tribes. The Kordshuli have various traditions about their origin, such as entering Persia before, or with, the Qashqa'i. Other traditions see them as a breakaway Qashqa'i or Bakhtiari group, the latter being more likely as they speak the Lur dialect of Farsi and not the Turkic of the Qashqa'i. At least two *tirehs*, or sections, were formerly Bakhtiari sections. Early in the twentieth century, they were an independent tribe. They were considered part of the Khamseh Confederation from 1943 but they did not formally get recognition as members until the 1970s, and political power is concentrated in the leaders of the sections.

In the mid-1970s they numbered 353 households, of which 296 were nomadic — or 1,700 nomads. The 57 settled households were landowners or agricultural laborers living in the summer pasture area and still integrated with the tribal structure. The Kordshuli consider the *sarhad*, or the summer pasture area in northern Fars, to be their homeland ,or *vatan*; it is the Shadkam Valley and lies 120 kilometers (75 mi.) north of Shiraz. They have villages, the largest of which is Khongesht, established in the valleys — although the winters are too severe to keep the sheep there. The wheat and barley crops grown are important for bread and fodder respectively. Sugar beet and other crops are grown for sale.

Nomadism

During the summer, the nomadic majority take their sheep into nearby mountain pastures daily and their time is productive in terms of carpet weaving. In summer they live in a *hajir*, or light tent, open on the south side. Poorer Kordshuli do not migrate but winter in the *vatan*, keeping their small flocks in shelters, but they spend the summer camping with their nomadic kinsmen. The nomads migrate with the onset of cold weather in September.

The Kordshuli do not feel at home in the winter pastures some 250 kilometers (150 mi.) to the south. Their six tribal sections, or *tirehs*, winter widely separated from each other, camping in the mountains at around 1,000 meters altitude, near Mobarakabad and Jahrom, south of Fars. In this area they compete for the lower pastures with the Qashqa'i, 'Arab, Basseri and the local nomadic pastoralist Kuhaki people, who live in tents there all year round; the police have to adjudicate in disputes. They spend the winter in their *chador*, or heavy black goat-hair ridge tent with loose stone walls around the base. A wall made of the household stores divides the interior, and half is used for lambs and kids and half for the family. Carpets are laid or the pebble floor, and the most honored position for a guest is to sit against the baggage in the center. The camp, or *beilah*, are formed of both close relatives and more distant kin who share the same pasture. The members refer to each other as *hamsayeh*, or of the same shade, but each "tenthold," or *huneh*, is economically independent and they tend to co-operate only in leading the pack trains on migration and in digging wells.

The spring migration begins at the Iranian New Year, and is a time for joy for most nomadic peoples. The Kordshuli pack their donkeys and lead them between two brushwood fires as a symbolic "gateway" to the new year, and it is considered unlucky to look back at the site of the winter camp. Their migration route, which is shared with the Basseri, takes them across a plain where there is now much irrigation agriculture and less pasture, and the livestock become weak due to being driven past the planted fields. Animal theft, both from other nomads as well as from local farmers, is also a constant problem. They also have to use the verge of the Shiraz-Esfahan highway, which has heavy traffic. The migration takes between 30 and 50 days. On the return journey in September stubble can be found en route on which to feed the sheep.

The men do the herding, shearing, sewing, buying and selling and the gathering of the firewood. By the time he is a teenager, a son will be in charge of the whole flock. Marriage is preferred with first cousins, and most marriages are at least within the same *tireh*. Levirate marriage is also a duty. When a man marries the new couple lives with his parents for about a year, but a high proportion stay on. The women are responsible for cooking, milking and making the dairy products such as yogurt, buttermilk, curdballs, clarified butter and whey.[53] There is no known Christian contact with them.

KOMACHI

In southern Iran, this is the pastoral element of a larger group, numbering in the 1980s about 120 households of some 550 persons. The name possibly comes from *komaj-i*, meaning "bread-like," referring to the gifts of unleavened bread they once gave to an Imir. Their tradition claims that they are descendants of three distinct lineages from different parts of Iran, who formed a tribe early in the twentieth century. A third of them, according to Bradburd's survey, came from other pastoral communities that have since disintegrated.[54] Their location is the Kerman region of southern Iran, that has traded with Europe in cashmere shawls and woolen carpets since the seventeenth century.

Nomadism

International trade caused the Komachi to shift the composition of the flocks to sheep in the last third of the twentieth century. They used to use camels as pack animals, but today they hire trucks and use motorcycles instead of horses. The Komachi also prospered from the rise in oil prices in the 1970s, for this resulted in a higher standard of living for the population of Iran and greater mutton consumption. Meat prices rose while grain prices were still controlled. Kerman is a very poor region, and flocks take three times longer to reproduce themselves on the poor pasture than those of the Yomut Turkmen in the north of the country.

Their winter pasture, that they call *garmsir*, is situated on the plain near the Gulf of Hormuz, around the town of Manujan, 110 kilometers (70 mi.) east of the major naval port of Bandar Abbas. They have occupied this area during the winters since 1960, when their previous winter camps in Jiroft became too crowded — a change of nearly 200 kilometers (125 mi.). In the 1970s, the government succeeded in pacifying the area from brigandage and malaria. Now there is intensive production of dates, oranges and lemons for Teheran and other northern cities. In theory, the land beyond the irrigated fields of the villages is state land open to all who receive a permit for grazing. In practice, permits are limited to those who have the capital to sink wells and develop the land.

The lambs and kids are born in November and initially the milk is given to them, until they are gradually weaned so that the milk can be diverted to dairy production. The early and late rains in December and February affect the extent and quantity of the milk production. The women are busy all day in February milking, making yogurt and churning butter. The area is too arid and in the spring it is too hot for effective pastoralism.

In April, they migrate 300 kilometers (200 mi.) northwards into the Zagros Mountains. The flocks take about 30 days for the uphill journey from the 100-meter altitude of the winter pastures to 3,000 meters. As the valleys they pass through have already been grazed all winter by Lak, Lurak and other tribes, the Komachi cannot delay on the journey. These valleys are linked by a Wadi called the "River of Thieves," and then higher up by another called the "Defile of Death." They have to pass through the Esfandagheh Valley, where there are Lori and Luri tribes who migrate only within the valley. The Komachi are able to trade dates they have carried from the coastal plain for sale. After crossing a 3,000-meter (10,000-ft.) mountain pass, they arrive at their summer pastures.

The Komachi feel that their *sarhad*, or summer pastures in Kerman, is their "homeland," where they are relatively free from state interference. Soon after arrival there, by the beginning of June, the dairy work begins to trail off and work switches to weaving goat-hair tents and bags. The summer is the time for shearing, the sale of wool and of surplus animals. Summer is also the time for rites of passage and other ceremonies, and wedding negotiations particularly engage everyone's attention, even of those not involved — like observing a soap opera, Bradburd suggests.

The camps are called *ehshams*, or "retinues," and consist of between three and 12 households in tents. Those who have joined the groups most recently serve as hired shepherds for a number of years and, together with those who have lost their flocks, continue as a lower class, whose tents are pitched separately and are poorer in size and quality. The relationship between these two classes is tense, as most of the work is done by the hired shepherds, yet they continue to get poorer and are treated as socially inferior, while the owners have a relatively leisurely life, enjoying a better diet and imported goods.[55] The migration cycle closes with the autumn journey, with the flocks being driven first. The families of the owners of the flocks follow in hired trucks, taking only about two days for the journey.

Religion

The Komachi are Shiite Muslims and believe that to be a Komachi one has to be a nomadic pastoralist, but to be a real person or human one must be a Shiite. They speak Farsi, so available Bible translations are adequate.

AFSHAR

There are 290,000 Afshar in the Kerman province, with about 40 sub-tribes of pastoralists in the region of Baft, Bann, Jiroft, Kahnooj and Sirjan. There are 5,000 in Afghanistan. The Afshar are the largest living group in a large territory west and southwest of Rafsanjan, and they migrate south to Bolook Orzooyeh in winter and north to Bolook Aghtae for the summer. They are of Turkic origin and speak Afshari, close to South Azeri. There is no Christian witness among them and there is one gospel cassette in their language.

BALUCH or *Balochi*

Baluchistan covers the adjoining parts of southeastern Iran, Afghanistan and western Pakistan. There are about 5,000,000 Baluch, including 3,000,000 who make up 3% of Pakistan's population.[56] The Baluch appear to have been formed from a number of different peoples, and historical evidence for the present people only goes back to the seventeenth century. There were, however, other earlier groups in other parts of Iran with the same name. The Persian government only started to control the region at the end of the nineteenth century, and many Baluch fled to Turkmenistan. Reza Shah banned the Baluch language and dominated them by military force.[57]

They are united by language and a common culture, and the name *baluch* has the connotation of a tent-dwelling nomadic pastoralist, although most of them have never lived like that. The Baluch practice different combinations of agriculture and pastoralism — some are settled cultivators, some semi-nomadic agropastoralists, and about 25%, or 650,000 of them, are pure nomads.[58] The varied environments have prompted them to adopt a variety of lifestyles between agriculture and nomadism.

Nomadism

The Baluch are gregarious and value the extended family of both their fathers' and mothers' relatives to provide a network of relationships. They enjoy being in a large camp and a number of herding groups may camp together if pasture and water supply allow. The herding group, or *halk*, usually consists of related families, but can also include others. The practical needs of pastoralism and other sources of income limit its size. The groups on the plains tend to be larger, having perhaps ten households, each with smaller flocks of 16 because they are also able to exploit other sources of income. On the Sarhad Plateau in the north, the groups are smaller with as few as three households, but each family owns a flock of around 40 animals. Camels are few and kept only to carry the camp equipment.

The sheep and goats belong to each household, and the *halk* is organized around an unwritten, yet formal, contract with a *shwaneg*, or shepherd, who supervises the flocks of the families together, and is paid in kind or in cash. The shepherd may be either a member of one of the families of the *halk* or an outsider. This arrangement frees the other members of the *halk* to form work groups to share other tasks, such as tending cultivation, repairing huts or dams, tending the camels, visiting markets or guarding the camp.

Marriages are often arranged when the bride is only a few days old. Outsiders are seen as a threat, and for this reason the Baluch are reluctant to settle in villages. Both sons and daughters inherit equally. The women never leave camp and work together in carrying water, cooking for visitors, caring for children, combing, spinning and weaving wool.[59] Some nomads are more prosperous than the sedentary Baluch.

Baluchistan is divided into a number of different zones, but all have a very unpredictable rainfall. Eighty per cent in Iran are oasis farmers with semi-nomadic livestock breeding. To the north, on the 1,500 meter-high Sarhad Plateau, there is often sufficient rain to provide pasture for sheep and goats as well as for growing crops. In the north, the Baluch are organized in tribes while in the south they have a feudal hierarchical society.

In the north there are four major tribes: the *Rigi, Ismailzai, Gamshadzai* and *Yarahmadzai* or *Shah Nawazi*.[60] The suffix *-zai* means "descendants of." The *Yarahmadzai Baluch* number about 5,000 and live on the Sarhad Plateau.[61] The three territorial sections of the tribe are divided into about 60 lineages led by headmen, who have most of the political responsibility. The cultivation of grain and date palm plantations in their three oases supplement the economy, but this has to be augmented by caravans to fetch grain. Non-tribesmen or former slaves do the cultivation, as the Yarahmadzai consider manual work beneath their dignity.

The Yarahmadzai pastoralists winter in fixed camps of tents, keeping the animals warm by placing the sheep and goats in tents and placing blankets on the camels. From March to May, they make as many as ten excursions to pasture the flocks and find fresh grass. During the summer many of the men, as owners or as laborers, travel some distance for the grain harvest. Then, during August to October, as many as possible leave the camps and flocks on the plateau to travel 160 kilometers (100 mi.) down to the Hamun-i Mashkel Basin, to pollinate and harvest their date palm groves.[62]

In southern Baluchistan political and social life is, or was, in the hands of a non-Baluch elite. The nomads have historically provided the military forces in power struggles within the towns or oases. Pakistani officials now replace the power of the elite. The Baluch form a class of independent farmers and pastoralists in the middle of society, between the elite and a caste of menial workers or former slaves. The river valley and plains have scattered farms using irrigation. These farmers are called *shahri*, in contrast to the term *baluch*, which is reserved for the pastoralists. The Baluch have tribes, or *kom*, but these have little actual authority, compared to their local headman and their patron among the elite.

Southern Baluchistan has three distinct regions: the southeast, the central south, and the southwest. Beyond these is the Makran coastal region, where the Baluch fishermen live.[63] To the southeast of the Sarhad lies the lower Saravan River Valley, which follows this pattern, where the Baluch are settled and cultivate fields and date palm plantations as well as being pastoralists of sheep and goats.

Southern Baluchistan is shut off from the Arabian Sea by the jagged Makran Mountains, and what little rain there is has to be caught in temporary dams. Goats and date palms are the only reliable sources of subsistence. A camp consists of the tents of the families of the herding group, or *halk*, positioned at easy distance from a surface source of water and their small cultivated plots. These plots are formed from sediment collected in dammed wadis, and they have to be irrigated daily with the meager water supply available. Here each family may grow a few date palms, peach trees, onions and pomegranates, as the supplementary means of subsistence to the pastoralism. The migration patterns of the pastoralists in the south are more irregular than elsewhere. They tend to move between their relatives in the more fertile areas, where they have shares in small plots of farmland, and these form the fixed points in their migrations as they try to find pasture created by flash floods and patchy rainfall.

The rain falls from December to February and the Baluchi camps have to be clear of the riverbeds, because of the flash floods, and be ready to migrate in the spring to exploit the new pasture. Thirty sheep and goats and a pack-camel or donkey for moving camp are sufficient for a family to survive, but in the spring the camp has to be near pasture, so that the goats can be milked twice a day. Many of the nomads have an arrangement to supply butter to the agricultural Baluch in exchange for dates and grain. In autumn the goats are taken further from camp with a few family members, while the rest of the family move to the village for the date palm harvest. In the Makran, the nomads are also able to gather the white hearts of the wild dwarf palms.[64]

In the southwest region of Baluchistan lies the huge Jaz Muriam Depression that is 400 kilometers (250 mi.) across and contains both desert and pasture. Here the Baluch have adopted camel pastoralism, and they breed some of the world's fastest camels, which are capable of speeds of 40 kilometers (25 mi.) per hour for an hour or more.

Others work in truck driving, farming in river valleys and fishing on the coast, and many take employment in Karachi, Bahrain, the U.A.E., Kenya and Tanzania. They have a considerable political influence in western Pakistan. Most of Afghanistan's Baluch have always been nomads or have reverted back to nomadism since the civil war from 1978.[65]

Religion

The Baluch are Muslims of the Hanafi sect. Most them have faith in the *pirs*, or "saints," and their descendants, who are believed to attain union with Allah by mystical experience, gaining spiritual power by long periods of fasting in order to kill carnal desires. They tend to be independent of the official Islamic establishment.[66] The *pir* has power to heal, save from drought, or defeat human enemies or evil spirits. *Pirs* go to visit their clients or followers regularly and receive considerable gifts. In southern Baluchistan, Zikrism is common. This is a sect that considers the teachings of a sixteenth-century Mahdi, Syed Mahmud, to supersede those of the prophet. The Sunnis have persecuted them and many have moved to be near Karachi. Many of the Baluchi fishermen are of this faith.

Literacy is low, and possibly lower among the pastoralists, though Balochi, as it is spelled in Pakistan, is a major language and has some literature.

Outreach

Bible portions are available in Western and Eastern Balochi, which are distinct from one another. The New Testament was available in Southern Balochi in 1998.[67] A fifteen-minute Christian program is broadcast twice a week in Balochi. Access to Baluchistan is relatively easier for local Christians.

BRAHUI

There are 1,500,000 Brahui living in Pakistan, 10,000 in Iran and 200,000 in Afghanistan. They claim to have originated in Syria, but they are probably the original Dravidian inhabitants of Baluchistan, where they number about 576,800, or 25% of the population. They form a confederation of 29 different ethnic tribes divided into four groups including the eight "True Brahui Tribes" in Kalat and the others in southern Kalat. Some Pushtun and Baluch have been absorbed into their tribes and many non-Brahui have elected to be adopted into a lineage to be part of the tribes, but they all use the same language. Their lifestyles vary — from sedentary farmers, some of whom migrate to the plains for the winter, to camel-riding pastoral nomads.

Nomadism

The Brahui migrate between Kalat, on the plateaus of Sarawan and Jhalawan at 1,800 meters (6,000 ft.), and the Kachhi plain, northern Sind, which lies at 150 meters (500 ft.). Many Brahui are semi-nomadic — that is, they cultivate their crops of cereals, fruit and vegetables from March to October, then migrate in November to the plains with their flocks of goats. Others are true nomads, who only spend a brief summer in Kalat. They raise mainly sheep for wool, as well as camels for wool and transport and a few goats for their hair. While the Suliaman and Kirthar ranges cross their path, the Bolan Pass helps to shorten the journey so that the horizontal distance is only 130 kilometers (80 mi.). Summer lasts from April to October on the plains, and there is very little pasture when the Brahui arrive in mid-November. The plains do not provide enough natural pasture, but local farmers control the six rivers with dams during the hot summer, so that there is pasture and stubble in the fields for animals to feed on during the winter until mid-March. Here the Brahui live in tents and seek to sell their cattle and handicrafts or look for work as laborers.

The plains soon becomes too hot in spring for the sheep, goats and camels, and the Brahui migrate back to Kalat in March where the melted snow provides enough moisture for summer pasture. Back on the plateaus the nomads move camp every few days, keeping within a few miles of the nearest water supply. The sheep have to be milked twice a day, so the whole camp keeps up with the flocks to help with the work of milking. By June the grass dries up, as does the milk, and the camps are able to remain in one place while the flocks are led further afield with some of the men. The families not needed to shepherd the flocks are free to work in the fields, and their summer diet changes as milk is replaced with wheat.

The size of flocks and the grazing groups is determined by the difficulties of finding sufficient natural pasture in both summer and winter locations. The camps form voluntary associations called *khalk*, and their size seems to be determined by the size of the flocks, rather than by relationships among the families. There seems to be a minimum flock size for the group of 250 animals, and the average holding of livestock of a household is about 80 sheep. Each household tent is economically independent, but the *khalk* provides protection and co-operation in the pastoral tasks. Leadership tends to be a matter of reaching a consensus among members. A household agrees to join such a group for the year's migration cycle, but after that is free to leave. Co-operation between the women in the milking often brings tents together. Often the migrating Brahui groups are accompanied by two or more *Luri* as minstrels. This voluntary nature of the groups in the face of the limited pasture means that families are constantly changing their lifestyle, and due to improved irrigation many are staying in Sind as farmers.[68]

Outreach

The Brahui speak their own language and some are bilingual, speaking Balochi as well. There is some Christian literature in Brahui, and there are Scripture portions in Arabic and Roman scripts. The New Testament and Genesis were published 1998.[69] A radio broadcast began in 1997. The Church Mission Society has worked among this people for some decades.

Peripatetics in Southwest Asia

There are a number of traditionally itinerant groups in Afghanistan that are called Jats, Zott, Zatt, Djatt and derived terms by outsiders. They themselves consider it derogatory and may use it themselves to describe other nomadic groups. There is no agreed understanding of the origin of meaning of the term *Jat*, but while an Indian origin of some of these groups is likely, they are not connected to the Jat farmers of the Punjab. It is in common use for very different groups who happen to have a similar nomadic lifestyle. The popular connotations of being dirty, thieving, inferior, rude, lazy, outsiders, bad Muslims, or having bad habits only show the prejudice of settled society.[70]

GHORBATI or Kurbat or Qorbati

They are also known as *Koli* or *Kowli*, the Farsi term for all "Gypsy" type peoples, which often has a derogatory sense. But its origin is probably from the Romani *kalo*, "black," and they call themselves *Kauli-ye Girbalbend*, which means Sieve-maker Koli. The term *ghorbati* is derived from the Arabic for "stranger" or "outsider."[71] They are probably related to the Luti.

Ghorbati, Iran

They are Gypsy tinkers and smiths, who are dispersed throughout Iran and also attach themselves to pastoralists like the Basseri and Qashqa'i, and to the Kurds in Iraq.[72] They prefer to call themselves *Haddad*, iron-worker, rather than *Kauli-ye Girbalbend*, Sieve-maker Koli. They imitate the clothing and customs of their adopted people, in order to hide their identity. They serve as flautists and drummers, fortunetellers and beggars, at the social occasions of the pastoralists. They also travel into Pakistan, India, Afghanistan and Kuwait. They are to be found in Baluchistan (see Luti, below).

Nomadism

They live in the villages during the winters, but groups of ten to 60 families or "tents" attach themselves to the Basseri, Qashqa'i and other pastoral nomads in the spring. They have no sheep or goats, but manufacture or repair horseshoes, spindle whorls for weaving, sheep shears, pots and pans, and so on. Their women move between the camp groups selling their wares and passing on news and gossip, but otherwise there is little communication between the two ethnic groups.[73]

Language

They probably speak their host language, Qashqa'i or Farsi, and Kurbat, a dialect of Domari. They are nominally Muslim and probably no specific Christian work has been attempted among them.

Ghorbati, Afghanistan

According to a legend, they believe that they are descended from a Persian king who disrespected the prophet Mohammed and so they were condemned to the nomadic life. They seem to have spread out from Kandahar, where there is a community that does not remember living in tents. Others moved on to Herat at the end of the nineteenth century and towards Mazar-e

Sarif about the middle of the twentieth century. They are now found in a large area all around the country, except in the mountains of the Hindu Kush, from northwest of Herat to Fayzabad in the northeast, Nimruz and Helmand in the south and around Gazni, Kabul and Jalalabad in the east.

Society

They have three major tribal divisions. There are the *Faray*, who are settled in Karbul with a hundred families in Peshawar. Their other two tribes are mostly nomadic — the *Syawun* in the east and the *Kayani* in the south and west. The Syawun became nomadic because their houses were demolished in the early twentieth century. The Ghorbati are called Jat, which has a poor connotation, implying they are dishonest and quarrelsome. They are considered social inferiors because they are poor and work with leather, and they often try to hide their identity. In most villages they would have difficulty settling, even if they wanted to, because they are despised. Only in Kabul do they feel secure enough to settle and change their occupation, to shopkeeper or paid employment.

Nomadism

The Ghorbati's main occupation is the manufacture of drums and sieves that are made and sold by the men. They also repair shoes, make bamboo birdcages and flutes and sell animals. The women peddle cloth and haberdashery bought from wholesalers, around an itinerary of regular customers. Older women also do bloodletting. Many of their goods can be made locally, so to settle would soon result in a saturated market. But their trade cannot be increased either by producing more of their traditional wares or by traveling further. The only work open to the women is to hawk bought goods like cloth, but this brings hostility in a Muslim society.

The typical migratory cycle starts with the sale of hides and sieves that have been prepared during the winter. In March they buy raw materials for their goods. During May the Ghorbati move from their houses to living in tents and migrate in family groups to higher altitudes, climbing some 2,000 meters, with each lineage and family following its own circuit of customers. Through the months of July to the end of September they travel constantly, making sieves and tambourines, and selling or leaving goods on credit. During October and November they retrace their journey, collecting debts from farmers and so on, after the harvest. By the beginning of December they have returned to their winter camps or houses. Most live in tin huts in communities in the winter, but some still use tents all year round, gathered in camps near the large towns.

Family

A tent represents a marriage, since a man does not have one until he is married, but he may have to provide another tent if he marries a second wife. Previously they used to make their own conical tents, but today they buy white or khaki ridge tents made in Pakistan. Inside there is no division between men and women, but the place of honor for guest is near the central pole. The men are responsible to erect the tent, in contrast to the Koochi, whose women do this. It is important to align the tent so that as one enters one is facing west towards Mecca, and also so that passers-by can see the people inside and feel they can receive traditional hospitality.

The women arrange the interior, build clay brick walls along the sides, cook the meals and wash clothes, it is said, on Thursdays. The women tend to have a stronger economic position than that among other Muslim groups, because they inherit their customers from generation to generation. They can be more successful in selling goods in contrast to the varied demand for the men's craft items. Some women can take decisions even contradicting those of their husbands. The children gather firewood, but the wife tends the fire. It is put out every night, and in winter the family sleeps under an eiderdown and also uses a charcoal heater.

Religion

The Ghorbati are Muslims but, like others in Afghanistan, husbands and wives sleep together. They consider sleep like death, so it is important to sleep with the body oriented in the right direction. Mothers give birth turned towards Mecca and the child sleeps in a hammock or cradle in the tent with its head to the south. They consider that two babies born close together in the same camp can cast spells on each other, and this is averted by the two families exchanging gifts of salt and bread before they are allowed to enter each other's tents. The dead are laid out with the head to the north and the right hand laid pointing to Mecca.

Like many peripatetics, they have myths that suggest misconduct to explain their misfortune or low social status. Allah needed a sieve to separate the dust to make Adam's body, and Satan taught an angel to make one, who sneezed with the dust. Therefore it is unlucky to be a sieve maker. Alternatively, their ancestor making the first sieve fell over when it rolled away from him, and so cursed all his descendants who would be sieve-makers. In fact, the Ghorbati learned the craft from another group in Kandahar.[74] There is no Christian media or witness among them.

The *Ghorbati* are also found in Baluchistan, Pakistan.

LUTI

The Luti live in Iran and prefer not to be called Luri (pron. Lori). They may be the same as the Ghorbati. Luli and Luti are common Persian names for any Gypsy-like people, so that there is no necessary connection between these people and modern Gypsies. The name may have come from the town in Sind, from which they may have originated.[75] They live in southwest Iran and in Baluchistan and Pakistan, where they call themselves Dom, and some travel with Brahui nomads. Others in southern Sind are called Lori.

They are itinerant musicians. They have a tale to explain how they came to Persia to be nomads, and also their disdain for farmers and the settled life. Once upon a time in the fifth century, Bahram Gur the king of Persia requested musicians, Luri, from India and 10,000 were sent. The king was so pleased with their music that he gave them all land, cattle and grain to settle as farmers and serve as his minstrels. But they were ill-prepared for a farmer's life, and the Luti promptly consumed both cattle and grain. This so angered the king that he turned them off their lands and condemned them to their nomadic existence with nothing but a donkey and their musical instruments.[76]

The Luti only marry among themselves. Muslims consider them ritually "unclean." The Lur pastoralists traditionally invite them to play and entertain at circumcisions, marriages and funerals, but the Islamic revolution banned the music between 1979 and 1989, and they suffered great hardship. However, since then the situation may be improving for them.[77] The Luti speak Lur and what some consider a "secret" language among themselves, which is possibly the Kurbat dialect of Domari.

SHADIBAZ

They are hawkers of cloth, perfume and haberdashery, who travel and live in tents. They also train monkeys and bears. Their women peddle bracelets and bangles. Their range of migration is in the east of Afghanistan around Kabul, Gardez and down to Jalalabad.[78]

JALALI

They beg and sell fruit, make cheap jewelry and have bears and monkeys. They travel in the north of Afghanistan, around Aqchah, Mazar-e Sharif, Kunduz eastwards to Feyzabad, and live in tents or houses according to need.

JOGI

They are fortunetellers and beggars; they usually travel by truck or bus.[79] The Jogi have a legend that says they are nomads because of misfortune, which is paradoxical for fortunetellers. Their ancestor attempted to seize another's piece of land, but the archangel Gabriel revealed this to the prophet Mohammed and the Jogi were cursed to wander forever.[80]

VANGAWALA

They are itinerant sellers of cloth, perfume, images, animals and hosiery. But they also specialize in conjuring. The women tend to peddle bangles. They live in tents during the summer, returning to houses in winter. They travel in three areas — around Konduz and Feyzabad; Gazni, Kabul and Jalalbad; and in a smaller area of Qalat and Durani in the south.[81]

PIKRAJ

They are traveling horse dealers and conjurers. Their women peddle cloth and bangles. They live in houses and tents in the north of Afghanistan around Mazar-e sharif, Konduz and Feyzabad, and also around Herat.[82]

"BALUCH"

They live from prostitution, in Afghanistan, right across the north of the country from Herat to Feyzabad.

SHEIKH MOHAMMADI

They are groups of peddlers in eastern Afghanistan. The names of the main groups are *Tela Khel*, *Nadaf Khel*, *Patragar*, *Babar Khel* and *Faqir*. The *Maskurahi* and *Chaharbaghi* are named after villages in Laghman province, 60 kilometers (37 mi.) from Jalalabad. The *Kolukhi* are so called because their huts look like mounds of earth. They continue to itinerate living in tents all the year, though some now spend the winters in houses. Their traditions claim descent from Sheik Mohammed as their spiritual father, who lived in the region, but the groups are not related by descent and they probably have been formed from different ethnic origins. Their unity appears to consist in speaking the Adurgari language, which resembles Kohistani in Pakistan. This is deliberately learned as a private second language to Farsi. One group is described as an example:

The *Maskurahi* number about 150 families and are also called Balatumani, or "More-than-Twenty," and Siyahpayak, or "Black Footed." They are peddlers of bangles, hairpins, thread, and so on, but the more wealthy sell cloth. They spend the winters in their own houses in Laghman, but as the spring wheat is harvested in June they peddle their goods in the villages around their own area. The harvest is the time not only when people have something to exchange, but also for celebrations and weddings, when the people dress up and consider buying a few simple luxuries that the peddler brings. Leaving Laghman in July they migrate about 200 kilometers (125 mi.), first westwards through Kabul and then north into the Koh-i Daman region, just south of Charikar, one of the main grape-growing areas of Afghanistan.

The journey takes over two weeks. Because the journey is to a lower altitude the harvests of wheat, maize and fruit are in July to October, and the grapes ripen in August. The peddlers can thus trade to receive some of the produce in return. A number of related families will camp together for about four months. They prefer to camp together even when there is not enough trade for them all. One reason is security against attacks from the villagers. They take the return journey to Laghman at the end of November. On the way they sell both the grapes and wheat given in payment in Kabul and other markets. Back in their village for the winter and spring they continue to trade in the local area, including making trips northeastwards to Kohistan. The rice and maize harvests in Laghman are in November, and the peddlers return in time to seek customers at this season. The spring is their slack time.

The Maskurahi are an example of nomads exploiting the times of relative plenty in two separate areas due to the different climatic conditions caused by a difference of altitude of 1,000 meters. Trade in each area is directly linked to the times of the various harvests. Each family is economically independent, with the boys learning to trade when they are old enough to defend themselves and carry the agricultural produce given in exchange. Groups migrate together for security. Most men become a separate business after they marry. Usually the women do household work, although widows may be forced to take up peddling. The economic returns may vary from the different harvest periods, but the families do more than just subsist. This means that no poor family is forced out of the group to take up other work. Some of the more successful families, however, are able to invest in a shop in the bazaars in Jalalabad, and they can give credit to their relatives to start the year's trading cycle again. Most do not have surplus to buy new stock.[83]

Religion

They are Muslims. They believe the world began with the sons of Sheik Rohari, a holy man, but they fell in vices such as gambling and are condemned to nomadism because of this. There is no known Christian contact among them.

BADAKHSHI TRADERS

They originated in Badakhstan, part of Tajikistan, but travel in Afghanistan from both urban and rural bases. A few have settled in the Wakhan. They are Tajik or Uzbek and speak Dari, Wakhi as well as their own language. They are important marketers of wool, felt and mutton to cities like Jalababad and Kabul. Tea and opium are also important commodities.[84]

KOUCHI TRADERS

These are possibly Pathans, not Gypsies (see entry above). They dress differently, and many only keep sufficient cattle and donkeys for domestic use. They enter the towns to beg. There are three million in Afghanistan who speak Pashto.[85] However, the terms *kouchi* and *maldar* more usually refer to pastoralists, and *jat* to the peripatetics.[86]

JATS

These are 1,000 Gypsies in Afghanistan. *Zott* is the Arabic form of Jat, which seems to have been the term the Arabs gave to anyone from the Indus River Valley. Their language is Jakati, which is not related to Rom, according to the *Ethnologue*. They work as iron-smiths, peddlers, fortunetellers and musicians. They do not call themselves Rom. They are also called *Charwala*.[87]

CENTRAL ASIA

Central Asia includes southern Russia and the Turkic republics into northwest China. This is the western half of a vast area reaching across Mongolia. It consists of steppe almost at sea level, in contrast to the eastern half, which is plateau at an altitude of around 1,500 meters. The dominating influences here in the west have been Muslim and Russian, while to the east the influences are Buddhist and Chinese, which we deal with in the next section. The peoples of these regions were united, however, in domesticating the horse as a pack-animal around 4000 BC and later for riding. This has revolutionized the world. By the tenth century BC, being able to ride on horseback transformed the sedentary range farming in the valleys into nomadic pastoralism ranging right across Central Asia — a cultural feature that unites the various peoples.

The Turkic peoples in western Central Asia have occupied the center of Asia for centuries and have felt the cultural and imperial influence of the surrounding civilizations of China, Russia, India and Persia.[1] Today they find themselves in the middle of a struggle for economic and cultural influence between the Islamic powers of Turkey, Iran and Saudi Arabia. The Russian Federation appears to continue to have the dominant economic influence, but some of its own minorities are restless. After the traumas of collectivization and being treated as "backward" and inefficient, the nomads are experiencing a cautious revival

as key figures in forming the new national identities of the independent countries. They are also learning to work on a more commercial basis. A modified semi-nomadism is taking shape, combined with other livestock raising methods such as keeping cattle in stalls. The key problems are the lack of water (many stations rely on water trucks), inadequate veterinary services, the environmental damage from the dust storms and salt spreading from the Aral Sea. Food and medical services are also harder to obtain in rural areas. Problems of quality and transportation need to be solved before they can compete with the heavy international competition for the export of wool.[2]

Through history there have been various religious influences such as Shamanist, Buddhist, Manichaean, Nestorian Christian and the present Islamic domination. Islam is being revived with new mosques in the towns and seeking to increase its political influence in all the republics. Its main success is in Uzbekistan. Orthodox and Catholic Christians, as the majority of Protestants, tend to belong to the non-Turkic peoples. There was a bishop and 33 Roman Catholic priests in Central Asia in 1994.[3] UBS and IBT have about 40 joint translation projects under way for the republics of Central Asia.[4] The Turks have been considered a key people for reaching Central Asia, but others suggest that Christian progress may develop from Central Asia first.

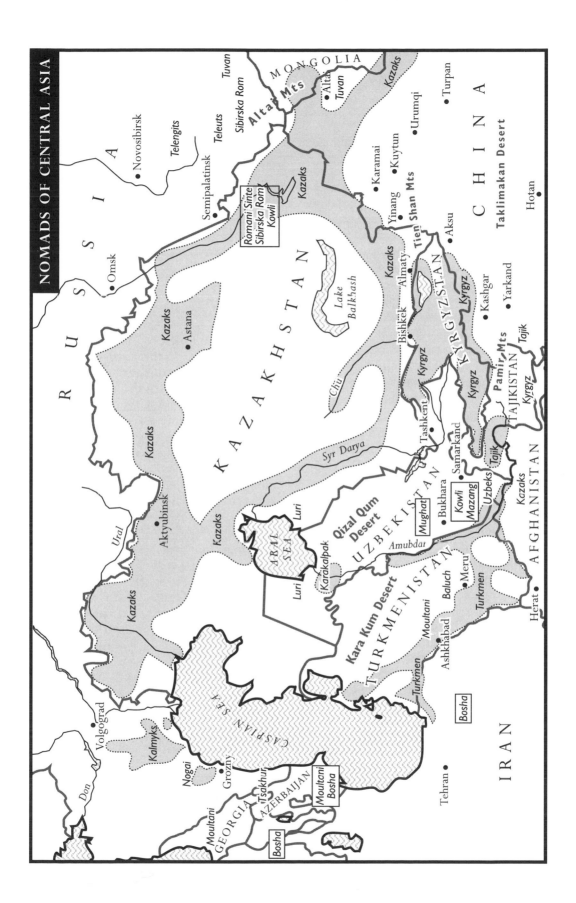

NOMADS OF CENTRAL ASIA

RUSSIA

Tuvan
Sibirska Rom
Teleuts
Tuvan
Teleuts
Telengits
• Novosibirsk
• Omsk
• Semipalatinsk

MONGOLIA

Altai Mts
• Altai
Tuvan
Kazaks

Kazaks

Romani Sinte
Sibirska Rom
Kowli

CHINA

• Turpan
• Urumqi
Taklimakan Desert
• Kuytun
• Karamai
• Yinang
Tien Shan Mts
• Aksu
• Hotan
Kazaks

Kazaks
Lake
Balkhash

KAZAKHSTAN

Kazaks
• Astana

Chu

Bishkek
Almaty
Kazaks
Kyrgyz
KYRGYZSTAN
Kyrgyz
Kyrgyz
• Kashgar
• Yarkand
Pamir Mts
Tajik
TAJIKISTAN
Kyrgyz

Kazaks
• Aktyubinsk

Ural

Syr Darya

Tashkent
Samarkand
Tajik
Mughat
Bukhara
Kowli
Mazang
Uzbeks
Kazaks

Luri

**ARAL
SEA**
Karakalpak.

Qizal Qum
Desert
UZBEKISTAN
Amubdar

AFGHANISTAN

Luri

Kara Kum Desert

TURKMENISTAN

Baluch
• Meru
Turkmen
Turkmen

Moultani
Ashkhabad

• Herat

• Volgograd

Kalmyks.

Nogai
• Grozny
Tsakhur
GEORGIA
AZERBAIJAN
Moultani
Bosha

Don

Bosha

CASPIAN SEA

Bosha

• Tehran

IRAN

Moultani

KALMYKS or *Khalmyks*

There are 174,000 Kalmyks in the Kalmyk Republic, Russia. They are related to 100,000 *Torguts* in Xinjiang, and 166,000 in Qinghai, China. The Kalmyks are the descendants of the Oirats, or Western Mongols, who migrated from Jungaris between the Altai and Tien Shan Mountains and settled in the lower Volga basin. Traditionally they are cattle breeders and they call their yurts *kibitka*. In 1771, the Kalmyks attempted to migrate back to Mongolia to help defend the main body of Oirat Mongols against the Chinese. On the way and on the return they were attacked by the Kazaks and Baskirs and many died. "Kalmyk" means "those who remain."

One group of Kalmyks did not attempt to return to Mongolia but settled in the Don River area. They are divided into **Derbet**, or **Durbet**, **Torgout** and **Khosheut**, based on an old military structure called *ulus*. The Derbet dialect forms the basis for the literary language. During the Second World War, most were deported for alleged collaboration and were not allowed to return to the Kalmyk ASSR until 1960.[5] They are Lamaistic Buddhists.[6] There is reportedly a Kalmyk community in the United States, in New Jersey. Their language is understood by the Buryats.

Since the end of Communism, the Kalmyks are reviving their Tibetan Buddhist religion, rebuilding temples and sending men to train in India as monks. The first Christian outreach was probably by the Moravians, who established a "model" town called Sarepta opposite a camp of the sick and outcasts in 1768, but the work was hampered by the Moravian ignorance of Buddhism and the indifference and constant migrations of the Mongols. At that time there was a religious division between the two branches of Shamanism. Black, or Bookless, Faith of Shamanism had its *ougon* or idols of felt or cloth and the *obos*. The more sophisticated Yellow Faith of the Gelugpa monks, with their books and learning, had a hierarchical organization going back to Tibet. The three converts the Moravians made were compelled to be baptized in the Orthodox Church. The migration of the Kalmuks to Mongolia ended the settlement.

Outreach

The Bible Society and, briefly, the London Missionary Society, worked among the Kalmyks in the early nineteenth century. A new translation of the New Testament is underway, and the Gospels and Acts have been published.[7] In this translation, the Buddhist term for "divinity" used in previous translations is being replaced by the phrase "Lord of the World" to make clear that God is not a deity among others, but unique. A children's Bible was published in 1998. CMA, Canadian Campus Crusade and Swedish Slavic Mission are working among this people. There are a number of believers who face persecution.

NOGAI or Noghaylar

The Nogai numbered 76,000 in 1989, but the population is said to be increasing rapidly. The 30,000 Black Nogai are the former nomadic cattle breeders who live in the Caucasus on the semi-desert Nogai Steppe between the Kuma and Terek rivers in northern Daghestan. The others are the White Nogai farmers. The Nogai separated from the Golden Horde of the Mongol invaders in the fourteenth century. In the sixteenth century their pastures were east of the Volga, but as a result of conflicts with the Russians, Kalmyks, Crimean Tatars and Cossacks they moved to the Cherkes area of the northern Caucasus.

The Black Nogai originated from the intermarriage of various Turkic and Mongol groups mixed with the Turkic Polovtsy, whose language they adopted.[8] Many of them were being absorbed into the

Circassians and the Kumyk, but during the twentieth century they appeared to be successful in maintaining their own identity. They were traditionally nomadic, but they are presently settled. They have their summer pastures in the mountains on the Kalmykia border, and this has caused disputes over land rights. They are still involved in cattle breeding and agriculture on former collective farms. They are Sunni Muslims. They speak Nogai, a west Turkic language. There are Bible portions available and the translation of Luke has been started, but there is no known Christian work among them.

There are a number of agropastoral peoples in the northern Caucasus who still follow their traditional sheep raising economy, based on villages, but agriculture is often limited. These are the *Avars* or *Maarulah*, with 596,000 in Daghestan and Azerbaijan; and the *Darghins*, *Dargins* or *Dargwa* (369,000). The *Laks*, *Laktsy* or *Kazikumukhs* in southern Daghestan, along with other widely separated groups, number 112,000. Traditionally the men shepherd and milk the sheep and the women the cattle. The 347,000 *Lezghis* live in southeast Daghestan and Azerbaijan. All of these peoples are literate in their own languages, though a majority also speak Russian as a second language. They are all Sunni Muslims. There are scattered Christians among them. The *Jesus* film has been translated into some of these languages. All the languages mentioned here have translation projects, with the Gospels published or about to be published.

JYKHI

This is what the *Tsakhur* or *Tsakhuri* call themselves. They live in the Caucasus and totaled 13,500 in 1989 and now probably number 16,000. They have doubled their population in Daghestan since 1956, to 7,000. Akiner shows their population in Azerbaijan revived since 1959 when there were 2,876, compared to 8,546 in 1979.[9]

The Tsakhur are an indigenous mountain people of sheep breeders, living in 12 different villages in the mountains by the River Samur, in southern Daghestan, in the Caucasus. They have maintained their Tsakhur language and culture. Those in Azerbaijan have been assimilated. They are Sunni Muslims.

The local Academy of Sciences has taken on the project of translating the Bible into the languages of Daghestan, but it is not clear whether this involves the Tsakhur language, which is unwritten. Possibly the translation of the Bible could also help to develop a Tsakhur literature. The people are said to have a good knowledge of Russian and use it for literary purposes. There are Christian broadcasts five days a week in Azerbaijani.

TURKMEN

The Turkmen are a major Turkic people of Central Asia found in Turkmenistan (2,918,000); Afghanistan (380,000); Iran (950,000); Russia (41,000); and Syria (98,000).[10]

The Turkmen may have migrated from the Altai region and settled in present-day Turkmenistan. They conquered the Arabs but converted to Islam. These Turks were called Oghuz. Other Turkic clans moved further to occupy Azerbaijan and Asia Minor. Those centered on Merv became a distinct ethnic identity, the Turkmen, considering themselves the "True Turks." They established their own empire based in Merv and invaded Iran and Afghanistan. They also adopted Islam. They, in their turn, were submerged by the invasions of the Mongols, but they re-emerged as a distinct people by the fifteenth century.

The Turkmen consist of five or more main tribes, and many sub-tribes. Of the tribes, the *Yomuts*, are found mostly in the north and northwest, and the *Ersari* in the northeast and east, in the Lebap district. The tribes on the northern side of the Kara-Kum Desert came under the influence of the Uzbeks. In the south, the politically dominant *Tekke* and other tribes have been influenced by Iran. These two groups of tribes were semi-independent of each other before the Soviet Union was formed, and there is still intertribal prejudice and hostility, but many today are valuing Turkmen unity.

Nomadism was their way of life before the Soviets came, and it provided an effective way of raiding farmers and traders, as well as avoiding submission to invaders, taxation and retaliation. The Kara-Kum Desert, which covers the heart of Turkmenistan, formed a refuge for them from outsiders. Russia increasingly dominated them from the mid-nineteenth century. The Soviets enforced collective farms on the nomadic Turkmen in 1929, and mosques and Islamic schools were closed. The Turkmen were forced to settle to work on cotton fields that became the exclusive crop in the planned economy. Many Turkmen became what they considered "modern" Turkmen, speaking mostly Russian and rejecting "religion." Since then, the desert has been found to contain vast reserves of natural gas.

Today, most of the Turkmen are agropastoralists, except for the *Balkan Ata*, *Maggyshlak Chovdor* and *Abdal* tribes, who are pure pastoralists. The majority are farmers living in oases around the desert, but it has been traditional for some of the cultivators to move out into the desert with the pastoralists in spring, to milk and prepare cheese and then return to their villages for the harvests. But the flocks were permanently led by *chopans*, or shepherds, who are often young men working to raise enough for a bride-price. They spend the winter in small family groups.

Turkmenistan has about the same ratios of livestock and human populations as Kyrgyzstan, where 80% of the population is involved with livestock. In the northwest, the flocks are in the winter pastures (*gyshtag*) in valleys from March to May, when they are driven to the spring grounds (*yaylag*) until the sun dries the grass. In the summer, the pastoral social unit is made up of a number of related families numbering between 50 and 200 persons. The summer pastures around the wells are occupied from June until November.[11] In the Kara Kum the pastoralists are semi-settled, as the desert gives some vegetation at all seasons, just a short distance from their villages. The Turkmen in the southeastern Akhal, with its fertile grassland and good water supplies, are the most settled.[12]

Now, with independence as Turkmenistan, the Turkmen are reviving their language and traditions. They are adopting a variety of approaches to this new situation. Some, being "modern" Turkmen, learn more of their own language, and other "traditional" Turkmen learn Russian and even English. Their attitude to Islam is also varied. For some, to be "Muslim" is popular, and new *madrassas* and mosques are being built. However, many consider religion to be more for old people, and they resent the influence of Muslim countries like Iran on Turkmenistan.

Religion

The Turkmen are proud that their religion is different from Islam elsewhere. Through intermarriage with Shiite women, it has become a unique synthesis of Sunni Islam with strong Sufism, Shamanism, ancestor worship and the continued influence of their former animism.[13] The Qur'an is hardly known. But even the more secular Turkmen will sacrifice lambs as a way to get God's attention on special occasions in the family and honor the ancestors and provide for them.[14]

Outreach

The first translation of the New Testament was presented to representative authorities in Ashkhbad, the capital of Turkmenistan, in 1995. A number of leading academics praised the work, saying that it is important to have the *Injul* in Turkmen. These included a mullah who admitted he had never read it.[15] Bur it is in the Cyrillic script and cannot be read by the Iranian Turkmen. The Old Testament translation is in progress with a number of books already published.[16] The *Jesus* film is available in Turkmen. The Unification Church and Bahai sects are also active in Askgabat.

The *Akto Turkmen* are 2,400 semi-nomadic shepherds based in two villages south of Kashgar, Xinjiang, China, at the western end of the Taklinmakan Desert. They are sometimes confused with the Kyrgyz but are distinct. They have a unique dialect with similarities to Uygur. They are Sunni Muslims who observe both Kyrgyz and Uygur Islamic festivals and customs. No Christian work has been done among them.[17]

Nomadism

The *charwa* raise sheep and goats for sale in town markets. Their migration pattern is limited and is not determined by the change of season according to altitude. William Irons brings out this contrast. When the pasture dries up during the summer and autumn they stay in camps near the permanent water sources. With the rains they disperse their camps, moving short distances to use the growing grass. During the summer near the water sources shepherding is less labor intensive, and the flocks are left in the hands of the younger men, while other members of the family engage in limited cultivation. Some *charwa* are beginning to own plots of land in *chomar* areas. Prosperity levels vary continually and are often related to the number of workers in a family, the fertility of the flock and the sale of animals, wool and carpets.

Society

The *charwa* society is strongly patrilinear.[18] The migratory groups, *obas*, are usually formed of related families, but others can join with the agreement of the members. Co-operation between relatives in different camps and *obas* is common. The independent families of sons remain as members of the father's *oba*.

Marriage is often between first cousins. Sons are married in order of age, with a bride-price of ten camels or the equivalent in sheep and goats given to the bride's father. This not only gives value to the women, but also is an expense representing years of work. There is a three-year "engagement" period when the bride and groom stay with their respective families before the wedding. When a nuclear family

has children old enough to help with the work, it splits from the father's household. The sons do this in order of age, but usually they are at least thirty years old. The daughter leaves around eighteen years of age. The youngest son inherits what is left of the father's estate and household. The fathers gain considerable help from their sons, therefore, for a period of 12 to 15 years.

Men without sons can adopt younger men, or hire a Yomut shepherd. Men of very poor households can be amalgamated with a more prosperous relative's family, or be hired as shepherds to others, but they only hire or work for other Yomuts.

a)Iran

The Charwa Turkmen, in northern Iran, come from different tribes — half of them are *Yomut* and the others are *Goklan* or Gokleng. They are semi-nomadic.[19] The Yomut are divided geographically 500 kilometers (310 mi.) apart — into those west of Khiva in northwest Turkmenistan and those on the Gurgan Plain in northern Iran, just southeast of the Caspian Sea. This region has been difficult for Iran to control, and the Persians built refuge towers against the Turkmen raids. The raids, called *alaman*, were the means to demonstrate Turkmen manliness. Both the Shahs and the Islamic Revolution of 1979 have clashed with the Turkmen. As other Turkmen, they are divided between *chomar* agriculturists and *charwa* pastoralists. The *Yomut* live in the west on the Gurgan Plain and the Goklan or Gokleng are situated east of Mashhad, near the Afghan border.

b)Afghanistan

Turkmen in Afghanistan are situated along the border that divides them from Turkmenistan. This border was set between the British and Russians in 1895. Before 1979 and the Soviet invasion, there were estimated to be less than 400,000 Turkmen, but many have moved back to Turkmenistan since they gained independence. They raise sheep and goats, horses and camels and cultivate wheat and barley. Some are semi-nomadic and have succeeded in being exempt from taxes, conscription and the national life of the country. Their social life has seen few changes, and they still have male-dominated extended families.[20]

BALUCH and BRAHUI

In Turkmenistan, this pastoral community of 19,000 moved into Central Asia in the 1920s and continued to be nomadic with flocks of sheep and goats, living in goat-hair tents near Merv. Some were still semi-nomadic in the 1980s. They tend to identify themselves as Turkmen, and the children attend local schools and speak and write Turkmen. The Brahui consider themselves the Brahui clan of the Baluch, although they still speak Brahui. A smaller group have been assimilated in Tajikistan.[21]

KARAKALPAK

The name means "black hat," and 409,000 of them live on the southern shores of the Aral Sea, Uzbekistan, and on the border in Tazhauz, Turkmenistan. Others are found in Iran and Turkey. They are divided into clans, or *koshe*, of several extended families claiming descent from a common ancestor, but they appear not to have a strong national identity.[22] They are surrounded by Kazaks and ethnically and linguistically they may be related, and usually they only intermarry with them.

Traditionally the Karakalpaks are agropastoralists. They have continued to live in yurts for a long time after becoming settled farmers. They decorate the yurts ostentatiously with rugs and wall hangings and are excellent craftsmen. They live in or near oases in the delta of the Amu Darya River and desert. Oxen are more important to them than the horses much loved by other Turkic peoples. They use the oxen to plow, turn water wheels and to thresh. When the rivers around the southern end of the Caspian Sea flooded, the Karakalpaks did what they considered an obligatory migration in ox-carts for a short distance with their cattle. During the winter most of the livestock were sheltered and fed with fodder.[23] Today they are farmers working in

cotton production or are industrial workers. Not many have been assimilated into Uzbek culture.

The 62,000 *Karakalpak*, in Turkey, live in the mountains near the Murat River, west of Mount Ararat, in the eastern part of the country.

The 36,000 *Karakalpak*, *Oarapapakh*, in Iran, live to the west of the River Zarineh running into Lake Urmia, in the northwest of the country between Kurdish and Azerbaijani areas.

They are relatively poorer than other Turkic peoples. They are Sunni Muslims, but they meticulously follow shamanistic rituals as rites of passage. The four Gospels have been published in the language.[24] The *Jesus* film is available. There were some believers among them in the 1990s.

UZBEKS

The Uzbeks were mostly non-nomadic, and by the twentieth century only those in the semi-desert of the Sherabad Darya River in the southeast of Uzbekistan were nomadic pastoralists. The latter believed that sheep came from heaven, and shepherds were held in great respect. In winter they stayed within two or three kilometers (1 or 2 mi.) of their villages, but for the summer they went to the nearest hills.

The Uzbekistan government has imposed restrictions on Christian work in general, as well as limiting political and media freedom.[25] The New Testament, with Genesis and Psalms, was published in 1999.[26] *Jesus Friend of Children* in Uzbek is available from the IBT in Stockholm. New Opportunities anticipate helping this people. On most days of the week there is a Christian broadcast in Uzbek.

KAZAKS, or *Kazakhs*

The Kazaks prefer the former spelling, with the name possibly coming from Arabic and meaning "outlaws." But they have called themselves Kyrgyz for centuries (see below). They are one of the major Turkic peoples who supported themselves by nomadic pastoralism on the Central Asian steppe. They have a population of 8,136,000, living

22a

22b

22c

22d

22 Kazaks:
  a. A Kazak family inside their yurt (Photo: R Spraggett).
  b. A Kazak elder, China (Photo: Block).
  c. A Kazak lady weaving belts to secure felt on her yurt (Photo: Block).
  d. A Kazak lady welcomes us to her yurt (Photo: R Spraggett).

22e

22f

22g

22 e. This mother has owl down on her son's cap to distract demons (Photo: Block).
    f. A mother presents a sheep-skin full of dairy produce (Photo: Block).
    g. Making a Kazak rope from wool and horse hair (Photo: Block).

mainly in Kazakstan, Xinjiang and western Mongolia. Many migrated to Kazakstan after independence, and with the high birth rate they should soon better their present 42% of the population of their new country.[27]

History

The Kazaks originated from a mixture of diverse, unrelated Mongol and Turkic tribes. They became a distinct people in the fifteenth century, when two sons of a khan, Janbek and Kirai, led them to independence from their Uzbek overlords and later Qasim Khan (1511-23) united them. They soon attained control, first of southeast Kazakstan, then of the whole of the south and finally of most of present-day Kazakstan.

The history of the Kazaks has been shaped by their powerful neighbors. In 1730, the western Kazaks appealed to Russia for help, because the Kalmyks were forcing them from their lands. This resulted in Russia steadily gaining control over what is now Kazakstan. In 1861 the Russian peasants were released from serfdom and many sought their own land on the open Kazak pastures in Kazakstan, forcing large numbers of Kazaks to move into Xinjiang.

By 1876 the Kokhand, the leader of Kazak resistance, surrendered and Russian control was complete. This resulted in more Russians settling the area and Russian farms gradually limited the pasture for the Kazak herds. A "land reform" gave more pasture to peasants in 1912, forcing a further 300,000 Kazaks to move temporarily into China. In 1916, Russia attempted to conscript Kazaks into the Czarist army. This provoked a rebellion that was severely crushed by the Russians.

From the 1920s, Soviet rural policy disregarded nomadic pastoralism as a valid way of life and many pastoralists were forced to become farmers without training, inclination or tools. They were forced to settle in *kolkhozes*, or farm settlements, and their herds and flocks were concentrated on inadequate pastures. Between 80% and 90% of the livestock was slaughtered by the Kazaks as a protest in 1932. In the resulting

famine, between one and three million Kazaks, or a third of the Kazak population, died. The remaining stockbreeders were expected to fulfill quotas for dairy and meat production as if the reduction in livestock had never occurred. Typhoid epidemics and famine resulted in many deaths. The Kazaks became serfs in a state-feudal system run by outsiders, without the ameliorating effects of paternalism that the old system had. The effects of collectivization have been described as a Kazak holocaust.[28]

Later Russian policies have also been disastrous for the Kazaks. For example, the Virgin Lands policy in the 1960s to turn northern Kazakstan into a grain prairie merely produced a dust bowl of the pastures and left much of it unsuitable for cultivation. Germans and other exiles from other parts of the USSR were resettled in the Republic. These and other Russian projects have made the Kazaks a minority in their own land.

The Soviet period has left a large area affected by radiation from nuclear weapons testing, the equivalent of 20,000 Hiroshimas — the latest being in June 1995. The area was further polluted because it served as the base for the Russian space program. Intensive irrigation and the use of fertilizers for the cotton fields has dried up the Aral Sea, caused the salinization of vast areas of farm land and ruined the health of a large section of the population, including children who have helped in the fields.

Finally, a brutal massacre in December 1986 of Kazaks protesting about the removal of the only Kazak in the government provoked the revival of Kazak nationalism. This led to the end of the Soviet Union in Kazakstan, and independence was declared on December 25, 1991. The democratic forces are not yet well organized and have failed to influence events. This is probably because President Nazarbayev has adopted a presidential neutrality from political parties and has been accused of authoritarian methods.[29]

Society

From this process soon emerged three confederations of tribes, usually called hordes, but more accurately *zhuz*, or hundreds. These imply regional military alliances, rather than common descent. The *Ulu Zhuz* (Great Hundred) migrated along the Chu, Talas and Ili rivers in the southeast and passed the summers in the Ala Tau Mountains. They are renowned as shepherds.

The *Orta Zhuz* (Middle Hundred) lived in central Kazakstan with winter pastures along the Syr Darya River and spent summers in the central steppe near the Sarysu, Tobol and Ishim rivers. This *zhuz* is considered to produce the best writers and poets, but it is also the most influenced by Russian settlement.

The *Kichi Zhuz* (Small Hundred) resides in the western part of the country, with winter camps along the lower Syr Darya and Ural rivers and migrating in the hills around the tributaries of the Ural and Tobol. They were reputed to be great warriors. The hordes used to be led by khans who claimed descent from Genghis Khan or from those who had made the pilgrimage to Mecca. The aristocracy was called "white bone," in contrast to all the commoners, who were called "black bone." Each tribe was led by a sultan, and its member clans by *biis*, or magistrates, elected from among the *aksakal*, or "white beards" of the extended families.

In spite of the tribes not being closely related, they have a common culture shaped by nomadic pastoralism. To be a Kazak one must be able to trace one's ancestry back seven generations, which identifies the Kazak within the tribal, clan and family structure. Despite Russian colonization, the Communist era and their settlement in houses, the Kazaks have retained their local tribal organization. This organization originated from the making of decisions in nomadic pastoral management, such as allocating available ranges of pasture. This means that each Kazak is known both according to his lineage and by a particular location of camps and pasture, even after he has moved out of pastoralism.

Both the tribes and clans are called *uru*. Key tribes in the Orta Zhuz, for example, are the Kerey and Nayman, present in both Kazakstan and Xinjiang. The Kerey is divided into 12 lineages and the Nayman nine, each of these being named after a common ancestor. Within each clan there were *auls*, that is, villages of 30 or 40 related families under the leadership of an *aksakal*, or "white beard."[30] A tribe might have about 100 *auls*. At this level being related is important. As a Kazak proverb puts it, "he who separates from his relatives will be eaten by wolves."

a) Kazakstan

The Kazaks have traditionally considered that to be a Kazak is to be a nomad; livestock is their life, their wealth and well-being, and land was to be used rather than owned. Their oral traditions are about mounted warriors whose horses are as much key characters as the men themselves. Modern Kazaks still enjoy the steppe, symbolized by the fragrance of the wormwood growing there. A sprig of wormwood is put into their children's cradles, so that they might grow up loving the free openness of the steppe. They have derogatory terms like *jatak*, or idle person, to describe one who does not migrate as a nomad.

Nomadism

The Kazaks have deliberately maintained herds of mixed stock of sheep and goats, horses, cattle and camels for security. During the nineteenth century the composition of the herding groups, as distinct from the lineages, grew considerably smaller until they had only about half a dozen yurts or households. This was to save trampling and overgrazing the pastures with the joint herds of the former larger groups. They spent four months of winter in a camp of yurts and huts in an area sheltered by hills or woods from the wind and snow. There they made and repaired their equipment and pastured the flocks. One problem in winter is *jut*, when ice covers the grass so that the animals are unable to feed.[31]

Both the Kazaks and the Kyrgyz consider Wednesdays and Fridays auspicious to start the spring migration, which requires them to take a bath and wear their best clothes and even to cover their baggage with carpets or fine blankets. A feast is held on the eve of the journey. The livestock has to be "cleansed" by being driven between two fires. The girls on horses used to take the lead, followed by their mothers with the younger children, but today trucks have replaced the camels to transport the camp.

Along the route, the *auls* often stopped at holy trees and stones to offer prayers or sacrifices. Mounted messengers, or "long ears," would run between the *auls* to give news, or to plan the migrations so that herds would not encroach on each other, but today radios are used. Distances traveled would be short every few days in spring, determined by the slow growth of the grass and the number of wells along the route. Traditionally the yurts would be erected in a circle with the doorways facing the center, where young animals would be penned. On arrival at the summer camp, or *jailu* or *jailau*, the pastures would be "cleansed" again by a fire being lit, and another feast held to ensure "good luck." Summer camp was moved a number of times as the pasture was used up between June to September.

The *kokteu*, or migration of the old days, was disrupted by collectivization, but since independence many still practice it in a modified form, and with the present-day economic uncertainties, others will do so to survive. The length of the migration may vary between 200 kilometers (125 mi.) for the tribes of the Great Horde to as much as 1,000 kilometers (620 mi.) for the others, moving roughly north and south according to the seasons. On the steppe to the west the Kazaks practice a "horizontal" pastoralism, but in the mountain areas to the southeast of Kazakstan, and in the Altai and Tien Shan mountains of Xinjiang, the migrations are shorter and take advantage of the change in growth according to altitude of the mountains.

In the 1990s about 20% of the population of Kazakstan, or over three million people, were in agriculture. This is equal to the number in industry. They worked on over 7,000 state or collective farms, with an average size of more than 35,000 hectares (135 sq. mi.). About 82% of the land is suitable only for grazing, and a third of the remaining cultivated 18% provides fodder for the pastoral sector. The Kazak pastoralists in southern Kazakstan used to produce 22% of the wool and 7% of the meat for the USSR. Fortunately there was a well-established practice of private agriculture and livestock raising on private plots alongside the state and collective farming, and these used to contribute 30% of the meat and 43% of the milk in Kazakstan during the final years of the USSR.

Today, privatization of the collective farms has taken place more slowly than expected, but most pastoralists appear to prefer to rent land that remains in the hands of the state.[32] Fortunately the old collective farms tended to follow the lineages and tribal structure of their traditional lands, so restoring social and pastoral patterns is easier.

Different forms of sheep pastoralism are practiced, such as stall feeding or pasturing near the farms during the winter with either close or distant pasturing during the summer. Herding on seasonal pastures is also done all year round, with winter camps in arid semi-desert, mainly breeding sheep for wool. Dairy cattle, usually kept in stalls, are often combined with sheep.[33] Camps of the herders are set up now near the electricity lines so that they can have television in the yurts, even if they do not have running water! Isolated shepherds are helped by family members staying with them for periods of time, as well as by having contact with centers for health and herding help.

The way of life of the herders and their families is returning in many ways to the traditional way of the nomadic pastoralist. The yurt is often preferred to the fixed house, even in the settlements. The herding camp, or *awiel*, consists of the family of leader, or *bastiq* (white beard), in the central yurt, the families of his sons to the right, and the yurts of other attached families to the left. The men herd the animals, shear the sheep and make the frame of the yurt and its furniture. Men also make saddles and do any cultivation.

Lifestyle

There is a general revival of Kazak traditions and language, while they are also seeking the advantages of modernization. Ninety-five per cent of Kazaks speak Kazak, and most are loyal to their pastoral and shamanistic roots. There are Kazak fishermen on the Caspian and Aral seas. They are considered a distinct people group, who have abandoned their ancestors because they have given up keeping livestock. The Communists may have sought to exaggerate the distinction between the fishermen and the rest of the Kazaks.

Today Kazaks see themselves as divided between *Traditional Tazas*, *Modern Tazas* and *Russified Kazaks*. Taza is a Kazak word which means "pure."

Traditional Tazas are Kazaks who live in the countryside, speak mostly Kazak, dress in a traditional way and still value the old ways. For them the basic social unit is the family, or *uey*, living in a yurt (or today in a house in a village), which once formed a brigade, or subdivision of a collective farm. Rural Kazaks are now able to migrate to the towns, encouraged by the more general use of the Kazak language, and look for work or get education. Young people in school can get residential permits for a place in a dorm, otherwise they must live with a "relative." Some move to the edge of town so that they can grow produce and keep some livestock. They retain strong links with the countryside.

The Kazaks have large families. Weddings are the key celebration in Kazak society, and they involve the gathering of clans and sacrifices, horse races and the exchange of a bride-price in livestock, and the gift of a yurt to the couple. The marriage is arranged perhaps years beforehand by the parents, between lineages, which creates strong links across society. Both a dowry and bride-price

are given, as well as many other gifts. Polygamy and levirate marriage are practiced.

The women were usually, and still are, the key people in a household. They milk the animals, make the butter, cheese and yogurt, and make the felt from wool for clothing and to cover the yurt. On migration the women dismantle the yurt, load the pack animals and put up the yurt again. The women also prepare the meals, sew and embroider and make clothes. The divorce rate is about 50%, and alcoholism is endemic.

The *Modern Tazas* are Kazaks who have had an education, live in larger towns, and speak both Kazak and Russian. But they observe the Kazak customs and prefer to speak Kazak to stress their Kazak identity. Speaking Russian was once essential for higher education, but now ability in Kazak is a necessary social qualification for student places and employment. Since independence these modern Kazaks prefer modernization and urbanization, but without identifying themselves with the Russians. They are perhaps the key people both for the future stability of Kazakstan and also for evangelism. They have a more Eastern world view. They consider themselves atheist but also follow Folk Islamic practices.

Russified Kazaks speak Russian but are now having to teach their children Kazak. They consider themselves as part of the Russian world.[34] But the divisions between the Kazaks themselves, as well as bad feeling for the Russians, may yet create conflict in the new Republic. The traditional Kazaks refer to the Russified as *Shala*, or half-breed, because they no longer prefer to keep Kazak customs or to speak Kazak, and consider the traditional ways as backward. Even the more secular Russified Kazaks believe in spirits, astrology, ancestor worship, shamans or faith healers and the evil eye.

Religion

The Kazaks made a token conversion to Islam in the eleventh century, but this affected only the "white bone," or social elite, and those in the towns. Being nomads right up to the twentieth century meant the majority of Kazaks had little contact with the institutions of Islam, except for the Sufi holy men who traveled among them. Being a Muslim meant the acceptance of Allah as head of their pantheon of lesser beings, in a struggle between good and evil. Islam was merely added to the "good." These beings include the spirits of the dead and animals residing in nature, and especially in the livestock, that can be persuaded by gifts to counter evil power.

Today Islam is mixed with Shamanism in a religious revival in which shamans attract great crowds through their miracles, due to the fear of spirits and by promotion on television. Much of this is a reaction against Russian influence. Their religion permeates their language and dominates their literature and art. In the traditional Kazak view, the world is considered to be a four-sided hill and the side showing presently is blue, so the sky is that color.

Sacrifices and fat poured on fires encourage the ancestors to help the living, and prayers are offered to various spirits in time of crisis. Animals, too, are to be driven to holy sites to be cured as all ill health is considered to be caused by evil spirits. A shepherd's staff and the strings to tie young animals used to be considered to have magical power. The shoulder blade and the elbow bones of a sheep foretell the future or protect from spirits.

The Kazaks are the least Islamic of the Central Asian Turkic peoples. The Kazakstan government has adopted a conciliatory attitude to the Muslim clergy to avoid their radicalization. It has established its own Islamic Board to replace the Muslim Religious Board of Central Asia established by the Soviets, which was used to control religious groups.

Other groups are working for a greater Islamic influence in Kazakstan. The Pan-Turkic Turkistan Party, for example, is working for a wider Islamic unity, while a number of literary figures are founding an Islamic Party. Both Iran and Turkey are seeking to influence and beam TV programs directly to Kazakstan. The Turkish clergy are training Kazak clergy in a number of towns, but demands for an Islamic state are not well organized. The shaman healers are trained and registered by the government. Bahai, Hare Krishna and New Age teachings are being actively spread.

Outreach

There are many Christian agencies working in Kazakstan, but little work as yet is being done among the rural Kazaks. Most of the Christian interest in Kazakstan has been centered in the south on the *Ulu* horde, until recently. There are 36 churches in Almati, the old capital, and they are now using the Kazak language, which is essential for traditional Kazaks. The traditional Kazaks in the villages are not only more religious but more responsive to Christianity than the Russified Kazaks. However, in one group there has been a response from both traditional and Russified Kazaks, and both the Russian and Kazak languages are used. Christians distributed 81,000 gospels in Kazak in 1994. Over 100 are known believers, and some are returning to their villages.

The *Jesus* film is available in Kazak and the Russian version, and Christian videos with Kazak dubbing, have been on TV a number of times. Kazak oral traditions of storytelling are important, so Gospel Recordings are working on cassettes to meet this need.[35] Eighteen books of the New Testament, together with Genesis and some Psalms, have been published and are popular, and the first Kazak Old Testament translation is in progress. The Children's Bible, produced by IBT and UBS, is very popular.[36] TWR and FEBA broadcast five times a week in Kazak.

b) Former USSR

Kazaks in Russia number 630,000; and there are 800,000 in Uzbekistan; 87,000 in Turkmenistan; 38,000 in Kyrgyzstan; and 11,000 in Tajikistan. Many of these prefer to leave their traditional lands, that have been placed on the wrong side of the border, to live in Kazakstan where they can find their Kazak identity. There are also Kazak communities in Iran, Azerbaijan, Moldova and Turkey. The latter are refugees from China. Each of these communities needs to be reached with the gospel.

c) Mongolia

Kazaks in Mongolia are called **Hasaq**, and total 100,000, or 4% of the population.[37] They live as pastoralists and farmers mainly in the Bayan-Olgiy Aimag. This is in the far west of the country, in the Altai Mountains, and close to those in Xinjiang, Kazakstan and Russia. Immediately after the collapse of Communism in the USSR and Mongolia, there was a trend to migrate to Kazakstan, which was seen as their homeland. More practical economic reasons have since curbed this, and many prefer to stay in eastern Mongolia.

d) Xinjiang, China

There are 1,400,000 Kazaks in Xinjiang, China.[38] Most of them live in the mountain grasslands of North and East Xinjiang, in Ili, Borkal and Mulei Kazak Autonomous Prefectures.[39] They moved eastwards in the latter half of the nineteenth century. The Mongols, who had fled to the Volga Valley in 1654 because of a Chinese attack, returned to what is now Xinjiang, and the Kazaks there sided with the Chinese to expel them and so came more closely under Chinese control. A small number are agriculturists. They have resisted assimilation into Chinese life, and they will live only with their relatives, continuing a semi-nomadic lifestyle, on the north slopes of the Tien Shan or in the Altai Mountains.

Nomadism

The migratory cycle in Xinjiang has differed from that in Kazakstan, as they use these mountain ranges for summer pasture in a "vertical" transhumance involving distances of 150 kilometers (95 mi.). During the winter they will live in adobe or log houses on their winter pastures, or *qistaw*, in the valleys. In spring, their pastures mature on the Tien Shan at the end of March and in April on the Altai Mountains, and the nomads move to their spring pasture, or

köktew, on the lower slopes. They move gradually upwards in May to the higher summer pasture, or *jaylaw*, moving again in July. An *aul* might have anywhere from 20 to only one or two yurts, with as many as 5,000 sheep, hundreds of horses and cattle and perhaps 100 camels, although trucks are replacing the latter. Sheep shearing is done in the autumn pastures, or *kuzin*, in September.

The Kazaks on the Tien Shan are more prosperous because they have a direct connection by road to the markets of Urumqi at the foot of the mountains, and also because summer and winter pastures are a short distance from each other due to the rapid rise of the northern slopes. The communes were abolished in 1985, and the Kazak households own mixed herds and have pasture rights and transit rights to re-establish nomadic migrations. Privatization has resulted not only in a higher standard of living for many of the nomads, with links to the urban markets for their products, but also in healthier livestock with dramatically lower mortality rates and larger herds. Schooling and health services appear to have improved, but there is a need for marketing skills so as not to be disadvantaged by Uighur merchants.[40]

The Kazaks, whose summer pastures are in the Altai Shan, enjoy some of the best grassland in Xinjiang. It was here that, centuries ago, Genghis Khan had the military headquarters of his empire. The mountains are only 4,300 meters high, so they are covered in grass and patches of forest. The harsh winters in these mountains, however, with deep snowfalls, means they have to travel more than 250 kilometers (150 mi.) to their winter pastures in the Junggar Desert. The spring and autumn migrations each take three months. Most families spend the winter in, or near, the towns such as Altay or Kuerte, where some have simple houses kept by their elderly members.

The Chinese have organized the families into numbered herd production teams. After the failure of its scheme to establish irrigation farming near the town of Altai, the Chinese government seems to recognize that nomadic pastoralism is the only way to use the land. It has set up education and health care, and it sees the need to use pastoralism as an economic resource as well as to carefully manage the pastures.

Each family used to have a train of four to six camels to carry the yurt and domestic utensils, and of necessity the yurt is now much more Spartan. Each family may have about two dozen cattle, and for this reason they will stop for two days at each camp for the cattle to graze. The young men travel separately with the sheep and goats, traveling light with a felt tent. Horses are their pride and joy, and those that are not being ridden are driven separately. These Kazaks play their traditional games of polo, in which two teams on horseback try to grab a sheep's carcass and carry it over a line. There is also the game of chasing and kissing the women on horseback while the women wield their whips on the men.

During most of the year the Kazaks are found in their yurts in groups in the mountain valleys to get protection from the winds, each erected at the same spot each year. Hospitality is usual and teenage sons are often sent to invite visitors. The yurt is about ten meters in diameter and five meters high, with an essential stove with a pipe chimney in the center. Blessings are exchanged by holding the palms of the hands towards the other person.

A visit is a cause for celebration, with the slaughter of a sheep, and all but the fleece and skin is served. The guest is expected to carve the boiled sheep's head and enjoy the eyes; the ears go to the youngest son. Guests are expected to show appreciation by enthusiastically clearing the dish. Yogurt, which comes in hard white blocks, is served along with tea, from tea leaves shaved from a compressed brick of tea embossed with a Communist emblem. Afterwards entertainment is provided by exchanging stories, composing poems and singing and clapping songs.[41]

In 1990, two-thirds of the Kazaks in Xinjiang were thought still to be involved in pastoralism. Chinese policy is to see nomads and all ethnic minorities as primitive and as needing the guidance of the Han Chinese to settle and gain the advantages of education and wage labor in the cities. When the communes were dismantled the Kazaks had their livestock returned so they could herd and sell the products. But if they wished to own the livestock they had to buy the animals. Pastures have to be rented from the government and the funds were supposed to go into range improvement, but this has not happened. Most Kazaks are reluctant to change their methods — not because of conservatism, but because pastoralism is so much part of their identity within an alien culture, and the alternatives offered give little improvement.[42]

Religion

In Xinjiang, the mullahs are also shamans.[43] There are many causes for nationalist unrest in Xinjiang, such as the Chinese repression of Muslim riots, the one child per family policy, the environmental threat from nuclear testing above ground until 1983, and the closure of borders with Kyrgyzstan.[44] They use Roman and modified Arabic scripts for Kazak. The Swedish Mission church was crushed under persecution in the early twentieth century. The Little Flock has attempted to reach them by moving Chinese Christians to the area. New Opportunities has a team there as well.

Kazaks also live in Kazak Autonomous regions in Gansu and Qinghai, China. They have a tragic history.

In 1939, during the civil wars in China caused by the various warlords, a group of 10,000 Kazaks fled southeastwards into Qinghai. But they were harassed by Mongols and were forced further south, where they had to fight a local warlord until only 700 of them were left. They avoided further loss by their nomadism. When they attempted to leave the People's Republic in 1953, 12,600 out of 15,000 were killed. Today, about 2,000 live in yurts as semi-nomads raising sheep, horses, cattle and camels. During the winter they live in houses near Golmud, the second largest city of the province. Their language differs from that spoken in Xinjiang, being influenced by Mongolian.[45]

e) Afghanistan

There are 2,000 Kazaks in Chahar Dara District, west of Kunduz, northern Afghanistan, who are reported to be nomadic.[46]

KYRGYZ

The name Kyrgyz may mean "tribes descended from forty maidens." They used to be called the Kara-Kyrgyz, or True Kyrgyz, to differentiate them from the *Otez Oghul*, or so-called Kyrgyz-Kazak, who are the present-day Kazaks. The simplest way of differentiating between them is to consider the Kyrgyz as the mountain-dwellers, who developed a transhumant nomadism in Kyrgyzstan, Xinjiang, the Pamirs and the Fergana Valley, while the Kazaks were those who developed a culture and nomadism on the open steppe.

Today the Kyrgyz number 2,450,000 in Kyrgyzstan. There are 64,000 in Tajikistan, although 20,000 have left for Kyrgyzstan as refugees. There are 175,780 Kyrgyz living in Uzbekistan, and 141,600 in Xinjiang, China. In the 1970s there were 1,900 in the Wakhan, Afghanistan, but most of these were resettled in Turkey, leaving only about 500.

Society

Kyrgyzstan is a small nation, and in any small meeting of Kyrgyz at least two people will find that they are related, because they have preserved their tribal structure. This structure is divided into two confederations: the *Otuz Uul*, or Thirty Sons, and the *Ich Kilik*. The Ich Kilik confederation consists of scattered tribes and clans, some of non-Kyrgyz origin. The Otuz are divided into an Ong Kanat (Right Wing) and a Sol Kanat (Left Wing). The major tribes of the Ong Kanat are the Tagay, with 13 clans including the Bugu and Salto, which have raised many Kyrgyz politicians and intellectuals within their ranks. The Tagay live in the Issyk Kul and eastern Naryn oblasts. Also of the Right Wing are the Adigene tribe with six clans, and the Mungush with two clans, in the

eastern part of the Fergana Valley. But one Adigene clan, the Kungrat, is separated from the rest at the extreme eastern end of Lake Issyk Kul. The Sol Kanat has eight tribes in western and central Kyrgyzstan.

Traditionally a Kyrgyz should be able to trace seven generations of his genealogy to prove to which lineage, or *oruq*, he belongs. The *kechek oruq*, or lineages, serve to identify both individuals and the *oeylar* (sg. *oey*), or households, and their names can be used as surnames. Through the period of Soviet collectivization, the local leaders tended also to be the leaders of the *oruq*. They are led by a *aqsaqal*, or "white beard," noted not only as a successful shepherd but also as an impartial judge and advisor. His position is by consent of the leaders of the camps or extended families in his lineage, who are considered his equals.

History

The Kyrgyz are an example of a sedentary people who became pastoralists and then became partially sedentary again. Originally the Kyrgyz were farmers and miners on the upper Yenisei River in central Siberia, who with the invention of better saddles and river bridges came to extend their pastoralism across the vast grasslands. They moved west and south in the fifteenth and seventeenth centuries, retreating from the attacks by the Kalmuks, to the area of present-day Kyrgyzstan, a land they call Altyn Beshik, or "the Golden Cradle," surrounded as it is by the snow-covered mountains that they call the Wings of the Earth.[47] During this long journey they converted to Islam, and their epic poem *Manas* tells of the religious wars that they fought. They finally settled on the mountains around Lake Issyk Kul and have many legends about the lake.

The Kyrgyz resisted the expansion of Czarist Russia by attacking the Russian towns and farms right across Turkistan, but they were weakened by a severe winter in 1859. Russia took over large areas of what is now Kazakstan and Kyrgyzstan for Russian farmers. The Kyrgyz joined the Turkmen in revolt again in 1916, participating in a

23a

23b

23c

23d

23 Kyrgyz:
   a. A family group of Kyrgyz shepherds in the Tien Shan Mountains.
   b. The last of the *kumiss* is offered to the visitors.
   c. Sheep and cattle are driven to a new pasture.
   d. The rest of the family follow on horseback.

massacre of local Russian settlers. In a dramatic encounter on horseback on a moonlit night, the Kyrgyz leaders urged the pioneer Moravian missionary Hermann Jantzen (1866-1959) to persuade the neighboring German villagers to join them in revolt. But Jantzen, aware of the strength of the more modern Russian forces, persuaded the Kyrgyz leaders to flee, before Russia took revenge, to the mountains to the south where many of them remain today. Later, when he was accused by the Communists of being a "counter-revolutionary," he too found sanctuary among the mountains in the yurts of those same Kyrgyz.[48]

When collectivization was forced on the nomads in 1924, the Kyrgyz slaughtered their flocks and many fled into China rather than submit. They kept their culture alive because it was possible to live in the natural conditions only in the traditional Kyrgyz way. Traveling storytellers (the chief entertainment in the winter) maintained the traditions by moving from camp to camp, so that Communism did not succeed in eradicating nomadism. But the collective farms tended to use the traditional Kyrgyz social structure and keep to the traditional land allocations, and so they became quite decentralized organizations keeping local clans and families intact.

In Kyrgyzstan, Russian and Uzbek settlers took the best land and the best jobs and now make up 34% of the population, and ethnic Kyrgyz make up only 53%. As their former lowland winter pastures were turned into Russian farms they moved to the valleys in the low highlands, and the Kyrgyz were forced to change their pastoralism. They had to increase the size of their flocks, switching to the Merino breed to produce fine wool, and they were forced to rely on imported fodder for the winter. While flocks within the Kyrgyz highlands would follow a transhumant pattern, those in the Clui Valley would be taken by train or truck to Kazakstan for the winter, while in return Kazak and Uzbek flocks would be transported to mountain pastures in Kyrgyzstan for the summer.

Sheep farming is still the most important industry after mining, and it is being given priority by the government. Kyrgyzstan, with its ten million sheep and goats and 2 million other livestock, is capable of producing enough buttermilk, yogurt and cheese to supply the entire former Soviet Union.[49] About 43% of the land of Kyrgyzstan is mountain pasture, and 80% of the population live in rural *kolkhoz*, or village settlements.

Since the dismantling of the Soviet Union, the return to a private economy has been difficult. By 1994, the livestock owned by families increased from 22% under the USSR to over 43%, and the creation of private farms increased by 16%. But independence has also brought a decline in fodder production and lack of fuel to transport the animals to distant pastures, resulting in a 50% decline in livestock numbers and the overgrazing of the lower highland pastures. It has also brought taxation for using the pastures.

Nomadism

Today, the people follow different forms of pastoralism. They mix stall feeding or pasturing near the farms during the winter with either close, or distant, pasturing during the summer, similar to the old nomadic method. So transhumant pastoralism is still practiced, with members of the families living in camps of yurts on the mountain summer pastures. While the men do the herding in the mountains, the women are often working on the farms in the valley doing the dairy work and making textiles, but they will visit the pastures to fetch the mare's milk to make *kumiss*. *Kumiss* is the fermented mare's milk enjoyed and drunk in large quantities. A family needs a minimum flock of about 35 animals for basic subsistence, providing milk for *korut*, or cheese balls, *kumiss* and wool to make felt for their clothes, and rugs and a yurt if they need one. Most flocks are much smaller and the owners hand them over to the few full-time shepherds in their village. Many of the new sheep holdings also have some land for cultivation as well as for keeping cattle. Most families survive because they are not taxed and have their children to work for them growing vegetables or fruit.

November to mid-April is spent in the low highland valleys at the settlement, or *kyshtoh*, or winter camp, where the cows and young animals are kept. The sheep might be taken to where there is less snow, but they are usually brought into a fold at night because of predators. Horses can paw away the snow and so can tolerate snowy areas, and the other species often follow behind them. Lambing can take place in heated shelters at the end of winter, and the lambs are reared in *sakman*, or age groups, until they join the flock when they are four weeks old.

The Kyrgyz migrations to their summer pastures in the Tien Shan mountains at an altitude of 3,500 meters are, or used to be, between 100 and 200 kilometers (60 and 125 mi.). The beginning of the spring migration is a time of celebration, and it is relatively leisurely. The spring pasture, at a middle altitude, is the place for shearing and lambing. The sheep are kept in flocks according to age and breed. The shearing is done in June with mechanized shears that increases production five times over a skilled hand shearer. Goats are sheared earlier in April.

A camp in the *jayloo*, or summer pastures, is called *qorow* (literally a kraal for sheep and goats), or *aul* (the people of the camp), and consists of a family, or *oey*, with the largest flock and usually other smaller, related *oeylar* with smaller or no flocks. The eldest male of the leading family is the leader, or *bii*, and guests are usually entertained in his yurt, although a guest is considered a guest of the whole camp, and everyone co-operates in the hospitality. They will help each other, and if an *oey* is on its own, a neighboring camp will help in times of sickness, death or celebrations. According to the viable pasture, the *aul* may divide up for a season.

The *aul* that arrives first on the *jayloo* hosts the others to a meal and games. Summer is the time to make yogurt, cheese and felt, and to make sure that the animals

are well fed to face the winter. Women also help with the herding at night. After a brief stationary period from June to mid-July, the flocks are moved about the summer mountain pastures during July and August. The descent begins slowly in September, using the spring pastures again on the way, because the grass has grown during the summer. But, with the sudden onset of frost in mid-October, they make a rapid return to the winter camp.

The horse is vital for nomadic pastoralism and is celebrated in Kyrgyz traditions as the protector of its rider and of the sheep. In the stories, the name and personality of the horse is a vital part of the plot. The Kyrgyz boast that their children can ride before they can walk.[50] How a person treats a horse is considered a sign of his or her attitude to the people and to nature.

Traditionally mountain pasture was not allocated to herds, but used according to tribe, on a first come basis. This is inadequate, and the Constitution of 1993 has made all land state-owned and 49-, 25- and five-year leases are being given by local government authorities or *raions*, in return for taxes. It has taken some time to establish a consistent system and to find alternative ways to migrate the sheep, for example, on foot, after the breakup of the collective farms. Methods for shearing and sorting the wool and marketing need to be improved.

Kyrgyzstan, although the second lowest in urbanization of former USSR states with 38% in 1991, now leads the list in Central Asia for rural migration to its towns. Many rural Kyrgyz are migrating to Bishkek and other towns. In the first quarter for 1993 there were over 30,000 registered migrants. The reasons for this movement are over-population in the countryside, the fall in agricultural production, and the dissatisfaction of the young with life in the villages where they have little prospect of full employment or a better life, although they often fare little better in the town.

By 1994, the rural migrants formed 10% of population of Bishkek. Now the city is ringed by squatter settlements equaling the area of the rest of the city. The typical rural migrant to Bishkek is a young couple in their early twenties, with usually one or more brothers or sisters living with them. They maintain strong links with their family in the countryside and find the town to be an alien environment that is unsympathetic to them, and to their close family ties. It is estimated that between 60% and 90% are without employment. Many have attempted unsuccessfully to establish small farms on their house plots. Criminal, or semi-legal, activities and casual day laboring are the only sources of income open to them. Many live in shacks, sheds, dugouts or incomplete houses. The suburbs lack roads, drains and water and power supplies.[51]

a) Xinjiang, China

There are 141,600 *Kyrgyz* living in Kizilsu Kyrgyz Autonomous Prefecture, western Xinjiang, and over the border from Kyrgyzstan.[52] They moved into Xinjiang to avoid conscription and a massacre by the Red Army in which 30% of the Kyrgyz died. The capital is Artux, in an oasis 40 kilometers (25 mi.) north of Kashi on the Pamir plateau, and has a population of 30,000. They are only partly nomadic due to government policies, but they keep camels, yaks, sheep, goats and, especially, horses.

Their pastures, in the Pamirs on the borders of Tajikistan and Kyrgyzstan, are the highest in Xinjiang. Here they live in yurts the whole year at 3,400 meters and move higher in summer to sparse pastures on two mountains around 4,200 meters. They keep the grass at lower altitude cut for winter fodder. But pasture is so scarce that they cannot develop better herds, and one of the results is a lack of work for the younger generation. The Chinese are trying to enforce a land allocation scheme, but this is not working because it is alien to Kyrgyz culture. They make their own rugs and felt from wool and import only flour, as they have no crops of their own. The government has provided schools and health care. They have few mullahs or mosques of their own, and drunkenness is a serious problem.[53]

b) Afghanistan

The Kyrgyz in northeast Afghanistan went there after the Chinese Communist Revolution, with others moving on into Pakistan. In the past the Pamirs were usually uninhabited, and used only as summer pasture occasionally by a few Kyrgyz. However, political events and the closing of the Soviet and Chinese borders have forced the Kyrgyz to live permanently in this restricted area from 1949. Denker credits the leadership of the Khan for their successful adaptation to this very high altitude pastoralism, which was possible only by changing their migration patterns, and increasing pasture and winter fodder by irrigation, and by extending traditional livestock sharing methods. Shanrani estimated there were 1,825 Kyrgyz in 333 families, or *oey* units, living on the Great and Little Pamir ranges in the Wakhan in 1978.

The Kyrgyz are divided into four main tribes, or *zor oruq* (major roots), named after four ancestors: the **Teyet**, **Kesak**, **Qephaq** and **Naiman**. The Teyet and Kesak have 17 and 14 lineages respectively. These lineages, or *kechek oruq*, form semi-autonomous political and social units, which have their own pastures and administer their own pastoral affairs, and are usually identified by their location. Living at 4,500 meters, they are totally dependent on their herds. This is one of the most rigorous environments, both in terms of altitude and temperature. They have developed a relationship with the Wakhi, who provide agricultural produce in return for animal produce.

They have mixed herds of between 100 and 500 sheep and goats and 20 yaks to each "household," or *oey*, of six adults and children. A yak is ridden to herd the sheep. A few families have no animals and live and work, almost as members of the extended family, for the wealthier families. They value horses as transport but these have to be bought from the Wakhi in the valley as neither horses nor cattle, including the *dzo*, breed easily at high altitude. This means there is no *kumiss* in the high Pamirs. The

Kyrgyz tend not to drink fresh milk, but they turn it instead into *mai* (clarified butter) and *qroot* (dried yogurt) for use in the winter.

After the Soviet invasion of Afghanistan had driven them into refugee camps in Gilgit, Pakistan, they suffered from the low altitude, the loss of their herds, malaria and the heat. They first explored the possibility of moving to Alaska, but collective visas for the whole tribe were refused. But Turkey agreed, and about 1,130 of these Kyrgyz were resettled in Karakondoz, in Van Province, in 1982.[54] They were provided with concrete houses with cattle stalls, and schooling. Their resettlement was difficult because the sheep did not produce large amounts of wool. This move gave them their first contact with the West, but they still also retain contact with Kyrgyzstan and Xinjiang.[55]

c) Heilongjiang, China

There are also Kyrgyz in Emin and Fuyu, Heilongjiang, China, but they have been assimilated with the Mongols and have adopted Lamaist Buddhism. They live in yurts all year round, but some have small one-room adobe huts for the winter. The Kyrgyz usually marry in their teens, and the ideal is to have three sons to be comfortable. A family will be on their own for nine months, but they have a chance to camp with others in the summer. Thirty per cent of the children die in their first year, due to the long winters and poor diet.[56]

The Kyrgyz dress their children alike until the boys are circumcised at age six or seven. The reason for this is to confuse the evil spirits. A baby is kept hidden for a time after birth, and moonlight must not be allowed to fall on young children so as not to bewitch them. On special occasions, the unmarried daughters wear red headdresses, and the wives white ones.

Kipchak, the Kyrgyz language, is close to Kazak, but until the twentieth century it was not a literary language. About 30% of Kyrgyz speak Russian as a second language.

Religion

The Kyrgyz are Sunni Muslims and Islam was spread, not by conquest as in neighboring Uzbekistan, but by Sufi wandering teachers, so that it became syncretized with earlier Kyrgyz beliefs. Many people go to the city of Osh on pilgrimage to the many Muslim sites, including the supposed tomb of the biblical Job. They maintain their shamanist beliefs and lax practice of Islam. Nine, for example, is considered to be a magic number. For the Kyrgyz, loyalty to one's tribe and Kyrgyz identity is far more important than unity with other Muslims. Kyrgyzstan is allowing religious freedom against Muslim opposition, "to satisfy the religious needs of citizens to profess and spread their faith."

The Kyrgyz believe human beings are an integral part of nature, in a landscape that is inhabited by the *arbak*, or ancestors, and other spirits. Nature is always seeking to return to a harmony in which humans ultimately fade away into it. The Kyrgyz world view is orientated to the past and, because history is considered cyclical, the past can always give guidance on how to act in the present. They consider it essential to consult the ancestors and appease them in order to benefit from their wisdom.

The Kyrgyz are steeped in Spiritism and Shamanism, which are served by many programs on TV and advertisements in the press.[57] Fear of spirits is so pronounced that it reduces industrial production by absenteeism. A shaman, or *bugsa*, can be called in to heal or be consulted about the future. A female demon with crooked feet called Albarste is considered responsible for a difficult childbirth, but holding a copy of the Qur'an over the mother, firing guns and barking dogs are thought to scare her away. The construction of a yurt is accompanied with special rituals and sacrifices. Butter is smeared on the poles of the yurts and bundles of grass, salt, onions and other things are hung on the latticework to ensure prosperity.[58]

24a

24b

24c

24d

24 Kyrgyz (continued):
    a. + b. Another shepherd uses a cottage, counting the sheep out in the morning and back into the fold at
            nightfall.
    c.   A yurt being assembled.
    d.   A Kyrgyz shepherd (Photo: R. Spraggett).

Outreach

The New Testament translation is archaic, but younger Kyrgyz can read the Scriptures in the similar Kazak language. The revision of the Kyrgyz New Testament is in progress, and parts of Old Testament are also being published.[59] The Lion Children's Bible has been translated and distributed.[60]

There is a growing community of 1,000 believers, who suffer persecution — especially away from the capital but have contacts with families in the countryside. Christianity is seen as a Russian religion and not compatible with being Kyrgyz. In 1995, the Orthodox and the Muslim clergy joined in calling for restrictions on ministry other than their own. There is a Christian broadcast six days a week in Kyrgyz. Half the students in the "Ray of Hope" Mission Bible school in Bishkek are Kyrgyz. A number of agencies are interested in reaching out to the Kyrgyz in the Russian-speaking cities, but outreach to the rural Kyrgyz is only beginning. The Back to Jerusalem Band and Gospel Recordings have an interest in Afghanistan and Turkey.[61]

TAJIK

There are 3,360,000 Tajik living in Tajikistan (3,360,000); 4,000,000 in Afghanistan (4,000,000); 34,000 in Kyrgyzstan; and 28,000 in Kazakstan. There are 1,007,000 in Uzbekistan, but with more who are counted among the Uzbeks.[62] Uzbeks and Tajiks lived together in Turkistan until the USSR created Tajikistan, leaving out two major cities of Tajik culture, Samarkand and Bukhara. For centuries the Tajiks controlled part of the Silk Road from these places. Since independence, a civil war between Islamic and other elements has exasperated deep tribal divisions. The people are a mixture of Persian, Mongol and Greek ancestry.

The countryside of Tajikistan consists of 93% of the Pamir, Tien Shan and Kun Lun mountains, with glaciers watering deep fertile valleys of wheat fields and orchards. The world's largest yaks and sheep are bred here, as well as the largest bears and, of course, the yeti! Nomadic Pastoralism was developed between 1500 and 500 BC by

Sarts, or Tats, moving north from Persia. Both the Persians and Greeks under Alexander conquered the area, driving out the Scythians.

A transhumant pastoralism is practiced by the settlements in the higher altitudes, because the livestock cannot thrive in the summer pasture all year round. Therefore the shepherds use spring and autumn pastures at the foot of the mountains and spend the winters in the valleys, where they stay in enclosures for six or eight months. Families live in yurts or *chaparis*, less-substantial tents, on the pastures.[63]

In Afghanistan they are semi-sedentary, but spend several weeks of the summer away from their villages during which the men take the flocks to high pasture and the women tend their high-altitude wheat fields. They make bread out of anything that can be ground into flour. They tend to refer to themselves according to the area in which they live, rather than use the name "Tajik."[64]

The UBS reported that 1,000 copies of the Tajik Bible were distributed in 1993.[65] There is also a new translation of Matthew's Gospel. The Children's Bible has been produced by the IBT Stockholm. HCJB and TWR broadcast in Tajik two to six days a week.

There are also 26,500 Tajik shepherds in Xinjiang, China. They have been forcibly moved to poorer pastures recently. As they are both non-Turkic and non-Chinese they have to speak Mandarin, Uighur or Kyrgyz. There are daily broadcasts in Uighur and Kyrgyz from FEBC.

TELENGITS

The Telengits are one of a group of nomadic Turkic tribes grouped together like the Altais. There are 3,500 concentrated along the Chulyshman, Chuja and Argut rivers in Gorno Altai Autonomous Province of Russia. They used to be called Uryankhai Kalmyks, which erroneously implied that they are Mongols. They are now settled in former collective farms for animal husbandry, living in wooden houses but using yurts in the summer. They speak an unwritten dialect of Altai that is related to Kyrgyz. Shirin Akiner considers them to be Christians.[66] An Altai

New Testament translation is underway, with the Gospels complete.[67]

TELEUTS

The Teleuts are a small group of about 2,000 Turkic people settled along the Great and Little Bachat rivers in the Kemerovo Oblast, Russia, with a few in the Gorno Altai Autonomous Province. They were originally nomadic, but most now work on farms or in mining. They are sometimes called White Kalmyks, which would imply that they are Mongols, which they are not. They speak an unwritten southern dialect of Altai, but they read Russian and Altai.[68] The first Altai New Testament is being translated.[69]

Peripatetics of Central Asia

MUGHAT, Tsygany or Central Asian Gypsies

Mughat, meaning "fire worshipper," is their own name and is derived from Farsi. They do not call themselves Rom. They are called Tsygany in Russian. They live in small, widely scattered groups. They are said to have moved into the region to escape Muslim persecution in India in the tenth century. They were nomadic until the 1930s, spending the winters camped near the towns. They have since settled, forming their own Gypsy quarters, but most still work as peddlers, tinkers, beggars and musicians, and some continue to travel — especially during the brief summers. Others have received education and work in industry or as teachers.

They speak Uzbek or Tajik, although they have their own cant, or way of speaking, called *lavzi mughat*. Many do not speak Romani. There are a number of sub-groups:

The *Mazang* were, or are, woodworkers and live separately from the others. They now live in the towns and have ordinary sedentary employment. They are Sunni Muslims, but the women do not wear the veil. There are said to be 11,000 in Uzbekistan, but estimates are difficult to verify. Some of these declared that they had their own language. This may indicate that another group related to the Romani is included in this total.[70]

Bosha, or *Lom*, is the Armenian version of Rom. There are 100,000 in Armenia, Turkey, Iran and Azerbaijan. Their language is Lomavren.[71]

The *Kowli* in Kazakstan and Uzbekistan are nomadic and speak Russian, Uzbek and Romani Kowli. They are related to the *Qorbati* in Iran. Gardaneh-ye Kowli Kosh is a pass in the Zagros Mountains, north of Shiraz, meaning "Kowli or Gypsy Killer" because of the dangers of making the passage. The latter are probably not Muslims.[72]

Luri or *Luli*: there are 400,000-500,000 in Turkmenistan, to the east and west of the Aral Sea. Some are in Afghanistan. Luli is the Uzbek name, according to Shirin Akiner. They are nomadic and Muslim.[73] They speak Russian, Turkmen and a Romani dialect. It is not certain that they are pastoralists.

There are 100,000 *Moultani* and *Qaraci* or *Karaci*, who are mainly nomadic, in Turkmenistan, Azerbaijan, Georgia. They speak a form of Caucasus Romani sometimes called Domari, as well as Russian.[74]

There are 200,000 *Romani Sinte* living in Kazakstan.

There are 11,600 *Sibirska Rom*, or Siberian Gypsies. From 1557 they were expelled from Germany to Poland to become *Polaska Roma*, or "lowland Gypsies" from Poland. Many were then expelled from Poland to Russia in the seventeenth century. They also include *Servi*, or Ukrainian Gypsies. Later arrivals were two groups of *Lovara*, the *Ungrike Rom* from Hungary and the *Bundaska* from Poland. Still later came the *Kalderash*, via Greece and Moldova. They used to travel with a tent and cart, but now most are settled and work as horse dealers, herders, farm laborers or drivers. In the 1970s some still traveled in the Altai Mountains and Kazakstan with covered horse-drawn wagons.[75]

INNER ASIA

This region covers the Mongolian and Tibetan plateaus and the connected parts of Siberia and so embraces Mongolia, Inner Mongolia, the Tibetan regions and the northwest of China. The Mongol peoples dominate the eastern half of the Central Asia steppe. The Mongolian plateau contrasts with western Central Asia as it is higher, at an average altitude of 1,500 meters (4,900 ft.).

The three areas of Tibet — U-Tsang, Kham and Amado — practice what is considered high-altitude pastoralism at a height where crops cannot be grown.

Agriculture is only possible at a subsistence level in the valleys below 4,000 meters. About 45% of the land area can only be used as high-altitude pasture, so that pastoralism is important economically in these regions.

The main political involvement of both the Mongols and the Tibetans has been with China, and they are united in sharing Lamaistic Buddhism. Nomadic pastoralism is concentrated in north Xinjiang, the southern Chang Tang, the Kham and Amdo regions, central Mongolia and eastern and central Inner Mongolia.

Nomadic Pastoralists of Inner Asia

UIGHURS

The Uighurs of the present day do not have any true links with the historical Uighur people. The term began to be used again about 1922 after the establishment of the Republic of China. The reintegrated Turkic peoples settled in what was Eastern or Chinese Turkistan, now Xinjiang.[1] Although they were herders centuries ago, the present Uighurs have long since adapted to a sedentary oasis lifestyle as farmers. They are the dominant ethnic minority in Xinjiang. There are two nomadic pastoral groups among them.

The *Keriya Uighurs* are named after the seasonal river on which they depend for water. Whether these are Uighurs in the present sense of the term, or whether they are of another origin is not clear, because they have their own customs and culture. They are considered primitive compared to other Uighurs. There were about 822 persons in 169 families in 1990, living as nomads with camels, sheep, goats and

donkeys based on an oasis in the delta of the Keriya River, in the southern Taklinmakan Desert.[2] There is only surface water in the river twice a year, first as spring melts the ice higher up the river to the south, and then later when the summer sun melts the snow in the Kun Lun Mountains. For the rest of the year this community uses salty water from shallow wells. Strong winds and shifting sand dunes can cover vegetation and water supplies.

A recent government attempt to introduce them to cultivation has failed, and their sole subsistence is by raising sheep and goats. Traveling peddlers from the town of Keriya bring them flour and other goods. They gather medicinal herbs for sale as another source of income. The families live scattered about two kilometers apart, in simple log cabins made from the local poplar wood, with an enclosure alongside where the flock is kept in winter. Each family probably uses on average about 4 square kilometers (2.5 sq. mi.) of land for pasture in the summer, and for cutting grass

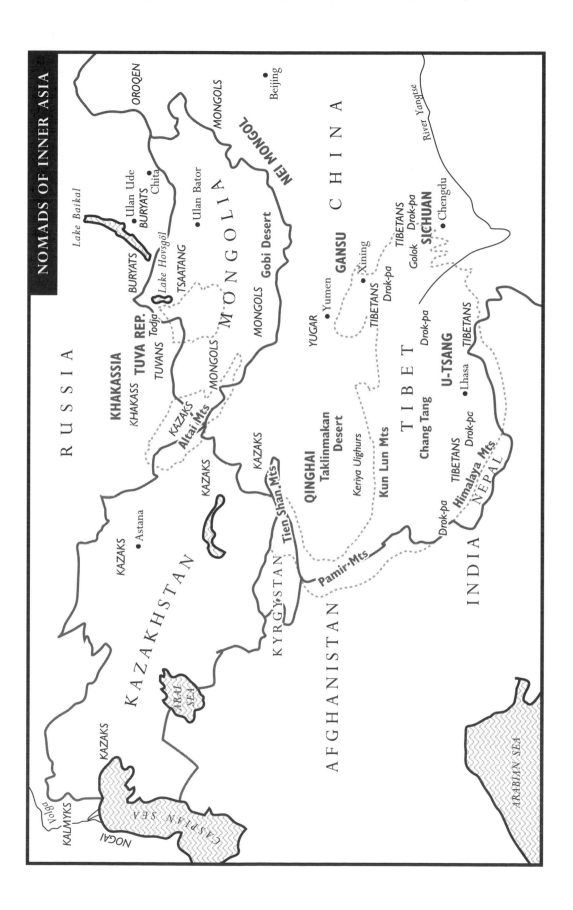

NOMADS OF INNER ASIA

to feed the flock in winter. There is a 15-minute gospel broadcast in Uighur, and the shepherds have radios and tape recorders.

Uighur herders live in narrow, barren valleys in the Kun Lun Mountains that rise towards the Chang Tang Plateau of Tibet. There are no roads linking them to the outside world, and meager resources limit the population of the villages. The villagers keep sheep and yaks, supporting themselves by mutton and dri's milk from the yak herd, and the small harvests of grain that can be grown in the irrigated terrace fields. About 15% of a flock and the wool and yak hair may be sold each year in Khotan.

The entire population follows a transhumant lifestyle, living in the villages in the winter and moving to pastures at over 3,000 meters in the summer. They use neither yurts nor tents, but dig a rectangular room into the mountainside, roofed over with branches and turf, plastic or felt. They bring carpets, rugs and utensils from the village. The women and children collect dung for the fire. Some families have few animals of their own, and must herd for the others, or collect jade in the riverbeds, which brings a greater income than pastoralism.[3]

KHAKASS

The Khakass live in the Khakass Autonomous Oblast, Russia, between the Ob and Yenisey rivers, and form a rural minority in their own territory of about 81,500. They are divided into five tribes, all of different ethnic origin, but they are united in calling themselves Khakass. The *Beltirs* are of Tuvinians origin and are farmers and cattle breeders. The *Kachin* are semi-nomadic herders on the east of the Abakan River. The *Kyzyl* and *Koibals* are herders of reindeer on the Abakan Steppe. The *Kacha* are the dominant group and most of the Khakass speak that language, which is also the literary language.[4] They practice a mixture of Shamanism and Russian Orthodoxy. A Bible translation is under way, with the Gospels nearly ready. There are no known Christians among them, but a number of agencies are committed to this people, including the Russian Pentecostals and Canadian Campus Crusade.

TUVANS, *Tuwa,* or *Tuvinians*

The Tuvan population in the Tuva Republic, Russia, has increased since 1944 to 309,000. There are 24,700 Tuvans in Mongolia who speak Russian as well as Tuvan, and there are about 4,000 in Xinjiang, China.

Environment

The Tuva Republic forms a distinct area, in the center of Asia. It is bordered by the Sayan Mountains to the north, and mountains separate it from western Mongolia to the south. Most of it consists of mountain steppe and the people practice mixed livestock nomadic-pastoralism, but the northeast is an area of taiga supporting reindeer herding.

History

These peoples were dominated by the Oirat, or western Mongols, from the thirteenth century, and they were nominally part of China, because of the latter's control of the Mongols. But starting in 1630 they also had to pay tribute to Russian invaders and fur traders, and Russian influence increased until by 1913 the 64,000 Russian settlers exceeded the local population.[5]

In the early Soviet period Tuva was divided, and part of it was led by nationalists pursuing pro-Buddhist and anti-Russian policies. A coup in 1930 by young Tuvans trained in Moscow, however, eliminated the nationalists and destroyed organized religion. The Communists attempted to impose collectivization, but although three-quarters of the Tuvans were members of collectives for a short time, 93% of their livestock continued to be owned by nomads. In fact, between 1933 and 1937, most Tuvans abandoned the collectives to continue a nomadic way of life. But a Stalinist terror campaign in 1937 and the conscription for the Second World War destroyed this semi-independence. A third of their horses and tens of thousands of cattle were confiscated for the war effort.

Tuva was made an "Autonomous" Province of Russia in 1944. The Tuvans continued to resist collectivization by slaughtering their animals, and they did not give up their tents until 1958. European Russians were settled to "modernize" the region by building the capital, Kyzyl, and the local pastoralists were trained as builders. Their children received the mixed benefits of boarding schools. Large areas of the steppe were plowed up in an attempt to establish agriculture in the region, where it was a complete novelty.

Nomadism

The western Tuvans are the majority (as much as 80%) and are nomadic pastoralists of the steppe and mountains, having flocks of sheep and goats and herds of cattle and camels. They also plant grain in the valleys using primitive irrigation systems, and sowing and harvesting are part of the migration cycle. The larger the herd, the greater the distances they travel. They have customary wintering camps in the mountains and live by using melted snow. In spring they move in stages to their summer pasture and villages in the river valleys. Horses are highly valued.[6]

The *Todja*, or eastern Tuvans, are, or were, either semi-nomadic hunters and horse breeders or reindeer nomadic pastoralists on the taiga, but most now live on former collective farms.[7] The eastern side of the republic is remote, and while they were once forced into collective farms, the lives of the shepherds and reindeer herders are not so different from their nomadic past.[8]

Religion

The Tuvans have been Lamaistic Buddhists since the seventeenth century, but their original shamanism flourished until recently.[9] The deities of both religions are considered to co-exist, and some Buddhist monks have also been shamans, although usually the shamans outnumber the monks. Like other Turkic shamanists, the Tuvans sacrifice animals to propitiate the spirits and gain their help. The shamans hold seances in which they diagnose and remove spirits causing illness by traveling to the spiritual world, with the help of animal spirits, in order to retrieve the souls "stolen" from the patients by the spirits. They could also send a spirit against a person to make him or her ill, and even after death a shaman is thought to cause harm, so that most of the Turkic Siberian peoples venerate dead shamans.[10]

Language

The Tuvan language has affinities with the Turkic group, since the Kyrgyz once dominated a mixture of Sanoyedic, Turkic and Mongolian nomads in the Altai and Sayan Mountains, who called themselves Tuba or Tuva. Most Tuvans speak their own language, and about 60% are bilingual in Russian.

Outreach

The first Tuvan New Testament translation has begun and Mark has been published.[11] A Central Asia Fellowship team went to Tuva in 1993. The laws of the USSR were still being applied against Christians in 1991, even after Communism's demise.[12] There are perhaps 50 Christians among the eastern Tuvans, but one or more were murdered around 1990. There is a need for workers and translators of Christian literature. A Swedish church is praying for them.[13] There is a mixed Tuvan and Russian church in Kyzyl, and the Swedish Slavic Mission has two workers in the villages.[14]

Uraankhays is the name given to two groups of Tuvans in Mongolia: in Tsengel sum, Bajan-Ulgiy, Kobdo and Buyant sum. They speak Tuvinian.[15]

The *Tsaatang* are Tuvan reindeer herders in central north Mongolia (see below).

Kök Monchaks is the Kazak name for groups of Tuvans in Xinjiang, China. They are found in Habahe, Burjin, Altai, Koktogai, Chingil and Buruultogai in the Altai district of Xinjiang. Estimates of their population vary because China does not recognize them as a nationality. The origin of these Tuvans is shrouded in mystery: either they are indigenous to Xinjiang, or they came to

Xinjiang during the conflicts between the Manchu and Dzungar empires over 200 years ago. Some fled there when the Soviets took over Tuva in 1921. They are not nomadic, but live in Russian-style houses, with market gardens attached. Their main income is from breeding and herding sheep, goats, cattle and horses. Their diet is that of a pastoralist with meat and milk, grain and some vegetables. They prize marriage, because it unites them together when they marry outside their own clan, and because the economic unit is the family. The Chinese policy that limits the number of children applies to them.

They speak Kazak and Mongolian well, and they attend schools in these languages. Although the Kazaks and Mongolians consider the Tuvans as "brother" groups, the Kök consider themselves very much as Tuvans and speak a dialect of their own language at home, which is readily understood by Russian Tuvans. Their houses, however, contain mostly Kazak carpets and furnishings. They are very concerned to preserve their language and willingly listen to a half-hour broadcast each evening. However, they have no literature in their own language. Few of them speak Chinese.

SOYOTS

The Soyots are a tiny, almost extinct, people, related to the Tuvans and Tsaatang. They were once reindeer herders living in the Sayan Mountains. The Soviet regime compelled them to be farmers. They number about 200 in the Oka District of the Buryat Republic. They have intentions to revive their identity, culture and reindeer breeding and have had contact with Native American organizations.[16]

TSAATANG

These are Tuvan reindeer herders, estimated to be between 100 and 500 strong, east of Lake Hovsgöl in northern Mongolia. They were self-sufficient nomads in the northern forests, except for bartering reindeer hides for ammunition for hunting. In 1959 they were forced to hand over their herds to a collective and then work as employee herders. Since about 1970, most have been encouraged by the government to settle in a new village, where they make up about half the population. They also do logging and fishing, and export reindeer antlers to make a medical remedy. About 50 continue to be nomadic, living in wigwams made of birch poles, reindeer hide and tarpaulin. They winter in a sheltered valley, but in April they move back into the forests, constantly moving camp every two or three weeks so that the reindeer can find the silver-white moss for fodder.[17] They are shamanists.

BURYATS

The Buryats are a branch of the Mongol people who moved northwards in the thirteenth century. They live in the Buryat Republic, Russia. Their population in 1989 was 423,436, and so they form the largest indigenous nationality in Siberia. The Buryat Republic, or Buryatia, has 250,000 people — only 24% of the population. There are 77,330 living in the Irkutskaya; 66,600 in Chitinkaya; and 8,500 in Yakutiya Oblasts. There are 48,000 in Mongolia and 10,000 in Hulun-Buyr, Inner Mongolia, China.[18] Buryatia can claim to be the birthplace of Mongol nationalism, culture and Shamanism, because Genghis Khan's mother was a Buryat and he is buried there.

The Buryats were colonized early by Russian fur traders who arrived in the area around 1640. In the early twentieth century, there was an attempt to establish a pan-Mongolian republic that would have been neutral between Revolutionary Russia and Imperial China. Characteristically, the West gave no recognition or support to this venture, and the Communists destroyed it in 1919. When Stalin incorporated the Buryats into the Soviet Union, many of them fled to Mongolia and some went as far as Harbin, in China. Stalin demanded their arrest and all the Buryat men over twenty-five years of age, who had fled, were executed in 1929. These events halved the Buryat population. The Soviets rewrote their history in an attempt to make them a separate race from the Mongols, and many of them forgot their own language.

West Buryats: The *Bulagat*, *Ekherit* and *Khonodor* tribes are agriculturists. They were forcibly incorporated into the Irkutsk Republic and became Russian Orthodox, but in spite of this they developed a more elaborate form of Shamanism, featuring 99 deities. Fire was especially revered and "white" shamans rode hobbyhorses to serve the heavenly sphere and "black" shamans "traveled" in the underworld. White horses were sacrificed to the sky-god Tengri, and their skin was put on a pole.

East Buryats: The *Tabunut*, *Atagan* and *Khori* tribes live east of Lake Baikal and continue to be pastoralists with horses, cows, sheep, goats and camels. Once nomads, they were "collectivized" and many were resettled around the headquarters of large collective farms. There is also a community of 500 Buryats with flocks of sheep on Olkhon Island, on Lake Baikal, among 3,000 Russians. Lake Baikal is said to contain 20% of the world's fresh water, more than North America's Great Lakes, because it is 1,600 meters deep. It is often swept by storms or frozen over, and even today the Buryats "bribe" the gods of the lake and of storms for protection.[19] Some Buryats work in industry in Baikalsk, Irkutsk and Ulan Ude; industrial pollution affects these areas.

Religion

While the Buryats originally brought Buddhism with them from Mongolia, they lapsed into Shamanism and late in the eighteenth century the Gelugpa Sect made a successful missionary effort to convert them back to Buddhism. The first Buddhist temples were mobile, in *gers*. The monks had more influence with their learning and "international" organization across Asia, and they conducted healing not only with magic but also with herbal medicine, which was often more effective. Shamanism went into decline because its claims to heal by casting out demons could not be substantiated. It is interesting to note that if Christian missionaries had been there to practice the Western medicine of the time, they would not have been any more effective. Buddhism was recognized as the religion of the Buryats by a Russian decree in 1741, and it excelled in literature, architecture and propagation, but the folk religion remained a syncretism with Shamanism.

A systematic persecution of the Buryats in the 1930s resulted in the closing of schools, the destruction of Buryat culture, shrines, buildings and books, and the death of many practicing Buddhists. While art and music were encouraged as "folklore" under the Soviets, religion was suppressed, and the Buddhist hierarchy was appointed by the Communist Party. Buryatia was divided by districts being given to the Irkutsk and Chita Oblasts. Most Buryats were reported to have accepted a materialistic world view by the 1970s. However, beneath a veneer of accepting Communism, and because Buddhist teaching was limited, many revived shamanistic ritual and beliefs. The rituals at the *ovoos*, or cairns, on mountain peaks revived.[20]

After the fall of Communism in 1990 the Buryat Republic established direct international contacts. The Buryats have returned to Lamaistic Buddhism, with shamanism also making a powerful comeback. The *Datsang* training center and monasteries at Ulan Ude receive pilgrims from throughout Central Asia and do not have room for all those wanting to attend. Mongolians, Tuvans and others study Buddhism there. There are movements to reunite all the Buryats into one Buryat-Mongol republic, with "Sunday schools" to revive the Buryat language and culture.

Language

A high proportion of Buryats have had a university education; 72% speak Russian, and Russian has supplanted the Buryat language in the schools.[21] Although most Buryats can speak Russian, 89% consider Buryat their native language and most use it at home or for cultural activities. This percentage is increasing. Equal numbers use the eastern and western dialects, but the eastern is used for literature. It is a literary language influenced by Russian and Mongolian, and there are many scholars that write and teach in the language. The Buryat Scientific Institute is reviving Mongolian for both Russians and Buryats. The Buryats can understand the Mongols speaking the Khalkha dialect, but the Mongols in the Republic have difficulty understanding the Buryats.

Outreach

The London Missionary Society pioneered Christian work in Irkutsk, and then in Selenginsk and Khoden, between 1818 and 1841. It took advantage of the brief interest of Czar Nicholas I in the Bible, during the attack of Napoleon on Russia. The Russian Bible Society received imperial support so the Buryat made a contribution to it, and this "loyal" gesture to the expanding Russian power was mistakenly interpreted by the missionaries as a desire for the Bible. They were unprepared for the sophisticated Buddhist opposition to their work. But they produced a Bible translation between 1817 and 1830, which they partly printed in Siberia. Twenty Buryats were converted.[22]

A new Buryat Bible translation is in progress by UBS with the Institute of Bible Translation, Stockholm. The Gospels and Acts have been translated and Mark, Luke and John were available from 1999.[23] The Slavic Mission distributed 180,000 children's New Testaments in 1994. The *Jesus* film is available in Buryat, but many prefer Russian.[24]

Friedenstimme has supported the former Ukrainian prisoner of conscience, Andrei Yudintsev, to work among the Buryats.[25] Other pastors among the Russians are also contacting them, and there is a growing number of Buryat Christians. Most of the believers have learned about Christianity in Russian, rather than in the Buryat language. A theological training by extension is beginning, as well as a small residential course; these use the Russian language, which is the medium for most Buryats.

MONGOLS

The Mongols prefer not to be called Mongolians. The population of Mongolia is 2,660,000.

Other Mongol peoples outside Mongolia

People	Population	Location(s)
Mongols	5,200,000	Inner Mongolia, Lianoning, Jilin, Heilongjiang, Qinghai and Gansu, China
Mongols	8,000	Buryat Republic, Russia
Daur	94,000	Heilongjiang, Xinjiang and Inner Mongolia, China
Kalmyks	40,000	Xinjiang, China
Kalmyks or Khalmyks	174,000	Kalmyk Republic, Russia (see Central Asia section)
Tu	59,000	Qinghai and Gansu, China

Other related peoples:

People	Population	Location(s)
Buryats	390,000	Buryat Republic, Russia.
Buryats	5,000	Inner Mongolia.
Ewenki	30,163	Russia (see Arctic section)
Ewenki	2,000	Inner Mongolia
Oroqen	4,500	Eastern forests of Inner Mongolia, China
Yugar	10,000	Gansu
Tuvans	166,000	Tuva Republic, Russia

The 1,277,000 rural Mongols are estimated to make up 48.2% of the population.[26] Beall and Goldstein calculate that 40% of Mongols are nomadic pastoralists, or *arat*.[27] Nearly half of the rural population spends part of the year moving with their herds.[28] Many otherwise settled people have become new nomads. Müller estimated that the provincial towns lost up to 30% of their inhabitants, who moved off to the steppe with their animals because town facilities deteriorated after the fall of Communism.[29] This transition was made easier by the fact that most Mongols still live in *gers* (called

25a

25b

25c

25d

25 Mongols:
   a. A Mongol lady (Photo R. Spraggett).
   b. Mongols are renowned for their horsemanship (Photo R. Spraggett).
   c. Making a herding pole in a Mongol camp (Photo R. Spraggett).
   d. A Mongol gentleman (Photo R. Spraggett).

yurts elsewhere), even in the capital, Ulaan Baatar, where they retain contact with the pastoral life by visits to relatives or by keeping animals. The ideals of nomadism have been successfully combined with the material advances of urban life and modernity, rather than being dismissed as archaic.[30]

Mongolia is known as the "Land of the Five Animals" and, as the most important pastoral country in the world, its major wealth is from sheep, goats, cattle, horses and camels. The horse is particularly important in Mongol culture, and they have many terms for different types of horses. Horses are ridden and milked but never used as draft animals. Livestock outnumber the people by twelve to one.

Environment

The landscape of the Republic and Inner Mongolia, or Nei Mongol, in China, is basically a large plateau at an average attitude of 1,500 meters with severe winters and hot summers. Four-fifths of Mongolia is steppe or natural grassland, are there are large stretches without a tree in sight. There is little moisture and the plains are dusty. There are three types of territory: the Gobi and semi-desert of the south; the grasslands of the central and eastern parts; and the forest and mountain steppe of the north and west. What rain there is, is usually in the summer. Nomadic pastoralism is the most obvious and successful way to make such a vast area productive.

Mongolia is now developing its rich mineral resources, such as the extraction of phosphate from the western shore of Lake Hövsgöl. There are fears that this will not only pollute the lake but will also break the permafrost of the meadows and threaten the wildlife. Nomads winter on the lake's shores. The lake also affects the Buryats' environment, for at present it supplies unpolluted water to the already polluted Lake Baikal.[31] The government of Mongolia is also encouraging international tourism, and one wonders at the effect of this on both pastoralists and wildlife.

The Mongol has a great sense of the worth of the environment and the need for careful human management of natural resources, and the appropriate rituals involved. Anyone who does not do this is socially censured. Traditional sports are based on the life on the steppe. There is horse racing, often bareback, by children over some 40 kilometers (25 mi.), as well as archery and wrestling. The ties to traditional grazing lands have been restored, and so have the religious ceremonies. The revival of Lamaism will almost certainly play an increasingly important role in the integration of communities at all levels.

Privatized pastoralism

Traditionally the nomads have lived as almost self-sufficient from their herds. Collective ranching was introduced in 1950, but was resisted by the herders. The collectives and a minority of state farms held on average 5,000 square kilometers of land and between 50,000 and 70,000 animals.[32] Wages were paid to the workers, who also benefited from new wells, veterinary services and winter fodder production. The system did allow for 27% of the livestock to be in private herds alongside those of the collectives. Provided the collective's quotas were met, the surplus products from the private animals could be sold to the government, or through a parallel private market system.

The local communities in Mongolia were mostly preserved in the collectives, in contrast to what happened in Russia. This gave a measure of stability after the chaos of the revolution and helped to give a higher standard of living and improved health services in new networks of settlements. The Mongol family is the first line of help in time of hardship. When privatization came, the Mongol's extended family ties were able to maintain co-operation and grazing rights on a greater scale.

But the collapse of the central economy, once supported by the USSR, has caused a social change as great as that when the Communists took over in 1921. The collectives are being changed into share-holding companies, or *kampan*. Government policy has been to distribute about 30% of livestock to member families of the former collectives and 70% to the stockholding companies. These companies then lease their animals to individual member families, who are in turn paid for products delivered to the company. By the end of 1994, 91% of livestock was privately owned and half of nearly 300 companies had been established.

But the new companies have not been effective, as they lack marketing structures and sales have been reduced to barter at the local level. Outside companies may buy up large numbers of stock to slaughter, or the herders themselves slaughter them and rely on relatives or other contacts in Ulaan Baatar to arrange the sales. The herders now have to decide the composition of their herds for themselves and market them without government guarantees or planning. Even with the free distribution of livestock, a differentiation between wealthier and poorer families has once again developed. Those unable to adjust to free market pastoralism, along with many young people, have moved to the towns — but many are very poor. The new system cannot yet provide the services as formerly. State relief in severe winters has stopped, and the veterinary service has become less effective. Many households suffer hardship without the ability to weather disasters, and some are destitute.

The "street children" phenomenon of abandoned children living by begging is now a serious problem. The inadequacies of the present system were cruelly demonstrated in the very severe winter of 1999-2000, when half the livestock died in some areas due to wealthy herders increasing their herds at the expense of others, and overgrazing resulting after drought. A quarter of the population is considered at risk, according to the UNFAO.[33]

But, in spite of these difficulties, the uncertainties of the town life with the collapse of the planned economy are greater. So a large number of people have left the towns to return to pastoralism. Some professional people or officials who never owned livestock under Communism have turned to livestock and use hired nomads to support themselves as the state could no longer pay their salaries. These new pastoralists are bringing in new attitudes and practices and are paying much needed income to nomads to herd for them.[34]

The proportion of camels and sheep has recently declined in favor of cattle and goats. The production of milk, cheese, curds, yogurts and fermented milk, as well as meat, leather and cashmere, form a large part of Mongolia's foreign earnings. Trade with Xinjiang may replace that with Russia.[35] Traditional dairy products, such as colostrum (coagulated fresh milk),[36] *orom* (fat and protein balls), yogurt, cottage and hard cheese, curds and the famous *airag*, or fermented mare's milk (*kumiss* in Turkic areas), are important.

Milk production is concentrated early in the year, when the animals are born, and the government treats this industry as part of the national heritage.[37] Animals are slaughtered at the beginning of the winter, and the meat is dried for use during the lean time of the year. Mongols eat more meat than other people, using every part of the animal.[38] A popular way of keeping meat is to dry it in strips in the sun as *borts*. These can be boiled, perhaps years later, and swell up to make a stew.

Nomadism

In present-day Mongol pastoralism, two or three families work together as a unit, or *ail*. A typical *nutag*, or migration, involves a spring camp for April and May; a summer pasture area in which camp may be moved four or five times; an autumn pasture where again camp may have to move a number of times, before the return to the winter camp, where they have stone shelters and corrals. Both the migration cycles and the size of the *ail* vary according to the terrain. Different types of terrain can be distinguished, such as steppe, forest steppe, desert steppe and mountain desert steppe.

In the open desert steppe of the southeast, the route has to be radically changed on average every third year to cope with the variations in the pasture, and camp has to be moved between eight and 20 times a year, at distances of five to 50 kilometers (30 mi.). Drought is a serious factor, and every move is determined by the availability of separate wells for humans and animals, combined with the quality and quantity of the pasture. The herding group does not hold together in such areas, because the families have to disperse to find pasture. The change in altitude of the *nutag* is little, staying around 800 meters above sea level.[39]

In the more mountainous areas of central Mongolia there is a greater certainty of finding sufficient pasture each season. Therefore each family may move camp only four or five times in a year. The altitude range of movement is greater, between 2,700 and 2,000 meters, and the distances traveled are much shorter in these cases — autumn and winter camps being only about two kilometers (a little over a mile) apart. It is rare that a *nutag* has to be radically changed, and the same families stay together for years.

In central and northern areas of Mongolia, the lower valleys are too exposed and the pasture can be covered by deep snow for over 100 days. Therefore each community has a winter camp higher up in the smaller valleys, which are both protected from the winds and have pastures that only receive a thin covering of snow. These pastures are always reserved for the winter.

In spring the nomads seek protection from the north winds on the southern slopes of the mountains, because of the weak state of the herds after the long winter. The spring can be associated with death rather than new life, because a cold spell or the wind can kill off animals that have barely survived the winter. More animals die of the cold than are taken to market each year.

In summer they move to the valleys where, because of the abundance of grass, the camps do not have to move far. The lower valleys are more fertile as summer pasture, because they are watered by rivers and streams and the same areas can be used most years. During the short autumn they expose the herds to the wind to rid them of insects, before moving back to their mountain valley camps for the winter.

Migration routes for pasture and watering places have been a matter of traditional agreement. A herder will leave a sign, such as a heap of manure, in front of a camp to show that he will return. In the past a local noble policed this arrangement, although the nomad could change his noble and therefore his route, and as he prospered he could gain access to more pasture. Under Communism, the collectives took over the role of the nobles.

Today there is a tendency to allow the traditional rights to continue, and many are able to return to traditional grazing areas. The Mongolian Buddhist practice of non-violence is said to contribute to these traditional rights being respected. The grasslands have not suffered as in Inner Mongolia, because there is not the same pressure of population and because mobile pasturing continued throughout the Communist era, but help in range and herd management are needed. The breakdown of the winter fodder supply has resulted in the livestock being in poorer condition, and there is conflict for pasture in some areas.

Family life

The Communist government encouraged large families.[40] The women are responsible for most of the work in the camp, including milking and dairy production. The men herd the larger animals, hunt and repair the equipment. The comprehensive welfare state benefits, health care and guaranteed salaries and pensions through the collectives have ceased, and so each family is responsible for its members.[41] Health and nutrition problems persist. Attendance at primary and secondary school was near 100%, and a literacy rate of near 90% was achieved. This standard continues and many nomads have children in university, and even professionals will retire to keep herds. The nomads are eager for help to complete schooling of children who left to help with the livestock and also for reading material.

Language

The Mongolian language is spoken by 1,883,300 people, or 89.7% of the population of Mongolia, according to the *Ethnologue*, in three main dialects: Khalkha (Halh or Xalx) and Tsahar which are mutually understandable. The 2,101,400 *Halh* or *Khalkha* Mongols make up 79% of the population of the Republic of Mongolia. The third dialect, western Mongolian or Oirat, differs considerably from the other two.

Religion

It is said that Lamaistic Buddhism was first introduced to "tame" the nomads. A *ger* often has a Buddhist shrine with a picture of Genghis Khan, statues of the "five animals" and family photos inside opposite the door. In the past, the interior of the *ger* was divided in two. The *xoimor*, or the "upper" half beyond the fire, was for people of higher status. The "lower" or "junior" half near the door was for dirty boots and "sinners," meaning usually people who had killed animals. But the two halves were divided again, with ritually pure males to the left and ritually unclean females to the right. Guests or older Mongols were seated near the shrine. However, the Buddhist images are becoming less common, as this hierarchical society has largely been discredited by Communism.[42]

Shamanist practices continue even today. The door of a *ger* faces south not only to protect from the prevailing wind, but also because sun worship was part of their original Shamanism. But if a sacred mountain is near, then the door faces that way and that direction is "south," even if it is something else on the compass. A pile of stones, called an *ovoo*, on mountain summits or at passes, is a place for prayer flags and sacrifices to the local lord or *ezed* of the locality. Every where these lords or keepers are thought to bring rain or other good fortune or be angry. Every day of the month is either the auspicious or wrong day to carry out certain activities. But Buddhist shrines are rare in the *gers*, replaced by family photos. A cult of Genghis Khan, who is often thought of as a personification of *tenger*, is now very popular. Meals are offered to his picture before being eaten by the family.

Outreach

The London Missionary Society's work among the Buryats at Irkutsk and then at Selenginsk on the east side of Lake Baikal between 1818 and 1841 was originally conceived as ultimately opening the "backdoor" to the Mongols of China and so to China. This strategy was erroneous on a number of counts. But, at the time, access through Chinese ports and through India, where the British East India Company was opposed to missions until 1813, plus a temporary evangelical interest by the Czar, encouraged this over-optimistic strategy.[43] The LMS revived its mission to the Mongols with James Gilmour, who in 1870 journeyed from Peking to Irkutsk and learned the language among the nomadic western Mongols. However, the work developed instead among the eastern settled Mongols, due to lack of workers willing to travel with the nomads.

Since the fall of Communism, many groups have begun to work in the capital, Ulan Bator, but work in the rest of the country is minimal. The New Testament was translated in the early nineteenth century. A new Mongolian New Testament has been published, and the entire Bible was available from AD 2000.[44] A new Oirat New Testament is also being prepared.

There are about 30 Christian churches along with the revived Shamanists, Russian Orthodox Church and a mosque. The Mongol welcomes change, but has difficulty in being committed to any one church or ministry. A congregation from the church in Erdenet has been established in Bulgan, with eight baptisms in 1994.[45] Aviation should soon be available to reach country areas. Medical Ambassadors are training personnel in all the districts of Mongolia.

Peoples Republic of China

Mongols in the People's Republic of China probably number about 2,720,000 in Nei Mongol, or the Inner Mongolia Autonomous Region.[46] Five million are said to live in China, but this figure must include Buryats and Tuvans, who are included in the Mongolian Official Nationality by China.[47] The situation is critical for pastoralism, because the Chinese government has encouraged Han Chinese to settle in Nei Mongol, and irrigation works have allowed large areas of grazing land to be converted to agriculture, which has resulted in the loss of traditional grazing areas.

Nomadism

A typical family in Inner Mongolia may have a mixed herd of between 75 and 200 sheep, two to forty cattle and yaks, two to sixty horses and three Bactrian camels.[48] The camels are used for baggage, and they have become more popular recently because of the high price of fuel. The cattle and yaks are used for transport and milk and leather. Other breeds of cattle are also now being introduced.

China had a system of collectivization in which families could bid for a particular pasture in return for a number of animals given to the state. But the government's policy is to allow each family between 20 and 30 square kilometers (12-18 sq. mi.) of pasture called *kulums*, or enclosures. These are not large enough to provide both winter and summer forage and, coupled with demand to meet commercial meat quotas, they have caused the pasture to rapidly suffer decline. The nomads have been forced to plant crops to feed their livestock.

All the herders have become semi-sedentary, with houses, animal pens and hay barns. They own their animals and animal movements are few. Inevitably some have become wealthier than others, while others struggle. With privatization, help in a disaster must come from one's relatives and friends.[49] The Mongols also have to compete with the Han Chinese, who have taken up settled animal rearing, resulting in the destruction of pasture near to the towns and villages. Yet while the grassland is poorer, the standard of living has improved as the prices of livestock and their products have risen.

Language

The Mongols can understand the Hahl language spoken in Mongolia, but there are significant differences and they use an Inner Mongolian script. The Bible needs to be translated in this script to be understood, and the lack of the Old Testament means that Mongols have difficulty in believing that God the Father is the Creator. The daily radio programs from FEBC are appreciated, and Christian literature is being placed in libraries. Deaf people also attend Christian services, so Mongolian sign language has to be learned and taught to both the deaf and other believers.[50]

TORGUT

The Torgut are a Mongolian people related to the Oirat and Kalmyks. There are 100,000 on the grassland bordering Kazakstan in Xinjiang, China. They speak a version of Oirat but consider themselves a separate tribe.

OIRAT

The Oirat (pron. Ooi rut) are 166,000 pastoralists in northern Qinghai, China. Percy Mather was the first missionary to these people in 1914 and compiled a dictionary for their language, Kalmyk Oirat.

SOGWO ARIG

The Sogwo Arig are 35,000 Mongolians in Tongde, He'nan County, eastern Qinghai, China. Isolated among Tibetans, they claim to be the descendants of a Mongol king sent to keep the Tibetans in check in the seventeenth century. Their area is a snow-covered plateau at over 3,500 meters (11,500 ft.). They speak Amdo Tibetan and follow Tibetan religious practices and have never heard of Christianity.[51]

26a

26b

26c

26d

26 Mongols (continued):
    a. Mongols walking around an *ovoo* or sacred place (Photo R. Spraggett).
    b. A mural displaying the Mongol's past prowess (Photo R. Spraggett).
    c. As Buddhists, Mongols prostrate themselves in prayer (Photo R. Spraggett).
    d. A Mongol riding boot (Photo R. Spraggett).

TIBETANS

The *Drok-pa* (nomads) and *Sa-ma-'drok* (semi-nomads) make up about one-third of Tibetans, but 43% of Tibet's land area is used only by them. *'Drok-pa*, *'brok-pa* or *dog-pa* means "wilderness" or "high pasture people," that is, "nomad," but they prefer to consider themselves pastoralists. A complimentary greeting between them is "Hail, untamed son." The term is used for nomadic pastoralists across the three regions of U-Tsang, or Western Tibet, Amdo and Kham. These do not correspond to Chinese provinces.

The Drok-pa dialect may contain elements of the original Tibetan, because it seems to be mutually intelligible to the nomads in all three regions, while other Tibetans of these regions are unable to understand one another. Their three cultures and languages — Lhasa, Kham and Amdo Tibetans — also seem to share common features. The nomads gather together in the summer for horse races and again at the New Year. They have their own style of singing, called *droklu*. There are many subdivisions and tribes that have varied authority to decide some pastoral practices. For example among the Amdo Tibetans 550,000 are Drok-pa and 270,000 are settled peoples.

The Chang Tang: The *Drok-pa* who live on the Chang Tang at over 4,900 meters (16,000 ft.) are the world's highest society. The Chang Tang, or Tibet's Northern Plain, lies between the Kun Lun Mountains in the north and the Himalayas to the south, both rising to over 7,000 meters. This plateau is vast, being 1,300 kilometers (800 mi.) wide, with series of treeless valleys and plains at an altitude of between 4,600 and 5,500 meters (15,000 to 18,000 ft.). There are rivers, but the land becomes increasingly arid as one goes west. The valleys are divided by mountains and connected by high passes, which must be crossed by the nomads. High winds sweep the area and even on summer nights the temperatures are just around freezing.

The little and unpredictable rain falls in "summer," from June to August, usually as snow or hail. As the growing season is so short there is no competition by farmers, because only grass grows! This area forms a large part of the Tibetan Autonomous Region and it consists of 69% pastureland. There are 500,000 people, or 24% of the population, who are nomadic pastoralists.[52]

Nomadism

The *Drok-pa* live in widely scattered camps. They are semi-permanent camps in the winter, but the men move constantly with the livestock, living in small tents from April to October. The camps consist of two to eight tents, each with an average of four to five persons and herds of yaks, dzos, sheep, goats and horses.[53] Each family has a main tent covering a pit a meter deep and with stone wall windbreaks. The tents are woven of yak hair and are porous to let in air and light in dry weather, but they swell to be waterproof in wet weather. The nomads also build permanent stone houses for storing barley and tools. They trade in animals, salt, wool and pelts in exchange for barley, flour, timber and rice, but cashmere has become the most important product.

Families usually split up to tend to the animals. Often the elder members of the household stay here all year round, while younger members or hired shepherds migrate with the livestock and set up temporary camps on the pastures, sleeping in the open with only a windbreak. The spring and new grass draw the non-milking animals away from the main camp, and a temporary camp is set up a day's walk away. The milking animals are pastured closer to the camp. During the winter, sheep and goats are kept near to the main camp on pasture left fallow during the summer for the purpose. Lambing takes place in winter. In contrast, the yaks spend the winter up on the mountains browsing on sedge.

Other nomads live in the Amdo area of southeast Qinghai Province and the Kham areas in western Sichuan. This is area of plateaus at between 3,500 and 4,500 meters. In Qinghai, thousands of families as well as the monasteries and schools are still

27a

27b

27c

27 Drok-pa, the "high pasture ones" of Tibet:
   a. A Tibetan Drok-pa couple welcome us to their sod hut (Photo: R. Pyykkonen).
   b. Drok-pa children in their tent (Photo: R. Pyykkonen).
   c. A high plateau camp with black yak-hair tents (Photo: R. Pyykkonen).

engaged in herding yaks, and they still live in yak-hair tents.[54]

In winter the nomads camp nearer the villages, and some of the family members may move into houses in the villages, especially older family members and the schoolchildren. The female yaks are kept near camp, but the men will herd the males to further pasture.

As soon as the snow melts in May, the herds are taken away from the winter pastures to preserve as much as possible of the grass for the next winter. The families live in the summer pastures, at higher altitudes, until the end of October. The women care for the young animals and gather and make dung cakes for fuel sufficient for the winter, while the men herd the larger animals. The fat animals are sold at the beginning of winter so that the family faces the bad weather with a minimum herd.[55]

Long periods of heavy snowfall struck areas of eastern Tibet, such as Yushu, Qinghai Province and Nagchu (300 km. north of Lhasa) between 1997 and 1999. The deep snow meant that even yaks could not forage by pawing away the snow. But this was also accompanied by the destruction of the grass roots by pika, or burrowing marmots, which meant that there was insufficient pasture in the summer as well. An estimated 250,000 yaks died. The nomads gave their own food to the yaks. The fewer yaks could not produce enough dung for the nomads' fires, so frostbite became a widespread problem. The resulting lack of milk and dung meant that the pastoralists could neither eat nor keep warm. Thousands of herdsmen died. Aid agencies sought to replace the livestock and supply grain and fuel.

The monasteries and powerful landowners and officials used to own most of the livestock and hired the Drok-pa to look after the animals. Before 1959, the Chang Tang nomads were feudally bound to the Panchen Lama in Shigatse and powerful landlords. They demanded taxes and limited the nomads' movement. There is an underclass of poor nomads who do not own animals but act as herders for the others.

Communism removed this feudal system, probably for good, and the Tibetan leadership in exile recognizes that there was a need for major social and economic changes. The Chinese set up a commune system for the poorer pastoralists, and each family received a few animals. However, each household remained economically independent and could sell the produce as it wished. The relatively wealthy nomads were forced to pay higher taxes and higher wages to the hired nomads. But when the commune system was to be imposed on all the nomads they rebelled, killed a number of pro-Chinese officials and set their own government — declaring religious and economic freedom. Without modern weapons they were quickly defeated and all their animals were confiscated. The nomads then became laborers for the commune and their households lost economic control and independence. The commune even supplied their food.

After 1981 the communes were abandoned for administrative units, or *dzugs*, consisting of up to nine households. Pasture has to be allocated locally according to flock size and season. The animals were divided equally per person, so that family flock size was according to the size of the family at the time. Each person received about 42 animals, and an average family had four to five members. The number of older children and adults available to work with the animals limits the size of the family flock. New couples set themselves up as independent camps or join other relatives, so this also limits the size of the family flock and the subsistence of the family. Pastoral skill also if a key factor. When the communes were abandoned skill paid off, and some families were soon able to develop herds of 200 or more animals while others soon sold off their animals and took up other work.

The Kham-pa have fought the Chinese through the centuries, repelling the Nationalists and then rebelling against the Communists, conducting a guerrilla war for 17 years in the 1950s and 1960s. The government has attempted to force the

Kham to settle in "model" villages as communes, but these were a failure, and pastoralism has reverted to the natural high pastures.[56]

Valley Pastoralists: The ***Sa-ma-'drok*** are semi-nomads who live in villages surrounded by small fields in the valleys. They only migrate with their animals during the summer. *Sa* refers to the soil. Their herds have more lowland breeds of cattle than yaks or sheep, than those of the Drok-Pa. They maintain close social links with the farmers; they do not consider themselves autonomous or completely mobile. However, many turn to year-round pastoralism, and some eventually join the Drok-pa. The Drok-pa maintain the distinction from the Sa-ma-'drok by calling themselves *aDrok Chen*, meaning "High-pasture great" and *aDrok Ngo Ma*, or "High pasture the real." The Drok-pa feel disdain towards the *Yul Pa*, *Rong Pa* and *Grong Pa* (country, deep valley and village people, respectively). Their lifestyle and exclusive attachment to pastoralism sets them apart from surrounding people, as these features do for many other nomads in the world.[57]

Religion

Religious freedom was restored in 1990, and the people considered religion as a defense against government interference.[58] The nomads have made donations to restore local monasteries, and monks visit the camps. As Buddhists, their lives are directed to gaining merit through the use of prayer wheels, flags and pilgrimages. They also enlist local gods against the powers of evil.[59] About one per cent of the people are avowed followers of Bon, which claims to be the pre-Buddhist religion of Tibet, but many different religious practices are mixed together. It is thought that many Bonpo hide their identity, however, and in the face of Chinese hostility many Buddhists attempt to claim that to be Tibetan is to be Buddhist.

Outreach

One of the challenges for Christian workers is to find terms and art forms that can be modified to lose their Buddhist connotations. Caris Faith Sy has explored analogies between Christianity and Tibetan Buddhism.[60] The Tibetan New Testament was available in 1991, the Old Testament revision is 80% complete and Exodus and Esther were published in 1991.[61] There are daily 30- and 15-minute broadcasts from FEBA and TWR. The *Jesus* film is available in Amdo and Central Tibetan.

Goloks are nomads among the Amdo Tibetans in Qinghai and Sichuan provinces, China. The total population of the area is about 100,000, of whom probably 90,000 are pastoralists.[62] The term refers to both the area and the people, but means "those with their heads on backwards," implying they are rebels. They are fiercely independent and have the reputation of being unwelcoming to outsiders. A myth tells of them being sent to this region to defend Tibet's borders in the seventh century AD. The 4,000 *Hdzanggur* are one of the fiercer tribes of Golok.

The Golok fought off the Communist army to secure a truce and greater freedom within their area. They speak a version of the Amdo dialect and cannot understand the other forms of Tibetan. Their families are often divided between the farmers, who may keep a few dzos for milk, and the nomads with, say, 40 yaks, 20 sheep and a dozen goats. They live in houses during the winter and the animals are kept in enclosures. In the summer they walk two days into the mountains and live in yak-hair tents. They are able to sell the wool to local yak wool factories, but they keep the milk and other dairy products. Animals are exchanged for outside goods.

Marriage can be both polygamous and polyandrous, and many children do not know who their father is. The women, who may leave the camps perhaps only for two or three days in the year, do most of the work. The women do not normally get drunk. Promiscuity, especially before marriage, and alcohol are serious problems for the men.

They wear traditional nomadic dress and may still keep their hair in 108 plaits, which has a mystical significance to Lamaistic Buddhists. They worship Maqen Bomra, the god of the highest peak of the Anyemaqen Mountains in Qinghai, and the deity Gar tsi, of Gyaring Lake, and are in fear of many different spirits. Buddhism is now more prevalent because of the restoration of six major Buddhist monasteries in the area. There are no known Christians and no Scripture in their language.

The *Yonzhi* are 3,000 pastoralists who are probably related to the Golok. They live as nomadic pastoralists in Heha Chen Valley, Gonghu County, Qinghai, China. This is a largely inaccessible snow-bound area. Pastoralism is the only method of subsistence. They worship both their own mountain god, Amni Druggu, and Anye Machen, whose mountain peak is just to the east. There are no Christian contacts among them.[63]

The 35,000 *Ergong*, *Hor-pa* are a Tibetan people engaged in agropastoralism in the Xinlong, Luhuo and Danba areas of Sichuan, China. Massive watchtowers are characteristic of their settlement. They were originally part of the ancient Qiang people and have been assimilated to Tibetan customs and religion. Their language is the Qiang dialect, which is related to Jiarong.[64]

The 5,000 *Zhaba* may call themselves Buozi. They are a partly pastoral people of Qiang origin living to the west of the Ergong. Their religion seems to be more Bonism than Buddhism.[65]

The 49,000 *Litang-pa* live in the Shiluli Shan Mountains in southwest Sichuan and consider themselves distinct from other Kham-pa Tibetans. This distinction seems to have been fueled by a struggle against the ascendancy of the Gelugpa order and the third Dalai Lama over local monasteries.[66]

There are 3,000 Tibetan yak-herding refugees in the north of Bhutan. The Bhutanese farmers, called *Drukpa*, and forest slash and burn *Monpa*, or *Dakpa*, are culturally related. The *Monpa* in eastern and southeast Bhutan differ from the Tibetans and may be the survivors of pre-Tibetan indigenous peoples.[67]

See the South Asia section, below, for Tibetan-Burmese peoples in India and Nepal.

YUGUR, Sarygh Uygur, Sari Yogar or Yuku

These are 12,300 herders of sheep, in nine different tribes in Sunan Yugur Autonomous District, and Jiuquan, Gansu, China. They used to live in yak-hair tents, but many now have wooden huts. Some speak a Turkic language called Yohur, while others speak Enger, a Mongolian language, and others only Chinese, but most are able to understand Chinese. Ancestor worship and the cult of the Khan of Heaven are popular among them, along with Lamaistic Buddhism. The pastoral co-operatives have been set up to sell wool and domesticate the wild deer. Primary and secondary schooling are available.[68] There is no Christian work among them and no known Christians.

Non-Pastoral Nomads of Inner Asia

There is no information available on peripatetic groups in this region.

28a

28b

28c

28 Drok-pa (continued):
    a. Mother and son (Photo: R. Pyykkonen).
    b. Mother and daughter ready for the cold (Photo: R. Pyykkonen).
    c. Mother milking a *dri* or female yak (Photo: R. Pyykkonen).

SOUTH ASIA

South Asia includes eastern Pakistan, India and Nepal. This region, even with the world's highest density of population, has a number of areas that are marginal for habitation and agriculture, and which are suitable for nomadic pastoralism. The high and often arid pasture areas all along the Himalayas and the forests of their foothills are used by peoples of Tibetan origin and others for transhumant pastoralism and for pack animal trading.

Throughout history, Pakistan has been the access route to South Asia from Southwest and Central Asia for peoples on the move, both conquerors and nomads. The Tharparkar area of Sind is estimated to have 600,000 pastoralists, and there are 460,000 in other areas as well. The Thar or Great Indian Desert straddles the India-Pakistan border and covers 200,000 square kilometers (77,000 sq. mi.), most of which is in Rajasthan, India. The growth of the cities in Pakistan has attracted nomads, along with many other rural people, to at least temporarily settle in them in small tribal groups, by squatting or purchasing cheap land and building houses. Others have more transportable tents and huts. But even these people have continued a seasonal migration pattern, visiting the villages at harvest time to practice their traditional nomadic occupations. They also shift camp periodically to make better use of day laborer opportunities within the urban areas.[1]

Many communities in India consider themselves migrants in some sense and have traditions and folklore to tell of this. India was considered a "field," and each community in its history has moved or spread out.[2] In India there are many more peripatetics, or service nomads, than in any other region in the world. Both the rich ethnic diversity and the division of society by specialized occupations have created a complex mosaic of different groups which makes classification according to ethnic, linguistic or the usual criteria difficult. Robert Hayden suggests that this is because Hinduism generates a society of endogamous castes, each with a traditional hereditary occupation, which become virtually distinct societies of their own. The concepts of degrees of prestige and sanctity or uncleanness associated with various occupations have played an important part in creating these divisions. The ties of patronage between the higher and lower castes, to particular landowners or customers, have assured subsistence to many different groups resisting any change to a more equitable system. The third factor contributing to the existence of so many nomadic groups is the Hindu attitude that it is meritorious to give to beggars.[3]

India has 18% of the world's cattle stock but produces only 6% of the world's milk. One-third of the population is vegetarian, so their need for animal protein can be supplied with milk. Policies are being considered that allow the cultivated land to concentrate on grain crops for human consumption, instead of the present mixed farming of animal husbandry and cultivation, in which grain is fed to the cattle. Meat and dairy production would be concentrated on the grasslands to use coarse fodder for the cattle. Such a separation would help the economic position of the various cattle-herding castes, many of which are semi-nomadic. Such policies could be based on developmental pragmatism rather than sentiment, and be realistic in planning for an uncertain future.[4]

Nepal is like a rich sandwich filling between Tibet and India, with a great variety of peoples as well as an awe-inspiring landscape. The country is divided topographically and ethnically into three zones running along its length. The Terai are hot plains near the Indian border. The people are close to those of India and up until recently the land was covered in jungle, but now it is being increasingly cultivated. Along the center of the country are the highlands, where the peoples who dominate Nepal, from a mixture of Tibetan and Indian origins, live. They are also Hindu and contribute most to the Nepalese identity and nationalism. All along the Himalayas, in quite isolated valleys, are the Bhotia peoples, who originated in Tibet and still consider themselves Tibetan. This forms the third zone. In many areas roads are still rare and the difficult terrain ensures that enterprising pack animal owners are needed to provide the transport.

Nomadic Pastoralists of South Asia

KHIK, or *Guhjalis* or *Gojal*

The Khik live in Hunzakut, northern Pakistan, in the Karakoram Mountains, bordering on China. The 6,000 Khik, as they call themselves, are village-dwelling agropastoralists. About half of them leave the villages with hundreds of yaks, cattle, sheep and goats for the high mountain pastures in mid-May. They load their yaks with sufficient household gear for a substantial camp where they stay until late October, returning to the village for the winter. The rest of the population stay in the village to tend the crops. They are one of many settled peoples following a transhumant lifestyle. They are Ismaili Muslims. The Khik, or Guhjalis, speak Wakhi, and some of the men speak Burushaski (Brushaski) and Urdu. There are evangelistic cassettes for all these languages and a Bible translation has been started.[5]

LADAKHI

There are 97,000 living on the Ladakhi plateau, or Land of Passes, in Kashmir, between India and Pakistan. The Ladakhi are a mixture of races and are influenced by Tibetan culture and religion.[6] They are farmers of terraced fields, but they measure wealth by the size of the herds of sheep, goats, yaks and horses.[7]

The Balti, lower down the Indus valley in Baltistan, Pakistan, are Muslims, who converted about 500 years ago but retain aspects of Bonism and Buddhism. There are Bible portions and cassettes available.

There are also two Tibetan minority groups, referred to as *Brok-pa* and *Chang-pa* (see below). They were nomadic and arrived from the east looking for grazing, and were probably the first to arrive.

CHANG-PA

This is a nomadic group of 7,000 Tibetans in the upper Indus valley on the Chang Tang Plateau, Ladakh, northeast Kashmir, India. Any Tibetan pastoralist living on the Chang Tang or Northern Plateau can be called by this name, but here the name is used of a particular group, found dispersed in at least five areas near the Chinese border, east and southeast of Leh. They raise sheep, goats, yaks and horses. A typical family has about 50 sheep and goats, 15 yaks and some horses. Each clan has traditional grazing areas and fines are demanded of families whose herd or flock strays on to the pasture of other families.

Social status is decided both by the size of the flock and by the size of their yak-hair tents. Quite a number of families live in their tents throughout the winter, and those few that have village houses only occupy them for about three months in winter. The tent is erected over a pit, which gives it a lower profile against the cold winter winds as well as giving more headroom for the occupants. They weatherproof the yak-hair cloth of the tent by covering it in yak butter. The tents are so heavy that, for transit from camp to camp, they are divided into sections to be carried by a number of yaks,

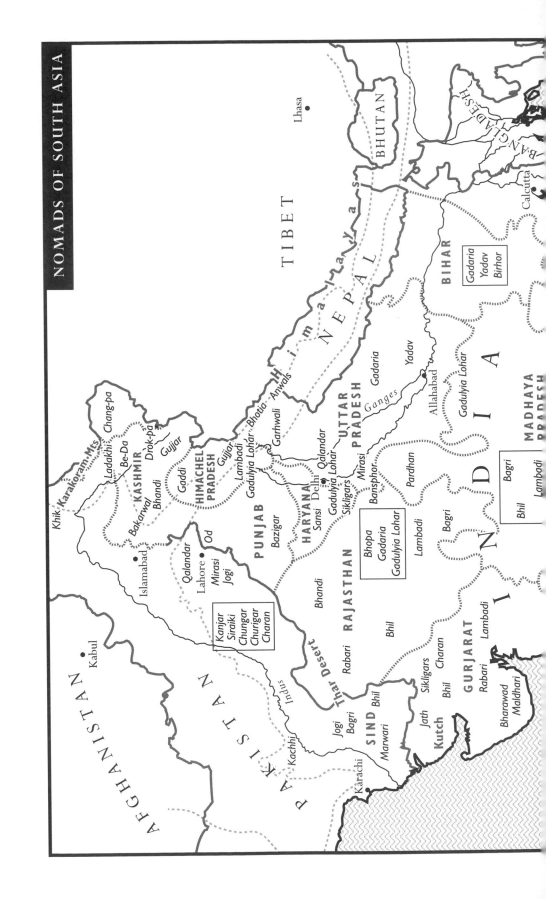

AFGHANISTAN

Kabul

PAKISTAN

Islamabad

Lahore

Karachi

Karakoram-Mts

Khik

Ladakhi
Be-Da
Chang-pa
Drok-pa
Gujjar

KASHMIR

Bakarwal
Bhandi
Gaddi

Gujjar

HIMACHEL
PRADESH

Gujjar
Lambadi
Gadulyia Lohar

Bhotia
Garhwali
Anwals

TIBET

Lhasa

N E P A L

BHUTAN

BANGLADESH

Calcutta

BIHAR

Gadaria
Yadav
Birhor

Gadaria

Ganges

Yadav

Allahabad

Gadulyia Lohar

I N D I A

MADHAYA
PRADESH

Bagri
Bhil
Lambadi

Qalandar
Lahore
Mirasi
Jogi
Od

Qalandar

Gadulyia Lohar

Sikligars

Mirasi
Bansphor

Pardhan

PUNJAB

Bazigar

Delhi

HARYANA

Sansi

UTTAR
PRADESH

Bhopa
Gadaria
Gadulyia Lohar

Lambadi

Bagri

Kanjar
Siraiki
Chungar
Churigar
Charan

Bhandi

RAJASTHAN

Bhil

Rabari

Thar Desert

Indus

Kachhi

Jogi
Bagri

Marwari

SIND

Bhil

Sikligars
Bhil
Charan

Jath
Kutch

Rabari

GURJRAT

Lambadi

Bharawad
Maldhari

Himalayas

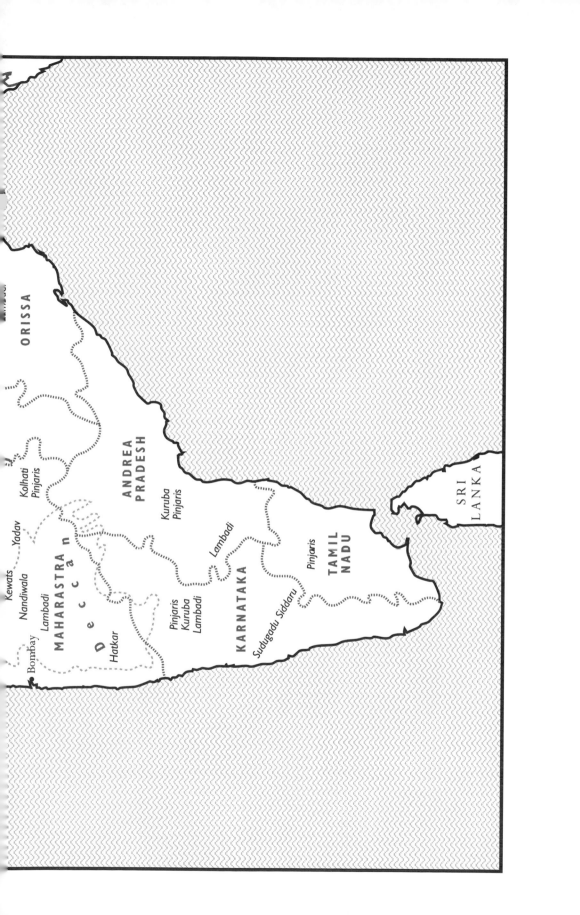

and the sections have to be sown together again each time they are re-erected.

Nomadism

The clans travel between four pasture locations each year. In the summer the nomads move every few days with their herds in the higher pastures. Wild asses compete for pasture and have to be driven away. Wolves, foxes, snow leopards, bears and a unique sub-species of wild dog are the predators that attack the flocks. Wolves are trapped in pits, with a goat provided by each family in turn as bait, then stoned to death. As a people who live under clear skies, the Chang-pa can identify the stars and plan their moves according to an astral calendar. They sometimes move without warning to avoid being ambushed on the journey, as used to happen in the past. In November, the Chang-pa travel down to the lower valleys for the long winter.

Their diet is yak and goat milk, butter and barley. The women and girls are responsible for the tent, cooking and milking. The wife controls the production of milk, yogurt and yak butter and the sale of milk-giving animals. They prepare yogurt in the stomachs of slaughtered sheep.

The men are responsible for herding and for collecting the sparse supply of firewood and yak dung for the fire in the hearth. The men are literate in Tibetan. The men are also responsible for butchering and preserving meat, but they get others to slaughter their animals, often by suffocation. This method has the advantage of saving all the blood, which is poured into the cleaned intestines and served as black pudding sausage. They find a use for most parts of the carcass. They also weave the yak wool into cloth.

Children are prized, and the babies are carried in their mothers' sheepskin coats. Ground up goat droppings within a sheepskin baby-carrier help to absorb the "droppings" of the baby! The Chang-pa also use yak butter as a remedy for chapped skin. Hygiene among these hardy people needs to be improved.

Religion

As Lamaistic Buddhists, they seek merit and forgiveness to obtain a better reincarnation. A man will pay to light a thousand lamps of yak butter before a shrine to secure forgiveness for his sins. Prayer wheels and flags are in constant use, and the monks' powers of divination are often consulted for important decisions. Quite a number of young sons and daughters are given to be monks and nuns as a way of gaining merit. But Lamaistic Buddhism is dominated by the occult, and charms and repetitious prayers and rituals are as much to guard against the *nagas*, or evil spirits.

The killing of animals is a sin that is important to avoid. The men are responsible for butchering and preserving meat, but they get others to slaughter their animals, often by suffocation. As the men work on the meat they mutter prayers for forgiveness for having killed the goat or sheep. When fish were caught in a marsh that was drying up because the water was being diverted by local villagers for their agriculture, a Lama led some nuns to rescue the fish, which are considered to be semi-sacred. They were released again where there was more water. The Chang-pa also consider the local black-necked crane as sacred and dance and sing about it.

The main contact the Chang-pa have with the outside world is through their trade in wool, especially the much sought after cashmere or pashmina wool, as well as yak butter and salt, which they gather in the high-altitude marshes, with a village of *Zangskari*. They exchange these items for barley and other products they cannot produce. The Chang-pa journey to camp near the village in the autumn, arriving and departing without prior warning. The Zangskari are themselves a distinct sub-group of Tibetans settled in villages in the southern end of the Kargil district of Zanskar, to the south of Ladakh. Each clan or family seeks out the same merchant family that they trade with for generations. The traders refuse to give cash, always bartering goods.

The region is undergoing change, not only from the tourists that visit it, but also from development. The Indian government has provided primary schools, but only the Zangskari boys tend to go to school. The Chang-pa do not benefit from them. The Chang-pa fear that the new road in Ladakh will take the young people away from their way of life.[8]

Outreach

Contact with the Chang-pa requires one to travel with them at least for short periods. It is difficult to find them. Anyone trying to make friends with the Chang-pa must be very fit for living at high altitudes and immune to very low temperatures! The Moravians formed a church in Leh, the capital of Ladakh, between 1886 and 1950, and produced a Tibetan translation of the Bible. YWAM and a local hospital connected with the Ludiana ministry have visited the area. There are two Christian converts among the Chang-pa.[9]

DROK-PA, Brog-Pa, Dog-pa, or Srin Shrin

These are 3,000 Tibetan nomads living in the high mountains on the Ladakh plateau, in eastern Kashmir. But neighboring Tibetans call this group Dog-pa and do not fully accept them as Lamaistic Buddhists because: 1) Dards are a people of an Indo-European origin with Iranian features in their language and therefore contrast with Tibetan-Mongol peoples; and 2) they have a syncretistic version of Lamaistic Buddhism with animism (although both religions are syncretistic, the Tibetans see their syncretism as a whole and they object to the foreign elements in Dog-pa religion). They are settled pastoralists who arrived in the twelfth and sixteenth centuries. They have Indo-Aryan features but perform Tibetan music and dance called *Brok-chos*.[10]

They are traditionally pastoralists and traders, but they have become exclusively goat herders because the scarce agricultural land is occupied by the neighboring Balti people. Like the Chang-pa they have lost about a third of their territory, due to the Chinese occupation of Aksai Chin in the

Indian-Chinese war of 1962. It is claimed that true nomadism has been abandoned, and some of them work as laborers for the government. Most now own land and have become agriculturalists. They speak the Shina or Shrina language at home, but they speak Ladakhi and Urdu with other people.[11]

PURIK-PA

They were originally known as *Potricksha*, or "people ruled from Tibet." A Tibetan once ruled a substantial area south of Kargil in Jammu and Kashmir, India and Kashmir, and his people established a fort at Shargol, 35 kilometers (20 mi.) southeast of Kargil. There are 600 of them living in Gar County, in Tibet. They speak a mixture of Ladakhi Tibetan and Balti called Purikskad. It is estimated that there are 148,000 who speak this language, but they are probably of mixed ethnic origins. They identify themselves with Tibet, but are Shiite Muslims. The New Testament is available in their language.

GUJJAR, or *Gujar*

They total 300,000 in Pakistan, 539,000 in India, and less than 2,000 in Afghanistan, giving an overall total of over 840,000.[12] In India the total may be 2,024,000, with 42,181 in Himachal Pradesh, and estimates of those in Jammu and Kashmir between 700,000 to 1,522,512. Others are also found in Uttar Pradesh, northeast Rajasthan, the Punjab, Haryana and Madhya Pradesh. Many are not registered as Indian citizens because they do not own property. In Pakistan all pastoralists, including the Gujjars, tend to be wrongly called Afghans.[13] In India the term has been loosely used for other herdsmen who are not nomads.

The Gujjars did not originate in Afghanistan as is commonly assumed, however there seems to be a small community of them, who use the highest pastures in Nuristan and Badakshan, in Afghanistan. It is also claimed that the Gujjars originated in Central Asia and came into India in the fifth century with an invasion of Huns and established a kingdom in Rajasthan until they were defeated by the

Muslims. They then settled in Gujarat, which provides one explanation of the name, but this idea is contested.[14] The first Gujjars are referred to in the seventh century as warriors, who later migrated to the mountains for pasture for their animals.

It is more certain that they migrated from Rajasthan to what is present-day Kashmir, Punjab and Himachal Pradesh during the sixteenth century. As pastoral nomads and to avoid conflict with the Jats, or farmers on the plains, they settled in the marginal land of the forests and mountains. Some have always owned land, but they have not been good cultivators.

Nomadism

The Gujjars are buffalo herders in scattered communities in every part of northwest India and northern Pakistan. Each family owns between 15 and 20 buffaloes, and though most of them in India are Hindus they still prefer buffaloes to cows.[15] Morton says that the Gujjars in Pakistan tend to move considerable distances at the same altitude to find pasture, in contrast to the Baluch who go to higher altitudes.[16] They use horses as pack animals and also keep sheep and goats. They live in black tents during the migration to their summer pastures, which they call their *tók*. Their buffaloes are seen as friends, being the offspring of animals owned by their ancestors, and are never slaughtered. The Gujjars tend to be vegetarian. Because of this, the only way the Gujjars can survive is by exchanging milk and other dairy products with nearby villagers.

The Gujjars are often in conflict with local villagers who are left with little pasture for their sheep, because a buffalo grazes eight times the pasture of a sheep. The Gujjars do not have the marketing contacts to develop the growing market for their dairy products. They are also usually at a commercial disadvantage with the village middlemen. They are exploited when selling or exchanging their dairy products, and they live in debt. There are also the pressures of competition from commercial dairies.

They consider the forest pastures that they have used for centuries to be communally owned. In recent decades their pastures have been depleted by the demand for farmland, and parts of the hill summer pastures have been taken up by apple orchards. The forests have been depleted for timber. The nomads are also accused of being against forest conservation, and to avoid the destruction of the forests and overgrazing, they often have to rely on outside supplies to get fodder. Pasture has been allocated to the Gujjars by the government on a family basis. These allocations are based on smaller herds than what the Gujjars actually have, and the system has led to overgrazing because they are not able to be nomadic.

Many have abandoned migrating with the buffaloes and taken up farming. Most own land as peasant farmers, and their crops are more successful than they have been in the past. Most families continue to rear buffaloes. Many family members have taken up other employment, such as sacking and loading grain and laboring, and others are in government service. Others estimate that about a fourth of the total Gujjar population is still nomadic, giving a total of 115,000 or more, with 5,000 to 18,000 nomads in Himachal Pradesh; and 1,500 to 7,300, or possibly 10,000, in Uttar Pradesh. There are a very few Gujjar who do not have animals and so have to work driving mules or as agricultural laborers. Certainly by tradition they are nomadic pastoralists.

In Kashmir, their "villages" are formed of scattered houses or *kars*, meaning "homestead," or *chula*, meaning a "hearth." Each *kar* represents a nuclear family as an independent social unit. In the Punjab Kandi, the villages are made up of *beras*, or open areas or streets for each extended family, off which each nuclear family has a house.[17] Some have a little land and part of the family stays on the plains to care for the crops, while the rest migrate with the buffaloes. As a people that live in isolated families for long periods, they value the network of relations on both sides. They have traditions of helping each other in hard times.

Religion

Initially they were all Hindus, but were converted to Islam by conquest, so that 75% were Muslim. Most of these fled into Pakistan at partition. The names of their sub-castes are similar to those of the Rajput, indicating that they were originally Hindu. They are now divided between Muslims and Hindus, the former being in Pakistan and along the foothills of the Himalayas. Some argue that the Hindu Gujjars are a different ethnic group. The Muslims and Hindus do not intermarry, and form two separate communities, but even the Muslims have *gotras* like the Hindus. A *gotra* is a lineage grouping within a caste or tribe that claims descent from a prestigious and mythical ancestor and who cannot intermarry, but take their spouses from outside the *gotra* (the idea is copied from the Brahmins). In the other Indian states they are Hindus, such as on the plains in Uttar Pradesh and those in agriculture on the plains of Punjab. The Hindu Gujjars are usually divided into three groups: *Gujjar*, *Dodhi Gujjar* and *Bakarwal*.[18] The latter are considered a separate group and even dress differently (see below).

The Muslim Gujjars are divided into two sections, the *Bhatariye* and the *Bhanariye*, who do not usually intermarry. Many Gujjars who have been in government service have become Sikh. Most Gujjars have a clan *than*, or place to worship a Muslim *pir*, in or near the house of the oldest clan member. Here they light a lamp every Thursday. They also have a *satiam*, or shrine, to honor an ancestress who committed *sati* (committed suicide on the funeral pyre of her husband).[19]

The Gujjar marry a partner from a different *gotra*. Monogamy is the rule, except when the wife is barren, but this is also a ground for divorce. Yet divorce is a matter of a woman leaving to take up residence with another man, the first husband being compensated by the second. The Gujjar have a high regard for parenthood and consider the family an essential training ground for each generation. The baby's face is covered to protect it from the evil eye, and it is purified from the influence of evil spirits by burning incense.

As among all Muslims, care is taken that the first thing that a newborn child hears is "God is Great" whispered in their ear. Circumcision takes place at age five for boys, accompanied by sacrifices of goats, sheep or chickens, and the boy's head is shaved. They value schooling for their children. Sons become independent soon after marriage and receive their share of the family's livestock, and disagreements cause them to separate from their parents. The youngest son inherits the residue of the father's house and herd, and the mother continues to live with him.

Women have a special place in Gujjar society, and Muslim restrictions do not apply. Unlike many other peoples, pregnant Gujjar mothers are given a period of rest and forbidden to do heavy work. Their daughters also own buffaloes and keep them through marriage and possible divorce. When there is no son, the daughters inherit after the death of the mother. It is reported that the women do not know how to sew or embroider. In the division of labor, one of their many tasks is to lop off the branches to feed the livestock on the leaves, and many women fall from the trees. A mother dying in childbirth is considered to haunt the child. Death involves mourning by the whole lineage or village. They believe that the soul is admitted to the realm of the dead on the fortieth day after death.

Their language is called Gojri, or Gujari. Literacy is negligible, and they tend to keep apart from others so few have learned other languages. Since Gujari is close to Pahari and Urdu, and most Gujjar men also speak Urdu (the lingua franca). They are becoming politically conscious and aware of their solidarity as Gujjars across India. They have convened All India Gujjar Conferences attended by both the president and the prime minister of India. The Indian government has provided development projects establishing education, electricity and healthcare at least for the settled Gujjar. The nomadic pastoralists tend to still lack basic services. Almost no schooling has been provided, and there is a need for teachers who are able to understand the difficulties of the Gujjar.

Outreach

CMA workers contacted some tent-dwelling Gujjar near Murree, north Rawalpindi, in Pakistan, some years ago.

Gujjars live in Pakistan in southern Chital, Swat and Dir Kohistan (20,000), eastern Hazar, Kashmir. In some areas, like Peshawar, almost any herdsman is called Gujjar, regardless of their ethnic origin. They are also found in the Jamuna, Chibbal and Hazara hill country north of Peshawar. They speak a dialect of Hindi. There are many Christian broadcasts in Hindi. A Christian medical team has worked there and the *Jesus* film has been shown. New Opportunities has a team working among them.

There are an estimated 700,000 *Gujjars* in Jammu and Kashmir. In dry, tropical Jammu they tend to be all Hindus, but in the higher and more fertile Kashmir they are Muslims. There are 43,100 in Udhampur district and 23,000 in Jammu district, and also in Saharnpur and Gwalior. They are divided between *Dudh*, or *Dodhi*, meaning "milk" (who are nomadic with their cattle) and the *Zamindar*, or "landowner," who are sedentary. The Dodhi often own some land. Both of these groups are divided into sub-castes to regulate marriage. Gujjars insist that wives must always be taken from a sub-caste different from that of the husband.

The Dodhi migrate twice a year, with their families, to higher altitudes for the summer. Each family group follows a particular route, traveling some 200 or 300 kilometers (125 or 190 mi.). Those with fields leave a member of the family to look after their house and crops. In the Punjab, government policy is to provide them with land in order to settle, and many are doing so, growing rice and maize, but the land is of poor quality.[20] In Jammu and Kashmir they are not a "Scheduled Tribe" and so do not receive government grants (scheduling under the constitutions of 1949 in Pakistan

and India tried to emancipate both untouchable castes and tribes and give them government benefits, education, etc.). Mobile primary schools have been provided and many have gone further in education and taken up skilled occupations.[21]

Gujjars in Himachal Pradesh, India, live mostly in the northwestern Chamba District in two villages, in the central districts of Mandi, Bilaspur, Sirmaur, and scattered in other parts of the state. They may number up to 34,000. They are mostly Dodhi Gujjars, being nomadic, moving between high and low pastures with herds of buffalo, and living from selling milk and dairy products. Few own any land. They have been declared a Scheduled Tribe and therefore receive government grants.[22] The pastoral Gujjar in Himachal Pradesh and Uttar Pradesh are usually of the *Baniyara* caste, which is divided into exogamous castes.

Gujjars in the Punjab Kandi, India, live in some 155 settlements at the foot of the Siwali Hills that form the border with Himachal Pradesh. They are settled farmers.[23]

Gujjars in Uttar Pradesh are found in both the Himalayan foothills and on the plains to the south in the Rohilkhand Area of the Moradabad and Bareilly Districts. Groups camp in the forests of the Dehra Dun and Saharanpur districts in the winter, from November to March. Their population of 20,000 in this part of the state seems to have stayed stable during the twentieth century, but other estimates are half this number. Each family has, on average, between 22 and 32 buffaloes. They migrate with their herds to summer Himalayan pastures in the Shimla district of Himachal Pradesh, or in Teri Garwhal and Uttarkashi, Uttar Pradesh for the months from April to October.

In mid-April, they congregate to await permission to travel, which is given by the provincial government far away in Lucknow. The journey takes ten to twenty days on fixed routes away from roads and villages, as the summer pastures are at 2,500 meters (8,000 ft.) and higher. On the route, they are able to graze their herds on the stubble of the villagers' fields, but conflict often arises as they have to obtain wheat and other supplies by exchanging milk with villagers. On the return journey, many take the cattle of the villagers to care for them on the plains and return them in the spring. They are an isolated people except for commercial contacts with others, and they are in danger of dying out. Most are Muslims and fear provoking wider conflict between Hindus and Muslims.[24]

The 732,000 *Gujjars* in Western Malwa and Chambal Valley, Madhya Pradesh, have abandoned pastoralism for settled agriculture, and they live in their own exclusive settlements.[25]

BAKERWALS or *Bakarwa(a)ls*

There are 20,219 Bakerwals, who are usually thought to be Gujjars. They travel high in the mountains of Kashmir, India, with sheep and goats rather than with buffaloes. However, many consider them a distinct group from the Gujjars; the name means simply "goatman."[26] They use horses to carry their household goods and sometimes rear animals for other people. They sell their livestock, milk, wool and hides during the summer. The women make rope and rugs from goat hair and wool.

They marry within their own clans, and cross-cousin marriages are common. The men wear a distinctive turban called a *dastar*, and the women wear a special cap. They speak Gujari, Kashmiri, Punjabi and Urdu, and some understand Pashto. They are Sunni Muslims.[27] Their pastoral life has inhibited their acceptance of development and education programs.

The Gujari Bible translation is in progress. The Kashmir Evangelical Fellowship says there are about 100 Christians, and New Opportunities has a team working among them.

PURIK

There are 148,000 Purik in Suru Valley, Kargil, Jammu and Kashmir, and 600 in China. The name means "of Tibetan origin." Winter snow cuts them off from India and China. They are animists that have converted to Shiite Islam. Their language is a mixture of Ladakhi and Balti. The Central Asian Mission worked here during the first half of the twentieth century, and there were three converts.

MARKAWAN

This is a group of horse breeders living in Kashmir.[28]

GADDI

These shepherds live in western Himachal Pradesh, India, and total 115,000. The name refers to the Gadderan mountain area in the Chamba and Kangra Districts, where they have their villages. Their transhumant lifestyle is similar to that of some of the Berbers.

Nomadism

The Gaddi take their flocks to the plains of the Punjab to spend the winter, and many families accompany them by closing their village homes. Those family members not needed to tend the flocks get work on road building or construction projects, while others enter domestic service.

In the spring they migrate back to their villages in Gadderan to avoid the heat and to plant crops on their terraced fields.[29] The women and children stay in the villages to tend the fields, especially if they have spent the winter on the plains. But the men, after a stay of only two weeks at their home, climb further with the flocks to the mountain pastures in Lahoul, at some distance from their villages, and they may be away for three months. The local people of Lahoul, who are of Tibetan origin, tend to use the nearer pastures for their own yaks, so the Gaddi go to the highest pastures at 4,900 meters (16,000 ft.). Once the flocks are on the summer pastures, only a few men are needed as shepherds and so the rest of the men descend to the villages in Gadderan to rejoin their families and attend to the fields. The shepherds carry their food and cooking utensils on their backs and usually sleep in the open, or in crude stone shelters, among the sheep. They have dogs to warn and defend against wild animals. The shepherds have learned to administer injections of antibiotics to their sheep for pneumonia, and they put splints on the animals' broken legs. Because of the shortage of pasture in Himachal Pradesh some men take their flocks to Gharwal, in northern Uttar Pradesh, and are away from home most of the year. The Gaddi are aware of the hardness of the nomadic life; 92% consider it to be inconvenient and undertake it only to find pasture for their animals.

Society

A distinguishing characteristic of Gaddi dress worn by both men and women, as well as children, is the *dora*. This is a circular woolen rope, about 15 to 20 meters long, looped around the waist. Although it is said to be strong enough to lift a sheep, it is more likely to be used as a pillow or for warmth. The men wear a distinctive hat with an embroidered strip around the front. The women wear full skirts made from 15 meters of cloth. The Gaddi exchange brides from villages on opposite sides of the Dhauladhar Range, and there are songs of homesick brides asking the mountains to bend to allow them a glimpse of their home villages. They have a mini caste system among themselves which affects how they greet and relate to each other.[30]

Religion

The Gaddi traditions claim that the Muslims drove them from the plains to take up pastoralism in the mountains, but they have probably always been a pastoral people. As Hindus they consider pastoralism to be their *dharma*, or duty, required of them by the Hindu high god Shiva, who is said to reside on Mount Kailash. Their myths tell of how Shiva, being tired of trekking over the Himalayas, lost his temper and drew dirt from his body and cast it on the ground. This turned into sheep and goats, which found a path down from the mountains for the gods. In gratitude, Shiva charged the Gaddi with looking after them. Shiva is considered to migrate in winter, and the Gaddi think of themselves as in some sense

accompanying him. Their songs are of Shiva and his consorts Sati and Parvati. Each year pilgrims come from the plains to bathe in the "sacred" lake on a mountain in their summer pastures. Every 12 years a *Mela*, or fair, is held at the lake attended by 2,000 pilgrims, and this traffic on the narrow mountain paths interrupts the migration of the flocks.

It is claimed that the Gaddi are less animistic than other mountain people, and have both Brahman and low caste priests. They worship various deities, who are considered to be evil spirits who have become gods. "Ram Ram" is the popular greeting, asking for that god's blessing. Animal sacrifices are made for special occasions in life — for building a new house, for the fertility of the fields, or for setting out on a journey to appease the spirits. If the animal trembles at the point of sacrifice it is considered to have been accepted by the god or goddess. Each mountain pass is believed to have a fickle goddess who needs to be propitiated with sacrifice. A spirit called Gunga is believed to cause disease in the cattle and needs to be propitiated with the blood of a he-goat sprinkled on iron in the cowshed. They believe they can be molested by the *Avtar*, who are the spirits of childless couples. The Gaddi erect stones to stop these spirits from disturbing them with their crying. They believe that the dead haunt the living unless small houses are built for them on the outskirts of the village. They have healers or shamans, called *Gardi chela*, who enter into trances to reveal the future to clients for a payment. Black magic is practiced against enemies and rivals.

Adopting a better breed of sheep and feeding them better for increasing wool production would help their future prosperity. This in turn would help to develop cottage industries to spin and card the wool themselves, rather than depending on the monopoly of the dealers. There is also a need for a marketing agency. The world demand for woolen goods is increasing, and it seems ridiculous that India has to import wool from Australia. India's own producers need to be encouraged by giving the benefits directly to them. The Gaddis' poor fields should not be divided further by inheritance, and help should be given to enable the Gaddis to produce most of the food they need. The production of better hay and silage would help to eliminate the winter migration to the plains for both livestock and the people.

Outreach

Hindu writers recognize that the Gaddi need help to overcome alcoholism and their dependence on animal sacrifice. Medical and educational help is also needed. It is becoming the practice to have one family member stay in the village all year round with the school-age children so that their education is not interrupted by the migrations. They speak Bharmauri or Gaddi, a language close to Dogri-Kangri, but about a third of the Gaddi are bilingual in Hindi. A Bible translation is in progress. Outreach would require a traveling ministry, although there would be sufficient people in the villages during the summers. SGM has published Bible portions, there are gospel cassettes, the *Jesus* film is available, and there is a radio program in the language.[31] The Gaddi are in a sensitive border area, and some travel restrictions apply for foreign workers.

GARHWALI or Pahari Gashwali

The Garhwali total 1,600,000 in Garhwal, Dehra Dun, Uttarkashi and Terhi Districts in the extreme northwest part of Uttar Pradesh, India and also in Jammu and Kashmir. They migrate annually to make the most of the mountain slopes of the Himalayas for both pastoralism and subsistence agriculture, using terraced fields. Other Garhwali live in towns and some are in various professions.

They speak Garhwali, which is related to Rajasthani. Because of the mountains, the communities are very isolated and there are many variations in the eight dialects. But the main dialect, called Srinagari, is considered the standard. There is very little literature in the language.

The Garhwali District contains the sources of the sacred rivers the Yamuna and the Ganges, and the mountains have many shrines to various Hindu gods and goddesses. The Garhwali are Hindus who also placate spirits in the natural features of the landscape. Malnutrition and alcoholism are common. They consider Christianity a Western religion and reject it as "shallow" and defiling. Indian Christians and missionaries are often hated as "foreigners." A conversion is very rare, but some do listen to Christian radio broadcasts. A translation of the New Testament was completed in 1827 but has been out of print for some time. A revision is being done and portions are available. There are about five agencies active in Garhwali, including the Indian Evangelical Mission, SGM and Campus Crusade. There are about 400 Christians, but because of the remoteness of many of the villages only a small proportion of the rural Garhwali have been evangelized. These Christians should be encouraged to reach others.

ANWALS

They live in Uttar Pradesh, India, and in Nepal. They originated from various areas in Garhwal, Danpuri and Nepal and have formed three geographical endogamous groups in the Darma valley, Pithoragarh, and in the Himalayas, Uttar Pradesh.[32] Bhotia, who as farmers had all the limited arable land under their control, had already settled this region. The only economic opportunity for the Anwals was to be hired shepherds to the Bhotia's flocks. In this early period they developed the skills of semi-nomadic herding, which they had not known, and they also managed to raise flocks of their own. The Anwals became pastoralists and traders with considerable numbers of sheep and goats and migrated to lower altitudes during the winter. They also became subordinate traders into Tibet for the Bhotia, although they lacked the trade contacts and knowledge of the language.

Nomadism

After 1960 the border with Tibet was closed, and the Bhotia were no longer able to trade with Tibet or to improve their flocks with sheep from Tibet. They increasingly turned to agriculture and government service. This gave the Anwals the opportunity to develop their pastoralism still further, and to increase wool production to weave blankets, garments and mattresses for sale. During the summers, most of the families work on cultivating the limited plots they have constructed higher up the mountains above the Bhotia's fields. These produce potatoes, wheat and chilies, although only the potatoes are of commercial value and are sold in Darcula, just over the Nepalese border. Others take the flocks higher up the valleys gradually as the snow melts and the mountain pastures grow. Some also provide pack animal transportation for the Bhotia in this region.

At the end of September, with the arrival of snow at high altitude, the shepherds bring the flocks down to be near the villages in preparation for the migration. Their annual migration cycle involves going down to the region around Mahendra Nagar in southwest Nepal during November. They travel in extended family groups to give more co-operative labor for their pastoralism. One or two male adults stay in the town with the pack animals to run a transport service to the surrounding mountain villages carrying the goods of the local Nepali merchants. The rest of the Anwals spend the winter pasturing the flocks in the region. Many families knit woolen garments and sell them in nearby markets. Through these various activities they are able to buy salt, cereals and molasses to take back with them into the mountains. The Anwals return to their villages in the Darma valley with the onset of the rains, because the trails in Nepal become impassable and this is the start of the growing season in their fields.

Outreach

There is no known Christian contact with them. They have shown an amazing ability to adapt their lifestyle to the available economic opportunities, and they could be helped to develop these further.

BHOTIA

Bhotia is Hindi or Nepali for "Tibetans," derived from *Bod-pa*, people of Central Tibet. However, in Nepal it tends to have a derogatory meaning implying "hill-billy." Nepali Tibetans might be a better term, as they still consider themselves Tibetan although some have absorbed some Hindu and Nepali culture. There are 400,000 Bhotia in northern Nepal in the remote and isolated valleys along the Himalayas.[33] They have come from different parts of Tibet and still consider themselves Tibetan, and are divided between those who have been in Nepal for centuries and more recent migrants. The earlier settled groups came for trade, or land, or to avoid persecution before Nepal was a united country with defined borders. Others, like the Drok-pa, are more recent arrivals due to the oppressive Chinese policies.

Because of the difficult terrain, the Bhotia live in widely separated valleys and have formed at least 20 separate societies of a few thousand people, each like a little country of its own. Each speaks its own Tibetan dialect and they still observe some of the older forms of Tibetan religion, because Buddhism has undergone reforms since they left Tibet. Each society tends to make class distinctions between itself and its near neighbors according to who has the best or only viable fields, or who dominates trade. Distinctions are also made between full Tibetan speakers and those with their own variation of the language.

Nomadism

The Bhotia have traditionally been yak herders, shepherds and farmers in the Himalayas in the summer. In the winter, they often trade animal products and Tibetan salt to the lowland peoples for grain. They live in villages linked together by mountain trails, in two-story stone houses stepped up the mountainside, with adjoining terraced fields. Each family has herds of between five and 100 yaks. Because the pasture for nomadism is so scarce in the Himalayas, they have developed a semi-sedentary lifestyle, living in a permanent village but moving to temporary villages lower or higher on the mountains for seasonal grazing. The yaks are usually grazed with the herds of other families, both to save work and to share the meager pasture equally between herds, and the herds are moved according to a monthly cycle. While the men look after the yaks, the women and children look after the sheep and goats, which have to be grazed separately from the yaks.[34] A village may have pastures scattered over an area of 320 square kilometers (200 sq. mi.), or in a few cases they have more fertile fields nearby with year-round grazing. The herders have to spend weeks living in tents or in caves or temporary stone huts. For many, nomadic pastoralism is still part of their culture.

The Bhotia have kept their Tibetan culture distinct from the Nepalese and have remained Tibetan Buddhists. But Nepalese policies and the education system are undermining the culture, even changing the children's names, to favor the Hindu-oriented, Nepalese culture. Aid given to improve their cultivation has not reached them. Foreigners who want to help the Bhotia need permits from the Nepali government to visit border areas. Some of the Bhotia have prospered through contacts with the outside world for trade and tourism, and they feel less pressure to be assimilated with Hindu Nepalese culture and may well emphasize a more "secular" Tibetan identity.[35]

We give here eight examples of those involved in nomadism of different forms, describing them from west to east: *Khampa*; *Jad, Tocha, Marchha* and *Johris*; *Humli-khyampa*; *Dolpo-pa*; *Nye-shang*; *Nar*; and the *Sherpas*. Their nomadism usually takes the form of trading using their animals.

The *Khampa* are traveling traders in Himachal Pradesh totaling about 1,300. They are called *Bodh* in some places and *Tibetan* in most others. Their traditional occupation is shepherding, although the majority now own land to cultivate. The women are noted for weaving carpets, shawls and blankets. They are mostly Lamaistic Buddhists, and the Lama decides the way of disposing the dead including cremation, leaving the body on the mountain or throwing it into a river. They worship family gods represented by slabs of stone. A minority of Hindus among them is growing. They speak the Khampa dialect among themselves, and they have a well-developed tradition of folk songs and tales. Nearly half are literate.[36]

The *Jad*, *Tocha*, *Marchha* and *Johris* are 40,000 Hindu Bhotia who live in Uttarkashi, Chamoli and Pithoragarh districts, in Uttar Pradesh. There are seven major groups of them, each with their own language, in seven separated valleys.[37] Until the Tibetan border was closed in 1962, they were primarily caravaners, with links to the Tibetan *mandis*, or trading centers, exchanging Tibetan wool in the Terai for Indian rice, sugar and brass ware back to take back to Tibet. Their societies were divided between traders, weavers and shepherds who worked for the traders. They migrate between summer villages at 3,500 meters, close to the border, and their winter villages at 1,200 meters. With the collapse of the trade, only some of the families could find grazing for pastoralism and settled at their winter villages as farmers. Most are seeking various types of employment, and the young men travel to the plains for work. The children are attending school but have little interest in returning to a nomadic life, even if it were economically possible.[38] They have a Hindu caste system and their religion seems to have a predominant Hindu form, with Buddhist elements. Tibetan names are now replaced with Hindu ones.

The *Jauhar*, etc., are Bhotia originating from Tibet who control the area where the Anwals live and who forced them to become herders. There are 4,000 living mainly in four communities in 19 villages within narrow valleys — the Jauhar, who do not intermarry with the others, and the Darma, Byans and Chaudas Valley Bhotia. Their lifestyle is that of transhumant agropastoralists.[39] They have summer high-altitude villages at between 2,400 and 4,000 meters and winter villages at between 50

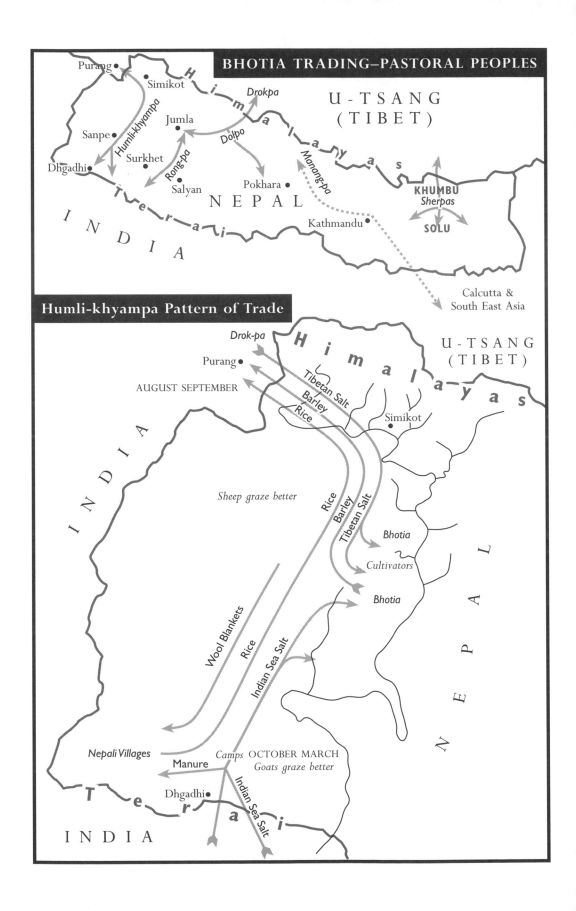

BHOTIA TRADING–PASTORAL PEOPLES

Purang

Simikot

Drokpa

U - T S A N G
(T I B E T)

Himalayas

Jumla

Humli-khyampa

Sanpe

Dolpo

Manang-pa

Surkhet

Rong-pa

Dhgadhi

Salyan

Pokhara

N E P A L

Terai

KHUMBU
Sherpas

SOLU

I N D I A

Kathmandu

Calcutta &
South East Asia

Humli-khyampa Pattern of Trade

Drok-pa

Purang

AUGUST SEPTEMBER

Himalayas

U - T S A N G
(T I B E T)

Tibetan Salt

Barley

Rice

Simikot

I N D I A

Sheep graze better

Rice

Barley

Tibetan Salt

Bhotia

Cultivators

Bhotia

N E P A L

Wool Blankets

Rice

Indian Sea Salt

Nepali Villages

Manure

Camps OCTOBER MARCH
Goats graze better

Terai

Dhgadhi

Indian Sea Salt

I N D I A

and 150 kilometers (30-90 mi.) distance. The entire population migrates with their livestock between these two locations each year. More than 90% of their livestock is made up of equal proportions of sheep and goats, because they do not need imported fodder or to be kept in stalls. They use the *dzo*, or *jhupu*, cross of the yak and cow as their draft animal. There is no known Christian contact with them.

The **Humli-khyampa** are a 1,000-strong community in the Humla region, in far western Nepal. They are one of a number of groups in Nepal and India that call themselves *Khyampa*, which means "wanderer," but the Nepalis consider them part of the Bhotia. Their 170 "households" live in tents all year round and migrate together, transporting salt and rice on their sheep and goats. Their domestic goods are carried by cows, or on their few horses. Their trade route reaches from Purang in Tibet to near the Indian border through the Kuwari, Kurna and Buriganga valleys in four districts of far western Nepal.

The Humli-khyampa took up trading, exploiting an economic niche, because they had no land to grow wheat and settle themselves, since the long-established Bhotia had all the fertile land. The Bhotia and Tibetan Drok-pa lacked rice, and Nepal lacked salt. The Drok-pa nomads in Tibet used to exchange Tibetan salt for Nepalese rice that the Humli-khyampa brought north in August each year. The exchange between rice and salt increased in favor of salt, of course, the further they were from Tibet. The Humli-khyampa then traveled south as far as Sanpe, where they used to camp for the winter, trading in Tibetan salt.

However, when Indian sea salt became available at the Indian border, the value of the Tibetan supply was reduced. The trade of the Khyampa was also affected when, in 1962, the Nepalese government began to control the trade. Since 1964, the Chinese have also controlled the trade in Tibet. Some of the farmers in the Sanpe area also began to travel to the south for Indian imports, including salt, for themselves.

The Humli-khyampa responded to this challenge by extended their winter migration further south than Sanpe to barter Nepalese rice for Indian salt in the Terai, the southern lowlands of Nepal. The Indian salt has to be paid for in Nepalese currency, which is obtained by selling blankets they make from their own sheep's wool to the Nepali villagers near Dhangadi and Chaumuhal. To do this, the Khyampa disperse into groups of four to six tents and establish a permanent camp where their women, children and elderly spend the winter. Those families with fewer animals have to go further and make four round trips to gather the Indian salt, while those with more animals need to make only two trips.

They then transport the Indian salt northwards into Nepal. When the caravans return with Indian salt they use the camps as a base and trade the salt in the villages around the area. The villagers not only exchange rice, vegetables and other goods for the salt, but they also allow the traders' sheep and goats to manure the farmers' fields. Both sides form a "brotherhood" of trade with a feast, and they persuade their relatives to trade with the same customers.

In March they start to move north, collecting the stored rice that was exchanged for the salt. The brief summer is the only possible time for trade over the Tibetan border as it is an arduous journey for the sheep and the tracks are closed by snow for most of the year. When they arrive in Purang, Tibet, in August, as much of the rice as possible is exchanged for Tibetan salt, trying to realize the highest price. The return journey southwards starts in September. Two of their families live permanently in Gömpa, where they trade the Tibetan salt with the other Bhotia farmers who have land on which they grow barley and wheat. In Banjur District south of Gömpa, about half of the Khyampa families have profited sufficiently to own small fields. The barley is used for themselves during the summer, and one of the men also transports the surplus to Purang for trade. This way they save as much rice as possible to exchange for either Indian or Tibetan salt.

On both the spring and autumn migrations the sheep are shorn and the short wool washed, spun and woven into blankets. The wool is short because the animals carry loads much of the time.[40] Their sheep and goats tend to complement each other because the sheep graze well in summer and autumn in the mountain pastures and are therefore stronger at that time, while goats find better forage in the Terai. The average flock size is about 50 to 80 animals. As far as is known these people have no Christian contact, although visits have been made there.

The **Dolpo-pa** are 5,000 agropastoral traders with yak herds, living in the Dolpo, north of Juphal and west of Mustang in the northern part of western Nepal.[41] They have had close ties with Mustang and Tibet, but they have their own language. The majority live in mountain villages of stone houses, less elaborate than those of other villages because timber (heavy beams for the roofs and doors) has to be transported over the mountains. Mountain streams irrigate their terraced fields, but the fields are so arid that they yield only a meager harvest. The field of the lama receives the water first, and then the rest benefit according to the throw of a dice.

Most families have a herd of yak, which they take progressively higher up to their summer pastures and live in yak-hair tents between April and September. They also take the yaks of those too poor to have a tent. When the Chinese border was open the Dolpo-pa used to send their yaks to winter in Tibet, but now they take their herds to the Tibrikot region to the west in Nepal. Other families camp, pasturing the sheep and goats at various sites near the village, or at *desas* on the mountains, with stone enclosures for the sheep and goats. Shearing the sheep in June and weaving and spinning occupy both the men and women in camp. The pastures are owned communally and they allocate their use by lot. Haymaking is essential for the herds to survive the winter, as the ground is arid and covered by heavy snowfall.

But the Dolpo-pa must purchase their other supplies by caravaning, using their yaks as carriers. The caravans are a strange sight, with some 2,000 yaks in groups of 50 to 150 animals winding their way over the mountains. They go north into Tibet in July to trade with Drok-pa nomads in Kyata Chongra, exchanging their grain for Tibetan salt. They also carry potatoes, cheese and imported radios and watches from Nepal. In return, besides the salt, the Dolpo-pa can gain sheep, fabrics and Chinese tea from Tibet. Unfortunately, the Chinese now control the exchange rates to the disadvantage of the Dolpo-pa. On the return journey, they off-load some of the salt in their own villages and then in October they travel on further south to Chuma or to Tukche in Nepal, to exchange the remaining salt for grain.

This trade illustrates the complex pattern of ethnic groups in the Himalayas, for the Dolpo-pa trade with four different groups to the south and west of them. Both they and the people of Mustang trade with the Thakali to the south. The *Thakali* of Thak Khola are sedentary farmers of unknown ethnic origin, although they claim to be related to the Tamangs. They built up their wealth through being middlemen for trade to the north and south of them. Between the Thalkali and Mustang are the *Baragaon*, in 13 villages of Tibetan origin and culture, although it is now fashionable for them to claim (dubiously) to be related to the Gurungs. The Baragaonlis run mule caravans, carrying Tibetan salt down to Pokhara and returning with Nepalese grain. The Dolpo-pa exchange Tibetan goods with both of these groups.

The Dolpo-pa also trade the Tibetan salt with the Rong-Pa (see below), to the west of them. They are divided into two groups as well. The traders of eastern Dolpo are clients of Tarakot, six villages on the left bank of the Bheri river, most of which are inhabited by the *Taralis*, a people with their own language called Kaike. The western Dolpo-pa trade with Tibrikot and other nearby villages, which are outposts of Hindu Nepalese. They also take the opportunity to feed their yaks on the stubble of the more fertile fields of the Rong-pa in the valleys. Even in this microcosm of pastoralism, the farmers can refuse to allow the Dolpo-pa's yaks to graze on the valley fields in winter and can force them to accept a poor rate of exchange for their salt.

The roundtrip journey takes the Dolpo-pa six months. The families on the journey sleep in the open, behind a windbreak of baggage. The route involves passes at over 5,000 meters (16,500 ft.). Some of the women stay in the village to tend the fields while the men are away caravaning. The women wear a characteristic headdress of the region, called *tik-pu*, consisting of silver and brass plates bound with leather thongs. Children will take responsibility for the animals from the age of four. The Dolpo-pa are Lamaistic Buddhists, and their contacts with the Rong-pa bring Tibetan and Indian culture into contact with one another.

Thakuri: Rong-pa is the Tibetan term for "low-pasture," or "deep valley people," in contrast to Drok-pa, "the high pasture people." However, these are not Tibetans but Nepalese. They are *Thakuri*, a subdivision of the Chetri caste in Nepal, and they are Hindus. They are shepherds and continue the trade route southwards over arduous terrain into central Nepal, carrying red beans and salt and using their sheep as pack-animals. Each owner can recognize his animals even without markings. There are no known Christians among either of these peoples, and they are considered very resistant to spiritual change.

Nyeshang-pa or *Manang-pa*, Nepal, are a community of 4,000 Bhotia in Nye-shang, in the upper Maryangdi Valley, north of Pokhara and southeast of Mustang. Manang is merely one of seven villages there. The valley lies north of the Annapurna Range, which cuts off most of the rain and makes the valley very arid. The people live in three villages and grow limited crops, which are barely sufficient to support themselves and also herd sheep, yak and dzos. The villagers feud with each other, and the Tibetans are quick to point out that the Manang-pa are of mixed descent. They claim to be Gurungs, but the latter dispute this.

The Manang-pa have turned to international trading, for which they used to be given special royal privileges. The men walk to the Indian border in the autumn to take the train to Calcutta and then a ship to Burma or Singapore to return in the spring. They are supposed to have started the trade by passing off cheap beads as semi-precious stones, but their business has developed into bringing stones and silks into India on the return trip. Today they deal in gold, silk and electronic goods, and allegedly drugs, and some have become rich and live in Kathmandu and have invested in land there. In contrast to other Buddhists they eat a lot of meat and their temples are in disrepair. Tibetan refugees have settled in the valley and may have an influence in reviving Buddhism. Their language differs quite a bit from Tibetan, but a full linguistic analysis is yet to be made.[42]

Nar is the valley to the east of Manang with a Bhotia community that has a transhumant lifestyle. The Bhotia live in the permanent high-altitude villages of Nar and Phu, where they spend the summers, plant their crops and take their yak herds to higher pasture. The summer pastures are scattered over an area of 500 square kilometers (310 sq. mi.) for about 2,000 yaks, the herds being divided and using the pasture in rotation to avoid overgrazing. The yaks find their own pasture, and the herdsman's work is to stop the yaks from going too far. The herds usually come back to Nar for the mid-summer festival. They leave the villages for more basic housing at lower altitude in two abandoned villages called Meta and Chaku in early January, to avoid the deep snow on the pastures. During the winter they have to supplement the yak herd's diet with hay. Some families keep cows, as well as sheep and goats, for a milk supply when the yaks are away. Each clan has a yak that does no work and is dedicated to the gods. Drok-pa refugees from Tibet, as recent arrivals, have difficulty finding pasture, and they have to camp in areas not used by the Bhotia.[43]

Sherpas: There are 35,000 Sherpas, including 14,000 in Nepal and 19,000 in

India. They are the Tibetan *Shar-pa*, or eastern people, who came originally from Kham, and now form a group of the Bhotia people in Solu, Pharak and Khumbu, eastern Nepal.[44] They concentrate on animal husbandry and so are distinguished from the Helambu Sherpas north of Katmandu, who are farmers. Solu does not have sufficient altitude for yaks, compared to Khumbu, so the herders have to take their herds both to nearer winter pastures (*gunsa*) and to high-altitude summer pastures (*yersa*). They specialize in the yak-cattle cross-breeds for sale to those outside the area. Their lives have materially improved and the population increased because of the successful introduction of the potato, which they also export to other areas. Tourism and trekking have allowed many of them sufficient income to employ others, such as local Drok-pa, in both herding and serving the tourists as mountain guides.

Sherpa society is divided into two higher and lower groups of clans. Polyandrous and levirate marriages are practiced. They are Tibetan Buddhists and worship either at the local *gompa*, or temple, or at a *mani*, a house with a giant prayer wheel. Wealthier families have their own brightly colored chapel rooms in their houses. They eat meat but do not kill animals themselves. There are a few Christians among them and many are aware that Christianity exists.

Tibetans and *Khambas* are recent refugees, or migrants, from central and eastern areas of Tibet, who now live in the territory of the Bhotia, in Nepal. They have fled from collectivization and the Chinese theft of their flocks. There are camps of Drok-pa, nomads from Western Tibet, living permanently in tents and paying a fee to the Bhotia for their grazing. They also do trading work as farm laborers with the permanently resident Bhotia. Many *Khambas* settled for a time in Mustang among the Bhotia, and some intermarried with them, but being more anti-Chinese the Nepali government moved them further into Nepal.[45]

Each Bhotia people is unique and largely isolated from the others. Each needs Christians to befriend and help them spiritually and materially. There are said to be 840 Christians among the Bhotia.

GURUNGS

The Gurungs are a Tibetan-Nepalese people with a population of 740,600, living in the hills of Lamjung and Kaski north of Pokhara, Nepal. This is the people from whom most of the Gurkha solders have been recruited into the Nepalese and British Armies. They are not a nomadic people. Most are farmers living in villages with terraced fields, but many of them work as a herders of sheep and goats, taking their flocks to mountain pastures during the monsoon. They are proud to be Buddhists, but their practice has an admixture of Hinduism. Their houses are recognizable by the Tibetan prayer flags they display. There are 97,100 living in India, including 13,780 in Sikkim and 49,500 in West Bengal. There are 11 known Gurung Christians.

BAGRI, *Bagdi* or Baghri

These are a nomadic people migrating in the Punjab, Sind and Rajasthan between Pakistan and India. There are 100,000 in Pakistan, including 15,000 in Sind and 1,055,000 in India. In Rajasthan they number 33,700, with the majority in Jhalawar District. Madhya Pradesh has 149,000, where they speak Malvi and Hindi. The women rear the cattle and sell the milk. Some rear buffaloes and goats.[46] They own no land and their major source of income is in rearing buffaloes and goats, and they now have cattle bought under a development program. Many work as day laborers.

In Rajasthan they have six exogamous clans and live in extended families. Men normally only have one wife, from their own local community. They speak Bagri and Hindi and literacy is about 5%. Their trade language in Sind is Sindhi. They are animists rather than Hindus and have their own priests. They eat beef and pork.

The Conservative Baptists work among them in Pakistan. There are about 400 Christians in Rajasthan. Christian Believers Assembly fellowship and others have varied contact with them in Rajasthan. They are in need of health, clean water supplies and educational help. There are no Scriptures in Bagri, or cassettes or the *Jesus* film or radio programs for this people.[47]

BHIL, *Bheel,* or *Bhili*

The Bhil are in Sind, Pakistan and north India, and some are semi-nomadic. There are 100,000 **Dhatki Bhil** living in Tharparkar and Sanghar districts of Sind, Pakistan. The total in India is about 3,000,000 in Gujarat, Rajasthan, Maharashtra, Madhya Pradesh, Andhra Pradesh and Bihar. They were once semi-nomadic hunter-gatherers, and the name Bhil comes from a word meaning "bow," because they are famous for their skill in archery. The Bhil follow different lifestyles according to their location, and small numbers keep camel herds.[48] In Punjab the Bhil are urbanized and educated and the southern Bhil are slash-and-burn cultivators. When they settle, they claim Rajput rank because some Bhils served as soldiers in the past.

The Rajasthani Bhil are semi-nomadic and are divided between **Palia Bhil**, who are organized into *pal* or groups of *phala*, or exogamous groups, usually forming a village community. These consider themselves pure Bhil. The others are **Kalia Bhil**, who have mixed origin and have adopted surrounding cultures. Among them, polygamous multiple families have a higher social status. They are animists and Hindus. The Bhakti movement and the Bhagat religion are strong among them. A Christian church was started 100 years ago, but it has not grown. There are some Bhil Christians in Kawaria. Eighty Bhil attended a training program in 1997. FEBA and TWR each broadcast once a week in Bhili. The New Testament and cassettes are available in two of the dialects.[49] An outreach to the Bhil in the area of Chittaurgarh, Rajasthan was initiated by the Rajasthan Bible Institute in 1978.[50]

RABARI, Reika, Dewasis, Rebari or Rubari

The Rabari are about 250,000 strong, living in the Thar Desert of western Rajasthan and in Gujarat, India. They originated in Marwar. They have three main geographical groupings: 1) the Rajasthani in Chunwalia, also called **Rahwari** and **Raika**; 2) the Central Gujarat in Patanwalia, also called **Bhopa**; 3) those in Kaichchh, having a number of names including **Wagadia**. There are also the Garasia Rabari, who are groups of settled agropastoralists.[51] They claimed in 1991 to have 200,000 *families*, which of course raises the estimate of their total population considerably. They, together with other groups such as the *Sindhi Muslims*, represent about 5% of the population of Rajasthan but have 50% of the livestock. Dewasi means "those governed by ten rules." The name comes from *rahabari*, "he who lives outside" — there are a number of myths to explain this, but the probable meaning is "he who lives beyond the confines of cultivated land," with the sense now of "master shepherd." The Rabari are also divided into two occupational sections, the superior **Maru**, who breed camels, and the low-class **Chalkia**, who keep sheep.

Legend has it that they were created by the god Shiva, to care for the first camel his consort had made, in the district of Marwar in Rajasthan and then radiated out from there. Few are found in Marwar today. Historically the Rebari took up camel breeding in the fourteenth century to meet the demand from the local princes for warfare and trade. The name *Raika* used to be reserved for those Rabari who breed camels, and they prefer this name in Rajasthan. The term was also used for camel-riding messengers, considered to be very trustworthy. They see themselves as itinerant wanderers, though in fact they are sedentary much of the time.

Nomadism

Today the Rabaris' largest herds are of goats and cattle, but they also have sheep, water buffalo and camels. They form traveling bands called *dhung*, or *dang*, which can include from 25 to 50 families (200 people), and drive between 2,000 and 10,000 sheep and goats with camels for transport. They consist mostly of men, for self-defense, due to conflict with the farmers who also have their own flocks and herds. Each shepherd knows his own flock, and calls them out to separate them during the day, but at night the flocks come together for collective protection. The herders sleep around the perimeter of the animals to guard against predators and thieves. The police and bandits demand protection money from the shepherds.

They live in their villages from July to October during the rains, but they travel with their flocks the rest of the time. Some of each family stay in the villages with herds of camels and buffalo and have small plots of crops near to their houses. The houses are round, made of mud brick, with conical thatched roofs. In Gujarat, the Rabari are known as cattle breeders, associated with the long-legged Kankregi breed. Traditionally they supplied dung in return for grazing rights from farmers, but irrigation schemes are increasing the amount of land turned to cultivation and the grazing areas, and conflict with local people is common. Irrigation is also encouraging two crops a year, leaving no opportunity to graze on the stubble. They used to migrate for pasture from October to June, in groups of five to 15 families in northwest India, mainly in Rajasthan State. More recently, however, because of the limits of pasture due to increased human and animal population, they have migrated further to the north, east and south through the states of Gujarat, Madhya Pradesh, Uttar Pradesh and the Punjab, making 1,000-kilometer (620-mi.) circuits for eight months of the year.

The *Raika* of Rajasthan are concentrated around Jodhpur and live in separate *dhani*, or *bas*, or settlements on the edges of the villages. These consist of about four to 20 families who specialize in breeding camels. Camels are important as draft animals in Rajasthan for carts or plowing, so that every peasant has one or two, and the Raika breed and graze camels for others. Lack of local grazing has forced them to be semi-nomadic. The young men will be away from the village to supervise the camels,

especially during the breeding season between November and March, and in the rainy season from July to September, to stop the camels from damaging the crops. At other times the herds are allowed to roam freely, going perhaps hundreds of kilometers. The camels are marketed in the big fairs in the region, but camel wool and milk are used only for the Raika. They seem to have a taboo on a commerce in milk, but often the young herders will live on nothing else when they are migrating in the spring. There is a network of informing about lost animals which reaches even across the Pakistani border. They can always be traced, because the herdsmen can recognize the tracks of their own animals. During the summer they take the herds up into the Aravali Range, but this has become restricted due to a new nature reserve. The lack of pasture has forced them to take the camels westward into Haryana, Uttar Pradesh and Madhya Pradesh.

Both the herds and the Rabari are continually sick, requiring medical and veterinary help, and they often walk five miles out of the way to attend a clinic, or 20 miles extra to pray at a temple. Trypanosomiasis afflicts most of the camels, and they have to rely on traditional remedies as modern treatment is not available. While the demand for camels continues, the lack of suitable grazing is making production very difficult. They lack political leadership, but in 1991 the Rajasthani government promised to allocate pasture to the Raikas at the side of the Indira Gandhi Canal.

Society

Women are treated as equal to men and are allowed to trade and own property.[52] Their marriages are held only on Krishna's birthday, at midnight, in their main camp or village. Child marriage is common although illegal. Camels are important in wedding rituals and are exchanged as dowries, because the Raikas do not sell or buy camels among themselves. The dowry includes elaborately embroidered costumes prepared by the bride's mother. They enforce the veiling of young wives in the presence of male in-laws. The Kuchchhi Rabari women wear black all year round and enormous ivory bangles on their wrists. Children are named on the night of the full moon, with drum beating and chanting to induce their priests into a trance to utter the name of the child. The men wear very short, finely embroidered, jackets.[53]

Religion

They are practicing Hindus and their usual response to disease is to do *puja*, or worship, to the local gods, but they have a special devotion to Krishna. Their myths claim that the god Shiva commissioned them to look after the camel. They gather at night in camps to sing devotional songs called *bhajans*. The Rabari keep a sacred camel called Mata Meri and worship Ramdev Pir, the mother goddess. Their deities include a goddess whose shrine in Baluchistan they used to visit before partition. They speak Gujarati but are illiterate, and they are classed as a Hindu caste of sheep and goat herders. The Ten Rules include a taboo on killing and eating camels, making curds or butter. They seem to have a taboo about eating and handling any meat. Milk is considered a gift of the gods and so should be given away, which hardly helps their commercial prospects.

Outreach

FEBA and TWR broadcast daily in Gujarati and Sindhi. The Indian Evangelical Mission have a clinic and outreach which may have contact with the Rabari.

SINDHI MUSLIM

They form castes in Rajasthan, India, and there are a number of different groups engaged in full-time pastoralism with large camel herds near the Pakistan border. (Cf. *Rabari* and *Bhil*.)

JATH

Jath refers to about 20 groups of Muslim herders who arrived in Kuchchh, Gujarat, 500 years ago. They are not to be confused with "Jat" with a hard "t," who are Hindu cultivators in the Punjab. The **Dhanetah** rear cattle and buffaloes, and some goats and sheep. They are the largest and most nomadic of the groups. The married women wear black clothes and a heavy nose ring, a *vindho*, that has to be supported by a strap hooked into their hair. The **Fakirani** were once sadhus and beggars, but they have turned to cattle herding. They live in collapsible huts made of reeds in the coastal area of Lakhpat. Other smaller Jath groups are the **Madhani** and **Karujath**. The *Garasia Jath* are former nomads who have settled as farmers.

The smaller groups in Banni, Gujarat (some are as few as 100), are the **Haliputra, Raisiputra, Mutwa, Node, Hingorjah, Bhambha, Cher, Jath, Junejah, Kaskalee, Korar, Ladai, Nuhani, Pathan, Baluch, Samejah, Sumra** and **Tabah**. They live in villages near water holes, but they migrate considerable distances in the dry season. They are all Muslims and tend to live separate lives from the Hindus. Their practice of Islam includes the veneration of *pirs* at their tombs. Groups of Meghwal knackers and tanners have attached themselves to these groups.[54]

BHARAWAD

They are found mainly in the Sanrashtra or Kathiawar region of southern Gujarat, India, and are sometimes referred to as **Ahir**. It is said that 65% of them are involved with cattle and the others work in agriculture. They keep cattle, sheep and goats and some specialize in selling milk in the towns. The *Gadaria Bharwad* are a section of Bharawad that rear only sheep. They used to migrate from north Gujarat to the humid south for ten months of the year. There, around Surat, they found stubble for grazing during the rainy season. They could not keep their mixed herds in the rains for long, because the goats got hoof rot. Their pastoral migrations return annually to the temple in Tarnetar in Surendranagar. This pastoralism provided subsistence and also created a surplus for the exchange of ghee. Their society is divided into two parts, **Motsa**

Bhai and *Nana Bhai*, with about 100 clans in each.[55]

The men and women wear embroidered jackets or bodices and shoes, and the bride's mother gives her an elaborately embroidered costume as part of the dowry. The younger men often wear a red scarf knotted around their heads, while the married men wear white turbans. They all have distinctive earrings in the top of the ear. This people are noted for their happy, extrovert disposition even in adversity. This is often expressed in music and dancing, including their renowned dance called *dandiya ras*.

Salzman describes a community of Bharawad that are now squatters in Surat who have given up the nomadic life to keep buffaloes as part of an urban dairy. They have achieved a modest income from seizing this opportunity of sedentary dairy production. Each nuclear family owns a few buffaloes. The buffaloes are kept in stables, so fodder has to be gathered by cutting grass from the grounds of colleges and hospitals, etc. Surplus calves are sent to the animal shelter, not the butcher, because as Hindus they say "the calves are like our children."

As is usual in India, each group of a caste forms a distinct community, differentiating itself from other groups even within the same caste. This dairy group is vegetarian and abstains from alcohol, wears distinctive clothes, and the women have tattoos. They are endogamous. Other groups of Bharawad also have their own distinctive styles, and remain nomadic.[56] They are Hindus and especially worship Krishna. Literacy has been increased to about 10% through the work of a voluntary organization. It is unknown whether there is a specific Christian outreach among them.

MALDHARIS

The Maldharis are a nomadic cattle-breeding caste situated in southern Gujarat, India. They raise the Gir breed, which has been exported successfully to Latin America as the Gyr. They also rear a breed of buffalo called Jaffabadi. The government set up a dairy plant in the hope that they would settle nearby to market the milk, but they have proved to be too nomadic. A policy is needed to market milk, when they are near to the dairy, and ghee when they are at some distance away.[57]

LAMBADI, Labana, Lamanis, Laman, Sugali or Sukali

There are 1,500,000 Lambadi. *Ghormati* or *Gormati* is their own name and means "people of the cattle." They are known by different names in different states, and some who are not of the Ghormati speakers and society are included with them. The non-Ghormati are often called Vanjari. "Lambadi" refers to them being carriers of salt. In South India they are known as Sugali.

Banjara is a common name of some of them and refers to anyone working with bullock caravans, because they are considered a subdivision of the larger group of that name. But the Banjara Conference only recognizes those who are Ghormati. They used to carry grain and salt on pack bullocks, and in colonial times they supplied the British army. They are found in Himachal Pradesh (9,043); Gujarat (41,000); Rajasthan (227,000); Delhi (15,900); Uttar Pradesh (290,550); Maharashtra (1,116,100); Andhra Pradesh (1,785,300); and Karnataka (916,260). They total about 4,830,000. They also live with the *Ahargari* in Pakistan, Iran and Syria.

They may have begun as traveling bards and genealogists, which gave them an aura of sanctity, and so they were entrusted with carrying goods on their itineraries and they extended this to carrying other goods. Some are shepherds, but many became seasonal agricultural workers, as the trade in bullocks decreased. They are nomadic in the forests and hill areas away from towns and villages in many states of India, from Himachal Pradesh to Tamil Nadu, and from Gujarat to Orissa.

The Banjaras have Hindu, Muslim and Sikh sections, but they also have their own Bhagat (priests), who specialize in either white or black magic. The Banjara revere their pack animals and one ox is kept as sacred — it never carries a load, nor is it slaughtered. It is decorated with red silk streamers and leads the caravan and, wherever it rests, the Banjara camp. They make vows or ask for healing at the feet of this ox. They have an ancestor called Lakha Banjara who was supposed to be very rich with many *lakhs* (100,000s) of rupees. Their goddess, Banjari Devi, is thought to reside in the horns of the cattle. They hang a saddle up in their camp-huts in her honor.

Because of the pressures of migrating, Banjara wedddings are held in the rainy season, which is forbidden to other Hindus. Banjaras insist on young wives covering their faces when their male in-laws are near. The married women have bangles on their arms above the elbow, and the girls below the elbow, and they wear rings on their shins. They wear pleated skirts and plaits of hairs down either side of the face. Their language is Gorboli. Banjara camps have occupational groups like Dhadi genealogists and bards, Dhalia musicians, Badi singers, Sonar goldsmiths, Navi barbers, Rohidas cobblers and Bharava ornament makers.[58]

The *Lambadi*, in Uttar Pradesh and Nepal, trace their origin from Rajasthan and resemble the Banjaras there. They travel into Nepal to sell grindstones and ropes they have made. Most have bought land and cultivate, but many are still traveling traders in cloth and cosmetics. The Muslim Banjaras are mostly cattle traders who speak Banjari.

The *Lambadi* in Rajasthan believe they became nomads when they deserted the service of the Rajputs. Thought many have land, they also work as cattle herders or traders. They speak Bagri.

The *Lambadi* in Maharashtra have their home settlements in the mountains of Ahmednagar and Bhir districts. There they are called Lamans. They have four main clans: *Rathod*, *Ramhar*, *Chauhan* and *Vadatya*. They live in groups called *thandas*, or camps, although the term means "bullock caravan." These settlements are high up the mountains, out of sight of the villages below, and they are always some distance from their water source. They consist of low-walled houses facing east, laid out in the order of a transit camp. When the family inheritance is divided between the sons the doorway is blocked and new doorways made in the wall, one for each son. In the past they were allowed to use only the infertile common land high in the mountains, and more recently have been buying this land to secure it for pasture. During June to November they provide casual labor and a traditional veterinary service for the villagers.

Nomadism

The traveling *thandas* are made up of combinations of families from different settlements. Two days before setting out, the families practice camping in the open. Whatever the order of traveling, the camps have the same layout of two rows of baggage with all but the young inside them. The young men sleep outside with the cattle. No tents are used. Not everyone goes on migration, although to participate regularly is important for every individual's identity as a Ghormati. They travel about 15 kilometers (9 mi.) per day. The men make ropes in transit to barter for goods, and the villagers en route ask the Lambadi to camp on their fields so they can have the dung for fertilizer and fuel.

They carry grain to the Konkan, or Western Ghats, and on arrival they divide up into different groups according to the business "contracted" — selling bulls, hiring oxen, charcoal carrying, and wood cutting. The most important consideration is to diversify the sources of income even within the same family. For months they may live without even a tent as shelter, and families are often split up, but it is also a time for negotiating marriages to be carried out on return to the home settlement.[59] A radio program has produced fruit for the gospel in a village in Yarvatmal District, resulting in a small congregation being formed.

Lambadi, or *Nakkala* are a nomadic community in Andrea Pradesh and Tamil Nadu. They call themselves *Vaghriwala*, or *Vaghri*. They are found mostly in the southwest upland districts of the state. They speak Telegu with other people, but Banjara or Lamani at home. They hunt foxes and jackals and sell the skin and teeth as well as eat the meat. The women are involved in all the work, are expert embroiderers and make bead necklaces. They also perform religious roles. Cattle and chicken are often sacrificed to appease their gods. Their names have suffixes of Nayak, Naik and Bai. Both sexes attend school up to secondary level and many have professional jobs. The Indian Evangelical Mission has had workers with them in Bheemaram, Andrea Pradesh since the 1980s.[60]

There are 807,561 **Lambani**, or *Banjara*, in six districts of Karnataka — most are in the north of the state.[61]

Religion

They are considered Hindus and believe in the ancestors of the clans, but they do not worship cattle and consider that they have a religion distinguished from that of others, having borrowed from Sikh and Muslim sources. They even worship a Baluchi goddess. Their languages are called Ghormati or Lambadi, spoken by more than half, and Banjari, spoken by 25%. These languages use different scripts.

Outreach

The Telegu dialect version of the New Testament was published in 1996 and the Old Testament translation was published in 1999.[62] The Banjari or Lambadi New Testament is in print, and the Gospels and Acts are on cassette. The Lambadi New Testament was to be published in 1999. The *Jesus* film is also available. There are radio programs in Lambadi and Banjari. A radio broadcast in Marathi has been effective, and a church has been established.[63] A number of agencies are working among them, including the Indian Evangelical Mission, Linguistic Recordings and Campus Crusade. The tiny minority claiming to be "Christian" has declined recently, as has the number considering themselves Hindu. But there are reports claiming 10,000 Banjaras have been converted since 1992. A Christian training course was attended by 45 people

from this group in 1997. A consultation of 50 leaders, including some Banjaras, to co-ordinate outreach took place in 1999.[64]

AHIR

The 56,000,000 Ahir are livestock breeding and herding castes in India, and some migrate for pasture. About 11,000 claim to be Christian.

The 31,000,000 **Yadav**, or **Dhangar Ahirs**, are the largest group of the Ahir, working as buffalo herders and milkmen in Bihar, Uttar Pradesh and many other states of India. In Madhya Pradesh they number 3,642,700. They prefer to call themselves *Dhangar Ahirs* in Maharashtra. *Bhainpal*, or "buffalo breeders," would be a better name. They are poor and considered a backward caste, but they are politically active in these states. The chief ministers of Bihar and Uttar Pradesh belong to this community. They identify themselves with the god Krishna when he, according to the myth, lived in the city of Mathura as a cowherd. They celebrate especially the eighth day after his birth. There is a theory that their ancestry is connected with the Jews. There is no known specific outreach among them, although there are reports of these 11,000 Christians.[65]

The **Gadaria**, or **Pal**, are shepherds in Rajasthan, Uttar Pradesh, Bihar and Madhya Pradesh, India. *Gadri* just means "shepherd," so there is confusion because many castes have some shepherds, but there are three distinct castes of shepherds in northern India under this name, such as the Dhangar or Maratha and the Kurumwar of Telegu. In fact they tend cattle as well as sheep and goats, and they once roamed in the jungles for pasture. Many still maintain sheep and goats and sell milk, but most practice agriculture. They are very poor. Other Ahirs treat them as inferiors.

There are groups in the Punjab and Rajasthan. In Uttar Pradesh they are found from Saharanpur district in the northwest to near Varanasi in the east. While these people are not nomadic now in the usual sense, they are widespread and accessible in many parts of Uttar Pradesh.

In Madhya Pradesh they number

472,800, but many have taken up other occupations, such as masonry, and live near large towns. In this state they also have some interesting customs not practiced in Uttar Pradesh. For example, an uncle must present clothes to a baby fifteen days after its birth. On the thirteenth day after a death, the children of the deceased must visit the relatives saying, "Oh God give us bread."[66]

Religion

They are Hindus and worship both the main deities and the village and family gods. They engage in magic and do various *pujas*, or rituals, to keep evil spirits away from their animals. Most are vegetarian. In Gwalior, north of Varanasi, and other places, the god *Jakh* is worshipped by treating trees as sacred. Lights of ghee are lit at the festivals of Diwali and Holi to keep the cattle healthy. Chickens are sacrificed at weddings to ward off evil spirits from the new home. The bones of the dead are thrown into the Ganges. It used to be the custom for hundreds of relatives to gather on the thirteenth day after a death, but the expense of entertaining such large groups has discouraged the custom.[67] A survey is needed to reach them as a distinct occupational and ethnic group.

ORAON or *Dhangar*

They are an agricultural caste, but some groups are pastoral. They are possibly the original people of Mirapur, Bihar, India. Dhangar means "cattle raiser," and they are probably the same as *Kurukh*. There are 1,393,900 in Bihar and 20,000 in Uttar Pradesh, of which a few hundred are in animal husbandry. There are also 177,900 in Sambalpur and Sundargarh Districts of Orissa.[68] In Madhya Pradesh they number 503,000 and are agricultural laborers. Literacy is about 33% for men and 6% for women. There is no Scripture translation.[69] They believe in a supreme deity and propitiate local gods.[70]

HATKAR DHANGARS or *Khilari-Dhangars*

They live in southwest Maharashtra, India. They are one of many groups who call themselves Dhangars, some of which are not pastoralists, that share similar cultural traits but do not have the same ethnic origins. They call themselves *Hatkar* to be distinguished from other Dhangars who weave blankets. They believe that a god commissioned them to look after sheep after the blanket-weaving Dhangars failed in this duty. The Hatkar are distinguished from other Dhangars by wearing a red turban, earrings and a coarse blanket and carrying a staff. Their women wear a considerable number of rings, necklaces, nose rings and ankle bangles.

Nomadism

Their main camps (*vadis*), where they spend the monsoon from June to September, are situated between 15 and 30 kilometers (9-18 mi.) west of Pune, on the Deccan Plateau. These are situated either on their own or on the outskirts of a non-Dhangar village. Some of the Dhangars in these villages concentrate on agriculture but the majority are in pastoralism. This preference for pastoralism is proven by the poor Dhangars who, having taken other employment, often invest their income in sheep to return to the traditional way of life. Each family can own over 50 sheep with two or three goats to lead them, and these are kept in a walled enclosure between the family huts in the village.

They migrate westwards to Konkan after Diwali in October or November. A dance is performed and a soothsayer goes into a trance to reveal the date of departure on migration. The women and children drive the horses ahead with the camp equipment, while the men follow driving the sheep, keeping each family's flock separate from the others. They use the same campsites at the roadside each year and maintain good relations with the farmers en route by allowing the flocks to manure the fields. The milk yield is negligible, and the Dhangars rely on the sale of mutton and the income from laying manure on the fields.

During February or March the Hatkar men make a return visit to the Deccan Plateau to repay debts incurred earlier. The families and flocks do not return to their villages until May or June. On arrival, the Dhangars receive extra income from the farmers for the sheep manuring the local fields just before the rains begin. If there is opportunity, according to the rainfall, they take the flocks to different pastures in the area. But if the rain is sufficient they will stay in their settlement for as much as four months of the monsoon.

Religion

The Hatkars are Hindus with their own particular customs.[71]

KURUBA, *Kurba* or *Kuraba*

The Kuruba live in Karnataka and Andhra Pradesh States, India. The term means "shepherd." They are Hindu and practice magic, and their mediums have trances.

In India there are a number of other groups who were originally pastoralists: *Idaiyan* and *Yadiva*, are cattle breeding castes (see *Ahir*).[72] There are *Vaidus* shepherds, and other groups such as the *Kaikadi*, *Vadar* and *Madari*.

Non-Pastoral Peoples of South Asia

BEDA

The Beda are a community landless families living as small groups in Ladakhi villages in India. They can trace their ancestry back four generations, to form *gyuts*, or groups of related families that are committed to help each other and worship the same deities. The trend is towards having one wife. Many are nomadic, supporting themselves as musicians at festivals and by begging. The majority are Lamaistic Buddhists, but some in the Nubra Valley are Muslims. Many of the folk songs are dedicated to the monastery. Those who have settled are wage laborers and have benefited from housing, water supplies and education. The Ladakhis do not accept them on an equal social basis. They speak Ladakhi.[73]

MON

The Mon are traveling musicians among the Ladakhis, in Jammu and Kashmir. They are not to be confused with the Monpa, a group of shifting cultivator peoples further west. They travel with the Beda, but they live in

small family groups along the Indus Valley at high altitude, or in Ladakhi villages. They provide the music for all the festivities of the Ladakhis. They are of Aryan origin and are Lamaistic Buddhists who speak Ladakhi. They have received education from schools established by Christian missionaries, according to Singh.[74]

QALANDAR

The Qalandar, in the Punjab, Pakistan, are some 900 families of animal trainers, acrobats, jugglers, magicians and impersonators. There are others traveling in North India leading Himalayan bears, monkeys and other animals and beating a drum. There are probably many more of these groups in South Asia. They think of their nomadic life as *parytan*, which means "purposeful planned movement to carry out specialized skills." They once traveled Rajasthan and other northern states of India, but the partition of the country has now confined some to Pakistan. Being unable to cross the border, they have lost

29   The Qalandar are itinerant animal trainers in Pakistan and India.

the custom from Hindu pilgrims and festivals. Others travel in India.

The Qalandar live and work in small groups called *dehra*, formed according to the combination of skills that the members have. They will often hire other specialists to work with them, such as the **Mirasi**, to entertain the customers. Each family forms a separate economic work unit called a *puki*, and the *dehra* is usually known by the name of the most successful head of a *puki* in the group. Each family camps in bender tents, which are owned by a married couple. Many families are identified by their tent, even from a distance. If the couple separate, the wife keeps the tent. The size of a tent tends to decide the number of adults that form a *puki*, and dependent relatives usually form another *puki* alongside, but may also be supported by loans from the family.

They have varied myths of descent from some famous religious leader to enhance their identity as a people. One tale connects them with the time of Alexander the Great, when a woman among their ancestors refused to give food to a beggar. The beggar cursed them to always wander like hungry stray dogs. They believe this curse has never been revoked, so that they are condemned to be nomads. In both India and Pakistan, they are Sunni Muslims and are followers of various *pirs*, or Muslim saints, and make pilgrimages to their tombs, but the claim that they are followers of Bu Ali Qalandar, who died in 1323, is to be discounted.[75]

The solidarity of the Qalandar is maintained by an ethic based on a contrast between brotherliness and shame. The brotherliness must be demonstrated by co-operation and toleration within the *dehra*. They view the sedentary life with disdain, and consider peasants to be nothing better than slaves to patches of dirt. Therefore shame is derived from any contact with those outside of the Qalandar such as by marriage, or through seeking help from the police, and this shame can bring lethal retribution on the culprit. Yet this code can be broken, as when their wives give sexual favors to gain influence with patrons for the economic benefit of the *dehra*. There is a

taboo on mentioning this, and the husbands dislike it. This shows the total weakness of the peripatetic in the face of unfavorable sedentary people. The Qalandar each belong to a tribe, or *qöm*, that arbitrates in disputes. They have their own secret cant with many Persian words.[76] There are no known Christians among them.

MIRASI, Hukiya, Langa, Pakhwali or Kanwal

They are bards, impersonators, genealogists, singers, dancers and storytellers like the Bhat in the Punjab, Pakistan and in northwest India. The name comes from the Arabic *miras*, or "inheritance." In India they are called Dom Mirasi. They usually identify themselves as *Mir Allam*, scholars of genealogies, to outsiders.

The Mirasi specialize as *bhand*, or comedians, with a repartee of satire of religious and political leaders. They will even publicly ridicule their host until he gives them a higher fee! Teams of Mirasi musicians and singers perform songs of romantic love. The dancers are boys dressed in women's clothes wearing their hair long, to avoid the Muslim taboo on women dancing in public. Both in Pakistan, in the Muslim environment, and among Muslims in India, the *Marasins*, or female dancers, also dance, but only to entertain the women.

In India, they serve the Muslim communities in Rajasthan and Gujarat as genealogists, maintaining lists of ancestry, and advising on property and family disputes. They travel in small groups from village to village, carrying their instruments.[77] There are also Mirasi in Uttar Pradesh, a sub-division of the *Shilpkar*, who travel to entertain with music and dance, or peddle bangles, combs and mirrors. They are also called Hukiya after the small drum they use, and are famous for their songs in the Kumaon district.

Nomadism

They are usually grouped together in *khandans* of related families. They have lived, and many still live, in bender tents on vacant ground, but some have bought houses as well as using the tent for their season of migrations. But their personal belongings are few, perhaps carried in a metal trunk, and the women make mud brick shelves and cupboards wherever they are. Many migrate to the villages for the wheat harvest in April and May and the rice harvest in October and November, where they will work on the harvest as well as performing their traditional occupations. In between they will return to the urban area, where the wedding season runs from October to March. They are in conflict with landowners who evict them from urban sites, but also with other Mirasi who take patrons from them. They are proud of the independence that their semi-nomadic lifestyle gives them. They often live close to other semi-nomadic peoples, such as the Qalandar.

Society

Their society consists of patrilinear clans, or *biraderi*, of a number of *khandans* who provide a network of relatives over quite wide areas. The elders decide marriages and other matters. Women are married early to cousins in another *khandan*, and go to live there with the parents of the husband. Their earnings at weddings and other family celebrations of their patrons are higher in the winter months. Many today are moving into all forms of unskilled work in building, farming, laboring or portering, as well as begging. They also sell balloons or work as day laborers. Mirasis have a low literacy level around Lahore.

Religion

Almost all the Mirasis are Muslims, but practical religion is a matter of seeking help from living or dead saints, called *pirs*, or holy men called *faqirs*, who are thought to perform miracles. They go on pilgrimages to the tombs of the saints for guidance in life's problems, to appease supernatural powers and for healing. Amulets are given out for different problems, such as success in business or illness. The springtime anniversary of the death of Shah Hussain

and Madho is a great celebration for the Mirasi, with a festival of music and dancing. They fear spirits and demons, and many of their practices are animistic.

Outreach

Some had intermittent contact with Christian missionaries before the partition of the country and retain some Christian teaching. A group near Lahore read their Bibles regularly, but they have received little support.[78] The Association for Community Training Services does humanitarian work, such as literacy, educational and community health programs among this people.

KANJAR

In Pakistan, they are nomadic makers of *papier mâché* or terracotta toys and paper flowers. They travel carrying their goods on donkeys or in mule carts. The women tour the streets calling children to take the toys in exchange for money or some food. The women are aggressive sellers and account for most of the income. They tend to be dominant in Kanjar society and are considered a threat in Muslim areas. The Kanjar men supplement the income from the toys and flowers by giving children rides on small merry-go-rounds and Ferris wheels at their camps, while the adults will be entertained by the women dancing and singing. The men usually provide the music. Begging and prostitution are also regular sources of income. The Kanjar avoid thieving, so as not to prejudice a return to the neighborhood.

The Kanjar have a concept of brotherliness of co-operation and mutual support that binds the "tents" or households traveling together. The composition of a traveling group is more on the basis of shared skills in the group, rather than by shared descent. Because all the members, including very young children, contribute to the income, decisions are taken together. They live in a tent of grass or reed mats, which the wife owns. This is a simple structure that can be rolled up and carried by a donkey or in a cart. In relation to the public the men are expected to be supportive but the women aggressive, yet within the camp there is a remarkable equality between them. The bride-price for a Kanjar is high, equal to several years of earnings. This leads to many first-cousin marriages, presumably because the money circulates back to the parents from the uncles. Their children who show the most talent as musicians and dancers are sold into professional Kanjar communities in the larger cities as entertainers and prostitutes. These can go on to be prosperous.[79] There is no known Christian witness among them.

SIRAIKI, or the Riasiti Gypsies

The Riasiti are 15 million non-pastoral Gypsies in Pakistan. Their other name is *Siraiki*. The Riasitis were the original inhabitants of Bahawalpur, the southern part of the Punjab. When the Punjabis moved south in the early twentieth century, many Riasitis sold their land for cash, and then were reduced to a peripatetic life as shepherds, migrant farm laborers, basket weavers, trinket sellers, circus workers, breeders of hunting dogs, and trainers of bears and monkeys. They are constantly mobile, so sustained contact with the same family group is often difficult. They are Muslims, but they trust more in *taweez*, or amulets, and *pirs*, or holy men. Their language is Siraiki, which is spoken by many others totaling about 35 million. A Bible translation is underway and the books of Genesis and Jonah are ready. Only about 20% of the Riasitis can read, but there is an active literacy movement. A Baptist church and SIM are ministering to them. Community health care is also a need that is being met.[80]

MARWARI

The Marwari travel selling toys and knick-knacks such as razors, soap and combs in the region around Hyderabad, Pakistan. There are about 50,000 people who speak Manwari in Sind and Rajasthan, most of them agricultural workers for Muslim landlords. They are both Hindus and Muslims. Bible portions are available and there are a number of Bhil Christians.[81]

SIRKIWAS

They are traveling basket and broom makers in Pakistan, but outsiders call them Chungar. They also make and sell toys of cloth and reeds. But most Chungar are beggars and scavengers of iron, glass, paper and rags in major urban areas. They sell what they collect to manufacturers. In the harvest times they will travel between the villages to sieve the grain. They live in tents constructed of woven grass or reed mats.[82]

CHURIGAR

In Pakistan, they are peddlers of bangles and jewelry. They are based in a town and move periodically around a circuit of villages, living in a small tent at night.[83]

JOGI, or *Saperas*

In Punjab and Sind, Pakistan, they are itinerant snake charmers, medicine makers and peddlers. They camp in bender-tents owned by the wives. There are many itinerant specialized sections including the *Bharatri*, who are wandering bards and their families; the *Manihari* peddlers; the *Rita Bikanath* who make and sell soap; and the *Patbina* who make thread and string bags in honor of the god Shiva. The *Vaidu* are beggars and sellers of traditional medecines and the *Nath* are snake charmers and conjurers. They tend to constantly change their routes to find crowds that have not seen their entertainment before. They also show hunting dogs. They are both Hindus and Muslims.[84]

BE-DA

Be-da, thought to mean "those separated," are peripatetics in Ladakh, living by begging. They claim that their ancestor renounced his inheritance and separated from his family, and so they are condemned to wander.

CHARAN

They are nomadic unskilled agricultural laborers and carriers traveling through the villages in the Punjab and Sind, Pakistan and the Indian Punjab. The name *charan* is

30a

30b

30 Riasiti:
    a. Riasiti Gypsies originated as dispossessed farmers in Pakistan in the early twentieth century.
    b. Riasiti children (Photos: G. Feldmann).

derived from *charana*, "grazing," or the Sanskrit for wanderer. They are often considered to be part of the Banjaras. In Gujarat they are found in all the districts and are divided into four groups totaling 1,500. In the past they were attached to princely courts and acted as guards to accompany travelers, because it was considered bad luck to kill them. They are cattle herders and agriculturalists. Some groups travel as bards and genealogists, and are also called Gadhavi. The Charan are often carriers, and Berland considers them to be the same as the Banjaras in India.[85] They have close relations with the Bharwad and Rabari. They speak Gujarati and are Hindus.[86]

SANSI

They are a people of nomadic unskilled laborers traveling from village to village to help with the harvest in Pakistan and India. There are 21,500 in Haryana who work on construction sites and canals. The Sansi sell natural remedies and charms against illness, and some are genealogists, but most of their income is from begging. In Lahore they work as hunters and scavengers. The nomadic Sansi look down on those that have become sedentary. They believe that they became nomadic to avoid conversion to Islam. In Punjab, they consider that they came from Rajasthan and were expelled by the Muslims. In Rajasthan, they work in cycle repairing, shoe shining and prostitution. They speak Sansi, which has similarities to Uru, but in Madhya Pradesh they use Hindi.[87]

BARAR, Burar, Berar or Bard

They are makers of baskets, combs, reed mats, wheat separators and winnowing fans. They also beg. They live in the Punjab in Pakistan and India (5,000) and Himachal Pradesh (3,000). They are landless.[88]

LALI FAQIR

They are beggars in the Punjab, but they now work as cardboard and paper collectors, as day laborers and in public services such as the railways and water and sewage works, and also selling fruit. Some own houses,

land and buffaloes, but some, like other nomad groups, have similar wealth in portable form such as jewelry. They often claim to be either Muslims or Christians, having made a group decision for one or the other at some time in the past, but they have little or no contact with the institutions of these religions. Along with Muslim amulets and vows to *pirs*, they continue to hold to Hindu and animistic ideas.[89]

BHANDI, Bahurupia and Naqqal

They are jesters, storytellers, quick-change artists and mimics who are both Muslims and Hindus in Kashmir. The 12,000 in Rajasthan now work in other employment. They speak Manwari, Punjabi and Hindi.[90]

CHANGAR

The Changar in Pakistan are nomadic reed weavers of baskets, winnowing pans, brooms and fishnets.

GOGRA

The Gogra are scavengers in the major towns and cities of Pakistan and northern India and resell the gathered paper, iron, rags and glass. They also work in the harvests. They are both Hindu and Muslim.[91]

BAZIGAR

They are traditionally acrobats and jugglers. Their name comes from *Bazi*, which is an annual show. Often the name is used as a synonym for the Nat in India, but a popular distinction is that the Bazigars are said to be more tumblers rather than tightrope artists. The Bazigar travel in Lahore and the Indian Punjab, where they are called *Badi* and their community totals between 120,000 and 180,000. Some are sedentary but travel to fairs and festivals. There are 84,724 in Haryana, 2,083 settled in Chandigarh, and 696 in Delhi. There are 1,716 in Himachal Pradesh, where they are said still to migrate using portable reed huts. In Chandigarh half are still performing, but in Himachal Pradesh they have ceased to do acrobatics to live from begging and hawking. In Rajasthan there are 30,888, where they form a community of dancers, singers and acrobats, but it is unknown whether they are itinerant. Acrobatics is still a major occupation in the Punjab. In Bihar there are 33,112, but many of them have given up doing acrobatics. Some Bazigar in Lahore are Muslims.[92]

OD, Beldar, Oud or Oudh

They are families of vagrants seeking casual labor, especially in digging or road-building and masonry, but many have turned to agriculture and are more settled. There are 55,000 living in the state of Haryana, and neighboring parts of Punjab (6,500), Himachal Pradesh and Chandigarh. In the south they are called Odde. The men do the digging and the women carry away the earth. They change marriage partners freely, many men are polygamous, and the women are said to be only restricted to up to 18 husbands! They allow a widow to remarry up to seven times. They have a vow to explain their nomadism, that they are never to drink from the same well twice, and so either have to dig or move on. They bury their dead, instead of cremating them, because they say their ancestor dug a well so deep that he was buried alive. Some are Hindus and others Muslims. The Od in Punjab speak Odki, and some Hindi or Punjab. Those in Haryana speak Haryanvi. There appears to be another group called Oudh who are pastoralists and caravaners.[93]

TALABDA KOLI SALAT

In Gujarat and Rajasthan, these are traveling millstone makers, the Salat, who also make images and other domestic articles. There are other sections of the Salat, such as the Sompura, who are temple sculptors.[94]

BHAT, Bhata, Raja Bhat or Bhatrazu

They travel in Gujarat, Rajasthan and Madhya Pradesh and Orissa. They have many names, and in Gujarat they are also known as Bahrot. In the south they are called Bhatrazu. The name is derived from *bhatta*, "lord," because they were originally Brahman who took up a secular life as genealogists. When they worked for a prince

they received a tenth of his income and so are also called Dasaundhi, or "tenth people". The *Charan* are part of the caste. Traditionally they are puppeteers and sellers of bangles. They also enact a play-horse dance of a bridegroom going to his wedding. There are a large number of sub-sections with different names and traditional functions, such as flag bearers, ushers, drummers, anointers, gardeners, and so on, and most beg as the accepted method of payment. Most are Hindus, but there is a Sunni Muslim minority practicing a mixture of both religions.[95]

PADHAR

They live near Lake Nal in Gujarat. They work as fishermen from August to January, and they migrate to collect roots, birds and wild animals the rest of the year. The tribe has a dance in which the women whirl about balancing a *thali*, or metal dish, on their open hand by centrifugal force.[96]

TURI

The 17,000 Turi are genealogists, drummers and dancers in Gujarat. The *Barot Turi* keep the family records of castes like the Chamaar, by visiting their clients every two or three years. As traveling entertainers, they enact the play called *Bhavai*. Their language is Gujarati. The *Betra Turi* are also itinerant basket makers and make many other articles in bamboo. The Turi are also in West Bengal (38,000), Oriisa (10,000), and Rajasthan (2,700). In Bihar they number 117,000, where they speak Sadri, and Christian cassettes are available. They are Hindus and there are about 300 Christians.[97]

KALBELIA, Madari, Garudi, Wadi or Vadi

They are traditionally nomadic and number 41,000 in southern Rajasthan. The *Daliwal Kalbelia* men are nomadic snake charmers, snake catchers, fortunetellers and magicians traveling in rural parts of Gujarat (12,000), Rajasthan (11,200), and in Bombay, where they are called Garudi. Those in Delhi and Rajasthan total over 30,000, and are called Kalbelia or Dalwal. They claim that they were Jogi who turned to a nomadic life because their guru, Gorakh Nath, commanded it.

They have two clans, or *wadis*, named after two ancestors, Lal and Phul. They travel in nuclear families and catch snakes, monkeys and bears for traveling shows. They will beg from door to door with the animals. After a conjuring trick they will say that "This is not *judu* (magic), but sleight-of-hand." The Kabelia also prepare and sell herbal medicines. Many now have other occupations, such as stone cutting. The women both play music and dance with their faces veiled, mimicking the movements of the snake. They are usually found in the marketplaces and avoid a settled life and own no land. They are monogamous and prohibit divorce, but when there is a divorce the wife is compensated. The **Mewara Kalbelia** are grindstone makers.

They are followers of Zinad Shah Madar, who lived in the eleventh century and is supposed to be still alive, and gives protection from snakebites. The Madari are shunned by other castes as dirty, and they live isolated lives. They have lost out in education and welfare programs because of their nomadism.[98] Their language is Mawari, for which there is an old New Testament translation which is out of print. Portions of a new translation for new readers are ready.[99]

MEGHWAL

These people dispose of the carcasses of animals, tan the hides and make articles from the leather, including shoes. They have four tribes, which are in turn divided into clans: *Marwar* or *Sodha Meghwal*, *Gujarat Meghwal*, *Charania Meghwal* and *Mahishree Meghwal*. There are 178,000 living in Kutch, and Jam Nagar in Gujarat, where they originated. There are 890,000 in northwestern districts of Rajasthan, where they are also known as Meghbangsi, or Megh. There are 30,000 living in the towns of Maharashtra and 16,000 in the Khargone District and other western districts of Madhya Pradesh. The number engaged in their traditional work varies from place to

place. Their language is Gujarati. The *Jesus* film is available in Gujarati. There are 3,000 Christians in Gujarat, 225 in Madhya Pradesh and 6,000 in Rajasthan.[100]

NAT

There are 30,900 Nats living in Rajasthan; 5,300 in Haryana; 124,400 in Uttar Pradesh; 58,700 in Madhya Pradesh; 33,000 in Bihar; and 5,000 in West Bengal and most parts of India. In Rajasthan, they are dancers, acrobats and singers and have three divisions called Mala, Bidu and Chaddi, each divided into clans. The unmarried girls often practice prostitution. They have many myths to explain their lifestyle with the similar theme of a prince once demanding that their ancestors perform some nearly impossible feat. When they were close to performing it, the prince had them killed. They worship Hanuman, the monkey god, and Hulki-Mai, the goddess of cholera, as well as Kali. They also revere their acrobatic equipment. In Uttar Pradesh and Madhya Pradesh, they tend to do agricultural work, metal work and menial jobs. In Bihar, they have changed from acrobatics to peddling herbal medicines and begging, although more than half work in agriculture. Their language is Hindi. There are less than 200 Christians in Uttar Pradesh.[101]

JOKHARA, VAIDU, BAIDYA and SINGIWAL

Jokhara are traveling Muslim medicine men, who breed leeches (*jonk*) which they carry around in earthen pots to bleed their patients. *Baidya* and *Vaidu* are occupational terms for medicine men who come from a number of different castes, and they seem to be associating closer together as a group in some places. The Baidya diagnose by feeling the pulse, "reading" the face and divination, and they prescribe herbal remedies. *Singiwala*, meaning "man with a horn," suck blood with a horn and treat snake bites.[102]

GADUL(Y)IA LOHARS, Gadia Lohar, Lohpitt, Chittoriya Lohar, Bhubalia or Kunwar Khati

They are a traveling blacksmith community in north India. The name comes from the

ANNUAL CYCLE OF THE GADULYIA LOHAR, NORTH INDIA

March	April	May	June	July	August	Sept	Oct	Nov	Dec	Jan	Feb
Hot season			*Rains begin*	*Heavy Monsoon Rains*		*Less Rain*	*Some Rain*	*Dry, cool to cold with chilly nights*			
Poor time for blacksmith work			Family groups on circuit 2-4 families together	Muddy Roads		Visit fairs to trade in bullocks		Small family groups scatter to client circuits for 5 months at roadside working as blacksmiths			
Breeding and selling bullocks to villages											
District groups camp together (c. 200 families together)			Winter crops harvested	District Group camps together				Minstrels for weddings and Hindu festivals			
			Farmers can pay to repair tools	Panchayat council Marriages etc. arranged							

31a

31b

31c

31 Gadulyia Lohar:
   a.   Two families of Gadulyia Lohar in Uttar Pradesh, India – the ox cart in the background is their home.
   b. + c. Many Gadulyia Lohar are born, live and die in and around their ox cart.

Hindi *loha*, meaning "iron," and they are to be distinguished from the many sedentary blacksmiths. They claim to be Rajasthani, because they originated there, but they form a distinct people with their own traditions and way of life. They call themselves the *Gadulyia* in Rajasthan and *Shilpkar* in Himachal Pradesh and Uttar Pradesh. Often the *Shilpkar* are considered a separate group.

Family life

The name *Gadulyia* is derived from the *gadis*, referring to the open bullock carts in which they travel and live. To be a Lohar one must have been born one — when camped at the roadside in or under the ox-cart. The carts are of a distinctive construction, with heavy wooden wheels, and the sides have inset panels. The family live at the roadside, where they also work. They either sleep in tents of black tarpaulin at the side of the cart or in the carts with a covering awning. Usually the Lohar construct low mud brick walls for some privacy.

They marry only other Lohars, but from another band. They are monogamous and divorce is rare. All marriages are arranged years beforehand, often when they are still children, with the partners not even knowing each other. Bangles are worn as tokens of marriage. The remarriage of widows and divorced women is common, although other Hindus frown it upon. The women grind the grain, bake and raise the children, but unlike many Indian women they have contact with other people, including men. This is because the women share the iron working equally with the men. A wife often swings the hammer or works the bellows for her husband until her sons are old enough to help. The Lohar supplement their income by the sale of bullocks and cattle. Some Lohar use camels.

The Lohar shun idleness, often working a ten-hour day for a meager income. Keeping a household and business on the roadside is difficult and unhealthy. Many of their prime camping sites for business have been taken for other purposes. Some villages have given them a plot of land to build a one-room house as a local base. Even those who have

houses tend to store the equipment in the house and camp outside it. Otherwise they travel and live in or by their bullock carts. The male Lohar wears a large red turban while his father is alive, white when he is dead. He wears a full mustache, but no beard.

Each family is economically independent, and they consider that five people are needed to do the work, so that most of the family are involved in one way or another. They make and mend all kinds of agricultural implements, tent pegs, cartwheel rims, shoes for horses and bullocks, and a variety of iron and copper bowls. They are renowned for "fixing the English iron," which means inserting new edges into old ax blades. Circular air bellows serve the small forge.

Nomadism

They are found in small nomadic family groups in Gujarat, Rajasthan, Punjab, Haryana, Madhya Pradesh and Maharashtra. Such groups can be seen in places like Rishikesh, south Delhi and Ghaziabad, and they are known to travel as far as eastern Uttar Pradesh. They are also found in Sind, southwest Pakistan, but are called Lori. The majority travel in rural areas. They number 146,000 in Himachal Pradesh alone. The Shilkar in Uttar Pradesh number 684,786, divided into various occupational divisions, of which some are Lohar, but these are not related to the Gadulyia who are said to total 21,000 in the state. A survey of these different groups is needed.

The families are formed into bands that belong to a district group and that take the name of the region. Each band has its own route within the region according to the annual cycle. After six months on the road and living by the roadside, they spend from March to May camping together and concentrating on selling bullocks, because this time is poor for blacksmith work. In June each group divides up into bands of three to a dozen families, each family with a cart. Each band has its own circuit of about 80 kilometers (50 mi.) with a regular schedule of visiting certain sites in towns and villages for a few days. This is a good time for custom because the farmers have their winter harvest gathered, and so have funds and need implements repaired to sow their next crop. News of their arrival in an area spreads quickly. They form long-term patron-client relationships with farmers, and if a family group cannot fulfill the schedule, another family band takes their place.

During the monsoon in July-August, the district group congregates together again near towns or villages — partly because this is a poor time for the smith's work, and partly because the roads are impassable. As many as 200 families may camp together, and it is a time to renew family ties and make new tools. September is the time to arrange marriages and settle bride-prices, which often involves the councils. Each band or clan will have its own *panchayat*, or council of leaders or representatives — one from each traveling family group. These settle disputes about work, bride-prices and even clothing styles. In September they visit the bullock fairs to trade in bullocks, after which they divide up into their family groups to work around the route of work sites and patrons until February, when the district families gather to camp together again.

Traditions

The Lohar are nomads who are conscious of once being settled and who took up nomadism in special historical circumstances. Their traditions claim that they were originally Rajput warriors and weapon makers in the fort of Chittaurgarh, southern Rajasthan. When the fort was under siege by the great Muslim leader Akbar in 1568, they saw defeat was inevitable and fled by a secret doorway. For this reason, they believe the goddess Kali uttered a curse on them and condemned them to a wandering life.

As a nomadic people they took five vows. They are never to return to Chittaurgarh, never to live in houses, never to use a light at night, never to sleep in cots, and never to use a rope to draw water. They believe the goddess Kali Mata might kill

them if they settle. In practice, the only vow kept today is never to live in a house. This notion of misbehavior in the historical past as the motive for nomadism appears to be a pattern found in many peripatetics.

Religion

They are a fervent Hindu community and participate in all the Hindu festivals, especially through music. They worship Ram as a hero god and have a special relationship with the goddess Kali Mata of Chittaurgarh. They carry a small image of her in the *thalia*, or cupboard, on their carts, where they keep stores and valuables. In addition each band worships its own deity and each family offers daily prayers to the god of the anvil. They worship new tools and say Shiva gave them the anvil. They use rotary blowers to avoid using cowhide bellows, which they see as unclean. They probably emphasize their Hinduism in order to be anti-Muslim. The caste system places them at different levels according to the district they move in. Their status means that their women cannot draw water from the wells of the very villagers that depend on them for their craft.

In 1955 the Indian government attempted to settle all nomadic groups, starting with the Lohars. A convention brought the Lohars back to Chittaurgarh for the first time in four centuries. Prime Minister Nehru led the Lohars in procession into the city, so breaking their vow. Their women feared the men would die, but nothing happened to them! A dozen colonies were established, but many families found it too expensive to build houses. Most did not take to farming. The scheme foundered because of lack of resources, poor land, and the Lohars' inadequate retraining as farmers. However, they are aware that the specialized economic niche that they have had for centuries is becoming more limited and that their own standard of living is declining compared to that of some rural settled people.

Language

Gade Lohar or Farasi is their language, which is a mixture of Marwari, Mewari and Gujarati, although a full survey of this language is yet to be done. Some claim to speak Adiwasi Girasia, a Bhil language from Rajasthan, among themselves. They readily speak Hindu to outsiders. Literacy is low, but one recent report claims it has increased considerably among them.

Outreach

No specific Christian outreach is being done among them. The Lohars blend into the roadside scene, yet because they are mobile a special effort has to be made to contact and befriend them. Because of their short stays and the social barriers between them and the other castes, they have little contact with the few Christians in north India. Unless someone makes it their special ministry to reach them, they will not hear the gospel. A study of their schedules and sites and the befriending of specific families is needed, including following groups to their different sites. There is a need to discover ways of making their itinerant work more economically viable, and to provide hygiene and basic health care. Some have been sub-contracted by industry to make articles for the factories. They value education for their children, so this, too, is a need.[103]

Lohar, Madhya Pradesh: A backward caste of *Lohar* or *Panchal* of Madhya Pradesh who number about 758,000, they are found in most districts of the state. Some of them travel from village to village as blacksmiths, although they may not be related to the Rajasthani people above.[104]

Lohar, Pakistan, is a similar traveling caste of nomadic blacksmiths and tinkers.

SIKLIGARS, Saqalgar, or Bardhia

They are traveling blacksmiths specializing in cold forming techniques, repairing domestic utensils, grinding knives, making locks and keys and also cowbells for the pastoralists in Kuchchh. They are also found elsewhere in Gujarat, in Rajasthan, around Delhi (8,500), in Haryana (6,400), Punjab (4,400), and in Himachal Pradesh (800). Their original occupation was polishing armor and sharpening weapons. They have occupational subgroups such as the *Siyahmaliya*, working in black ironwork, and the *Kachloyiha*, working in impure iron. They use donkeys for transport rather than ox-carts. Only the men and boys work, the girls being kept at home to do domestic work with their mothers. They speak Punjabi and Hindi and are Hindus, except in Himachal Pradesh where they are Sikhs.[105]

BANSPHOR, Benbansi Bansphor, Dhulia or Burud

The name means "bamboo-splitters," and they travel making and selling baskets, birdcages, cane chairs and cradles, sieves and fans, and mats in Uttar Pradesh (18,500), Rajasthan (4,700), Arunachal Pradesh and Assam. They are called Dhulia or Burud in Maharashtra. They consider themselves to belong to the large Dom caste and also have a number of totemistic sects or clans. They speak Bhojpuri and Hindi. There are a few recent conversions among the Bhojpuri people, who speak that language. The *Dharkar*, *Munjkut* or *Vanvat* are rope makers.[106]

RAJIS

They live in Pithoragarh, Uttar Pradesh and Nepal. They have between 60 and 78 families and some 24 of these have been settled in villages since 1980. They make wooden bowls, pots and rope from grass and products of the forest, which they exchange for other commodities. Because of their limited slash-and-burn cultivation in the forests, they have been driven out by the forest department.[107]

BAJANIYA, Bajenia Nat, Karnat, or Kannala

They live in Uttar Pradesh and Delhi, northern India, and are traditionally troupes of acrobats and tightrope dancers. Some are landless and still itinerant, but at least half have settled and have their own agricultural plots. They claim to have been warriors in Rajasthan, but moved eastwards to avoid

32 The Peripatetics or Commercial Nomads are often forgotten as they blend into rural and urban life. South Asia has many different such groups, for instance these basket makers living at the roadside in Uttar Pradesh, North India.

being forcibly converted to Islam. *Baja* is the music the men beat on drums and the women sing. The women and girls dance on a portable tightrope and perform acrobatics. They used to engage in prostitution. The men show films with a bioscope. They speak their own language of Banjania among themselves. They are Hindus and also worship their ancestors.[108]

CHAMAARS

This is a populous "untouchable" caste who were leather workers, but who are now mostly agricultural laborers or day workers in the towns. In Uttar Pradesh they number over 13,000,000; in Rajasthan 2,500,000; in Bihar 4,000,000; in West Bengal 945,700; and in Orissa 146,000.[109]

There are a number of nomadic sub-castes:

The first is the **Siyar Marwa**, or jackal killers. The jackal is usually killed by setting a trap with a small explosive device in it, or by imitating the distress call then clubbing those that respond. They cut the meat into strips, preserve it by drying it, and eat it as required.

The **Chamaar Mungta** make a living by begging, both in the cities and in villages. They travel in small family groups, camping in a village for days at a time. They also earn some money by working as ear cleaners in the cities, plying that trade in busy areas such as railway stations. The ear-cleaning method involves the use of oil and hand-made cotton swabs. Apparently they are territorial, with each family group being assigned a particular group of villages from which to make their living.

The **Kangkali** are traveling musicians. The **Patharkat** make grinding stones and hawk various goods around the villages. These groups never build huts but camp under trees and stay for a few days, especially at harvest time. Each village on the north India plains has at least one large grove of mango trees in an open space. This functions as a sort of village square or public area. Here farmers often build their haystacks of rice straw, wheat straw, and so on. Peripatetic groups camp here under the trees. The size of these groups is unknown.[110]

NANDIWALA

There are 2,500 Nandiwala in Maharashtra, India. They were primarily entertainers with trained bulls, and they do acrobatics and tell fortunes. More recently some of them have moved into trading the bulls. They are still nomadic. Every three years they camp in tents together outside the village of Wadapuri, Pune District, even though they have no other connection with it. The villagers benefit from the dung of thousands of bulls for fertilizer and fuel and tolerate the cutting of grass for fodder in return. They take the cattle of the villagers in the Deccan, which often suffers drought, to distant pastures for fattening. They speak a dialect of Telegu among themselves, although they speak Marathi to outsiders. They are Hindu but non-vegetarian. Each family sacrifices a pig twice a year to the spirit of Ram Mamma, a Nandiwala who was killed in about 1920 by fellow caste members. They eat the pork, which results in them not being considered a clean caste.[111]

KOLHATI, Dandewala or Bansberia

The Kolhati of Central India are acrobats who use bamboo poles, similar to those of the Nats. Their women are nimble dancers.[112]

DURGIMURGIWALA

They travel around as families, displaying ornamented idols of the gods in return for offerings. The idols are carried in painted boxes on buffaloes or on the heads of their wives. The box is set down and opened to reveal the god, and while the wife drums, the man sings Hindu hymns and whips himself until he draws blood, while the children collect the alms. The performance is considered to please the gods.[113]

GONDHALI

They travel as begging musicians in Maharashtra and other central states of India. They are employed to provide entertainment at weddings and other occasions. The name refers to a dance of confused noise that is dedicated to the goddess Devi. Four men perform it, two drummers and a dancer making fun of the fourth, the bearer of the "sacred flame." Men from other castes can join the Gondhali to fulfill a vow to the goddess, going around begging on Tuesdays, but otherwise continuing in their original occupations.[114]

PARDHAN or *Dewar*

They are a caste of semi-nomadic street singers, snake charmers and monkey trainers. They also buy and sell household garbage and rear pigs. There are 6,600 living and traveling around Chhattisgarh, northwest Madhya Pradesh. They are a section of the Gond and act as their priests and minstrels, and they have a three-year itinerary to visit their Gond patrons. They say they became nomadic because the queen of their Raja died in tragic circumstance. Most are now only seasonally nomadic. They worship their *sarangi* stringed instrument. When they move camp, their idols are carried in baskets above the heads of a man and a woman, and they sacrifice a goat to the god of marriage. Holi, the spring festival, is their most important gathering, which they celebrate in their home villages. They are completely different from the Dewar of Orissa, who are fishermen.[115]

BIRHOR

The Birhor, also known as *Mankind*, are an example of nomadic rope makers in Bihar, Orissa and Madhya Pradesh, India. Their myths claim that they have to wander because their ancestor, the eldest son and heir of a king, was beaten in a horse race by his younger brother and so lost the throne.

Nomadism

Like the Gypsies, they consider that for them to be dependent on a sedentary employer is demeaning, and in Indian society this would involve being in a low caste. Therefore they maintain their "self-employed" status by trade with sedentary

people. They get resources in the forests, by hunting or gathering, and turn them into products such as horns, bones and skins sold for their supposed medicinal or magical properties. Some Birhor claim to have magical power, gain followers, and go around begging. They also hunt monkeys, hares and porcupines for sale.

Each household is economically independent and can migrate alone or with other related families. They walk everywhere, and the head of the family will carry most of their belongings on the ends of a pole across his shoulders. The itinerary of each family is unique and usually circular, but determined by access to the forest and to new customers. They camp in one place for perhaps two to four weeks, except during the monsoon when they stay in one place for longer. The winter is the best time for their trade and for the gathering of products in the forest.[116]

BHOPA, CHITRAKATHI, GARUDA and KILLEKEYATA

For centuries, traveling families in India have acted out religious plays and stories in the open air. They recite the stories of the gods and the exploits of traditional heroes, holding up painted sheets or scrolls. The sheets and scrolls are handed down from generation to generation in the family. Nowadays they also depict many secular and modern themes, such as Indian political heroes and contemporary events. The actors stimulate the interest of the crowds by introducing variations into the well-known stories, which often allude to local personalities or events.

The *Bhopa* are one such group of actors in Rajasthan, who begin and end each performance with an act of worship. The stories tend to be about heroes on horseback, painted on cloth sheets about two meters wide and some ten meters long. A special group paints the sheets. They do not paint the story in the right sequence, so the performance has an element of surprise to it. The storytellers, often a man and his wife, run backwards and forwards to point to various parts of the pictures. At night the wife will illuminate only the relevant part of the panel with a lamp. It is bad luck not to complete the story. A musician accompanies the story with song and dance.

The *Garuda* are a section of priests from some castes that travel, putting on the plays in Gujarat. Their scrolls are on paper only about 30 centimeters wide and between three and six meters long. The actor slowly unrolls the scrolls as he relates the story.

The *Chitrakathi*, literally "people with picture stories," travel in Maharashtra. The men paint their own pictures and their women dance with a brass plate that make a droning sound. They are also called *Haridas* after their god, Hari.

The *Jarana patachitra* in Bengal paint their own scrolls on paper.

The *Killekeyata*, or *Katbu*, travel giving shadow theater in Karnataka and Andhra Pradesh and southwards. They perform parts of the main Hindu poems, the *Ramayana* and *Mahabarata*, telling the story using the shadows of figures cut out of hide on a screen silhouetted from behind by a lamp.[117]

KEWATS

Found in a number of states, they are traditionally boatmen and fishermen, but many have turned to other trades. For example in the Allahabad Division of Uttar Pradesh, the traditional fishermen and ferrymen took up sari weaving, after a dam was built which reduced the water in the Ganges. Here we describe a semi-nomadic group of about 5,000 jute weavers in northern Maharashtra State. They are thought to be found only in the Aurangabad, Buldhana and Jalgaon districts of the state.

The Maharashtra weavers are said to have come to the state 300 years ago, as part of an invading army from Rajasthan, and stayed to become a caste of jute basket weavers. It is not known whether this is a case of a nomadic group adopting a new occupation. During the monsoon they live in 42 different villages, most in Aurangabad, to weave their bags and sacks. Each village has about 20 families. They have adopted the dress of the surrounding people so that they are often indistinguishable, except for their ornaments using designs from Kathiwad or Kathiawar in Gujarat. They also wear the sari in a different way from the local women. These Kewats appear to be a case of nomadic adaptation to a new area, while still maintaining their own distinctiveness.

Nomadism

Their main customers are the semi-nomads with animals, such as the Vaidus, Laman, Dhangar shepherds, and other groups such as the Kaikadi, Vadar and Madari and others. Many of these may camp for months near a village and also work as farm laborers. These Kewats themselves do not keep any animals, but they travel to the places where the nomads meet annually, such as the fair at Madhi, in Maharashtra State. This is the only time that these semi-nomads are in one place for any length of time, when they renew their vows to their gods, bathing the images and offering sacrifices of goats. The councils, or *panchayats*, of elders decide various disputes at the fair. The Kewats spend their time here selling jute bags, rugs and carpets. Therefore the Kewat continually travel to fairs and markets and wherever the pastoralists gather.

In winter, the Kewats grow their own jute for the basket weaving. As they do not own any land themselves, they have to hire wasteland from villages within 80 kilometers (50 mi.) of their own village to grow the jute. They camp near their crops for three months, from November to January. They harvest the jute and soak it in a nearby river to separate the fibers, then they dry and store it in their houses.

The Kewats' summer activity is cultivating watermelons and other vegetables on the riverbanks in a different area. Whole groups of families camp for the months of March and April near these plots. These plots are in areas where the river level has receded during the hot weather. Since they are cheap to rent, the income from selling these crops to wholesalers around the markets is a worthwhile supplement to the jute weaving. Neither the jute nor the watermelons require very fertile soil or ties of land ownership or long-term rentals. The Kewats therefore illustrate the common features of a nomadic people — systematic exploitation of marginal resources, dovetailing together different resources according to the season, and having no permanent ties with the surrounding society. They combine the typical seasonal work with opportunistic flexibility. The growing areas are all within the three districts within 80 kilometers (50 mi.) of their villages.

After the sale of the melons and other fruit they return to their villages to spend the rainy season from May to October weaving baskets, pack bags for animals, sacks for grain, carpets, mattresses and seed bags. The headman of each family travels over a much wider area of the whole of Maharashtra to sell both melons and the woven goods. He hires the plots of land and arranges sales at the fairs and markets, and spends most of the year away from his family. He may often travel along with the nomadic groups that are his customers, especially the Dhangars or shepherds. Products are often exchanged in return for woolen goods. The rest of the family does the planting, harvesting and weaving.[118]

They speak Rajasthani among themselves and Marathi as a trade language. It is not known whether these people have any contact with Christians.

GYPSY

These include groups such as the *Luri* and *Dom*. There are a number of totally unrelated castes or tribes called Dom, and these are not to be confused with the caste that traditionally cremated the dead. The *Dom*, or *Dombara*, have many other names and are nomadic groups distributed over Tamal Nadu. Traditionally they are acrobats and tumblers who migrated from Gujarat and speak Kachhi among themselves. Their usual performance is the pole-dance, accompanied by loud music. They are also farm workers, scavengers and pig breeders. They are divided between the *Kudi Dombara* and the *Reddi Dombara*. The former claim

superior status and do not carry their belongings on donkeys or use ankle bands when performing. Women have considerable equality among them. They are Hindus.[119]

PINJARIS, *Nadafs*

They are found mainly in four states, Maharashtra and Karnataka, and they are called **Dudekula** in Andhra Pradesh and **Panjukottai** in Tamil Nadu. Their population is estimated at about 500,000, or 1.2 million for Karnataka alone. There are said to be 10,000 in Bijapur city in Karnataka. The Pinjaris are of very mixed origins, such as Afghans, Jats and Maratas, who were once soldiers and officials in the Moghul Empire. They are said to be semi-nomadic carders of cotton to stuff pillows and make mattresses, and so on. Most are seeking other work and are very poor. They speak Kannada, Telegu, Tamil and Marathi according to the area. Literacy among them is less than 1%. They are Sunni Muslims of the Hanafi school, and there are also Hindus among them. Tribal Transformations-India is seeking to help them.[120]

SUDUGADU SIDDARU or *Siddha*

They are a semi-nomadic beggar tribe of about 9,000 found in northern Karnataka, India. They used to live in Hindu burial and cremation grounds, with a reputation for practicing witchcraft and sorcery. *Sudugaradu* refers to the grounds, and *siddha* to magical powers. They were considered the "masters" of the disposal of the dead and collected fees for every body buried.

Most Siddha are now based in government settlements with cultivated plots in the southwest of the state, but they are itinerant, seeking alms especially at harvest time, on behalf of their own god, Siddappaji, from whom they are said to be descended. He was supposed to have been resurrected when brought for burial. The men wear saffron *dhotis*, cover their heads with "holy ash," and stand on beds of nails and make predictions about the future. Most of them work, at least for part of the year, in agriculture. Tribal Transformations-India is working among them and are seeing good results. They are also establishing work among needy children.[121]

"GYPSIES"

There are 700 Telegu-speaking peripatetics based around Thambuttegama, Sri Lanka. They work as entertainers, snake charmers, magicians and fortunetellers. In Sri Lanka, a number of them lead a nomadic kind of lifestyle. They work as palm readers, snake charmers, tattoo artists, and so on, and travel from village to village to earn money. The others are more or less settled in different villages, employed as laborers. It is believed that these Gypsies migrated to Sri Lanka from India in the eighteenth century. They speak the Telegu language. They also speak Tamil and Sinhala. About 200 have become Christians through the outreach of a student from Lanka Bible College. He continues to work among them with the help of a local pastor.[122]

Other Examples of Peripatetic Groups in India

The *Baul* are wandering minstrels in Bengal, and are Muslims and Hindus belonging to a mystical sect that draws inspiration from Buddhism, Hinduism and Sufi Islam. They wear ochre robes and are clean-shaven. The *Kamad* are a small caste of traveling jugglers using cymbals in Rajasthan. The *Dhadi* are a caste of balladeers and singers of public eulogies for their patrons, and were once sponsored by a Sikh Guru. They travel in the Punjab. The *Manganiyar* are groups of Muslim genealogists and musicians who play a variety of instruments, including blowing into an earthen pot. They travel mostly in Rajasthan. Although Muslims, the patrons of the *Manganiyar* are Hindu Meghwals and other castes. The **Vaghri** are peddlers in a two-way trade of taking factory goods to rural bazaars to exchange them for rural articles and clothes for the town. The *Vansfoda* bamboo splitters make and sell baskets of all sizes and shapes.[123] The *Kuravar*, Sri Lanka, are a few hundred snake charmers, palm readers, and monkey dancers who speak Telegu and seem to be of Tamil origin. Some have been taught trades and have settled.

BANGLADESHI BOATMEN

Bangladesh has 8,000 kilometers of navigable rivers, covering 30% of the country in the dry season and 70% in the rainy season from June to September. The Delta formed from the Ganges and the Brahmaputra Rivers, called Patma, or Lotus, is probably the world's most complete system of inland waterways. Humankind discovered early that a hundred times more could be carried afloat than what could be transported on the backs of pack-animals or men.[124]

They have the world's largest fleet with the biggest impact on the surrounding society of Bangladesh. There are many different styles of boat, from large schooners that trade across the Bay of Bengal to small canoes and punts on the inland canals. A boat owner and captain is called a *majhi*, and local pilots are *sareng*. These men have a certain status in the river communities. Many of them are nomadic in that they travel the river systems for long periods. Their families live in riverside villages or sometimes on board. Various types of boat, such as the high-prowed *goloi*, the humble *piragua*, or large bamboo rafts 300 meters long, are moved about the rivers. They depend on shippers, called *dalal*, who organize the cargoes and charter them as carriers.

When other national economies are affected by fuel prices or shortages, the poor economy of Bangladesh will be able to continue, because a large part of its transport system relies on its boatmen working with sails, oars and muscle. The crew is often used to pull the boat from the bank in narrow channels. Cargoes of fish, silt (to make bricks or just to make the land), vegetables, reeds, cattle and expensive timber are all precariously balanced on overloaded boats or towed alongside the boats. Monsoons cause the rivers to be turbulent, and in the dry seasons rivers may silt up. There is fog in winter, and on average five major ferries sink every year with about a hundred people drowned. The boatmen are both Muslim and Hindu.

BADHJA, *Bahi* or *Badhi*

River Gypsies form about 50% of all the riverboat people of Bangladesh. They are low-caste Hindus. They migrate from one river to another as extended families selling jewelry and herbal medicines. During the monsoon they take advantage of the high water level to penetrate the remoter villages to peddle their wares, but towards the end of the year the clans come together around rivers such as the Mirpur, Savar and Dhakeswari. They spend most of their lives in their small boats and are noted for keeping them tidy.[125]

SOUTHEAST ASIA

The region of Malaysia, Thailand, Indonesia, Brunei and the Philippines consists of many complex peninsulas and archipelagos, which lend themselves to boat nomadism. But as we have already found, this type of nomadism is not unique to this region.

SEA NOMADS

It is thought that these peoples are remnants of societies that were living in the area prior to the coming of the Malays and Indonesians. They managed to have a continued influence on the latter's rulers by dominating trade between the islands until the arrival of the European colonizers. They could not establish the same relationship with the Portuguese and Dutch and so turned to piracy as a way of resisting colonialism. The names of these groups are functional and are used by many groups of sedentary fishing peoples living near the nomads. So the sea nomads are simply referred to by the name of the land peoples, or as the people of a particular island. The term "Bajau" is often used for all these groups. Another people, the *Bugis*, are a sedentary people in southwest Sulawesi, but the men trade in *praus*, their traditional sailing vessels, for most of the year. The families like to travel and visit relatives, but this does not make them nomadic.

Many communities are still nomadic, traveling in small related groups under the leadership of an elder, traveling considerable distances to fish. Others live ashore, but spend part of the year afloat. They spear fish or hunt sea and coastal animals for sale to Chinese traders. Their contacts with outsiders tend only to be for trade, and they meet prejudice as "outsiders," primitive, "without culture," and are suspected of being pirates and practicing magic. Governments see them as hindrances to modernization and have programs to settle

them. The sea-nomads tend to act to substantiate these fears and maintain their distinct identity. They usually marry only within their own group and live in small communities of related families.

Muslims consider them to be "unclean" because they eat wild pig, keep dogs and have a traditional animistic religion. There are both Muslims and Christians among them.[1]

The *Moken*, *Moklen* or *Mawken* are groups of sea peoples totalling about 5,000 on the Mergui Islands of southern Myanmar and the southwest coast of Thailand. The name means "drowned peoples."[2] A Bible translation for them is in progress.

The *Urak Lawoi*, or "sea people," total about 4,000 and live among the islands on the southwest coast of Thailand. The New Testament was published in Urak Lawoi in 1998.

The *Orang Laut*, meaning "sea peoples," are a group of nomadic boat communities. The *Orang kuala*, or "estuary people," are groups found along the north coast and islands of Sumatra, Indonesia, and southwest Johar, Myanmar. The *Orang suku laut* live on the Riau Archipelago off Singapore and the Anambas Islands, in the South China Sea. The Sekah live on the Bangka and Billiton Islands off eastern Sumatra.

The *Bajau* or *Sama-Bajau* live in boat communities in five different countries: Myanmar, Malaysia, Singapore, Indonesia, and the Philippines. The name refers to a wide range of tribes and communities, with many sub-groups. About 45,000 live in the Sulu Islands of the southern Philippines, and 10,200 are found on the west coast of Brunei and 55,800 on the west and east coasts of Sabah, Malaysia, and Kalimantan. There are 35,000 living in Sulawesi, Indonesia and Nusa Tenggara and southern Moluccas. The total estimated number of the Suku Bajau is about 500,000.

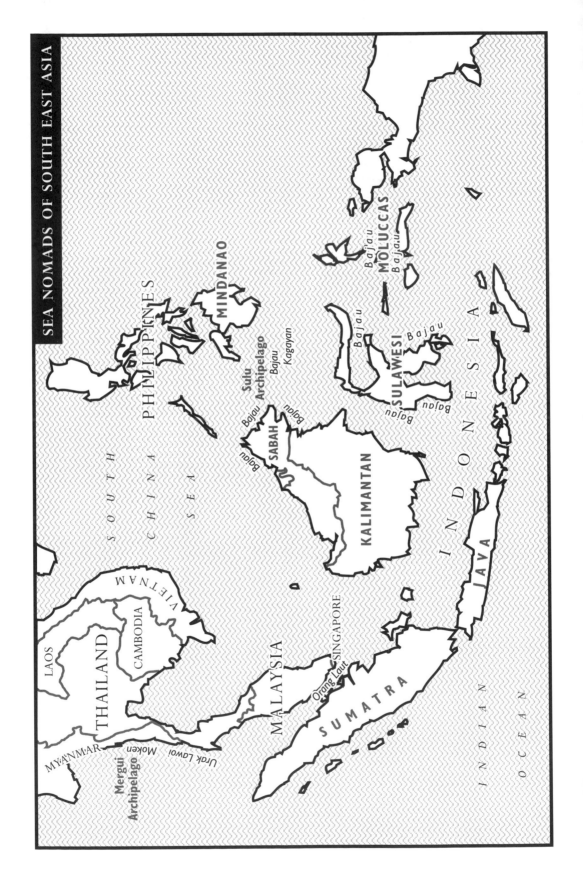

SEA NOMADS OF SOUTH EAST ASIA

Their origins are obscure, but they were once fishermen and pirates and have diversified into forestry, sea trading and some farming. The boat nomads and pirates now live both in boats and in houses on stilts in small villages around the coasts. The men do the seafaring and fishing while the women weave and make pottery. Those that still live in boats will periodically return to a common anchorage to meet relatives, but they spend long periods as nuclear families of five or six people in a boat ten meters long and two meters in the beam. They fish for sea slugs for the Chinese market and many other species. The majority, in contrast to the tradition of piracy, are timid and avoid conflict. They have been pressured by the Indonesian government to settle in coastal villages, but they still continue their maritime pursuits. There are a number of different Bajau languages.

The **Bajau Kagayan** live in the Sulu Islands between Mindanao and Sabah. They have simple villages of houses built on piles, but they spend much of their time in their fishing boats. As other Filipinos have taken over the fishing, they have forced many of the Bajau to move to Sabah to live and fish.

They are Sunni Muslims, but the boat communities have little regular contact with the practices of Islam. Christian radio programs and the *Jesus* film are available. They speak various dialects of Sama or Bajau.

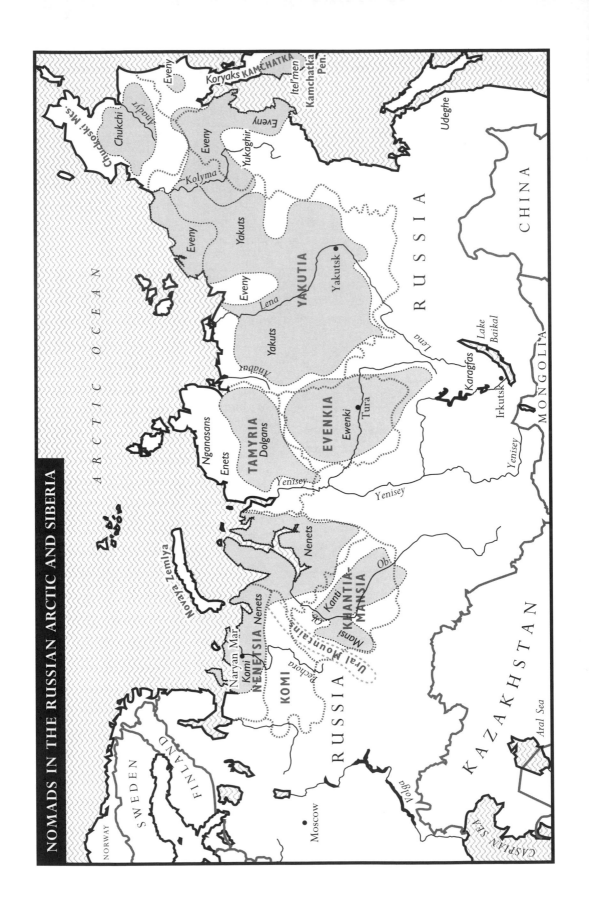

NOMADS IN THE RUSSIAN ARCTIC AND SIBERIA

The RUSSIAN ARCTIC and SIBERIA

"Don't forget those outside the 10/40 Window" warns *Ungodly oppdrag* (YWAM Norway). The Russian Arctic and Siberia, although the same size as the USA and Europe combined, have been inaccessible, and almost unknown, to the modern missionary movement. Even today the southern peoples of the old USSR, the Turkic and Mongol peoples, get more attention than the 26 indigenous non-Russian peoples in the Arctic with a population of about 1,050,000. The concept of the 10/40 Window, the most unreached area of the world, left out this region and should be redefined as "10/80"!

These peoples are nomadic hunter-gathers, pastoralists and fishermen, for the terrain is best used for nomadism. This fragile environment is described by the Russians as *taiga*, meaning birch and conifer forest on permanently frozen ground with very low rainfall, and with too-short summers when the surface is boggy and useless for cultivation. To the north of the tree line is the *tundra*, or rocky open country supporting grasses, mosses and lichens, alternately boggy in the brief summer and frozen the rest of the year, with permanently frozen subsoil.

This region had its colonial period of exclusive Russian expansion, so that it did not benefit from contact with the rest of the world as other post-colonial areas have. Its peoples have been disadvantaged and submerged by an alien and excessively dominant culture, in a situation similar to that of the American Indians. The Soviet period was hostile to the nomadic native peoples of Siberia. Even the identity of the peoples was tampered with, as new "nationalities" were created such as Khahas from the Kachas, Sagais, Beltirs, Kyzyls or Koibals, and the Altaians from seven small Turkic groups. Traditional rituals, art, music, costumes and dancing were revived, as folklore art forms but without their indigenous and religious meanings.[1]

Agriculture, industry and urbanization were imposed where possible, and pastoralists were reorganized into collective farms. This resulted in the widespread slaughter of livestock, the substitution of Russian huts for tents, and boarding schools for the children where they learned the Russian language and culture, and were taught to dislike the traditional way of life. Small settlements were forcibly closed and the population was concentrated in large centers, mostly for bureaucratic convenience.

The collective farms restricted herding with inappropriate ideas of industrial production as the men became state employees of a centralized bureaucracy, and the herds were enclosed in fenced areas. While the advantages of education, medical care and modern transport came through the Soviets, the native societies were demoralized and disrupted. In the post-Communist era, Russia's economy requires the rapid development of oil and natural gas in the region, with resulting transport systems, population invasion and damage to the fragile environment.

Since the end of Communism all groups are ready to exploit their new freedoms within the Russian Federation. Young leaders grieved at the injustices under Communism are determined to re-establish their identities and self-confidence as peoples, and they are open to outside trade and partnership.[2] Anyone seeking to befriend them must seek to share their involvement with their environment. The paternalistic and oppressive experience with Communism serves as a warning to how we witness and adapt to their culture and revived nomadic lifestyle.

A number of Christians are now working among these peoples. The Slavic Mission,

Sweden is co-operating in a Urals Bible School to train a number of CIS nationalities such as Mari, Komi, Chuvashian, Tatar, and son on.[3] YWAM wants to establish a School of Frontier Missions in Norway which will train workers for the Arctic.[4] Russian

churches need to be culturally sensitive in reaching out to these peoples. They need to be effective not only in evangelism, but also in helping to bring about reconciliation between the indigenous and "white" races after centuries of Russian domination.

Nomadic Pastoralists of the Arctic

NENET, *Nentsi* or *Yurak Samoyeds*

They number 38,000 (34,665 Nenets according to the 1989 census), and about 10,000 still herd reindeer in the tundra and forest of northwest Siberia, Russia. Their territory stretches from the White Sea in the west to the Yenisey River in the east, a distance of over 1,500 kilometers (930 mi.), and includes the island of Novaya Zemlya. Even the Nenets call the Yamal Peninsula "the ends of the earth," and over 50% of the 9,000 people living there are nomadic reindeer herders using half of the area as pasture.

They are related to the *Enets*, *Sel'kep* and *Nganasan* — all of whom are Samoyedic peoples. They have been in the region for 1500 years, but they were forced further north by Khants and Selkups. The latter were displaced into Nenet territory by Russian fur trappers and settlers moving into valleys of the Ob and Yenisey rivers. But the Nenets, although dominated militarily by Russia, have never been integrated into Russian society. They maintain their independence by replacing hunting with reindeer herding.

The Communists treated the nomadic life and culture as backward and implicitly recommended an unobtainable Russian lifestyle and culture. Initially they established tent schools, or "Red Chums," to travel with the Nenets to teach both literacy to the children and ideology to the adults. *Chum* is the Nenet term for their wigwam of birch poles and reindeer skins. But when collectivization was imposed, the reindeer became state property and the children were

sent to boarding schools. Many of the Nenets killed their herds in protest, resisted the anti-shamanist propaganda and refused to pay taxes in order not to submit to an alien regime. These measures meant that the men would spend six-week shifts with the herds without their families, who were placed in settlements with craft factories and schools.

The young had primary education and became literate, but the disruption of their lifestyle lead to the demoralization of family life. The increase of the Nenet population by 29% between 1959 and 1979 may be explained by people of mixed marriages preferring to claim to be Nenet rather than Russian or Komi.[5] In the 1970s they still largely wandered in family collectives without the central administrative headquarters so loved by the planners.

The Nenets face a number of threats to their way of life, because Russia sees their territory as a national resource for the development of industries that do not contribute anything to the local people's welfare. Very large natural gas and oil reserves are being developed in the area, causing serious pollution of the ground and the air. The Russians estimate that 2,500 square kilometers (1,550 sq. mi.) of pasture will be destroyed by oil field exploration, and this is due to double when production begins.

A railway to the Yamal Peninsula for the oil field has destroyed the environment and separated the Nenets' winter and summer pastures. The summer grazing areas to the south, in the *taiga*, are being spoiled by the pollution of the streams and rivers from

33a

33b

33 Nenets:
   a. Western Siberian reindeer herders on the tundra (Photo: E. Rønningstad).
   b. The stove is the central feature inside a Nenet tent (Photo: Mark Dotson).

33c

33d

33 c. A Nenet camp on the tundra.
    d. A Nenet family relaxes at home (Photo: Olga Koskova).

industrial developments. Half a million hectares of pasture have been lost, and these industrial developments have been carried out despite local political protests.[6] Large numbers of outsiders have moved into the area so that the Nenets make up only about 10% of the population in their own area.[7] These problems have created overgrazing, and only a few hundred now work as herders. Many who have been forced to live in the villages under Communism have lost the skills necessary to be able to live on the tundra. Some have been encouraged to join a Russian commercial fishing enterprise, and others seek to support themselves by hunting and fishing, but most are unemployed.

Two hundred *Nentser*, probably Nenets, were discovered to the north of Yorkuta in 1997. Undetected by the authorities throughout the Communist era, they had resolved to "disappear" into the tundra when they heard of the effects of collectivization on their neighbors. They have sustained themselves by reindeer herding and hunting, and by reviving the ancient skills of making their own cloths and tools.[8]

Nomadism

The Nenets' pastoral methods differ from those of the Saami (Lapps), in that they guard their reindeer near the camps all year around and do not milk or ride them. The Saami let them roam free. The Nenets travel north in the spring on sleds, taking the herds onto the tundra close to the sea, and in autumn they move southwards again to the *taiga*, south of the tree line. Other Nenets migrate within the forest all year round. The length of the pastoral migration routes between summer and winter pastures varies from 500 to 1,000 kilometers (310 to 620 mi.). In 1996 the collectives still owned most of the reindeer, but the size of the private herds is increasing. The average herd contains about 2,000 reindeer.

There are about 50 "brigades" of extended family herding groups. A typical group is about five to ten herders, with their families, who live in *chums*, or tepees, and

the men spend as much as 24 hours a day with the reindeer. Typically the group is responsible for between 3,000 and 6,000 reindeer, half belonging to the families and half to the state farm. In the past they have supplied the farmers with meat, but the system is disintegrating and the price is too low. To the west of the River Pechora the men leave their families in the villages and live in smaller tents on sleds. Often the families join the men at their camps for the summer, but during the rest of the year they return to the settlement for the children to go to school. The men can be away from the villages for four or five months.

The reindeer are sold for meat and the skins are still used for winter clothing and footwear. Lassos are made from strips of hide. Wounded animals are strangled and can be eaten raw, and the blood drunk. The blood is considered a defense against scurvy. The men and children have priority over the women for the first portions.

There are many social and moral problems among the Nenets, especially in the few urban centers. Egil Rønningstad says, "Much loneliness, despair, criminality and alcoholism come out of this school system." The drunkenness results in violence, suicide, child abuse and accidents.[9] With the influx of Russian industrial workers on short contracts, many Nenet women became their temporary wives. Life expectancy for the Nenets is only 47 years. A special problem for all the families is the alienation the children feel from their parents and their way of life because of their Russian education.

Their language, Nenets, is spoken by about 80% of the Nenets, but fewer and fewer of the younger generation speak their language. All speak Russian, but some also speak Komi. There is very little literature in the Nenet language, which means it is difficult for them to maintain their identity. But they sing traditional epics that last for three or more days.

Religion

After a forced conversion to Russian Orthodoxy in the nineteenth century, the

Nenets synthesized it with their own Shamanism, which they still practice. They also believe in a good sky god or creator called Num, who is in conflict with Nna, or Earth. They carry images of the spirits on their sleds. Although little Shamanism is being practiced today, what remains is a spiritual problem for the people. A pioneering evangelical work among them in the 1920s left few Christians.[10]

Outreach

A Bible translation is still in the early stages, but portions of Luke became available in 1995.[11] The New Testament is available in both Komi and Russian. YWAM has an international team centered in Naryan-Mar, the central administrative town beyond the Arctic Circle with a population of 29,000,[12] and the Russian Baptists have a witness there too. There are gospel cassettes available. There are two small congregations of Nenet Christians. Issues such as dealing with the biblical injunction against drinking blood, abstinence and rehabilitation from alcohol abuse, and indigenous forms of evangelism and discipleship need solutions.

There is a temptation to consider accepting or rejecting Christianity as part of a "superior" culture. Some of the young people who show interest have had to leave the area to study or work. A long-term Christian witness is needed by those willing to live simply in the cold climate and to work in the Nenet language, although short-term workers can use Russian. Meals are being provided for students of vocational courses in Naryan-Mar. There is an urgent need for all types of medical and dental work, as well as veterinary and other forms of help.

KHANTI and MANSI

There were 22,521 Khants and 8,461 Mansi in 1989. These are two related peoples living east of the Urals, on the west and east sides of the River Ob in Siberia. The Mansi live in eastern Khantia Mansia, and the Khanti in the west and north.[13] The Khanti call themselves *Hant*, and the Mansi the "People of Mansi," but previously the Russians called

them Ostyaks and Voguls. They are related to the Magyars and were originally horse breeders on the steppe, to the south in Central Asia, like the Kazaks and Mongols. They migrated to northern Siberia in the fifth century at the same time the Magyars moved into present-day Hungary.

The region is a vast plain divided by many rivers and lakes and covered in forests that are very rich in wildlife. The waters contain salmon, sturgeon and other varieties of fish. The Khanti and Mansi have developed differing lifestyles appropriate to the environment. In the north, they are reindeer herders, with herds of 25,000 deer. The reindeer were used at one time for transport in hunting, but they are now domesticated for meat and hides; they are not milked. In the autumn and spring the people still hunt, taking their families with them and using reindeer for transport. Others herd and hunt in the dense coniferous forests in the central part of the region. They are very poor.

In the south, they specialize in hunting and fishing and have provided as much as two-thirds of the Siberian fish for the Russian market. Whole families leave the village in the spring to live in houseboats that they have towed to various central locations. They live in the houseboats and go out on fishing excursions in motorboats. When they go further from the houseboat, they often live in temporary wigwams of turf or bark. They only return to the settlements for the winter. They have supplemented their diet by keeping cattle and growing some crops. Often today the cattle have replaced the reindeer and only a few hunt.[14]

Under the Czars, Russian merchants exploited these peoples in an unequal trade of exchanging furs for necessities. The Communists forcibly resettled them in collectives in 1930, but this was not a success, and the people reverted to a semi-nomadic lifestyle. But collective centers were set up for both the fishing groups and herders to provide services such as schools, clinics and houses for about 600 people. They also gained hunting and fishing rights.

Their environment has been spoiled by extensive oil field development since the 1960s and by gravel extraction since 1984.[15]

Khanti and Mansi are Finno-Ugric languages, but the different regions have developed six dialects that are barely understandable to each other.

Religion

Nominally they are Orthodox Christian, but they are animists in practice. Until recently, they celebrated the bear as a son of their supreme god, Numi-Torem, with special feasts. They propitiate tree spirits, but the shaman is less important for them than among other Central Asian peoples. They practice ancestor worship and believe that every man has five souls — but women have only four!

Outreach

British and American Christians have provided basic materials for poorly equipped schools or kindergartens, as well as books for a village library. No Russian Christians visit the area. Lifewater International is involved in providing wells.[16] IBT is working on a translation of the Gospels and children's Bible portions.[17]

ENETS (*Ents*)

They are related to the *Nenets*. According to James Forsyth there were 340 left in the 1970s, speaking their own language, and aware of their ethnic distinctiveness. They have been assimilated either with the *Nganasans* to the north, a hunter-fisherman group, or with the Nenets to the south. Intermarriage has been common. In the summer they move close to the Yenisey Gulf and migrate southwards to spend the winter near Lake Pyasino. Most are bi- or tri-lingual, since Enets are taught in the schools in order to learn Russian, which is the language of instruction after the first year. Only between 90 and 200, mostly middle-aged, people speak the Enets language. The IBT has begun Bible translation and short portions were available in 1995.

NGANSANS, or *Avam* and *Vadeyev*

There are 1,300 Ngansans living on the Taymyr Peninsula, between the Enets and Dolgans. They speak Dolgan and have contact with the eastern Nenets. They used to hunt wild reindeer and fish, but they have since developed reindeer herding. They were organized into four collectives. Although one of the smallest people groups in Russia, they maintain a strong sense of ethnic identity. They are shamanists and believe in the myths that the gods came from the Sun Mother melting the Ice Mother. They seem to believe in a form of reincarnation. Russian Orthodox missionaries attempted to convert them before Communist times; there are no Christians among them.[18]

DOLGANS

They are 7,000 reindeer herders near the Taymyr Peninsula, Russia.[19] Originally related to the Evenks and Evens, they migrated eastwards and came under the influence of the Yakuts and adopted much of their Turkic language. They have adopted a number of skills from their different neighbors, such as the domestication of reindeer for riding, pack-carrying and sleigh pulling, and the use of herd-dogs. This made them efficient enough to supply furs and run a reindeer sleigh service between the Yenisey and Anabar rivers for the Russians. During the 1930s they could not avoid being collectivized, and at that time their population was only 1,445.

The social conditions in which many of this people live are considered to be well below standard, with a high level of infant mortality. Apathy and alcoholism is common. A measure of social stratification has developed, with some families being very wealthy and others very poor.[20] One-parent families have become common, as Russian development workers use local women as concubines. The non-ferrous metal complex at Norilsk has also polluted a vast area of their territory. They speak Dolgan, which is sometimes mistakenly described as a Yakut dialect. It is in fact a distinct language that is also spoken by the Ewenki and local Russians. The Gospels have been translated and published by the IBT.

EWENK, *Evenki* or *Tungus*

There are 30,163 Ewenki, most of whom are in Russia, between the River Ob and the Pacific. There are 27,300 of them that form 42% of the population in the Yakut Republic, Russia. There are 8,000 east of Lake Baikal, 1,310 in the Irkutsk Province and 3,239 in the Ewenki National Region. There are 2,000 living in Chenbaehru Qi, Inner Mongolia, China. They are related to the *Even*, or *Lamuts*. They are divided into tribes that live in the forests separated by great distances, and therefore they have had no political unity.

They live by reindeer herding and hunting, with some cattle and horse rearing and agriculture.[21] Originally they were serfs to herd owners, but under the Soviet and Chinese regimes their herding was collectivized. The Ewenki Autonomous Region succeeded in getting a hydroelectric scheme rejected, the lake of which would have covered over 6,400 square kilometers (4,000 sq. mi.) of their pasture, but a large part of their territory was taken for timber cutting in 1987.[22]

A few were reported to be still nomadic in the 1980s.[23] In recent decades, the Ewenk have migrated three times a year, spending the winter in a camp with warehouses, animal sheds and power-operated wells. In spring they move to a pasture area for lambing and then in the summer on to the better grazing land. During the summers they still live in tents of poles and straw. Perhaps 99% of the children attend school, and this is undermining their pastoralist culture. The co-operatives provided medical centers.

Religion

The Ewenki practice a syncretism of Russian Orthodoxy and Shamanism, believing in the spirits of campfires, the bear and the wolf. There are 26 dialects of the Evenki language, but there is a literary language based on Podkamennaya Tunguska. In 1979, 43%

spoke their own language. A new translation of the New Testament is being prepared by UBS and IBT, and Luke and portions of the other Gospels were published in 1996, but this script cannot be read in China.[24] Two churches are reported, with about 100 Evenki claiming to be Christians. A children's Bible in Russian is also used.

Ewenk, Solons or *Yakuts*

There are 26,300 Ewenki in China of which 21,000 are Solon, living as reindeer herders and hunters in the forests of western Heilongjiang and Morindawa and Oroqen Qi, eastern Inner Mongolia. They moved into China in the seventeenth century, because many of them were being compelled to convert to the Russian Orthodox faith. They used to be called Solons Tunguses, or Yakuts. *Solon* is their own name that means "people of the upper river" but as an officially recognized minority in China they are called Ewenki.

Traditionally they move every two weeks, living in tents or tepees covered in cloth in the summer and with hide and birch bark in the winter. However, many of the women have settled in villages to enable the children to attend school. They trade in meat and antlers and use birch bark for utensils. They are shamanists, and there are no known Christians among them.[25] Their spoken Evenki language differs significantly from that spoken in Russia, and they use Chinese as their written language.[26]

Tungus or *Khamnigan Ewenk*: 1,600 live in northeastern Inner Mongolia, China. They are shamanists except for those influenced by the Mongols to adopt Buddhism.[27]

There are two or three thousand *Ewenk* in Mongolia, where they speak Halh Mongolian.

KARAGFAS, Tofa, Tofalar or Karagass

They call themselves *Tubalar* (sg. *Tuba*), and are closely related to the Tuvans, some of whom live among them. The Karagfas have been more receptive to Russian influence than the Tuvans. They are 731 reindeer herders and hunters dwelling in the Irkutsk

34a

34b

34 Evenki:
   a. Evenki in traditional dress at a summer festival in the birch forests of the *taiga*, eastern Siberia (Photo D. Hazell).
   b. An Evenki boy smart in his complete winter suit, made by his mother from reindeer skins (Photo: D. Hazell).

Republic, southern Siberia, Russia, situated northwest of Lake Baikal. They are divided into five lineages. Traditionally they were nomadic, living in birch-bark tepees. The Soviets collectivized them into three villages, but this period was catastrophic for them and resulted in a great decline in their population, and this decline continued as they merged with the Russians.

They roam with the reindeer over a large area of the East Sayan Mountains. The men spend as much as two years at a time away from their families, but this is done in relays, so that some men are at home for a period. The Karagfas know all their animals by name and use euphemisms when they die, or are killed, showing that they are reluctant to kill them.[28] They speak a language that has a mixture of Turkic and Mongolian elements. In 1986 they were given their own alphabet of 42 letters, but they use Russian as the literary language. Although converted to Russian Orthodoxy and given Russian names in the sixteenth century, they continued to pay tribute to Genghis Khan. This is no known Christian outreach among them.

SAKHA, *Yakuts*

Sakha is their own name and 382,255 live in Yakutia between the Lena and Kolyma rivers in Russia.[29] It is the coldest place on earth, near the Arctic coast. They appear to have originated from the mixture of Turkic people being pushed north by the Mongols and the indigenous peoples of the region. The Sakha have been part of the Russian Empire since 1638. They are an example of a people who were forced out of their territory, adapted to new livestock and exchanged tents for huts in order to preserve their Turkic society and language. The Sakha fought a four-year war against the Soviets.

The northern Sakha, or Yakuts, are traditionally reindeer herders, who were allowed to revert to a semi-nomadic life after a disastrous attempt at collectivization. The Soviet government was forced to recognize the reindeer herding economy as an important food supply for the various mining and other projects in the region. The

southern Sakha are cattle and horse breeders.

Diamond mining, hydroelectric schemes, natural gas, coal mining, salt production and the resulting immigration of other peoples have changed their territory and reduced the Sakha to being only a third of the population in their own territory. This is in spite of the fact that their population had increased by 62%. However, as the newcomers are concentrated in only a few areas, the Sakha have remained a majority in other parts of the territory.[30] They were still largely rural (79%) in 1970.[31]

Religion

Shamanism has always had a great influence among the Sakha. The shaman (*oiuun*) and also shamanesses (*udagan*) claim to be able to heal, curse and predict the future. Since the late seventeenth century, when the Sakha underwent a "conversion" to Orthodoxy, the shamans have been persecuted by the Russians. They are very much mediators who alone have access to the spirit world, and their supposed effectiveness gives each one a reputation as either a good or poor medium. They heal by expelling the evil spirit that is thought to cause the disease and by returning the patient's soul to his or her body. They believe in a whole cosmology of the spirit world in a three-tier universe. The spirits are housed in wooden images into which the shaman is said to breathe life.[32]

The shaman heals by imploring the helper spirits with incantations, to induce a trance-like state. They bang their drum, calling it their "mount" on which to travel and feed food to the spirits. These spirits are thought to be in the forms of birds or animals, and they protect the shaman as he or she travels to either the lower world or the sky world of the spirits. Many of the Yakut shamans are birdmen and dress in gowns to resemble their particular species. The shaman will impersonate his spirit, making animal or bird noises and movements to suggest traveling to the netherworld or to the sky. The spirit's qualities as a bird, such as the ability to fly, its eyesight, or the fierceness of the bear, are deemed necessary to make the journey to retrieve a soul "lost" by sickness. The people are considered to vary according to their susceptibility or resistance to the influence of the spirits and shamans. Laughter therapy is used after the seances. The curses can appear to work with people becoming ill or dying soon afterwards. Prediction is done by the shaman having a "magical" dream. Shamans also engage in spiritual warfare, fighting against other spirits.

While only a few claim to be shamans today, it is said that many more people are having "shamanist sickness," that is, experiencing the trance-like call to be a shaman. Still more believe in Shamanism and also have contact with Evenk and Even shamans, who are said to be more powerful. The Sakha are reviving their epics as dramas, so that they are not forgotten. Each year the Sakha have a spring festival, which is a state holiday, to celebrate fertility, when eagle images on poles are set up in the streets. They drink *kymys*, or mare's milk, and eat horse meat kebabs in honor of an ancestor warrior-shaman. The Yakut protect the eagles and consider them to be children of the sky-god.

During the Communist era, some enterprising political and religious Russian deportees learned the Yakut language and educated them. The Yakut have recently developed their own newspapers, literature and radio programs. Yakuts have become vocal about the lack of local government freedom and the persecution of their leaders throughout the twentieth century. They have managed to get dam projects shelved in their region. Many have become nominal Russian Orthodox believers, but most Yakuts remained animists and Shamanists at heart.[33] Yakut is a Turkic language. A storybook version of Luke and Acts, *Jesus and the Early Church*, has been in circulation for a few years. A new translation of the New Testament is in progress and Luke and Acts have been published. The *Jesus* film is also available.[34]

Yakut, China: This is an isolated community of 1,700 semi-nomadic reindeer pastoralists living in northeastern Inner Mongolia. Alcohol abuse is a serious problem. There is no Christian witness to these shamanists.[35]

EVENY (sg. is *Even*, pron. Evén), *Lamut* or *Orochen*

They are reindeer herders and hunters. There are 21,000, according to a 1997 estimate, in Yakutia (the Sakha Republic) and the Kamchatka Peninsula, Russia, of which 7,500 are estimated to be nomadic. There are four groupings and dialects of the Eveny, *Anyuy*, *Omolon*, *Kolyma* and, further west, the *Uyandino*. They may have originated in Manchuria and are related to the Evenki.

No agriculture is possible in this mountainous and frozen region, and the ground below the surface is permanently frozen. Grass is slow to grow, and the time the herds are in any one area must be limited. The reindeer have to cover greater distances than in more temperate zones. It is a mountainous region where larch trees grow on the south-facing slopes, but there is little vegetation on the northern slopes. During the brief summer a slight thaw produces boggy ground that breeds many mosquitoes.

Nomadism

The Eveny used to live in scattered settlements of tents, and the herding used to be a family affair. Their herding was collectivized by 1962 and they lived together with Ewenkis and Yakut on state farms.[36] A brigade is responsible for about 2,000 reindeer, which need constant supervision as they are half-wild and can scatter and be lost. They migrate six times a year, although this does not include many short moves — every ten days in summer. Only a few of the reindeer are domesticated to be ridden and to pull sleds of provisions. The best can be used for sled races and may be flown by helicopter from one race site to another. Calving is in April, and the herds are corralled to check the animals. In the long days of summer the herds must be watched continuously, and the men can be too busy to sleep or eat. In the winter the men can visit the villages, because the ground is frozen and the herds do not travel as far in the semi-darkness of the Arctic. They produce meat, antlers and fur to fulfill the farms' quotas.

The Soviets forced the nomads to live in villages with Yakut, Russians and others to "civilize" them. The children were sent to boarding schools and the wives were given work in villages. This system has caused a whole generation not to learn the skills of herding. This has also resulted in the destruction of family life. Recently the state boarding schools have been closed and replaced by village schools, to keep the families together. Out of a population of hundreds, less than 100 are herders. Herding is done by assigning about six men to "brigades," irrespective of family ties, and the herds belong to "the farm" rather than to family units. The herding is usually done by the younger men, who lead a bachelor existence and spend as much as ten months without their families. Wives are often involved in teaching, administration and the manufacture of reindeer clothing. Although manufactured clothes are worn in the short hot summers, the people still rely on reindeer skin for working garb and wear boots made in the villages. Many spend the short summer holidays staying with the men in the herding camps.

The Eveny see the possibility of having modern facilities and education incorporated into their reindeer nomadism, which most recognize to be so important for their self-identity. Decollectivization into family and other small ownership groups began in 1989, but central administration was still the rule in the mid-1990s. About 60% of the herd now belongs to a product company; the rest of the animals are privately owned by the herders. With the free market, mobile meat processing plants are projected to reach the international markets, but one of the biggest problems is transport of products, since the helicopters once used are now very expensive.

The Eveny have become politically aware of the problems of the Arctic as a whole,

and not just of their own problems, and they have taken encouragement from how Scandinavian and Canadian Arctic peoples are responding to the modern world. They are demanding local ownership and administration to replace state control of their own territory, in order to develop their herding. They want a nomadic school system to restore their culture and family life. They are also protesting against industrial and nuclear environmental damage in their region. Their young people are divided about assimilation, or maintaining the traditional lifestyle. They use Russian and Yakut as literary languages, and they are reviving the Eveny language as a school subject. Local political reactions are mixed, from advocates of "closing down" the Arctic to those who are encouraging a modern nomadism.

Religion

Many Eveny still respect the spirits. In camp, at the beginning of a meal, a portion is thrown into the campfire or stove to feed the spirit of fire. The shamans used to be the focus of Eveny cultural life, but the Communists destroyed their power. There is a revival of shamanistic dances as part of a new sense of pride in folklore, but this is unlikely to include a desire to restore belief in the old religion, or the power of the shaman. They bury their dead. The IBT has begun a Bible translation and published portions of Luke.

CHUKCHI, *Chuckchee*

According to the 1989 census, there were 15,184 Chukchi living in the extreme northeast of Siberia, Russia. They are divided between reindeer herders and sea hunters. Although their lifestyle is similar to the Eskimo's, they and their language are not related to any others except the Korak.[37] The reindeer herds provided most of their needs, in spite of the fact that the Chukchi failed to domesticate the reindeer or their dogs for more efficient herding. They lived in large tepees, as big as eight meters in diameter, fitted with an inner sleeping compartment lined in furs. They had no central authority or organization beyond the small clan of a herding group.

They were the last Siberian people to submit to Russian overlords. Although the Chukchi numbered only 9,000, they defeated a Russian force in 1729. The Russians responded with a revenge extermination campaign, claiming it was "with the help of Almighty God." After 1764, when the Russian commander was killed, the Russians attempted more peaceful methods of establishing trade, having calculated that the war was costing 41 times more than the value of the fur trade. The coastal Chukchis had contact with American and Japanese whaling ships in the nineteenth century.

Over 70% of the Chukchis were still nomadic in 1934, until 1936, when about 20 collectives of reindeer herders were formed, involving only 11% of the Chukchis. Many left the vicinity of the Russians in the Anadyr River basin for the tundra of the Chuckoski Mountains to the north, and were joined by coastal Chukchi who abandoned seal hunting for herding. However, by the 1950s all the reindeer were state owned. Herds of between 10,000 and 20,000 reindeer were formed into collectives which also allowed some movement for pasture. These were supposed to be "mixed economy" centers, but the fishing side has been overtaken by modern fishing ships manned by Russians. The small settlements were closed down, nomadism banned and the Chukchis concentrated in the collectives. Today they use helicopters and snowmobiles to control the herds, but many are reduced to menial jobs around the Russian military installations in the area, and the young people are seeking Russian jobs in the towns.[38]

Much of the area has been contaminated by radioactivity from nuclear tests in Novaya Zemlya. The herding culture tended to prevail over the coastal hunting culture, and most of the Chukchi children no longer recognized the distinction by 1970. Yuryi Rytkhen is a published Chukchi writer who at first believed the Soviet propaganda about the good treatment of native peoples, but he has since become disillusioned and has advocated that the northern people create their own adaptation to modern life rather than have it imposed.[39]

The Chukchi marry only within their group, usually with cousins. But polygamy and a restricted promiscuity are common. Any disputes are usually over women. Many women have a number of children by different Russian fathers who were among the development or military personnel during the 1960s.

An attempt after 1815 to convert them to Russian Orthodoxy failed. Their own traditions showed their constant fear of malicious spirits, called *kelet*. The shamans healed and placated the spirits. Reindeer and dogs were sacrificed and the blood and fat "fed" into the mouths of effigies of the spirits. The shamans continued to have great influence well into the twentieth century. They opposed the education and medical services provided by the collectives because they were thought to offend the spirits.[40] The Communists conducted a campaign to undermine the authority of the shamans, and the few children that attended the schools had to report on the shamans' activities and ridicule them. It was widely thought that the murders of some Communist Party officials may well have been instigated in revenge. Tragically, cultural degradation has set in. There are no Christians among them, but a Bible translation has been started with portions of Luke made available in 1995.[41]

KORYAK

The 1989 census reported 9,242 Koryak divided between coastal fishing and reindeer herder Koryaks. There were originally nine groups of Koryaks.[42] They live in Koryakskiy Avt, Kamchatka Peninsula and make up 25% of the population. There are also Cossacks and other Russians who are likely to remain in the area. Collectivization was carried out during the 1940s and 1950s, and they had 200,000 reindeer in 11 collectives that had interbred with wild reindeer. These farms are now privatized, with six herders to every 2,000 reindeer. The migration route includes spending the winter on the western side of the peninsula and, in late May, taking about two months to cross it to spend the summer on the eastern coast. Here the reindeer find it necessary to drink salt water. Upon returning to their winter camps, they have the festival of Hololo when the surplus reindeer are slaughtered.[43]

The Koryaks have been opposed to rapid development projects such as mining, because they are aware of the ecological consequences. The Koryak National Association was formed in 1991 to protect their economic interest in herding and fishing and to encourage appropriate development. The major difficulty is the lack of transport, either by air, sea or land, to export the venison. There is now no internal market in Russia for the meat. The local people lack the experience to develop an export market. American and Japanese trawler-fishing at sea has damaged the salmon life cycle sufficiently to disrupt the Koryaks' river fishing.[44] In 1986 the Koryak village of Paren was threatened with closure and the enforced removal of the population from reindeer herding because it was considered "unprofitable." Local political and media protests reversed the decision.[45]

The Koryaks seem to have preserved their own identity, although the Russian language is used in the schools because their own language has so many dialects. Half the population is under the age of sixteen, and they are increasing. The children attend 32 different boarding schools. There is a nucleus of Koryak professionals, such as doctors, teachers, writers and engineers. The young adults are bilingual in Russian and also understand Chukchi. But the very young speak only Russian, and the old only know Koryak, which has eight different dialects, some unintelligible to each other.[46]

They believe in a remote creator god, who sent a being called Black Raven to bring humankind out of chaos and to defeat evil spirits. This Raven then left or was turned into stone. The Koryaks keep and still believe in their totem idols, which are kept in their tents or huts. These are crude flat woodcarvings, roughly in the shapes of dolls. They are "fed" with fat to help them drive away evil spirits. The Koryaks cremate the dead after stabbing the corpse, and then return home by a zigzag route to make sure the spirit does not follow. They believe that they each have three souls: "soul," "breath" and "shadow."[47] The Bibelmission has visited the Kamchatka area.[48] The IBT is involved in a Bible translation, and part of Luke has been published.

Non-Pastoral Nomadic Peoples in the Russian Arctic

KOMI

They are a hunting and fishing people, in northern Russia, who have been nominally Orthodox for centuries. The New Testament in Komi is available. There is one known Christian among them.

YUKAGHIR or *Yukagir*

The Yukaghir are 1,100 traditional hunters, near the Kolyma River in eastern Yakutia or Magadan, Russia. They have, or had, a highly-developed shamanist cult worshipping the ancestor spirit of each clan.[49] Their language has two dialects that are not mutually intelligible, but only a few older people speak it. Most are bilingual in Russian and Yakut. Some speak Even. Portions of Luke have been translated and published.[50]

UDEGHE, or *Udege*

There are 1,600 hunters in the Sikhote Mountains and on the coast of the Primorsky Territory, 500 kilometers (310 mi.) northeast of Vladivostok. They are probably related to the Ewenkis, but they have no reindeer. They travel on skis and sleds and live in bark tepees. Only the older generation speaks Udeghe, and 70% of Udeghe acknowledge Russian as their language. Jansi Kimonko is a Udeghe writer with published work. The state forestry threatened the survival of the Udeghe by giving a contract to a Cuban company to fell the forest, until a ban was imposed in March 1990.[51]

ITEL'MEN

There are 2,500 Itel'men, who are fishermen and hunters in the central western Kamchatka Peninsula, Siberia.[52] Most of them have been absorbed into the *Kamchadals*, a mixed racial group. They have been relocated to collective farms and reduced to being day laborers. Yet an increasing number, possibly 1,600, still claim that their nationality is Itel'man.[53] The Itel'men language is taught in school at primary level, but nearly all are bilingual in Russian. Instruction in reindeer breeding and fur farming is given.[54]

LATIN AND NORTH AMERICA

The American continent had, and still has, many hunter-gatherer peoples, and others combining seasonal cultivation with hunting; in the past they wandered on the plains and forests in small family groups, with little or no overall social organization. Today most are restricted in their movements. In the open country of the plains to the north and south, these peoples migrated on foot until the introduction of the horse by the Spanish before 1600. The horse gave them considerable mobility and facilitated both the hunting of wild buffaloes and warfare in North America. The popular image of the Plains Indian riding a horse in North American folklore was a very late development. For a brief period, hitherto village-dwelling Indians took to a nomadic hunting life with portable tepees, but they did nothing to domesticate, or conserve, the stock of bison in a genuine pastoralism. The European invaders soon established pastoralism conducted in ranches, and the Spanish and Portuguese pioneered the concept of the cowboy, both in Mexico and on the pampas to the south. Today there are a few examples of semi-nomadic pastoralist peoples.

With the upheaval of rapid urban growth, and the migration of country people to the shantytowns, there are probably other migrating groups, especially peripatetics within the urban areas, that have yet to be clearly identified. There is a popular misconception that primal peoples in Latin America are tribes within the forests. But just one people of nomadic pastoralists, the Guarjiro, total more than all the existent hunter-gatherer and agricultural Indian tribes still in South America.

Nomadic Pastoralists of the Americas

INUPIAT

These are 8,000 Alaskan Eskimos who live on the Seward Peninsula, Alaska and around the northern coast to Mackenzie, North West Territories, Canada. The Inupiat, formerly hunters of caribou, herd reindeer near the coast. It was feared in the 1880s that the indigenous caribou would be hunted to extinction. Therefore the Presbyterian missionary, Sheldon Jackson, imported reindeer and brought over Sami instructors to teach the local people herding. He recognized that pastoralism of managed herds would keep the Inupiat self-sufficient, or at least from dying of starvation. He also claimed that bringing the Inupiats from the wild hunter stage to a herder stage was a "great step out of barbarism towards civilization." It would also mean that the people would remain close to mission schools to become Christians.

This was a gallant attempt to change hunters into pastoralists as a more stable form of subsistence, but it proved premature because the decline of the caribou was not as rapid as predicted. However, the Inupiats did lose access to whales along the shore due to the increased activity of whaling ships. The development of local herders was painfully slow and many reindeer remained in the possession of the mission, and Jackson was forced to resign. Legislation in

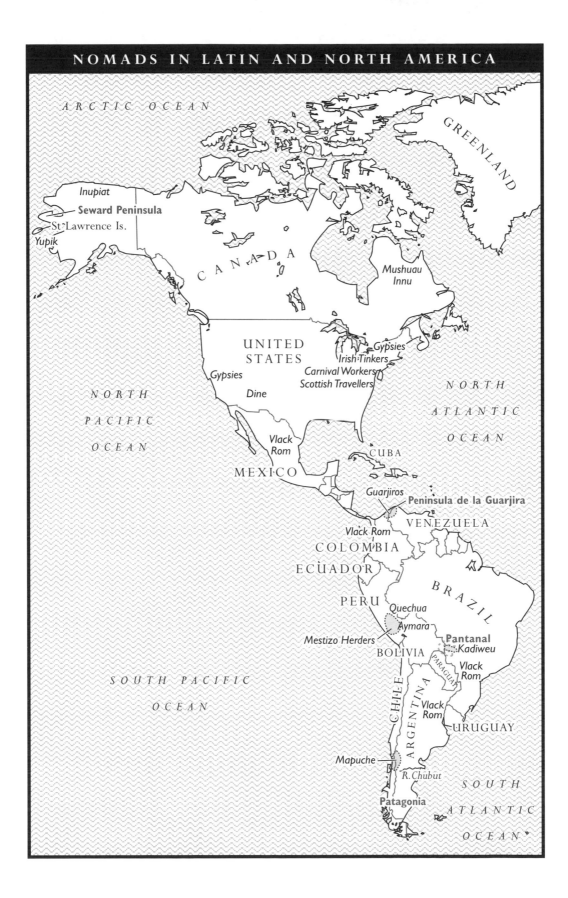

NOMADS IN LATIN AND NORTH AMERICA

ARCTIC OCEAN

GREENLAND

Inupiat
Seward Peninsula
St. Lawrence Is.
Yupik

CANADA

Mushuau
Innu

UNITED
STATES

Gypsies
Irish Tinkers
Carnival Workers
Scottish Travellers

NORTH
PACIFIC
OCEAN

Gypsies
Dine

NORTH
ATLANTIC
OCEAN

Vlack
Rom

CUBA

MEXICO

Guarjiros
Peninsula de la Guarjira

VENEZUELA

Vlack Rom

COLOMBIA

ECUADOR

BRAZIL

PERU

Quechua
Aymara

Pantanal
Kadiweu

Mestizo Herders

Vlack
Rom

BOLIVIA

PARAGUAY

SOUTH PACIFIC

OCEAN

CHILE

ARGENTINA

Vlack
Rom

URUGUAY

Mapuche

R. Chubut

SOUTH

Patagonia

ATLANTIC

OCEAN

1937 limited reindeer ownership to the indigenous people of Alaska. To the north, the other related Inuits, called the **Nunamiuts**, are traditionally nomadic caribou hunters, but they have settled in Anaktuvuk, in the Endicott Mountains — an area called the Gates of the Arctic — and they continue to hunt the caribou.

Nomadism

There is sufficient pasture for the Inupiat to have larger herds, but the poor method of herding limits the size of the herds. In Alaska they have neither learned to partially tame the reindeer for sleds, nor use the lasso and the relative taming of the animals so that they can be herded to particular areas, as the Sami have done. In early summer the wild reindeer are corralled for de-horning. The horns are sold to Asian buyers for traditional medicines. For five months of the summer, the grazing grounds of the Inupiat are clear of snow, but the terrain is very difficult for following running reindeer. The reindeer are then left free to roam until early winter, when they are rounded up for selective slaughter. The herders' camps of cabins or tents are near the shore, so that they can be contacted by helicopter that is able to land on the beach or sea ice.

An aerial infrared survey has helped to identify the limited winter pasture of lichen to develop a five-year grazing migration plan. The pasture could be used far more productively if the owners co-operated to put their herds together, instead of individual owners being allocated large areas for their herds to roam at will. The reindeer mix and join the caribou herds and are lost. At present there is no incentive to develop their herds, because caribou meat is freely available by hunting. The people can subsist better by hunting and fishing, and using the reindeer only to supplement this through the sale of antlers, rather than through the sale of meat.

Suicide and alcoholism among the Inupiat are said to be the worst in the country. Their language is Inuktitut, but less than half of them speak it. The younger people tend to speak English. The New Testament was published in 1968, and the Old Testament is in draft form. A Christian bookstore opened in Nome in 1979.[1]

YUPIK

The Yupik are found on St. Lawrence Island, 180 kilometers (110 mi.) off the Alaskan coast. They are hunters who supplement their diet from reindeer herds. They are related to the Yupik in southwest Alaska. There are also 1,500 living on the Chukotskiy Peninsula, Siberia. The Presbyterians brought the gospel to them in 1894, and we have already referred to the restocking of the reindeer herd in Alaska. The Yupik have recently evangelized the Yupik in Siberia. WBT has developed a written form of the language and a bilingual education curriculum has been established. There are 13,000 who speak the language, though most also know English. The New Testament translation was completed in 1956 and the Old Testament is also ready. A Bible translation in the Siberian dialects is in progress and portions are available, but only the older people speak the language.[2]

DINE or *Navajos*

There are 219,000 Navajo living on the Colorado Plateau where Utah, New Mexico and Arizona meet. They exemplify the adaptation of a people who changed from being hunter-gatherers in Canada seven centuries ago to being sheep pastoralists in northeast Arizona. They have also learned agriculture from the Pueblos and silversmithing from the Mexicans. In the nineteenth century, uncontrolled pastoralism has led to the limitation of the herd in modern times. But although the flocks are still small and not for commercial production, they have increased according to family size, rather than according to the grazing capacity of the land. This is because there are no alternative ways to support those unemployed and marginalized by the surrounding society.[3] Because of this the livestock has come to symbolize the values of co-operation and generosity, because herding requires sharing and the help of others. The sheep are a means of maintaining family prestige, in exchanging gifts within the society and special inter-family transactions, and without adequate stocks the breakdown of relationships is only averted by buying consumer goods for exchange. Hence, livestock play a vital part in the social and cultural fabric of the Dine as well as being economic goods.

The herds are individually owned but the land belongs to the community, and there is no organization to stop overgrazing.

Each Dine is a member of one of 60 clans, determined by descent through his mother. A voluntary state program with payments to reduce the number of sheep was carried out in the 1970s. There is heavy snowfall in winter, while the summers are hot, which makes sheep farming difficult. They supplement their pastoralism by horticulture, and they have been able to exploit the mineral resources of their reservation profitably. Many individual Navajo are at poverty level, and alcoholism and suicide are common problems.[4] They have developed their own educational institutions.

Religion

The Dine, or "People," believe that humans must maintain the harmony of creation established by the gods, through ritual and a code of behavior that includes being wary of non-Dine. Central to this belief is the "changing woman," a deity who created humankind and provided them with corn. The Native American Church accepts a syncretism of Christianity, Navajo animism and a pan-Indianism. The Navajo New Testament was published in 1997.

GUARJIROS

They live as herders of sheep, goats and cattle on the arid La Peninsula de la Guajira, Colombia and Maicao, Venezuela. This covers an area of 9,325 square kilometers (3,600 sq. mi.). The boundary divided the Guarjiros so that there are 135,000 in Colombia and 170,000 in Venezuela.[5] They probably moved into the desert centuries ago to avoid colonization, and paradoxically learned to herd cattle — either from the

Spanish or from their African slaves. The Guarjiros had their own slaves until about 1950. So their nomadism saved them from elimination during the Spanish Conquest, as happened to most of the original Amerindians.

Cattle are highly valued and are taken to a shaman if sick.[6] The Guarjiros migrate constantly in small groups with their herds of goats or cattle, for pasture and social reasons, sheltering in flimsy *ranchos*. Their stable diet is corn gruel, and they sleep in hammocks. They have also shown flexibility by adding the harvesting of sea salt to their pastoralism. They go down to the coast twice a year to do this and sell it to the Latinos to buy the goods they do not produce themselves. They are also great fishermen, selling shellfish as far away as Bogatá. There are bands of outlaws and drug traffickers in the desert who have attacked the Guarjiros, most of whom are armed.

The Guarjiros have seven clans, structured according to descent through the mother, and many marriages are polygamous. These clans used to be constantly in conflict. They only marry women outside their own clan or group, and they have to give a dowry of goats for her. They have become citizens of both Colombia and Venezuela. In Maicao they are provided with employment as day laborers, and there are schools and clinics for them, to help them make a transition to urban life. But this has tended to change their culture to being male-dominated, because their wives are left on the peninsula. A school for 300 children is run by Spanish Capuchins at the Nazare oasis, and some of the men have learned to speak Spanish.[7] They use Spanish words as names, so that their real names are kept secret.

Outreach

Their language is Wayuu, and the New Testament translation is complete with portions of the Old Testament also available. SIL has produced a 700-page grammar and readers, needed because of the high level of illiteracy. The Gospel of Mark was translated and published in the 1940s. The South

America Mission, Inc. was the only mission working with these people, and overcame their resistance to contact with outsiders. A group of believers started to gather in 1980. The Foursquare Church has established an outreach to Guajiro *civilisados* and professionals who have settled. The SAM established five primary schools in 1989, and these also help Guajiro primary teachers to come up to Colombian standards.[8] The Ocaña Bible Institute, led by TEAM, was established in 1981 with two Guajiro students, and others have since been trained. Christian cassettes are available and daily radio broadcasts have been transmitted from Maicao since 1983 in Guajiro or Wayuu.

QUECHUA

Quechua is a linguistic classification of various ethnic groups in Peru, and many are without clear ethnic differentiation. Quechua was the lingua franca of the Inca Empire. The rural Quechua live in self-contained local communities and marry within that same community. The farmland is distributed to individuals from a common ownership. They practice subsistence agriculture and herd llamas and sheep on the surrounding natural pasture, which is very poor. It is not clear how many herders might be semi-nomadic. The fluctuations in environmental conditions cause pastoralists to migrate between the *puna*, at 3,800 meters and higher, to the high mountain valleys below at 3,200 meters. But they also sometimes migrate down to 1,000 meters above the coastal plains. In Peru the pasture can support two or more animals per hectare, but in Bolivia it is so arid that 20 hectares are needed to support one animal. Llama and alpacas are easily herded because they flock together naturally, so that one family can herd 300 animals. These animals also have the extraordinary habit of evacuating their bowels in the same place every day, which means it is easy to collect the droppings for use on the fields. The animals are used to transport their own dung to the crops of potatoes that give an alternative subsistence.[9]

AYMARA HERDERS

The Aymara are transhumant llama pastoralists in the districts of Caillona, Arequipa, Puno, Cuzco, Aputmas and Ayacucho, in Peru. Aymara is the second major language of the Sierra Indians, but there is no major ethnic difference between them and the Quechua groups. They are true pastoralists, they do not practice agriculture, and their lives and beliefs center around their herds of alpacas, llamas and sheep. They live in dispersed extended family groups and produce their own clothes from their wool. They can travel great distances to trade their surplus wool and meat to buy agricultural products for food. They probably speak Aymara. They are nominally Catholic but essentially pre-Christian, and they make offerings to the powers in the mountains.[10]

The *Quechua Boliviano*, a revised Bible translation with a concordance, and the *Quechua Ancash* New Testament were published in 1993. The New Testament in *Quechua Canar* is 70% complete. The *Quechua Imbabura* Bible is complete. The New Testament in Spanish Simple Language Scripture for Children is available and the Old Testament is ready.[11] HCJB broadcasts a number of programs in various forms of Quechua daily.

MESTIZO HERDERS

In rural areas, Mestizos have a higher social position than the pure Indians and gain office in local government; in the past they often acted as go-betweens for the Indians in their relationships with the urban population. The Mestizos form a number of communities of pastoralists in the High Sierra on the western side of the Andes in southern Peru. They consider themselves distinct and accuse the Aymara herders, as well as town dwellers, of stealing their livestock. They practice a transhumant pastoralism, moving between three very different climatic zones — the High Sierra, the lower High Sierra and the *puna* (dry altiplano) — that are only about 15 kilometers (9 mi.) apart horizontally. The lower High Sierra lies between 2,500 and 3,400 meters (11,150 ft.). It is an arid region with sparse vegetation for most of the year, but it is transformed by a limited seasonal rainfall to give pasture from November to April. But above 3,400 meters, up to 3,800 meters, the High Sierra receives six times the rain (250 mm.) and has much more varied and permanent vegetation. This High Sierra is below the altitude of the Aymara llama herders, who keep to the *puna*.

Nomadism

Some of these Mestizo herders living in the Asana Valley, Department of Moquegua, Peru, serve as an example of their lifestyle. Each nuclear family is economically independent with its own herd, of mostly goats with some sheep and a few cows. There is little common identity between them as pastoralists, and grazing disputes are common. The father takes the herding decisions and has to be away bartering with farmers or at the market in Moquegua. The whole family works with the animals, but a few families are also prosperous enough to do some cultivation as well. The herds range in size, with between 120 and 900 goats, about 30 sheep and five to ten cows of the local breeds. The emphasis is on goats because of the nature of the terrain and the available forage.

The herds graze in the lower valleys between November and July, then move up to the area of permanent vegetation of the High Sierra during the dry season. This is usually a distance of about 15 to 20 kilometers (9 to 12 mi.), but a change in altitude of a 1,000 meters. Although the distances are small, some families move to live with their livestock according to the seasons, while others have a permanent location where some of the family live for most of the year. Theft and predators cause great losses, so the families always camp with the animals. In both wet and dry seasons these camps have to be moved only once or twice, so they are quite well established for weeks in between.

At least one year in ten they have to move to new areas because of poor rainfall.

At these times they will slaughter as much as 50% of their herds. These families value their herds for the prestige they confer as much as for economic subsistence, which requires them to keep herds of fit animals that are as large as possible. Like pastoralists elsewhere, they value animals as a herd rather than for meat. While they do not form a separate society, and some would claim they are not true nomadic pastoralists, they are nomadic in the sense that they utilize the seasonal and local variation in forage growth according to altitude. They occasionally migrate out of their area more than 100 kilometers (60 mi.) to exploit pasture there.[12]

Religion

They are Folk Catholics with many Amerindian practices. It is not known whether these people have contact with evangelical Christians.

FLETEROS, *llamero, cargucho* or *arrieres*

They are llama caravan drovers in parts of the Andes in Bolivia, Chile and Peru. In Chile, groups trade between Isluga, near the Bolivian border with Iquique, and others trade from the Cordillera de Lipez in southwest Bolivia into Chile — some 150 kilometers (90 mi.). In Bolivia, caravans still trade from around Lake Titicaca to lower mountain valleys. In the 1970s, caravans were operating in the area between Oruro and Potosi. Others are found in Paratia and Collaguas.

As castrated male animals are best for transporting, the herds have five males for every two females, compared to one male for every 20 or more females for those in wool production. Therefore the Fleteros are occupationally, but not ethnically, distinct from the wool herders, since they use the animals for trade and for hiring to farmers for transport. For those living above 3,800 meters the Fletero is important, for marketing the products of the pastoralists and bringing food products back up to them.

A drover travels about 15 to 20 kilometers (9 to 12 mi.) per day with about

15 to 20 animals, guiding them by whistles, calls and stones from a sling. They stop early in the afternoon to allow the animals to forage. Journeys can last up to two or more months. The droves stop with well-established trading partners on the route. Boys learn to be drovers between eight and twelve years of age, first with a relative and then with friends of his father, to build up his experience and develop partnership between the drover families. The enforcement of school attendance in Bolivia has reduced the number of boys learning the trade. The lead-llama has bells around its neck, and flags and tassels will be added at the end of a successful trip, and are part of rituals to ensure good luck. A ceremony before the journey is led by the eldest Fletero, asking the gods of the animals to allow them to go and seeking protection from evil spirits on the way.[13]

KADIWEU

They live in the Pantanal, between Conrumba and Campo Grande, in western Mato Grosso do Sul, Brazil. They are about 1,200 nomadic horse breeders, descended from the *Guaicuru*. In the seventeenth century they soon acquired horses from their Spanish enemies and developed great skill as horsemen as well as basic veterinary ability. The Kadiweu possessed thousands of horses and vast herds of sheep and cattle on the Gran Chaco, and they were reputed to be fast runners to catch the animals. They also used to capture the offspring of other tribes, rather than have the inconvenience of pregnancy.

The Kadiweu sided with Brazil in the war against Paraguay in the last century and were awarded their territory within Brazil, but this has since been given to cattle ranchers. Their reservation is very fertile, but it does not benefit the Kadiweu at all because it is leased to Brazilian ranchers by the FUNDAI, the government agency that is supposed to protect the Indians. This situation was confirmed in a court case between Mato Grosso State and the Brazilian Supreme Court, and their land is still leased to the cattle ranchers to the detriment of the Indians. They work as cowhands on the ranches and have a depressed culture. Lévi Strauss, the anthropologist, lived with them for a time. In the past they allowed the Jesuits to work among them and are nominally Christian.[14] SIL have a literacy and Bible translation program.

MAPUCHE, Mapudungi

There are 40,000 in Argentina and 400,000 Mapuches south of Santiago in Chile. Those in Argentine are recent migrants from Chile. They are transhumant sheepherders in the hills of the provinces of Nenquén, Rio Negro and Chubut. They want to be integrated into Chilean society. Their language is called Mapudungun. A Bible translation in progress, and SAMS is working there as well as SIM, developing a TEE course as well as providing preventative health care.[15]

PATAGONIANS

These consisted of at least five groups. The *Yaghan* were once shellfish-gathering nomads and the *Ona* were hunters in Tierra del Fuego, but only a few individuals are left. The original people were the *Puelche* and *Querandí* to the north on the pampas, and the *Tehuelche* to the south of the River Chubut in Patagonia. They were hunter-gathers, but they soon acquired horses and the necessary skills from the Spanish. They hunted the wild guanaco and rhea, following them as they migrated from the high ground to sheltered valleys near the coast in winter. This amounted to a parallel form of nomadic pastoralism, as both the Tehuelche's horses and the wild guanacos moved according to the seasonal growth of pasture and changes in climate. They never domesticated the animals, however. They traded in skins and rhea feathers with the Spanish and with the Welsh at Trelew, in the Chubut Valley. The Welsh Non-Conformist settlement at Trelew was established in 1862, and they soon learned from the Tehuelche how to live in their new environment by going on hunting trips. Due to Puelche attacks on settlers, a war of ethnic cleansing wiped out most of the Indians, even though the Tehuelche had non-aggression treaties with the Argentineans, and by 1890 the surviving Indians were in two camps. Their hunting grounds were converted into huge sheep farms.

This vast region is so infertile that two to four hectares (5 to 10 acres) are required to support one sheep. The large sheep *estancias* of the region use *mestizo* shepherds from Chiloe Island in Chile. They are separated from their families for long periods with only a horse for company. Also *Araucan* Indians, who originally were driven from Chile in the nineteenth century, work in traveling gangs as sheep shearers.[16]

Examples of Non-pastoral Nomads in the Americas

ESKIMO, *Inuit*

While the term Inuit has been adopted to describe all the Eskimos in Canada, the Inuit only represent about 60% of them, and perhaps the term Eskimo is still to be preferred. The related non-Inuit peoples are the *Aleut* (2,000) and *Yupik* (21,000).[17] They are traditionally hunter-gathers north of the tree line from Siberia (1,300), Alaska (33,000), Canada (24,000) and Greenland (43,000). They form, or formed, small communities of a few hundred according to the subsistence available, most dividing up for nearly all the year and following an annual migration between the sea, ice hunting for polar bear and seals, and the inland areas for river fishing and caribou. A few groups stayed inland living off caribou, hares and berries all the time.

Moravian missionaries from Greenland entered Labrador in 1770 and encouraged the Inuits in European-style fishing and trade. A literacy and school program was successful, but the influence of European settlers was negative overall. Generally the influence of the fur trade encouraged the Inuit to give up hunting. When schools were established the people moved near to the trading posts that had the schools. This has had the effect of reducing the infant mortality rate, but has also created a generation gap between the young wanting Western amenities and the parents preferring the old ways. Attempts have been made to domesticate the caribou, import reindeer and market Inuit crafts — with little success. What is preferred is a mixed economy of hunting and fishing with salaried employment. The northeast part of the Northwest Territories became the new Territory of Nunavut in 1999, with its capital at Iqaluit (Frobisher Bay), and the Inuit population gained a large role in the administration.

In August, the *Napaaq turmiut* of western Alaska take all their belongings and ascend the Noatak River in their large hide boats for river fishing and caribou hunting. The hides of the caribou in autumn are best for making clothes, and at the end of September they move into sod or log half-underground shelters for the winter, where they stay unless food starts to run out. Then they split up into small family groups, constantly moving to find caribou or hares. In mid-March they return to their shelters, pack all their belongings on sleds and go to the Chukchi coast, to live and hunt on the sea ice. When the ice breaks up they move ashore and hunt seal, whale and walrus by kayak. When the ice is clear from the coast all the scattered camps travel along the shore, gradually forming one large party of over 1,000 people to have a fair or gathering for games, dancing and feasting. In August the process starts again up the river. The whole migration pattern is an example of careful exploitation of seasonal conditions and resources.[18]

There are 10,000 *Mushuau Innu* living in Nitaassinan or northern Quebec and

Labrador, Canada. Traditionally they were hunters of the 600,000 caribou, but many now have part-time employment. NATO low-level flying training has been a nuisance and has encouraged human rights activity among the Innu. Because many of them were moved from their traditional homeland in Labrador to Davis Inlet to start a fishing industry, the change provoked cultural collapse and communal suicides.[19] They are hoping for a second move back to be near their old hunting grounds. They are shamanists, believing in supernatural "animal masters" who control the caribou and in a goddess who lives in the depth of the sea. Fear, rather than belief, is the way they describe their religious attitude. Their language is Eastern Inuktitut or Eastern Canadian Inuit. The Bible was translated in 1826.[20] There were 900 conversions to Christianity reported in 1988.[21] The Diocese of the Arctic, Episcopal Church (originally BCMS) serves them.

The *Thule Inuit*, Greenland, have a new commitment to their ethnic identity not only in the old skills as hunters, but also at home and at school. They are able to pay for imported food, clothes and other goods by selling the skins and furs of the animals they hunt. The Danish government provides medical services and loans for items such as motorboats. Caribou have been reintroduced to Greenland, but they also hunt seals and bears on the ice for short periods in winter darkness, and longer periods as summer approaches when the sea ice is treacherous, as currents and tides underneath melt it. In the summer they hunt by motorboat for three months. They live in two-room wooden houses. Some of them are also now teachers, carpenters or nurses. Depression affects the adults as the days shorten to a few minutes in autumn, and heavy drinking and suicide are problems. The Danish Lutheran church is present among them.[22]

CARNIVAL WORKERS, USA

Each year, as many as 85 million Americans attend thousands of carnivals or fairs held by 300 to 500 traveling groups of operators. The permanent traveling staff of a carnival may range from a few families to as many as 800 people. They work as performers or operator-owners of the rides, side shows and food stalls. The composition of the staff varies constantly because each show or ride has a different contract for different periods, so that staff of the same owner may be in different places at the same time. About 80% of the workers have never worked anywhere else except in the carnival business, and 13% were born into a carnival family. They are therefore a distinct people with a different approach to life from other Americans. They tend to be considered of lower rank to circus performers, and the carnival provided a less united or stable social environment compared to the circus. However, 11% have worked from time to time in both. Some of them are able to settle in retirement.[23]

IRISH TRAVELERS or *Tinkers*

They arrived in America early in 1847 and initially traveled as tinkers. As that market declined, they switched to horse and mule trading between 1860 and 1920. They do not consider themselves Gypsies. Since then they have traveled selling linoleum and doing spray painting. The men travel most of the year in groups, with their families joining them in the summer.[24]

SCOTTISH TRAVELERS

There are about 4,000 in Scotland and 4,000 in the United States. The latter still itinerate from a fixed base. Their language is Scottish Traveler Cant.

ROM or GYPSIES

The first Gypsies to arrive in the United States came from the British Isles, but later others came from the Mediterranean, along with the general shift of immigrants from northern to southern Europe. Among these were Rom, who had moved out of Romania and Moldova in the middle of the nineteenth century, traveling through Austria-Hungary, Italy and the Balkans, to arrive in New York in 1881. Most were able to travel on European passports. They managed to avoid the discrimination against them that they had met in Europe, because of the many immigrants and the size of the country. But soon after this, immigration restrictions were introduced on those identified as Gypsies, and these have not been repealed. After World War II, many of the Rom tried to emigrate to the United States, but most did not succeed.

There are now different groups in North America that have little felt unity between them, each even considering the others not to be true Gypsies. But they do claim to be Gypsies, and they maintain the Gypsy purity laws.[25] (See the description of the concept of pollution in the Europe section, below.) There are, of course, barriers in the form of the Gypsy's and the American's stereotypes of each other that affect relations between them, especially for Gypsy children who attend school.

American Gypsies use rented houses in the winter close to their relatives and customers and to store equipment for roofing and laying tarmac. Fortunetelling is usually profitable in poorer areas. They all tend to advertise in the press, the Rom also using radio and TV. Laws against Gypsies and the costs of housing and licenses are important factors when they consider their location. Local law enforcement and laws requiring a license to settle, trade or practice fortune telling vary according to the state or county.

The **English Gypsies** or **Romnichels** crossed to North America from 1850 onwards, and they now number about 20,000. They hawk linoleum, carpets, clothes-lines, lace and baskets, but they have more recently concentrated on paint spraying. They live in houses during the winter.[26] They seek to operate within the law with all the necessary permits. They speak a Romani vocabulary with English syntax. They consider themselves Protestant and many have become Pentecostal, and they also continue to maintain the Gypsy purity laws.

Ludar or **Rudari** or *Romanian Gypsies* arrived in the United States in the 1880s, via Bosnia and other areas now independent of the Ottoman Empire. They earned a living as bear and monkey trainers in the tradition of their Romanian role, and others worked as showmen and woodworkers, traveling by horse and wagon. They went through a period of nomadism before mainly settling their extended families in the shantytowns of New York City, Philadelphia and Chicago. They now work making furniture, roofing and in carnivals. They speak a Romanian dialect, not Romani. Their religious preference is Romanian Orthodoxy, or Roman Catholicism as a second best.[27]

Rom or "Serb" or "Russian" Gypsies number about 20,000 and have spread across North America in large family groups and tend to stay together. They have tried to continue in fortune telling, but they soon moved on to roofing and car sales, traveling in trailers and mobile homes. Metal work is one of the preferred activities of the men — in car body repairs, scrap collecting, car sales and occasional coppersmithing, but more often they do roofing, paving and home improvements. They often now compete with each other. The women tell fortunes and sell cheap goods around the houses.

Anne Sutherland describes the **Machwaya** and **Kalderash** in California.[28] These are two of the four main "nations" or tribes of the Rom. The Machwaya are more prosperous and consider themselves better Rom and "cleaner" than the Kalderash. The two "nations" divide up the state of California between them into territories in which each claims exclusive rights to Gypsy sources of income. The Kalderash claim that the "superior" Machwaya often tries to encroach and even take over their territories. They divide into related households which are often extended families, living in rented houses for short periods, usually on the main streets for business contacts, where they will spend about half the year. The rest of the time they travel constantly to visit relatives, ply their trade and fulfill religious ceremonies.

Households will also move because of conflict due to a breach of the purity laws, or poaching on the trade of another group. Each territory has a leader, *rom baro*, or "big man," who deals with problems with non-gypsies, distributes the economic opportunities within the territory and settles disputes. They are usually Serbian Orthodox but many are now Roman Catholic. *E Nevi Vastia*, the Kalderash New Testament, has had two translations both published in France.

The **Lovara Rom** are more recent immigrants and are integrating into the Rom above.

VLACK ROM

In Mexico, the Vlack Rom total 53,000, divided into various groups. The Mexican groups are well-armed to guard against any revenge attacks. One group, the *Xulupeste*, was driven out of Mexico to Argentina after street fights, and a vendetta against them is still in force. They all invoke Our Lady of Guadalupe for protection and keep her festival, as do millions of other Mexicans.[29]

They show films with traveling cinema equipment, or do metal work, to earn their income. They usually rent their homes or live in shanties built on vacant ground, often with a wall and gate that can be locked. Buildings with more than one story are avoided, because a woman upstairs might stand over a man downstairs and so defile him. The walls are covered with brightly printed drapery with photos and pictures pinned to it. One corner is reserved as *santuario*, with an image of Our Lady of Guadalupe and other "saints." There are usually no internal walls, only curtains, separating sleeping spaces. Food is cooked on a charcoal fire and eaten sitting cross-legged around a low table.

The parents of a couple who marry maintain a special relationship of friendship and co-operation as long as the marriage lasts. They have neither Catholic nor state marriages and divorce is frequent, as is having children by a number of partners. Usually they live as nuclear families, except when a new wife of a son is being "indoctrinated" into the customs of the husband's clan, because she has come from another clan. The women are distinguishable by their long dresses and aprons. The married women also wear a kerchief as a sign of marriage. Education is restricted to a limited ability to read and write. When a member of the family is sick, the whole family tends to be disrupted; they have no confidence in *gaje*, or non-Gypsy doctors, but consult their folklore for cures.

Though claiming to be Catholic, the Rom have little knowledge of its rites, and they tend not to be interested in religious issues. Beneficial powers in the world are considered to be personified as Catholic "saints," but evil forces are impersonal. But they fear death and the dead.

There are also between 100,000 and 210,000 Vlack Rom in Argentina, Brazil and Colombia. They are probably sedentary, except for some groups working as mobile tradesmen and craftsmen in Argentina. Their world total is 1,500,000.[30] There are 500,000 living in Europe. A Brazilian Rom, Hugo Caldeira, is probably the first Gypsy to write a book about the Bible entitled *La Bibbia e gli Zingari* (*The Bible and the Gypsies*) in 1994. William Mitchell, UBS, reported requests for Bible translations from Gypsy churches in Brazil, Argentina, Chile, Peru and Ecuador. Some Bible portions in Kalderash are available in Chile.

EUROPE

While Europe has a few nomadic pastoralists, the rest of its nomadic peoples are peripatetics. Both suffer from the encroachment of a highly urban and industrialized society. The high density of population puts pressure on common lands that could be used for pasture or camping. The traumas of European history have further generated movements of people pressed to leave because of social or ethnic intolerance. Legislation unfavorable to traveling peoples has added to this, because they have few votes and little influence.

Europe is probably the place that is most intolerant of nomadic peoples, and it probably has the fewest reasons for being so. In other places, hostility between the settled and the nomad has deep historical motives, but in Europe nomads have never been a threat to the state or society. Rather, the hostility is rooted in unfounded fears of those who do not wish to conform to the assumed "civilized" lifestyle, suspicion of the unknown and misunderstood, and in highly developed administrative organization which resents what seems to be unaccountable. The increased sophistication of entertainment and the industrialization of services also counts against what the peripatetics can offer. But political integration and rapid transport systems should encourage the survival of nomadism, and the trend towards uniformity should encourage the demand for simpler alternatives. Tourism and the desire to "opt out" tend to encourage the preservation of alternative simpler lifestyles. Nomads have used their mobility to find more profitable economic opportunities and lower social profiles.

Nomadic Pastoralists of Europe

SAMI, *Saami Samer* or *Lapps*

"Lapp" comes from the Finnish, but the name is considered derogatory and is no longer used in the area. In Norwegian the Sami were called Finns and Norway's most northern county, where many Sami live, is called Finnmark. Ethnically they are related to the Finns, Hungarians, Khants and Mansi, but it is not clear that they also migrated from Siberia. They may have been the original inhabitants of Finland, whose language was influenced by Finnish.[1] Estimates of the Sami population vary as there is no official ethnic category for a census, but it is accepted that 30,000 live in northern Norway; 20,000 in northwest Sweden; 8,000 in northern Finland; and 2,000 on the northern half of the Kola Peninsula in Russia. Out of these, 45,000 live north of the Arctic Circle and the rest in mountain villages near the Norwegian-Swedish border south of the Circle.[2] In some areas they are outnumbered by the Scandinavians, being less than 3% of the population. There are also large communities in Oslo and Stockholm.

History
The Sami once occupied the whole of Finland and the northern half of Sweden, and were known to the Romans as hunters traveling on skis. They originally had a diverse economy as hunter-gatherers, farmers and fishermen, but they had to adopt reindeer hunting, and later

pastoralism, from the thirteenth century onwards, as they were forced northwards by the advancing Nordic and Finnish peoples. Having no central political structure of their own, they became subject to Scandinavian overlords, paying them tribute. Around the fifteenth century, because hunting with guns quickly depleted the reindeer stock, the Sami adopted pastoralism by herding the reindeer and domesticating some of them for transport and milk. The scarcity of pasture in the Arctic encouraged them to travel with the herds, and to develop the nomadic life using migration routes that led to the coast or the mountains in summer. In this way, using all the products of their reindeer, the Sami managed to be largely self-sufficient, in spite of losing the best lands. The treaty of 1751, that confirmed the borders of the Scandinavian kingdoms, recognized the rights of the Sami, including their nomadic migrations across the borders. But when Norway and Sweden were united between 1814 and 1905, the Sami suffered as a result of development, the settlement of the north and racial disparagement.

Nomadism

Today about 10% of the Sami are transhumant reindeer herders, or "Mountain Lapps," and most combine this with other sources of income, which as we have seen is characteristic of most nomadic peoples. The herders are found scattered all over the Sami area, where the majority of Sami are farmers with cattle and crops in the valleys, and along the Norwegian coast many Sami engage in fishing. So while only some Sami have reindeer, to own and herd them gives a certain prestige, because this is central to Sami culture.

The characteristic herding group is the *siida*, consisting of several related families, and provides loyalty and mutual support between the families. The herds of a *siida* usually belong to the member families, as well as to settled Sami. The Sami farmers can be prosperous and keep flocks of sheep and herds of cows, but they welcome the extra income from owning some reindeer. For a family to be self-sufficient, supported only

by reindeer, requires a herd of 350 animals. This is possible in Norway and to a lesser extent in Sweden, but much smaller herds are the norm in Finland. In Sweden the Sami have herding co-operatives called *samebys*, but the laws controlling membership have resulting in fewer Sami being able to engage profitably in herding.[3]

The reindeer are owned individually by men, women and children. Sami boys and children build up their herds as their parents and relatives give them reindeer on birthdays, at their confirmation and on other special occasions. The youngest son, not the eldest, inherits what is left of the parent's herd. In return, he is expected to stay at home and care for the aged parents. Women are considered equals and have always participated in both herd ownership and herding. Daughters can have substantial herds by the time they are ready to marry, so consent for marriage is not easily given, since the family's herd is diminished when her animals leave to form a separate herd. Wooing, therefore, involves careful negotiations!

In the winter the reindeer live on lichen on the tundra and on the trees; the latter is particularly important for their survival when the ground is frozen or the snow too deep to paw away. In the spring, the herds are rounded up and driven to special areas reserved for calving. They are also separated into herds according to their owners for branding. They are then herded across country to the summer grass pastures, which are on the coast in Norway, or in the mountains to the west in Sweden. The journey is around 200 kilometers (125 mi.) long and takes about two weeks. It used to take much longer, using the *pulka*, or boat-shaped sled pulled by reindeer. Today the men migrate on snow scooters, usually traveling at night because the snow is frozen and therefore firmer for the reindeer. With the snow scooters, time is not needed to round up and carefully load the pack reindeer before moving on each day. The scooters can also pull five times the load of a reindeer. Two men can now control a herd that used to take a dozen men. The scooters also make it easier to guard against the most common predators, the lynx and wolverine, and the eagles and foxes that go for the calves. In addition, the scooters enable some herders to travel ahead of the herds and set up camp before the others arrive.

The scooters also mean that the herders can make rapid visits to trading posts in a matter of hours, over distances that once took days to cover. Fishing, which once supplemented their diet, has now become a commercial sideline, as they use scooters to deliver fresh trout to the roads. It is delivered from there to the villages and towns. But the pack reindeer is coming back into use, because when there is no snow the herder has to walk. Also, the expense of the snow scooter and the cost of fuel means that reindeer have to be slaughtered and sold for meat to pay for them. It is also claimed that the reindeer have become more timid with the noise and pollution of the scooter.

In the past, the families used to travel with the men, but the reindeer sleds moved too slowly to keep the children warm on the long journeys. Today, the families travel to the summer pastures by bus or car to spend the summer in huts, many of which have most of the amenities of modern houses. In September the herds are rounded up again and about a fifth of the animals are selected for slaughter. This cull for the commercial meat market enables the Sami to buy modern goods such as clothing, domestic utensils and a variety of food. The rest migrate back to the tundra for rutting in October and for winter pasture.

The Sami are reviving their cultural consciousness, and assimilation to the surrounding Scandinavian culture has slowed down. They are increasingly aware of being exploited, and they often resent the attention of tourists, journalists and anthropologists. The thousands of tourists affect not only the humans, but also the countryside, and reindeer herding has become impossible in some areas. The building of roads, the damming of rivers, oil exploration, timber felling and mining have all adversely affected the environment. Conservation is construed as preserving only non-human processes, and ignores the role the Sami have had in creating or modifying the landscape. The nomadic pastoralist is a range manager who in time modifies and recreates the landscape and has to be included as part of the conservation. This is made difficult when tourism requires the herder to use only traditional methods, cloths and equipment, as if in a time lock of the past.[4] Another problem for the herders is that radioactive fallout from Chernobyl has seriously affected the reindeer in the southern Sami regions.[5]

But because unemployment is a problem in the far north, the Sami have been versatile in taking seasonal work in tourism or forestry. They also help each other by moving to work with relatives. Those along the Norwegian coast have adopted Norwegian ways, often separating themselves from their fellow Sami.[6] A few thousand work in industry, in the civil service, and as teachers and nurses, and so on. Alcoholism is a problem among them. To deal with their affairs, Sami parliaments were formed in Finland in 1976, in Norway in 1989 and later in Sweden. How their traditional way of life and its continuing pastoralism are integrated into the modern Scandinavian society is a test case for pastoral peoples elsewhere.

There are four Sami languages, but Northern Sami is spoken by 75% of the Sami.[7] Sami is usually only spoken at home, and some parents speak Norwegian to the children, which they learn at school, because it is felt this will be more useful to them. In some areas schooling from kindergarten to college level is taught in Sami, and there are radio and some TV programs in the language. It has only become a literary language in the last 100 years. In Russia the Sami speak three different dialects, which are not understandable to each other. An attempt to create a unified form of the language failed, and Russian serves as the literary language.[8]

Religion

The Sami were originally shamanists, but most of its practices were removed through

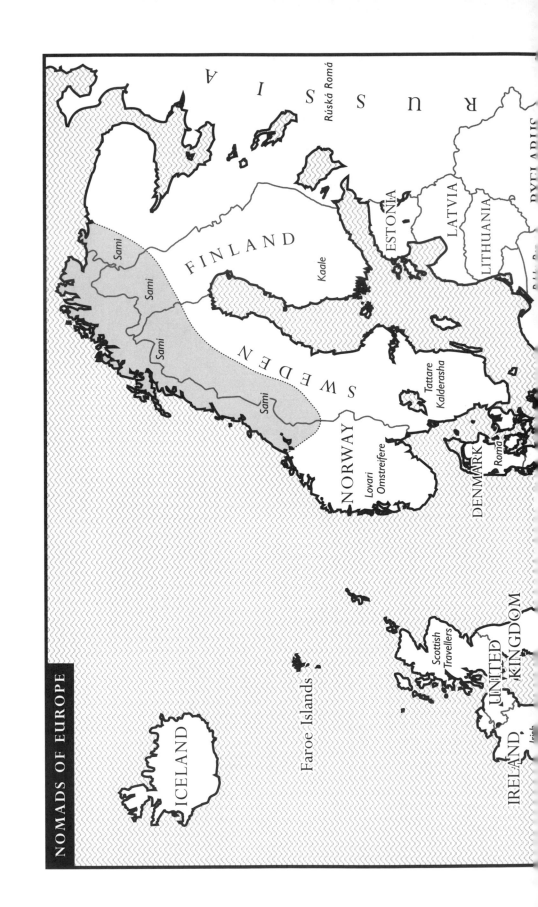

RUSSIA

Rúská Romá

FINLAND

ESTONIA

LATVIA

LITHUANIA

BYELARUS

Sami

Sami

Sami

Sami

Kaale

Sami

SWEDEN

Tattare
Kalderasha

NORWAY

Lovari
Omstreifere

DENMARK

Romá

ICELAND

Faroe Islands

Scottish
Travellers

UNITED
KINGDOM

IRELAND

Irish

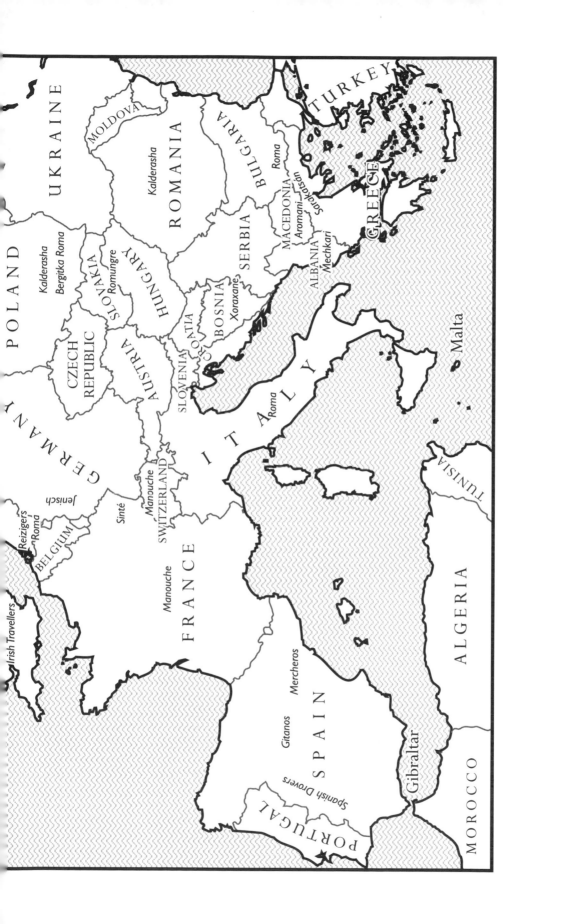

the ministry of Lutheran and Russian Orthodox missions during the seventeenth century. Christianity had the misfortune of being associated with suppressing Sami culture in the nineteenth century, and there is a need to demonstrate that a Sami Christianity is possible. Most Sami are Lutheran, and for this reason the Lutheran Church is stronger in Finnmark than in any other part of Norway. In the nineteenth century, Joakim Stockfleth volunteered for missionary work among the Sami, traveling through out the region and living with the nomadic groups. A Swedish mission provided schools for the Sami. A Swedish Sami pastor founded the Laestadian movement around 1850. Its ministry in northern Sweden had a transforming effect on the poorer people. It protested against the use of Norwegian in worship and the vices of alcohol, but it tended to excesses and exclusivism after the founder's death. Where the Laestadian lay movement is strong, the Lutheran Church is strong.[9]

Outreach

The first Northern Sami New Testament translation was published in 1755, with the whole Bible in 1811. The Southern Sami Bible followed in 1895. A new translation in Northern Sami is expected to be complete in 1998. A new translation of Mark's Gospel in Southern Sami was published in 1993.[10] A translation program in Lule Sami has only just begun.

The Sami have a special form of singing called *yoik*, which involves a wordless refrain in ballads somewhat like a Swiss yodel. After being discouraged by the churches in the past as somehow being connected with Shamanism, Sami Christians are beginning to use it in worship. There are both nominal and evangelical Christians among the Sami, but there is a great need for spiritual revival and for an openness to allow other Christians to minister.[11] YWAM supports Sami evangelists in missions among other indigenous peoples and in church planting in northern Norway.

AROMANI, *Arumuni, Koutzovlack, Aromanian* or *Vlach*

They are found in Greece, Serbia, Macedonia, Albania and Bulgaria, with a total of 1,500,000 Aromani worldwide. "Vlach" is used by the Greek villagers to refer to any shepherd, and they use the word Koutzovlack, which means "lame shepherd" (presumably because of the way they spoke Greek), to distinguish this group from other shepherds.[12] The Romanians call them Macedo-Romanians. In Macedonia they are also known as *Cincari*. The *Aromani*, their preferred name, are a distinct ethnic people. Since they are often known to the outside world as Vlachs, they are confused with the Gypsy groupings from Wallachia, also called Vlach, who migrated to many parts of Europe during the nineteenth century.

The question of their origin has given rise to various theories, but they are possibly the descendants of a Thracian tribe who intermarried with Roman colonists. When the Roman Empire retreated, they took refuge in the Carpathian Mountains as shepherds. This means that they are related to the Romanians. Some migrated southwards to the Pinus Mountains in the Balkans in about the twelfth century. Many of these have maintained their Latin-based culture by keeping largely to themselves as pastoralists in the mountains, at least until the twentieth century.

In the past, the Aromani controlled the overland trade between Greece and the Balkans. They were involved in the struggles in the Balkans at the end of the nineteenth century when Greece and Bulgaria laid claim to the area as the Ottoman Empire weakened. Many were Hellenophile, having had Greek schooling, and were influential within the Orthodox communities in the towns and supported Greek independence. The shepherds in the mountains, however, were pro-Bulgarian. But others in Macedonia leaned towards Romania, which supported them and provided Vlach schooling. Many migrated to Romania and advocated an independent Macedonia in 1918. During the

German occupation of Macedonia and Greece, some Vlachs led a short-lived, self-styled fascist state. When Macedonia was part of Yugoslavia under Communism, the ownership of large flocks and herds was banned, and many of the Aromani chose to settle in the villages.

a) Greece

The majority of the Aromani are in northern Greece, living in scattered rural communities and appear nearly assimilated so that their population cannot be estimated. There were 40,000 recorded in the 1951 census in Greece, but the number must be far higher — probably about 100,000. They are seasonally nomadic as shepherds, with most of the men spending the winters on the plains with the flocks, while their families continue to live in their mountain villages. In the summer, the men also pursue sedentary occupations, such as taxi driving, law and medicine. Greeks resent them using their language, Aromani, which has similarities to Romanian. In the 1980s, local cultural organizations were formed to guard against the extinction of the language. Generally, those who feel their distinction from Greeks strongly have emigrated so that separatist ideals are stronger outside Greece. Those who remained in Greece have tended to accommodate themselves to their minority status, in spite of an undercurrent of hostility from the Greeks.[13]

b) Albania

Traditionally they have kept large herds of cattle, which the men take up into the mountains in the spring and spend the summer there. There are perhaps 200,000 of them. These are probably the people referred to as *Karagounis*, black capes, the *Arvanitovlachi*, *Albanovlach* living in both the northwest Pinus Mountains of Greece and southern Albania. Their Aromani language is mixed with Albanian.[14] The Aromani tend to live apart from the Albanians, although both Albanian and Yugoslav governments have forced assimilation on them. Colonies of them live in towns in the southeast of

Albania, such as Kastoria, Florina, Manastir, Ohrid and Korça. There is another concentration of them around Vlora, where the marshes have been drained, and other groups have settled for agriculture, forcing the Vlachs to assimilate. The Vlachs formed an association in 1990 and held a conference in 1992.[15] They prefer to live in the hilliest parts of these towns. There is a plan to reopen Aromani speaking schools and the Romanian Orthodox churches that Romania encouraged before the Communist era. Under Communism the Vlachs were "settled," but they have begun to move with flocks again, traveling in the mountains around Korça in the summer and to Greece for the winter.[16] The Aromani New Testament was published in 1986 and Bible portions are available. Little Christian work is being done among them, but some Christians in Romania are interested in working with them.

c) Former Yugoslav Republic

The **Aromani** in the former Yugoslav Republic of Macedonia are concentrated around Bitola, Resen and Krusevo. The population is declining, mainly due to assimilation, which is hastened by the migration of the young people to the larger towns for work in industry. In the 1981 census about 6,400 declared themselves Aromani, but the number who still consider themselves as a distinct ethnic (Aromani) group is far greater. They appealed to a Balkan Foreign Ministers Conference in 1988 to be recognized as meriting separate Aromani education.[17]

SARAKATSÁN

They are a distinct ethnic group in Greece, often confounded with the Aromani as "Vlachs." There is no accepted explanation of their name, or knowledge of their origins. While other nomadic peoples invaded and settled in the Balkans, the Sarakatsán appear to have continued to be nomadic throughout their history. They are often called *adespotoi*, "master-less," because they keep to themselves. And, being completely nomadic, they tend not to have close connections with Greek society. The Sarakatsán are more mobile than the Aromani, as the latter live in village houses for half the year. The two peoples differ in many other ways, too, and often compete for winter pastures, have a disdain for each other, and do not intermarry.

The Sarakatsán appear to be of Greek origin, although they have been nomadic shepherds for centuries. It is estimated there may be 80,000 of them, scattered in groups over most of mainland Greece, from the Adriatic to Thrace and Greek Macedonia. They practice transhumant pastoralism, considering their summer pasture in the mountains their homeland, although typically they have no infrastructure there — paradoxically, though, their houses (if they have them) are on the plains, which serve as their winter pastures. The Sarakatsán rent pastures from villagers, like the Yörük do in southeastern Turkey.

Until the breakup of the Ottoman Empire, many of them traveled each year into Bulgaria and across into Asia Minor for pasture. A group in Vlora, southwest Albania have become assimilated since the Second World War. There are quite a few groups who have settled, due to the closing of borders and the denial of grazing rights, but even after two or three generations still claim to be Sarakatsán.[18]

Nomadism

The sheep are considered the mainstay, or "guard," of each family. Each migration can take four weeks. They use pack-horses to carry their belongings from camp to camp. They live in beehive huts of branches and wickerwork of rushes, and whole "villages" of these huts are sometimes built near the pasture. Typically the men wear black double-breasted waistcoats of black goats' hair, a black sash, and a black kilt with leggings and pointed shoes. A man is never separated from his crook, even when resting. The women wear distinctive clothes decorated in black and white geometrical designs of triangles and saw-tooth patterns. The wife is considered the servant of the husband, and she is generally referred to by

the female form of his name. Only a woman's husband and her immediate relatives call her by her real name.

The Sarakatsán have set traditions and customs concerning every aspect of their lives. Each family belongs to a clan or *stani* (fold), led by a *tsellingas*. Each family considers itself a corporate unity, so that a marriage is a "mixing of blood" to make a new unity, and sons- and daughters-in-law are referred to by being related to the father. Children are highly valued. The family jointly owns property, although the men administer it. Divorce is very rare, though the Greek Orthodox Church allows it.[19] Married brothers usually do not divide up to form separate families until all their sisters have been married and belong to other families.

Maintaining the honor of the family is vital. A man must maintain a certain reserve outside the family, and all members are intensely loyal, admitting to no faults. Honor depends on the "manliness," or the potency and status of the man, to stand up for the good name of the family and be a successful shepherd. A woman's honor is based on her sexual purity. Ideally, a girl who is not a virgin on marriage should be killed.[20]

Their diet consists of milk and black bread that they bake themselves. The hearth and fire inside their huts are considered to be sacred, and the fire is kept lit to ward off evil spirits. They are reluctant to slaughter their animals and tend to eat meat only on special occasions and when they receive visitors. They are fond of horse racing and wrestling.

Religion

They speak only a distinctive dialect of Greek that differs from the local dialects, implying a long stable history as part of Greece. They are nominally Greek Orthodox, but they have their own belief in a hierarchy of "saints" and both good and evil spirits, all presided over by Aï, the Holy, who is both God the Father and Jesus. St. George's day is the beginning of the summer migration, and a black lamb is sacrificed to him. On Easter, which is less important to them, a less prestigious white lamb is sacrificed. The pastoral winter begins with St. Demetrius' day. Both of these saints are worshipped as horsemen, and John the Baptist is worshipped because of his traditional rustic garb. There are shrines to Elijah, corrupted to St. Lios, on the peaks of the mountains. He is worshipped as a fertility deity, and as a mountain person like the nomads themselves. Each *stani* has its patron saint, but much effort is spent in warding off the various evil spirits that are thought to attack them or their animals in every aspect of life. Death is imagined to be continually present, and each adult carries with them a new set of cloths for burial, in case they should die on migration.[21]

SPANISH DROVERS

These men drive 30,000 head of cattle and 300,000 sheep and goats each spring from Extremadura in the southwest to León, northwest of Madrid, and then return in the autumn, a round trip of 700 kilometers (430 mi.). They make the trip in order to avoid the hot summers. The journey takes about two weeks, and they leave a parched south for pastures where it is still spring when they arrive. They follow ancient rights of way called Caminos Reales, or Cañadas, that were established before Christ and given recognition in 1273 AD. The last part of the journey is the most difficult, over the mountains on steep tracks of loose stones. The herds remain in the summer pastures for five months. The herders control the cattle on horseback and are said to be the inspiration for the American "cowboys," as the Spanish colonists in Latin America copied their methods. The herders sleep in the open next to the horses, and donkeys or trucks carry their basic supplies.

Perhaps another pointer to the general future of nomadic pastoralists is that the Spanish Drovers, although threatened by modern enclosures and roads, are now recognized as of historical and cultural value to Spain, so that legal protection for some 30,000 of the 125,000 kilometers (18,600 to 77,600 mi.) of "roads," and the drover custom is to be maintained. They are hardly a nomadic ethnic group, but it is possible for Christian tourists to join the droves for a holiday with an opportunity to witness to the men.[22]

Peripatetics in Europe

ROM, Gypsies, Travelers

There are probably between five and twelve million Travelers in Europe, depending on whether other indigenous traveler groups are included. The Gypsy Research Center, Paris, estimates there are between 7,000,000 and 8,500,000 in Europe, including Russia and the Ukraine.[23] We have tended to use their minimum figures in the sections below.

Non-Gypsies use the term "Gypsy," but many of these related groups call themselves *Rom* (pl. *Roma*), as reflecting their ethnic unity. *Rom* means "man." The people are called Romany, and their language is called Romani. The term *Rom* is used either of all East European Gypsies, or of those nomadic races that spread across Europe in the nineteenth century, like the Kalderash. The major division of Eastern European Roma is between the traditionally Orthodox and the Muslim Roma. In Western Europe, Gypsies tend to refer to themselves by the more local group names such as *Manouche* or *Sinte*. They have a growing self-awareness of their identity and origins as an international people.

Being conscious of being a separate people, all relationships with non-Gypsies are limited to commercial or exploitative transactions. There are varied degrees of disdain expressed in their terms for non-

35a

35b

35c

35d

35 Romanys:
    a. A large people group scattered around the world (Photos: M. Rodger).
    b. Romany children are happy although disadvantaged in lacking education (Photo: M. Rodger).
    c. Few use the horse-drawn *vardo* today like this Romany family (Photo M. Rodger).
    d. Outreach to a Romany family in England (Photo: M. Rodger).

Gypsies that they call the gadzé (sg. gadzo) or gadjo, gazé, or gorgio. In Spain non-gypsies are called payo. Many of the various communities are transnational, and it is a matter of debate whether we can describe the Roma by national subdivisions, such as English Gypsy or French Gypsy, but we divide this section by country perhaps more for gadzé (non-Gypsy) convenience to find them!

The Byzantine Greeks called them Alzinganoi, meaning "untouchables," after a completely unrelated Greek sect of magicians and minstrels. The name has stuck, in modified form, as their name in many languages, such as tsigan in the Balkans, tsiganes in French, Zigeuner in German or cigano in Portuguese, and so on. The English term "Gypsy" comes from "Egyptian," because when they first appeared in Europe they were often considered to come from there.

The constant conflict between the small states of India, and the invasions from the northwest, created an unstable situation for people to think of moving out of India. One of the invaders in the third century AD, Persia, attracted many different types of workers from India. In the fifth century, the Shah invited others as musicians. There are some who would say that the Banjaras and Dom castes were originally Gypsies. All these Indians formed a lower class distinct from the native Persians, and they intermarried and continued some of the earlier forms of Hinduism. These and later groups are possibly the origin of the Dom (see Middle East section, above), or Rom.[24]

History

It is generally accepted that the Gypsies are descended from groups of people who emigrated from northwest India, at least those moving from the ninth century AD onwards, under various names such as Luri, Luli or Zott. Their routes have been traced through the origins of many loan words from Persian, Turkish, Armenian, Greek and Romanian in their Romani dialects. Romani appears to have separated from the Sanskrit language about the same time as

Hindustani, around 900 AD.[25] Romani has European, Armenian and Asiatic branches. The Armenian branch includes the Bosha, or Lom, dialects. The Asian branch includes dialects such as the Nawar and Kurbat of the Levant and the Karachi of Turkey. When they arrived in Europe they were still aware of their origins in India.

European Roma have formed a complex pattern of various communities, during three great periods of migration, in the fifteenth and nineteenth centuries, and in the upheavals caused by the Second World War. These many groups have different histories and more than 60 Romani dialects. No common or standard Romani has developed, because the Roma have been constant travelers and highly adaptive to their surroundings, and they had no literature until the twentieth century.

The first migration of Roma into Europe was probably in the fourteenth century, as they moved out of the collapsing Byzantine Empire and ahead of the invading Ottoman Turks. As they advanced across Europe they gained a reputation for sorcery, fortunetelling and popular entertainment. Their presence was recorded in Germany and France by the early fifteenth century, and in Britain and Scandinavia by the beginning of the sixteenth century.

Those traveling further into Europe adopted the pose of pilgrim penitents, as the only way to get alms and to escape persecution as "heathen" in Catholic Europe. Having escaped the Turks, many ended up as slaves of Christian states. For example, in Tudor England Gypsies could be executed or sold into slavery, just for being "Egyptians." Other Gypsies were transported in Scottish, and probably English, ships and abandoned on the Norwegian coast from 1544 onwards.[26] Many lost their lives because they were accused of being pagan, sorcerers, spies or thieves. Portugal deported Gypsies to Africa, Brazil and India in the fourteenth century, and later Britain sent them to the West Indies. Others spread eastwards into Russia by 1501 and were reported in Siberia by 1721.

These first migrations established the long-standing communities of Gypsies in the various countries of Europe, the majority of whom have become settled for generations. The *Sinti* are in German-speaking Europe; the *Calé* or *Gitan* are in Spain and southern France and Latin America, the *Ciganos* in Portugal, the *Mantouche* in the rest of France, the *Romanichal* in England and from there to English-speaking countries around the world. The *Romungre* are in Austria-Hungary, and the *Kaale* in Finland. The attitude of the host societies differed greatly between Eastern and Western Europe.

West of the Czech Republic, the Gypsies were considered a nuisance and tended to be driven out, which persuaded them to remain nomadic. But, in the east, the Gypsies were often seen as cheap labor by a still largely feudal society, and they got long-term employment as peasants, musicians and soldiers. They were often persuaded to settle, or were enslaved. In this way there developed large sedentary communities of Gypsies in Eastern Europe, who continued to live in tents or huts. A minority continued to be nomadic and to speak Romani.[27]

In spite of the pressures to be assimilated, most Gypsies maintained their identity and economic independence, resourcefully adapting to the changes of industrial revolution that came rapidly in Britain, and more slowly in the rest of Europe. In the Hungarian Empire, Russia and Spain they developed a reputation as musicians. Many worked in rural communities as itinerant craftsmen and hawkers, until the better communication systems of the nineteenth century resulted in the rural communities getting wares and services from the towns. The Gypsies responded by moving to camps on the outskirts of the towns, while going back to the country for seasonal work in the harvests, or for horse races. These well-established groups did not welcome the new arrivals of the second migration, because they attracted unfavorable attention from governments and from the public.

This second large migration left Wallachia in Romania and neighboring areas in the mid-nineteenth century. Since the sixteenth century, they had been slaves on the estates of the landlords, princes and monasteries in Moldova and Romania. As the Austro-Hungarian Empire shrank, they won their emancipation in 1864. These new migrants called themselves *Rom*, meaning "man" in Romani, although other groups had preceded them also using that name. Their Romani language is heavily influenced by Romanian. These migrants formed a number of distinctive groups of Gypsies, who are called Vlach Rom. Although they are often referred to as just Vlachs, they have no connection with the Aromani, who are commonly called Vlachs by non-Greeks. Vlach in this connection refers to Wallachia, but in reference to the Aromani, as we have seen, it is the common Greek term for any shepherd.

As former slaves, these new Gypsy migrants had been classified according to their owners and occupations. They formed new *Rom* groupings such as the *Kalderash*, or coppersmiths; the *Lovara*, or horse-dealers; and the *Curara*, or sieve makers. There are claimed to be about seven million Kalderash worldwide. These groups, or "nations," have developed their own dialects of Romani such as "Russian," "Greek," Romanian and Serbian Kalderash, Lovari, Curari, and, in the United States, the *Macvano* or *Machwaya* dialect. Other groups from the Balkans also began to move westwards. Some of these new mobile groups did not speak Romani, such as the Romanian-speaking *Boyash*, or "gold-washers," and the *Rudari*, or "miners." These migrations were just part of a greater movement of people within Europe which took advantage of better roads and the growing railway network, as well as the attractions of employment in the industries of Western Europe and the United States. Many traveled living in tents, but this was the time when the *vardo*, or horse-drawn living wagon, came into use — again an example of the Gypsy adopting an idea, for the design originated with non-Gypsy carriage-builders in Western Europe.

The third major migration was during the upheavals of the mid-twentieth century, and this resulted in new communities moving and being formed across Europe. In the interests of what it called "racial hygiene," the Nazi regime exterminated "asocials," including between 250,000 and 500,000 Gypsies from all the territories they occupied. The regime merely capitalized on the legislation, prejudices and racial theories current as a reaction to the second migration in the previous century. The Gypsies call the Holocaust "the Devouring." It is a bitter irony that this regime persecuted as "dirty," or antisocial, the two peoples, the Jews and the Gypsies, who practice the most elaborate systems of ritual cleanliness and social solidarity. It is a warning not to allow negative stereotypes to fester in the popular imagination, as they still do against the Gypsies.

After the war, the changed Polish borders, the exodus of Germans from Eastern Europe, the return of deportees and the uprisings against Communist regimes were all events that affected movements of both the Rom and the settled communities. The Iron Curtain had an escape hole through Yugoslavia, and the **Xoraxame** or Turkish Gypsies from Bosnia and Montenegro, who speak a non-Vlach Romani, moved first to Italy — a case of people becoming nomadic after having been settled.

Other more recent migrations have been from Ireland to England, and from Portugal to Spain in the 1960s and 1970s. Gypsies still often experience attitudes of hatred, and they suffer expulsions, arson attacks and abuse and, in many cases, murder. An Eastern European prime minister, alluding to Gypsies in terms reminiscent of the Nazis, said it was necessary to curtail "the socially unadaptable and mentally backward population." In a time of the nation states feeling their way to European integration, they are intolerant of a people who have always seen Europe as integrated without national boundaries!

Society

In most parts of Europe, the Gypsy population is made up of different communities that originated during these main periods of migration. Dialect, origin, religion, local organization, customs and traditional occupational specialization have led to a patchwork of different groupings in Europe that are difficult to trace precisely. Much of what follows is tentative.[28] The different groups have slightly different customs and rituals, as well as different dialects that are often not mutually intelligible. The majority of Gypsies are settled, but a high percentage in some countries practice various degrees of nomadism, either as itinerant workers or for seasonal work. Any halt, however long, is considered temporary. "A Gypsy at rest remains a traveler" because "nomadism is a state of mind more than a state of fact." They see the houses they use as big tents and prize the flexibility that comes from having a number of skills.

These major divisions or tribes of the Rom are called *natsia* (nations), or race, which have a unity in dialect and basic customs. But the individual Rom tend to identify themselves by their *vitsi* (pl. *vitsa*), or clan — a group of related extended families, or *familias*, often named after an common ancestor. The *familia* in turn is made up of a number of *tsera*, or households, made up of a nuclear family of three generations. It is within their *vitsi* that they look for mutual support and for wives for their sons. The *vitsi* does not travel or work together, but they do gather for weddings and funerals.

Nomadism and their work strategies require them to form smaller working groups called *kumpania*, made up of *tsera* who are not necessarily related, perhaps from different clans under the leadership of a *rom baro*, or "big man." These respected leaders lead by consensus. They administer disputes about territory for hawking and trading between the tribes and clans. Sanctions such as fines are imposed by consensus. Decisions are taken by *diváno* (discussion) or more rarely, in serious cases, by *kris*, or trial by clan elders.

The first preoccupation of two Gypsies when they meet is not to merely accept that they are both Gypsies, but to establish each other's *vitsi* and identify as many as possible of their common acquaintances. The identity of the individual is determined both by genealogy and by belonging to temporary travailing groups, or *kumpania*. They modify their genealogies as necessary to maintain the fiction of unity by descent and marriage.

They are conscious of being different, so loyalty to their own people is decisive. To a lesser extent, they also feel a loyalty to similar groups. It is said the Romani language has no word for "work." A Gypsy will never be employed, not even by another Gypsy. All enterprises are considered associations or co-operatives, sharing the benefits with the family, rather than being a source for personal profit. Group honor is important — the individual belongs to his extended family and to his traveling group and the wider tribe. His or her behavior is determined by knowing what is good for the group.

Marriage is arranged by the parents, ideally between second or other degrees of cousins, and sometimes between brothers and sisters between two families. The couple can refuse the choice. Among some of the Rom, the custom of bride-price still operates. The solidarity between the families often means that every effort is made to encourage a troubled marriage to continue, so divorce is rare.

Pollution laws

The Gypsies have their own system of purity, as elaborate as that found in the Old Testament. *Marime* is pollution, dishonor or uncleanness. Food, and anything that touches food, has its own separate regime. Cleanliness depends on keeping the upper part of the body separate from the lower part, with its polluting emissions. They use separate soap and towels for the two parts. Anything to do with entering the body, such as food utensils, is washed separately.

Clothes covering the lower body must not be brought in contact with food or utensils used for food. Food is shared only with those who keep these standards. The feet and the ground are considered most unclean or polluted.

Similarly the stages of life are classified according to pollution: marriage is considered to be especially polluting, while old age is revered and looked forward to as "clean." Many of these rules fulfill the practical needs of hygiene in toiletry and food preparation in a more consistent way than those practiced by the *gadzé*.

Maintaining non-pollution determines one's membership in the family and the group. Any relationship or behavior that affects the honor of the groups is either "clean" or "unclean." To become polluted is to undermine the status of one's family with other Gypsies, and is considered a cause of illness and misfortune. Behavior is therefore controlled by the opinion of the group according to these concepts. The Gypsy fears two things — the *mulo*, or ghost of the dead, returning to haunt them, and being a social outcast from their clan. They also fear supernatural sanctions, and expulsion from the group spells spiritual and moral death to the Gypsy. These concepts of pollution mean that non-Gypsies and Gypsies do not drink from the same cups or sit in the same seats, and the outside surroundings of Gypsy homes and vans are untidy with *gadzé* scrap or rubbish, while inside the homes are clean. Some Roma do not accept other Gypsies, because they are consider them to be faulty in this system of cleanliness.

The Gypsies see the *gadzé* as immoral, without family loyalty, and unhygienic. The Gypsies' relationship to the *gadzé* is determined, therefore, by this code of cleanness. Contact with non-Gypsies is inherently polluting. When eating in a non-Gypsy environment, disposable plates and cups are preferred, because it is polluting to use utensils that have not been cleansed the Gypsy way. Gypsies will occasionally deliberately act according to stereotyped misconceptions, such as appearing to be dirty, lice-ridden, rude, untidy, or feign madness — contrary to their own self-image — to keep the non-Gypsies away and so maintain their own ritual cleanness.

To maintain these standards, visitors will be served with special crockery and sit in a place reserved for those outside the rules of purity, but hospitality that is offered should be accepted by the *gadzo* as honoring the Gypsy hosts. Gifts of food, clothing or housing will be treated as polluted and will need cleansing. Needless to say, this system has been counterproductive in creating harmonious relationships with society as a whole. Conversation, also, will inevitably touch on subjects in current affairs, history or religion that the Gypsy construes, often with good reason, as anti-Gypsy. A Christian worker has to have knowledge of this regime, and be sympathetically persistent to have realistic contact with the Roma.

Religion

Gypsies tend to adapt the religion of their surroundings to their own beliefs. Shashi says the essence of Gypsy religion is that human beings were created free to exercise love, and even a minimum of loving acts justifies creation. Gypsy religion is animistic, with Muslim or Christian additions, marked by a number of taboos — although these vary between the *vitsa*. The Hindu goddess Kali, or Durga, is believed to be reincarnated as the Catholic St. Sarah, patron saint of Gypsies in many parts of the world. The word for "trident," the symbol of the Hindu god Shiva, is used for the cross.

The Roma think that the spirit of a dead relative, or *mulo*, must be honored each year so that it can eventually join the sky spirits, who are considered protectors of Gypsies. Good intentions to protect the living are usually attributed to the *mulo*. Dying as an evil person, or in an untimely way, can lead to the mulo becoming a vampire to haunt. Moral wrong is associated with the purity system, so young children and old people, not being sexually active, are considered pure or innocent. Friday is considered the devil's day, and owls are a portent of death. The spirits cause some diseases. Evangelism and claims about having the truth contradict the Gypsy's syncretistic view of the world.

Gypsies love storytelling and the most immediate events, however trivial, are retold with fictional additions. Most Gypsies are unaware of their own history, as they consider history to be the earliest memories of the oldest living persons they know. Only recently have some Romani scholars found value in developing an ethnic history and investigating the traditions of an origin in India. Various myths explain their wanderings as originating with their unwillingness to give hospitality to Joseph and Mary, with the infant Jesus, during their exile in Egypt, or because they are descendants of the blacksmith who forged the nails for the crucifixion.

Outreach

Early Christian efforts to help them often seemed to confuse "civilizing" with conversion, aiming to turn them into settled domestics. But there were exceptions. George Borrow, who was a Bible Society worker in Spain in the 1830s, befriended Gypsies there and in Britain his writings influenced the establishment of the Gypsy Lore Society in 1888. Converts to Christianity in the past have been encouraged to leave the Gypsy life. The converted Gypsies Cornelius and Rodney Smith were famous evangelists in the late nineteenth and early twentieth century, but they claimed that the Gypsy people were not ready for the gospel in their day. They concentrated on very effective evangelistic tours among the *gadzé* in the English-speaking world.[29]

Christian work, especially Bible translation and distribution, is hampered by such factors as the many different dialects; different orthographies even within the same dialect; the lack of interest in books, especially books in Romani; and the fact that the distribution is not connected to the nomadic Gypsy lines of communication. There has been a lack of enthusiasm for Romani translations not only because of the discouragement from publishers, who tend to avoid the expense of minority language editions, but also because Christian Gypsies fear disruption of their unity due to their different dialects. The argument is that most Gypsies are fluent in one or more European languages anyway. There is a New Testament, however, as well as radio programs and the *Jesus* film in Kalderash. Another argument against more translations is that most Gypsies are fluent in one or more European languages anyway.[30]

TWR is providing five or more broadcasts from Tirania each week, in Romani, to Gypsies throughout Eastern Europe.[31] The Cooperative Baptist Fellowship has eight couples committed to Radio Bible Studies and other ministries to the Gypsies in Europe and elsewhere.

a) Scandinavia and Finland

There are 500 **Lovari** here. The **Omstreifere**, or wanderers, may be a mixture of Germans and long-established Gypsies. Some speak Rodi or Traveller Norwegian, which is based on Norwegian, Northern Romani and German, and is not understood by English Romanis.[32]

Sweden has 8,000 people called **Tattare**, or **Resande**. They are probably non-Gypsy in origin, but they use Romani. Gypsies are called *zigenare*, of which there are 5,000 **Kalderash**, or Coppersmiths, who arrived about 1900, organized in eight clans. They survive by doing various jobs in the summer. Volunteers have tried summer tent schools for the children, but these were not satisfactory. Many of the adults are also receiving basic education.[33] The latter have been evangelized by one of their own people.

There are 7,000 **Kaale** who are said to be semi-nomadic, working in various trades such as horsesellers, veterinary work, blacksmithing and coppersmithing, lace making and seasonal agricultural work. Many are now concentrating in the Helsinki area, and 2,000 have migrated to Sweden.[34] There are 300 who have converted to Christianity. The Gospel of John was published in 1971 in Finnish Romani.

There are 1,500 here. Some Gypsies were transported to Denmark by James IV of Scotland in 1505. The Gypsies in Denmark speak a language called Traveller Danish.

b) Britain

There are over 45,000 Gypsies in Britain, possibly as many as 90,000, divided between 7,700 Gypsy families. Another source estimates 50,000 with 12,000 caravans. In England they prefer to call themselves Travelers, and sometimes *Didikois*, meaning "tent dweller" or "horse trap people," which can have both a fond appreciative sense of "true" Gypsy, or a derogatory sense. To be accepted as a Gypsy, both of one's parents must have been Gypsies, and those of a mixed marriage are accepted if they marry a Gypsy. A number of *gaje* families are found traveling with the Gypsies, but they are not fully accepted and are often exploited for labor.

To be accepted as a Gypsy one must not only have at least one Gypsy parent, but one must also must keep the traditions of cleanliness. In England, the inner body and anything that touches the mouth and food are clean. Anything that is unsuitable for the inside of the body is *mochadi*, or polluted, such as a chipped cup or a bowl that has had more than crockery washed in it. The outer body and the outside of the van is less "soiled," or *chikli*. The inside of the van is kept spotless, but the outside of the van is a temporary "no-man's land" where anything considered unfit or unclean is thrown. This division of clean and polluted areas creates much misunderstanding, because the non-Gypsy wants to give a good impression on the outside and hide away unacceptable things. The Gypsy considers sinks and toilets as too soiled for the inside of the van. They also prefer to be on view to other Gypsies and so have their vans facing each other in circles, while non-Gypsies prefer the anonymity of being in rows.[35]

Among the Gypsies are 16,000 **Romanichals** and 200 **Kalderash**. The latter are descended from two couples who originally came from Greece. They have settled in London and, according to Sashi, pass themselves off as Greeks and make a living from fortunetelling or itinerant blacksmith work.

After the Second World War many Gypsies gravitated to the countryside around London, attracted by the affluence and increasing population. In spite of the fact that many have lived in a house at some time, traveling is still a necessary qualification for being a Gypsy, along with keeping the cleanliness code and having some knowledge of Anglo-Romani. Some were so impoverished that they still slept in tents in the 1970s; others had vans. It used to be possible to travel the length of England, working in turn the cherry, hop, apple, potato and sugar beet harvests, but this work is now done by machines. The Gypsies consider traveling, even in a congested urbanized area, as healthier than settling, which they believe quickly leads to sickness and death.

Because of legislation against non-Gypsy travelers, local authorities are being discouraged from providing campsites. In 1990 there were 270 public sites and many more private ones. The Gypsies themselves buy some sites, but they often fail to get permission to establish their camps on them. It is becoming common for the travelers to live in mobile homes but to also have a small van to take on the road for seasonal work. Gypsies living in one place still resist moving into houses and becoming part of the *gaje* way of life. The Romany Guild and the Gypsy National Council for Education, Culture, Welfare and Civil Rights are organizations that are defending the right of the Gypsies to lead at least the semi-sedentary way of life, as an essential part of a distinct ethnic identity. Illiteracy among them is still around 70% in spite of various schemes to provide education.[36]

There are about 200 official campsites provided by central government, but these are not sufficient for even half the Traveling population. The Criminal Justice Legislation passed in 1995 has removed the obligation of local government to provide camping places for them and has empowered local authorities to remove them from their customary sites. But as legislation also requires that welfare examinations be carried out before they are evicted, delays in them moving on can be protracted. However, the effect has been to force many to settle and even join local government housing lists.

Outreach

The French Mission Evangélique des Tziganes started evangelism among Travelers in Britain in 1952, and today there are about 5,000 Christian Gypsies. Davey Jones of the Light and Life movement has seen thousands of conversions in Britain and Ireland. The gospel presents a moral challenge in terms of honest relations with the non-Gypsy, in abandoning some traditional ways of making a living, in keeping sites as tidy as the insides of their vans, and most of all in reconciliation with other Gypsies. Conventions are held at which as many as 600 vans will gather. Gypsies for Christ works not only in the U.K., but is also helping Gypsies in Romania. There is a part-time Gypsy Smith training school for pastors and evangelists. Local *gaje* churches are being encouraged to contact local Gypsies, but it is said, "the only person that understands a Gypsy is the Lord." The Gypsy and Travelers Evangelical Movement has four pastors working among the Gypsies, and there are others in training. SGM has produced a translation of the parable of the prodigal son included in a booklet called *The Drom*, or "The Way."[37]

Converts to Christianity in the past have been encouraged to leave the Gypsy life. We have already referred to the Smiths, converted a hundred years ago, but a real conversion of Gypsies has only taken place more recently. A Pentecostal initiative was launched in 1978, and there are a number of Gypsy congregations. It is said that one in eight Gypsies in Britain are now Christians. Gypsies for Christ provides a mobile Bible teaching ministry for Romani Christians in England and is encouraging an outreach to Romania. SGM has an Anglo-Romani translation program and has published selections from the Kalderash New Testament.

c) Belgium and Germany

There are 10,000 Gypsies in Belgium and 35,000 in the Netherlands. The **Roma** had formed Christian fellowships by 1981. Near Eindhoven, 5,000 *Manouche*, in villages set up by the government, have been reached.

There are over 110,000 **Sinté**, or *Sinti*, and **Roma**. The Sinté (sg. Sinto) are the long-term residential Gypsies of the German-speaking countries, but even after centuries they are not considered German, because of the continued influence of the concept of Germanness, or Volk. Some moved to Russia in the nineteenth century and were deported to Kazakstan by Stalin. Between 250,000 and 500,000 Gypsies were killed by the National Socialist regime in the 1940s, having previously been "scientifically" classified as "antisocial," "criminal" and subhuman. Today, in Germany, the names Sinté and Roma are used to refer to these people, although the terms are of separate sub-groups. At least this is better than Zigeuner, which was used during the Nazi era, when Gypsies were branded with a "Z." But so often, both to the public and the law, even these names imply unwanted asylum seekers rather than a European ethnic group entitled to rights.[38] About 50,000 *Sinté* are confined to camps. The Sinté are spread from the Netherlands to Germany and even as far east as Kazakstan. There are probably about 500,000 of them. They follow strict cleanliness laws, and any profession or activity involved with the body or blood is considered impure. The Sinté do not allow their dialect of Romani to be written down. SIL is undertaking a translation in cassettes.

There are also groups of *Kalderash* in the eastern Länder. There are 70,000 Romanian Gypsies, who entered Germany in the early 1990s and are being returned to Romania, even when they were driven out by arson attacks. Some of the attacks on "Turks" were in fact on Gypsies. A German Pentecostal minister has led an outreach among them. Mark's Gospel has been published in Sinté/Manouche, and the Gospels and Acts are being prepared for publication.

The **Sinté**, or **Manus**, are a distinct endogamous subgroup in Alsace and the Rhineland of Germany and Switzerland. Their lifestyle varies from nomadic living in caravans all year round, to semi-nomadic traveling only in the summer months, to those who live in houses all year — but all these groups can change as economic opportunities present themselves. They speak German as a second language, but their language, Manus, has many German and some Greek words.

They claim to be Catholic but in fact have a system of belief of their own. The Supreme Being, *Baro Devel*, has a special relationship with the Sinté, having created them specially. The Mother of God or Holy One is important, and her statue is in every caravan, but Jesus is of no importance. Many Sinté go to Lourdes. They believe that evil powers surround humans, and small children are particularly at risk of being kidnapped and substituted by an evil look-alike. Ghosts also can be either a threat or a help. The Sinté believe that as they sleep they are in active contact with these beings and that the mouth is a gateway for the spirits, so they must wash out their mouths before they do anything else in the morning. The devil has a hell, or "kitchen," but the Supreme Being does not let the Sinté go there. The devil is responsible for madness and epilepsy.

The Sinté observe similar purity and shame rituals as other Gypsies, as described above. Their first act in setting up camp is to light a fire so that it shines into the door of each van. Death is considered to pollute, and the dying may be placed in a tent bought for the purpose that can be destroyed afterwards.[39]

d) Poland

There are over 50,000 Gypsies here. Polska Roma arrived in the fourteenth century and settled in northwestern Poland. They showed themselves hostile to later migrants and have stressed their Polish culture. Bergitka Roma entered Poland in the fifteenth and sixteenth centuries, moved to the southern part of the country and later became sedentary. Some 15,000 lived in the region of Warsaw while it was still a village, without a city government.

After 1860 Vlachs, Ursari and Hungarian Gypsies moved into Poland, being resented by the long-established "Polish Gypsies," or the Polska and Bergitka, who were poor and sedentary. Yet the newcomers quickly exerted their domination. Large numbers of Romanian Gypsies still migrate to Poland and Slovakia during the summer months for seasonal work and then return again.

The Vlachs were divided between Kalderash, Lovara and Churara. The Kalderash absorbed the other smaller groups, except for the Lovara, and preferred not to identify themselves as Gypsies in order to disassociate themselves from the Polska. The Kalderash were itinerant coppersmiths, and their language is influenced by Romanian.

The Lovari are traditionally horse dealers. Their dialect has been influenced by Hungarian, but they can understand the Kalderash. There may be about 500,000 of them around the world. There are about 5,000 in Poland. These groups have varied rules, called *romania*, to maintain purity from non-Gypsy pollution. The smallest social unit, the nuclear family, is the *tsera*, a number of which form a *familia*, or a co-operative group of related families. An itinerant group is a *tabor*, but with the legislation that forced them to settle they have formed *kumpania*, or associations.[40] A Bible translation is being prepared in the Lovari dialect. They tend to be Catholic in Poland, but Protestant in Hungary and Romania.

e) Czech Republic

The Czech Republic has 250,000 Gypsies, and Slovakia 480,000. Slovak Roma migrated here as part of a movement from Wallachia, now part of Romania, in the sixteenth century, and may become the majority by 2075. These Gypsies are found elsewhere in Europe, such as in Italy. There have been examples of persecution and racism against Gypsies in the Czech Republic and Slovakia due to exaggerated fears of the growth of their population, and this led to the deaths of 26 Roma in 1993.[41] Two books of Bible stories are available, and John's Gospel in Slovak Romani will be published soon.

f) Hungary

Romungre or Hungarian Gypsies were among the first Gypsies to establish themselves in Europe, and they quickly lost much of both Romani and their culture to adapt to the Hungarian way of life. They became famous as minstrels among both humble peasantry and the nobility, and groups of violinists are common today playing in restaurants, and so on. Many live in western Slovakia. They occupy about 2,000 settlements in appalling conditions. Some even live on a derelict arsenic mine at Rudnany. There are 65,000 in Budapest. In the area of Nograd in northern Hungary, where a third of the population of the town of Nogradmeyer are Roma, housing has been provided and most Gypsies have employment.

g) Former USSR

There are 10,000 Rom in Belarus and 6,000 in the Baltic Republics. There are about 4,000 Lotfítka Romá in Latvia and Estonia. A translation of the New Testament in the Balt-Slavic dialect is being prepared.

Russia and the Ukraine have perhaps 500,000 Cigan. The Gypsy Research Centre estimates that there are between 270,000 and 460,000, but some of these are in Central Asia. About 77% speak Romani as their first language, and most live in urban areas. Rúská Romá are in northern Russia. The Ukraine had a mixed population of settled and nomadic Rom in the early eighteenth century, working as ferriers, horse dealers, sieve makers, tinkers and bear trainers. Often their leaders would collect taxes for Russian authorities, and in this way they were tolerated. Gypsy music became very popular in Russia, and every noble house would have its Gypsy orchestra, and the music and dances spread to the popular level through minstrels traveling around the inns and as written music for the new pianos became popular. Tolstoy admired Gypsy music and women, and his brother married a Gypsy. They were treated as state peasants, which gave them some freedom to move around the country.

Lovari Rom moved into Russia from Poland at the beginning of the twentieth century. Initially the Communists were positive towards the Gypsies and they were encouraged to speak Romani, but this led to enforced settlement which they resisted, and from then on Gypsy culture was suppressed. Krushchev had policies to "reconcile vagrants to work"! Under Gorbachev a cultural revival developed, and the Romani National Union was formed in 1989.[42]

h) France

There are 280,000 or more *Manouche*, and *Gitans*, in southern France, are the long-term residents. There are also Rom, mostly *Kalderash* and *Xoraxane*. The Manouche are amusement and side show carnival owners, who operate as separate family units traveling independently of each other.[43] A remarkable spiritual movement among the Gypsies in Europe has resulted in the conversion of about 70,000. This began in 1950 in Lisieux, Normandy, after a Pentecostal pastor had given a tract to a Gypsy woman. By 1958, 3,000 conversions had resulted among the Manouche. The Christian conventions are important within this movement, with as many as 2,000 vans attending. One problem was that nomadic preachers could not be taught in a sedentary Bible institute. This movement has spread to Spain, Italy and many other countries. The work spreads along tribal lines, with Manouche and Sinté evangelists working with their own tribes. They have discouraged fortunetelling.[44] *E Nevi Vastia*, the Kalderash New Testament, has had two editions, both published in France. A translation of the Old Testament has yet to be published.[45]

i) Spain, Portugal, Switzerland, Austria and Italy

Kalé, or "Black," is the name the 500,000 to 650,000 people, who are mostly *Gitanos*, have for themselves. Gitan is derived from "Egyptian." The Gypsies were first recorded

in Spain when bands of them, under "Counts" John and Thomas of "Little Egypt," were given safe conduct as pilgrims in 1425 by the king of Aragon. The attitude turned unfriendly when others soon began to arrive from Greece. By the 1700s only a few were still nomadic. For a period they were made slaves, and a Spaniard could be sent to the galleys for even helping a Gypsy, but this policy ended when it was recognized that they were indeed law-abiding, legally married, and receiving the church sacraments when allowed to do so. The Gitanos developed the flamenco song and music. Flamenco was a term for Gypsy.

Many have formed local Gypsy communities, called *gitanerías*, in cities like Madrid, Cadiz and Seville. Since 1966, the Catholic Church has formed secretariats to provide vocational training and housing aid for Gypsies, and to counteract the prejudice against them. A number of university students raised funds for Gypsies to build the La Alegría community, in Madrid, with a school, nursery and vocational training center. Because the Gypsies here pay only a nominal rent, they are able to pursue traditional occupations, whereas elsewhere those fortunate enough to live in apartments have to be in full-time employment to pay their expenses. They are also able to go to "Peru," by which they mean various countries in Latin America, for periods of months or years, to accumulate income to improve their standard of living. Others work in the vintage in Castille each summer.[46]

There are a number of local groupings of Gitans, although differences between them are more a matter of social class and economic level. *Béticos* are Gypsies who solved the ban on owning land by constructing caves in which they still live, in Granada and Guadix. They work as hawkers, smiths, waiters and entertainers. *Castellanos*, or Gypsies of Castille, keep themselves apart from other Gypsies and work in typical traveler trades. *Cafeletes* are families of the above groups who settled in Catalonia during the twentieth century. About 5% of the Catalans may still be nomadic — the rest may be sedentary, but hardly "settled," and are usually without work. Only about 15% have employment. Many live scattered in San Roque or close together in Hostafranchs, Barcelona. The latter have been settled for five generations and have a better standard of living than those in San Roque. Lineages in San Roque arrange to migrate to gather beans and grapes in French Catalonia from the middle of May to the end of October. In between the two harvests, the men make baskets that the women sell around the villages. This income helps to settle debts.

Húngaros, or Hungarians, is the local name for the Kalderash in Spain and probably came from France and Greece. They are also called *zingaros*. They consider themselves different from the Gitanos (the latter do not see them as Gypsies either).

Spanish Romani, or Calo, is different from other forms of Romani. George Borrow, a Bible colporteur, first contacted the Gypsies in Spain in 1836, and he translated the New Testament into Calo. There are 500,000 registered Gypsies in Spain, and 200,000 of them are associated in some way with the Philadelphia Evangelical Church. This growth, the major success of the gospel among a nominally nomadic people, has been facilitated by conversions through extended families and lineages. There is a need to consolidate the work among the churches by Bible teaching. A French Manouche went as a missionary to Spain in 1966, holding conventions among Gypsies. Over a ten-year period there have resulted some 8,000 conversions and 68 churches, and a Bible college has been founded. After conversion, many Spanish Gypsies, until recently illiterate, became the best customers in the CLC bookstores.

There are 40,000 here. The first Gypsies, or *Ciganos*, appear to have arrived from Spain in 1521. Portuguese policy was to banish them to its African and Brazilian colonies. Paradoxically, some were sent to India. Some Spanish Gypsies led a ministry in Lisbon so that by 1978 there were 500 Portuguese Gypsy Christians.

Switzerland: There are 30,000 Gypsies here. MRG reports that children have been taken away from their parents by the authorities and raised as "orphans." French Manouche Christians have evangelized the Travelers and Gypsies since 1972.

Austria: There are 20,000 here. Since the civil war caused by the breakup of Yugoslavia, some 30,000 Roma from Bosnia and Serbia have requested refugee status in Austria.

Italy: There are 90,000 here, including *Sinté* (*Manouche*) and *Rom*. An Italian brought the gospel to some of the latter in 1977, and in three years there were 120 conversions. There is a Bible reading plan in Romani published by Editione Romani.

j) Balkans

Bosnia has 40,000, and Serbia-Montenegro 400,000. The name *Xoraxane* means "Turks" (sg. Xoraxanó), to signify being Muslim. Communist Yugoslavia did not force settlement on its Gypsies, and laws prohibiting discrimination against the Rom were enforced. So they have been able to remain nomadic, and until about 1970 they traveled in horse-drawn carts and lived in tents, spending only the winter in their own or rented houses. They worked mostly as coppersmiths. With the improvement of the economic lot of the rural population their market has contracted. Many have now migrated to Western Europe, turning to scrap metal collecting, hawking household articles, and living on welfare. Most do not learn the local language and cannot get work. Often they get temporary accommodation in cities, sharing it with other non-Gypsy groups. They come to "gather" and "ask," that is, to thieve and beg.[47]

k) Albania

There are 90,000 Gypsies here. The Roma have been in the country for over 500 years. The *Mechkari* are the largest grouping and are nominal Muslims. The Romani dialect of the *Kabudji* tribe has more Turkish words. The *Chergari*, or "Tent-dwellers," are Turkish Gypsies found in Albania, Macedonia and elsewhere. In contrast to the Albanians, who want to identify themselves with a wider European and Western world, the Roma identify themselves with their own extended family. They accept living in Albania as their lot, rather than having any feeling of patriotism. They also see speaking Romani as essential for their Gypsy identity, but they are mostly illiterate. Some that Fonseca visited were once nomadic basket weavers who settled in the 1960s to work on a farm which has since been abandoned. Because they are desperately poor, the rural communities of Gypsies are often no more than settlements of plastic bags and packing cases.[48]

Southern towns such as Korça are 20% Romany. Once settled in flats under Communism, they have now taken to tents and itinerant work, such as horse and mule trading, tinkering, selling jewelry, street sweeping and money-changing. Carver describes how a woman with a dancing bear chained the bear outside a hospital while she went inside to give birth. He relates how evangelical missionaries have helped in cases where girls were kidnapped for prostitution and in a case of a girl killing her father after being sexually abused by him.[49]

Arnúta, or *Xoraxané*, means, says Piasere, "Albanised Serbs." They speak Albanian, have market stalls in Korça and are quite prosperous. Caribbean YWAM is reaching them, efforts are being made to find a common form of Romani, and a translation of Ephesians in an Albanian dialect is available. A Serb Romani New Testament is available.

The *Yevkos* may well have been longer in Albania than the Roma, who refuse to accept them as Gypsies and nickname them *sir*, or "garlic." They claim to have originated as Egyptian slaves working as grooms for the Ottoman army. There is also evidence to show that 300,000 Egyptians came to the Balkans in the fourth century. They are considered the poorest group in Albania and many live by begging in Tirana and other towns. They are also in Macedonia and claim a community of 20,000 or more. In 1990 they built a mosque for themselves near Lake Ohrid in the

southwest. Many in Ohrid and Struga renounced being Roma, and declared themselves *Egipcani* in the 1991 census and formed the Egipcani Association, with some 4,000 members. In Kosovo 100,000 claim to be Yeukos and have a similar association. They are probably of Gypsy origin, but they do not speak Romani.[50]

There are other groups that are not recognized by the Roma as Gypsies but are similar, such as the **Ashkali** and **Mango** in Montenegro, Kosovo and Macedonia and the **Rlia** in Albania. These are said not to speak Romani.[51]

l) Former Yugoslavia

In the former Yugoslav Republic of Macedonia, the **Roma** are 56,000 strong according to the 1991 census, but the real number is far higher — probably over 220,000, according to Gypsy Research Centre. The township of Shuto Orizari, outside Skopje, has some 40,000 Gypsies, and claims to be the only place on earth where the Gypsies are in the majority. About 80% of them speak three different dialects of Romani, but the Arlija dialect is used in education. Popularly they are called *cigane*, as a term of abuse.

They have their own political party, the PSER, whose demands for Roma education are being met in primary schooling. The PSER has also called for a new Roma state called Romanistan. This would not be within Macedonia as such, but as a dramatic way to highlight the disadvantaged Roma elsewhere in Eastern Europe, perhaps so that they be declared an "indigenous people" in United Nations terms and so merit the protection of the international community.

Since the breakup of Yugoslavia they gained sympathy in the ministry of education. A Romani primer and a Romani-Macedonian dictionary have been published, a program for two hours of lessons in Romani in the schools is in place, and a Romani faculty in the university was set up in 1993. There are 30-minute programs in Romani on TV and radio.[51]

m) Greece

Estimates of Roma, called **Djambazi**, vary between 160,000 (Gypsy Research Center) and 500,000. Greece refuses to officially recognize ethnic minorities in its territory, and Poulton cites attempts to convert Muslim Roma to Greek Orthodoxy.[52] Non-settled Gypsies are called *Yifti*. The ministry of a French Manouche and others have reached the 40,000 nomadic **Roma** in Thessalonica. The Orthodox Church has difficulty accepting that it does not have exclusive rights to minister in Greece, so this work has met with opposition.

n) Moldova and Romania

There are 20,000 Roma in Moldova (see also *Jakati*, below). A Gypsy "king" was buried here in 1998 with his computer, mobile phone and television — a modern version of the Rom tradition of getting rid of the possessions of the dead.

In Romania there are between 1,800,000 and 3,000,000 Gypsies in a population of 23,000,000, so they make up about 13%. Official figures put the total as low as 470,000 — probably to quell the anxiety of Romanians and Hungarians about having the largest Gypsy population in Europe. The European Union Commission cites 800,000, and Fraser estimates there are more than a million. Up to 36,000 Romanian Gypsies, mostly from nomadic groups, died during the Nazi era. Even as recently as the 1990s they were considered as subhuman, and the term "Gypsy" implied "slave."[53]

The Gypsies who have assimilated the least are the 200,000 **Kalderash**, who are considered both by themselves and others as a sort of "true Gypsy" aristocracy. They have established a "monarchy," more as a reaction to persecution than as a genuine Roma institution. The self-defeating divisions between Gypsies are seen in Romania as elsewhere, undermining any progress they might make for justice.

The Communist government attempted to forcibly integrate the Gypsies, moving them into new areas, which the local inhabitants resented. This included the 5,000 Gypsies that returned from the concentration camps, forcing them on reluctant local communities prejudiced against them. After the fall of Communism many people, including the long-time sedentary Gypsies, lost their jobs under the transition to a free market economy. But many Gypsies who had maintained their itinerant skills as car traders, or who had family businesses such as cafés, and so on, became relatively prosperous as they adapted to the opportunities of hitherto prohibited free enterprise. Some still work making baskets, brushes and wooden utensils.

Right across Romania, as well as in other parts of Eastern Europe, hostility flared against the Gypsies. The new Romanian government in 1989 declared students and Gypsies as "enemies of democracy," and mobs of miners attacked them. The Gypsies suffered racial discrimination, arson attacks, being driven from their homes and murdered of reported mob violence in 35 places during 1990, with little or no pretext. There have been many unreported attacks out of envy, or to find a scapegoat for the troubles of the time. Both those who have been settled for centuries and others forcibly settled by the Communists were targets for abuse. "Democracy" was considered to be the self-determination of the majority! The judiciary has failed to bring the perpetrators to justice. Many Gypsies migrated into Western Europe, especially Germany. There were 50,000 who were repatriated from Germany to Romania in 1992, and German aid was given to create work for them.[54]

There are 5,000 Christian Gypsies. Many have been beaten and otherwise persecuted for Christian activity.[55] A translation of Mark is available and a draft of the New Testament is ready in the Vlach Gypsy dialect of Transylvania. The Gospel of Matthew has been published in installments in a Romani newspaper.

o) Bulgaria

There were 313,000 **Tsigani** who declared themselves to be Gypsy in 1992, but the real number is probably over 700,000, which makes Bulgaria the country with one of the highest percentages of Gypsies. They have been in Bulgaria for 600 years in various cities such as Sofia, Sliven, Septemvri, Straldzha, Razlog and Smoljan.[56] They probably arrived with the Ottoman imperial forces, some settling and others developing a semi-nomadic lifestyle — the most popular occupations being blacksmith and musician. There were entire villages of Roma farm workers. Many runaway Gypsy slaves from Wallachia and Moldova settled in Bulgaria, and when slavery was abolished large numbers came south again.

The town of Sliven has a population of 100,000, and half of it is Gypsy. While discriminated against, they have managed to have a significant role in the Bulgarian society and economy. When forced to settle at the beginning of the twentieth century and in the 1950s, they formed settlements outside the cities.

Gypsies have tended to change their religion according to the political power. In Bulgaria they are divided between the settled Orthodox Christian Gypsies and the "Turkish" Gypsies, which means they are Muslim. The Christian Gypsies have always had Bulgarian names and are more prosperous. The Muslim Gypsies were forced to be semi-nomadic during the summers, working as basket makers, tinkers and ironworkers. They are very much poorer, living in ghettos, or *mahalas*. Many of the Gypsies have, over a long time, claimed to be Turks so as not to be discriminated against as Gypsies. With the upheavals accompanying Bulgarian independence in the 1880s, many moved westward to Britain and the United States. The **Grastari**, or **Lovara**, were nomadic until the mid-century, trading in cars and gold. They maintain the strict five-fold purity laws and never marry with other Gypsies, and they refuse to live as settled people, even when they own houses.

The Communists attempted the complete assimilation of the Gypsies and legislated them out of existence by first outlawing nomadism in 1958 and resettling them by scattering families in different parts of the towns, and in 1960 they forced those with Turkish names to adopt other names. The term Tsigani was banned in 1970. Romani and Gypsy music and dances were also banned between 1984 and 1989 because of their Turkish origins. Because most Gypsies are Muslim, the government banned headscarves, closed mosques and prohibited Muslim practices. However, they persisted in their cultural gatherings and language. Since the fall of Communism, economic discrimination has replaced political restrictions, and many have taken up nomadic occupations again. Gypsy street children are also a serious problem in Sofia and other large towns, living on drugs, sniffing glue and living by petty crime.

Although most are sedentary as far as residence is concerned, they travel widely with their special occupations, being away from home most weekends, or up to a month at a time. Many have weekday unskilled jobs but travel at every opportunity with their traditional work. Many work on the railways and use their free travel concessions to further Gypsy trading. Under Communism, the Gypsies benefited in terms of housing and education. Family life in Bulgaria may begin with elopement, and the bride-price has been replaced by a dowry of gifts, displayed at the time of the engagement, called a *ceiz*. A wife may be abandoned after a year if she has not produced a child. They have four to six children, on average.

There are a number of groups with names reflecting differences of dialect, religion, or occupation that consider themselves Rom. They combine more than one source of income, but many work as peddlers at any public gathering selling baskets, brooms, trinkets, shoes and combs, and some are traders in horses and other animals.

Kopanari or **Rudari** or **Ludari**, Bulgaria: Kopanari is the term for Christian Orthodox Gypsies. These Romani work as entertainers and sell wooden artifacts. Some also work as animal trainers, usually of bears and monkeys. Bulgarians have many superstitions about bears, and there used to be a tradition that a fair could not take place without one. They supplement the performance of the animals by singing accompanied on homemade instruments. Groups of Gypsy musicians almost have a monopoly on performing at weddings and other family functions. They are usually well paid and can combine this with a regular job.

The **Kalajdzhii** are coppersmiths that work from door to door.

The **Kovacki** are blacksmiths who make, repair and sell tools, bells and shears for sheep. They are usually Muslim and bilingual in Turkish and Romani. They are concentrated in Madan, southern Bulgaria.

The **Millets** are *Xoraxane* Turkish-Gypsies, in southern Bulgaria. The term "millet" comes from the Ottoman Empire that established self-regulating communities for those of different religions within the empire. There were Jewish, Orthodox and Armenian millets, each with their own leaders who represented the community to the authorities and their own schools and laws. They are not nomadic.

The Millet religion is a mixture of Muslim, Christian and pre-Christian rites and beliefs. There has been a significant work by the Holy Spirit as the first known breakthrough among Turkish-speaking people. There are estimated to be at least 4,000 believers from this ethnic group in Bulgaria. In 1991 it was estimated there were up to 2,000 believers, but recent reports highlight the need for a fresh survey. As more mission work is done, so it will become more evident just how many Christians there now are among the Turkish-speaking population. Dreams have been important in some cases in helping Muslims to accept the authority of the Bible. In one case a man dreamed that Jesus offered him a glass of water. Some time later, he opened his Bible and came across John 4:10, where Jesus offers living water. The Adventist Press has produced *O Neeve Zaveti*, or a New Testament translation in a local dialect, and Matthew has been re-circulated in "Central Bulgarian" Romani.

IRISH TRAVELERS or Tinkers

They call themselves *Travelers*, and they are indigenous to Ireland, having traveled the island since probably the twelfth century, before the arrival of the Gypsies. The latter tend only to visit Ireland for relatively short periods. There were said to be about 6,000 in the Irish Republic and under 400 in Northern Ireland, but 30,000 in Britain and 50,000 in the United States. Another estimate gives 800 Irish Traveler families in England and Wales. Some were sent to the West Indies plantations or pressed into the Royal Navy as a "punishment" in the seventeenth century.

They traveled in rural areas doing tin smithing, peddling and horse-dealing until the mid-twentieth century. Three-quarters of them traveled all year round, but usually only covering two or three counties. The others only traveled for about three months of the year. Most would prefer to live in one place but not to live in houses. They traveled in "open lots," that is, horse-drawn wagons covered with a barrel canopy. A few had motor trailers, but about 45% were so poor they only had a bender tent and pony cart in which to live and travel.

An Irish government commission in 1963 made many enlightened recommendations to help them, but few of these were implemented. They formed their own representative organization, called Itinerants Action International. In the last 40 years they have moved into bigger towns to trailer camps and live by scrap-dealing and begging. When about 60 families attempted to construct their own school near Dublin, they were evicted and the building demolished.

The Travelers cross regularly to South Wales and the English Midlands and attempt to continue their traditional trades. They think that they can find a better life in Britain. They are found in many places in southern England, some in permanent council and private sites. Today most have cars or motor trailers and modern caravans and trade in linoleum, household goods, artificial flowers, horsehair and feathers.

36a

36b

36 Irish Travelers:
a. + b. Irish Travelers may have originated as displaced peasants. Many are found in England (Photos: M. Rodger).

Many work laying tarmac or collecting iron, brass and copper scrap and rags. Others deal in horses and other animals, and many get their main income from begging.

Some intermarry with Romanies, but the couple has to make the choice whether to integrate with the Travelers or the Gypsies. They have their own cant, or language, called Shelta, or Gammon.[57] A man is a *fean*, and a married woman a *beyor*. The road is the *tohar*, in contrast to the Romani *drom*.

Most are nominal Catholics and observe the sacraments, but do not attend church otherwise. The clergy have often reflected the suspicion of their congregations against the Travelers. The attitude towards them in Northern Ireland has been even less enlightened. There is a small and growing number of evangelical Travelers in Ireland.

SCOTTISH TRAVELERS

They were reported in the twelfth century before the arrival of the first Gypsies in Britain and probably originated among the Scots. There are about 4,000 of them. They are not related to the Gypsies, although they have adopted Romani words and have similar attitudes and values. To be a Traveler one has to have had at least one Traveler parent and be committed to their values. There are also other traveling groups in Scotland not accepted by the Travelers, but Gypsies have never established themselves in Scotland. Some Travelers continue to be nomadic, especially in the summer. Those who have settled tend to hide their identity because of continual persecution and harassment. Estimates of numbers are varied, one reason being that they have no social organization beyond the local groups, except their attachment to their culture.

The travelers are deeply suspicious of the sedentary population, who they call Flatties, and consider themselves superior to it because of their versatility in finding independent means of income. Flattie society is considered bound by conventions and restrictions of dress, employment, prejudices and many material possessions. Even a prosperous Traveler lives simply and appears poverty-stricken, his wealth being

used to entertain other Travelers and so gain status. The women are considered to be close to the supernatural, with powers of divination and fortunetelling. They do not share the men's interest in status, but they follow a system of purity and impurity similar to that of the Gypsies, separating anything to do with food from clothes. Families usually camp together because of their fear of spirits. Marriage is simply by cohabitation, and each couple is considered a separate economic unit. Children are highly valued and often get the best food and are treated very leniently.

Until the Second World War, they traveled by cart or van in small family groups, in rural areas serving the rural population, settling only for the winter months. They worked as casual farm workers, tinkers and horse traders. Now they are concentrated in large urban areas as squatters in disused buildings or on waste ground. They change their town at least once a year and move their location within each town several times, so that at any one time most will have lived in more than a dozen places within the last 12 months. They work collecting scrap metal, rags, hawk small domestic items, beg and do seasonal farming work. They avoid employment by Flatties — not because they are lazy, but because this puts them in an inferior position. They are willing to work on a self-employed basis.

Paradoxically the closing of sites, intended to curb nomadism, has forced some to be more nomadic as they seek a place to settle. The traditional trades by which a family was able to maintain its independence have been curbed by legislation. Even when they succeed in buying land, planning permission to build on it is usually refused. Their language is a Scottish Cant, a mixture of Romani and Elizabethan English. Travelers would send their children to school and Sunday school, if it were not for the hostility shown by the rest of the population. They see value in arithmetic, reading and writing, but not the rest of the curriculum.[58]

ENGLISH TRAVELERS

The Gmelchs' survey in England shows that families tend to have different practices — some moving only around one locality, others in a region, but some ranging throughout the country. Collecting scrap metal, laying tarmac, visiting fairs, or picking fruit are activities that can be carried out at widely separated locations. Selling carpets requires traveling the longest distances.[59] The latter tend to move in large groups of as many as 40 vehicles and 100 people for protection against eviction, because the local sites are usually already occupied by local New Age Travelers (drop-outs from the British population). But often a move of location is preceded by months of commuting to seek customers.

REIZIGERS or Woonwagenbewoners

They are non-Gypsy Travelers in Belgium and the Netherlands, who originated in Brabant or in Westfalen, in Germany, in the eighteenth century. Most are sedentary, living in trailers dealing in scrap, second-hand cars and peddling cloth. They are being reached in Ostend.

JENISCHE or *Yénisches*

They are a non-Gypsy group of Travelers in the Rhineland, Germany, who speak a mixture of Yiddish, Romani and German. They are known as *yéniches* in France and Belgium. They used to travel hawking baskets, sieves and working as knife grinders and tinkers.[60]

MERCHEROS, Quinquis, Quinquilleros

The Mercheros, or Tinkers, are a closely related and exclusive group numbering about 150,000. They prefer to be called *Mercheros* (mercers) or *Moinantes*. They are less well known than, but quite unrelated to, Gypsies. They probably originated from landless peasants that took to nomadism in the sixteenth century, and continued in that life until the mid-twentieth century. They used to be disliked by the Gypsies and *payos* (non-Gypsies) alike.

Nomadism

They traveled mainly in northern Spain, from Galicia through Castille to the Ebro Valley and as far south as northern Estremadura. Their hallmark was their bright yellow horse-drawn carts covered with a hooped awning. Their belongings were hung in bags under the cart, and copper pots were hung on the tailboard. Each cart was home to a family, often of three generations, with the father having supreme authority. They only married other Quinquis, without a wedding ceremony, and unfaithfulness was punished by expulsion from the family. Beyond the family they had little organization. Although they followed a Gypsy-like lifestyle and the women wore long dresses, in appearance they are indistinguishable from other Spaniards.

New laws in the 1950s against nomadism forced them to become squatters in shantytowns for a time, until these were demolished without provision of other housing. At this time plastic containers removed the need for tinkers. Most now live in the slums of Madrid, Barcelona and Bilao. Most, being unskilled, cannot get suitable work. They have a reputation for being involved with petty crime. But others have become well-established and reasonably affluent as market traders in clothes and haberdashery. Some are still seen traveling with their carts.

Religion

They believe in a Supreme God, but as the Catholic church closed its doors to them as much as the landowners closed camping sites, they never keep the sacraments, nor are they orthodox in their beliefs.[61] They speak an old form of Castilian with their own cant, called Quinqui, but most are illiterate. There is no Bible translation in their language, but the Spanish Bible is available. In most places there is probably no Christian outreach to them. But a local church, including WEC workers, contacted some of them in Torrente, near Valencia, and an extended family was converted. From this a Quinqui Baptist church has resulted with its own Quinqui pastor. A number of Christians have been trained at the Baptist seminary and are serving elsewhere.

JAKATI, *Jati* or *Jat*

There are 154,000 living in Moldova. They are considered a "Gypsy" people, but they are not related to the Rom and speak their own language based on Arabic, not Romani.[62] They are Muslim. There is a group of families totaling about 1,000 people in Afghanistan. Little is known about their lifestyle, but presumably it is similar to that of the Gypsies.

NOTES

Part I: Characteristics of Nomadic Lifestyles

JESUS AT HOME IN THE TENTS

1. Rev. 7:15ff.

CHAPTER 1: WHO ARE THE NOMADS?

1. The term derives from the Greek *nomas*, meaning "wandering shepherd," and is related to *nemein*, "to feed or pasture;" see P. Salzman, "Movement and Resource Extraction among Pastoral Nomads," *Anthropological Quarterly* (n.d.), 185ff.

2. N. Dyson-Hudson, "Inheriting and Extending Man's Oldest Technique of Survival, Nomads Find Freedom and Identity in the Life they Follow," in *Nomads of the World* (Washington: National Geographic, 1971), 10-24. An accurate definition of nomadic pastoralism is essential to understanding them and has only been available since 1970, according to Malcolm Hunter, *Appropriate Development for Nomadic Pastoralists: A Study of the Waso Borana of Northern Kenya Illustrating the Value and Meaning of Holistic Development Amongst Nomadic Peoples* (The Open University and the Oxford Centre of Missions, England, 1996), ch. 1. Hunter is the "mentor" of the Nomadic Peoples Network sponsored by Global Connections in the United Kingdom, and has had over 30 years of experience with 27 different pastoral groups in Ethiopia and Kenya with SIM International.

3. See Claude Poulet, "Home on the Range," *The Royal Geographical Society Magazine* (June 1997), 56-62.

4. Joseph C. Berland, "*Parytan*: 'Native' Models of Peripatetic Strategies in Pakistan," *Nomadic Peoples* 21/22 (Dec. 1986), 189-205, 195.

5. For a number of articles on the peripatetics see A. Rao (ed.), *The Other Nomads* (Cologne: Böhlau, 1987), and esp. Rao's article "The Concept of Peripatetics: An Introduction," 1-32.

6. Oliver Leach, "The 'Monde du Voyage': French Carnival Nomads' View of Peripatetic Society," *Nomadic Peoples* 21/22 (Dec. 1986), 71-8.

7. Cf. Richard V. Weekes (ed.), *Muslim Peoples* (Westport, CT: Greenwood, 1978), 325.

8. Salzman suggests multi-resource nomadism in "Movement," 185ff. Dawn Chatty is quoted as defining these nomads as semi-nomadic in Marina Leybourne, Ronald Jaubert and Richard N. Tutwiler, *Changes in Migration and Feeding Patterns among Semi-Nomadic Pastoralists in Northern Syria* (Pastoral Development Network Paper 34a, July 1993).

9. Wendy Wilson, "The Fulani Model of Sustainable Agriculture: Situating Fulbe Nomadism in a Systematic View of Pastoralism and Farming," in *Nomadic Peoples*, 36/37 (1995), 35-52.

10. Probably three-quarters of West African nomads may be in this situation according to Malcolm Hunter. The majority of Saudi Bedouin are working away from pastoralism.

11. Michael J. Casimir, "On the Formation of the Niche: Peripatetic Legends in Cross-Cultural Perspective," *Nomadic Peoples* 21/22 (Dec. 1986), 89-102.

CHAPTER 2: TO WHERE THE GRASS GROWS GREENER

1. Malcolm Hunter, "Nomadic Pastoralists — Who are they?" (unpublished paper, 1993).

2. Stephen Sandford, *Size and Importance of Pastoral Populations* (Pastoral Network Paper 1c; Agricultural Administration Unit; London: ODI, 1976), 2-3.

3. *Mongolia Challenge Report #3* (Lynwood, WV: Issachar, 1984), II/3iii.

4. Paul Baxter, "Pastoralists are People," *REB* (AERDD, University of Reading, April 1994), 4, 5.

5. J.K. Campbell, *Honour, Family, and Patronage* (Oxford: Oxford University Press, 1964), 26f., 268ff.

6. Richard Widdows (ed.), *Family of Man* (London: Marshal Cavendish, 1974), 1968.

7. John Galaty, "Dreams, Symbols and Totems," *New Internationalist* (April 1995), 28-9.

8. Thomas J. Barfield, *The Nomadic Alternative* (Englewood Cliffs, NJ: Prentice Hall, 1993), 9ff.

9. Weekes, *Muslim Peoples*, 135.

10. Paul Riesman, "Aristocrats as Subjects in a Multi-ethnic State," in *Image and Reality in African Interethnic Relations: The Fulbe and Their Neighbors* (ed. Emily A. Schultz; Williamsburg, VA: College of William and Mary, 1981), 21-9.

11. Widdows (ed.), *Family*, 811.

12. Baxter, "Pastoralists," 4.

13. Angelo B. Maliki, *Joy and Suffering among the Wodaabe* (JCMWA; Jos, Nigeria, 1984).

14. Carole E. Devillers, "Oursi, Magnet in the Desert," 525.

15. Dyson-Hudson, "Inheriting," 10. Animals cannot be killed "wantonly," that is only for food, but must be also sacrificed and distributed to kin (Widdows (ed.), *Family*, 659). As Buddhists, the Tibetan nomads also are reluctant to kill their animals (M. Goldstein and C. Beall, "The Remote World of Tibet's Nomads," *National Geographic* [June 1989], 761).

16. Cf. K.A. Gourlay, "The Ox and Identification," *Man* 7.2 (June 1972), 244-54. Gourlay illustrates this from the Karimojong.

17. Galaty, "Dreams." Cf. Vincent J. Donovan, *Christianity Rediscovered: An Epistle from the Masai* (London: SCM Press, 1982), 20.

18. Isle Köhler-Rollefson, "The Raika Dromedary," *Nomadic Peoples* 30 (1992), 74-83, 79.

19. Daniel Stiles, "The Gabbra Nomad Survival Kit," *Msafiri* (n.d.), 48-51.

20. Donald P. Cole, *Pastoral Nomads in a Rapidly Changing Economy: The Case of Saudi Arabia* (Pastoral Network Paper 7e; London: ODI, 1979), 16.

21. *Mongolia Challenge Report #3*, ii/3ii.

22. S. Vainshtein, *Nomads of South Siberia* (Cambridge: Cambridge University Press, 1980), 65.

23. Ellwood, "Nomads," 7-10.

24. Marie Herbert, *The Reindeer People: Travels in Lapland* (London: Hodder and Stoughton, 1976), 114.

25. Chris Wallis, SAMS.

26. Cf. W.W. Swidler, "Some Demographic Factors Regulating the Formation of Flocks and Camps Among the Brahui of Baluchistan," in *Perspectives on Nomadism* (ed. William Irons and Neville Dyson-Hudson; Leiden: E.J. Brill, 1972), 69-75, 74.

27. V.H. Matthews and Don Benjamin, *Social World of Ancient Israel 1250-587 BCE* (Peabody, MA: Hendrickson Publishers, 1993), 52-66.

28. Stiles, "Gabbra Nomad," 48-51.

29. Leybourne et al., *Changes*, 7.

30. Bruce Ingham, *Bedouin of Northern Arabia — Traditions of the Al-Dhafir* (London: KPI, 1986), 48.

31. Stiles, "Gabbra Nomad," 48-51

32. A knowledge of these traditional allocations is necessary for the planning of development projects. John Morton says a knowledge of the subtleties of traditional land tenure among pastoralists is lacking in Pakistan for making good developmental decisions ("Pastoralists in Pakistan," *Rural Extension Bulletin* [April 1994], 33-6). M. Hunter stresses this for missions ("What of the "Nomadic Pastoralists?" [unpublished paper, 1993]).

33. Marina Leybourne, Ronald Jaubert and Richard N. Tutwiler sum up: "It appears that rather than settling, the semi-nomadic population of Northern Syria, who are based in the steppe, have become more nomadic in recent years, unless other forms of income can be found. The present constraint to their settling is a lack of available grazing; they are forced to move in order to find enough grazing for their flocks. The migration and feeding patterns have changed in that much more emphasis is on crop residues and stubble, rather than natural grazing. In fact the sheep are now grazing rangeland for about a month each year, and during this time their diet is still supplemented with hand-fed feed" (*Changes*, 18).

34. Goldstein and Beall, "Remote World," 752ff. George B. Challer, "Tibet's Remote Chang Tang — In a High and Sacred Realm," *National Geographic* 184.2 (Aug. 1993), 62-87.

35. K.S. Freudenberger, "Don't Fence Me In," *New Internationalist* (April 1994), 14-16.

36. Salzman, "Movement," 185ff.

37. Freudenberger, "Don't Fence," 14-16.

38. J.B. Wychoff, "Planning Arid Land Development Projects," *Nomadic Peoples* 19 (Sept. 1985), 59-69.

39. This contains 88.3% of the rangeland. "The chief characteristics of the pastoral area are: vast land with sparse population; many different nationalities; density of live-stock and a minority of most livestock species and little farmland. Consequently, this broad area is not suitable for the development of cereal production, but it can be used to develop animal husbandry, especially pastoral systems." Shen-Chang-jiang, *Pastoral Systems in Arid and Semi-Arid Zones of China* (Pastoral Network Paper 13b; London: ODI, 1982), 4.

40. Robin Hanbury-Tenison, "Reindeer Nations of Siberia," *Geographical Magazine* (Feb. 1998), 15-29.

41. N.P. Ivlev and M.N. Ivlev, "River Crossings and Bridges of Nomads," *Central Asian Survey* 13.3 (1994), 417-24.

42. Goldstein and Beall, "Remote World," 764.

43. Leybourne et al., *Changes*.

44. Salzman, "Movement," 185ff. The only nomads who appear to be self-sufficient are the hunter-gatherers, such as the Pygmies, Amazon Indians, Aborigines and Bushmen. Trader and craft nomads such as the Gypsies are interdependent with the sedentary population providing skills that the latter lack or are unwilling to provide for themselves (Richard Evans, "Born to Roam Free," *Geographical Magazine* [March 1991], 22-3).

45. Cole, *Pastoral Nomads*, 4.

46. Cole, *Pastoral Nomads*, 18.

47. Han van Dijk, "Farming and Herding after Drought: Fulbe Agropastoralists in Dryland Central Mali," *Nomadic Peoples* 36/37 (1995), 65-84.

48. Salzman, "Movement."

49. Philip Carl Salzman, "Labor Formation as in a Nomadic Tribe," *Nomadic Peoples* 13 (July 1983), 35-59. Added to these is work as building laborers in Iranian and Pakistani cities (*Geographical Magazine* [March 1991], 22-3).

50. Widdows (ed.), *Family*, 2111.

51. Goldstein and Beall, "Remote World," 767.

52. Jim Carrier, "Gatekeepers of the Himalayas," *National Geographic* (Dec. 1992), 79.

53. S.L. Pastner, "Co-operation in Crisis among Baluch Nomads."

CHAPTER 3: WHO YOU KNOW, NOT WHAT YOU OWN

1. Widdows (ed.), *Family*, 811.

2. Mary Zuppan, "Need Herders and Farmers Quarrel?" *REB* (April 1994), 12-16.

3. Wilson, "Fulani Model," 37.

4. Lynn Teo Simarski, "The Desert Meets the Sown," *Aramco World* 46.2 (March-April 1995), 2-9.

5. Eric Valli and Diane Summers, "Himalayan Caravans," *National Geographic* (Dec. 1993), 5-35.

6. Wilson, "Fulani Model," 35-52.

7. Dyson-Hudson, "Inheriting."

8. Goldstein and Beall, "Remote World," 758. Tomasz Potkanski, "Mongolia: Reworking the Revolution," *REB* (April 1994).

9. Pastner, "Co-operation."

10. An example are the Dogon, who lost a year's grain harvest to Fulani cattle during a drought (*The Alliance Witness* [26 Feb. 1986]).

11. Baxter, "Pastoralists," 4.

12. See Richard Tapper's discussion in *Pasture and Politics* (London: Academic Press, 1979), 1-17.

13. Widdows (ed.), *Family*, 2396.

14. Stiles, "Gabbra Nomad," 48-51.

15. Pastner, "Co-operation."

16. For more information on these meetings, see the profile on the Gadulyia Lohar in ch. 13, below.

17. Cole, *Pastoral Nomads*, 17-18.

18. Hunter, "Nomadic Pastoralists."

19. See, e.g., the Turkana in Cathy Watson, "Kenya, Turkana: Women Coping," *REB* (April 1994), 23-8.

20. Daniel Bradburd, *Ambiguous Relations: Kin, Class and Conflict among the Komachi Pastoralists* (Washington, DC: Smithsonian Institution, 1990), 96.

21. Clare Oxby, "Inequality in Pastoral Society and Response to Drought — The Tuareq and Wodaabe of Niger" (unpublished paper; University of Khartoum).

22. Pastner, "Co-operation."

23. Ellwood, "Nomads," 9.

24. P.C. Salzman, "Are Nomads Capable of Development Decisions?" *Nomadic Peoples* 18 (June 1985), 47-52.

25. Barfield, *Nomadic Alternative*, 16-17.

26. Franz-Volker Müller, "New Nomads and Old Customs," *Nomadic Peoples* 36/37 (1995), 175-94, 189.

27. Melvyn C. Goldstein and Cynthia M. Beall, "Change and Continuity in Nomadic Pastoralism on the Western Tibetan plateau," *Nomadic Peoples* 28 (1991), 105-22.

28. Chris Wallis, SAMS.

29. Cole, *Pastoral Nomads*, 16.

30. C. Humphrey, M. Monguish and B. Telengid, "Attitudes to Nature in Mongolia and Tuva: A Preliminary Report," *Nomadic Peoples* 33 (1993), 51-61.

31. Hildegard Diemberger, "Gangla Tshechu, Beyul Khenbalung: Pilgrimage to Hidden Valleys, etc.," in *Anthropology of Tibet and Himalaya* (ed. C. Ramble and M. Brauen; Zurich: Ethnological Museum of the University of Zurich, 1993), 60-72.

32. Marku Tsering, *Sharing Christ in the Tibetan Buddhist World* (Upper Darby, PA: Tibet Press, 1988), 101.

33. See particularly Tsering: *Sharing Christ*, ch. 5.

34. Hunter, "Nomadic Pastoralists" and "What of the Nomadic Pastoralists?"

35. *Christianity Rediscovered*, 41.

36. James Forsyth, *A History of the Peoples of Siberia* (Cambridge: Cambridge University Press, 1992), 288.

37. *Tribes of the Sahara* (Cambridge, MA: Harvard University Press, 1960), 163.

38. Widdows (ed.), *Family*, 132.

39. George Jennings, *Welcome to the Middle East* (Le Mars, IA: M.E. Missions Research, 1986), 86.

40. Goldstein and Beall, "Remote World," 766.

41. Robyn Davidson, "Wandering With India's Rabari," *National Geographic* (Sept. 1993), 64-93, and her book *Desert Places* (Penguin: Harmondsworth, 1997).

42. Pastner, "Co-operation."

43. Some 50% of the Tuareqs and Fulanis of Niger and Mali either died or moved into cities during the famine of the 1980s (private communication with Malcolm Hunter).

44. G. Robinson, *Native Peoples of the Soviet Arctic* (YWAM-Slavic Ministries, 1989), 2.

45. Goldstein and Beall, "Remote World," 752ff.

46. Weekes, *Muslim Peoples*, 211; Carl van Leeuwen, "Animal Husbandry in Central Asia," in *Nomads in Central Asia* (Amsterdam: Royal Tropical Institute, 1993), 9-36.

47. *Unreached Peoples '83* (ed. R. Dayton, et al.; Monrovia: Cal. Marc, 1983), 232.

48. Dan Boneh, "Returning to Pastoralism: Three Cases from the Negev Bedouin," *Nomadic Peoples* 15 (April 1984), 41-50.

CHAPTER 4: THE NEED FOR UNDERSTANDING

1. Evans, "Roam Free." Cf. Baxter, "Pastoralists," 5; and Zuppan, "Herders," 13. Zuppan says that Europeans hypothesized separate racial origins for pastoralists from agriculturists, and this resulted in colonial stereotypes.

2. Tony Banks, "Pastoral Land Tenure Reform and Resource Management in Northern Xinjiang: A New Institutional Economic Perspective," *Nomadic Peoples* NS I.2 (1997), 55-74.

3. Roger Boyes, "Czech Abuses Take Toll on Romanies," *The Times* (Nov. 16,1999).

4. Forsyth, *History*, 400.

5. See, e.g., "The Drying of India," India Today (June 22, 1998), 62-8.

6. Cathy Sanders, "Desert Storm," New Internationalist (April 1995), and the Urmul Trust, Rajasthan.

7. Ellwood, "Nomads," 8.

8. Ellwood, "Nomads," 8.

9. Freudenberger, "Don't Fence," 14-16.

10. Peter Fuchs, "Nomadic Society, Civil War and the State in Chad," *Nomadic Peoples* 38 (1996), 151-62.

11. *Encyclopaedia Britannica 1994 Book of the Year* (Chicago: Encyclopaedia Britannica Inc., 1994), 464; Robin Hanbury-Tenison, "Back to Nature," *Geographical* (Oct. 1997), 99.

12. Forsyth, *History*, 297.

13. Terence McCabe, "The Turkana of Kenya," in *Nomads* (ed. P. Carmichael; London: Collins, 1991), 66-95, 92.

14. This is usually related to 'The tragedy of the commons' (Ellwood, "Nomads," 9).

15. Nigel Cross, *The Sahel: The People's Right to Development* (London: MRG, 1990), 24.

16. Various articles in Pastoral Development Network Paper 36b (ODI, July 1994).

17. Hunter, "What of the Nomadic Pastoralists?".

18. Cole, *Pastoral Nomads*, 17.

19. Hunter stresses this after research among the Borana in Kenya (*Appropriate Development*).

20. Krisztina Kehl, *Die Tahtaci: vorlaufiger Bericht uber die Holzarbeiter in Anatolien* (Berlin: Frie University, 1988), 37-45.

21. Malcolm Hunter, "Nomadic Pastoralists and their Spiritual World" (unpublished paper at EMA Nomadic Pastoralist conference, Oct. 1993).

22. Donovan, *Christianity Rediscovered*, 22.

23. Ibid., 42f., 50.

24. Ibid., 47.

25. Ibid., 51.

26. Nik Repkin, "Why are the Unreached, Unreached?," *EMQ* (July 1996), 286.

Part II: The Missionary Challenge of Nomadic Peoples

CHAPTER 5: A JOURNEY WITH GOD

1. E.A. Martens, *God's Plot and Purpose in the Old Testament* (Leicester: IVP, 1981), 27.

2. The family may have been worshippers of the Moon god (D. Kidner, *Genesis* [TOTC; Leicester: IVP, 1967], 111).

3. 2 Sam. 23:1; Ps. 20:1; 46:7; 75:9; 76:6; 81:1-4, 84:8; 114:1, 7; 132:2, 5; 146:5; Is. 2:3.

4. Ex. 40:34-38. See Gordon Wenham, *Numbers* (TOTC; Leicester: IVP, 1981), 100.

5. D.J. Wiseman, "Abraham Reassessed," in *Essays on the Patriarchal Narratives* (ed. A.R. Millard and D.J. Wiseman; Leicester: IVP, 1980), 139ff. D.J. Wiseman, "They lived in Tents," in *Biblical and Near Eastern Studies* (ed. Gary A. Tuttle; Grand Rapids: Eerdmans, 1978), 195-200. See also Joyce Balwyn, *The Message of Genesis 12-50* (Leicester: IVP, 1986), 28. Nomads neither travel for the sake of it nor are adverse to using agriculture, as she suggests, as the many examples below show.

6. Barfield, *Nomadic Alternative*, 62; Michael Asher, *The Last of the Bedouin — In Search of the Myth* (London: Penguin, 1996), 64-5.

7. K.R. Veenhof in *The World of the Bible*, I (gen. ed. A.S. van der Woude; Grand Rapids: Eerdmans, 1986), 234-39, see also 264-67; John Bright, *A History of Israel* (London: SCM Press, 1972), 80.

8. This is not anachronistic, says Bright, *History*, 89; K.A. Kitchen, *The Illustrated Bible Dictionary* (Leicester: IVP, 1980), 88.

9. A camel, especially after a journey, can drink between 100 and 120 liters of water in one watering (Barfield, *Nomadic Alternative*, 59). This could take hours of work, so that later Moses' help made a significant difference (Ex. 2:18).

10. Bright, *History*, 80, 91. Cf. Gen. 25:20; 31:20; Dt. 26:5. Short descriptions of early biblical pastoralism are in Ralph Gower, *The New Manners and Customs of Bible Times* (Chicago: Moody Press, 1987), 24-7, 132-47 and John Bimson, *The World of the Old Testament* (London: SU Press, 1988), 47-52.

CHAPTER 6: THE PASTORAL GOD OF A TRAVELING PEOPLE

1. Alistair I. MacKay, *Farming and Gardening in the Bible* (Old Tappan, NJ: Spire Books, 1970), 233f.

2. History has seen other such organized movements of peoples. The Mongol empire had a mobile court, a *tumen*, with the *gers* of Genghis Khan and his entourage drawn by dozens of oxen on wheeled platforms across the steppe, accompanied by thousands of cavalry and tens of thousands of livestock ("The Mongols," map [loose inset] in *National Geographic* [Dec. 1996]).

3. Their complaints are those of any human group in a difficult environment, including: 1) the brackish water (Ex. 15:22); 2) hunger (Ex.16:3); 3) thirst (Ex. 17:3); 4) Moses' absence (Ex. 32:1); 5) more varied diet (Num. 11:1); 6) his Cushite wife (Num. 12:1); 7) military inferiority (Num. 14:1ff); 8) his unique authority, as Korah's challenge involves confidence in his ability to lead within the circumstances and the people's reaction (Num. 16 — 17); and 9) lack of water again (Num. 20:2f). If they had been totally inexperienced farmers or town dwellers, the complaints would have been on a vaster scale.

4. Deryck Sheriffs, *The Friendship of the Lord* (Carlisle: Paternoster, 1996), see 81, n. 32 for a breakdown of allusions to the Exodus.

5. J. Gary Millar, *Now Choose Life: Theology and Ethics in Deuteronomy* (Leicester: IVP, 1998), esp. 67-98.

6. D. Kidner, *Numbers* (Leicester: IVP, 1981), 57; O Böcher in *NIDNTT*, III (Carlisle: Paternoster, 1992), 1004. It has been argued that the wilderness journey was a forced refugee migration and not one of those experienced in pastoralism. However, the Israelites had also been forced into all types of field work (Ex. 1:14) and "field" (*sadeh*) is used of both cultivated land and the open country used for pasture, so that we have the phrase "the beasts of the field" meaning wild animals (Gen. 2:5, 20; 3:14, 18; Dt. 7:14). They also had large herds of livestock that played a significant role in events and not just a few family "pets" (Ex. 9:4-7; 10:9, 26; 11:7; 12:32, 38; 17:3). The sacrificial system envisaged *every family* contributing from self-reproducing herds and flocks, not from one or two animals.

7. Dt. 34:5. Israel took the symbolism of Elijah reversing the opening up of the Jordan, in order to return to God, to mean that God was not to be found in the land. Elisha not only established his credentials by returning in the same manner, but also demonstrated that the promise of the land was not irrevocably achieved by Joshua, but is exclusively for those who, like Elijah and Elisha, walk with God (2 Kgs. 2:8).

8. See, e.g., Chris Wright, *Knowing Jesus through the Old Testament* (London: Marshall Pickering, 1992).

9. William J. Dumbrell, "The Prospect of Unconditionality in the Sinaitic Covenant," in *Israel's Apostasy and Restoration: Essays in Honour of Roland K. Harrison* (ed. Avraham Gileadi; Grand Rapids: Baker, 1988), 141-56.

10. Ex. 19:1-6, set between the Exodus and the covenant and the law, "gives to Israel an identity and role as a priestly and holy people in the midst of 'all the nations' in 'the whole earth' which is God's." "They were to be teacher, model and mediator for the nations"... "the law was given to Israel to enable Israel to live as a model, as a light to the nations," argues Chris Wright ("The Ethical Authority of the Old Testament: A Survey of Approaches, Part II," *TynBul* 43.2 [1992], 203-31, 227). The call of Israel creates a sample applicable to all "to make visible [God's] requirements on the rest of the nations" (Chris Wright, *The Use of the Bible in Social Ethics* [Grove Booklet on Ethics 51; Bramcote: Grove Books, 1983], 16). The prophets disclose a centripetal mission for Israel with the law, and later a centrifugal mission to the nations at the coming of the Messiah (W. Vogels, *God's Universal Covenant: A Biblical Study* [Ottawa: University of Ottawa, 1979], 119, 147). Vogels suggests that the phrase "in the eyes of the nations" refers to them acting as legal witnesses, and in other contexts there is a call for a moral decision on the part of the nations (Dt. 4:6). It is often found in Ezekiel (ibid., 68). See Ez. 7:20; 9:8; 11:3; 12:36; Lev. 26:45. The witness of nature includes the nations (Dt. 4:26; 30:19; 31:28; 32:1).

11. Jeffrey J. Niehaus, *God at Sinai* (Carlisle: Paternoster, 1995), 141, 181.

12. Malcolm Hunter, in an unpublished article entitled "The Nomadic Church."

13. Even the widely held date for the Exodus, 1260 BC, allows for the use of the Tabernacle for 300 years.

14. Ps. 18:11; 27:5; 31:20; Amos 9:11.

15. W. White, "*rôeh*," in *TWOT* (ed. L. Harris, G. Archer and B. Waltke; Chicago: Moody Press, 1980), 852.

16. K.R. Veenhof, "History of the Ancient Near East," in *World*, I, 237f.

17. Matthews and Benjamin, *Social World*, 52-66.

18. T.C. Mitchell, "Nomads," in *The New Bible Dictionary* (Leicester: IVP, 1962), 892-95 and *The Illustrated Bible Dictionary* (Leicester: IVP, 1980), 1093-94, and his article on Arabia, 83-6.

19. E.W. Heaton, *Everyday Life in Old Testament Times* (London: Transworld Publishers, 1974), 59; H. Strathmann, "*polis*," in *TDNT*, VI (ed. Kittel and Friedrich; Grand Rapids: Eerdmans, 1965), 516-35, (or abridged edn 1985), 908.

20. C.H.J. Wright, *Living as the People* (Leicester: IVP, 1983), 59.

21. Martens, *God's Plot*, 105.

22. Chris Wright, *God's People in God's Land* (Grand Rapids: Eerdmans, 1990), 63f.

23. Bright, *History*, 109; John Paterson, "Resources: Conservation and Christian Responsibility," *Christian Graduate* (March 1971), 11-14.

24. Paterson, "Resources."

25. Matthews and Benjamin, *Social World*.

CHAPTER 7: COME, FOLLOW ME

1. Cf. F.F. Bruce, *The New Testament Development of Old Testament Themes* (Grand Rapids: Eerdmans, 1969), 100-114.

2. William Lane, *The Gospel According to Mark* (Grand Rapids: Eerdmans, 1971), 202.

3. Susan R. Garrett, *The Temptations of Jesus in Mark's Gospel* (Grand Rapids: Eerdmans, 1998), 53.

4. E. Earle Ellis, *The Gospel of Luke* (London: Marshall, Morgan & Scott, 1974), 148; Ernest Best, *Following Jesus* (Sheffield: JSOT Press, 1981), 15f.

5. Lane, *Mark*, 161.

6. Willard M. Swartley, *Israel's Scripture Traditions and the Synoptic Gospels* (Peabody, MA: Hendrickson, 1994), 96-7.

7. Lane, *Mark*, 39f, 52. His route is "geographically tortuous" says Best (*Following Jesus*, 138).

8. Swartley, *Traditions*, 44-94.

9. W.L. Liefeld, "Transfigure," in *NIDNTT*, 863; Nichaus: *God at Sinai*, 336ff.

10. Christina Noble met a shepherd who had lost one small lamb, and she climbed back an altitude of 800 m. (2,600 ft.) over a distance of 9 km. (5 mi.) searching for it. He was amazed to find that a non-shepherd like herself had bothered to rescue it (*Over the High Passes: A Year in the Himalayas with the Migratory Gaddi Shepherds* [London: Collins, 1987], 10). Janny van der Klis, AIM, worked on the Turkana Bible translation (*Failure is Not Final* [London: Marshall Pickering, 1993], 67).

11. Mark stresses the journey to death by relating predictions of the cross with "on the way" Mk. 8:27; 9:33f; 10:32 (Best, *Following Jesus*, 15). See also Leon Morris, who says that there is no doubt about the journey, but that we have difficulty in plotting its course. But Jesus is committed to the cross and his teaching and ministry is in relation to going to die (*Luke* [Leicester: IVP, 1974], 177). The material in Luke, but not in the other Gospels, may have been arranged thematically, or Luke may retain more the original setting and Matthew may have put some of the sayings together. However, there has been no attempt by Luke to remove the context of a journey towards the cross, even if the precise chronological and geographical details cannot be reconstructed. See Ellis, *Luke*, 146ff. See Swartley, *Traditions*, 98-126.

12. Rikk Watts, *Isaiah's New Exodus and Mark* (Tübingen: Mohr Siebeck, 1997), esp.123-36; Tremper Longman III and Daniel G. Reid, *God is a Warrior* (Carlisle: Paternoster, 1995), 91ff. Pastoral, sacrificial and servant themes are all prominent, so it is not adequate to describe Jesus as a warrior. Rather, through his obedience and death as God's servant he accomplishes God's victory.

13. R.H. Stein says the Jews did not understand Zech. 9:9 to be messianic until around AD 400 (*Jesus the Messiah* [Leicester and Downers Grove: IVP, 1996], 183). N.T. Wright stresses the journey of Jesus as fulfilling the return of God fulfilling the prophecies for after the exile (*Jesus and the Victory of God* [Minneapolis: Fortress, 1996], 639). However the return under Zerubbabel was an incomplete fulfillment and Jesus saw himself more as the regal agent of the Lord, with his deity implicit.

14. Swartley, *Traditions*, 126-45.

15. *Mongolia Challenge*, II/9v.

16. Best, *Following Jesus*, 49.

17. Noble, *High Passes*, 25. Davidson, "Wandering."

18. Richard B. Hays, *Echoes of Scripture in the Letters of Paul* (London: Yale, 1989).

19. John Sherwood, "The Missionary's Lifestyle," *EMQ* (July 1999), 334-37.

20. This is a translation issue. The emphasis is not on being hired and therefore not bothered for someone else's sheep, but that he is inexperienced as a shepherd.

21. Jn. 10:12. See Leon Morris, *The Gospel According to John* (New London Commentaries; London: Marshall, Morgan & Scott, 1977), 502.

CHAPTER 8: MISSION OF PILGRIMS

1. Vogels, *Universal Covenant*.

2. *The Missionary Nature of the Church: A Survey of the Biblical Theology of Mission* (New York: McGraw-Hill, 1962), 19.

3. John Piper, *Let the Nations be Glad* (Grand Rapids: Baker, 1993), 174-205.

4. K.L. and M.A. Schmidt, *TDNT* V, 853.

5. A parallel can be traced with the emphases on "pillars" of faith, fellowship, holiness and sacrifice in the ethos of WEC International, of which I am a member.

6. J. Breay, "Romany Christ," *JGLS* XLVII (1968), 34-7.

CHAPTER 9: CHRISTIAN NOMADIC PARTNERSHIP

1. Robert Fetherlin, "Going to Samaria," *The Alliance Witness* (CMA), (26 Feb. 1986), 18-19.

2. Hunter, "Spiritual World." Debra Braaksma discusses this in relation to the Orma, Kenya ("My Pastoral Neighbours are Hungry... What's the Missionary to Do?" [unpublished essay; University of Edinburgh, 1994]).

3. D. Gitari, S. Houghton and G. R. Mullenix, "The Unreached Gabbra: A Plan to Reach a Nomadic People," in *Unreached Peoples 1979* (Elgin, IL and Weston, Ont.: David C. Cook, 1978), 119-27.

4. Debra Braaksma, "Can Christian Development Work Fit on a Donkey's Back?" (Dissertation for Department of Christian Ethics and Practical Theology, University of Edinburgh, 1994).

5. Donovan, *Christianity Rediscovered*, 24, 138ff.

6. Talk given by Cash and Ann Godbold in 1994.

7. SIM Mursi Team, "Goals and Plans," 1997.

8. Louis J. Luzbetak, *The Church and the Cultures* (Techny, IL: Divine Word, 1970), 96.

9. Maureen Yeates.

10. L. and A. Vanderaa, *Global Prayer Digest* (Feb. and Mar. 1987), and "Strategy for Mission among the Fulbe" (paper).

11. Hunter, "What of the Nomadic Pastoralists?"

12. Personal communication with Malcolm Hunter.

13. Hunter, *Appropriate Development*, 253f.

14. Satya Pal Ruhela, "Bullock-cart Blacksmiths, Gaduliya Lohar Bring Forges to Rajasthan Villages," in *Nomads of the World* (Washington, DC: National Geographic Society, 1971), 26-51.

15. Carol Beckwith, "Niger's Wodaabe: 'People of the Taboo'," *National Geographic* 164.4 (Oct. 1983), 483-509; see also Marion van Offelen, *Nomads in Niger* (New York: H.N. Abrams; London: Collins; Paris: Ed. du Chene, 1983).

16. Valli and Summers, "Caravans," 5-35.

17. "Visiting the Kazakhs: A Photo Essay," *China Review* (Dec. 1989), 57-66.

18. Köhler-Rollefson, "Dromedary."

19. Herbert, *Reindeer.*

20. Davidson, "Wandering," and her book *Desert Places.*

21. Isabel Fonseca, *Bury Me Standing — The Gypsies and their Journey* (London: Chatto & Windus, 1995), 60.

22. Paul Riesman, *Freedom in Fulani Social Life* (Chicago and London: University of Chicago Press, 1977).

23. Lois Beck's full description is in the introduction to *Nomad — A Year in the Life of a Qashqa'i Tribesman in Iran* (University of California and London: I.B. Tauris, 1991), 15-27.

24. Brian Hugh MacDermot, *Cult of the Sacred Spear — The Story of the Nuer Tribe in Ethiopia* (London: The Travel Book Club, 1972).

25. R. Lovett, *James Gilmour of Mongolia* (London Religious Tract Society, c. 1890), 130.

26. Berland, "Parytan," 192; and *No Five Fingers Are Alike* (Cambridge, MA: Harvard University Press, 1982).

27. Judith Okely, "Gypsies Travelling in Southern England," in *Gypsies, Tinkers and Other Travellers* (ed. F. Rehfisch; London: Academic Press, 1975), 55-83, 67 and *The Traveller Gypsies* (Cambridge: Cambridge University Press, 1983) an excellent and practical survey of Gypsies in England in the early 1970s.

28. Okely, *Traveller Gypsies*, ch. 3.

29. Noble, *High Passes.*

30. Tapper, *Pasture*, 262-65.

31. T.S. Randhawa, *The Last Wanderers: Nomads of Gypsies of India* (Middletown, NJ: Grantha, 1996).

32. Bradburd, *Ambiguous Relations.*

33. John Pilkington, "Kyrgyzstan: A Tale of Two Journeys," *Geographical Magazine* (April 1993), 8-12.

34. Phil and Marion Grasham, WEC.

35. Hanbury-Tenison, "Reindeer."

36. Gitari, Houghton, and Mullenix, "Unreached Gabbra."

37. Secretary Anthony Matthew (Agricultural Christian Fellowship; 38, De Montfort St.; Leicester, LE1 7GP, England. acf@uccf.org.uk).

38. Malcolm Hunter, "General Guidelines" (unpublished paper).

39. YWAM Safari Trips, Apartado 109, E-29620 Torremolinos, Málaga, Spain.

40. *Christianity Today* (May 16, 1994).

41. *The Topper*, local newspaper, Nottingham, England (June 5, 1996).

42. Philip Andrews-Speed, "Herdsmen of Chinese Turkestan," *Asian Affairs* XXVII.1 (Feb. 1996), 53-61.

43. Vanderaa, "Strategy," 2.

44. Maliki, *Joy.*

CHAPTER 10: WORKING WITH NOMADS

1. Donovan: *Christianity Rediscovered* 17.

2. Derek Kidner, *Wisdom to Live By* (Leicester: IVP, 1985).

3. Melissa Llewelyn-Davies, "Two Contexts of Solidarity among Maasai Women," in *Women United, Women Divided* (ed. Patricia Caplan and Janet M. Bujira; London: Tavistock, 1978), 206-37, 207f.

4. Dawn Chatty, "Changing Sex Roles in Bedouin Society in Syria and Lebanon," in *Women of the Muslim World* (ed. Lois Beck and Nikki Keddie; Cambridge, MA: Harvard University Press, 1978), 399-415. See also the articles in this volume by Beck on Qashqa'i women, by Nancy Tapper on Shahsevan women, and by Emrys L. Petters on the Bedouin of Cyrenaica.

5. Okely, *Traveller Gypsies*, 66-104, 203ff.

6. Cf. Tsering, *Sharing Christ*, for contextualization of various points of the gospel for Mongols and Tibetans.

7. Salzman, "Development Decisions."

8. John Best, "Editorial," REB (April 1994), 2.

9. D. Michael Warren, L. Jan Slikkerveer and David Brokensha (eds.), *The Cultural Dimension of Development: Indigenous Knowledge Systems* (London: Intermediate Technology Publications, 1995).

10. Gufu Oba, "Environmental Education for Sustainable Development among Nomadic Peoples," *Nomadic Peoples* 30 (1992), 53-73, 55.

11. Hanbury-Tenison, "Reindeer."

12. Wychoff, "Planning," 60-66.

13. Salzman, "Development Decisions." The example he gives is the Yarahmadzai Baluch. This whole edition of *Nomadic Peoples* is given to this subject. See Gufu Oba's detailed example from the Rendille, Kenya ("Environmental Education," 60ff.).

14. Wilson, "Fulani Model," 43.

15. Goldstein and Beall, "Remote World," 766.

16. Cf. Claire Heffernan, *The Socio-Economic Impact of Restocking Pastoralists in Northern Kenya* (Reading: Department of Agriculture, University of Reading, 1997).

17. Geoff Thomas, "Evangelising the Eskimos Yesterday and Today," *Evangelical Times* (July 1996), 7.

18. Müller, "New Nomads," 190.

19. Dawn Chatty, *From Camel to Truck: The Bedouin in the Modern World* (New York: Vantage Press, 1986), 119-40.

20. C. Agnew, "Green Belt Around the Sahara," *Geographical Magazine* (April 1990), 26-38.

21. Prem Singh Jina, "Pasture Ecology of Leh, Ladakh" (Wissenschaftsgeschichte usw. in N.W. Indien; Dresden: Staatliches Museum for Völkerkunde, 1990), 171-80.

22. "Trees of Life," *SIM Now* (Sept. 1994), 12-13.

23. Sam David, interviewed by Bob Mann, "The Sahel: Drought, Trees and Livelihood," *REB* (Aug. 1993), 23-32.

24. *Wild about Animals* XII (Dec. 1990), 50.

25. Peter Newsham, "A Desert Dilemma," *Geographical Magazine* (April 1993) 33-8 and Joseph J. Hobbs, "Sinai's Watchmen of the Wilderness," *Aramco World* (May/June 1999), 13-21.

26. T. and D. Mangers, *In the Shadow of the Black Tents* (Tihama, no date).

27. Hunter, "Nomadic Pastoralists" and Robert Bowen and Miriam Andriessen, "Improving Animal Health through Paravets," *Footsteps* 34, Tearfund (March 1998), 1-2. VETAID, Centre for Tropical Veterinary Medicine, Easter Bush, Roslin, Midlothian, EH25 9RG, UK, gives help to those wanting to set up para-vet schemes. An information kit on Paraveterinary Medicine is available from YC James Yen Center, IIRR, Silang, Cavite 4118, Philippines.

28. Morton, "Pastoralists," 34.

29. Veterinary Christian Fellowship, c/o Professional Groups Secretary, 38, De Montfort St., Leicester, LE1 7GP, England and the Christian Veterinary Mission, 19303 Fremont Ave., N. Seattle, WA 98133, USA.

30. Michael Wood, *Different Drums* (London: Century, 1987), 64f.

31. *Mongolia Challenge* II/3, i, ii.

32. Wood, *Different Drums*, 118.

33. Simon Harragin, *Health and Healthcare Provision in North West Turkana, Kenya* (ODI Network Paper 36c; July 1994), 2-3.

34. Bernhard Helander, "Getting the Most Out of It — Nomadic Health Care Seeking and the State in Southern Somalia," *Nomadic Peoples* 25-27 (1990), 122-32.

35. Andrew Perkins, Mali, RSMT, says cataract and trachoma are the commonest conditions in the Sahel, but both are either operable or preventable. Cultural resistance must be overcome to establish public health standards (Cilla Perkins, "News from the Eye Clinic," *Islam Shall Hear* 3 (1991), 12-13.

36. See also Andrew Perkins, "Eye Work in Mali's Western Sahel," *Saving Health* (Spring 1994), 11-12.

37. Lovett, *James Gilmour*, 130f.

38. Cole, *Pastoral Nomads*, 11.

39. Caroline Dyer and Archana Choksi, "The Demand for Education among the Rabaris of Kutch, West India," *Nomadic Peoples* NS I.2 (1997), 77-97.

40. Dawn Chatty, "Boarding Schools for Mobile People: The Harasis in the Sultanate of Oman," a paper presented at a day conference, People on the Move: Education and Nomadism in the Late 20th Century, at the University of Warwick, 1999.

41. Chimah Ezeomah, "The Fulbe: Their Education and Settlement" (Doc. 25, Nomadic Education Unit; Jos, Nigeria: University of Jos).

42. P. Heron, "Education for Nomads," *Nomadic Peoples* 13 (July 1983), 61-68, 65.

43. Heron, "Education." 38% of Maasai children attend school (Wychoff, "Planning," 62). See also Anders Närman, "Pastoral Peoples and the Provision of Educational Facilities — A Case Study from Kenya," *Nomadic Peoples* 25-27 (1990) 108-21.

44. Juliet McCaffery, "Literacy among the Fulani Pastoralists of Northern Nigeria," 1999.

45. Heron, "Education" and Salzman, "Development Decisions."

46. An example is Mary Lar, *Aspects of Nomadic Education in Nigeria* (Jos, Nigeria: Fab Education Books, 1989).

47. Malcolm Hunter cites the successful case of the Catholic Mission to the Borana, in Merti, Kenya (*Appropriate Development*, 110-11).

48. Parallel editing and publication of ethnic history, ethics and traditions, etc., with biblical material for comparison, might be a possibility.

49. Frederick and Audrey Hyde-Chambers, *Tibetan Folk Tales* (Boulder: Shambhala, 1981), 27-70.

50. Maria Leach, *The Beginning* (New York: Funk and Wagnall, 1956), 200f., 198f.

51. Clinton Bailey, *Bedouin Poetry: From the Sinai and the Negev* (Oxford: Oxford University Press, n.d.).

52. Donovan, *Christianity Rediscovered*, 44.

CHAPTER 11: COMMUNICATING THE GOSPEL TO NOMADS

1. Rick Brown, "Communicating God's Word to an Oral Culture" (unpublished paper, 1998).

2. Widdows (ed.), *Family*, 2396.

3. *Mongolia Challenge*, II/9v.

4. John Mbiti, "'Cattle are Born with Ears, Their Horns Grow Later' and Appreciation of African Oral Theology," *Africa Theological Journal*, 8.1, 15-25. John Windsor, "Sitting Comfortably? Then I'll Begin," *The Independent* (London, 20 Aug. 1994). He reports on a storytelling festival and the importance of the ability to tell stories orally even in a literate society. He cites an example of the Ibos, Nigeria.

5. Timothy Lenchak, "The Bible and Intercultural Communication," *Missiology: An International Review* (Oct. 1994), 457-68. Working in the Amazon area, the author constantly met Brazilians who said they could not become evangelical Christians because they did not know how to read.

6. For example J.D. Wilson, "What it Takes to Reach People in Oral Cultures," *EMQ* (April 1991); J. Goldingay, "How Far do Readers Make Sense? Interpreting Biblical Narrative," *Themelios* (Jan. 1993).

7. Lenchak quotes Herbert Klem, saying that 70% of the world's population is unlikely to take an interest in the Bible if we insist that they must read it ("Bible," 462-4). Cf. Herbert V. Klem, *Oral Communication of the Scripture: Insights from African Oral Art* (Pasadena: William Carey Library, 1982).

8. Kenneth Bailey, "Informal Controlled Oral Tradition and the Synoptic Gospels," *Themelios* 20.2 (Jan. 1995).

9. Loveday Alexander, "Ancient Book Production and the Circulation of the Gospels," in *The Gospels for All Christians* (ed. R. Bauckham; Edinburgh: T. & T. Clark, 1998), 71-105, 73, 86.

10. Alexander, "Ancient Book Production," 101.

11. See, e.g., Keith Carey, "Reaching Buddhists through Wisdom Literature of the Old Testament," *International Journal of Frontier Missions* (Oct. 1985), 335-42 and Howard S. Olson, "The Place of Traditional Proverbs in Pedagogy," *Africa Theological Journal* 10:2 (1981), 28-35.

12. See Graeme Goldsworthy, *Gospel and Wisdom* (Carlisle: Paternoster, 1997).

13. Mohammed Abdillahi Rirash, "Somali Oral Poetry as a Vehicle for Understanding Disequilibrium and Conflicts in a Pastoral Society," *Nomadic Peoples* 30 (1992), 114-21.

14. Sylvia A. Matheson, *The Tigers of Baluchistan* (Karachi: Oxford University Press, 1975), 170.

15. Eddie Gibbs, *The God Who Communicates* (London: Hodder, 1985), 18, 140ff.

16. Charles H. Kraft, *Communicating the Gospel God's Way* (Pasadena: William Carey Library, 1979), 3; Gibbs, God.

17. Dell and Rachel Schultze, *God and Man* (Mandaluyong, Manila: 1984 and rev. Singapore: SBC-IMB, 1987).

18. Trevor McIlwain, *Building on Firm Foundations* 1-9, and cf. McIlwain, *Chronological Approach Seminar* (cassette and video, New Tribes Mission).

19. Richard Shawyer, "The Chronological Approach" (WEC Fula Ministry Conference, The Gambia, 1997).

20. Shawyer, "Chronological," 169.

21. Letter by Eugene Thieszen, *EMQ* (Oct. 1996), 393-94.

22. A book written for "motivated lay people" and others is Richard L. Pratt, Jr.'s *He Gave Us Stories — The Bible Student's Guide to Interpreting Old Testament Narratives* (Nutley, NJ: Presbyterian and Reformed, 1993). See Robert Alter, *The Art of Biblical Narrative* (New York: Basic Books, 1981) and Ronald F. Thiemann, *Revelation and Theology — The Gospel as Narrated Promise* (Notre Dame, 1985). Robert C. Tannehill, *The Narrative Unity of Luke-Acts* (Philadelphia: Fortress Press, 1986), is an example of a commentary, and Gabriel Fackre, *The Christian Story* (Grand Rapids: Eerdmans, 1984) is a revision of an older work presenting basic doctrine in a narrative form. See Goldingay, "How Far" and R.W.L. Moberly, "Story in the Old Testament," *Themelios* XI.3 (April 1986), 77-82, and "Sternberg on Biblical Narrative," *Themelios* XVI.3 (April 1991), 21-2.

23. Tremper Longman III, *Literary Approaches to Biblical Interpretation* (Foundations of Contemporary Interpretation 3; Grand Rapids: Zondervan, 1987), 151. Also Anthony C. Thiselton, *New Horizons in Hermeneutics* (London: HarperCollins, 1992), 32-5, 283-312, 471-86, and esp. 566-82; Grant R. Osbourne, *The Hermeneutical Spiral* (Downers Grove: IVP, 1991), 153-73. The latter two authors see the narrative form as conveying a truth-claim involving reference to real people and events that is conveyed by the literary conventions accepted by both authors and their original readers. They argue that this truth-claim cannot be ignored by treating Scripture as a solely literary composition or as fictional history.

24. *The Dramatised Bible* (Swindon: The British and Foreign Bible Society, 1989).

25. SAT-7 Project Office, P.O. Box 6760, CY-1647 Nicosia, Cyprus.

26. Eleanor Vandevort, *A Leopard Tamed* (London: Hodder, 1968).

27. Vanderaa, "Strategy," 5-7.

28. Riesman, *Freedom*, 217f.

29. Donovan, *Christianity Rediscovered*, 81, 83.

30. G. Swank, "The Evangelization of the Fulani," *Unreached Peoples '79* (1978), 107-17.

31. David Peterson, "Worship in the New Testament," in *Worship: Adoration and Action* (ed. D.A. Carson; Grand Rapids: Baker; Carlisle: Paternoster, 1993), 51-91, 52.

32. John Mallison, *Mentoring to Develop Disciples and Leaders* (Lidcombe, NSW, 1998), 25f.

33. See Richard Bauckham, "For Whom Were Gospels Written" and Michael B. Thompson, "The Holy Internet: Communication Between Churches in the First Christian Generation," both in *The Gospels for All Christians* (ed. R. Bauckham; Edinburgh: T. & T. Clark, 1998), 9-70.

34. Earl Anderson and David Cashin, "Responsive Somali Peoples in Kenya," in *Unreached Peoples '80*, 67-73.

35. Albert J. Wollen, *God at Work in Small Groups* (London: Scripture Union, n.d.). Jesus also taught larger groups (Mt. 5 — 7, etc.) without any of the trappings of modern church buildings.

36. Repkin, "Unreached?," 286.

37. Cf. David J. Phillips, *Divine Law as a Basis for Moral Community and Political Participation with Special Reference to Latin America* (unpublished PhD thesis; University of Wales, 1994), sections 1.5, 2.4, 4.6. The issue of Christ representing two groups: humankind, of which he is a member by voluntary incarnation; and the believers, with whom he is united by redemption and their faith, is dealt with in Ch. 2.

38. "200 Unreached Peoples in Our Midst," *Mission Frontiers Bulletin* (May-June 1994).

39. Vanderaa, "Strategy," 4.

Part III: Nomadic Peoples Survey

CHAPTER 13: A WORLD SURVEY OF NOMADIC PASTORAL AND PERIPATETIC PEOPLES

WESTERN SAHEL

1. Patrick Thornberry, et al. (ed. MRG; Harlow, Essex: Longman, 1989).

2. Ellwood, "Nomads," gave the estimate of 1 million.

3. Ellwood, "Nomads," estimated 300,000.

4. Thornberry, *World Directory*; see Cross, *Sahel*.

5. Charles Frantz, "West African Pastoralism, Transformation and Resilience," in *Nomads in a Changing World* (Naples: Istituto Universitario Orientale, 1990), 293-337.

6. Other estimates, such as 127,000 or 350,000 for Niger, and 683,000 or 190,000 for Mali, appear to be low. These are taken from, respectively, Patrick Johnstone, *Operation World* (Gerrards Cross: WEC International, 1993) and *Ethnologue Languages of the World* (ed. Barbara F. Grimes; Dallas: SIL, 13th edn, 1996).

7. Sources for the Tuareq are: Briggs, *Tribes*, 124-65 and 243ff.; Widdows (ed.), *Family*: "Kel Ahaggar" (1553-57) and "Tuareg" (2527-31). Also Jeremy Keenan, *The Tuareg — People of Ahaggar* (London: Allen Lane, 1977); V. Englebert, "Tuareg Men of the Veil," in *Nomads of the World* (ed. Robert L. Breeden; Washington: National Geographic, 1971), 110-33. Sara Randall and Michael Winter have described marriage customs in Mali in *The Reluctant Spouse and the Illegitimate Slave: Marriage, Household Formation and Demographic Behaviour amongst Malian*

Tamesheq from the Niger Delta and the Gourma (Pastoral Development Network Paper 21c; London: ODI, 1986). Barbara Worley, "Property and Gender Relations among Twareg (sic) Nomads," *Nomadic Peoples* 23 (1987), 31-5; M. and A. Kirtley, "The Inadan-Artisans of the Sahara," *National Geographic* (Aug. 1979), 282-98; Carol Beckwith and Angela Fisher, "Brides of the Sahara," *National Geographic* (Feb. 1998), 85-90; Donovan Webster, "Journey to the Heart of the Sahara," *National Geographic* (March 1999), 8-33.

8. Maurice Glover, private communication.

9. P. Marnham, *Nomads of the Sahel* (Minority Rights Group No. 33;1976). Victor Englebert, "Drought Threatens the Tuareg World," *National Geographic* (Apr. 1974), 544-71, Beckwith, "Wodaabe."

10. *The Economist* (13 Oct. 1990); and the summaries in *Keesings Record of World Events*.

11. Prayernet, World Horizons; *The Economist* (13 Oct.1990).

12. Grimes, *Ethnologue and World Translation Progress Report (WTPR)* (Reading: United Bible Societies, 1993 [published annually]).

13. *The Tuaregs and SIM's Work among Them* (SIM, n.d.).

14. *SIM Now* (Autumn 1992).

15. For more information, contact: Adopt-A-People Clearinghouse, P.O. Box 1795, Colorado Springs, CO 80901, USA; in the UK contact Nomadic Pastoralists, P.O. Box 4, High Wycombe, Bucks, HP14 3YX.

16. Grimes, *Ethnologue*.

17. Maurice Glover, SIM.

18. Amanda Lake, WBT.

19. Information resources on the Fulani include: Weekes, *Muslim Peoples*, 134ff., *Geographical Magazine* (Jan. 1971), 276. Widdows (ed.), *Family*; Adopt-a-People Clearinghouse, "The Fulani: A People who Need our Prayer," *International Journal of Frontier Missions* 11 (1 Jan. 1994), 9-10; Patience Sonko-Godwin, *Ethnic Groups of Senegambia* (Banjul: Book Production and Material Resources Unit, 1986). Elsie Kastner, *Let's Help the Fulani People* (London: SIM, 1978). Ron Nelson, "Some Crucial Dimensions of Ministry to Fulbe," *Missiology* XI.2 (April 1983), 201-18. Devillers, "Oursi"; George Gerster, "The Niger, River of Sorrow, River of Hope," *National Geographic* (Aug. 1975), 152-89. Robert Brain, *Into the Primitive Environment* (London: George Philip, 1972), 87-101. Ahmad von Denffer, *The Fulani Evangelism Project in West Africa* (London: The Islamic Foundation, 1980). W. and A. Williamson, "Fula Anthropology" (WEC notes). *Unreached Peoples '79*, 107ff. See also histories such as John D. Anderson, *West Africa and East Africa in the Nineteenth and Twentieth Centuries*, I (London: Heinemann, 1978).

20. Weekes, *Muslim Peoples*, 134.

21. A.H.M. Kirk-Greene, "Mawdo Laawol Pulaaku, Survival and Symbiosis," in *Pastoralists of the West African Savanna* (ed. Mahdi Adamu and A.H.M. Kirk-Greene; Manchester: Manchester University Press, 1986).

22. Maliki, *Joy*.

23. See Swank, "Evangelization." See also Victor Azarya, *Aristocrats Facing Change — The Fulbe in Guinea, Nigeria, and Cameroon* (Chicago: University of Chicago, 1978).

24. *World Translation Progress Report 1996* (Reading: United Bible Societies, 1995). Also, NT translations are in progress in Fulbe Jelgooji in Mali, and in Kano Bororro in Niger.

25. Swank, "Evangelization."

26. Colin Smith, Action Partners.

27. Wilson, "Fulani Model."

28. John Gordon, 1985, gives the higher figure and Gerald Swank the lower in "Evangelization."

29. Grimes, *Ethnologue*. Freudenberger, "Don't Fence." C. Santoir, "Peul et Aménagements Hydro-agricoles danes la vallée du Fleuve Sénégal," in Adamu and Kirk-Greene (eds.), *Pastoralists*, 191-213. See the detailed account in Cheikh Bâ, *Les Peul du Sénégal* (Dakar and Abidjan: Les Nouvelles Editions Africaines, 1986).

30. Kristine Juul, "Pastoral Tenure Problems and Local Resource Management: The Case of Northern Senegal," *Nomadic Peoples* 32 (1993), 81-90.

31. Larry Vanderaa, *A Survey for CRWM of Missions and Churches in West Africa* (Grand Rapids: CRWM, 1991).

32. Vanderaa, *Survey*, 79.

33. Larry Vanderaa, private communication.

34. John van d. Lewis, "Range Use and Fulbe Social Organization: The View from Macina," in *Image and Reality in African Interethnic relations: The Fulbe and Their Neighbors* (ed. Emily A. Schultz; Williamsburg, VA: College of William and Mary, 1981), 1-19.

35. Mirjam de Bruijn, "A Pastoral Women's Economy in Crisis," *Nomadic Peoples* 36/37 (1997), 85-104; van Dijk, "Farming."

36. *Alliance Life* (Sept. 20, 1995). Veterinarians willing to help are encouraged to contact Dr. Jay O'Leary, Wexford Veterinary Hospital, 10309 Perry Highway, Wexford, PA 15090, USA.

37. *Alliance Witness* (26 Feb. 1986), 18-19.

38. Riesman, *Freedom*, an excellent anthropological study.

39. Riesman, "Aristocrats"; Richard Smith, SIM, private communication.

40. G.A. Finnegan and C.L. Delgado, "Cachez la Vache: Mossi Cattle, Fulbe Keepers, and the Maintenance of Ethnicity," in Schultz (ed.), *Image and Reality*, 31-50.

41. Beckwith, "Wodaabe." Widdows (ed.), *Family*, 340ff.; John W. Sutter, "Commercial Strategies, Drought, and Monetary Pressure: Wo'daa'be Nomads of Tanout Arrondissement, Niger," *Nomadic Peoples* 11 (Oct. 1982), 26-59.

42. Zuppan, "Herders."

43. People profile compiled by Ben Webster, Dec. 1989.

44. Maliki, *Joy*.

45. V. Englebert, "Bororo Herdsmen of Niger Celebrate the Rains," in Breeden (ed.), *Nomads of the World*, 172-95.

46. Harold D. Nelson, et al., *Area Handbook for Chad* (Washington, DC: American University, 1972), 50.

47. Roger Blench, *Fulbe, Fulani and Fulfulde in Nigeria, Distribution and Identity* (Nigeria: Federal Department of Livestock and Pest Control Services, 1990).

48. *African Encyclopaedia* (London: Oxford University Press, 1974), 216.

49. Ezekiel H. Gigin, CAPRO.

50. M.O. Awogbade, "The Fulani of the Jos Plateau," in Adawa and Kirk-Greene (eds.), *Pastoralists*, 214-24.

51. Adopt-A-People, P.O. Box 6001, Jos, Nigeria.

52. Weekes, *Muslim Peoples*, 420-22. See *Unreached Peoples* '80, 191.

53. WEC Senegal.

54. Luc Greiner, WEC.

55. Richard and Carolyn Davey, WEC.

56. Warren and Diana Furey, WEC People Profile.

57. Vanderaa, *Survey*.

58. David and Sally Pritchard, SIL, 1998.

59. *WTPR*, 1999.

60. Vanderaa, *Survey*.

61. Ibid., 75.

62. Ibid.

63. Ibid., 3

64. Ibid. and Grimes, *Ethnologue*.

65. Blench, *Fulbe*.

66. Joyce Hendrixsen, "The Changing Significance of Ethnicity and Power Relationship, Sokoto, Nigeria," in Schultz (ed.), *Image and Reality*, 51-93.

67. Blench, *Fulbe*.

68. Paul Burkwall, "Homogeneous Ministry" (unpublished paper; WEC Library, Bulstrode, England).

69. Rick Smith, SIM.

70. Blench, *Fulbe*.

71. Jonathan Derrick, *Africa's Slaves Today* (London: George Allen & Unwin, 1975), 73-6.

72. Hugh Griffiths, RBMU, 1995.

73. Grimes, *Ethnologue*. See Devillers, "Oursi."

74. Grimes, *Ethnologue*.

75. Ulrich Braukämper, "Strategies of Environmental Adaptation and Patterns of Transhumance of the Shuwa Arabs in the Nigerian Chad Basin," *Nomadic Peoples* 39 (1996), 53-68.

76. Patience Ahmed, *Conquered by the Sword* (Jos, Nigeria: Capro Research Office, 1993), 165-69. Kyari Tijani, "The Shuwa Arabs," in Adawa and Kirk-Greene (eds.), *Pastoralists*, 62-73.

77. Tijani, "Shuwa Arabs," 71.

78. Derrick, *Africa's Slaves*, 63.

79. Grimes, *Ethnologue*

80. Ezekiel H. Gigin, CAPRO.

81. Agnes Wedderburn, "The Koyam," in Adawa and Kirk-Greene (eds.), *Pastoralists*, 74-83. Ahmed, *Conquered*.

82. Marguerite Dupire, "A Nomadic Caste: The Fulani Woodcarvers Historical Background and Evolution," *Anthropos* 80 (1985), 85-100.

83. Harold D. Nelson et al., *Area Handbook for Senegal* (Washington, DC: The American University, 1974), 85, 90,144f.; Sonko-Godwin, *Ethnic Groups*, 16f.; Dupire, "Nomadic Caste."

84. Sonko-Godwin, *Ethnic Groups*, 20f.; Dupire, "Nomadic Caste."

85. R.M. Dilley, "Itinerant Tukolor Weavers, Their Economic Niche and Aspects of Social Identity," *Nomadic Peoples*, 21/22 (Dec. 1986), 117-33; and Dilley, "Myth and Meaning and the Tukulor Loom," *Man* 22 (June 1987), 256-66; Yaya Wane, *Les Toucouleur du Fouta Tooro (Sénégal)* (Dakar: IFAN, 1969), 50-52.

86. Kirtley, "Inadan-Artisans." Dominique Casajus, "Crafts and Ceremonies: The Inadan in Tuareg Society," in Rao (ed.), *Other Nomads*, 291-310.

87. Riesman, *Freedom*, 23.

88. Harold Olofson, "Children of the Bowed Lute," *Anthropos* 75 (1980), 920-29.

89. P.T.W. Baxter, "Peripatetics in Africa: A Glance," *Nomadic Peoples* 21/22 (Dec. 1986), 103-15; and Michael Bollig, "Ethnic Relations and Spatial Mobility in Africa: A Review of the Peripatetic Niche," in Rao (ed.), *Other Nomads*, 179-228, 192.

90. Christiane Lauschitzky, "Sorogama Project" (SIL Report; 1992 and March 1998); Vanderaa, *Survey*, 75.

91. Bollig, "Ethnic Relations," 211.

EASTERN SAHEL

1. The ODI estimates 1,800,000 in Chad and 3,900,000 in Sudan. *The New Internationalist* (April 1995) gave 3.5 million.

2. Fuchs, "Nomadic Society," 151.

3. Cf. Fuchs, "Nomadic Society."

4. M.E. Abu Sin, "Sudan," in *Custodians of the Commons: Pastoral Land Tenure in East and West Africa* (ed. Charles R. Lane; London: Earthscan, 1998), 120-49, 121.

5. Jean Chapelle, *Nomades Noirs du Sahara: Les Toubous* (Paris: Editions l'Harmattan, 1982); Weekes, *Muslim Peoples*, 408-12; *Unreached Peoples* '80, 193; Nelson, et al., *Chad*, 47-8, 64-8.

6. Grimes, *Ethnologue*.

7. For more information, contact Adopt-A-People Clearinghouse, P.O. Box 1795, Colorado Springs, CO 80901, USA; in the UK contact Nomadic Pastoralists, P.O. Box 4, High Wycombe, Bucks, HP14 3YX.

8. Jean Chapelle, *Le Peuple Tchadeu*, 171-76.

9. William S. Ellis, "Africa's Sahel: The Stricken Land," *National Geographic* (Aug. 1987), 141-79.

10. Nelson, et al., *Chad*.

11. Braukämper, "Strategies," 53.

12. Colin Smith, Action Partners.

13. Grimes, *Ethnologue*; G.O. Swank, SIM; Harold D. Nelson, et al., *Area Handbook for the Democratic Republic of Sudan* (Washington, DC: American University, 1973), 82; and Michael Asher, *A Desert Dies* (Harmondsworth: Viking, 1986), 29.

14. Grimes, *Ethnologue* and G.O. Swank, SIM. A previous estimate in 1997 gave only 1,800.

15. For a detailed description, see Asher, *Desert Dies*, also his *In Search of the Forty Days Road* (Harmondsworth: Viking, 1984), and *Bedouin*, 250. He lived with the Kababish for three years, after three years as a teacher in a Sudan school. Erikki Viitanen, "Nomadism and Desertification: A Case Study of Northern Kordofan, Sudan," *Nomadic Peoples* 10 (April 1982), 58-64; Widdows (ed.), *Family*, 1446-48.

16. Widdows (ed.), *Family*, 645-47.

17. Widdows (ed.), *Family*, 1076-77; Sin, "Sudan," 131; Michael Asher, "How the Mighty are Fallen," *Geographical Magazine* LXIV.3 (March 1991), 24-26.

18. Grimes, *Ethnologue*; *AD200 & Beyond*; Asher, *Bedouin*.

19. Yeates, Grundy and Forrest, "Short Note on the Position of Beja Women" (July 1988).

20. *Global People Profile*; Widdows (ed.), *Family*, 281.

21. Grimes, *Ethnologue*; Widdows (ed.), *Family*, 365-67. See esp. Ahmed, *Conquered*, 33-8.

22. Ahmed, *Conquered*, 33-8; Widdows (ed.), *Family*, 365-67. Thor Heyerdahl used the *kadai* as evidence that the ancient Egyptians could have crossed the oceans on papyrus boats (*The Ra Expeditions* [Harmondsworth: Penguin, 1970], 61ff.).

23. Ben Webster, AIM/TEAM.

24. Grimes, *Ethnologue*; G.O. Swank, SIM and Nelson et al., *Sudan*, 82.

25. Widdows (ed.), *Family of Man*, 906-909.

26. Michael Asher: *Desert Dies*, 47.

27. Widdows (ed.), *Family*, 202-204; Robin Strachan, "With the Nuba Hillmen of Kordofan," *National Geographic* (Feb. 1951), 249-78.

28. Widdows (ed.), *Family*, 1182-84.

29. Joel M. Teitelbaum, "The Transhumant Production System and Change among Hawazwa Nomads of the Kordofan Region, Western Sudan," *Nomadic Peoples* 15 (April 1984), 51-65; A.S. El Wakeel and M.A. Abu Sabah, "Relevance of Mobility to Rangeland Utilization: The Baggara Transhumant of Southern Kordofan," *Nomadic Peoples* 32 (1993), 33-8.

30. John Ryle, *Warriors of the White Nile* (Amsterdam: Time Life, 1982); G. Lienhardt, *Divinity and Experience* (Oxford: Clarendon Press, 1961) (Religion of the Dinka); an extract is in "Diviners in Dinkaland," in *Sociology of Religion* (ed. Roland Robertson; Penguin Modern Sociology Readings; Harmondsworth: Penguin, 1969), 419-31. Widdows (ed.), *Family*, 658-61.

31. Grimes, *Ethnologue*.

32. Lienhardt, *Divinity*, 56-74; Joy Anderson, "Behold the Ox of God?", *EMQ* (July 1998).

33. *WTPR*, 1996.

34. *WTPR*, 1993.

35. Marc R. Nikkel, *The Origins and Development of Christianity among the Dinka of Sudan* (Edinburgh: University of Edinburgh, 1993).

36. Grimes, *Ethnologue*; see Widdows (ed.), *Family*, 2110-13.

37. Peter J. Newcomer, "The Nuer are Dinka: An Essay on Origins and Environmental Determinism," *Man* 7.1 (March 1972), 5-11. Aidan Southall argues for an earlier date in "Nuer and Dinka are People: Ecology, Ethnicity and Logical Possibility," *Man* 11.4 (Dec. 1976), 463-89.

38. For detail see E.E. Evans Pritchard, *Nuer Religion* (Oxford: Clarendon Press, 1956) and MacDermot, *Sacred Spear*. Vandevort, *Leopard*.

39. *WTPR*, 1999.

40. Jon Arensen.

41. Weekes, *Muslim Peoples*, 408-12; Steve Godbold, "A Church for the Teda," (1988), 88; Briggs, *Tribes*, 167-89, Nelson, et al., *Chad*, 56.

EAST AFRICA

1. Other estimates are 5 million in Ethiopia and 3.5 million in Kenya ("Nomads: The Facts," *New Internationalist* [April 1995], 18).

2. "No Pastures New," *The Economist* (Jan. 18, 1997), 59.

3. Widdows (ed.), *Family*, 12; Weekes, *Muslim Peoples*, 4; *Unreached Peoples '79*, 145ff.; Johan Helland, "An Analysis of 'Afar Pastoralism in the North East Rangelands of Ethiopia," in Helland, *Five Essays on the Study of Pastoralists and the Development of Pastoralism* (African Savannah Studies 20; Bergen: University of Bergen, 1980), 79-134; Victor Englebert, "The Danakil: Nomads of Ethiopia's Wasteland," *National Geographic* (Feb. 1970), 186-211; Ayele Gebre-Mariam, "Labour Inputs and Time Allocation among the 'Afar," *Nomadic Peoples* 23 (1987), 37-55.

4. Grimes, *Ethnologue*.

5. *WTPR*, 1994.

6. I.M. Lewis, *Social Culture, History and Social Institutions* (London: London School of Economics and Political Science, 1981); R.P. Jordan, "Somalia's Hour of Need," *National Geographic* (June 1981), 748-775; Robert Caputo, "Tragedy Stalks the Horn of Africa," *National Geographic* (Aug. 1993), 88-121; Johnstone, *Operation World*, 491f.; Dan R. Aronson, "Kinsmen and Comrades: Towards a Class Analysis," *Nomadic Peoples* 7 (Nov. 1980), 14-23.

7. Peter D. Little, "Traders, Brokers and Market 'Crisis' in Southern Somalia," *Africa* 62.1 (1992), 94-120.

8. Närman, "Pastoral Peoples."

9. *Unreached Peoples '79*, 147-48.

10. *Global People Profiles* (Colorado Springs, CO: GMP, n.d).

11. *Unreached Peoples '80*, 67-73.

12. Personal communication from AIM International.

13. Widdows (ed.), *Family*, 2394-96; Urs J. Herren, "Cash from Camel Milk," *Nomadic Peoples* 30 (1992), 97-113; *Unreached Peoples '79*, 233-35; *Unreached Peoples '80*, 67ff.; *Unreached Peoples '83*, 67f., 237.

14. Neville Firth, AIM International.

15. Grimes, *Ethnologue* and *WTPR*, 1996.

16. *SIM Now*, 1990.

17. Widdows (ed.), *Family*, 1968-71. David Turton, "Looking for a Cool Place: The Mursi, 1890s-1980s," in *The Ecology of Survival* (ed. Douglas Johnson and David Anderson; London: Lester Cook, 1988), 261-82, and "Constraints on Mursi Pastoral Production" (report for OXFAM, 1995). Leslie Woodhead, *A Box Full of Spirits* (London: Heinemann, 1991). He has made a number of TV films on the Mursi.

18. M. Hunter, private communication.

19. They were featured in two British Granada TV programs and by Woodhead, *Box*.

20. Peter Moll with Mohammed Amin, *Portraits of Africa* (London: Harvell, 1983), 28-30; *Unreached Peoples of Kenya* (Daystar Communications n.d.), 23, *WTPR* 1994 and Grimes, *Ethnologue*.

21. *Ethiopia: A Country Study* (ed. H.D. Nelson; Area Handbook Series; Washington, DC: The American University, 1980), 13, 86. See also Alan Tippett, *People of Southwest Ethiopia* (Pasadena, CA: William Carey Library, 1970).

22. John Kayser, *Prairie Overcomer* (March 1983), 133-35.

23. Moll and Amin, *Portraits*, 20-23. There are 69,000 in Kenya.

24. Grimes, *Ethnologue*, and listed according to Oromo language.

25. Gufu Oba, "Kenya, Boran: Sharing and Surviving," *REB* 4 (April 1994), 17-22. Oba is himself a Boran and has worked for UNESCO and the University of Uppsala. See Helland, *Five Essays*, 48-75.

26. Hunter, *Appropriate Development*, 97; W.F. Deedes, "The Well of Life," *Telegraph Magazine* (n.d.), 51-6.

27. Gufu Oba, "Perception of Environment Among Kenyan Pastoralists: Implications for Development," *Nomadic Peoples* 19 (Sept. 1985), 33ff., and "Kenya."

28. Hunter, *Appropriate Development*, 81-112; R. Hogg, "Re-Stocking the Isiolo Boran: An Approach to Destitution Among Pastoralists," *Nomadic Peoples* 14 (Nov. 1983), 35-40. See Oba, "Kenya."

29. Hunter, *Appropriate Development*, 114.

30. Moll and Amin, *Portraits*.

31. Bob Beak, Crosslinks. *UBS World Report* (May 1995).

32. Dyson-Hudson, "Inheriting," 10. See Howard La Fay, "Uganda — Africa's Uneasy Heartland," *National Geographic* (Nov. 1971), 708-35. Widdows (ed.), *Family*, 1516.

33. Dyson-Hudson, "Inheriting," 23. and Gourlay, "Ox."

34. Thornberry, *World Directory*, 276.

35. Barfield, *Nomadic Alternative*, 27.

36. R.M.C. Beak, Crosslinks.

37. Widdows (ed.), *Family*, 676-79. The families live in defended stockades.

38. Närman, "Pastoral Peoples," 110.

39. Widdows (ed.), *Family*, 2532-35; R. Dyson-Hudson and J. Terrence McCabe, "Water Resources and Livestock Movements in South Turkana, Kenya," *Nomadic Peoples* 14 (Nov. 1983), 41ff.; Jan Wienpahl, "Turkana Herds Under Environmental Stress," *Nomadic Peoples* 17 (Feb. 1985), 59ff.; Moll and Amin, *Portraits*, 184ff.; *Unreached Peoples '79*, 241.

40. McCabe, "Turkana," 88. The Turkana are well covered in the literature.

41. Watson, "Kenya."

42. Simon Arraign, *Health and Healthcare Provision in North West Turkana, Kenya* (Pastoral Development Network Paper 36c; July 1994).

43. *WTPR*, 1999.

44. United Bible Societies World Report (Sept. 1992), 265.

45. AIM International.

46. Stiles, "Gabbra Nomad."

47. Daniel Stiles, "The Gabbra: Traditional Social Factors in Aspects of Land-use Management," *Nomadic Peoples* 30 (1992), 41-52.

48. Moll and Amin, *Portraits*, 44-7. There is a need to articulate a "Theology of Herd Management" according to Gitari, Houghton, and Mullenix, "Unreached Gabbra" and AIM International.

49. Moll and Amin, *Portraits*, 138ff.; Anne Beaman, "Women's Participation in Pastoral Economy: Income Maximization among the Rendille," *Nomadic Peoples* (Feb. 1983); Neal Sobania, "Pastoralist Migration and Colonial Policy: A Case Study from Northern Kenya," in *The Ecology of Survival* (ed. Douglas Johnson and David Anderson; London: Lester Crook, 1988), 219-40; Oba, "Environmental Education."

50. R.M.C. Beak, Crosslinks.

51. AIM International.

52. A case in Orus is described by Art and M. Davis, AIM, Nov. 1994.

53. Elizabeth L. Heyerhoff, "The Threatened Ways of Kenya's Pokot People," *National Geographic* (Jan. 1982), 120-40.

54. *Together* (Oct. — Dec. 1983).

55. *Global People Profiles*.

56. Barbara A. Bianco, "Songs of Mobility in West Pokot," *American Ethnologist* 23.1 (1996), 25-42.

57. AIM International.

58. *Global People Profiles*.

59. Widdows (ed.), *Family*, 2002-04; Moll and Amin, *Portraits*, 116ff.

60. Pal Vedeld, "Household Viability and Change among the Tugens," *Nomadic Peoples* 25-27 (1990), 133-52, 138f.

61. Widdows (ed.), *Family*, 2308-10. See *A Call to Share: Unreached Peoples of Kenya* (Nairobi: SIL and Daystar University, 1995), 23.

62. Amin and Moll, *Portraits*, 148ff.; *Unreached Peoples of Kenya*, 49.

63. Braaksma, "Christian Development" and "Hungry."

64. Anders Närman, "Pastoral Peoples," 110; Melissa Llewelyn-Davies, "Two Contexts." See also S.S. Sankan, *The Maasai* (Nairobi: Kenya Literature Bureau, 1971); Cheryl Bentsen, *Maasai Days* (London: Collins, 1990).

65. *Economist* (Feb. 4 1995).

66. Gill Marais, "The Maasai: A People under Threat," *Traveller* (Autumn 1988), 22-5, 24.

67. Ellwood, "Nomads," 9; George Monbiot, "Back to No Man's Land," *Geographic Magazine* (July 1994), 32-4; Elliot Fratkin, "Pastoral Land Tenure in Kenya: Maasai, Samburu, Boran, and Rendille Experiences, 1950-1990," *Nomadic Peoples* 34/35 (1994), 55-68; John G. Galaty, "'The Land is Yours: Social and Economic Factors in the Privatization, Sub-division and Sale of Maasai Ranches," *Nomadic Peoples* 30 (1992), 26-40.

68. George Monbiot, *No Man's Land: An Investigative Journey Through Kenya and Tanzania* (London: Macmillan, 1994).

69. Neville Frith, AIM International.

70. Donovan, *Christianity Rediscovered*.

71. Grimes, *Ethnologue*; Daniel Ndagal, "Pastoralists and the State in Tanzania," *Nomadic Peoples* 25-27 (1990), 51-64.

72. Ellwood, "Nomads," 9.

73. Ndagal, "Pastoralists"; Arvi Hurskainen, "Levels of Identity and National Integrity," *Nomadic Peoples* 25-27 (1990), 79-92.

74. Bollig, "Ethnic Relations," 203-206; William A. Shack, "Notes on Occupational Castes among the Gurage of South East Ethiopia," *Man* 53-54 (March-April 1964), 50-52.

75. Bollig "Ethnic Relations," 193; Grimes, *Ethnologue*.

76. Bollig, "Ethnic Relations," 201-203; K.L.G. Goldsmith and I.M. Lewis, "A Preliminary Investigation of the Blood Groups of the Sab Bondsmen of Northern Somaliland," *Man* 251-252 (Dec. 1958), 188-90.

77. Michael J. Casimir, "In Search of Guilt," in Rao (ed.), *Other Nomads*, 373-90, 383.

78. Bollig, "Ethnic Relations," 206-208; B. Heine, *The Waata Dialect of Oromo: Grammatical Sketch and*

Vocabulary (Berlin: Reimer, 1981). Amin and Moll, *Portraits* (16-19) give examples.

79. Bollig, "Ethnic Relations," 211.

80. Maureen Yeates, "Reaching Nomads," RSMT 1 (2000).

SOUTHERN AFRICA

1. Widdows (ed.), *Family*, 1152-55; *The Namibians* (London: MRG No. 19, 1984).

2. *New International* (March 1998), 5.

3. AIM People Profile.

4. Bollig, "Ethnic Relations," 199; Widdows (ed.), *Family*, 2524-26.

5. Michael de Jongh and Riana Steyn, "Methodology on the Move: Studying Itinerants and their Children," *Nomadic Peoples* 1.2 (1997), 24-35; and Michael de Jongh, "Karretjie People, Agency and 'Karoo Culture'," *South African Journal of Ethnology* 23.1 (2000), 1-13.

NORTH AFRICA

1. Diana Stone, "The Moors of Mauritania," in Carmichael (ed.), *Nomads*; Briggs, *Tribes*, 211-36; Alfred G. Gerteiny, "The Moors," in Weekes (ed.), *Muslim Peoples*, 277-79 and *Mauritania* (London: Pall Mall, 1967); Peter Hudson, *Travels in Mauritania* (London: W.H. Allen, 1990).

2. Johnstone, *Operation World* and Grimes, *Ethnologue*.

3. Asher, "Mighty," 23; *Cultural Atlas of Africa* (ed. Jocelyn Murray; Oxford: Phaidon, 1981), 125; *The Western Saharans* (MRG Report 40; London: Minorities Rights Group, 1984); Nick Ryan, "A Forgotten War," *Geographical Magazine* (May 1999), 41-7.

4. *Unreached Peoples '83*, 249. *Western Saharans*, 6. Morocco claims that Spain forced 120,000 Saharawis out of the territory (*Encyclopedia Britannica Book of the Year* [1994], 389).

5. Sources on the Berbers: Widdows (ed.), *Family*, 296, 2527-31; Weekes (ed.), *Muslim Peoples*, 99-110; Carla Hunt, "Berbers Bribes' Fair," *National Geographic* (Jan. 1980), 119-29; Ernest Gellner and Charles Micaud, *Arab and Berber — From Tribe to Nation in North Africa* (Lexington: Lexington Books, 1972), esp. ch. 2 by Gellner.

6. Widdows (ed.), *Family*, 2367-69; Victor Englebert, "Trek by Mule Among Morocco's Berbers," *National Geographic* (June 1968), 50-75.

7. For more information, contact Adopt-a-People Clearinghouse, P.O. Box 1795, Colorado Springs, CO 80901, USA; in the UK contact Nomadic Pastoralists, P.O. Box 4, High Wycombe, Bucks, HP14 3YX.

8. Widdows (ed.), *Family*, 1975-76.

9. Briggs, *Tribes*, 190ff.

10. Family life described in Emrys L. Peters, "Women in Four Middle East Communities," in *Women of the Muslim World* (ed. Lois Beck and Nikki Keddie; Cambridge, MA: Harvard University Press, 1978), 315-32 and *Global Prayer Digest* (July 1984).

11. Frontier Fellowship, *Global Prayer Digest* (Oct. 1993).

12. Briggs, *Tribes*, 108-13; Grimes, *Ethnologue*; Gerteiny, *Mauritania*, 55f. Peter and Sandy Jorgensen, "Report on the Nemadi Language," SIL (Nov. 1995).

13. Briggs, *Tribes*, 113ff.; Grimes, *Ethnologue*; Gerteiny, *Mauritania*, 19, 174-78; Hudson, *Travels*, 157-68.

14. Briggs, *Tribes*, 234; Gerteiny, *Mauritania*, 53-54; "The Griots' Grievance," *West Africa Witness* (London: Afrimedia Int. Ltd., 16 April 1983).

15. Briggs, *Tribes*, 233; Gerteiny, *Mauritania*, 53.

16. Jasper Winn, "Blessed Balancers," *Geographical Magazine* (Sept. 1997), 19-26.

17. Cultural Map Supplement, *National Geographic* (July 1972).

18. C.F. Thomas, "The Dom of North Africa" (Vol. I.1; Dom Research Center; Jan. 2000).

19. V. Minorsky, "Les Tsiganes Luli et Les Lurs Persans," *SOAS Offprints* 13 (April-June 1931).

20. Dom Research Center, Bob van de Pijpekamp, "The Gypsy People Groups and Gypsy Tribes of the World" (Zeist: Euromission, 1990); Casimir, "Search."

21. Dom Research Center, John Walker, "The Gypsies of Modern Egypt," *The Moslem World* XXIII (July 1933), 285-89; B. Streck, "Über Sprache and Gewerbe der Niltalzigenar," *Giessener Hefte für Tsiganologie* 1 (1984), 26-57.

MIDDLE EAST

1. Priit J. Vesilind, "Water: The Middle East's Critical Resource," *National Geographic* (May 1993), 38-71.

2. Ingham, *Bedouin*, 48.

3. Cole, *Pastoral Nomads*; Alan Keohane, *Bedouin: The Nomads of the Desert* (London: Kyle Cathie, 1994).

4. See Barfield, *Nomadic Alternative*, 61f., and Israel Eph'al, *The Ancient Arabs* (Jerusalem: Magnes Press, 1982).

5. William and Fidelity Lancaster, "The Concept of Territoriality among the Bedouin," *Nomadic Peoples* 20 (March 1986), 41-7; Michael Asher disproves this myth from a number of countries in *In Search*.

6. Joseph Ginat, "Meshamas: The Outcast of Bedouin Society," *Nomadic Peoples* 12 (Feb. 1983), 26-47. Also Chatty, *Camel to Truck*.

7. Keohane, *Bedouin*.

8. Jennings, *Welcome*, 23ff.

9. *The Arabian Peninsula* (Amsterdam: Time-Life Books, 1985), 61-89.

10. Keohane, *Bedouin*, and esp. Donald P. Cole, *The Nomads of the Nomads — The Al Murrah of the Empty Quarter* (Chicago: Aldine, 1975).

11. Donald P. Cole, "Al Murrah Bedouin of Arabia's Empty Sands," in Breeden (ed.), *Nomads of the World*, 52-71.

12. Ingham, *Bedouin*.

13. Ibid., 8ff.

14. Ibid., 48.

15. Widdows (ed.), *Family*, 1149-51.

16. Leybourne et al., *Changes*.

17. Chatty, "Sex Roles."

18. Global Partners; Lisa Sykes, "The Human Factor," *Geographical Magazine* (Aug. 1996), 24-7. The lower figure may be more accurate.

19. For the educational system and its effect on the Bedouin life see Avinoam Meir and Dov Barnea, "The Educational System of the Israeli Negev Bedouin," *Nomadic Peoples* 24 (1987), 23-35.

20. Widdows (ed.), *Family*, 2022-25.

21. Aref Abu-Rabia, "Control and Allocation of Grazing Lands among the Bedouin Tribes," *Nomadic Peoples* 20 (March 1986), 5ff.

22. Fiona McKay, "A Pyrrhic Victory for Israel's Bedouin," *Middle East International* (March 3, 1995), 18-19.

23. Newsham, "Dilemma."

24. Dick Doughty, "Oasis in the Rock: The Gardens of High Sinai," *Aramco World* 46.2 (March-April 1995), 20-27.

25. Simarski, "Desert." See Wilfred Thesiger, *Arabian Sands* (Harmondsworth: Penguin, 1964), for an early description of Oman and the Empty Quarter.

26. Thesiger, *Arabian Sands.*

27. J. Wilson, WEC, reported contact with the Solieb tribe that claimed to be Christian in Syria, Dec. 1932.

28. Resources on Bedouin: Keohane, *Bedouin*; Weekes, *Muslim Peoples*, 29-50; Widdows (ed.), *Family*, 1042-46, 1149-51, 1441-45, 1972-74, 2135-38; Ingham, *Bedouin*; William Lancaster, *The Rwala Bedouin Today* (Cambridge: Cambridge University Press, 1981). See also the following articles in *National Geographic*: Thomas J. Abercrombie, "Ibn Battuta: Prince of Travellers," (Dec. 1991), 2-49; T.J. Abercrombie, "The Persian Gulf: Living in Harm's Way," (May 1988), 648-71; Marianne Alireza, "Women of Saudi Arabia," (Oct. 1987), 423-53; T.J. Abercrombie, "Arabia's Frankincense Trail," (Oct. 1985), 474-513; Harvey Arden, "Eternal Sinai," (April 1982), 420-61.

29. See Dawn Chatty, "The Harasis: Pastoralists in a Petroleum Exploited Environment," *Nomadic Peoples* 24 (1987), 14-22.

30. Thesiger, *Arabian Sands*; F. Stark, *Southern Gates of Arabia* (London: John Murray, 1936); W. Phillips, *Unknown Oman* (London: Longmans, 1966); *Area Handbook for Persian Gulf States* (Richard F. Nyrop, et. al.; Washington, DC: The American University, 1977), 53, 66, 354; *Area Handbook for the Yemens* (ed. Richard F. Nyrop, et. al.; Washington, DC: The American University, 1977), 11, 30f., 52, 72.

31. Thesiger, *Arabian Sands*; F. Stark: *Southern Gates of Arabia*; W. Phillips: *Unknown Oman*; *Gulf States Area Handbook*, pp. 53, 66, 354; *Yemen Area Handbook*, pp. 11, 30f, 52, 72.

32. Daniel G. Bates, *Nomads and Farmers: A Study of the Yörük of Southeastern Turkey* (Ann Arbor: University of Michigan Press, 1973). Weekes, *Muslim Peoples*, 494-8. Nina Hyde, "Wool: Fabric of History," *National Geographic* (May 1988), 562f., 584f.

33. See Jean-Paul Roux, "The Tahtaci of Anatolia," in Rao (ed.), *Other Nomads*, 229-45; and Grimes, *Ethnologue.*

34. Christopher Hitchens, "The Struggle of the Kurds," *National Geographic* (Aug. 1992), 33-60. For general information, see: Weekes, *Muslim Peoples*, 220-26; Widdows (ed.), *Family*, 1694f.; *Unreached Peoples '79*, 202; '80, 164; '83, 226; *People Without a Country: The Kurds and Kurdistan* (ed. Gerard Chaliand; London: Zed, 1980); Sheri Laizer, *Into Kurdistan: Frontiers Under Fire* (London: Zed, 1991); N.R. Izady, *A Concise Handbook: The Kurds* (London: Taylor & Francis, 1992); the Ethnos Profile is available from: Postfach 620 662, 10796 Berlin, Germany.

35. Kehl, *Die Tahtaci.*

36. Roux, "Tahtaci"; *Ethnic Groups in Turkey* (ed. P. Andrews; Tübingen: Reichert, 1988).

37. Michael J. Casimir, "On the Formation of the Niche: Peripatetic Legends in Cross-Cultural Perspective," *Nomadic Peoples* 21/22 (Dec. 1986), 89.

38. Carol Delaney, *The Seed and the Soil: Gender and Cosmology in Turkish Village Society* (Berkeley: University of California Press, 1991), 105.

39. *Global Prayer Digest* (May 1991); Bart Dowell, *Gypsies: Wanderers of the World* (Washington, DC: National Geographic Society, 1970).

40. Pijekamp, "Gypsy People" (unpublished paper); Angus Fraser, *The Gypsies* (Oxford: Basil Blackwell, 1995), 41.

41. G.A. Williams, "The Gypsies of Cyprus," Dom Research Center (March 2000).

42. G.A. Williams, "The Gypsies of Lebanon," Dom Research Center (April 2000).

43. G.A. Williams, "Dom of the Middle East: An Overview," Dom Research Center, 1.1 (Internet article, Jan. 2000); Amoun Sleem, "The Dom Community of Jerusalem," Dom Research Center, 1.2 (Spring 2000).

44. William and Fidelity Lancaster, "The Function of Peripatetics in Rwala Bedouin Society," in Rao (ed.), *Other Nomads*, 311-21.

45. William and Fidelity Lancaster, "Nomadic Fishermen of Ja'alân," *Nomadic Peoples* 36/37 (1995), 227-43.

46. Phillips, *Unknown Oman*, 173.

SOUTHWEST ASIA

1. Morton, "Pastoralists," 35.

2. *Independent*, London (May 18, 1989).

3. Richard Tapper, *Frontier Nomads of Iran* (Cambridge: Cambridge University Press, 1997), 349-55.

4. Shirin Akiner, *Islamic Peoples of the Soviet Union* (London: Kegan Paul, 1983), 262.

5. Lois Beck, *The Qashqa'i of Iran* (New Haven & London: Yale University Press, 1986).

6. Tapper, *Pasture*, and *Frontier Nomads*. Weekes, *Muslim Peoples* pp., 357-62; Widdows (ed.), *Family*, 2337-9; *Unreached Peoples '80*, 186.

7. Tapper, *Frontier Nomads*, 309-13.

8. Ethnos Profile (Berlin, 1998).

9. Ethnos Profile (Berlin, 1999); *Area Handbook for Afghanistan* (ed. Harvey H. Smith et al.; Washington, DC: The American University, 1973), 72-3; Weekes, *Muslim Peoples*, 8-12.

10. Cultural Map, Supplement *National Geographic* (July 1972); Widdows (ed.), *Family*, 1130-33 and Mousavi, *Hazaras*, 62.

11. Mousavi, *Hazaras*; Hafizullah Emadi, "The Hazaras and their Role in the Process of Political Transformation in Afghanistan," *Central Asian Survey* 16.3 (1997), 363-87; Grimes, *Ethnologue*, 499; *Unreached Peoples '82*; Weekes, *Muslim Peoples*, 163ff.; Akiner, *Islamic Peoples*, 372.

12. Mousavi, *Hazaras*, 34; Ethnos Profile (Berlin, 1999).

13. Sayed Asker Mousavi, *The Hazaras of Afghanistan* (London: Curzon Press, 1998), 75f .

14. *The Independent* (18 May 1989). See also Ruth Lyon, *The Migration Patterns of Afghan Refugees* (unpublished paper, May 1987). Berland, *No Five Fingers*, 59.

15. Thomas J. Barfield, *The Central Asian Arabs of Afghanistan: Pastoral Nomadism in Transition* (Austin: University of Texas, 1981).

16. Grimes, *Ethnologue*.

17. People Profile, World Centre of Missions; Weekes, *Muslim Peoples*, 262-67. Ethnos Profile (Berlin, 1999).

18. Grimes, *Ethnologue* cites various estimates of speakers of the language.

19. Widdows (ed.), *Family*, 1472-76.

20. Grimes, *Ethnologue*.

21. Grimes, *Ethnologue* and *100 Peoples of the Soviet Union: A Fact File, Prayer Manual* (1990).

22. Figures from Grimes, *Ethnologue* and Akiner, *Islamic Peoples*.

23. Widdows (ed.), *Family*, 1219f. See *Unreached Peoples '79*, 188. *Adopt a People Profile*.

24. M. Nazif Mohib Shahrani, *The Kirghiz and Wakhi of Afghanistan* (Seattle and London: University of Washington Press, 1979), 55-85; Widdows (ed.), *Family*, 1612-16. *Adopt a People Profile*.

25. The source for these Kyrgyz is Shahrani, *Kirghiz*, 86ff.

26. *Unreached Peoples '80*, 176; Widdows (ed.), *Family*, 2202-06; Weekes, *Muslim Peoples*, 323ff.

27. Johnstone, *Operation World*.

28. Richard Tapper, "Golden Tent-Pegs: Settlement and Change among Nomads in Afghan Turkistan," in *Cultural Change and Continuity in Central Asia* (ed. S. Akiner; London: Kegan Paul, 1991), 198-217; Birthe Frederiksen, *Caravans and Trade in Afghanistan* (London: Thames and Hudson, 1996), 45f.

29. Widdows (ed.), *Family*, 733-37. See also *Nomadic Peoples* (Dec. 1986), 164, for references.

30. Evans, "Roam Free," 22-3.

31. See Beck, *Qashqa'i* for a history of how these policies affected the Qashqa'i.

32. Grimes, *Ethnologue*; Widdows (ed.), *Family*, 212-16; Weekes, *Muslim Peoples*, 60-64; *Unreached Peoples '80*, 136; J.-P. Digard, *Techniques des Nomades Baxtyri d'Iran* (Cambridge: Cambridge University Press, 1981), reviewed in English by Richard H. Meadow in *Nomadic Peoples* 13 (July 1993), 73-80.

33. Minorsky, "Tsiganes."

34. Lurs in *Unreached Peoples '80*, 166; Weekes, *Muslim Peoples*, 231-7; J. Black-Michaud, *Sheep and Land: The Economisc of Power in a Tribal Society* (Cambridge: Cambridge University Press, 1986).

35. There are 680,000 according to Grimes, *Ethnologue*. See Weekes, *Muslim Peoples*.

36. *Unreached Peoples '80*.

37. Beck, *Qashqa'i*, 259.

38. Weekes, *Muslim Peoples*.

39. Inge Demant Mortensen, *Nomads of Luristan* (London: Thames and Hudson, 1993).

40. See the descriptions in Mortensen, *Nomads*.

41. Beck, *Qashqa'i*, 179ff.

42. Ibid., 204.

43. Ibid., 144.

44. Beck, *Qashqa'i*, esp. the map on p. 4. Beck has also provided us with a detailed account of a year in camp and on migration with a Qashqa'i family in *Nomad — A Year in the Life of a Qashqa'i Tribesman in Iran*. See also Vincent Cronin, *The Last Migration*

(London: Hart-Davis, 1957), for a fictionalized account of a migration in the 1930s.

45. M. Bahmanbegui, "Hardy Shepherds of Iran's Zagros Mountains: Qashqa'i Build a Future Through Tent-school Education," in *Nomads of the World*, 94-108.

46. Beck, *Qashqa'i*, 277.

47. For a detailed history of the Qashqa'i until about 1983, see Beck, *Qashqa'i*.

48. Grimes, *Ethnologue*; *Unreached Peoples '80*, 179.

49. See William Irons, "Variation in Economic Organisation: A Comparison of the Pastoral Yomut and the Basseri," in *Perspectives on Nomadism* (ed. William Irons and N. Dyson-Hudson; Leiden: E.J. Brill, 1972), 88ff.

50. Fredrik Barth, *Nomads of South Persia: The Basseri Tribe of the Khamed Confederacy* (Boston: Little, Brown & Co., 1961), 15. See also Irons, "Variation," and Tapper, *Pasture*, 240-61 for comparisons with the Shahsevan.

51. Barth, *Nomads*, 6.

52. Ibid., 135-52.

53. Gary M. Swee, *Sedentaization: Change and Adaptation among the Kordshuli Pastoral Nomads of Southwestern Iran* (Michigan State University, 1981).

54. Bradburd, *Ambiguous Relations*.

55. Ibid., 94-6.

56. Johnstone, *Operation World*. Sources on the Baluch: Widdows (ed.), *Family*, 238f.; Weekes, *Muslim Peoples*, 64-9; *Unreached Peoples '80*, 137; Akiner, *Islamic Peoples*, 359-63; Robert G. Wirsing, *The Baluchis and Pathans* (No. 48; Minority Rights Group; n.d.); Richard F. Nyrop, et al., *Area Handbook for Pakistan* (Washington, DC: American University, 1975); Matheson, *Tigers*.

57. Ethnos Profiles (Berlin, 1998).

58. Morton, "Pastoralists," 33.

59. Philip C. Salzman, "Kin and Contract in Baluchi Herding Camps" (Naples: Istituto Univeritario Orientale, 1992).

60. Philip C. Salzman, "Adaptation and Political Organisation in Iranian Baluchistan," *Ethnology* X (Oct. 1971), 433-44.

61. Salzman, "Labor Formation," *Nomadic Peoples* 13 (July 1983), 35-59, and "Movement." See also Philip Salzman, "Multi Resource Nomadism in Iranian Baluchistan," *Journal of Asian and African Studies* VII (1972), 60-68.

62. Salzman, "Development Decisions," 50.

63. Stephen Pastner, "Baluch Fishermen in Pakistan," *Ethnology* XVIII (Jan. 1979), 31ff.

64. Brian Spooner, "Nomadism in Baluchistan," in *Pastoralists and Nomads in South Asia* (ed. L.S. Leshnik and G.-D. Sontheimer; Wiesbaden: Otto Harrassowitz, 1975), 171-82. See also Pastner, "Co-operation."

65. *Geographical Magazine* (March 1991), 22-3.

66. Stephen L. Pastner, "Power and Pirs Among the Pakistani Baluch," *Journal of Asian and African Studies* XIII.3-4 (July-Oct. 1978), 231-43.

67. *WTPR*, 1999 and Grimes, *Ethnologue*.

68. Weekes, *Muslim Peoples*, 115-18; W.W. Swidler, "Some Demographic Factors Regulating the Formation of Flocks and Camps among the Brahui of Baluchistan," *Journal of Asian and African Studies* VII (1972), 69-72; Bart McDowell, *Gypsies: Wanderers*

of the World (Washington: National Geographic, 1970), 85.

69. *WTPR*, 1999.

70. Aparna Rao, *Les Gorbat d'Afghanistan: Aspects Economiques d'un Groupe Itinérant 'Jat'* (Paris: Institut Français d'Iranologie de Tehran, 1982), 23-7.

71. Dom Research Center.

72. McDowell, *Gypsies*, 163.

73. Barth, *Nomads*, has a chapter on the Ghorbati; McDowell, *Gypsies*, 162-64, 170.

74. Rao, *Gorbat*.

75. Minorsky, "Tsiganes."

76. Casimir, "Formation," 89. The legend is referred to in Fraser, *Gypsies*, 35; McDowell, *Gypsies*, 160; and Randhawa, *Last Wanderers*, 28. Donald Kenrick argues against this origin and says that they are not related to the Romani Gypsies (*Gypsies from India to the Mediterranean* [Toulouse: Gypsy Research Centre, 1993], 38). However, the fact that they speak Baluchi is not evidence against this as such people assimilate languages as well as religion as they move.

77. Mortensen, *Nomads*, 373.

78. Aparna Rao, "Roles, Status and Niches: A Comparison of Peripatetic and Pastoral Women in Afghanistan," *Nomadic Peoples* 21/22 (Dec. 1986), 153ff; Rao, *Gorbat*, 30f.

79. Rao, "Roles."

80. Casimir, "Formation," 89.

81. Rao, "Roles"; Rao, *Gorbat*, 30f.

82. Rao, "Roles"; Rao, *Gorbat*, 30f.

83. Asta Olesen, "Peddling in East Afghanistan," in Rao (ed.), *Other Nomads*, 35-63.

84. Shahrani, *Kirghiz*, 195f.

85. Pijekamp, "Gypsy People."

86. Rao, "Roles," 169.

87. McDowell, *Gypsies*, 166f.

CENTRAL ASIA

1. Aba Al-Hada, "The Uighurs of Xinjiang," *International Journal of Frontier Missions* (Oct. 1985), 377.

2. van Leeuwen, "Animal Husbandry."

3. Jonathan Luxmoore, "A Bishop to the Lost People of the Steppes," *Catholic Herald* (Sept. 16, 1994), 3.

4. Fiona M. Garratt, UBS (Nov. 1994).

5. *100 Peoples of the Soviet Union* (Spring 1990). Ronald Wixman, *The Peoples of the USSR* (London: Macmillan, 1984), 90. See C.R. Bawden, *Shamans, Lamas and Evangelicals: The English Missionaries in Siberia* (London: Routledge & Kegan Paul, 1985) for a description of the Moravian work.

6. Central Asia Fellowship (Dec. 1, 1992). The total given was 174,000.

7. *WTPR*, 1994.

8. *100 Peoples of the Soviet Union*; H. Krag and L. Funch, *The North Caucasus — Minorities at a Crossroads* (London: MRG, 1994), 23.

9. Akiner, *Islamic Peoples*, 168-71; see also 115, 169.

10. Joshua Project 1997; Johnstone, *Operation World*. See Ethnos Profile (1998).

11. Tatjana Emeljaneko, "Nomadic Year Cycles," in C. Leeuwen, T. Emeljanenko and L. Popova, *Nomads in Central Asia* (Amsterdam: Royal Tropical Institute, 1995), 37-67.

12. Emeljaneko, "Nomadic Year," 41-4.

13. Akiner, *Islamic Peoples*, 313-27.

14. *The Turkmen* (Littleton, Colorado: The Caleb Project, 1995).

15. Institute for Bible Translation, Box 20100, S10460, Stockholm, Sweden, reported by UBSWR (Nov. 1995).

16. *WTPR*, 1994.

17. Asian Minorities Outreach, 1999.

18. Weekes, *Muslim Peoples*, 427-33.

19. Global People Profile. Irons, "Variation."

20. Ruth Lyon, *Afghanistan: Country Summary* (unpublished paper, 1989).

21. Akiner, *Islamic Peoples*, 359ff.; Wixman, *Peoples*, 25-6.

22. *100 Peoples of the Soviet Union*.

23. Emeljaneko, "Nomadic Year," 45f.

24. *WTPR*, 1999.

25. *Economist* (July 16, 1994), 64; *Open Doors* (Sept. 1994); *Pulse* (July 22 and Aug. 19, 1994); *News Network International* (June 14, 1994).

26. *WTPR*, 1994; *Unreached Peoples '80*, 160; Akiner, *Islamic Peoples*, 338ff.

27. *Impact International* (Sept. 1994); Ethnos Profile, Berlin; *The Kazak Report* (Caleb Project, 1992).

28. Ahmed Rashid, *The Resurgence of Central Asia* (London: Zed Books, 1994), 115.

29. Mehrdad Haghayeghi, "Islamic Revival in the Central Asian Republics," *Central Asian Survey* 13.2 (1994), 249-66.

30. *Kazak Report*; Alfred E. Hudson, *Kazak Social Structure* (New Haven: Yale University Publications in Anthropology; Toronto: Burns & MacEachern, 1938, 1964). Yurts are now made in factories by the thousands in Ushtobe, Kazakstan (Leeuwen, Emeljanenko and Popova, *Nomads in Central Asia*, 31).

31. General information can be found in the following: Widdows (ed.), *Family*, 1546-49; Weekes, *Muslim Peoples*, 210ff. The traditional society of the Kazaks is described in Alfred E. Hudson, "Kazakh Social Structure," in *Anthropology* 20 (New Haven: Yale University Press, 1938); Martha Brill Olcott, *The Kazaks* (Stanford: Hoover Institution Press, 1995); Emeljaneko, "Nomadic Year."

32. Cynthia A. Werner, "The Privatisation of Agriculture in Contemporary Kazakstan," *Central Asian Survey* 13.2 (1994), 295-303.

33. Emeljaneko, "Nomadic Year," 71-2.

34. *Kazak Report*.

35. *Sounds* (Spring 1993); *Kazaks: The Time is Now* (Caleb Project, c. 1995), is a 36-page prayer guide.

36. *WTPR*, 1994.

37. Grimes, *Ethnologue*.

38. 1990 census (Grimes, *Ethnologue*).

39. *China: A Guidebook to XinJiang* (Xinjiang, 1988) and Andrews-Speed, "Herdsmen," 58f.; Ingvar Svanberg, "The Nomadism of Orta Zuz Kazaks in Xinjiang 1911-1949," in *The Kazaks of China: Essays on an Ethnic Minority* (ed. Linda Benson and Ingvar Svanberg; Upsala, Sweden: Studia Multiethnica Upslaiensa, 1988), 107-40; Banks, "Pastoral Land";

Linda Benson and Ingvar Svanberg, *China's Last Nomads* (New York and London: M.E. Sharpe, 1998).

40. Barfield, *Nomadic Alternative*, 173.

41. Description in *China Review* (Dec. 1989), 57-66.

42. Benson and Svanberg, *China's Last*, 180ff.

43. *Unreached Peoples* '81, 184.

44. "Arc of Crisis," *Economist* (April 14, 1990). However the one child rule, it is said, applies only to Han Chinese in Eastern China. See Rick Gore, "Journey to China's Far West," *National Geographic* (March 1980), 292-331; *Unreached Peoples* '81, 184; Benson and Svanberg (eds.), *Kazaks of China*, is a detailed study.

45. Wong How-Man, "Peoples of China's Far Provinces," *National Geographic* (March 1984), 283-333, 296-99; *China's Minority Nationalities* (ed. Ma Yin; Beijing: Asian Minorities Outreach, 1989), 152.

46. Lyon, *Migration Patterns*. There are 1,300 Kyrgyz refugees from Afghanistan listed in *Unreached Peoples* '83, 232. See also Charlotte McPherson, "Uralic-Altaic Studies, Its Significance and Methods of Research and Issues Important to Me," (unpublished degree paper; Istanbul University, Istanbul, Turkey c. 1990), who discusses health care and education projects among various peoples in northeast Afghanistan.

47. Rashid, *Resurgence*, 136-57.

48. Hermann Jantzen, *Im wilden Turkestan* (Giessen: Brunnen Verlag, 1988).

49. Emeljaneko, "Nomadic Year," 71-2.

50. Ibid., 37-67.

51. Irina Kostyukova, "The Towns of Kyrgyzstan Change their Faces: Rural-urban Migrants in Bishkek," *Central Asian Survey* 13.3 (1994), 425-34.

52. 1990 census, Grimes, *Ethnologue*. For general information on the nomadic life, see: Widdows (ed.), *Family*, 1612-16; Weekes, *Muslim Peoples*, 215-20; Akiner, *Islamic Peoples*, 327ff.; *Unreached Peoples* '80, 162.

53. Andrews-Speed, "Herdsmen," 59f.; Debra Denker, "The Last Migration of the Kirghiz of Afghanistan?", *Central Asian Review* 2.3 (Nov. 1983), 89-98.

54. Rashid, *Resurgence*, 156.

55. *Scan Profile* (People International, 1988); Widdows (ed.), *Family*, 1612-16; *Unreached Peoples* '83, 232.

56. Shahrani, *Kirghiz*, 87-212.

57. NNI (Sept. 23, 1992). Report the German Kyrgyzstan newspaper.

58. Emeljaneko, "Nomadic Year," 61f.

59. *WTPR*, 1994.

60. *WTPR*, 1994.

61. *Scan Profile* (People International, 1988).

62. Johnstone, *Operation World*. Rashid, *Resurgence*.

63. Emeljaneko, "Nomadic Year," 48.

64. Weekes, *Muslim Peoples*, 389-94. *Unreached Peoples* '80 featured the 15,000 Tajiks in Iran.

65. UBSWR (May 1993). This translation was produced by the IBT.

66. Akiner, *Islamic Peoples*, 434-35.

67. IBT, 1992.

68. Akiner, *Islamic Peoples*, 435-36.

69. *WTPR*, 1994.

70. Akiner, *Islamic Peoples*, 371-72.

71. Fraser, Gypsies, 41; Grimes, *Ethnologue*; Pijekamp, "Gypsy People."

72. McDowell, *Gypsies*, 162.

73. Pijekamp, "Gypsy People."

74. McDowell, *Gypsies*, 162; Fraser, *Gypsies*, 38.

75. V.J. Sanaroy, "The Siberian Gypsies," JGLS (3rd Series) XLIX (1970), pt. 3-4, 126-37.

INNER ASIA

1. Weekes, *Muslim Peoples*, 451-53; Al-Hada, "Uighurs"; Gore, "Journey."

2. Yang Yichou, "A Green Corridor in the Sand," *China Pictorial* (Jan. 1990), 4 pp.; Andrews-Speed, "Herdsmen." See also Bao Xiu and Wang Miao in *Xinjiang Tourism* (Xinjiang People's Publishing House, n.d.), 28, 82ff.

3. Andrews-Speed, "Herdsmen."

4. Wixman, *Peoples*, 101; Akiner, *Islamic Peoples*, 405; IBT and *World Christian News* (Spring 1995).

5. Forsyth, *History*, 279; Vainshtein, *Nomads*.

6. Vainshtein, *Nomads*, 42, 84ff.

7. Grimes, *Ethnologue*.

8. Forsyth, *History*, 373f.

9. Akiner, *Islamic Peoples*, 400ff. See also Vainshtein, *Nomads*.

10. N.A. Alekseev, "Shamanism among the Turkic Peoples of Siberia," in *Shamanism in Soviet Studies of Traditional Religion in Siberia-Central Asia* (ed. M.M. Balzer; London: M.E. Sharpe, Inc., 1990), 49-109.

11. *WTPR*, 1999.

12. Swedish Slavic Mission (Nov. 1990).

13. Swedish Slavic Mission (Nov. 1990).

14. Newsletter from the Slavic Mission, Sweden (July 7, 1994).

15. Marina Monguish is a Tuvanian scholar from Russia, "Tuvanians in China: Problems of History, Language and Culture," *Central Asian Survey* 14.4 (1995), 543-51.

16. Natalya L. Zhukovskaya, "Religion and Ethnicity in Buryatia," *Central Asian Survey* 14.1 (1995), 25-42, 37f.

17. Jean-Christophe Grange, "Cold Comfort for the Last of the Few," *Telegraph Magazine* (London: April 27, 1991), 22-37, with a number of large photographs by Pierre Perrin. *Mongol Messenger* (Dec. 15, 1992); also *Frontier Fellowship* (Dec. 1984), although their sketch map places the Tsaantang wrongly. *Friends of Turkey* (Feb. 1985) classifies them as a Turkic people.

18. Central Asia Fellowship (Dec 1, 1992). Asian Minorities Outreach gives an estimate of 65,000, see their Profile in *50 of the Most Unreached People Groups of China and Tibet* (Chiang Mai: Asian Minorities, 1996), 7.

19. Don Belt, "Russia's Lake Baikal: The World's Great Lake," *National Geographic* 181.6 (June 1992), 2-39; Jasper Becker, *The Lost Country — Mongolia Revealed* (London: Sceptre-Hodder, 1993), ch. 10.

20. Forsyth, *History*, 378; Zhukovskaya, "Religion."

21. Slavic Mission, Sweden (Nov. 1990).

22. C.R. Bawden gives a detailed study of this in *Shamans*.

23. *WTPR*, 1994.

24. Slavic Mission, Sweden (July 7, 1994).

25. Andrei Yudintsev, "My Willing Exile in the Soviet Wilderness," *Christian News World* (Sept. 1990), and "Reaching out to the Buryat Buddhists," *Friedenstimme Partners* (Sept.-Oct. 1990).

26. Thomas B. Allen, "Time Catches up with Mongolia," *National Geographic* (Feb. 1985), 242-69; "Nomads: The Facts," *New Internationalist* (April 1995), 18, gives 40%.

27. C. Beall and M. Goldstein, "Past becomes Future for Mongolian Nomads," *National Geographic* (May 1993), 126-35.

28. *Mongolia Challenge* II/3i. *Nomadic Peoples* 33 (1993) produced a special edition with a number of articles on pastoralism and ecology under the general theme of "Mongolian Pastoralism on the Threshold of the 21st Century."

29. Müller, "New Nomads," 180f.

30. Terence Hay-Eadie, "Tents in the City," *New Internationalist* (April 1995), 30.

31. Martin Harper and Craig Bennett, "Pumping in New Life," *The Geographical Magazine* (May 1996), 18-20.

32. Müller, "New Nomads," 176.

33. Paul Mooney, "Orphans of Change," *Asiaweek* (Nov. 27, 1998), 54-6; "Living in a Manhole," *Economist* (Jan. 22, 2001).

34. Müller, "New Nomads," 181.

35. Beall and Goldstein, "Past becomes Future," 126-35. See their book *The Changing World of Mongolia's Nomads* (Hong Kong: The Guidebook Company, Ltd., 1994) as the best presentation of pastoralism in west Mongolia.

36. Colostrum is usually defined as the thin secretion of white blood cells that precedes and follows the milk from the teat.

37. Jeremy Swift, "Traditional Pastoral Milk Products in Mongolia," *Appropriate Technology* 18.1 (June 1991), 14-16.

38. *Mongolia Challenge* II/3i.

39. Robin Mearns, "Territoriality and Land Tenure among Mongolian Pastoralists: Variation, Continuity and Change," *Nomadic Peoples* 33 (1993), 73-103.

40. "Eyewitness: Mongolia Steps Out," *Asiaweek* (July 14, 1989), 37-43; Allen, "Time"; Widdows (ed.), *Family*, 1569-73. There were special awards for couples that had five or more children (*Mongolia Challenge* II/3iii).

41. Potkanski, "Mongolia"; Mearns, "Territoriality."

42. See Caroline Humphrey, "Inside a Mongolian Tent," *New Society* (London: Oct. 31, 1974), 273-75.

43. C.R. Bawden calls this a "grand design," which was based on false premises. For example, it was thought that learning Mongolian would lead to an ability in Manchu, which was assumed to be the language of the educated classes of China. In fact, only the Chinese Imperial court used it (*Shamans*, 14f.). This was a clear case for more thorough mission research!

44. *WTPR*, 1996.

45. Swedish Slavic Mission (July 7, 1994).

46. Grimes, *Ethnologue* and K. Sinclair, *The Forgotten Tribes of China* (London: Merehurst, 1987). *50 of the Most Unreached People Groups of China and Tibet* gives 4,807,000.

47. Ellwood, "Nomads."

48. Steven Seidenberg describes a group in eastern Nei Mongol and at various points we have used his article ("The Horsemen of Mongolia," in Carmichael (ed.), *Nomads*, 96-125.

49. Ellwood, "Nomads," 8, but esp. see the number of articles in *Nomadic Peoples* 33 (1993).

50. Mark and Gill Newham, "Country Life is Demanding," *Fellowship Missionary News Digest* (July 1996), 9-10.

51. Asian Minorities Outreach.

52. Goldstein and Beall, "Change and Continuity," gives an excellent survey of the past and present of the Phala nomads. Strictly speaking, "yak" refers to an ox of the species, a castrated bull. The bull is a *boa.* and *dri* is the female, so that dairy products are strictly dri's milk, etc. The *dzo* is a cross between a yak and lowland cattle. The female is a *dzamö*.

53. "Nomads: The Facts," *New Internationalist* (April 1995), 18-19, gave the nomadic pastoralist total for Tibet as 500,000 for all peoples.

54. Richard P. Cincotta, Zhang Yanqing and Zhou Xingmin, "Transhumant Alpine Pastoralism in North-eastern Qinghai Province," *Nomadic Peoples* 30 (1992), 3-25.

55. Friends of China Foundation, 1996.

56. Fred Lane, "The Warrior Tribes of Kham," *Asiaweek* (March 2, 1994), 30-38.

57. Robert B. Ekvall, *Fields on the Hoof: Nexus of Tibetan Nomadic Pastoralism* (New York: Holt, Rinehart and Winston, 1968), 21-2. All of Ekvall's books are out of print, including his two fictional studies, but they are excellent and still valuable. There are many excellent studies on the Drok-pa, esp. Merwyn C. Goldstein and Cynthia M. Beall, *Nomads of Western Tibet* (London: Serindia, 1989) that concentrates on their pastoralism and political changes, and Kazuyoshi Namachi, *Tibet* (Hong Kong: Local Colour Ltd., 1993), which gives much on religious customs.

58. Goldstein and Beall, "Remote World," 752ff. Mentioned as the Drok-pa trading with the Dolpo yak herders from Nepal (Valli and Summers, "Caravans").

59. Windsor Chorlton, *Cloud-Dwellers of the Himalayas: The Bhotia* (Amsterdam: Time-Life, 1982). Sources on Tibetan religion include: Guiseppe Tucci, *The Religions of Tibet* (London: Routledge and Kegan Paul, 1980), ch. 6 is on folk religion, ch. 7 on Bonism. See also Hildegrad Diemberger, "Gangla Tschechu"; Krystna Cech, "The Social and Religious Identity of the Tibetan Bonpos," in *Anthropology of Tibet and Himalaya* (ed. Charles Ramble and Martin Brauen; Zurich: Ethnological Museum of the University of Zurich, 1993). See also Helmut Hoffman, *Tibet: A Handbook* (Oriental Series Research, Institute for Inner Asia; Bloomington, IN: Indiana University Press, 1986), 93-125.

60. Caris Faith Sy, *A Study of Tibetan Culture and Religion and of Potential Redemptive Analogies which would Heighten the Tibetan's Receptivity to Christianity* (MA thesis; International School of Theology, 1987).

61. *WTPR*, 1996.

62. Galen Rowell, "Nomads of China's West," *National Geographic* (Feb. 1982), 244-63.

63. Asian Minorities Outreach.

64. Asian Minorities Outreach.

65. Asian Minorities Outreach.

66. Gyurme Dorje, *Tibet Handbook* (London: Footprint Handbooks, 1996), 496.

67. Widdows (ed.), *Family*, 712-16; 2478-80.

68. Yin (ed.), *China's Minority*, 129ff.

SOUTH ASIA

1. Wayne McClintock, "Nomadic Tribal Peoples of Lahore," (Working Paper 2; Lahore: Social Research Unit, Association for Community Training Services, Aug. 1986).

2. K.S. Singh, *People of India: An Introduction* (Calcutta: Anthropological Survey of India, 1992), 103.

3. Robert Hayden, "Conflicts and Relations of Power between Peripatetics and Villagers in South Asia," in Rao (ed.), *Other Nomads*, 267-90, 268.

4. Shanti George, "Nomadic Cattle Breeders and Dairy Policy in India," *Nomadic Peoples* 19 (Sept. 1985), 1-19.

5. Grimes, *Ethnologue*; S. and R. Michaud, "Trek to Lofty Hunza — and Beyond," *National Geographic* (Nov. 1975), 644-69.

6. Abbas Kazmi, "The Ethnic Groups of Baltistan," and Amelie Schenk, "Inducing Trance: On the training of Ladakhi Oracle Healers," in Ramble and Brauen (eds.), *Anthropology*, 158-163 and 331-339, respectively. Nigel J.R. Allan, "Building Blocks of Balt Ethnicity," and Timothy Malyon, "Ladakh at Crossroads," *Himal* (Sept.-Oct. 1993), 12-15.

7. Widdows (ed.), *Family*, 1715-18. In 1975, 20% of the men were Buddhist monks of the Nyingmapa sect, or "red hats," in contrast to the Gelugpa, or "yellow hats," who are dominant in Tibet. Thomas J. Abercrombie, "Ladakh: The Last Shangri-la," *National Geographic* (March 1978), 333-59. For a description of missionary work in this area in the 1920s see Jock Purves, *The Unlisted Legion* (Edinburgh, Banner of Truth, 1977).

8. *The Desert in the Sky* (Nareshi Bedi, Producer and Director, Bedi Films, associated with Channel Four TV, UK, 1995). See Jina, "Pasture Ecology," for environmental problems.

9. *Unreached Peoples '81*, 168. WEC People Profile.

10. Widdows (ed.), *Family*, 1715.

11. K.S. Singh, *People of India*, III: *The Scheduled Tribes* (Calcutta: Anthropological Survey of India, Oxford University Press, 1994), 200-202. *Unreached Peoples '81*, 173.

12. Grimes, *Ethnologue*. *Languages of India* (Madras: IMA, 1997) gives 566,000 in India and *World Christian Encyclopedia* II (ed. David Barrett, et al.; Oxford: Oxford University Press, 2001), 102 gives 633,640. Trilok Nath Pandit claims there are millions in India ("A Note on the Gujar of North-west India [Kashmir]," *Wissenschaftsgeschichte und Gegenwärtige Forschungen in NW Indien* [Dresden: Staatliches Museum für Völkerkunde, 1990], 107-12).

13. Morton, "Pastoralists," 33.

14. R.S. Negi, "Population Structure of a Pastoral Nomadic Community of the Himalayas," 42-51; and R. Sarkar, V. Sarkar and M.K. Raha, "The Gujjars and their Society," 65-74, both in *Nomads in India* (ed. P.K. Misra and K.C. Malhotra; Calcutta: Anthropological Survey of India, 1982); Calinda E. Hallberg and Clare F. O'Leary, "Dialect Variation and Multilingualism among Gujars of Pakistan," in unknown source, 91ff.; Pernille Gooch,

"Transhumant Pastoralism in Northern India: The Gujar Case," *Nomadic Peoples* 30 (1992), 84-96.

15. Randhawa, *Last Wanderers*, 89.

16. Morton, "Pastoralists," 34.

17. Compare J.G. Sharma, "Communicational and Educational Problems of Gujjars: A Pastoral Nomadic Tribe," in Misra and Malhotra (eds.), *Nomads*, 271-76, with Sarkar, Sarkar and Raha, "Gujjars," for the differing descriptions of villages.

18. Sarkar, Sarkar and Raha, "Gujjars." *Unreached Peoples '81*.

19. Darshan Singh Manku, *The Gujar Settlements: A Study in Ethnic Geography* (Delhi: Inter India, 1986), 48.

20. Sarkar, Sarkar and Raha, "Gujjars"; Sharma, "Communicational."

21. Pandit, "Note."

22. V. Sarkar, R. Sarkar and M.K. Raha, "Planning for the Rehabilitation and Development," in Misra and Malhotra (eds.), *Nomads*, 304-13; Pandit, "Note"; *Go into All Haryana* (Madras: IMA, 1995).

23. Manku, *Gujar Settlements*.

24. R.S. Negi, "Population Structure"; Gooch, "Transhumant Pastoralism." See also David E. Sopher, "Indian Pastoral Castes," in Leshnik and Sontheimer (eds.), *Pastoralists*, 199.

25. *Madhya Pradesh Unreached Peoples Harvest Handbook* (Jabalpur, 1995).

26. Randhawa, *Last Wanderers*, 91.

27. Pijekamp, "Gypsy People"; Singh, *Scheduled Tribes*, 82-3; Randhawa, *Last Wanderers*, 91, 102-109.

28. Randhawa, *Last Wanderers*, 91.

29. S.S. Shashi, *The Gaddi Tribe of Himachal Pradesh* (Delhi: Sundeep Prakshan, 1977) and *The Shepherds of India* (Delhi: Sundeep Prakshan, 1978). Noble, *High Passes*; Sarkar, Sarkar and Raha, "Planning." Minoti Chakravarty-Kaul, "Transhumance: A Pastoral Response to Risk and Uncertainty in the Himalayas," *Nomadic Peoples* NS I.1 (1997), 133-49.

30. Randhawa, *Last Wanderers*, 61, 73f., 89-90, 99.

31. *Languages of India* (1994 edn).

32. Jagdish Chandra Das and Manish Kumar Raha, "Ecology, Economy and Transhumance: A Study of an Immigrant Society of the Himalayas," in Misra and Malhotra (eds.), *Nomads*, 58-64.

33. Chorlton, *Cloud-Dwellers*, 5.

34. See Sikkimese in Widdows (ed.), *Family*, 2388-90; Tsering Shakya, "Whither the Tsampa Eaters?" *Himal* (Sept.-Oct. 1993), 8-11; Tshewang Lama, "Who Cares for Humla," *Himal* (Sept.-Oct. 1993), 16-18; Widdows (ed.), *Family*, 312-15.

35. Charles Ramble, "Whither, Indeed, the Tsampa Eaters," *Himal* (Sept.-Oct. 1993), 21-5.

36. Singh, *Scheduled Tribes*, 498-500.

37. S.S. Shashi, *The Nomads of the Himalayas* (Delhi: Sundeep Prakashan,1979), 58-86.

38. Subrat Sharma and H.C. Rikhari, "The Bhotia: The Disruption in Lifestyle of a Nomadic Community in the Indian Central Himalayas," *Nomadic Peoples* 36/37 (1995), 167-74.

39. Nehal A. Farooquee and Annpurna Nautiyal, "Livestock Ownership Patterns among Transhumants in High-altitude Villages of the Central Himalayas," *Nomadic Peoples* 39 (1996), 87-96 and see Shashi, *Nomads of the Himalayas*, 58-86.

40. Hanna Rauber-Schweizer, "Trade in Far West Nepal: The Economic Adaptation of the Peripatetic Humli-Khyampa," in Rao (ed.), *Other Nomads*, 65-87.

41. Grimes, *Ethnologue*; Valli and Summers, "Caravans," *National Geographic* (Dec. 1993), 5-35; David Snellgrove, *Himalayan Pilgrimage: A Study of Tibetan Religion* (Oxford: Bruno Cassirer, 1961), and C. von Fürer-Haimendorf, *Himalayan Traders* (London: John Murray, 1975), 132-222. FMC for Himalayan Peoples have produced a People Profile.

42. Andrew Hall, "Himalayan Exodus: Nepalese Migrant Groups," *Asian Affairs* XXVII.2 (June 1996), 131-41; Dor Bahadur Bista, *People of Nepal* (Kathmandu: Bhotahity, 1996), 197-202; Snellgrove, *Pilgrimage*, 204-26.

43. Chorlton, *Cloud-Dwellers*; Snellgrove, *Pilgrimage*, 226-40.

44. Carrier, "Gatekeepers," 79. This article gives some basic information on Lamaistic Buddhism. See C. von Fürer-Haimendorf: *The Sherpas Transformed* (New Delhi: Sterling Publishers, 1984).

45. Chorlton: *Cloud-Dwellers*, 144-65.

46. *Let My People Go*, Rajasthan (Madras: IMA, 1995); K.S. Singh, *People of India*, IV: *The Scheduled Castes* (Calcutta: Anthropological Survey of India, Oxford University Press, 1993), 69ff.

47. *Let My People Go*, Rajasthan; World Vision Profile.

48. Brief reference in Morton, "Pastoralists," 35. Adopt-a-People Clearing House has a profile from 1992.

49. *Languages of India*.

50. *Global Prayer Digest* (March 1985).

51. Randhawa, *Last Wanderers*, 195.

52. Davidson, "Wandering," and *Desert Places*; P. C. Salzman, "Shrinking Pasture for Rajasthani Pastoralists," *Nomadic Peoples* 20 (March 1986), 46-61; Köhler-Rollefson, "Dromedary."

53. Randhawa, *Last Wanderers*, 18, 64, 115ff., 196, 213, 214.

54. Randhawa has rare photos of these groups, *Last Wanderers*, 94, 95, 123-27.

55. Singh, *Scheduled Tribes*, 113-15; Randhawa, *Last Wanderers*, 64, 91-2, 122.

56. P.C. Salzman, "From Nomads to Dairymen: Two Gujarati Cases," *Nomadic Peoples* 24 (1987), 44-53.

57. George, "Nomadic."

58. Randhawa, *Last Wanderers*, 18, 25, 137-39.

59. C.H. Childers, "Banjaras," in Leshnik and Sontheimer (eds.), *Pastoralists*, 247-65.

60. *Outreach*, IEM (May 1986); Singh, *Scheduled Tribes*, 1091-92.

61. *Let My People Go*, Karanataka (Madras: IMA, 1996).

62. *WTPR*, 1999.

63. Tony Hilton and Lazarus Lalingh, *Banjara: A People of India* (Chennai: People India, PO Box 2297, Chennai Ayanavaram, TN 600 023), 23.

64. Ibid.

65. *Madhya Pradesh*; Shashi, *Shepherds*, 46f.

66. *Madhya Pradesh*.

67. Shashi, *Shepherds*, 29-36.

68. Singh, *Scheduled Castes*, 421f. and *Go into all of Orissa* (Madras: IMA, 1994); *Let My People Go*, Bihar (Madras: IMA, 1995).

69. *Languages of India*.

70. *Madhya Pradesh*.

71. Gunther D. Sontheimer, "The Dhangars," in Leshnik and Sontheimer (eds.), *Pastoralists*, 139-70.

72. See George, "Nomadic."

73. Singh, *Scheduled Tribes*, 102-104.

74. Singh, *Scheduled Tribes*, 816-18.

75. Berland, *No Five Fingers*, 74.

76. Berland, "Parytan"; Casimir, "Search," 382; Randhawa, *Last Wanderers*, 166, 175.

77. Randhawa, *Last Wanderers*, 142f., 159.

78. Wayne McClintock, "The Mirasis of the Punjab" Profile and *The Mirasi People of Lahore: An Ethnography* (Lahore: Nirali Kitaben, 1991), and other titles; Randhawa, *Last Wanderers*, 166.

79. See Berland, "Parytan" and also his "Kanjur Social Organisation," in Rao (ed.), *Other Nomads*, 247-65.

80. Personal communication, SIM 1998.

81. Grimes, *Ethnologue*; Berland, "Peripatetic Strategies in South Asia: Skill as Capital among Nomadic Artisans and Entertainers," *Nomadic Peoples* 13 (July 1983), 17-34; Roger Pomeroy, "The Marwari Bhils of Pakistan," *Evangelical Times* (Nov. 1997), 13.

82. Berland, "Peripatetic Strategies."

83. Ibid.

84. Ibid.; Randhawa, *Last Wanderers*, 19, 41, 142, 166-67.

85. Berland, "Peripatetic Strategies."

86. Randhawa, *Last Wanderers*, 42, 144; Singh, *Scheduled Tribes*, 208-10

87. *Haryana*; Singh, *Scheduled Castes*, 1147-56; Grimes, *Ethnologue*.

88. Singh, *Scheduled Castes*, 145-49.

89. McClintock, "Nomadic."

90. Randhawa, *Last Wanderers*, 162f.; Singh, *Scheduled Castes*, 234f.

91. Berland, *No Five Fingers*, 59.

92. Singh, *Scheduled Castes*, 194-202; *Let My People Go*, Rajasthan and *Let My People Go*, Bihar.

93. Singh, *Scheduled Castes*, 1006-10; Randhawa, *Last Wanderers*, 26, 46, 57, 63; *Haryana*.

94. Randhawa, *Last Wanderers*, 181, 188.

95. Singh, *Scheduled Castes*, 250ff.; Randhawa, *Last Wanderers*, 141f., 155.

96. Randhawa, *Last Wanderers*, 87; Singh: *Scheduled Tribes*, 957-59.

97. Randhawa, *Last Wanderers*, 180; Singh, *Scheduled Castes*, 1274-80; *Let My People Go*, Bihar, 54-5; *Let My People Go*, West Bengal (Madras: IMA, 1995), 80-81.

98. Singh, *Scheduled Castes*, 657-61, 811-13; *Let My People Go*, Rajasthan, 60-61; Randhawa, *Last Wanderers*, 87, 88, 166.

99. *WTPR*, 1996; Grimes, *Ethnologue*.

100. *Let My People Go*, Gujarat (Madras: IMA, 1995), 22-3; *Madhya Pradesh*, 82-3 and *Let My People Go*, Rajasthan, 14-15; K. S. Singh *Castes*, pp. 937ff; T. S. Randhawa: *The Last Wanderers*, p. 128.

101. Randhawa, *Last Wanderers*, 25, 165, 170-71; *Let My People Go*, Uttar Pradesh (Madras: IMA, 1995), 42-3.

102. Randhawa, *Last Wanderers*, 183.

103. Sources: Singh, *Scheduled Castes*, 802-806; Ruhela, "Bullock-cart"; P.K. Mistra, "Mobility — Sedentary Opposition: A Case Study of the Nomadic Gadulia Lohar," *Nomadic Peoples* 21-22 (Dec. 1986), 179-87, and "The Gadulia Lohars," in Leshnik and

Sontheimer (eds.), *Pastoralists*, 235-46; Randhawa, *Last Wanderers*, 36, 179, 185f.

104. *Madhya Pradesh*.

105. Randhawa, *Last Wanderers*, 127, 180, 186-87; Singh, *Scheduled Castes*, 1213-19.

106. Singh, *Scheduled Castes*, 137; Randhawa, *Last Wanderers*, 48, 180; *Let My People Go*, Uttar Pradesh, 76-7.

107. Sarkar, Sarkar and Raha, "Planning."

108. Singh, *Scheduled Castes*, 83-7; and YWAM, Pune, India.

109. See G.W. Briggs, *The Chamars* (New Delhi: DK Publishers, 1995) for general information on this caste.

110. Personal conversation with a Chamaar.

111. Hayden, "Conflicts."

112. Randhawa, *Last Wanderers*, 165.

113. Ibid., 46, 144, 171.

114. Ibid., 143, 159.

115. Singh, *Scheduled Castes*, 415-19; Randhawa, *Last Wanderers*, 30, 161.

116. A.K. Adhikary, "Nomadism, Economy and World View of the Birhors of Orissa," in Misra and Malhotra (eds.), *Nomads*, 247ff.

117. Randhawa, *Last Wanderers*, 163-65.

118. S.B. Khomne, S.K. Hulbe and S.T. Vetschera, "Kewats and Their Economic Activities: A Semi-Nomadic Group of Weavers in Maharashtra," in Misra and Malhotra (eds.), *Nomads*, 93ff.

119. Singh, *Scheduled Castes*, 477-82.

120. Tribal Transformations-India, Bangalore.

121. Tribal Transformations-India; Singh, *Scheduled Castes*, 1241f. Maurice Glover visited the Siddhi in 1998 to do a survey of the language.

122. *Overseas Council Update* (Oct-Dec. 1998) and the Sri Lanka Bible College.

123. Randhawa, *Last Wanderers*, 144, 159, 161, 187.

124. *Lonely Planet Guide to Bangladesh*, 33; Video: The Last Sailors (North Harrow, England: DD Video, 1998); T. and G. Baldizzone, *Brahmaputra* (New Delhi: Timeless Books, 1998).

125. Alex Newton, Betsy Wagenhauser, Jon Murray, *Lonely Planet Guide to Bangladesh* (Oakland, CA: Lonely Planet Publications, 1996), 33.

SOUTH EAST ASIA

1. Lioba Lenhart, "Recent Research on Southeast Asian Sea Nomads," *Nomadic Peoples* 36/37 (1995), 245-52; H. Arlo Nimmo, "Gentle People of Gentle Seas, the Boat-dwelling Bajau Still Roam Philippine Waters," in *Nomads of the World*, 72-91; Widdows (ed.), *Family*, 208-15.; Grimes, *Ethnologue*; cf. David Hogan, "The Names of God in the Urak Lawoi," *The Bible Translator* (Oct. 1984), 405-15.

2. Walter G. White, *The Sea Gypsies of Malaya* (London: Seeley, Service & Co., 1922).

THE RUSSIAN ARCTIC AND SIBERIA

1. Forsyth, *History*, 364f.

2. Robin Hanbury-Tenison, "Reindeer Nations of Siberia," *Geographical Magazine* (Feb. 1993), 15-19.

3. Slavic Mission (July 7, 1994).

4. Darryl Krause, UIO, 2312 Ottestad, Norway. There is a 3-month training period followed by an initial field placement for 12 months.

5. Forsyth, *History*, 355.

6. Nikolai Vakhtin, *Native Peoples of the Russian North* (London: Minority Rights Group International, 1992), 24.

7. Fen Montaigne, "Nenets Surviving on the Siberian Tundra," *National Geographic* (March 1998), 120-37; Widdows (ed.), *Family*, 2030-31. Egil Rønningstad, "The Nenets: A Presentation of the People and of YWAM's Involvement" (unpublished paper; Borgen, Norway: WYAM); Debbie Hershmann and David Dektor, "Last of the Nomads," *Geographical* (Sept. 1998), 6-15.

8. *The Times* (10 Sept. 1997).

9. Rønningstad, "Nenets," 5.

10. *100 Peoples of the Soviet Union: A Fact File* (1990).

11. WTPR, 1996.

12. Darrel Krause, YWAM, Norway.

13. Wixman, Peoples, 102, 131; G. Robinson, *Native Peoples of the Soviet Arctic* (YWAM-Slavic Ministries, 1989).

14. Forsyth, *History*, 390; Widdows (ed.), *Family*, 1574-77.

15. Vakhtin, *Native Peoples*.

16. Widdows (ed.), *Family*, 1574-77; David Lewis, "Back to Siberia," *Christian Herald* (July 8, 1995), 8.

17. WTPR, 1996.

18. Grimes, *Ethnologue*; *Global Prayer Digest* (June 1994); Robinson, *Native Peoples*.

19. Grimes, *Ethnologue*. See Akiner, *Islamic Peoples*, 420ff.

20. Forsyth, *History*, 310.

21. Widdows (ed.), *Family*, 801-804. They use traditional tepees of birch bark or skins, as well as log huts. The Soviets organized collectives for hunting and herding.

22. Forsyth, *History*, 414; Vakhtin, *Native Peoples*.

23. Forsyth, *History*, 383.

24. WTPR, 1996.

25. *Unreached Peoples '81*, 176.

26. Grimes, *Ethnologue*, and IBT.

27. Asian Minorities Outreach.

28. Becker, *Lost Country*, 251ff.; Grimes, *Ethnologue*; Wixman, *Peoples*, 192f.

29. 1989 census and Grimes, *Ethnologue*.

30. Forsyth, *History*, 379.

31. Akiner, *Islamic Peoples*, 390-97.

32. Alekseev, "Shamanism"; and Marjorie M. Balzer, "Siberian Shamanism," *American Anthropologist* 98.2 (1996), 305-18.

33. Robinson, *Native Peoples*; Widdows (ed.), *Family*, 2653.

34. WTPR, 1999.

35. Asian Minorities Outreach.

36. Forsyth, *History*, 382. But see esp. Piers Vitebsky, "The Reindeer Herders of Siberia," in Carmichael (ed.), *Nomads*, 126-54; Vanora Bennett, "On Shifting Ground," *Choices* (New York: UNDP, Jan. 1998), 13-17.

37. Forsyth, *History*, 71.

38. Ibid., 366.

39. He has written an autobiography entitled *The Time when the Snow Thaws*. He also discusses Canadian policies (Forsyth, *History*, 366, 397f.).

40. Forsyth, *History*, 288.

41. *WTPR*, 1996.

42. Widdows (ed.), *Family*, 1660.

43. Hanbury-Tenison, "Reindeer." Widdows (ed.), *Family*, 1660, gives four collective farms. Christina Dodwell, *Beyond Siberia* (London: Hodder, 1993), mentions eleven state farms.

44. Hanbury-Tenison, "Reindeer."

45. Vakhtin, *Native Peoples*.

46. Forsyth, *History*, 367.

47. Dodwell, *Beyond Siberia*, 59.

48. *Will and Way* (Oct. 1994).

49. Forsyth, *History*, 75. He says there were only 600 in the 1970 Census.

50. Grimes, *Ethnologue*.

51. Forsyth, *History*, 412; Vakhtin, *Native Peoples*.

52. Hanbury-Tenison, "Reindeer."

53. Forsyth, *History*, 368.

54. Vakhtin, *Native Peoples*.

LATIN AND NORTH AMERICA

1. Hugh Beach, "The Reindeer-Caribou Conflict in the Nana Region of Alaska: A Case Study for Native Minority Rights Issues," *Nomadic Peoples* 17 (Feb. 1985), 1-22; Prit J. Vesilind, "Hunter of the Lost Spirit," *National Geographic* (Feb. 1983), 151ff.; Paul Lindholm, "Christians on Top of the World," *Floodtide* (June 1984), 9-11; S. Jackson, "Annual Reports on the Introduction of Domestic Reindeer into Alaska" (U.S. Office of Education, 1890).

2. Thomas, "Eskimos," 7; *WTPR*, 1996, *In Other Words* (Sept. 1989), and Beach, "Reindeer-Caribou."

3. John J. Wood, "Navajo Livestock Reduction," *Nomadic Peoples* 19 (Sept. 1985), 21-31.

4. Widdows (ed.), *Family*, 2005-2008. Geoffrey Zwirikunzeno Kapenzi, "Shona and Navaho — A Comparative Study of Beliefs and Practices," *Missiology* (Oct. 1974), 489-95.

5. Grimes, *Ethnologue*.

6. Widdows (ed.), *Family*, 1012-16. J.H. Stewart and L.C. Faron, *Native Peoples of South America* (New York: McGraw-Hill, 1959), 359-60.

7. Loren McIntyre, "Touchy and Self-sufficient as Their Goats, Guarjiros Toughen on the Scrubland They Wander," in *Nomads of the World*, 154-71.

8. IFMA, 1989.

9. David L. Browman, "Camelid Pastoralism in the Andes," in *Nomads in a Changing World* (ed. C. Salzman and J.G. Galaty; Naples: I.V. Orientale, 1979), 395-437.

10. Chris Wallis, SAMS.

11. *WTPR*, 1996. See Widdows (ed.), *Family*, 2273-76.

12. Lawrence A. Kuznar, "Transhumant Goat Pastoralism in the High Sierra of the South Central Andes," *Nomadic Peoples* 28 (1991), 93-104.

13. Browman, "Camelid."

14. Widdows (ed.), *Family*, 1465-1467.

15. *SIM Log* (June 1995).

16. Widdows (ed.), *Family*, 2198-2201.

17. Ernest S. Burch, *The Eskimos* (London: Macdonald, 1988), 13f.

18. Ibid., 73-87.

19. *Encyclopaedia Britannica 1994*, 464; Julian Burger, *The Gaia Atlas of First Peoples* (London: Robertson McCarta, 1990).

20. Grimes, *Ethnologue*

21. *Interact*, SGM, 9-1988.

22. Wally Herbert, *Hunters of the Polar North: The Eskimos* (Amsterdam: Time-Life Books, 1981).

23. Marcello Truzzi and Patrick C. Easto, "Reflections on the American Carnival and Related Peripatetic Societies," *Nomadic Peoples* 21/22 (Dec. 1986), 79-88.

24. Matt T. Solo, "The Gypsy Niche in North America," in Rao (ed.), *Other Nomads*, 89-109; S.S. Shashi, *Roma: The Gypsy World* (Delhi: Sundeep Prakashan, 1990), 189f.

25. Solo, "Gypsy Niche" and also Matt T. Solo, "Peripatetic Adaptation in Historical Perspective," *Nomadic Peoples* 21/22 (Dec. 1986), 11-12.

26. Solo, "Peripatetic Adaptation."

27. Solo, "Peripatetic Adaptation" and "Gypsy Niche"; Fraser, *Gypsies*, 235.

28. Solo, "Peripatetic Adaptation" and "Gypsy Niche"; and Anne Sutherland, "The Gypsies of California," in *Face Values* (ed. A. Sutherland; London: BBC, 1978), 186ff. and "The American Rom: A Case of Economic Adaptation," in Rehfisch (ed.), *Gypsies, Tinkers*, 1-40; Fraser, *Gypsies*, 235-6; Shashi, *Roma*, 185-91.

29. David W. Pickett, "The Gypsies of Mexico," *JGLS* XLIV, XLV (1966), 6-17, 84-99.

30. Pijekamp, "Gypsy People."

EUROPE

1. Walter Marsden, *Lapland* (Amsterdam: Time-Life Books, 1976), 26.

2. Widdows (ed.), *Family*, 1737-41; Mervyn Jones, *The Sami of Lapland* (London: MRG Report 55, 1982); Thornberry, *World Directory*; Herbert, *Reindeer*; Nils-Aslak Valkeapaa, *Greetings from Lapland* (London: Zed, 1983).

3. Beach, "Reindeer-Caribou."

4. Hugh Beach, "Three Complementary Processes that Alienate the Sami from their Land in Sweden," *Nomadic Peoples* 20 (March 1986), 11ff.

5. MRG, *Minorities*, 96.

6. Jones, *Sami*, 5.

7. Jones, *Sami*, 10; Grimes, *Ethnologue*, lists Lule Sami as having 25,000 speakers and Northern Sami with 16,600.

8. Wixman, *Peoples*, 122.

9. Myrdene Anderson, "The Sami People of Lapland," *Nomadic Peoples* 14 (Nov. 1983), 51-9; Jones, *Sami*, 7; K.S. Latourette, *A History of the Expansion of Christianity*, Vol. IV (Grand Rapids: Zondervan, 1970), 118 and *Christianity in a Revolutionary Age*, II (Grand Rapids: Zondervan, 1959), 172.

10. *WTPR*, 1996.

11. *Unreached Peoples '79*, 204.

12. Hugh Poulton, *Who are the Macedonians?* (London: Hurst, 1996), 17.

13. MRG, *Minorities*, 130-31 and *Roma: Europe's Gypsies* (London: Minority Rights Report 14, 3rd edn, 1980), 9, mentions treatment of the Roma. See also Sutherland, "Gypsies," for a summary of the ideas of pollution and cleanness.

14. Patrick Leigh Fermor, *Roumeli — Travel in Northern Greece* (London: Penguin, 1983), 28.

15. Miranda Vickers and James Pettifer, *From Anarchy to a Balkan Identity* (London: Hurst, 1997), 201.

16. Robert Carver, *The Accursed Mountains* (London: Harper-Collins, 1999).

17. Poulton, *Macedonians?*, 136-7

18. Vickers and Pettifer, *Balkan*.

19. Campbell, *Honour*, 185ff.

20. Campbell, *Honour*, 193ff.

21. Fermor, *Roumeli*, passim; John K. Campbell, "Two Case Studies of Marketing and Patronage in Greece," in *Acts of the Mediterranean Sociological Conference* (ed. J.G. Peristany; Athens: Social Sciences Centre, 1963), 156-71, and Campbell, *Honour*.

22. Jasper Winn, "On the Wild West Trail," *Geographical Magazine* (April 1995), 28-31; Robin Hanbury-Tenison, "The Last Great Migration," *Geographical Magazine* (Oct. 1996), 5.

23. MRG, *Roma*, 7.

24. Kenrick, *Gypsies from India*.

25. Sources on Gypsies include Fraser, *Gypsies*; Liégeos, Gypsies; Shashi, Roma; McDowell, Gypsies; and Manfri Frederick Wood, *In the Life of a Romany Gypsy* (London: Routledge & Kegan Paul, 1973). Also Sutherland, "Gypsies," and Shashi, Roma, 95ff., for a summary of the ideas of pollution and cleanness. The Gypsies in Eastern Europe are described by Fonseca, *Bury Me Standing* and David M. Crowe, *A History of the Gypsies of Eastern Europe and Russia* (New York and London: I.B. Tauris, 1995).

26. Grimes, *Ethnologue*, 472.

27. Willy Guy, "Ways of Looking at Roms: The Case of Czechoslovakia," in Rehfisch (ed.), *Gypsies, Tinkers*, 201-30.

28. Fraser, *Gypsies*, 292f.

29. D. Lazell, *From the Forest I Came* (London, 1970 and older sources).

30. Paul Ellingworth, personal communication.

31. *Listening World* (Bristol: Transworld Radio, spring 1996).

32. Grimes, *Ethnologue*; Fraser, *Gypsies*, 298.

33. Fraser, *Gypsies*, 298; Shashi, *Roma*, 158.

34. Shashi, *Roma*, 166.

35. Okely, *Traveller Gypsies*, 66-104.

36. Okely, "Gypsies Travelling," in Rehfisch (ed.), *Gypsies, Tinkers*, 55-83; *Independent* (20 Nov. 1989), (21 Aug. 1992); *The Economist* (24 Aug. 1991); Pat Sinclair, "Casting out the Outcasts," *Geographical Magazine* (March 1993), 14-18.

37. W. Shenton, "God Working with Gypsies Despite High Court Injunction," *Redemption* (Oct. 1992), 20; Sue Locke, *Travelling Light: The Remarkable Story of Gypsy Revival* (London: Hodder and Stoughton, 1997).

38. Fonseca, *Bury Me Standing*, 228.

39. Aparna Rao, "Some Manus Conceptions and Attitudes," in Rehfisch (ed.), *Gypsies, Tinkers*, 139-67.

40. Ignacy-Marek Kaminski, "The Dilemma of Power: Internal and External Leadership. The Gypsy-Roma of Poland," in Rao (ed.), *Other Nomads*, 323-56.

41. Crowe, *History*, 64f.

42. Crowe, *History*, 151-94.

43. Oliver Lerch, "The 'Monde du Voyage': French Carnival Nomads' View of Peripatetic Society," *Nomadic Peoples* 21/22 (Dec. 1986), 71-8.

44. Joe Ridholls, *Travelling Home* (Basingstoke: Marshall-Pickering,1986); Clement Le Cossec, *My Adventures with the Gypsies* (Banglore: The Indian Gypsy Work Fellowship, 1991); Fraser, *Gypsies*, 315f.

45. Personal communication with Paul Ellingworth, who has given valuable information on Bible translations.

46. Teresa San Román, "Kinship, Marriage, Law and Leadership in Two Urban Gypsy Settlements in Spain," in Rehfisch (ed.), *Gypsies, Tinkers*, 169-99. Fraser, *Gypsies*, passim; Walter Starkie, *In Sara's Tents* (London: John Murray, 1953).

47. William G. Lockwood, "East European Gypsies in Western Europe: The Social and Cultural Adaptation of the Xoraxane," *Nomadic Peoples* 21/22 (Dec. 1986), 63-70. Leonardo Piasere, "In Search of New Niches: The Productive Organisation of the Peripatetic Xoraxané in Italy," in Rao (ed.), *Other Nomads*, 111-32.

48. Fonseca, *Bury Me Standing*, 75, 109.

49. Carver, *Accursed Mountains*, 77, 167.

50. Fonseca, *Bury Me Standing*, 22, 72f.; Poulton, *Macedonians?*, 141f.

51. Poulton, *Macedonians?*, 191ff.

52. Ibid., 194.

53. Crowe, *History*, 145ff.

54. Fonseca, *Bury Me Standing*, 140-97; Fraser, Gypsies, 279, 289-92.

55. "Growth for Gypsy Church in Romania," *Baptist Times* (Aug. 25, 1994); Dieter Grahl, "Heiligung unter den Roma in Rumänien," *Weltweit* 4 (1994), 8-9; "Glaugenserlebnisse," *Weltweit* 2 (1999), 18-19; and "Sieben Jahre Einsatz unter Roma in Rumänien," *Weltweit* 1 (2000), 18-19.

56. Carol Silverman, "Bulgarian Gypsies: Adaptation in a Socialist Context," *Nomadic Peoples* 21/22 (Dec. 1986), 51-62 and Elen Marushiakove and Vesselin Popove, "A History of the Roma of Bulgaria," in *Patrin* [web journal] (March 6, 2000), 1-3.

57. Fraser, *Gypsies*, 171, 296; and A.M. Fraser, "The Tinkers of Ireland," *JGLS* (3rd Series) XLIV (1968) Pt. 1, 38-48.

58. Fonseca, *Bury Me Standing*, 233; A. and F. Rehfisch, "Scottish Travellers or Tinkers," in Rehfisch (ed.), *Gypsies, Tinkers*, 271-83.

59. George Gmelch and Sharon Bohn Gmelch, "Commercial Nomadism: Occupation and Mobility among Travellers in England and Wales," in Rao (ed.), *Other Nomads*, 133-53.

60. Fraser, *Gypsies*, 298.

61. MRG, *Roma*; Fraser, *Gypsies*, 299; Kristina Bonilla, "The Quinquis: Spain's Last Nomads," *JGLS* I.2 (1976), 86-92.

62. Grimes, *Ethnologue*. Earlier editions listed them under Romany.

SELECT BIBLIOGRAPHY

Below are the more important sources on nomadic peoples in English (marked with *), as well as all the sources cited with short titles in the notes. Many sources are found in the specialized journals listed below.

BOOKS

*Adamu, Mahdi, and A.H.M. Kirk Greene (eds.), *Pastoralists of the West African Savanna* (Manchester: Manchester University Press, 1986).

*Ahmed, Patience, *Conquered by the Sword* (Jos, Nigeria: Capro Research Office, 1993).

*Akiner, S. (ed.), *Cultural Change and Continuity in Central Asia* (London: Kegen Paul, 1991).

---. *Islamic Peoples of the Soviet Union* (London: Kegan Paul, 1983).

Asher, Michael, *The Last of the Bedouin — In Search of the Myth* (London: Penguin, 1996).

---. *A Desert Dies* (Harmondsworth: Viking, 1986).

---. *In Search of the Forty Days Road* (Harmondsworth: Viking, 1984).

*Azarya, Victor, *Aristocrats Facing Change: The Fulbe in Guinea, Nigeria, and Cameroon* (Chicago: University of Chicago, 1978).

*Balzer, M.M., (ed.), *Shamanism in Soviet Studies of Traditional Religion in Siberia-Central Asia* (London: M.E. Sharpe, Inc., 1990).

*Barfield, Thomas J., *The Central Asian Arabs of Afghanistan: Pastoral Nomadism in Transition* (Austin: University of Texas Press, 1981).

---. *The Nomadic Alternative* (Englewood Cliffs, NJ. Prentice Hall, 1993).

*Barth, Fredrik, *Nomads of South Persia: The Basseri Tribe of the Khamed Confederacy* (Boston: Little, Brown & Co., 1961).

*Bates, Daniel G., *Nomads and Farmers: A Study of the Yörük of Southeastern Turkey* (Ann Arbor, MI: University of Michigan Press, 1973).

*Bawden, C.R., *Shamans, Lamas and Evangelicals: The English Missionaries in Siberia* (London: Routledge & Kegan Paul, 1985).

*Beck, Lois, and Nikki Keddie (eds.), *Women of the Muslim World* (Cambridge, MA: Harvard University Press, 1978).

*Beck, Lois, *Nomad: A Year in the Life of a Qashqa'i Tribesman in Iran* (University of California and London: I.B. Tauris, 1991).

---. *The Qashqa'i of Iran* (New Haven and London: Yale University Press, 1986).

Becker, Jasper, *The Lost Country: Mongolia Revealed* (London: Sceptre-Hodder, 1993).

*Benson, Linda and Ingvar Svanberg (eds.), *The Kazaks of China: Essays on an Ethnic Minority* (Uppsala, Sweden: Studia Multiethnica Upslaiensa, 1988).

*Benson, Linda, and Ingvar Svanberg, *China's Last Nomads* (New York and London: M.E. Sharpe, 1998).

Berland, Joseph C., *No Five Fingers Are Alike* (Cambridge, MA: Harvard University Press, 1982).

Best, Ernest, *Following Jesus* (Sheffield: JSOT Press, 1981).

*Black-Michaud, J., *Sheep and Land: The Economic of Power in a Tribal Society* (Cambridge: Cambridge University Press, 1986).

*Blench, Roger, *Fulbe, Fulani and Fulfulde in Nigeria: Distribution and Identity* (Federal Department of Livestock and Pest Control Services, Nigeria, 1990).

*Braaksma, Del and Debra, "Can Christian Development Work Fit on a Donkey's Back?" and "My Pastoral Neighbours are Hungry... What's a Missionary to Do?" (dissertations submitted to the Department of Christian Ethics and Practical Theology, University of Edinburgh, 1994).

*Bradburd, Daniel, *Ambiguous Relations: Kin, Class and Conflict among the Komachi Pastoralists* (Washington, DC: Smithsonian Institution Press, 1990).

*Breeden (ed.), *Nomads of the World* (Washington, DC: National Geographic Society, 1971).

*Briggs, Lloyd Cabot, *Tribes of the Sahara* (Cambridge, MA: Harvard University Press, 1960).

Bright, John, *A History of Israel* (London: SCM Press, 1972).

Burch, Ernest S., *The Eskimos* (London: Macdonald, 1988).

*Campbell, John K., *Honour, Family and Patronage* (Oxford: Oxford University Press, 1964).

*Caplan, Patricia, and Janet M. Bujra (eds.), *Women United, Women Divided* (London: Tavistock, 1978).

*Carmichael, Peter (ed.), *Nomads* (London: Collins and Brown, 1991).

Carver, Robert, *The Accursed Mountains* (London: Harper-Collins, 1999).

*Chatty, Dawn, *From Camel to Truck: The Bedouin in the Modern World* (New York: Vantage Press, 1986).

*Chorlton, Windsor, *Cloud-Dwellers of the Himalayas: The Bhotia* (Amsterdam: Time-Life Books, 1982).

*Cole, Donald P., *The Nomads of the Nomads: The Al Murrah of the Empty Quarter* (Chicago: Aldine, 1975).

---. *Pastoral Nomads in a Rapidly Changing Economy: The Case of Saudi Arabia* (Pastoral Network Paper 7e; London: ODI, 1979).

Cross, Nigel, *The Sahel: The People's Right to Development* (London: MRG, 1990).

*Crowe, David M., *A History of the Gypsies of Eastern Europe and Russia* (New York and London: I.B. Tauris, 1995).

Davidson, Robyn, *Desert Places* (Penguin: Harmondsworth, 1997).

Derrick, Jonathan, *Africa's Slaves Today* (London: George Allen & Unwin, 1975).

Desert in the Sky, The [video] (Nareshi Bedi, Producer and Director; Bedi Films, 1995, in association with Channel Four TV, UK).

*Donovan, Vincent J., *Christianity Rediscovered: An Epistle from the Masai* (London: SCM, 1982).

*Dowell, Bart, *Gypsies: Wanderers of the World* (Washington, DC: National Geographic Society, 1970).

*Ekvall, Robert B., *Fields on the Hoof: Nexus of Tibetan Nomadic Pastoralism* (New York: Holt, Rinehart & Winston, 1968).

Ellis, E. Earle, *The Gospel of Luke* (London: Marshall, Morgan & Scott, 1974).

*Emeljaneko, Tatjana, Carl van Leeuwen and Larisa Popova, *Nomads in Central Asia* (Amsterdam: Royal Tropical Institute, 1995).

Fermor, Patrick Leigh, *Roumeli: Travel in Northern Greece* (London: Penguin, 1983).

*Fonseca, Isabel, *Bury Me Standing — The Gypsies and their Journey* (London: Chatto & Windus, 1992).

*Forsyth, James, *A History of the Peoples of Siberia — Russia's North Asian Colony 1581–1990* (Cambridge: Cambridge University Press, 1992).

*Fraser, Angus, *The Gypsies* (Oxford: Blackwell, 1995).

Gerteiny, Alfred G., *Mauritania* (London: Pall Mall, 1967).

Gibbs, Eddie, *The God Who Communicates* (London: Hodder, 1985).

*Goldstein, Merwyn C., and Cynthia M. Beall, *Nomads of Western Tibet* (London: Serindia, 1989).

*---. *The Changing World of Mongolia's Nomads* (Hong Kong: The Guidebook Company, Ltd., 1994).

*Grimes, Barbara F., *Ethnologue: Languages of the World* (Dallas: SIL, var. edns.).

Helland, John, *Five Essays on the Study of Pastoralists and the Development of Pastoralism* (African Savannah Studies 20; Bergen: University of Bergen, 1980).

*Herbert, Marie, *The Reindeer People: Travels in Lapland* (London: Hodder and Stoughton, 1976).

*Hudson, Alfred E., *Kazak Social Structure* (Yale University: Publications in Anthropology; Toronto: Burns & MacEachern, 1938, 1964).

Hudson, Peter, *Travels in Mauritania* (London: W.H. Allen, 1990).

*Hunter, Malcolm, *Appropriate Development for Nomadic Pastoralists: A study of the Waso Borana of Northern Kenya Illustrating the Value and Meaning of Holistic Development Amongst Nomadic Peoples* (The Open University and The Oxford Centre of Missions, England, 1996).

Ingham, Bruce, *Bedouin of Northern Arabia: Traditions of the Al-Dhafir* (London: KPI, 1986).

*Irons, William, and Neville Dyson-Hudson (eds.), *Perspectives on Nomadism* (Leiden: E.J. Brill, 1972).

*Izady, N.R., *A Concise Handbook: The Kurds* (London: Taylor & Francis, 1992).

Jennings, George, *Welcome to the Middle East* (Le Mars, IA: M.E. Missions Research, 1986).

Johnstone, Patrick, *Operation World* (Gerrards Cross: WEC International, 1993).

*Jones, Mervyn, *The Sami of Lapland* (London: MRG Report No. 55, 1982).

Kazak Report, The (The Caleb Project, n.d.).

*Keenan, Jeremy, *The Tuareg: People of Ahaggar* (London: Allen Lane, 1977).

Kehl, Krisztina, *Die Tahtaci: vorlaufiger Bericht uber die Holzarbeiter in Anatolien* (Berlin: Frie University, 1988).

*Kenrick, Donald, *Gypsies from India to the Mediterranean* (Toulouse: Gypsy Research Centre, 1993).

*Keohane, Alan, *Bedouin: The Nomads of the Desert* (London: Kyle Cathie, 1994).

*Lane, Charles R. (ed.), *Custodians of the Commons: Pastoral Land Tenure in East and West Africa* (London: Earthscan, 1998).

Lane, William, *The Gospel According to Mark* (Grand Rapids: Eerdmans, 1971).

Languages of India (IMA, 1994).

*Lazell, D., *From the Forest I Came* (London: Concordia, 1970).

*Le Cossec, Clement, *My Adventures with the Gypsies* (Banglore: The Indian Gypsy Work Fellowship, 1991).

*Leshnik, L.S., and G. Southeimer, *Pastoralists and Nomads in South Asia* (Wiesbaden: Otto Harrassowitz, 1975).

Leybourne, Marina, Ronald Jaubert and Richard N. Tutwiler, *Changes in Migration and Feeding Patterns among Semi-Nomadic Pastoralists in Northern Syria* (Pastoral Development Network Paper 34a, July 1993).

*Liégeos, Jean-Pierre, *Gypsies: An Illustrated History* (London: Al Saqi Books, 1986).

Lienhardt, G., *Divinity and Experience* (Oxford: Clarendon Press, 1961).

*Locke, Sue, *Travelling Light: The Remarkable Story of Gypsy Revival* (London: Hodder and Stoughton, 1997).

Lovett, R., *James Gilmour of Mongolia* (London Religious Tract Society, c. 1890).

*MacDermot, Brian Hugh, *Cult of the Sacred Spear: The Story of the Nuer Tribe in Ethiopia* (London: The Travel Book Club, 1972).

*Maliki, Angelo B., *Joy and Suffering among the Wodaabe* (trans. Gordon Gorder; Jos, Nigeria: JCMWA, 1984).

Manku, Darshan Singh, *The Gujar Settlements: A Study in Ethnic Geography* (Delhi: Inter India, 1986).

*Marnham, P., *Nomads of the Sahel* (London: MRG Report No. 33, 1976).

Martens, E.A., *God's Plot and Purpose in the Old Testament* (Leicester: IVP, 1981).

*Matheson, Sylvia A, *The Tigers of Baluchistan* (Karachi: Oxford University Press, 1975).

*Matthews, V.H., and Don Benjamin, *The Social World of Ancient Israel 1250–587 BCE* (Peabody, MA: Hendrickson Publishers, 1993).

McDowell, Bart, *Gypsies: Wanderers of the World* (Washington, DC: National Geographic Society, 1970).

*Misra, P.K., and K.C. Malhotra (eds.), *Nomads in India: Proceedings of the National Seminar* (Calcutta: Anthropological Survey of India, 1982).

Moll, Peter, with Mohammed Amin, *Portraits of Africa* (London: Harvell, 1983).

Mongolia Challenge Report #3 (Lynwood, WV: Issachar, 1984).

*Mortensen, Inge Demant, *Nomads of Luristan* (London: Thames and Hudson, 1993).

Mousavi, Sayed Asker, *The Hazaras of Afghanistan* (London: Curzon Press, 1998).

Nelson, Harold D., et al., *Area Handbook for Chad* (Washington, DC: American University Press, 1972).

---. *Area Handbook for the Democratic Republic of Sudan* (Washington, DC: American University Press, 1973).

Niehaus, Jeffrey J., *God at Sinai* (Carlisle: Paternoster, 1995).

Noble, Christina, *Over the High Passes: A Year in the Himalayas with the Migratory Gaddi Shepherds* (London: Collins, 1987).

*Okely, Judith, *The Traveller-Gypsies* (Cambridge: Cambridge University Press, 1983).

*Olcott, Martha Brill, *The Kazaks* (Stanford: Hoover Institution Press, 1995).

Phillips, W., *Unknown Oman* (London: Longmans, 1966).

Poulton, Hugh, *Who are the Macedonians?* (London: Hurst, 1996).

*Pratt Jr., Richard L., *He Gave Us Stories: The Bible Student's Guide to Interpreting Old Testament Narratives* (Nutley, NJ: Presbyterian and Reformed, 1993).

*Ramble, Charles, and Martin Brauen (eds.), *Anthropology of Tibet and Himalaya* (Zurich: Ethnological Museum of the University of Zurich, 1993).

*Randhawa, T.S., *The Last Wanderers: Nomads and Gypsies of India* (Ahmedabad: Mapin, 1996).

*Rao, Aparna (ed.), *The Other Nomads: Peripatetic Minorities in Cross-cultural Perspective* (Köln and Wien: Böhlau, 1987).

*Rao, Aparna, *Les Gorbat d'Afghanistan: Aspects Economiques d'un Groupe Itinérant 'Jat'* (Paris: Institut Français d'Iranologie de Tehran, 1982).

*Rashid, Ahmed, *The Resurgence of Central Asia* (London: Zed Books, 1994).

*Rehfisch, F. (ed.), *Gypsies, Tinkers and other Travellers* (London: Academic Press, 1975).

*Ridholls, Joe, *Travelling Home* (Basingstoke: Marshall-Pickering, 1986).

*Riesman, Paul, *Freedom in Fulani Social Life* (Chicago and London: University of Chicago Press, 1977).

*Robinson, G., *Native Peoples of the Soviet Arctic* (YWAM-Slavic Ministries, 1989).

Roma: Europe's Gypsies (London: MRG Report No. 143, 1980).

*Salzman, C., and J.G. Galaty (eds.), *Nomads in a Changing World* (Naples: I.V. Orientale, 1979 [1990]).

*Sankan, S.S. *The Maasai* (Nairobi: Kenya Literature Bureau, 1971).

*Schultz, Emily A. (ed.), *Image and Reality in African Interethnic Relations: The Fulbe and Their Neighbors* (Williamsburg, VA: College of William and Mary, 1981).

Shahrani, M. Nazif Mohib, *The Kirghiz and Wakhi of Afghanistan* (Seattle and London: University of Washington Press, 1979).

*Shashi, S.S., *Roma: The Gypsy World* (Delhi: Sundeep Prakashan, 1990).

*---. *The Nomads of the Himalayas* (Delhi: Sundeep Prakashan, 1979).

---. *The Shepherds of India* (Delhi: Sundeep Prakashan, 1978).

*Singh, K.S., *People of India*, III, *The Scheduled Tribes* (Calcutta: Anthropological Survey of India, Oxford University Press, 1994).

*---. *People of India*, IV, *The Scheduled Castes* (Calcutta: Anthropological Survey of India, Oxford University Press, 1993).

*Snellgrove, David, *Himalayan Pilgrimage: A Study of Tibetan Religion* (Oxford: Bruno Cassirer, 1961).

Sonho-Godwin, Patience, *Ethnic Groups of Senegambia* (Banjul: Book Production and Material Resources Unit, 1986).

*Starkie, Walter, *In Sara's Tents* (London: John Murray, 1953).

Swartley, Willard M., *Israel's Scripture Traditions and the Synoptic Gospels* (Peabody, MA: Hendrickson, 1994).

*Swee, Gary M., *Sedentaization: Change and Adaptation among the Kordshuli Pastoral Nomads of Southwestern Iran* (Ann Arbor, MI: Michigan University Press, 1981).

*Tapper, Richard, *Frontier Nomads of Iran* (Cambridge: Cambridge University Press, 1997).

*---. *Pasture and Politics* (London and New York: Academic Press, 1979).

*Thesiger, Wilfred, *Arabian Sands* (Harmondsworth: Penguin, 1964).

*Tippett, Alan, *People of Southwest Ethiopia* (Pasadena: William Carey Library, 1970).

*Tsering, Marku, *Sharing Christ in the Tibetan Buddhist World* (Upper Darby: Tibet Press, 1988).

*Tucci, Guiseppe, *The Religions of Tibet* (London: Routledge and Kegan Paul, 1980).

Unreached Peoples '83 (ed. R. Dayton, et al.; Monrovia: Cal. Marc, 1983).

Unreached Peoples of Kenya (Nairobi: Daystar Communications, n.d.).

*Vainshtein, Sevyan, *Nomads of South Siberia: Pastoral Economies of Tuva* (Cambridge: Cambridge University Press, 1980).

*Vakhtin, Nikolai, *Native Peoples of the Russian North* (London: Minority Rights Group, 1992).

Vanderaa, Larry, *A Survey for CRWM of Missions and Churches in West Africa* (Grand Rapids: CRWM, 1991).

*Vandevort, Eleanor, *A Leopard Tamed* (London: Hodder, 1968).

Veenhof, K.R., *The World of the Bible*, I (gen. ed. A.S. van der Woude; Grand Rapids: Eerdmans, 1986).

Vickers, Miranda, and James Pettifer, *From Anarchy to a Balkan Identity* (London: Hurst, 1997).

Vogels, W., *God's Universal Covenant: A Biblical Study* (Ottawa: University of Ottawa, 1979).

*von Fürer Haimendorf, C., *Himalayan Traders* (London: John Murray, 1975).

*---. *The Sherpas Transformed* (New Delhi: Sterling Publishers, 1984).

*Warren, D. Michael, L. Jan Slikkerveer and David Brokensha (eds.), *Cultural Dimension of Development: The Indigenous Knowledge Systems* (London: Intermediate Technology Publications, 1995).

*Weekes, Richard V. (ed.), *Muslim Peoples* (Westport, CT: Greenwood, 1978).

Western Saharans, The (London: MRG Report No. 40, 1984).

*White, Walter G., *The Sea Gypsies of Malaya* (London: Seeley, Service & Co., 1922).

*Widdows, Richard (ed.), *Family of Man* (London: Marshal Cavendish, 1974; published in 98 weekly parts during 1974-76).

Wixman, Ronald, *The Peoples of the USSR* (London: Macmillan, 1984).

*Wood, Manfrid Frederick, *In the Life of a Romany Gypsy* (London: Routledge & Kegan Paul, 1973).

Wood, Michael, *Different Drums* (London: Century, 1987).

Woodhead, Leslie, *A Box Full of Spirits* (London: Heinemann, 1991).

World Directory of Minorities (ed. P. Thornberry and Minority Rights Group; Harlow: Longman, 1992).

World Translation Progress Report and Supplement (Reading, England: United Bible Societies).

Yin, Ma (ed.), *China's Minority Nationalities* (Beijing: Asian Minorities Outreach, 1989).

ARTICLES, UNPUBLISHED PAPERS AND INDIVIDUAL CHAPTERS IN BOOKS

Alexander, Loveday, "Ancient Book Production and the Circulation of the Gospels," in *The Gospels for All Christians* (ed. R. Bauckham; Edinburgh: T. & T. Clark, 1998), 71-105.

Alekseev, N.A., "Shamanism among the Turkic Peoples of Siberia," in *Shamanism in Soviet Studies of Traditional Religion in Siberia-Central Asia* (ed. M.M. Balzer; London: M.E. Sharpe, Inc., 1990), 49-109.

Al-Hada, Aba, "The Uighurs of Xinjiang," *International Journal of Frontier Missions* (Oct. 1985), 377.

Allen, Thomas B., "Time Catches up with Mongolia," *National Geographic* (Feb. 1985), 242-69.

Andrews-Speed, Philip, "Herdsmen of Chinese Turkestan," *Asian Affairs* XXVII.1 (Feb. 1996), 53-61.

Asher, Michael, "How the Mighty are Fallen," *Geographical Magazine* LXIV.3 (March 1991), 24-26.

Banks, Tony, "Pastoral Land Tenure Reform and Resource Management in Northern Xinjiang: A New Institutional Economic Perspective," *Nomadic Peoples* NS I.2 (1997), 55-74.

Baxter, Paul, "Pastoralists are People," *REB* (AERDD, University of Reading, April 1994).

Beach, Hugh, "The Reindeer-Caribou Conflict in the Nana Region of Alaska: A Case Study for Native Minority Rights Issues," *Nomadic Peoples* 17 (Feb. 1985), 1-22.

Beall, C., and M. Goldstein, "Past Becomes Future for Mongolian Nomads," *National Geographic* (May 1993), 126-35.

Beckwith, Carol, "Niger's Wodaabe: 'People of the Taboo'," *National Geographic* 164.4 (Oct. 1983), 483-509.

Berland, Joseph C., "*Parytan*: 'Native' Models of Peripatetic Strategies in Pakistan," *Nomadic Peoples* 21/22 (Dec. 1986), 189-205.

Bollig, Michael, "Ethnic Relations and Spatial Mobility in Africa: A Review of the Peripatetic Niche," in Rao (ed.), *Other Nomads*, 179-228.

Braukämper, Ulrich, "Strategies of Environmental Adaptation and Patterns of Transhumance of the Shuwa Arabs in the Nigerian Chad Basin," *Nomadic Peoples* 39 (1996), 53-68.

Browman, David L., "Camelid Pastoralism in the Andes," in *Nomads in a Changing World* (ed. C. Salzman and J.G. Galaty; Naples: I.V. Orientale, 1979), 395-437.

Carrier, Jim, "Gatekeepers of the Himalayas," *National Geographic* (Dec. 1992), 79.

Casimir, Michael J., "On the Formation of the Niche: Peripatetic Legends in Cross-Cultural Perspective," *Nomadic Peoples* 21/22 (Dec. 1986), 89-102.

---. "In Search of Guilt," in Rao (ed.), *Other Nomads*, 373-90.

Chatty, Dawn, "Changing Sex Roles in Bedouin Society in Syria and Lebanon," in Beck and Keddie (eds.), *Women of the Muslim World*, 399-415.

Davidson, Robyn, "Wandering With India's Rabari," *National Geographic* (Sept. 1993), 64-93.

Devillers, Carole E., "Oursi, Magnet in the Desert," *National Geographic* (April 1980), 512-25.

Diemberger, Hildegard, "Gangla Tshechu, Beyul Khenbalung: Pilgrimage to Hidden Valleys, etc.," in Ramble and Brauen (eds.), *Anthropology of Tibet and Himalaya*, 60-72.

Dodwell, Christina, *Beyond Siberia* (London: Hodder, 1993).

"Drying of India, The" *India Today* (June 22, 1998), 62-8.

Dupire, Marguerite, "A Nomadic Caste: The Fulani Woodcarvers, Historical Background and Evolution," *Anthropos* 80 (1985), 85-100.

Dyson-Hudson, N., "Inheriting and Extending Man's Oldest Technique of Survival, Nomads Find Freedom and Identity in the Life they Follow," in Breeden (ed.), *Nomads of the World*, 10-24.

Ellwood, Wayne, "Nomads at the Crossroads," *New Internationalist* (April 1995), 7-10.

Emeljaneko, Tatjana, "Nomadic Year Cycles," in Emeljanenko, Leeuwen and Popova (eds.), *Nomads in Central Asia*, 37-67.

Evans, Richard, "Born to Roam Free," *Geographical Magazine* (March 1991), 22-3.

Freudenberger, K.S., "Don't Fence Me In," *New Internationalist* (April 1994), 14-16.

Fuchs, Peter, "Nomadic Society, Civil War and the State in Chad," *Nomadic Peoples* 38 (1996), 151-62.

Galaty, John, "Dreams, Symbols and Totems," *New Internationalist* (April 1995), 28-9.

George, Shanti, "Nomadic Cattle Breeders and Dairy Policy in India," *Nomadic Peoples* 19 (Sept. 1985), 1-19.

Gitari, D., S. Houghton and G. R. Mullenix, "The Unreached Gabbra: A Plan to Reach a Nomadic People," in *Unreached Peoples '79* (Elgin, IL and Weston, Ont.: David C. Cook, 1978), 119-27.

Goldingay, J., "How Far do Readers Make Sense? Interpreting Biblical Narrative," *Themelios* (Jan. 1993).

Goldstein, Melvyn C., and Cynthia M. Beall, "The Remote World of Tibet's Nomads," *National Geographic* (June 1989), 752ff.

---. "Change and Continuity in Nomadic Pastoralism on the Western Tibetan plateau," *Nomadic Peoples* 28 (1991), 105-22.

Gooch, Pernille, "Transhumant Pastoralism in Northern India: The Gujar Case," *Nomadic Peoples* 30 (1992), 84-96.

Gore, Rick, "Journey to China's Far West," *National Geographic* (March 1980), 292-331.

Gourlay, K.A., "The Ox and Identification," *Man* 7.2 (June 1972), 244-54.

Hanbury-Tenison, Robin, "Reindeer Nations of Siberia," *Geographical Magazine* (Feb. 1998), 15-29.

Hayden, Robert M., "Conflicts and Relations of Power between Peripatetics and Villagers in South Asia," in Rao (ed.), *Other Nomads*, 267-89.

Heron, P., "Education for Nomads," *Nomadic Peoples* 13 (July 1983), 61-68.

Hunter, Malcolm, "Nomadic Pastoralists — Who are they?" (unpublished paper, 1993).

---. "What of the "Nomadic Pastoralists?" (unpublished paper, 1993).

---. "Nomadic Pastoralists and their Spiritual World" (unpublished paper at EMA Nomadic Pastoralist conference, Oct. 1993).

Irons, William, "Variation in Economic Organisation: A Comparison of the Pastoral Yomut and the Basseri," in Irons and Dyson-Hudson (eds.), *Perspectives on Nomadism*, 88-97.

Jina, Prem Singh, "Pasture Ecology of Leh, Ladakh," *Wissenschaftsgeschichte und Gegenwärtige Forschungen in NW Indien* (Dresden: Staatliches Museum für Völkerkunde, 1990), 171-80.

Kirtley, M. and A., "The Inadan-Artisans of the Sahara," *National Geographic* (Aug. 1979), 282-98.

Köhler-Rollefson, Isle, "The Raika Dromedary," *Nomadic Peoples* 30 (1992), 74-83.

Lenchak, Timothy, "The Bible and Intercultural Communication," *Missiology: An International Review* (Oct. 1994), 457-68.

Llewelyn-Davies, Melissa, "Two Contexts of Solidarity among Maasai Women," in Caplan and Bujira (eds.), *Women United, Women Divided*, 206-37.

Lyon, Ruth, "The Migration Patterns of Afghan Refugees" (unpublished paper, May 1987).

McCabe, Terence, "The Turkana of Kenya," in Carmichael (ed.), *Nomads*, 66-95.

McClintock, Wayne, "Nomadic Tribal Peoples of Lahore" (unpublished paper, 1986).

Mearns, Robin, "Territoriality and Land Tenure among Mongolian Pastoralists: Variation, Continuity and Change," *Nomadic Peoples* 33 (1993), 73-103.

Minorsky, V., "Les Tsiganes Luli et Les Luis Persans," *SOAS Offprints* 13 (April-June 1931).

Morton, John, "Pastoralists in Pakistan," *REB* (April 1994), 33-6.

Müller, Franz-Volker, "New Nomads and Old Customs," *Nomadic Peoples* 36/37 (1995), 175-94.

Närman, Anders, "Pastoral Peoples and the Provision of Educational Facilities — A Case Study from Kenya," *Nomadic Peoples* 25-27 (1990) 108-21.

Ndagal, Daniel, "Pastoralists and the State in Tanzania," *Nomadic Peoples* 25-27 (1990), 51-64.

Negi, R.S., "Population Structure of a Pastoral Nomadic Community of the Himalayas," in *Nomads of India*, 42-51.

Newsham, Peter, "A Desert Dilemma," *Geographical Magazine* (April 1993) 33-8.

Oba, Gufu, "Environmental Education for Sustainable Development among Nomadic Peoples," *Nomadic Peoples* 30 (1992), 53-73.

---. "Kenya, Boran: Sharing and Surviving," *REB* 4 (April 1994), 17-22.

Okely, Judith, "Gypsies Travelling in Southern England," in Rehfisch (ed.), *Gypsies, Tinkers and Other Travellers*, 55-83.

Pandit, Trilok Nath, "A Note on the Gujar of North-west India (Kashmir)," *Wissenschaftsgeschichte und Gegenwärtige Forschungen in NW Indien* (Dresden: Staatliches Museum für Völkerkunde, 1990), 107-12.

Pastner, S.L., "Co-operation in Crisis among Baluch Nomads," *Anthropological Quarterly* 44 (1971), 173-84.

Paterson, John, "Resources: Conservation and Christian Responsibility," *Christian Graduate* (March 1971), 11-14.

Potkanski, Tomasz, "Mongolia: Reworking the Revolution," *REB* (April 1994).

Rao, Aparna, "Roles, Status and Niches: A Comparison of Peripatetic and Pastoral Women in Afghanistan," *Nomadic Peoples* 21/22 (Dec. 1986), 153ff.

Repkin, Nik, "Why are the Unreached, Unreached?" *EMQ* (July 1996), 286.

Riesman, Paul, "Aristocrats as Subjects in a Multi-ethnic State," in Schultz (ed.), *Image and Reality in African Interethnic Relations: The Fulbe and Their Neighbors*, 21-9.

Rom·n, Teresa San, "Kinship, Marriage, Law and Leadership in Two Urban Gypsy Settlements in Spain," in Rehfisch (ed.), *Gypsies, Tinkers and other Travellers*, 169-99.

Rønningstad, Egil, "The Nenets: A Presentation of the People and of YWAM's Involvement" (unpublished paper; Borgen, Norway: WYAM).

Roux, Jean-Paul, "The Tahtaci of Anatolia," in Rao (ed.), *Other Nomads*, 229-45.

Ruhela, Satya Pal, "Bullock-cart Blacksmiths, Gadulyia Lohar Bring Forges to Rajasthan Villages," in Breeden (ed.), *Nomads of the World*, 26-51.

Salzman, Philip Carl, "Labor Formation as in a Nomadic Tribe," *Nomadic Peoples* 13 (July 1983), 35-59.

---. "Movement and Resource Extraction among Pastoral Nomads," *Anthropological Quarterly* 44 (1971), 185-97.

---. "Are Nomads Capable of Development Decisions?" *Nomadic Peoples* 18 (June 1985), 47-52.

Sanaroy, V.J., "The Siberian Gypsies," *JGLS* (3rd Series) XLIX (1970), Pt. 3-4, 126-37.

Sarkar, R., V. Sarkar and M.K. Raha, "The Gujjars and their Society," in *Nomads in India*, 65-74.

---. "Planning for the Rehabilitation and Development of the Nomads of Central and Western Himalayas," in *Nomads in India*, 304-13.

Sharma, J.G., "Communicational and Educational Problems of Gujjars: A Pastoral Nomadic Tribe," in *Nomads of India*, 271-76.

Shawyer, Richard, "The Chronological Approach" (unpublished paper; WEC Fula Ministry Conference, The Gambia, 1997).

Simarski, Lynn Teo, "The Desert Meets the Sown," *Aramco World* 46.2 (March-April 1995), 2-9.

Sin, M.E. Abu, "Sudan," in *Custodians of the Commons: Pastoral Land Tenure in East and West Africa* (ed. Charles R. Lane; London: Earthscan, 1998), 120-49.

Solo, Matt T., "Peripatetic Adaptation in Historical Perspective," *Nomadic Peoples* 21/22 (Dec. 1986), 11-12.

---. "The Gypsy Niche in North America," in Rao (ed.), *Other Nomads*, 89-109.

Stiles, Daniel, "The Gabbra Nomad Survival Kit," *Msafiri* (n.d.), 48-51.

Sutherland, Anne, "The Gypsies of California," in *Face Values* (ed. A. Sutherland; London: BBC, 1978), 186ff.

Swank, G., "The Evangelization of the Fulani," in *Unreached Peoples '79* (1978), 107-17.

Swidler, W.W., "Some Demographic Factors Regulating the Formation of Flocks and Camps Among the Brahui of Baluchistan," in Irons and Dyson-Hudson (eds.), *Perspectives on Nomadism*, 69-75.

Thomas, Geoff, "Evangelising the Eskimos Yesterday and Today," *Evangelical Times* (July 1996), 7.

Tijani, Kyari, "The Shuwa Arabs," in Adawa and Kirk-Greene (eds.), *Pastoralists*, 62-73.

Valli, Eric, and Diane Summers, "Himalayan Caravans," *National Geographic* (Dec. 1993), 5-35.

Vanderaa, L. and A., "Strategy for Mission among the Fulbe" (unpublished paper).

van de Pijekamp, Bob, "The Gypsy People Groups and Gypsy Tribes of the World" (Zeist: Euromission, 1990).

van Dijk, Han, "Farming and Herding after Drought: Fulbe Agropastoralists in Dryland Central Mali," *Nomadic Peoples* 36/37 (1995), 65-84.

van Leeuwen, Carl, "Animal Husbandry in Central Asia," in Emeljanenko, Leeuwen and Popova (eds.), *Nomads in Central Asia*, 9-36.

Watson, Cathy, "Kenya, Turkana: Women Coping," *REB* (April 1994), 23-8.

Wilson, Wendy, "The Fulani Model of Sustainable Agriculture: Situating Fulbe Nomadism in a Systematic View of Pastoralism and Farming," *Nomadic Peoples* 36/37 (1995), 35-52.

Wychoff, J.B., "Planning Arid Land Development Projects," *Nomadic Peoples* 19 (Sept. 1985), 59-69.

Zhukovskaya, Natalya L., "Religion and Ethnicity in Buryatia," *Central Asian Survey* 14:1 (1995), 25-42.

Zuppan, Mary, "Need Herders and Farmers Quarrel?" *REB* (April 1994), 12-16.

JOURNALS OFTEN CITED

Central Asian Survey (Basingstoke, England: Carfax Publishing-Taylor & Francis, Ltd.; quarterly).

Geographical (formerly *Geographical Magazine*; London: Campion Interactive, monthly).

International Journal of Frontier Missions (ed. Hans Weerstra; El Paso, TX: International Student Leaders Coalition for Frontier Missions, quarterly. The summer edition 2000, Vol. 17, No. 2 is a special edition on nomads.)

Journal of Asian and African Studies (Leiden: Brill).

Journal of the Gypsy Lore Society (Cheverly, MD: Gypsy Lore Society).

Man (London: Royal Anthropological Society).

National Geographic (Washington, DC: National Geographic Society; monthly).

New Internationalist (Hertford, England: New Internationalist Publications Ltd.; monthly special feature on nomads No. 266, April 1995).

Nomadic Peoples (Uppsala, Sweden: International Union of Anthropological and Ethnological Sciences-Commission on Nomadic Peoples; 2 issues/year).

Rural Extension Bulletin (University of Reading, England: Agricultural Extension and Rural Development Department; 3 issues/year).

Also the journals of many of the mission agencies have news of nomadic peoples including *Worldwide* (ed. Jean Goodenough; WEC International: Bulstrode, Oxford Road, Gerrards Cross, Bucks, SL9 8SZ, England; bi-monthly. A number of brief articles by the author.)

GENERAL INDEX

Bhotia, 12, *346*, 356-62, *358*
Bhubalia see Gadulyia Lohar
Bibelmission, 408
Bible narrative, 122-4
Bible Society, 300
Bible teaching, 121-2
biblical wisdom literature, 120
Bidan see Moors
Birhor, *29*, *346*, 386
Blauw, J., 75
Boa, see Bua
Bodi, *196*, 200-201, 203
Booboos see Toubou
Booth, W., 100
Borana, 15, 17, 27, 38, 120, 205-207
Born see Borana
Bororo see Fulbe, Wodaabe
Borrow, G., 435, 441
Bosha, *238*, *299*, 322
Boua, 186
Boudouma see Yedina
Bozo see Soroge
Braaksma, Debra, 84, 215
Braaksma, Del, 215
Bradburd, D., 95, 288
Brahui, *261*, *325*, 292-3, 304
Brog-pa see Drok-pa
Briggs, L.C., 38, 193
Bua (Bwa), *179*, 186
Bunna see Banna
Buryats, 115, *325*, 328-30
Bushmen, 8

C
CAFOD, 110
Caldeira, H., 420
Cameleers, 220
Cameroon, 164
Campus Crusade, 355, 368
Canadian Campus Crusade, 300, 326
CAPRO, 160, 161, 164, 165
CARE, 110, 224
Cargucho see Fleteros
Carnival Workers (USA), *29*, *411*, 418
Central Asia Fellowship, 327
Central Asian Mission, 353
Chaamba, *226*, 233
Chadian Ba Illi Missionary Training Centre, 160
Chamaars, 377, 385
Chambers, R., 15
Changar, 376
Chang-pa, 345-9, *346*
Charan, *29*, *346*, 374-6
Chenguin, 13
Children of the Bowed Lute, 173-4

Chilean Presbyterian Church, 145
Chitrakathi, 386
Christian Aid, 110
Christian Believers Assembly, 363
Christian College Coalition, 97
Christian Reformed Church, 89, 163
  see also CRWM
Christian Veterinary Mission (US), 111
Chukchi, 44, 115, *394*, 406-407
Chungar, *29*, *346*, see Sirkiwas
Church Mission Society (CMS), 215, 293
church
  as community, 128-9
  as pilgrim, 76-7
  structures, 125-6
Churigar, *29*, *346*, 374
CMA (Christian and Missionary Alliance), 151, 157, 177, 300, 352
COCIN (Church of Christ in Nigeria), 151, 158, 161, 166,186
Cole, D.P., 45, 113
collectivization (Communism), 32, 25, 38-9, 44, 298, 307, 309, 313, 316, 326-7, 336, 362, 396, 399, 404, 407
Conservative Baptists, 363
Cooperative Baptist Fellowship, 436
CPK (Anglican Church of the Province of Kenya), 207, 213, 214
Crosslinks, 207, 213
CRWM (Christian Reformed World Missions), 151, 155, 157
Cookinkoobe, 157

D
Daasanich, *197*, 204-205
Dadjo, *179*, 187
Daju see Dadjo
Dama (Bodi name for Mursi), *196*, 200
Dama (distinct from Mursi), 204
Danakil see 'Afar
dandi culture, 173
Darfur, 187, 189
Darghins, 301
Dar Hamid, 183, 187, *190*
Datoga, *197*, 216-17
Dausahaq or Dawsahaq see Idaksahak
David, S., 111

Davidson, R., 92, 103
Daza see Toubou
Degodia, 206
Dendi, 164
development projects, 45, 84, 106-11
Dewar see Pardhan
Dewasis see RabariDhadi, *389*
Dhangar see Oraon
  see also Hatkar Dhangars, Ahirs
Diida, D., 207
Dime see Dimi
Dimi, *196*, 201
Dine, 131, *411*, 412-13
Dinkas, 17, *179*, 189-191, *190*
Diocese of the Arctic Episcopal Church, 418
discipleship, 126-8
Djibo see Jelgoobe
Dodos see Dodoth
Dodoth, *197*, 208
Dog-pa see Drok-pa
Dolgans, *394*, 401-402
Dolpo-pa (Dolpo), 31, 91, 357, *358*, 360-61
Dom, *238*, 254, *255*, 256, 388
  see also Gypsies, Ghorbati
Donovan, V., 37, 48, 85, 126, 216
Dorze, *29*, *196*, 218
Drok-pa, 13, 24-25, 27, 31, 32, *325*, 338-41, *339*, *343*, *346*, 349, *358*
Durgimurgiwala, 385

E
education, 113-15
Elam Ministries, 265
EMS (Evangelical Missionary Society), 161
Enets, 396, 401, 419
English Travelers, *28*, *425*, 448
Episcopal Church, 191
  see also Diocese of the Arctic Episcopal Church
Ergong, 342
Eskimo, 417-18
  Aleut, *28*, 417
  Inuit, 417
  Mushuau Innu, 44, *411*, 417-18
  Napaaq turmiut, 417
  Thule Inuit, 418
  Yupik, *28*, 417
Ethnologue, 335
Ethiopian Orthodox Church, 205
Evangelical Church of West Africa (ECWA), 151, 161
Evangelical Free Mission, 151

Komi, *29*, *394*, 408
Kordshuli, *260*, 287-8
Koryak, *394*, 407-408
Kouchi traders, *29*, 297
Koutzovlacks *see* Aromani
Kowli, *29*, 284, 293, *299*, 322
Koyam, 165-6
Kraemer, H., 84, 85
Kuchi *see* Arab Koochi
Kuhaki, 287
Kundar Khati *see* Gadulyia
Lohar
Kuravar, 389
Kurbat *see* Ghorbati
Kurds, *238*, 270, 291
Kuruba, 370
Kyrgyz, 11, 18, 35, 39, 83, 92, 95, 115, 271, 272, *299*, 303, 304, 309, 314-21, *315*, *320*
Afghanistan, 318-19
China, *315*, 318, 319

L
Ladakhi, 345, *346*
Laestadian movement, 426
Laks, 301
Lali Faqir, 376
Lamans *see* Lambadi
Lambadi, *346*, *347*, 366-8
Lamut *see* Eveny
land, 13, 26-7
Israel's concept of, 65-6, 67
Langa *see* Mirasi
Language Recordings, 125, 213, 186, 214, 217, 230
Lanka Bible College, 389
LaoBe *see* Lawbe
Lapps *see* Sami
Lawbe, *28*, 139, *140*, 166-7
relationship with Fulbe, 166
leadership, 34-6
Lezghis, 301
Lienhardt, G., 191
Lifewater International, 401
Light and Life Movement, 437
Linguistic Recordings, 205, 211, 311, 368
Litang-pa, *342*
literary culture, 115, 119
Little Flock, 313
Livingstone, D., 69
Llamero *see* Fleteros
Loikop *see* Samburu
Lom, *29*, *238*, 254
London Missionary Society, 300, 330, 335
Lori, Lors *see* Lur
Lovara, 322
Lur, 11, 27, 34, 43, 273, 274, 275-8
Luri *see* Luti

Lutherans, 426
see also Finnish Lutheran Mission, Mekane Yesu Evangelical Lutheran Church, Norwegian Lutherans, Swedish Lutherans, US Lutherans
Lutheran Church of Christ in Nigeria (LCCN), 161, 180
Luti, 12, 13, *29*, *260*, 275, 295, *299*, 322, 388

M
Maabube, *28*, *140*, 167-70
Sanyaobe, 170
Maarulah, 301
Maasai, 18, 27, 31, 36, 37, 85, 103, 112, 114, *197*, 215-16
Maba, *179*, 186-7
McCabe, T., 209
MacDermott, B.H., 93
McIlwain, T., 121
Maccube *see* Maabube
Mahra, *239*, 250-51
Maldharis, *346*, 366
Manganiyar, 389
Manna, *29*, *196*, 219
Mansi, *394*, 400-401
Mapuche, *411*, 416
Markawan, 353
Marwari, *29*, *346*, 374
Masai *see* Maasai
Mather, P., 336
Maures *see* Moors
Mauritania, 153
Mazang, *299*, 322
Medical Ambassadors, 335
Meghwal, 378
Meidob, *179*, 183, *190*
Mekane Yesu Evangelical Lutheran Church, 204
Mercheros, 448-9
Merille *see* Daasanich
Mestizos, *411*, 414-15
Methodist missionary, 111
Midgan *see* Sab
Midob, 183
migratory system, 10-12, 22-6
Minorsky, V., 236
Mirasi, *29*, *346*, 372-3
Mission EvangÈlique des Tziganes, 437
Mitchell, W., 420
modernization, 43-6
Mohammed Reza, 274
Mon, 370
Mongols, 13, 15, *19*, *20*, 35, 36, 37-8, 44, *88*, 93, *102*, 110, 115, 312, *325*, 330-36, *331*, *337*
Oirat, 336

in People's Republic of China, *325*, 336
privatized pastoralism, 332-3
Sogwo Arig, 336
Torgut, 336
Moors, 12, *140*, 225-230, *226*, *229*, 235
moral issues, 99-100
Moravian Missions, 200, 300, 349
Mortensen, I., 277
Moses, 37, 58-9, 60, 63, 64, 67, 70, 72, 79
Moultani, *299*, 322
Mouride Islamic Brotherhood, 154-5
Moussa, *28*, *see* Ouloud n'Sidi Ahmed
MRG (Minority Rights Group), 441
Mu'allmin, *28*, *226*, 235
Mughat, *29*, *299*, 322-3
Müller, F.-V., 330
Mun *see* Mursi
Murle, *179*, 192
Mursi, 8-9, 17, 113, *196*, 200, 201-204

N
Naasaadinkoobe, 157
Nafusa Berbers, 232
Nakkala *see* Lambadi
Nandi, *197*, 213
Nandiwala, *29*, *347*, 385
Nat, 378
National Union of the Lawbe of Senegal, 167
Native American Church, 413
Navajos *see* Dine
Nawar, *29*, *238*, 236
Nazarbayev, President, 307
Nemadi (Namadi), *28*, *226*, 234
Nenets (Nentsi), 21, 24, *102*, *394*, 396-400, *397*, *398*, 401
New Internationalist, 15
New Jerusalem, 77-8
New Opportunities, 155, 163, 181, 185, 232, 233, 266, 268, 273, 278, 184, 304, 313, 353
New Tribes Mission, 121
Ngansans, *29*, 401
Ngaturkana, 31, 35, *197*, 208-209
Nicholas I, Czar, 330
Noble, C., 94
Nogai, *299*, 300-301
Noghaylar *see* Nogai
nomadic theology, 78-81
nomadism, 6-14

animals, importance of, 15-21, 126-7
  hunter-gatherers, 8, *28-9*
  migratory system, 10-12, 22-6, *23*
  non-pastoral resources, 27-30
  numbers, 15
  pastoralists, 8-9, *16*
  peripatetics, 9-10, *28-9*, *384*
  world view, 12-13
North African Mission, 249
Northern Chad, 139
North Nigerian Programme, 126
Norwegian Lutherans, 164
Norwegian Mission to the Santals, 163
Nubians, 183, 187, 236
Nuer, 17-18, 21, 27, 46, 93, 112, 126, *179*, *190*, 191-2
Nuristani, 270

O

Od (Oud), 377
Oirat, 336
Okely, J., 94
Omsteifere *see* Gypsies
Operation Mobilisation, 268
oral cultures, 118-20
Oraon, 369
Orebro Mission, 151
Organisation for Nomadic Affairs (ONA), 265
Orma, 214-15
Orochen *see* Eveny
Oromo, *196*, 205
Orthodox, 298, 300
  see also Greek Orthodox, Romanian Orthodox, Serbian Orthodox, Russian Orthodox, Ethiopian Orthodox Church
Ouaddai, 186-7, *190*
Ouloud n'Sidi Ahmed, *226*, 235-6
OXFAM, 110

P

Padhar, 377
Pahari Gashwali *see* Garhwali
Pal, 368, *see* Ahir
Pamiri, *261*, 271-2
Pardhan, *346*, 386
Pari Gashwali *see* Garhwali
Patagonians, 416-17
Pathans *see* Pukhtana
Paul, St., 54, 74, 89
peanut plantations, 44, 154-5
Pentecostals, 419, 437, 438, 440
  see also Russian Pentecostals

Peoples Database, 230
Peul *see* Fulbe
Philadelphia Evangelical Group, 441
Pikraj, 296
Pinjaris, *347*, 388
Pish-e Kuh, 277
Podi *see* Bodi
Pökoot *see* Pokot
Pokot, *197*, 209, 212-13
Polaska Roma, 322
Polo, M., 271
Porte Ouverte, 145
Potricksha *see* Purik-pa
Poulton, H., 443
Presbyterians, 412
  see also Chilean Presbyterian Church, United Presbyterians
prejudice, 33, 40, 42, 43, 46-8, 58, 64, 69, 72, 84, 92, 113, 133, 134, 187, 253
privatized pastoralism, 332-3
  see also collectivization
Pukhtana, *261*, 267, 268, 269, 272-3
  Durrani, 272
  Ghilzais, 272, 273
  Powindahs, 273
Pulaar Bozo, 175, 177
Purik, 353
Purik-pa, 349
Pygmies, 8

Q

Qalandar, *29*, 93-4, *346*, 370-72, *371*
Qashqa'i, 10, 25, 26, 27, 34, 43, 86, 93, 95, 100, 103, 104, 114, 122, *260*, 264, 273, 274, 275, 278-84, *279*, *282*, *285*, 287
Qorbati *see* Ghorbati
Quechua, 21, 36, *411*, 414
Quinqui Baptist Church, 448-9
Qinquis *see* Mercheros

R

Rabari, 18, 92, 113, *346*, 363-5
racism, 42-3, 439
Rajasthan Bible Institute, 363
Rajis, *29*, 383
Randhawa, T., 95
Rashaida *see* Rasheida
Rasheida, *102*, 195-9, *196*, *198*
RBMU (Regions Beyond Missionary Union), 164
Rebekah, 56, *123*
Reformed Church in America, 215
Reika *see* Rabari

Reizigers, *29*, *425*, 448
relationships
  external, 31-2, 42-6
  internal, 32-4
religious beliefs, 36-8, 104
Rendille, *195*, 211-12
Reshiat *see* Daasanich
Reza Shah Pahlavi, 43, 259, 274, 275, 280, 283, 284, 289
Riasiti *see* Siraiki
Riesman, P., 17, 93, 173
Rif Berbers, 231
Riimaybe, 157, 158
Rodda, D., 121
Roma *see* Gypsies
Rom Gypsies, 322, 418-420, *424*, 429-45, *430*
  Kalderash, 12, 419, *424*, *425*, 432, 436, 440, 443
  Lovara Rom, 420, *424*
  Ludar, 419
  Machwaya, 419
  Romnichels, 419
  Vlack Rom, *28*, *411*, 420
  see also Gypsies
Roman Catholics, 181, 209, 211, 216, 249, 298, 412, 419, 420, 438, 439, 440, 448
Romanian Orthodox, 419, 427
Romani Sinte, 322
Rønningstad, E., 399
RSMT (Red Sea Mission Team), 157, *195*, 199
Ruhela, S.P., 91
Russian Baptists, 400
Russian Bible Society, 330
Russian Orthodox, 321, 326, 329, 335, 399, 401, 402, 404, 405, 417, 418, 421, 426
Russian Pentecostals, 326

S

Saami *see* Sami
Sab, *29*, 218-19
Saharawi, *226*, 230-31
Sakha, 404-405
Sakuye (Sakuge), *197*, 214
Salale, 205
SALTLIC, 216
Salvation Army, 192
Salzman, P.C., 27, 366
SAMS (South American Missionary Society), 414, 416
Sa-ma-'drok, 341
Samburu, *197*, 211, 213-14
Sami, 8, 27, 92, 399, 421-6
Sansi, 376
Sanyaobe, 170
Saperas (Jogi), 374
Sarakatsán, 15, 18, 427-*28*

ALSO AVAILABLE FROM PIQUANT

OPERATION CHINA: Introducing all the Peoples of China
by Paul Hattaway

A reference book for the first time ever profiles ALL the people groups of China; with a prayer calendar and up-to-date ethnographic information plus 740 full-colour photographs. Foreword by Patrick Johnstone, author of *Operation World*.

"The most significant contribution to mission research in 20 years!"
Dr David Barrett, President of the Global Evangelization Movement

ISBN 0-9535757-5-6
Large p/b; 720 pp; 248x172 mm
Retail Price £20.00 / $35.00

Order directly from the publishers at info@piquant.net or visit our website www.piquant.net

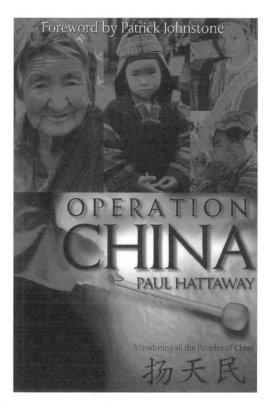

Available in the USA directly from William Carey Library, visit www.wclbooks.com

Piquant PalPacks:
Buy 2 copies and get the second half-price!!!

The Fifth Pillar: A spiritual journey
by David Zeidan

The real-life story of an Arab man's spiritual journey, from an upper-class and traditional Muslim background to faith in Christ and life in the West — ideal to gain an insight into Muslim culture and life in the Middle East.

0-9535757-4-8
P/b, 128 pp; 178x111mm
Retail price: £3.00 / $5.00

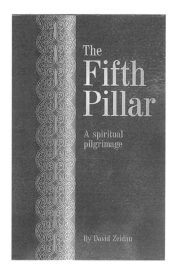

Polygamy: A cultural and biblical perspective
by Dr I. Gaskiyane

A Christian worker with 35 years' experience in Africa, also among polygamous people groups, proposes biblical solutions for a problem that the church has never yet adequately addressed — for pastors, mission workers and policy makers.

0-9535757-9-9
Pb, 64 pp, 178x111mm
Retail price £3.00 / $5.00

Piquant PalPacks:
Buy 2 copies and get the second half-price!!!

piquant

FORTHCOMING IN 2002

THE SHAPING OF MODERN CHINA:
The Life of Hudson Taylor
by A.J. Broomhall

Re-issued in two volumes: The definitive 7-volume
history of the life and influence of Hudson Taylor,
pioneer and missionary to China (1854–1901) and one
of the fathers of the modern missionary movement.

ISBN 0-903689-16-3
Large pb; 720 pp; 248x172 mm
Retail Price £29.99 / $45.00 per set

Advance orders to Piquant at info@piquant.net or visit
www.piquant.net
Also available in the USA from William Carey Library, visit
www.wclbooks.com

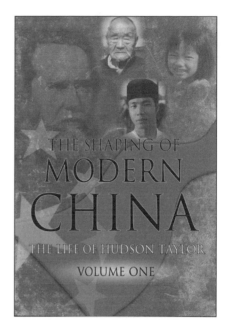